THORFIN AND GUDRIDA ON THE SHORE OF VINELAND

OUR COUNTRY.

A

HOUSEHOLD HISTORY

FOR ALL READERS,

FROM THE DISCOVERY OF AMERICA TO THE ONE HUNDREDTH ANNIVERSARY OF THE DECLARATION OF INDEPENDENCE.

BY

BENSON J. LOSSING, LL.D.

WITH OVER FIVE HUNDRED ILLUSTRATIONS,

BY

FELIX O. C. DARLEY.

VOLUME ONE.

NEW YORK:
JOHNSON WILSON & COMPANY.
1875.

Electrotyped by
SMITH & McDOUGAL.

Printed by
J. F. TROW & SON.

TO

THE HOUSEHOLDS OF

OUR COUNTRY,

WHEREIN PRIVATE VIRTUE SUSTAINS THE FABRIC OF OUR FREE INSTITUTIONS,

This Work is Dedicated,

WITH THE RESPECT AND AFFECTION OF

THE AUTHOR.

PREFACE.

OUR country, as known to civilized men, is young in years and without antiquity of Art, Science, Literature or Government, measured by the standards of other continents. It is in a *New World*, as the chroniclers have called it; its existence suspected by the ancients but proven only in the later periods of history. Yet its people possess the treasures of the experience of ages, and the results of the progress of the human race from pre-historic times. With these treasures they have bought wisdom wherewith to construct, with wonderful celerity, the fabric of a nation marvellous in its strength and resources developed and undeveloped.

It is only yesterday in the calendar of the earth's existence, when the fact was first made known to modern men, that our planet was a globe, and that in the waters between the western coasts of Europe and Africa and the eastern coasts of Asia, there lay a vast continent teeming with life, wealth and beauty. For generations after that discovery, it was wrapped in profound mystery, the subject of wild conjecture and tales of wonder. Then newly-awakened moral forces impelled brave and earnest men and women to venture across the Atlantic Ocean and establish homes in the virgin wilderness. So began the heroic age of our Republic, in which time were planted the germs of the great commonwealths that compose this nation.

The story of the growth of the Republic since the planting of those germs, is deeply interesting in incident and rich in suggestions. It is full of picturesque passages which give life and color to the less attractive details, making the whole a fascinating drama. I have endeavored, in the following pages, to unfold that story in language so plain and in form so simple, that whole households may be interested and instructed by the reading of it. Greater prominence than usual has been given to what may be called the romance of our history; and the pencil of the artist has been summoned to the aid of the pen of the author, in presenting those picturesque scenes. So may be diffused, it is hoped (especially amongst the young, who, as *readers* only, prefer such literature in this more attractive shape rather than in the stately figures which engage the *student*), a knowledge of the principal characters and events in our history, and impress them with a warm love for our free institutions.

The History of the United States may properly be arranged in six distinct periods, under the respective heads of (1) DISCOVERIES; (2) SETTLEMENTS; (3) COLONIES; (4) THE WAR FOR INDEPENDENCE OR THE POLITICAL REVOLUTION; (5) THE NATION; (6) THE CIVIL WAR, OR THE SOCIAL REVOLUTION. This work is, accordingly, divided into Six Books, each containing a record of events that occurred in corresponding periods of the six divisions. So is presented, in proper order, striking epochs that indicate the growth of the nation in its successive stages, and the unity of achievements by which the grand results that Americans now enjoy were reached.

In the First Book may be found a sketch of the several discoveries, actual and apocryphal, in America, which bear direct relations to the history of the Republic from the advent of the navigators of the North in the tenth and eleventh centuries, until Hudson and Champlain won their deserved honors. It also contains a history of the Indians found here.

In the Second Book is told the story of the several unsuccessful and successful efforts to plant settlements along the Atlantic coasts from Florida to the Gulf of St. Lawrence, and upon the banks of the great "River of Canada."

In the Third Book are narratives showing how the several settlements crystallized into organized communities and became permanent colonies—the originals of great States. The events which mark the foundation of these colonies, and of their growth to flourishing and powerful commonwealths when the French and Indian war, at the middle of the last century, compelled them to form a union for mutual protection, are carefully delineated in their most picturesque features. So the colonial history of each of the old thirteen States is given separately, to the period when this colonial union, and the political league of 1776, were formed.

In the Fourth Book may be found an account of the chief and most stirring events of the great struggle which resulted in the political independence of the United States, and the establishment of a national government in 1789, by the union of the several States under one supreme central power.

In the Fifth Book may be found an account of the progress of the new nation during a period of more than seventy years, until the beginning of the civil war in 1861. In this book the events of the Indian wars, the war of 1812–'15, and the war with Mexico from 1846 to 1848, are delineated.

In the Sixth Book may be found the exciting and deeply impressive story of the Civil War which resulted in a great social revolution by the abolition of slave-labor throughout the Republic. In it may also be found a general review of the progress of our country, from the inception of our nationality until the end of the first century of its existence in the year 1876.

In the preparation of this work I have availed myself of all new revelations concerning the history of our country made by recent investigations, which have fallen under my observation; and I have endeavored to make it a faithful picture of the Republic in all its phases, without any exaggeration in outline or coloring. In this labor I have been nobly seconded by Mr. DARLEY, the eminent American artist, who has, in every drawing illustrative of the text, consulted the best authorities for portraiture and costume, and followed their teachings. His spirited sketches of a vast number of events in our history, are, therefore, stamped with the insignia of truth, and are positively useful, not only as artistic embellishments, but as safe instructors. The spirit of these drawings has been admirably preserved by eminent engravers. To these gentlemen, and to the generous liberality of the Publishers in bringing out the work in a style of great elegance and costliness, the reader is largely indebted for the pleasure and instruction which these volumes may afford.

With these remarks, I submit the work to the households of Our Country.

BENSON J. LOSSING.

The Ridge, Dover, N. Y.

CONTENTS.

BOOK I.

DISCOVERIES.

CHAPTER I.

CHAPTER II.

CHAPTER III.

CHAPTER IV.

CHAPTER V.

CHAPTER VI.

CHAPTER VII.

CHAPTER VIII.

CHAPTER IX.

CHAPTER X.

CHAPTER XI.

CHAPTER XII.

CHAPTER XIII.

BOOK II.

SETTLEMENTS.

CHAPTER I.

CHAPTER II.

CHAPTER III.

CHAPTER IV.

CHAPTER V.

CHAPTER VI.

CHAPTER VII.

CHAPTER VIII.

CHAPTER IX.

CHAPTER X.

BOOK III.

COLONIES.

CHAPTER I.

CHAPTER II.

CHAPTER III.

CHAPTER IV.

CHAPTER V.

CHAPTER VI.

CHAPTER VII.

CHAPTER VIII.

CHAPTER IX.

CHAPTER X.

CHAPTER XI.

CHAPTER XII.

CHAPTER XIII.

CHAPTER XIV.

CHAPTER XV.

CHAPTER XVI.

CHAPTER XVII.

CHAPTER XVIII.

CHAPTER XIX.

CHAPTER XX.

CHAPTER XXI.

CHAPTER XXII.

CHAPTER XXIII.

LIST OF FULL-PAGE ILLUSTRATIONS.

VOLUME FIRST.

BOOK I.

DISCOVERIES

FROM 1002 TO 1609.

OUR COUNTRY.

CHAPTER I.

THE EXTENT AND CHARACTER OF OUR COUNTRY—THE FORM OF ITS GOVERNMENT—ITS DISCOVERY BY NORWEGIANS—ICELANDIC NAVIGATORS—THEIR ATTEMPTS TO FOUND A COLONY HERE—TRADITIONS RESPECTING OTHER DISCOVERIES—THE NORTH AMERICAN INDIANS IN THE SIXTEENTH CENTURY.

OUR COUNTRY occupies a large space on the Map of North America. It extends, in a broad irregular belt across the Continent, from the Atlantic Ocean on the East to the Pacific Ocean on the West. Its breadth is from far down each end of the Gulf of Mexico on the South to a line even with the northern shores of Lake Superior, with a large separate territory in the far northwest, on the confines of Asia. It comprises an area of more than three and a half million square miles ; equal to over twenty-two million farms of one hundred acres each, if it were all land. It contains almost forty million human beings, of whom more than twenty-seven million are natives of the land. The remainder are from almost every country on the globe. The latter, mixing with the native citizens, make us a strong people.

Over all this vast domain, favored with every variety of climate, soil and productions, great lakes and rivers, and the grandest and most beautiful natural scenery, now divided into many States and several organized Territories (the germs of States), is felt the benign influence of a free and enlightened government. It is a model government which the older nations of the Earth are gradually copying as the wisest and most sturdy on the globe. It is a government by the people. How? The people, the true source of all power in government, choose a few of their number to make laws for the whole, and others are chosen to execute those laws. It is therefore a Representative Democracy, or a government exercised by the whole people through their chosen representatives. Its wisdom and strength have been tested by the most severe strains: and the superiority of such a government, with an educated people as its basis, has been demonstrated.

In contemplating the majesty of our Republic, the question naturally arises in the mind, By what processes has this great and expanding nation been planted, nurtured, and strongly rooted here, where less than three hundred years ago brooded the darkness and solitude of a wilderness over the whole continent, peopled only by savage hunters or half civilized barbarians? The answer to this question will be the marvelous story which I am about to tell.

ALMOST nine hundred years ago, a famous Norwegian sailor named Eric—called Eric the Red because he had red hair and florid complexion—settled in Iceland, the northern shores of which touch the Arctic Circle. Whilst he was on a voyage westward from that far north country, he discovered Greenland and made it his home. His son Lief, an ambitious young man, wished to become a discoverer, like his father. He bought a ship—one of those queer little Norwegian vessels which were moved sometimes by sails and sometimes by oars. They were used by those old Sea-kings, as they were called, of Northern Europe, who spread terror by their piracies over the British Islands and the coasts of Western Europe from the Rhine to the Straits of Gibraltar, more than a thousand years ago.

Lief's ship was stout and tight. She had made many voyages safely. He furnished her with twenty-five strong men, and invited his father to go with him as the commander. Eric thought himself too old for such an undertaking, but was persuaded to go. Embracing his younger sons Thorwald and Thorstein, and his fiery daughter Freydisa, he bade them farewell, mounted his horse and rode toward the ship. The animal stumbled. Eric thought it was an omen of evil. "I do not believe it is given to me to discover any more lands, and here I will abide," said the old navigator, and he returned to his house.

Lief and his companions sailed southwesterly. It was in the early summer of the year of our Lord 1002. They were soon fighting the storms and waves of the North Atlantic Ocean between Greenland and Labrador, and were sometimes chilled by slow-drifting icebergs. At length they saw land. It was flat and stony near the shore, with high snow-capped mountains a little back from the sea. They did not land, but sailing southward they soon came to another country, flat, and covered thickly with woods. It had a broad beach of white sand sloping gently to the sea. The adventurers anchored their little ship, went on shore, and fed themselves with sweet berries. A few hours later they sailed away southward.

NORTHMEN DISCOVERING TRACES OF HUMAN HABITATION.

These bold seamen soon came in sight of another land. It was hilly—gently so—and mostly covered with trees. Its northerly shores were sheltered by an island. They found there an abundance of small fruits, delicious to the taste. No traces of human beings were found excepting some burnt wood and the bones of large fishes: and no sounds were heard but the songs of birds and the chirping of squirrels. Charmed by the soft climate, they sought a harbor, and found one at the mouth of a river where the vessel was swept by the tide into a bay. The waters were filled with the finest salmon, and wild deer abounded in the woods. The days and nights were nearly equal in length, at first. As they remained all winter, they noticed that when the days were the shortest, the sun rose at half-past seven o'clock and set at half-past four o'clock.

A young German of Lief's company, who was Eric's servant, was missing one day. They searched for him in all directions. He had wandered deep into the forest, and when they found him he was full of joy because he had discovered grapes, delicious and abundant, such as grew in his own country. So Lief named the country *Vineland.* He and his company built huts and wintered there, and in the spring they returned to Greenland. Eric had lately died, and Lief, his eldest son, came into the possession of his estate and patriarchal office. Eric's family were Christians, but Eric died a pagan.

Thorwald, Lief's younger brother, bought the good ship and, with thirty companions, sailed for Vineland. They passed the winter there, occupying the huts built by Lief and his companions, and subsisting as they had done, upon fish. In the spring, Thorwald and a part of his company explored the neighboring coasts, finding many sandy islands, on which there were no traces of wild beasts and few of human beings. The summer was spent in these explorations, and the next was passed at their old quarters in *Vineland.* Other explorations were made the following summer, by the whole company. In the early autumn they entered a large inlet. There were high lands on each side, thickly wooded. "Here," said Thorwald, "is a goodly place; here I will make my abode." They found there some natives—dusky people, of small stature, like the Esquimaux of Greenland. They were in canoes, and were timid and harmless. The Northmen caught them and cruelly put them to death, excepting one who escaped to the hills and aroused his countrymen. The angry savages went silently in their canoes and surprised Thorwald and his company. A sharp fight ensued. Arrows flew thick and fast. Thorwald was mortally wounded, but his companions escaped unhurt. The savages fled to the wooded hills, and Thorwald's companions buried the body of their chief on the promontory where he intended to settle, with a cross at its head and another at its feet. The survivors passed the winter in Vineland, in mortal fear of the enraged savages, and in the spring they returned to Greenland.

Thorstein, Eric's third son, on hearing of the death of his brother, sailed for Vineland, with twenty-five companions and his young wife, Gudrida, a beautiful blonde, to whom he had been married only a few weeks. Adverse winds drove their little vessel on a desolate shore of Greenland, far up the eastern border of Baffin's Bay. There the company suffered dreadfully, and were compelled to stay until spring. A contagious disease broke out among them, and Thorstein and a greater portion of his companions perished. Sadly the young wife carried home the body of her husband. So died two of the brave sons of the valiant Eric the Red, leaving their wayward sister, Freydisa, alone with Lief.

During the next summer, a rich citizen of Norway, young and comely, arrived in Greenland. His name was Thorfin. He saw and loved Gudrida, and demanded her in marriage, of Lief, her patriarchal brother-in-law. They were wedded; and the Norwegian, accompanied by his bride and five other young women with their husbands and other men, sailed for Vineland, to plant a colony there. They landed near the spot where Lief had passed the winter. Upon the shore, with the little Norwegian vessel anchored near, that company of sturdy emigrants presented a picturesque group. Thorfin, stout, but not very tall, was clad, on that occasion, we may imagine, in the costume of the Norwegian nobility. If so, over his linen shirt he probably wore a dark woolen tunic that descended to the knees, with long sleeves reaching to the wrists. The borders of the skirt, the collar, and the ends of the sleeves were ornamented with various colored cloth in a variety of devices. Around his waist was a girdle or belt of dressed leather, ornamented with bosses of silver and gold; and over all was a short cloak of rich stuff made of silk and woolen, of a purple color, fastened to his shoulder by a brooch of gold and precious stones. His legs were covered with white hose, bandaged with crossed fillets of gay colors from the ankle to the knee; and on his feet were black buskins, open in front, and secured by thongs of silk, with tasseled ends

DISCOVERY OF GRAPES.

depending from the top of the shoe. His long, dark wavy hair fell upon his back and shoulders, and his flowing beard covered his bosom.

The beautiful Gudrida, tall and slender but muscular and lithe, stood by the side of Thorfin, whilst he audibly thanked God for their deliverance from the perils of the waters; and near them in the shadows of great trees were gathered the rest of the company, silently uniting in the thanksgiving. Gudrida, we may imagine, was dressed in a manner befitting the rank of her husband. She might have worn, in the costume of that day in Norway, a white linen tunic that descended to the instep. Over this a black gown of silk reaching only to the knees, with short flowing sleeves that left half the arm bare below the elbow, and clasped by a golden bracelet. A broad band of gold embroidery extended from the waist to the lower edge and around the bottom of the gown, and also around the edges of the sleeves; and over all hung gracefully a gray woolen mantle of fine and light texture, fastened at the throat with a brooch of gold and pearls. It hung in graceful folds to her waist, in front, and behind as low as the gown. Upon her head was a veil or hood of silk, loosely and tastefully arranged over the portion back of the ears, and falling in folds upon her shoulders and bosom. In front of this hood hung her beautiful auburn hair in a rich profusion of curls and ringlets. On her feet were black buskins, their open fronts laced with silken cords, showing her white hose.

Thorfin remained with the colony in Vineland about three years, when he and Gudrida, with a part of the company, sailed for Norway, with specimens of fruits and furs which they had gathered in the new country. After making several voyages Thorfin settled in Iceland, where he built a fine mansion, and lived in a style unrivalled by the richest chieftain in that country. There Thorfin died. Gudrida, who had become the mother of a son, whilst she was in Vineland, then went with her boy, on a pilgrimage to Rome, where she told the stories of the adventurers in the ears of Pope Benedict. After her return, she entered a convent. Her son, whose name was Snorre, became, in time, master of his father's estates, and the ancestor of a long line of descendants. Among these was Albert Thorwaldsen, the great Danish sculptor of our day.

Those of Thorfin's colony who remained in Vineland, were joined by two brothers, named Helgi and Fiombogi, with about thirty followers. They were Icelandic chieftains, who fitted out their expedition in Greenland. Freydisa, the daughter of Eric the Red, obtained a willing permission to go with them, and share in the profits of the voyage. She was an artful, intriguing, deceitful and fiery-tempered woman, and Lief and his family hoped she would remain in Vineland and be decently buried there. She was a fury and a firebrand among the colonists. Where peace had reigned she enthroned discord. Quarrels ensued which ended in a fight and the death of thirty persons. Then Freydisa, finding her own life in peril, returned to Greenland, where she died universally detested.

Such is the substance of the accounts of these adventurers, given in the chronicles of Iceland. They reveal the fact that Norwegians discovered America almost five hundred years before Columbus sailed westward from Spain, in search of India. The stony land with the snow-capped mountains was, doubtless, Labrador. The flat, wooded land, with its white beach, must have been Newfoundland; and the time given of the rising and the setting of the sun at the winter solstice—the shortest day at about Christmas time—indicates some point on the New England coast between Boston harbor and Narragansett bay, as the spot where the German lad discovered the grapes, and Lief named the country *Vineland.*

Where Thorwald was buried, or where Thorfin and Gudrida landed and lived, nobody knows. The best informed students of the subject believe it to have been on Rhode Island, and that the mysterious stone tower at Newport, with its massive cylindrical walls resting on seven columns, whose foundation stones are wrought spheres, was built by these Norwegian colonists. It was there when the English settlers came, and the Indians had no knowledge of its origin. If the Northmen did not build it, who did? Perhaps Gudrida's son was born there. Who knows?

All positive traces of that colony in America, after the departure of Freydisa, are lost. Icelandic histories called Sagas, and poems called Eddas, give us glimpses of it for a few years, when it fades into utter forgetfulness. These histories and poems tell us that a navigator named Gudlief made a trading voyage from Iceland to Ireland at about the year of our Lord 1030. Whilst he was sailing along the western shores of Iceland, a strong wind blew his ship far into the Atlantic Ocean toward the southwest. After many days he and his crew saw land, anchored their ship in a safe harbor, and were made prisoners by dark-colored people who came from the woods in great numbers. Their captors took them into the forest, where they were met by a white chieftain who spoke to them in Icelandic, and procuring their release, advised them to depart immediately, for the dark people were cruel to strangers. He refused to tell them his name, but inquired after Snorre and other well-known persons in Iceland. Taking a gold ring from his finger, he asked Gudlief to present it to Thurida, Snorre's sister. Gudlief bore the jewel to the daughter of Gudrida. It was believed that the white chief was Bjorn, a famous Icelandic bard, who had been a lover of Gudrida and a rival of Thorfin, and who left his country in the year 998. If this story be true, Bjorn the bard and Lief the navigator, may fairly contend in the halls of Odin for the honor of having been the first of all Europeans to discover America.

It is also related that thirty years after the event just mentioned, a Saxon priest from Ireland, who had been laboring among the pagans of Iceland, went to Vineland, and was murdered there; and that a bishop of Greenland undertook the same vovage, and was never heard of afterwards.

ANCIENT TOWER AT NEWPORT, RHODE ISLAND.

From that time, for more than four hundred years, America lay hidden from the knowledge of Europeans, a wild, uncultivated waste. There are some traditions, that seem to have facts for their substance, that tell us of other voyages to this Western world, during that period. The most reasonable of these stories, is that of Prince Madoc of Wales, said to have been drawn from the chronicles of that country. It is believed by some historical students that Madoc, who was a son of Owen Gwynneth, disgusted with the domestic contentions about the rightful successor to his father, went on a voyage of discovery, with ships well manned, in the reign of King Henry the Second, of England; that he went westward from Ireland and found a most fruitful country, in the year 1170; that he returned home, and with a squadron of ten ships sailed for the same lands with a colony of men, women and children, to settle there, and that he was never heard of afterwards. It has been asserted by more than one traveller in this country, that light-colored Indians have been met by them who had many Welsh words in their language. Humboldt refers to this tradition; and Southey, the English poet, made it the theme of one of his finest productions. Until the translation of the Icelandic Chronicles revealed the story of the Norwegian voyagers, the Chronicles of Wales claimed for Madoc the honor of being the discoverer of America. There are traditions of voyages to this country in the fourteenth century, but they are so vague and improbable that I will not weary you with a recital of them.

During the centuries whilst America again lay hidden from Europe, great changes had taken place among the nations of the Eastern hemisphere. The wild tribes of this portion of our continent had evidently been subjects of great changes, too. Stronger bands of warriors and women had displaced the weaker ones; and when the Europeans again appeared on our shores, the dwarfed Esquimaux, whom the Northmen encountered, had been annihilated by a nobler race or driven toward the frozen regions of the Arctic Circle. There had evidently been great migrations from one part of the continent to the other, during which half-civilized barbarians had been expelled from fertile territories by savages, whilst once savage regions seem to have been colonized by sun-worshippers from Central and South America. They have left remains of art, in buildings and pottery, which tell of a rude civilization.

We know that in South America there existed a native empire that compared favorably with any one in the Eastern hemisphere at that time. We know that between the Rio Grandé, or Grand River, which divides our country from Mexico, to the Isthmus of Darien, there was an Empire whose rulers and people displayed many of the nobler virtues and some of the arts and sciences of civilized life, and whose laws evinced as profound respect for the great principles of morality as is to be found in the most civilized nation. We know, too, that the softening influences of that empire were beginning to spread among the ruder tribes of the North, when Cortez and his followers—civilized ruffians from Spain—overturned that empire. They extinguished the light that was beginning to shine in the darker regions within the present domain of our Republic. With professed Christian zeal they barred the way to the advance of a civilization more practically Christian than that which the Spanish conquerors displayed

Whence came these dusky inhabitants of our land? is an unanswered and seemingly unanswerable question. Out of isolated facts—facts like the following—bold theories have been formed. Remains of fortifications like those of ancient European nations have been discovered. An idol, composed of clay and gypsum, representing a man without arms, resembling one found in Southern Russia, was dug up near Nashville, in Tennessee. A

Roman coin was found in Missouri; a Persian coin in Ohio; a bit of silver in the Genesee country, New York, with the year of our Lord 600 engraved on it; split wood and ashes, thirty feet below the surface of the earth, at Fredonia, New York; a silver cup, finely gilded, within an ancient mound near Marietta, Ohio, and in a tomb near Montevideo, in South America, two ancient swords, a helmet and shield, with Greek inscriptions upon them, showing that they were made in the time of Alexander the Great, more than three hundred years before Christ. The mysterious mounds found in various parts of our country have made strange revelations: such as weapons and utensils of copper; catacombs with mummies; ornaments of silver, brass, and copper; stones with Hebrew inscriptions; traces of iron utensils wholly reduced to dust; mirrors of isinglass and glazed pottery, and other evidences of the existence of a race here far more civilized than the tribes found by Europeans. And nearly all of these modern Indian nations have traditions respecting their origin. Some of them told of a partial or universal deluge; and some said their particular progenitor came in a bark canoe after that terrible event.

These facts have been the texts of long argumentative discourses. One theorist tells you that they came originally from Phonecia; another that they are Egyptians, Hindoos or Chinese; while others insist with great pertinacity that they are the descendants of the ten "Lost Tribes of Israel," who made their way from Asia to our Continent, over the Aleutian Islands or across Behring's Straits. Others dismiss the question with the positive assertion that they are the products of this continent alone—that they originated here as did the plants and trees. "The land you sleep on is ours," said a Micmac chief, in Nova Scotia, to Colonel Cornwallis, of the British army, a century and a quarter ago. "*We sprung out of the Earth like the trees, the grass and the flowers.*" Who knows? Ethnology, history, revelation and reason are all dumb before the questioner concerning these mysteries. The pious and superstitious parson, Cotton Mather, of Boston, who wrote more than one hundred and fifty years ago, took a short method of solving the question by shrewdly guessing that "the Devil [whom he called the old usurping landlord of America] decoyed these miserable salvages hither, in hopes that the Gospel of our Lord Jesus Christ would never come here to destroy or disturb his absolute empire over them." But the mounds and their contents, the relics and the theories have not solved the great question. The mounds scattered all over the continent—huge interrogation points of deep significance—and the mound-builders are yet the subjects of sharp speculation; and we might show wisdom if we should follow the example of Parson

Mather, who, when the delusion of witchcraft had made him ridiculous, declared that the subject was "too deep for ordinary comprehension," and referred its decision "to the day of judgment." We can afford to dwell, without further inquiry for the present, in the dim light reflected by Bryant's soliloquy:

> "And did the dust
> Of these fair solitudes once stir with life
> And burn with passion? Let the mighty mounds
> That overlook the rivers, or that rise
> In the dim forests, crowded with old oaks,
> Answer. A race that long has passed away
> Built them; a disciplined and populous race
> Heaped with long toil the earth, while yet the Greek
> Was hewing the Pentelicus to forms
> Of symmetry, and rearing on its rock
> The glittering Parthenon."

CHAPTER II.

INDIAN POPULATION AT THE BEGINNING OF THE SIXTEENTH CENTURY—THEIR LANGUAGE, RELIGION, GOVERNMENT, RECORDS, LITERATURE, DOMESTIC AND MILITARY HABITS, AND THEIR PHYSICAL AND MENTAL CHARACTERISTICS—THE IROQUOIS CONFEDERACY—THEIR CIVIL AND MILITARY GOVERNMENT—THE FIVE NATIONS—THE STORY OF HI-A-WAT-HA—ORIGIN OF THE CONFEDERACY—GEOGRAPHICAL DISTRIBUTION OF THE INDIANS.

THE number of human inhabitants of the entire continent of America, from the Frozen Ocean to Cape Horn, did not exceed five million, it is supposed, when Columbus sailed from Spain; and that within the present domain of our Republic—THE UNITED STATES OF AMERICA—there were only a little more than one million souls, or one to each three and a half square miles of territory. The people of the latter region seemed to have all come from the same original stock, excepting some on the borders of the Gulf of Mexico. They had high cheek bones and broad faces; heavy dark eyes; jet black hair, lank and incapable of curling because of its peculiar structure; and skins of a dull copper color. They spoke more than a hundred dialects, or peculiar forms of expressing language, all springing, evidently, from a common root. They were all taciturn or habitually silent, in society, and could endure great mental or physical suffering without visible emotion. Their plan of government was simple, and there were very few transgressors of the law. Their theology or religious system was as simple as their civil government. They believed in a great GOOD SPIRIT and a great EVIL SPIRIT, each supreme in its sphere; and they deified, or made God, the sun, moon, stars, meteors, fire, water, thunder, wind, and everything else which seemed to be superior to themselves. There were no unbelievers among them. They had no written language, excepting rude picture-writings made on rocks, barks of trees or the dried hides of beasts. Their historical records were made upon the memory from parent to child, as were their legends, and so transmitted from one generation to another. Their dwellings were rude huts made of poles leaning to a common centre, and covered with bark or the skins of beasts. The men were engaged in war, hunting, and fishing, whilst the women did all of the domestic drudgery. The women also bore all burdens during long journeys; put up the tents, or the wigwams, as their dwellings were called; prepared the food and clothing; wove mats for beds, and planted, cultivated, and gathered the scanty crops of corn, beans, peas, potatoes, melons and tobacco, wherever these products were raised. In winter the skins of wild beasts formed the clothing of these rude people, and in summer the men wore only a wrapper around the loins. They sometimes tattooed themselves, that is, pricked the skin in lines to form shapes of objects, and making them permanent by coloring matter put in the punctures; and they were generally ornamented with the claws of bears, the pearly parts of shells, and the plumage of birds. Their money

THE DWELLINGS OF INDIANS.

consisted of little tubes made of shells, fastened upon belts or strung on little thongs of deers' hide, which was called *wampum*. These collections were used in traffic, in treaties, and in giving tokens of friendship. Their weapons of war were bows and arrows, tomahawks or hatchets, war-clubs, and scalping knives. Some wore shields of bark, and also corselets of hides, for protection.

The civil governor of a tribe or nation was called a Sachem; the military leader was called a Chief. They were naturally proud and haughty, and had great respect for personal dignity and honor. It was offensive to a Chief or Sachem to ask him his name, because it implied that he was unknown. Red Jacket, the great leader of the Seneca nation, was once asked his name, in court, in compliance with the legal form. He was very indignant, and replied: "Look at the papers which the white people keep most carefully"—(land cession treaties)—"they will tell you who I am."

Elevated as were their conceptions of the dignity of the men, they utterly degraded the women to the condition of abject slaves. They made them beasts of burden and mere objects of convenience. They were never allowed to join in the amusements of the men, but were permitted to sit, with their children, as spectators around the fires at war-dances or the horrid orgies after a victory. The husband had absolute control of the body and destiny of the wife, even to the taking of her life; and so far was she removed from a position of equality with the opposite sex, that there was no society for the cultivation of those refining qualities of woman which give the chief beauty and charm to civilized communities.

The mental characteristics, or the workings of the mind of the Indian, was the same everywhere. He subjected his body to the control of his will. He was schooled in taciturnity—taught to be a silent man—because it was necessary in a society where the sharp weapon was the quick response to an unguarded or insulting word. He was trained, too, to accept physical endurance as a virtue. Apparent insensibility to fear or pain was significant of most sturdy manhood. It was regarded as an evidence of weakness or cowardice for an Indian to allow his countenance to be changed by surprise or suffering. And so his nerves and muscles were steeled against fear or pain, and made absolute slaves to his will. An Inca or King of ancient Peru, caused some of his warriors to be instantly put to death because they had shown some surprise at the appearance of Pizarro's cavalry, the horse being a novelty and wonder to that people. "Coward!" exclaimed Pontiac, an Ottawa chief, when he saw one of his followers startled by muskets fired in the gloom of night by the English garrison at Detroit, and instantly cleaved his head with a tomahawk. "Squaw!" cried Cornstalk, the leader of the Shawnoese in the battle of Point Pleasant, when he saw one of his warriors hiding behind a clump of bushes, and immediately ordered him to be dressed in a petticoat and to carry a pappoose—an Indian baby.

The brain of the Indian seemed to be cast in a poetic mold. In his simple language—too poor to allow a profusion of words—he would express ideas in elegant and poetic forms, his figures of speech being drawn from the objects of nature around him. What he lacked in words, would be supplied by those figures. "I stand in the path," said Pontiac, haughtily, to the commander of a British force that marched into his country, signifying that he held kingly dominion over all that region, and defied the intruder's power. When Red Jacket, the Seneca chief, who became intemperate in his later years, saw all of his eleven children die one after another with consumption, he regarded the calamity as a punishment for his sin. To a lady who had known him many years before, and who, ignorant of his misfortune, enquired of his family, the old chief, with bowed head replied: "Red Jacket was once a great man, and in favor with the Great Spirit. He was a lofty pine among the smaller trees of the forest. But after years of glory he degraded himself by drinking the fire-water of the white man. The Great Spirit has looked upon him in anger, and his lightning has stripped the pine of its branches." At a council at Vincennes, over which Governor Harrison presided, Tecumtha, the great Shawnoese warrior, made a speech. When it was ended, it was observed that no seat was provided for him. An officer handed him one saying, in the foolish phraseology of talk with Indians, "Your father [meaning Harrison] requests you to be seated in this chair." "My father!" said the chief scornfully, whilst his eyes flashed with indignation. Wrapping his broad blanket around him, and assuming the most haughty attitude, he continued: "My father is the Sun, and the Earth is my mother. I will recline upon her bosom." And then he seated himself upon the ground.

Notwithstanding the Indians exhibited many of the nobler traits of human nature, they were, with a few notable exceptions, cruel savages, as a whole, throughout the entire country north of the parallel of Alabama, when the Europeans came and made permanent settlements here. Among these exceptions, the most conspicuous were the five nations who formed the Iroquois Confederacy within the domain of the present State of New York, and the dwellers in the softer climate around the shores of the Gulf of Mexico.

The Iroquois Confederacy was a remarkable fact in history. It was composed of five large families, each having the dignified title of a nation. These nations were named respectively, Mohawks, Oneidas, Onondagas, Cayugas, and Senecas. They were subdivided into smaller families or tribes, each having its symbol—coat-of-arms—such as the bear, the wolf, the eagle, the heron, the beaver, the deer, the turkey or the tortoise. They occupied a belt of country extending across the present State of New York from the Hudson River to Lake Erie, south of the Adirondack range of great hills, and north of the Kaatsbergs, or, as they are commonly called, the Catskill Mountains.

When Europeans became acquainted with the nations of this league and the form of their government, they were filled with admiration because of its wisdom and strength. They called these nations "The Romans of the New World," because they seemed to have many things in common with that ancient people, especially in military affairs. As in old Rome the soldiers were honored above all other citizens, so they were among the Iroquois; and the warriors, under their chiefs, were all-powerful in public affairs. Whatever was done in the civil councils of the separate nations, or of the confederacy, was subjected to review by the soldiery, who had the right to call councils whenever they pleased, and approve or disapprove public measures. And so careful were the civil authorities to pay deference to the warriors that general answers to questions of state policy were postponed until the opinions of the soldiers might be known. Therefore, in nearly every such council, decisions were made by unanimous consent.

As each of the confederated nations was divided into several tribes, there were thirty or forty sachems in the league. These had inferior officers under them, answering to our magistrates in towns; and so the civil power of the government was quite widely distributed. There was not a man who gained his office otherwise than by his own merits, and he held it only during good behavior. Any unworthy action was attended by dismissal from office and the penalty of public scorn. They, as well as the military leaders, accepted no salary, and gave away any perquisites of their offices in time of peace and their share of plunder in time of war. There was no bribery nor corruption in office, for they had not learned these arts of civilization. They felt themselves amply rewarded by the confidence and esteem of the people. Chosen by the voice of universal suffrage, and feeling the responsibilities which that trust imposed upon them, their deportment was as dignified as their position.

Each canton or nation was a distinct republic, entirely independent of the others in what may be termed the domestic concerns of the state; but each was bound to others of the league by ties of honor and of general interest. Each had an equal voice in the General Council or Congress of the league, and each possessed a sort of veto or prohibitory power, which was a guaranty against a central despotism. The powers and duties of the chief magistrate of the Confederacy were similar to those imposed upon the President of the United States. He had authority to "light the great Council Fire"—to assemble the General Congress—by sending a messenger to the sachem of each nation, calling him to a meeting. With his own hand he kindled a blaze around which the representatives gathered and each lighted his pipe. He had a cabinet of six councillors of state, whose powers were only advisory. In the Council, he was only the moderator or presiding officer. He had no power to control, directly, military affairs, nor interfere with the internal policy of the several states of the league. There was really no coercive or compulsory power lodged anywhere, that could act upon a state or individual, excepting that of despotic public opinion. There was a third party in the government, who exercised great influence. These were the matrons or elderly women, who had a right to sit in the councils and there exercise a negative or veto power on the subject of a declaration of war, or to propose or demand a cessation of hostilities.

Theirs was a highly conservative power. They were pre-eminently the peace-makers of the league, for their personal happiness depended upon peaceful pursuits. They modestly refrained from making speeches in the legislature, but they furnished materials for masculine orators, and so wielded a potent influence. And so it was that in that notable confederacy of barbarians, formed long before their contact with Europeans, woman was man's co-worker in legislation—a thing unheard of in civilized nations. It was a government the nearest to a pure democracy, and yet highly aristocratic—a government of the best of the people—that the world has ever seen. It had all of the essential elements of our form of government.

I have said that the soldiers of the league controlled the legislators. The military leaders, like the Sachems, derived their authority from the people, who recognized and rewarded their ability as warriors. They held the relations to the civil heads of the nations, similar to that of Roman generals to Emperors, whom they elevated to and deposed from office. The army was composed wholly of volunteers, for there was no power to conscribe men. Every able-bodied man was bound, by custom, to do military duty, and he who shirked it incurred everlasting disgrace. The ranks of the army were, therefore, always full. The war-dance and the assemblages for

AN INDIAN WAR-DANCE.

amusement were the recruiting stations, for there the veteran warriors, painted and decorated, recounted their brave deeds in wild songs, as they danced around great fires, singly or in a ring formed by clasped hands. These stirring war-songs inspired the young men with desires to emulate their example and win the honors of war. Sometimes young men—mere lads—seated among the women as spectators, inspired by these songs, would spring to their feet, and rushing out into the magic circle in a complete frenzy, would seize each other by the hand and dance and yell around the blazing pile, to the delight of the old warriors. Such was the method of "beating up for recruits" among all the barbarian nations of North America. In the perfect freedom of this voluntary system, lay the amazing strength of the league, for every servant of the state was an inspired and willing one. And so much did the people of this league reverence the inalienable rights of man, that they never made a fellow-man a serf or slave—not even their captives in war.

There is no positive proof as to the time when the Iroquois Confederacy was formed. It was probably at the beginning of the fifteenth century, or about a hundred years before Columbus crossed the Atlantic Ocean. When Europeans found it, it was powerful and aggressive. Like old Rome, the state was constantly increasing in area and population, by conquests and annexations. Had the discovery of America by Europeans been deferred a century longer, no doubt that republic would have embraced the continent; for the FIVE NATIONS, as the league was called, had already extended their conquests from the great lakes on our northern border almost to the Gulf of Mexico, and were the terror of all the other Indian tribes east and west of them. In unity was found their strength. For a time even the French in Canada, who had taught them the use of fire-arms, maintained a doubtful struggle against them. "Our wise forefathers," said one of their leading sachems to commissioners of Pennsylvania, Maryland and Virginia, in 1744, "established unity and amity among the Five Nations. This has made us formidable. This has given us great weight with our neighboring nations. We are a powerful confederacy; and by observing the same methods our wise forefathers have taken, you will acquire fresh strength and power. Therefore I counsel you, whatever may befal you, not to fall out with each other."

Like every other unlettered nation whose history is unrecorded in books, and whose origin is obscure, the Iroquois have colored their traditions of the beginning of the league with the hues of the supernatural or miraculous. Their story is only another form of the old story—older than the ages of history and as widespread as the race. It has come floating down the stream of time from Central Asia—the home of the true Hindoo—the Eden—the Paradise—the garden—which produced the root of the languages and the germs of the religion and laws of Europe and of the Caucasians of this continent. That teeming East is the mother of those historic myths in which figure, in divine grandeur, the founders of nations. Among these is *Hi-a-wat-ha*, the founder of the Iroquois Confederacy. Their traditions tell us that this personage, whom, in later years, they revered as the incarnation of wisdom, came from his serene dwelling in the skies, and took up his abode with the Onondagas, then the most favored of the Five Nations of the great Iroquois family, living within the domain of the present State of New York. The Onondagas occupied a central position, the Mohawks and Oneidas being east of them, and the Cayugas and Senecas west of them. *Hi-a-wat-ha* taught them the art of good living; the value and strength of mutual friendship and good-will, and the advantages of having fixed habitations and the cultivation of the earth. He was yet among them when a band of fierce warriors came down like an icy blast from the land north of the great lakes, slaying everything human in their path. He advised these related nations to call a council of their wise men for the purpose of forming a league for the common good, to oppose the destructive enemy. His advice was approved and immediately acted upon. The chief men of the Five Nations, followed by their women and children, gathered in great numbers on the banks of the Onondaga Lake. To the representatives of each nation was assigned a particular position in that council, with an appropriate title.

That was a notable gathering of gayly-decked savages at the dividing line between the woods and the waters. There the grave and dignified Mohawk of the east, met the fierce and fiery Seneca of the west, and all waited in silence for the presence of *Hi-a-wat-ha*, who appeared on the lake in a mysterious canoe with a beautiful and gentle maiden, his daughter. He landed on the pebbly shore, and as he and his sweet child ascended the bank, a strange sound was heard in the air—like a wind rushing by. In the far distant sky a white speck was seen, which grew larger and larger as it approached, in rapid descent, toward the spot where the great multitude stood. It assumed the shape of a monster bird. As it was evident that it was about to fall upon the council ground, the people fled in terror, all but *Hi-a-wat-ha* and his daughter. "Stand still, my child," he said, "it is cowardly to fly from any danger. The decrees of the Great Spirit may not be averted by flight." He had just ceased speaking, when the bird, an enormous white heron, with extended wings, fell upon the maiden and crushed her to the earth. Its fall was so violent, that its beak and head were buried in the ground, and the bird and the maiden both perished. *Hi-a-wat-ha*, though so suddenly and awfully bereaved, showed no signs of emotion. Not a muscle was moved by the calamity. He calmy beckoned to the warriors, who came forward and plucked the beautiful white plumes of the dead heron, and each placing one on his head, wore it as a commemorative decoration. Thenceforth, for many generations, it was the custom of the braves of the Five Nations to wear a white heron-plume on their heads when going out on the war-path, or as a national insignia and memento of the origin of the league.

On removing the body of the bird, no traces of *Hi-a-wat-ha's* daughter could be found. The disconsolate father was moody for awhile, and the

HI-A-WAT-HA AND HIS DAUGHTER.

people waited in respectful silence until he aroused himself and proceeded to the discharge of his grave duties. He placed himself at the head of the council and guided its action. He was seated on a mossy stone, and was clad in a wolf-skin mantle and a tunic of soft furs that hung from his waist. His arms and legs were bare, and without ornaments, and on his feet were rich moccasins. On his head was a cap formed of a band of soft deer-skin, covered with the small plumage of many colored birds. From this arose a stately pile of feathers of every sort, from those of the white heron and the gray eagle to the smaller ones of the golden oriole and the flaming scarlet taniger. Near him were seated the chief warriors and councillors of the tribes, who joined in the brief debates and listened with profound attention to the words of wisdom that fell from the lips of *Hi-a-wat-ha*. After listening to the discussion, he arose and addressed the people by nations, saying, as he pointed toward the heads of each:

"You (the Mohawks) who are sitting under the shadow of *The Great Tree* whose roots sink deep into the earth, and whose branches spread wide around, shall be the first nation, nearest the rising of the sun, because you are warlike and mighty.

"You (Oneidas) who recline your bodies against *The Everlasting Stone*, emblem of wisdom, that cannot be moved, shall be the second nation, because you always give wise counsel.

"You (the Onondagas) who have your habitation at the foot of *The Great Hills*, and are overshadowed by their crags, shall be the third nation, because you are all greatly gifted in speech.

"You (the Cayugas) the people who live in *The Open Country*, and possess much wisdom, shall be the fourth nation, because you understand better the art of raising corn and beans, and making houses.

"You (the Senecas) whose dwelling is in *The Dark Forest* nearer the setting sun, and whose home is everywhere, shall be the fifth nation, because of your superior cunning in hunting.

"Unite, you five nations and have one common interest, and no foe shall disturb or subdue you. You, the people, who are as the feeble bushes, and you who are a fishing people (addressing some who had come from the Delawares, and from the sea-shore), may place yourselves under our protection, and we will defend you. And you of the South and West may do the same—we will protect you. We earnestly desire the alliance and friendship of you all. Brothers, if we unite in this great bond, the Great Spirit will smile upon us, and we shall be free, prosperous and happy. But if we remain as we are we shall be subject to his frown. We shall be enslaved, ruined, perhaps annihilated. We may perish under the war-storm, and our names be no longer remembered by good men, nor repeated in the dance and song. Brothers, these are the words of *Hi-a-wat-ha*. I have said it. I am done."

The confederation was formed the next day. Then *Hi-a-wat-ha's* mission to the Iroquois was ended. He gave them more wise advice, and then announced his intention to return to his divine habitation. Whilst the multitude stood in silence and awe, he went down to the water's edge and entered his mysterious canoe. Suddenly the air was filled with delicious music, like the warbling of innumerable birds, that charmed the senses of the wondering people. Slowly the canoe and its precious burden arose in the air, higher and higher, until it was lost in the blue depths to the vision of eager eyes gazing after it until it vanished. *Hi-a-wat-ha* had returned to the region of the Blessed.

Atatarho, a chief of the Onondagas, and eminent for his wisdom and valor, was chosen President or Grand Sachem of the League. A delegation of the Mohawks were sent to offer him the honor. They found him seated in grim solitude in the dark recesses of a swamp, smoking his pipe, with drinking vessels around him made of the skulls of his enemies, as were those of the old barbarian Northmen centuries before Lief came to Vineland. The delegation could not go near his person, for he was clothed with hissing serpents, emblems of wisdom. The Mohawks stood at a distance under the branches of a tamarac, whilst their leader approached nearer and announced their errand. Atatarho arose, and with dignity accepted the office. The serpents were transformed into a mantle of bear's skin; and following the delegation, the president of the league went to the council and there declared that he would do the will of the sages and warriors of the confederated nations. From that time the Iroquois Confederacy was invincible until the white man came and, by craft and power, paralyzed its strength and finally destroyed it.

When the white man came, early in the sixteenth century, to make permanent settlements in our country, he found the dusky inhabitants, as we have observed, speaking about a hundred different dialects. But there were only eight radically distinct nations. They are known as the Algonquins, Huron-Iroquois, Cherokees, Catawbas, Uchees, Natchez, Mobilians or Floridians, and Dakotahs or Sioux. Algonquin was a name given by the French to a large collection of families north and south of the great lakes, who speaking dialects of the same language, seemed to belong to the same nation. These inhabited the territory now included in all Canada, New England, a part of New York and Pennsylvania, the States of New Jersey, Delaware, Maryland and Virginia, Eastern North Carolina above Cape Fear, a large portion of Kentucky and Tennessee, and all north and west of these States eastward of the Mississippi River. Within the folds of the Algonquin nation were the Huron-Iroquois in Canada, New York, Pennsylvania and Ohio; a few families in Southern Virginia and upper North Carolina, and the Iroquois Confederacy in the State of New York.

The Cherokees inhabited the picturesque and fertile region in the upper part of Georgia and its vicinity, where the mountain ranges that form the watershed between the Atlantic Ocean and the Mississippi River melt into the lowlands which border the Gulf of Mexico. They were called the mountaineers of the South, and were the most formidable of all the foes of the conquering Iroquois. Their neighbors on the east were the Catawbas, who dwelt upon the borders of the Yadkin and Catawba rivers on both sides of the boundary line between North and South Carolina. The Iroquois made incursions into their country, but they never brought the Catawbas under the yoke of that confederacy. The Uchees were only the remnant of a once powerful people. They were living in the beautiful land in Georgia between the sites of Augusta and Milledgeville, along the Oconee and around the head-waters of the Ogeechee and Chattahoochee. They claimed to be the descendants of a people more ancient than those around them, and they had no traditions, as all the others had, of having migrated from another country.

INDIANS SPEARING FISH.

The Natchez, who occupied a territory east of the Mississippi stretching north-eastward from the site of the City of Natchez, along the borders of the Pearl River to the head-waters of the Chickasahaw River, claimed to be an older nation than the Uchees. Like the other Indians of the Gulf region, they were fire and sun worshippers, and made sacrifices to the great luminary. The Mobilians or Floridians occupied a very large territory that bordered on the Gulf of Mexico. It stretched along the Atlantic coast from the mouth of the Cape Fear River to the extremity of the Florida peninsula, and westward to the Mississippi River. They also held jurisdiction up that stream to the mouth of the Ohio River. Their domain included the States of Florida, Alabama and Mississippi, all of Georgia not occupied by the Cherokees and Uchees, and portions of South Carolina, Tennessee and Kentucky. The nation was divided into three confederacies, known respectively as the Creek, Choctaw and Chickasaw.

Under the general title of Dakotas or Sioux, have been grouped a vast number of tribes west of the Mississippi River and the great lakes, with whom the earlier French explorers came in contact. They spoke, apparently, dialects of the same language, and were regarded as one nation. They inhabited the vast domain stretching northward from the Arkansas River to the western tributaries of Lake Winnepeg, and westward along that line to the eastern slopes of the Rocky Mountains. These have been arranged in four classes, namely, the Winnebagoes, the Assinniboins or Sioux proper, the Minetarees and the Southern Sioux.

Such was the general geographical distribution of the Indians when European settlements were begun among them. They were not stationary residents of a fixed domain; nor, with the exception of the Iroquois Confederacy, was there the semblance of a national government amongst them. They had wandered for centuries, and some of them had evidently traversed the whole continent. Yet they were not a nomadic race, or a people seeking pasture for cattle, living in tents, and having no fixed home for a month at a time. Neither were they agriculturists, steadily cultivating the soil. The horse, cow, sheep and swine were unknown to them. They had never tamed the buffalo nor the stately elk for labor or food; nor had they sheared a fleece from the great-horned Rocky Mountain sheep. Like primitive man, the Indian was a hunter and fisher, and depended for his sustenance chiefly upon the chase and the hook.

CHAPTER III.

THE INDIANS OF THE GULF REGION—THEIR RELIGIOUS CEREMONIES AS SUN-WORSHIPPERS—THEIR DOMESTIC HABITS, COSTUMES, DWELLINGS AND PRODUCTIONS—THEIR MILITARY DEFENCES AND WAR-LIKE OPERATIONS—THEIR MARRIAGE AND FUNERAL CEREMONIES—THE FATE OF THE INDIANS—EUROPEAN SOCIETY IN THE FIFTEENTH CENTURY—THEORIES RESPECTING THE SHAPE OF THE EARTH—DISCOVERIES BY THE PORTUGUESE—POPULAR TRADITIONS CONCERNING THE ATLANTIC OCEAN—CHRISTOPHER COLUMBUS: HIS THEORIES AND ASPIRATIONS—HIS FAMILY RELATIONS AND EARLY VOYAGES—HIS EFFORTS TO OBTAIN MEANS FOR MAKING A VOYAGE OF DISCOVERY—CONDUCT OF THE KING OF PORTUGAL.

IN the warmer region around the Gulf of Mexico dwelt a people having the same general hue of skin, form of features and texture of hair as those of the more northern countries. They were either the descendants of the Central or South Americans, or their habits of life had been modified by contact with the half civilized people of those countries. They were an athletic and vigorous race. The men were well proportioned, active and graceful in all their movements. The women were smaller, exquisitely formed, and some of them were very beautiful.

In the colder weather of the winter, the common men wore a mantle made of a sort of cloth manufactured of the soft inner bark of trees, interwoven with hemp or a species of flax. This was thrown gracefully over the shoulder, leaving the right arm exposed. Around the loins was a very short tunic, extending half way down the thighs, or only a wrapper. The richer and nobler sort of men wore beautiful mantles made of feathers of every hue, exquisitely arranged, or the skins of fur-bearing animals, with dressed deer-skin tunics wrought in colors, and moccasins and buskins of the same materials. The women of the better sort, at the cooler season, wore a garment of cloth or feathers or furs wrought like the mantles of the men. It was wrapped more closely around the body at the waist, and fell gracefully almost to the knee. The rest of the form was left bare excepting in the coldest weather, when they wore short mantles that fell from the neck to the hips. Their heads were always uncovered, but the men wore a skull-cap of cloth ornamented with beautiful sea-shells, the claws of beasts, or strings of pearls. It is related that a queen, on the banks of the Savannah River, took from her neck a magnificent string of pearls and twined it around that of De Soto, the early Spanish discoverer of the region. Sometimes they wore pearl pendants in their ears. In summer both sexes went without clothing, excepting a drapery of what is now known in that region as Spanish moss, gathered from the trees. This was fastened at the waist, and fell in graceful negligence to the thighs. The chiefs, and prophets, and other principal men, and their wives, painted their breasts and the front part of their bodies, with stripes of white, yellow and red; and some practiced a kind of tattooing. Sometimes the fops of this class might be seen promenading, at evening, in beautiful mantles of deer-skins and of the marten, which trailed on the ground, or were held by attendants; and if they were warriors, on their heads might be seen lofty plumes of the eagle and the flamingo.

SOUTHERN INDIANS.

The houses of the chiefs, spacious and airy, stood upon large mounds, natural or artificial, that were ascended by steps of wood or earth. These dwellings were built of timber, sometimes in the form of a great pavilion with a broad piazza around it, furnished with benches. They were covered with the leaves of the palmetto, or thatched with straw; and sometimes they were roofed with reeds after the manner of tiles. Their winter houses were daubed inside and out with clay.

The weapons of the Floridians for hunting and war were strong bows and arrows, and javelins. Their arrows were made of fine dried cane, tipped with buck-horn and pointed with flint, hard wood, or fish bones. They were carried in a quiver made of the skin of the fawn, cased at bottom with the hide of the bear or the alligator, and slung by a thong of deer's skin so as to rest on the hip. The warriors all wore shields in battle, composed of wood, split cane, or the hide of the alligator and buffalo. On the left arm they wore a small shield of bark to protect it from the rebound of the bow-string. They also had short swords made of hard wood. When a chief was about to declare war, he sent a party at night toward the town of the

DECLARATION OF WAR BY SOUTHERN INDIANS.

enemy, to stick arrows in the ground at the cross-paths or other conspicuous places near it. From these arrows waved long locks of human hair as tokens of scalping. Then he would assemble his painted warriors, and after some wild ceremonies, would turn reverentially toward the sun, with a wooden javelin in his hand, and invoking the aid of the great God of Fire, he would take a vessel of water, and sprinkle it around, saying: "Thus may you do with the blood of your enemies." Raising another vessel of water, he would pour it upon the fire which had been kindled, and as it was extinguished he would say: "Thus may you destroy your enemies and bring home their scalps." When the battle was over, the victors cruelly mutilated the bodies of their captives. Carrying their dissevered limbs and their scalps upon spear-points, into the public square, they were there placed on poles, and the people celebrated the triumph by dancing around these trophies and singing wild songs of joy. The widows of those lost in battle gathered around the chief with piteous cries, praying him to avenge the deaths of their loved ones, asking him for an allowance during their widowhood and permission to marry again as soon as the law would allow. Then they visited the burial places of their husbands, and cutting off their long tresses, strewed them over the graves. When their hair had grown to its usual length they were ready to marry again.

Hunting, fishing and the cultivation of the rich land were the chief employments of these people. The cotton plant was unknown to them, but hemp and flax were quite abundant. The women assisted the men in the fields, in the cultivation of corn, beans, peas, squashes, and pumpkins, which yielded enormous returns for the little labor bestowed. These productions were stored in granaries made of stone and earth and covered with mats, for winter use; also preserved meats. They obtained salt by evaporation, and the women were generally good cooks of the simple food. They made and used pottery for kitchen service, some of it skillfully constructed and quite beautiful. They were skillful artisans, as evinced by their arms, houses, beautiful barges and canoes, and ornaments. They had fortifications with moats or ditches; and walled towns; and some of their temples were grand, imposing and beautiful. Their roofs were steep and covered with mats of split cane, interwoven so compactly that they resembled the rush carpeting of the Moors. At the entrances to some of the temples, and in niches in the interior, were well-wrought wooden statues, some of them of persons who were entombed in the sacred place. Between these were shields of various sizes, made of strongly woven reeds adorned with pearls and colored tassels. Rich offerings of pearls and deer-skins, and the furs of martens and other animals were seen in these temples in great profusion, all dedicated to the Sun, the great God whom they worshipped.

The theology or religious system of these people was very simple. They regarded the Sun as the Supreme Deity, and venerated the moon and certain brilliant stars. In all their invocations of blessings upon their chiefs or upon themselves, the Sun was appealed to, as we appeal to God. "May the Sun guard you!" "May the Sun be with you!" were usual forms of invocation. At the beginning of March the men of a community selected the skin of the largest deer, with the heads and legs attached, which they filled with a variety of fruit and grain. It was served up, and appeared like the live creature in form. Its horns were garlanded with fruits and early spring flowers. Then the effigy was carried in a procession of all the inhabitants, to a plain, and placed at the top of a high post. There, at the moment when the sun appeared upon the eastern horizon, the people all fell upon their knees, with their faces toward the rising luminary, and implored the god of day to grant them, the ensuing season, an abundance of fruit and grain as good as those which they then offered.

The funeral ceremonies of these people, especially those on the death of a chief or prophet, were very peculiar. The body underwent a sort of embalming, when it was placed in the ground in a sitting posture by the nearest relatives of the deceased. Then food and money were placed by its side, and a conical mound of earth was piled over it, at the foot of which was

A CEREMONIAL INVOCATION.

made a paleing of arrows stuck in the ground. Around this tomb the people gathered in great numbers, some standing, some sitting, and all howling. This ceremony continued three days and nights, after which, for a long time, chosen women visited the tomb three times a day, morning, noon and night. The chief, whilst he was alive, was held in the greatest veneration, for, like the Assyrian kings, he was both monarch and pontiff—the chief magistrate and the high priest. A cruel sacrifice was made to him of every first-born male child, a custom learned from the Central Americans. It symbolized the devotion and surrender of the entire strength of the nation to the chief. Sitting upon a bench on one side of a large circle, a block two feet in height was placed before him. The child was brought by a dancing-girl and placed upon the block, and the young mother, weeping in agony, was compelled to stand near it, to make the offering. A prophet dashed out its brains, and then a group of girls danced around the altar of sacrifice, singing songs.

When a young chief desired to marry, he would send a few of his principal men to select from the daughters of the first families one of the youngest and most beautiful of the marriageable ones. The chosen bride was then painted and decorated in the most tasteful manner, preparatory to the nuptials. Brilliant colors, and costly pearls and shells, adorned her person. She was covered from her waist almost to her knees with a beautiful tunic of rich feathers. Then she was placed in a sedan chair, the top of which was an arch of green boughs festooned and garlanded with flowers. In that state she was conveyed to the presence of her future lord on the shoulders of six noblemen who were preceded by musicians and two men bearing magnificent feather fans, and followed by dancing-girls and the immediate relatives of the bride. When arrived at the residence of the chief, she was received by the lords in waiting, who conducted her to a seat by the side of her husband, on an elevated dais, where great pomp and ceremony were displayed by those in attendance. The bride and groom were constantly fanned by beautiful maidens, if the weather was warm; and they were regaled with the unfermented juice of the grape, in its season, or with a kind of sherbert made of orange juice, at other times. At near the sunsetting the chief and his young wife walked out into an open field, followed by all the people, and at the last parting ray of the luminary, they prostrated themselves toward the west and invoked the blessings of the Sun upon themselves and their children. From that moment until the stars appeared the people indulged in music and dancing—the music of the reed and a sort of tambourine and the dancing of young men and maidens—when the chief and his bride retired to their dwelling, there, with friends, to partake of a marriage-feast by the light of lamps.

Such is an outline picture of the people with whom the Spaniards first came in contact on the continent after the discoveries of Columbus and his cotemporaries. These, with the Iroquois Confederacy, are the two notable exceptions spoken of, to the general character and habits of the dusky nations who then inhabited North America. We now have a tolerably correct impression of these barbarian and savage communities whose history, down to the present time, forms an important part of that of our Republic. Some of them have gone up in the social scale, and others have gone down: some of them have disappeared, and other tribes have been discovered. All are gradually fading away from the earth; and the time cannot be far distant when the last of the dusky race may sit on the verge of the Pacific Ocean, with his face toward the setting sun, and chant the death-song of his people, saying:

"We, the rightful lords of yore,
Are the rightful lords no more.
Like the silver mists we fail;
Like the red leaves in the gale—
Fail like shadows when the dawning
Waves the bright flag of the morning."

CARRYING THE BETROTHED TO THE CACIQUE.

But they will leave behind them myriads of memories of their existence here, in their beautiful and significant names of our mountains and valleys, our lakes and rivers, our states, counties, villages and cities. We may say to our people,

"That, mid the forests where they warr'd,
There rings no hunter's shout;
But their name is on your waters—
Ye may not wash it out."

At this point in our story, the scene shifts, as in a dissolving view, to another continent, and presently appears the grand procession of discoverers who opened the way to settlements in this new-found land.

We have remarked that from the period of the visits of the Northmen to Vineland (America) until Columbus crossed the Atlantic Ocean, great changes had taken place in Europe. The empire of the Franks, founded by Charlemagne, had been succeeded by that of the more progressive Germans, in the mastery of Europe, with Otho the Great as the initial Emperor. The Crusades had broken up the inertia or stagnation of European society. They had unbarred the gates of the East, and let in a flood of light from the sources of science and philosophy. The Northmen or Normans had taken possession of some of the fairest regions of France (Normandy), and had invaded, conquered, and refined England. The feudal system—a system in which lands are held by a few nobles who farm them out as a privilege secured by military service—had given way to an established political system in the form of monarchies or powerful republics. Commercial cities were gathering and distributing the products of industry and flecking the seas with white sails, proving that the arts of peace are far more productive of happiness than the pursuit of war. Over all Europe, from the Carpathian mountains to the sea, and from the Mediterranean to the Baltic, there was wonderful intellectual, moral and physical activity at the middle of the fifteenth century. Trade had linked various peoples in bonds of mutual interest and sympathy, and Europe, with the birth of the printing-press at that time, was prepared to enter upon that new and bright era of scientific investigation and maritime discovery which speedily appeared. When Lief came to America, the gloom of the dark ages was most intense—it was the world's midnight. When at near the close of the fifteenth century Columbus crossed the Atlantic, the faint gleam was seen of the dawn of that glorious day in the history of civilization, whose sunrise was heralded by the bold assertion that man had an inalienable right to the free exercise of his reason in faith and practice, whether in religion, politics, or morality.

Early in the fifteenth century, commerce had stimulated maritime adventure which led to maritime discoveries. Its most wonderful activity was seen in the Mediterranean and Adriatic seas. For the control of this commerce, Genoa on the Mediterranean and Venice on the Adriatic, both in Italy, were powerful and zealous rivals. The commerce of India was very profitable, and for the monopoly of it, these rivals fiercely contended through diplomacy and arms. That commerce found its chief communications with Genoa by way of the Indus, the Oxus, and the Caspian and Black Seas. It found its chief communications with Venice by way of the Persian Gulf, the river Euphrates and the Red Sea to Syrian and Egyptian ports. To these and the ports of the Black Sea the Italian vessels resorted for the silks, and spices, and other rich commodities of the Orient.

In the sharp contests of these rival republics for commercial supremacy, the Venetians finally outgeneraled the Genoese. They acquired by diplomacy and business activity such influence over the ports of the Black Sea and the Levant, that the Genoese saw ruin before them; and they began to look in other directions for relief and continued prosperity. With the revival of learning which the Crusades (or the wars of Christians for the rescue of the Holy Sepulchre of Jesus, at Jerusalem, from the hands of the Turks) had been chiefly instrumental in producing, came into Europe a knowledge of the theories and demonstrations of the Arabian astronomers, concerning the globular form of the earth. Intelligent mariners and others had become satisfied that it was globular; and the idea was finally impressed as truth upon the minds of the Genoese merchants, whilst the clergy vehemently opposed it. Reason and Faith came into collision. Reason prevailed, and the Genoese merchants were willing to allow the navigators of their ships to sail westward in quest of India.

Meanwhile the merchants of Western Europe, who were wholly excluded from direct participation in the commerce of the East through the Mediterranean by the jealous Italians, were seeking other channels of communication with India. In this enterprise they had the powerful aid of Prince Henry, son of John the First, King of Portugal and the English princess Philippa of Lancaster, sister of King Henry the Fourth of England. Whilst Prince Henry was with his father on an expedition into Africa, he received much information from the Moors concerning the coast of Guinea and other parts that were then unknown to Europeans. He believed that important discoveries might be made by navigating along the western coast of that continent, and on his return home the idea absorbed his whole attention. He retired from court, and at a beautiful country seat near Cape St. Vincent, in full view of the ocean, he drew around him men of science and learning. Being a studious and profound mathematician himself, he had become master of all the astronomy then known to the Spaniards. With these scientific men and scholars, he studied every branch of learning connected with maritime art, and they became satisfied, from ancient chronicles and fair induction, that Africa was circumnavigable—that India might be reached by going around the southern shores of that continent. This idea was contrary to the assertions of Ptolemy, the standard geographer at that time, and of many learned men; but Prince Henry adhered to his belief in the face of threats of the priests and the sneers of learned professors.

Wild tales were believed of dreadful reefs and stormy headlands stretching far out at sea, and of a fiery climate at the equator which no living thing, not even whales in the depth of the ocean, could pass because of the great heat. It was believed that the waves rolled in boiling water upon the fiery sands of the coasts, and that whoever should pass beyond Cape Bajador would never return. Against every species of opposition Prince Henry persevered. His navigators scattered all these fallacies and tales to the winds by doubling Cape Bajador and penetrating the tropical regions. At length, in the year 1497, Vasquez de Gama, a Portuguese mariner who had been in Prince Henry's service in his youth, passed around the Cape of Good Hope (which he so named), with an Arabian chart directing his course, and crossing the Indian Ocean landed in India at Calcutta. Africa was circumnavigated, and a new way was opened to India by the ocean pathway of Pharaoh Necho. Prince Henry had then been dead twenty-four years. He saw the promises of this achievement from afar, but he did not live to enjoy this full triumph of reason. But a greater triumph had lately been achieved than when De Gama passed the Cape of Good Hope.

Just at the evening twilight of a beautiful day in October, 1485, a man about fifty years of age (tall, well-formed, and muscular; long visaged; a face of fair complexion, a little freckled and usually ruddy, but now pale and careworn in expression; an aquiline nose, rather high cheek bones, eyes a light-gray; his hair thin and silvery, and his whole demeanor elevated and dignified), might have been seen standing at the gate of the Franciscan Convent near Palos, in Spain, asking for a little bread and water for his pale-faced, motherless child, whom he was leading by the hand. It was CHRISTOPHER COLUMBUS, then in extreme poverty, making his way, with his boy Diego, on foot for the Spanish Court. While he lay sick near Belem, a mysterious voice had said to him in a dream: "God will cause thy name to be wonderfully resounded through the earth, and will give thee the keys of the gates of the ocean which are closed with strong chains." It was a prophecy of the imagination—a sequence of intense thought and weary study on the subject. To the mind of Columbus it had all the reality of a revelation from God.

Columbus was the son of a wool-comber in Genoa, where he was born about the year 1435. Like other boys with busy fancies in that maritime city, he showed a fondness for the sea at an early age, and his father, though straitened in means, sent him, for a short time, to the University of Pavia to study the sciences which might fit him to be a navigator. It was an age of rapid intellectual development. Learning was leaving the monasteries to take up its abode with the laity. Geographical discoveries had created an intense longing for geographical knowledge, and the writings of Pliny, Strabo and others, which the newly-discovered art of printing soon multiplied, were read with avidity.

Columbus became a passionate disciple of geographical teachers. He made his first voyage when he was only fourteen years of age. As his practical knowledge deepened with experience, and wonderful tales of mariners concerning mysterious lands seen in the far-off Atlantic fell upon his ears, his soul burned with an intense desire to penetrate the unknown waste of waters. There was then a popular tradition that there was a very large island in the Atlantic called Antilla, mentioned by Aristotle, which Carthagenian mariners had visited. There was also a tradition of another island, on which St. Brandon, a Scotch priest, landed in the sixth century, and found magnificent cities. Still another spoke of the Island of Seven Cities, on which seven Spanish bishops, who fled from Spain with an immense number of followers, on the invasion of the Moors, had settled and founded seven grand cities. Even the learned geographer, Martin Behm, whom the King of Portugal employed, placed these islands on a globe which he constructed as being contiguous to the eastern coast of Asia. And with the revival of letters, came from Greece the story of Atlantis, which Plato had learned from the Egyptians and told to his countrymen—a story which gave an account of an immense island in the Atlantic, in early times, larger than Asia and Africa

COLUMBUS AND HIS SON AT THE CONVENT GATE.

together, full of inhabitants, great cities and mighty kingdoms, which, by tremendous earthquakes, had been shaken from their foundations and swallowed by the sea. These traditions, the stories of the people of the Canary Islands concerning land frequently seen westward of them (a mirage?) and scores of other marvelous tales, fired the imagination of Columbus, and he conceived the grand design of attempting the discovery of unknown lands in the West.

Finding very little encouragement in his native city, and Prince Henry of Portugal being then engaged in his explorations of the western coast of Africa, Columbus went to Lisbon. He arrived there about the year 1470, when he was in the prime of his young manhood. There he was a strict attendant at religious services in the chapel of the Convent of All Saints. In that convent several ladies of rank boarded or resided. Among these was Doña Felipa, daughter of Bartolomeo de Perestrello, an Italian cavalier then lately dead, who had been one of Prince Henry's most noted navigators. He had discovered, colonized and governed the island of Porto Santo, one of the Madeiras. Columbus and Doña Felipa became acquainted. The acquaintance ripened into love and resulted in marriage.

Columbus and his bride resided with her mother in Porto Santo. Madame Perestrello placed in the hands of her son-in-law the maps, charts, journals and memoranda of her late husband. They opened new fields for the contemplation of the navigator, and inspired him with an irrepressible desire for attempting discoveries in the West. These desires were stimulated by facts that were given him by Pedro Correo, an eminent navigator, who had married a sister of the wife of Columbus. He told him of timber handsomely carved, and of immense canes such as it was said grew in India, that had been found floating on the sea, from the westward; also of the bodies of two men which had been cast ashore on one of the islands of the Azores by a westerly gale, whose faces were large and their skins a copper color. These things confirmed Columbus in a budding belief that he might reach India by sailing westward, and he formed plans accordingly. These he communicated to the eminent Toscanelli, of Florence, who wrote to him an encouraging letter, and sent him a map projected partly by Ptolemy and partly from descriptions of Marco Polo, a Venetian, who made an overland journey to China late in the thirteenth century, and was in the public employment of the Great Khan or Emperor of Tartary. With this map before him Columbus studied the narrative of Polo, and was impressed with the belief that by sailing westward he would find the rich country of Cathay described by that traveller (now known to be China) and the great island of Zipangi, supposed to be Japan. These were the subjects of his dreams, whilst cruising among the islands in American waters, many years afterward.

Columbus made voyages in the service of the Portuguese; and in 1477 he sailed to Iceland and beyond. There he doubtless heard the traditions concerning the voyages of the sons of Eric the Red, or listened to rehearsals of the sagas in which they were recorded. On his return he was filled with zeal for undertaking western discoveries. But comparative poverty was his portion. He was not able to fit out a ship, so he appealed to the King of Portugal for assistance. That monarch was too much engrossed in a war with Spain to listen to him. He waited patiently until his successor, the young John the Second, ascended the throne. John was endowed with the spirit of his great uncle, Prince Henry, and listened to Columbus gladly. The scheme of the navigator was referred to a junta composed of two eminent cosmographers or describers of the universe, and a learned bishop. They decided that his project was extravagant and visionary.

The king was not satisfied. He called a council of learned men, who also decided against the project. Still the king was not satisfied; when the bishop (who was his confessor) proposed to him a mean stratagem. It was that he should get from Columbus his plans, charts, proposed directions for sailing and all other necessary information, under the pretext that he cherished his propositions. Then he was to send a caravel (a small three-masted vessel) to the Cape de Verd islands on the pretext of carrying provisions there, with instructions to go as far westward as possible, to ascertain if there were any foundation for the navigator's theory. This was to secure advantages to the state without committing it to what might turn out to be a mere chimera. The king permitted himself to follow the advice of the bishop. The cowardly crew of the caravel did not go far, before they were frightened back by the great waves. Columbus discovered the infamous trick to defraud him of the honors of such a discovery, and with lofty pride he scorned all offers of the monarch to renew the negotiations. His wife was now dead. She had borne him a son, whom they had named Diego. The domestic ties which bound him to Portugal were broken, and turning his back upon the faithless king and priest, he took his boy and secretly departed from Lisbon late in the year 1484. Whither he went then nobody certainly knows. He first reappears in history in the south of Spain, standing, in the twilight of a beautiful October day, at the door of the Franciscan monastery near Palos, asking for a little bread and water for his famishing boy.

CHAPTER IV.

COLUMBUS AT THE CONVENT OF DE RABIDA—ASKS AID OF THE SOVEREIGNS OF SPAIN—THE SPANISH MONARCHY AT THAT TIME—COLUMBUS KEPT IN SUSPENSE—THE COUNCIL AT SALAMANCA—DELAYS AND DISAPPOINTMENTS—QUEEN ISABELLA RESOLVES TO FIT OUT VESSELS FOR COLUMBUS—HE IS APPOINTED ADMIRAL AND SAILS FOR PALOS—THE VOYAGE WESTWARD—DISCOVERS AN ISLAND SUPPOSED TO BE A PART OF THE EAST INDIES—LANDS, TAKES POSSESSION, AND CALLS THE NATIVE INHABITANTS INDIANS.

IT is supposed by some that Columbus, after leaving Portugal, applied for aid to the Republic of Genoa. If he did, he was unsuccessful; and so we find him at the gate of the convent near Palos, in Andalusia, which was dedicated to Santa Maria de Rabida. Whilst the porter was getting refreshments for his boy, the prior of the convent, Friar Juan Perez de Marchena, happening to pass by, was attracted by the dignified aspect of the stranger. He soon learned that he was on his way to the neighboring town, Huelva, to seek for his brother-in-law, probably Pedro Correo, already mentioned. He also learned, from a brief conversation, that the stranger was an extraordinary man, and he invited Columbus to remain as his guest. With increasing wonder and admiration he heard the lips of the navigator unfold his theories, his plans and his hopes. That such a man should stand a beggar at his convent gate was a marvel to Father Marchena.

The friar was learned in geographical science. Able, therefore, to comprehend the grandeur of the views of Columbus, he was deeply impressed with the wisdom of the navigator, which seemed to him like inspiration. Distrusting his own judgment, he sent for Garcia Fernandez, a scientific friend in Palos, to come and converse with his guest; and within the quiet cloisters of La Rabida, the project of Columbus received the most profound respect, such as powerful courts and learned philosophers in council had not deigned to bestow. There he was brought in contact with old and eminent navigators of Palos, whose stories of the sea confirmed his faith in his theory. Marchena, impressed with the same faith, and the importance to Spain of a successful result of an enterprise like that proposed by Columbus, not only offered to give him a favorable introduction to the court, but he also offered to take his son Diego into the convent, and there educate him.

It was now one of the most remarkable and brilliant periods in the history of the Spanish monarchy. Ferdinand, King of Arragon, and Isabella, Queen of Castile and Leon, had been joined in marriage. Their kingdoms were united, and formed a strong empire. So was consolidated the Christian power of the Spanish Peninsula, and gave a prophecy of a speedy conquest of the Moors who were confined to Grenada, the kingdom which they had set up on Spanish soil more than two hundred years before. To effect that conquest, the efforts of united Spain were now directed. The two monarchs were one in love, respect, interest, views and aims, and were happily united in their councils for the good of the realm, yet they ruled as separate sovereigns, each having an independent council, and sometimes holding court and exercising sovereignty at widely separate points at the same time. They were wise in council and brave in action. Sometimes they were both in the field at the head of troops in their warfare with the Moors; and the armor worn by the queen on these occasions may be seen in the royal arsenal at Madrid. The monarchs were a unit, however, in the general administration of the consolidated kingdoms. All acts of sovereignty were executed in the names of both; public documents were signed by both; their profiles were stamped together on the national coins, and the royal seal displayed the united arms of Castile and Arragon. They were both extremely religious and were warmly attached to the Church of Rome, then at the height of its temporal power, whose head claimed to be "King of Kings."

It was an inauspicious time for Columbus to lay his projects before the monarchs. The court was moving from place to place, and was continually surrounded by the din and pageantry of war. So the navigator remained quietly at La Rabida, the guest of Father Marchena, until the spring of 1486, when the court had arrived at the ancient city of Cordova, where the troops had assembled for a vigorous spring campaign against the common enemy. To that old city, and to the court of the young sovereigns, Columbus repaired, bearing a letter from Marchena to the friar's intimate friend, Fernando de Talevera, prior of the monastery of Prado and confessor to the queen. He was a man high in the royal confidence, and possessed great weight in public affairs. With bright hopes Columbus presented the letter. The prior read it carefully, listened patiently to the explanations of the bearer, and coldly shaking his head in token of his doubts, bade the disappointed mariner good morning. He was not favorably impressed with the project of Columbus, and it is probable that he did not even mention it to the sovereigns.

For a long time Columbus lingered in Cordova. He went no more to the priest, but found a friend and an advocate of his theory in Quintanillo, the controller of the finances of Castile. That officer obtained for the navigator the friendly aid of Mendoza, Archbishop of Toledo and Grand Cardinal of Spain. By that important personage he found admittance to the royal presence. The sovereigns listened with wonder and deep interest whilst he unfolded his theory and gave them corroborating facts. The prior of Prado

THE QUEEN'S CONFESSOR AND COLUMBUS.

was ordered to assemble a council of astronomers and cosmographers at Salamanca to confer with the navigator. There, in the Convent of St. Stephen, they listened to his theories and his arguments. These were confuted by the books of Moses, the Psalms of David, the prophecies, the Gospels and Epistles, and by the writings of the early fathers of the Christian Church. Plain reason confounded his wild notions. "If the earth is round," said the wise men of that council, "you will be compelled to sail up a kind of mountain from Spain, which you cannot do, even with the fairest wind, and you could never get back." The Grand Cardinal of Spain intimated that the theories of Columbus were irreligious; and the astonished navigator was really in danger of being consigned to the Inquisition, which was about to be revived, as a heretic, instead of receiving aid and honor as a discoverer.

Columbus was again doomed to long delay. Disappointed, wearied, almost in despair, he humbled his just pride and wrote a letter to the King of Portugal, whose overtures he had rejected, again asking aid. That monarch invited him to Lisbon. It was now the early spring of 1488. Circumstances had just then revived his hopes of help from the Spanish monarchs, and Columbus did not go. He was attached to Cordova, for there Beatrix Enriquez had borne him a son whom he named Fernando, and who became the historian of his father. But another year passed away before he was again summoned to confer with scientific men at Seville. The war was then at its height. The clangor of arms disturbed every peaceful occupation, and the conference was not held.

Another year passed away and Columbus, wearied by the suspense, pressed for a decisive answer to his petition. Another council of wise men decided that his project was vain, and beneath the dignity of sovereigns to engage in. Not so, secretly thought the monarchs. They were unwilling to reject his suit altogether, and they sent him word that so soon as the war should be closed they would treat with him on the subject. So encouraged, Columbus went to the court at Seville, but saw little prospect of success there. He felt impelled to seek aid at other European courts, but he did not wish to leave Spain. Diego was at La Rabida, and Beatrix and his infant son Fernando were at Cordova. So he turned from the monarchs to the rich nobles of Spain. But he found no one among them willing to embark in his enterprise. The Duke of Medina Celi, to whom he applied, advised him to make another application to the Spanish monarchs, and gave him a letter to the queen.

The proud spirit of Columbus would not permit him to again wait upon the court in the character of a suppliant. He had received an invitation from the king of France to come to Paris, and he resolved to go. He went to the convent for Diego, to place him with Beatrix, at Cordova. The good father, Marchena, was touched with tenderest pity when he saw that great man, after years of weary waiting, again standing at his gate as poor, almost, as when he first stopped at that portal and asked food for his famishing boy. The friar's patriotism was also enkindled when he heard from the lips of the disappointed navigator that he was about to leave the country forever, for he wished Spain to be a sharer with Columbus in the brilliant honors which would be acquired by the great discoveries which Marchena believed he would soon make. He summoned his scientific friends of Palos to a council for consultation. Among them came Martin Alonzo Pinzon, the head of a wealthy family of navigators there. Pinzon approved the project of Columbus, and showed his faith in the theory by offering to engage in a voyage of discovery, with his person and his purse, and to pay the expenses of another application to the court. Columbus was willing to delay his departure for France, but he would not be a suppliant again at the feet of the Spanish monarchs. So the warm-hearted Father Marchena resolved to seek a personal interview with Queen Isabella. He had once been her confessor, and he knew that persons of his sacred order found easy access to the presence of that devout woman.

Isabella was then at the military city of Santa Fé. Thither Marchena sent a letter to the queen by an eminent navigator, who, within a fortnight, brought back a note from her majesty summoning the friar to her presence, and giving Columbus the assurance that he might confidently expect royal aid. That note was laid before the little junta of friends at the convent, and produced much joy. Before midnight Marchena had saddled his mule and departed secretly for Santa Fé, where the sovereigns were superintending the close investment of the capital of Granada. An audience of the queen was readily obtained, when the friar pleaded eloquently in behalf of Columbus and Spain. His honest zeal and earnest eloquence secured Isabella's favorable attention. Her favorite, the Marchioness of Moya, seconded Father Marchena's pleading, and the queen requested that Columbus should be sent to her again. She forwarded money to him wherewith to purchase clothes, a mule for his journey, and to bear his traveling expenses.

With renewed hope Columbus journeyed toward the camp before Granada, where he arrived in time to see the Moors surrender to the Spanish power. He was soon admitted to the presence of the sovereigns. "What do you expect?" asked the king. "To be invested with the title and privileges of an admiral and viceroy over all the countries I may discover," Columbus replied. "Also one-tenth of all the gains either by trade or conquest," he added. One of the courtiers said: "By such an arrangement you would secure the honor of a command, without any loss in case of failure." Columbus instantly replied: "I will furnish an eighth of the cost provided I may enjoy an eighth of the profits." His terms were pronounced to be inadmissible. Others were offered. He refused to compromise, and the conference seemed fruitless. Columbus, again disappointed and heartily disgusted, turned with a heavy heart from the royal pavilion, resolved to go immediately to France. He mounted his mule and started for La Rabida. Some powerful persons who were zealous converts to his theory, learning of his departure, deeply deplored the event. One of these was St. Angel, receiver of the ecclesiastical revenues of Arragon. He obtained an immediate audience of the monarchs, and ably vindicated the judgment of Columbus. The king was not convinced; the queen was. "Our treasury," said Ferdinand, "has been too much drained by the war, to warrant us in engaging in the undertaking." "I will undertake the enterprise," said Isabella, "for my own crown of Castile, and, if necessary, I will pledge my jewels for the money." St. Angel said, with emphasis, "It will not be necessary."

FATHER MARCHENA DEPARTING FOR SANTA FÉ.

A courier was sent to bring Columbus back to the presence of the queen. He was two leagues away when the messenger overtook him at the bridge of Pinos. The often disappointed mariner hesitated. The injunction, "Put not your trust in princes," was deeply impressed on his mind. When he was assured of Isabella's earnestness, he turned back. An immediate audience was granted. The queen received him graciously. She was seated in a richly-cushioned chair by the side of her husband, whilst Columbus stood before her with St. Angel at his right hand. He was then fifty-six years of age; the queen was forty. In person she was of medium height, and exquisitely formed. Her complexion was fair, her hair a rich auburn color, and her eyes a clear blue. There was a mingled gravity and sweetness in her countenance which made it very winning, and a singular modesty which graced the firmness of her purposes, her earnestness of spirit, and her courage to do right. She possessed more genius and grandeur of soul than her husband; and could far better than he comprehend the theory of Columbus, and estimate the mighty results of his success should he achieve it.

The ambition of the navigator was lofty and noble. His piety was heartfelt; his religious convictions were deep and controlling, and his zeal was fed by an earnest desire to serve God and benefit mankind. And when, with a tongue that seemed to be touched with the flame of inspiration, he told the queen of his faith and hope,—a belief that he was ordained of God to bear the Gospel of Jesus to the heathen of unknown lands, and a hope that he should bring back to her the glad tidings of pagans converted to the true faith,—her face kindled with enthusiasm and beamed with angelic benignity. And when he spoke of giving to Spain the honors and emoluments of his anticipated discoveries, and promised to devote the profits of the enterprise to efforts for the recovery of the Holy Sepulchre at Jerusalem from the hands of the Paynim, the beautiful queen was transported with joy. She arose quickly from her chair, and stretching forth her clasped hands, sparkling with jewels, and with her soft eyes raised toward heaven, she fervently invoked the blessing of Almighty God upon the person and deeds of Columbus. The navigator stood in awe, with bowed head, before the seeming transfigured sovereign. The colder Ferdinand's soul was warmed, and to the uttered benediction he responded "Amen."

Isabella assented to all of the demands of Columbus, and urged him to depart on his great mission as speedily as possible. Ferdinand acquiesced in the arrangements. The contract was signed by the sovereigns, at Santa Fé, on the 17th of April, 1492. On the 30th of the same month, his commission of admiral and viceroy was signed by both of them in the city of Granada. By that instrument, the dignities and prerogatives of viceroy were made hereditary in the family of Columbus, and his heirs were entitled to prefix to their names the title of Don, a token of rank and estate. Early in May the queen appointed Diego, the son of Columbus, page to her majesty's son, Prince Juan or John. Then Columbus departed for La Rabida with a light heart, and was there received by the good Father Marchena with open arms.

The port of Palos had lately sinned against the monarchs, and the citizens had been condemned to serve the crown one year with two armed caravels—small three-masted vessels. Furnished with authority from the monarchs, Columbus went to the Church of St. George, in Palos, and in the porch of the fane, in the presence of the public officers of that sea-port town and many citizens, he caused a royal order to be read commanding the authorities to have two caravels ready for sea within ten days, and they and their crews placed at the disposal of the admiral. By the same order he was empowered to fit out a third vessel; and the people of that portion of the Andalusian coast were directed to furnish supplies for the three ships at fair prices.

When the destination of Columbus was made known, the greatest consternation spread amongst the seamen of Palos and their friends. The stories of the awful terrors of the far-western Atlantic, which everybody believed, made the stoutest hearts of the mariners quail. Many of them fled to avoid

QUEEN ISABELLA INVOKING BLESSINGS.

the service, and for weeks no progress was made toward the equipment of the vessels. Finally Martin Alonzo Pinzon, and his brother, Vincent Yañez, navigators of Palos, of great wealth and well-known courage and ability, having ships and seamen in their employ, came forward and not only engaged to furnish one of the vessels, but to go themselves with Columbus on the perilous voyage, each as master of a ship; Martin also agreed to furnish Columbus with the money to pay his promised one-eighth of the cost. These acts of the Pinzons had a powerful effect upon the people, soothing their fears and inspiring them with confidence; and very soon three vessels—all that were required—were ready for sea. Two of them were no larger than our river and coast sailing vessels—without decks, pierced for oars to be used in calms, with each a forecastle, and a cabin in the high stern for the accommodation of the ship's company. The largest, which was fitted expressly for the expedition, was decked, and was named *Santa Mariá* (or Holy Mary). She was the flag-ship of Columbus. One of the caravels was called the *Pinta*, and was commanded by Martin Alonzo Pinzon, who was accompanied by his brother, Francisco Martin, as pilot. The other caravel was the *Niña*, with lateen sails, and was commanded by Vincent Yañez Pinzon. There were three other pilots; an inspector-general of the armament; also a native of Cordova, Diego de Avana, as chief alguazil, an officer corresponding in his functions with our constable. Roderigo de Escobar was with Columbus as royal notary, an officer always sent with the armaments of the crown, as historian of the expedition. There were also a physician and surgeon, some private adventurers, servants, and ninety mariners; in all one hundred and twenty persons. After appropriate religious ceremonies in the Church of St. George in Palos had been performed, the expedition sailed on Friday the 3d of August, 1492. On the 9th, the little flotilla reached the Canary Islands, where they were detained more than three weeks, and early in September they passed the westernmost of the group, escaped some Portuguese caravels which had been sent out to intercept them, and sailed boldly toward the unknown. Columbus carried with him charts constructed on the basis of that which Toscanelli had formerly sent to him. Expecting to find the eastern coast of Asia, he also bore a letter from the Spanish sovereigns to the Grand Khan (Emperor) of Tartary, in whose service Marco Polo had been employed two hundred years before.

With wonderful endurance the three little vessels buffeted with the waves of the Atlantic. They encountered no heavy storms such as sometimes lash that sea into fury; nor did they observe any of the expected terrors of the trackless deep. Phenomena sometimes startled the mariners, and day after day they were agitated by alternate hopes and disappointments. The volcanic blaze of the peak of Teneriffe scared the sailors as it shot up behind them. When they were two hundred leagues or more westward of that peak, Columbus observed, for the first time in his life, a variation of the needle of his compass from a true line with the north star. It inclined five or six degrees to the northwest, and this variation increased as they sailed on with no sure guide but the stars. Very soon they encountered vast masses of sea-weeds, which retarded the vessels, and seemed like a green island hundreds of miles in extent floating on the bosom of the ocean. It was doubtless the mysterious Sargasso Sea, now so well known to mariners, and which probably gave rise to the legends concerning fertile islands in the Atlantic. Then they were cheered by the sight of a flying heron and a tropical bird which were harbingers of land. The sailors, who had been mutinous at times, were quieted by these promises of nature; but when they seemed to be deceptive, the crews again became stormy and almost ungovernable. They reproached their sovereigns for trusting the ambitious Italian, who would sacrifice their lives "to make himself a great lord;" and they resolved to retrace their course and seek the shores of Spain. With kind words, tempting promises of reward, and threats against the more mutinous, Columbus quelled the rising insurrection for the time.

For eleven days after leaving the Canary Islands, the ships had sailed before the easterly trade winds; now gentle breezes came from the southwest, and often diminished into dead calms. At early twilight one evening, Martin Pinzon, standing on the high stem of the *Pinta*, and pointing toward the southwest, shouted to the admiral, "Land! land! señor; I claim my reward"—a pension promised by the sovereigns to the first man who should discover land. Believing the report to be true, Columbus knelt and returned thanks to God; and his own crew and that of the *Pinta*, sailing close by, joined with the commanders in repeating the *Gloria in Excelsis*. Alas! the apparition was only a cloud which vanished before the dawn.

Days passed on, and the sun each evening set in the waves. Martin Pinzon believed that a more southerly course would be wiser, and he was confirmed in his opinion by seeing a flock of parrots flying toward the southwest. He advised Columbus to follow them, but the admiral kept on his due west course. The crews again became discontented and mutinous. They had lost all hope, and in their desperation they defied Columbus. With great dignity and calmness, and with the coolness of true courage, he said: "This expedition has been sent out by your sovereigns, and come what may I am determined, by the help of God, to accomplish the object of the voyage." "We will cast you into the sea and return to Spain," said the exasperated sailors; and just at sunset, on the evening of the 11th of October, they were about to carry their threat into execution, when a coast-fish was seen to glide by; dolphins played near the surface; a branch of thorn with berries on it floated near, and a staff, artificially carved, came upon the waters to testify of human habitations near. Such unmistakable signs of land close by hushed the voice of rebellion, and the tigers became as meek as lambs. After the vesper hymn to the Virgin had been sung at the close of twilight, as usual, Columbus addressed his crew in words of kindness and congratulation. Recounting the many blessings which they had received from God on the voyage, he assured them that a greater blessing was about to be bestowed upon them—that probably land would be seen in the morning. He enjoined them all to watch, and promised that to whosoever should first discover land should be given a doublet of velvet, in addition to the pension offered by the sovereigns.

COLUMBUS AND HIS MUTINOUS CREW.

Not an eye was closed. Eagerly every man watched far into the night. Columbus, sitting on the high poop of the *Santa Maria*, more eagerly than they, gazed upon the western horizon. At about ten o'clock he thought he saw the glimmer of a distant light. He called Gutierrez, gentleman of the king's bed-chamber, who was one of the private adventurers, and inquired whether he saw a light. "I do," said Gutierrez. Columbus then called Sanchez, another adventurer, and after a few minutes they all three saw it, gleaming like a torch in a fisherman's boat, rising and falling with the waves. At length, at two o'clock in the morning, whilst the vessels were continuing on their course, a gun fired on board the *Pinta* announced the joyful tidings that land had been seen. It was first observed by a mariner named Rodrigo de Triana, but, as Columbus had seen the lights several hours before, the award was given to the admiral. The land was clearly seen at a distance of about six miles. The vessels were laid to, and all waited impatiently for the dawn. When it came a beautiful picture was revealed. Wooded shores were in full view. The perfumes of flowers came upon the light land breeze. Birds in gorgeous plumage hovered around the vessels caroling morning hymns, which seemed like the voices of angels to the late despairing seamen. In spite of every difficulty and danger, Columbus had accomplished his object. "The great mystery of the ocean was revealed," says Mr. Irving. "His theory, which had been the scoff of sages, was triumphantly established; he had secured to himself a glory as durable as the world itself."

At sunrise, Columbus and his companions landed in small boats. Many naked men and one woman, with skins of a dark copper color, who had watched the movements of the Europeans with mingled feelings of curiosity, wonder and awe, now fled in alarm to the deep shadows of the forest. The admiral, dressed in gold-embroidered scarlet cloth and bearing the royal standard, first stepped upon the shore. He was followed by the Pinzons, each carrying the white silk banner of the expedition. It was pennon-shaped, emblazoned with a green cross, on one side of which was the letter F and on the other side the letter Y, the initials of Ferdinand and Ysabella, and each was surmounted by a golden crown. When the officers and crews were all landed, the whole company knelt, kissed the earth, and with tears of joy filling their eyes, chanted the *Te Deum Laudamus*. Rising from the ground, Columbus displayed the royal standard, and drawing his sword, took possession of the land in the name of the sovereigns of Spain. To the island (for such it proved to be) he gave the name of San Salvador—Holy Saviour. His followers crowded around him with the most extravagant demonstrations of delight. Those who had been most insolent and mutinous were foremost in the utterance of vows of faithfulness thereafter. Each gladly took an oath of obedience to him as admiral and viceroy, and the representative of Ferdinand and Isabella. Now the triumph of Columbus was complete.

The native inhabitants had watched the approaching ships since the dawn, with fear and awe, regarding them as monsters of the deep; and when they saw the white men come from them, dressed in gay colors, with shining lace and glittering armor, they supposed them to be superior beings who had come down from the skies. Each party was a wonder to the other. The naked people with dusky skins painted with a variety of colors and devices, the men without beards and both sexes having long black hair falling from their heads over their shoulders and bosoms in great profusion, were unlike any human beings of whom Columbus and his companions had ever heard. By degrees the alarm of the timid natives subsided, and they approached the Europeans giving and receiving signs of amity and good will. As the boats of the navigators moved along the shore, in an exploration of the coast of the island, the inhabitants of villages, men, women and children, ran to the beach, throwing themselves on the ground, and assuming attitudes of worship of the supposed celestial beings. They made signs for the Spaniards to land; and when they found that the boats kept on their way, many of them went into the sea and swam after them, and others followed in canoes. Believing that he was upon an island of Farther India, Columbus called these wild inhabitants *Indians*, a name which all the native tribes of America have since borne.

THE LANDING OF COLUMBUS.

CHAPTER V.

COLUMBUS DISCOVERS CUBA AND SAN DOMINGO—LEAVES A COLONY ON SAN DOMINGO—THEIR CONDUCT THERE—COLUMBUS RETURNS TO SPAIN—UNRIGHTEOUS AMBITION OF PINZON DEFEATED—COLUMBUS INVITED TO THE COURT—HIS BRILLIANT RECEPTION AT BARCELONA—HIS AUDIENCE WITH THE SOVEREIGNS—COLUMBUS AT THE FEAST GIVEN BY CARDINAL MENDOZA—HE MAKES OTHER VOYAGES AND DISCOVERS SOUTH AMERICA—HE IS FALSELY ACCUSED AND SENT FROM SAN DOMINGO TO SPAIN IN CHAINS—INDIGNATION OF ISABELLA—INGRATITUDE AND INJUSTICE OF FERDINAND—COLUMBUS DIES IN POVERTY AND NEGLECTED—HIS REMAINS—A MONUMENT TO HIS MEMORY IN GENOA.

THE native name of the island whereon Columbus landed was Guanhana. To the Spaniards and others it is yet San Salvador; but the English having given it the vulgar name of Cat Island, persist in calling it so. It lies about two hundred and fifty miles E.S.E. of the southern point of the peninsula of Florida, and is one of the larger of the Bahama group. After examining it, the admiral cruised among others of the same group, naming some of them. He also touched at outlying islands as he sailed southward, and on the 28th of October he saw the northern shores of Cuba. Entering a beautiful river, which he called San Salvador, he anchored, and in honor of Prince Juan (John), the son of Isabella, he named the great island Juana. But it has retained its native name of Cuba. He sailed northwesterly along its coast as far as the eastern entrance to Laguna de Moron, which was the nearest approach to the North American continent ever vouchsafed to Columbus. There he first saw a weed, the leaves of which the natives rolled into long slim packages, called *tobacco*, and smoked. It was the modern cigar. The Spaniards considered the habit a nauseous indulgence, and did not adopt it. They left to an Englishman, born fifty years afterward, the fame of introducing this use of tobacco to Europeans.

Columbus persuaded several of the native inhabitants of Cuba, of both sexes, to go with him to Spain, and at the middle of November he sailed in that direction. Head winds and rough weather caused him to return to Cuba. He signalled for the Pinzons to follow him. Martin Alonzo did not heed the order, and very soon the *Pinta* disappeared on the eastern horizon.

Early in December, Columbus saw the eastern end of Cuba, and a few days later, as he sailed toward Europe, the charming vision of beautiful

Hayti, now St. or San Domingo, burst upon his sight. The country so much resembled Spain in its natural features, that he named it Hispaniola—Little Spain. On its shores he lingered with delight many days. He received an invitation from one of the leading caciques or native rulers to anchor his vessels near his residence, and whilst sailing along the coast for the purpose of casting anchor in the harbor of the friendly chief, the *Santa Maria* was wrecked late on Christmas eve, in consequence of bad steering. Columbus and his crew took refuge on board the caravel *Niña*, commanded by Vincent Pinzon, where a matin hymn to the Virgin was chanted by the admiral and his followers in the morning twilight, and utterances of thanksgiving went up to God for their deliverance from great peril on that holy festival of the church. When the cacique heard of the disaster, he sent men and canoes in abundance to unload the vessel. It was soon done with willing hands, for a truly Christian spirit animated these pagans. "So loving, and tractable, and peaceable are these people," Columbus wrote to Ferdinand and Isabella from Hispaniola afterward, "that I declare to your majesties that there is not in this world a better nation or a better land. They love their neighbors as themselves. Their discourse is ever sweet and gentle, and accompanied with a smile."

Satan had entered that paradise. Many of the followers of Columbus asked permission to remain on the island. The *Niña* was crowded; and, delighted with the idea of planting the germ of a Christian colony there, the admiral gave his consent. Of the wreck of the vessel they built a fort, which Columbus named La Navidad—the Nativity, in commemoration of their having escaped shipwreck on Christmas day. A fort! What need had they of a fort among such a people? Alas! it was a sign of premeditated wickedness. Thirty-nine remained. Arana, the alguazil, was placed in command of them, and they were conjured by Columbus to act honestly and live united in good-fellowship. As soon as the admiral had departed, they broke every promise. Each, bent upon private gain and incited by a desire and expectation of acquiring great wealth in a short time, broke from the social tie and acted independently. The gentle natives were compelled to yield to their avarice and lust. The golden ornaments of the women were seized, and two or three of them were made wives by each of the Spaniards. Robbery and licentiousness marked every step in the career of these Europeans. They went to different parts of the island in search of reported treasures, and soon found an incarnation of retributive justice in the person of a fierce Carib chief who ruled much of Hayti, and who slew the Spaniards and burnt their fortress to ashes. These acts of the intruders were only the beginnings of similar performances, as the Spaniards colonized the West India Islands, and especially Hayti. These savage Christians made that Pagan Eden a wilderness and a land of unutterable woes, for the real Christian kindness of the so-called savages was requited by the most barbarous cruelty. Thousands of men, women, and children perished under the hardships imposed upon them as slave-workers in the fields and in mines, and many were made abject beasts of burden for the gain of their white conquerors.

Early in January, 1493, Columbus left La Navidad, in the *Niña*, and sailed for Spain. He soon saw the *Pinta*. The avaricious Pinzon had heard

CRUELTY OF THE SPANIARDS IN SAN DOMINGO.

of a region of gold, from one of the natives, and with a desire to secure the treasure for himself he had deserted the admiral. He had returned to Hispaniola, and there heard of the shipwreck of the *Santa Maria*, but he did not go to the assistance of Columbus because it might interfere with his own selfish projects. The admiral would have cruised longer among the islands, but this conduct of Pinzon, and the fact that the latter had kidnapped four men and two girls for the purpose of selling them as slaves in Spain, had destroyed his confidence in that commander, and he determined to hurry home and rid himself of so undesirable a companion. The *Niña's* prow was turned toward Europe, and the *Pinta* followed.

The caravels encountered dead calms and fierce tempests on that winter voyage, and were separated. In one of these storms, Columbus, fearing the destruction of the vessels and with them the loss of all knowledge of his discoveries, placed a written narrative of his adventures in a sealed cask, and committed it to the waves. The sailors, in affright, vowed that they would, if spared, attend mass in their shirts only at the first Christian church they should come to. That vow they performed at the Azores, which they reached in February. They were all saved. At dawn on the 4th of March, about eight weeks after she had left La Navidad, the *Niña* appeared off the rock of Cintra at the mouth of the Tagus, in Portugal, and soon afterwards she was anchored in the waters of that river.

Columbus immediately sent a courier with a letter to Ferdinand and Isabella, in which he announced his great discovery. He also wrote a letter to John, King of Portugal, who was then at Valparaiso. That monarch sent a cavalier to Columbus with his congratulations and an invitation for the admiral to come to his court. Columbus went and was treated with distinguished attentions. A numerous train of cavaliers escorted him back to his ship. He stopped at a monastery on the way to visit John's queen, who had expressed a strong desire to see the great discoverer; and on the 13th of March he again put to sea. Two days later, at noon, the *Niña* entered the harbor of Palos, where the admiral was received with the greatest demonstrations of joy. It was then seven months and twelve days since he left that harbor for the regions of the unknown, and out of those mysterious regions he had brought the wonderful tidings of a new-found world.

On the evening of the same day, the *Pinta* sailed into the harbor of Palos. Martin Alonzo Pinzon, her commander, after she had been driven into the Bay of Biscay by a storm, had entered the port of Bayonne, and from thence had sent a letter to Ferdinand and Isabella recounting his adventures and the discoveries, hoping to gain for himself the prepossessions of the Spanish court. He also expected to be hailed at Palos with great acclamations, and to receive royal honors from his sovereigns, for he supposed Columbus was yet fighting the waves of the Atlantic, or was engulfed in their bosom. When, therefore, he saw the flag of the *Niña* fluttering in the breeze at Palos, and heard the praises of him whom he chose to regard as his rival, Pinzon, jealous, and fearing the admiral as his accuser, sought seclusion until the discoverer had left the port. And when an answer to his letter was received from the monarchs filled with reproaches, and forbidding him to appear at court, his "heart died within him." Killed by disappointed ambition and mortified pride, the body of Martin Alonzo Pinzon was laid in the grave a few days after the reading of the royal epistle.

Columbus hastened to Seville, where he received a letter from the monarchs expressing their delight because of his great achievements, and inviting him to repair immediately to their court at Barcelona. The letter was addressed to "Don Christopher Columbus, our admiral of the ocean sea, and viceroy and governor of the islands discovered in the Indies." To their presence the honored Italian hastened, taking with him six of the Indians whom he had brought from Cuba—four young men and two beautiful maidens. Great preparations had been made for his reception, for his discoveries and the recent conquest of the Moors were regarded by the sovereigns as special indications of the favor of God. A procession was formed on a brilliant April day (such as may be seen only in Catalonia), composed of priests, nobles, and military men. In that procession, among the hidalgos, rode the admiral, richly dressed, the cynosure of every eye, preceded by music, soldiers, and brilliantly dressed Catalonian guards, and followed by the dusky natives of the West Indies. The latter wore handsomely embroidered white tunics, with jewelled bands around their heads bearing lofty plumes of gay colors, and golden circlets around their bare arms and legs. They carried birds of strange and brilliant plumage from the tropical islands. After them came the crews of the vessels of the expedition, carrying a crown of gold sent by the friendly cacique of Hispaniola, and many curious things, such as images of stone rudely wrought; a masque with eyes of gold; a living alligator; palm branches with the fruit dried on them; reed arrows winged with beautiful feathers, and a hundred other strange objects from those far-off lands. Over these waved the Green Cross banner which had floated over those mysterious islands of the sea; also the modest white banner of the admiral, bearing the arms which had been granted to him, namely, those of the Spanish kingdom quartered by a group of islands surrounded by billows, and inscribed with the words, in golden letters,

POR CASTILLA Y POR LEON
NUEVO MUNDO HALLO COLON:
"For Castile and for Leon, Columbus has discovered a New World."

In a vast hall open to public view and access, two thrones had been erected under a rich canopy of brocade, and near them waved thirty Moorish banners captured at Granada and Malaga, trophies of the recent conquest. Seated upon these thrones, Ferdinand and Isabella waited the arrival of the discoverer. He entered among a crowd of brilliant Spanish knights, his tall and erect figure, his flowing gray hair and beard, his lofty bearing, his benignant aspect and his great deeds making him appear, as he really was, the noblest champion of them all. The sovereigns arose to receive him, when a murmur of applause burst from the lips of the haughty grandees present. The admiral knelt before the monarchs, when the queen bade him rise. He then asked permission to kiss the hands of Ferdinand and Isabella, who, after God, had most favored him. The boon was granted, when the admiral took his seat among the nobles, and with a clear and steady voice he recounted the chief incidents of his voyage, exhibited gold and spices, and other productions of the country he had discovered, and then declared that all this was but the foreshadowing of greater marvels to be revealed. His words were listened to with the most profound interest and emotion. When they had ceased, the monarchs cast themselves upon their knees, and with tears coursing down their cheeks they fervently thanked God for so great a blessing. The whole multitude followed their devout example. As they arose to their feet, the choir of the royal chapel chanted the *Te Deum.* Every voice in the great hall took up the words of that glorious hymn of praise, "and it seemed," says Las Casas, "as if, in that hour, they communicated with celestial delights." The company were dismissed with the apostolic benediction by the Grand Cardinal of Spain, and the streets of Barcelona echoed and re-echoed with shouts of joy.

That Grand Cardinal of Spain, Gonzales de Mendoza, Archbishop of Toledo, who had hinted to a council that the theory of Columbus was irreligious, was now among the first, after the monarchs, to honor him. He invited the admiral to a feast, at which were gathered some of the highest prelates and nobles of Catalonia. To the navigator he gave the seat of honor at the table, and other marks of superior distinction. These attentions to one who was so lately a poor Italian mariner excited the envy of some of the guests. A courtier present, moved by a narrow feeling of personal and national jealousy, asked the admiral whether he thought that in case he had not discovered the Indies (which it was believed he had found), there were not men in Spain who would have been equal to the enterprise? Columbus immediately took an egg that was before him, and invited the courtier to make it stand on one of its ends. He could not. All the company tried in vain to do it. Then the admiral struck the egg upon the table so as to flatten the end by a fracture and left it standing. "Any one could do that," cried the courtier. "After I have shown the way," replied the admiral. "Gentlemen," continued Columbus, "after I have shown a new way to India, nothing is easier than to follow." The courtier was answered.

After giving an account of his voyage and discoveries in a letter to Sanchez, the treasurer of Spain (which was printed), Columbus, at the request of the monarchs, immediately fitted out another expedition to continue his researches in the western seas. The harbor of Cadiz was very soon

COLUMBUS AND HIS TRAIN ENTERING BARCELONA.

the scene of busy preparation, and late in September, 1493, the admiral left the bay with three large ships of heavy burthen, and fourteen caravels, with fifteen hundred men. We will not follow him in his subsequent voyages in detail, for they have no special bearing on the history of our country. It is sufficient to say that he made three others from Spain, and that during the last but one, he discovered the *continent* of America. When he left Cadiz on his second voyage in the autumn of 1493, his good fortune seemed to forsake him. His followers were largely selfish adventurers who went out in search of gold and other treasures. Quarrels and mutinies followed disappointed expectations. The chief blame was laid upon the shoulders of the admiral, and he finally became a victim to the intrigues of vicious men, who, envious of his fame and dignities, sought continually to build up their own fortunes out of the ruins of his character.

Columbus sailed on his third voyage, at the close of May, 1493, with six ships, from the port of San Lucar de Barrameda, near the mouth of the Guadalquiver. Passing the Cape de Verde Islands, he proceeded toward the equator in a southwesterly direction, and then sailed due west with the trade winds, in search of a continent. Supposing Cuba to be a great cape of Asia, he believed that under the equator he would find not only the main land, but every production of nature in greater profusion, perfection and preciousness, than elsewhere. He was not disappointed, for on the 1st of August he saw the continent, not of Asia, but of South America, near the mouth of the Orinoco River. That was not many days after Sebastian Cabot, an English navigator, discovered North America.

Columbus coasted for awhile near the shores of South America, and then, broken in health by his labors, anxieties and exposures, he sailed for his colony on Hispaniola. There he found everything in disorder; and in his efforts to bring order out of confusion, he so interfered with the selfish projects of leading adventurers there, that they determined to ruin him. Preferring malicious and false charges against him, at the court of Spain, they induced the sovereigns to send out a commissioner to inquire into the causes of the difficulties. Francisco de Bobadilla was sent. He was as ambitious and unscrupulous as any of the adventurers, and after deposing Columbus from the vice-royalty, he sent him in chains to Spain. Valleja, who was sent with the admiral as a sort of guard, and also the master of the caravel in which Columbus was conveyed, were grieved by this cruel treatment of the man whom they revered. They would have removed his irons, but Columbus would not allow them to do so. "No," he said proudly; "their majesties commanded me by letter to submit to whatever Bobadilla should order in their name; by their authority he has put upon me these chains; I will wear them until they shall order them to be taken off, and I will preserve them afterwards as relics and memorials of the reward of my services." It was done. "I saw them always hanging in his cabinet," said his son and biographer, Fernando, "and he requested that when he died, they might be buried with him."

When, after the arrival of the caravel at Cadiz, Isabella heard of the cruel treatment of Columbus, she was very indignant, and sent an order for his immediate restoration to liberty. The sovereigns wrote a letter to him couched in terms of affection and gratitude, expressing their grief because of his sufferings, and inviting him to the court. The people, too, were very indignant, and were loud in their denunciations of the treatment of such a benefactor of their country. When he arrived at Granada, in December, 1498, he was cordially received by the monarchs, who, disavowing the doings of Bobadilla as contrary to their instructions, promised that he should be dismissed from office. But the Spanish nobles, jealous of Columbus because he was evidently a royal favorite, persuaded the king, who was dissatisfied with the apparent unproductiveness of the admiral's discoveries, not to reinstate him in the vice-royalty. Another was appointed in the place of Bobadilla. After experiencing neglect, and alternate hope and disappointment, for almost four years, whilst others were reaping the harvest of his seed-time, the admiral was entrusted with the command of a small expedition to find a passage through "the sea" now known as the Gulf of Mexico, into the Indian Ocean. He sailed with four caravels and one hundred and fifty men, early in May, 1502, and after much suffering, returned to Cadiz in November, 1504, sick and dejected. Nineteen days after his arrival, the good Queen Isabella died. "She was one of the purest spirits

COLUMBUS IN CHAINS.

that ever ruled over the destinies of a nation," says Mr. Irving. With her died the hopes of the admiral, for he knew how cold and calculating was the disposition of the king. That ungrateful monarch, after torturing the discoverer with the cold politeness and evasive promises for which he was noted, rejected the legal and equitable claims of Columbus to the dignities and emoluments of vice-royalty which had been secured to him by royal contract; and this great and good man, then about seventy years of age, who had given more real honor and glory to Spain than had the whole line of her kings or the families of her nobles, was allowed to pass the remnant of his days in comparative poverty and obscurity. "I have," Columbus once wrote, "no place to repair to excepting an inn, and often with nothing to pay for my sustenance." At length, when he was utterly prostrated, and hopeless of justice, death came to his relief at Valladolid on the 20th day of May, 1506, as he was uttering the words, "Lord, into thy hands I commit my spirit." His remains were put into the convent of San Francisco, where, for seven years, no stone or inscription marked the place of his burial. Then the ashamed king, when the navigator's bones were removed to a monastery in Seville, ordered a marble tomb to be placed over them with the inscription:

A CASTILLA Y A LEON
NUEVO MUNDO DIO COLON.

"To Castile and Leon, Columbus gave a New World." He "asked for bread" and he gave him "a stone." More indelibly than on brass or marble, is the truth of that inscription engraved on the memory of mankind.

Columbus died with full faith that although princes might neglect him and wicked men might defraud him, God and eternal justice would vindicate his honor and his fame, and that the world would pay to him the just homage due for his services. He also died in the belief that he had discovered Farther India, and not an unknown continent; and such was the belief of all navigators and scientific men at that time.

In the year 1536, the remains of Columbus and of his son Diego, were taken to Hispaniola, and interred in the Cathedral at San Domingo. There they remained two hundred and sixty years, when, in 1796, they were conveyed with great pomp to Havana, in Cuba, where they now repose. A few years ago, a magnificent monument to the memory of Columbus, was erected in his native city of Genoa, in the centre of one of its public squares, where it is surrounded by flowers and shrubbery. It is composed of Carrara marble, and is about forty feet in height. On four panels between four pedestals are represented, in relief sculpture, four great events in his life, namely, his *Conference with the Council at Salamanca; the Landing in*

America; Presenting the Indians to Queen Isabella, and the *Admiral in Chains.* Upon each pedestal is a figure personifying respectively *Navigation*, *History*, *Astronomy* and *Wisdom.* On a round shaft which rises between these figures are sculptured in high relief the prows of ancient vessels. This shaft is surmounted by a slightly colossal statue of Columbus, resting his

MONUMENT IN HONOR OF COLUMBUS AT GENOA.

left hand on an anchor, whilst with his right hand he presents a naked Indian maiden, sitting modestly at his feet, holding in her hand a small cross upon which she is gazing intently, her head adorned with the plumage of birds. This figure represents *America;* and the faith of Columbus that the New World would receive the religion of Jesus Christ is indicated by the symbol of the Atonement.

In summing up the character of Columbus, Mr. Irving wrote: "In him were singularly combined the practical and the poetical. His mind had grasped all kinds of knowledge, whether procured by study or observation, which bore upon his theories; impatient of the scanty aliment of the day, 'his impetuous ardor,' as has been well observed, 'threw him into the study of the fathers of the church, the Arabian Jews, and the ancient geographers;' while his daring but irregular genius, bursting from the limits of imperfect science, bore him to conclusions far beyond the intellectual vision of his contemporaries. If some of his conclusions were erroneous, they were at least ingenious and splendid. And their error resulted from the clouds which still hung over his peculiar path of enterprise. His own discoveries enlightened the ignorance of the age, guided conjecture to certainty, and dispelled that very darkness with which he had been obliged to struggle. It has been said that mercenary views mingled with the ambition of Columbus, and that his stipulations with the Spanish court were selfish and avaricious. The charge is inconsiderate and unjust. He aimed at dignity and wealth in the same lofty spirit in which he sought renown; they were to be part and parcel of the achievement, and palpable evidence of its success; they were to arise from the territories he should discover, and be commensurate in importance. No condition could be more just."

We have now traced, in brief outline, some of the principal causes which led to the discovery of America, and the chief events in the career of the great pioneer of such discovery. He demonstrated the fact that the earth is globular, and that fertile lands might be found by sailing westward from Europe across the Atlantic Ocean. Having discovered and pointed out the way to these lands, he retired, and other navigators and discoverers appeared upon the scene. The exploits of some of them, we will now consider.

CHAPTER VI.

HENRY THE SEVENTH OF ENGLAND—HE COMMISSIONS THE CABOTS TO MAKE DISCOVERIES—VOYAGE AND DISCOVERIES OF SEBASTIAN CABOT—KING HENRY'S AMBITIOUS DESIGNS—CABOT IN SPAIN—AMERICUS VESPUCCIUS—HIS PRETENDED FIRST DISCOVERY OF AMERICA—HOW, BY FRAUD, OUR CONTINENT WAS CALLED BY HIS NAME—THE POPE'S GIFT OF AMERICA TO THE SPANISH MONARCH—VOYAGES OF CORTEREAL TO LABRADOR AND THEIR RESULTS—YOUNG COLUMBUS IN SAN DOMINGO—DISCOVERY OF CENTRAL AMERICA—PONCE DE LEON'S SEARCH FOR THE FOUNTAIN OF YOUTH, AND DISCOVERY OF FLORIDA—DISCOVERY OF SOUTH CAROLINA—CRUEL TREATMENT OF NATIVES AND THEIR REVENGE—ATTEMPTS TO COLONIZE CENTRAL AMERICA—THE SPANIARDS IN CUBA—THEIR INTRODUCTION OF CHRISTIANITY TO THE NATIVES OF THAT ISLAND.

WHEN Columbus was about to leave Portugal for Spain, he sent his brother Bartholomew to England to ask assistance of the British monarch. The ship in which he sailed was robbed by pirates, but he reached England, where he appears to have lived several years. For reasons not made clear by the chroniclers, he did not apply to the monarch until about the time when his brother was on his first voyage of discovery. Henry the Seventh was then King of England. He was the first of the Tudor dynasty, of which Queen Elizabeth, in whose honor our Virginia was named, was the last. He was an energetic and enlightened prince, and responded to Bartholomew's request promptly and generously. He sent him to Spain in search of his brother, and to invite him to the English court. At Paris, whilst he was on his way, the Italian heard the joyful news of the great discoveries by his brother, and of Christopher's return in triumph to Andalusia.

When King Henry heard of the marvelous success of Columbus, he felt a disappointment because he had failed to secure for his crown and country the renown and advantages which their assistance in the great achievement would have given. But he was not thereby discouraged nor deterred from assisting in further attempts at discovery, though such assistance was, at first, only a permission. By royal charter he gave to John Cabot (a Venetian merchant at Bristol), and his sons, in 1496, permission to explore any seas with five ships and as many seamen as they might choose to employ, at their own expense, "to discover and occupy isles or countries of the heathen or infidels before unknown to Christians, accounting to the king for a fifth part of the profit upon their return to the port of Bristol." It was then the favorite theory of both church and state that all lands occupied by pagans of right belonged to Christians. There is no positive evidence that the Cabots took advantage of this privilege, or that any of them engaged in a voyage of discovery before the year 1498, when John Cabot was dead.

All Europe was then ringing with the fame of Columbus, and excited by the wildest stories of the marvelous discoveries by Spanish navigators. Maritime nations and seamen everywhere were crazed with a desire to be discoverers of new lands and to gather immense riches from glittering mines. Englishmen caught the infection, and their ambitious and avaricious monarch was as eager as any to wear such laurels as then graced the brows of Ferdinand and Isabella, and to hold the key of a vast treasure-house. He was seeking to secure the hand of a daughter of the Spanish sovereigns for his eldest son Arthur, whose suit the cold King of Arragon repelled on pretexts of state policy. Piqued by this circumstance the proud Henry gladly promoted the English thirst for discovery, hoping by its results not only to gain riches and honor, but to either diminish the glory of his Spanish rival or win his favor by some splendid achievement in the new field of contest. So he listened with eager attention to a proposition of Sebastian, a young son of John Cabot, concerning a voyage of discovery.

Sebastian Cabot appears to have been an ardent student of geography and the kindred sciences, from early life. When he reached young manhood he was proficient in the theory and practice of the navigator's art. To him King Henry not only gave a commission to go on a voyage of discovery, but fitted out two small vessels for him, in the year 1498. The history of that event was given by Sebastian to the Pope's legate in Spain in a few quaint sentences. "When my father died," he said, "in that time when news were brought that, Don Christopher Colonus, Genoese, had discovered the coast of India, whereof was great talk in all the court of King Henry the Seventh, who then reigned, insomuch that all men with great admiration affirmed it to be a thing more divine than human, to sail by the west into the east where spices grew, by a way that was never known before; by this fame and report, there increased in my heart a great flame of desire to attempt some notable thing. And understanding by reason of the sphere, that if I should sail by way of the northwest, I should, by a shorter tract, come into India, I therefore caused the king to be advertised of my desire, who immediately commanded two caravels to be furnished, with all things appertaining to the voyage."

All accounts of that voyage are very meagre, and most of them are somewhat contradictory. Sebastian Cabot had probably sailed as far as Cape Farewell, in Greenland, on trading voyages in his father's ships, and knew of the cold, icy sea beyond. Now he voyaged in the same direction, hoping to make a passage to India during the warm summer time. Leaving Bristol in May, 1498, with the two caravels and a full supply of men, he sailed to the northwest until the ice pack in Davis' Straits barred the way. Turning southward, he discovered land late in June or early in July, which he named Prima Vista—First View. Whether this was the northern shores of Newfoundland, or the continent on the coast of Labrador, near Cape Charles, cannot be determined. Unlike Lief the Northman, who sailed southward after seeing the land, Cabot turned northward in search of a passage to

CABOT IN DAVIS' STRAITS.

Cathay, and followed the coast of the continent almost to the sixtieth degree of north latitude, when the ice would permit him to go no further. Although it was then about mid-summer, the weather was very cold; and seeing no prospect of an open sea further northward, Cabot sailed back, discovered a large island which he called New-found-land—Newfoundland—and observed the immense numbers of codfishes which have continued to fill the waters there ever since. He divulged this secret to Europe after his return, and within five or six years thereafter fishermen from England, Brittany and Normandy were off Newfoundland gathering these treasures of the sea. Leaving Newfoundland, Cabot coasted as far as the shores of Maine, and some writers think no farther; but if the reports of his conversation with Butrigarius, the Pope's legate, be true, he went as far as the Carolinas.

"There," he said to that functionary, "my victuals failing, I departed from thence and returned into England, where I found great tumults among the people and preparations for wars in Scotland, by reason whereof there was no more consideration had to this voyage. Whereupon I went into Spain, to the Catholic king."

Henry was then struggling for his throne against righteous claimants. Ferdinand refused to give his daughter in marriage to Arthur whilst these claimants existed. The unscrupulous Tudor beheaded two of them in the tower, and eagerly depressed and despoiled the old nobility who were adherents of the fallen house of York, his rival. These things caused the "tumults among the people," mentioned by Cabot. The king's eagerness to enrich himself by despoiling that old nobility; the agreement of Ferdinand to bestow his daughter Catharine upon Arthur, and the failure of Cabot to bring back gold from America, all caused the monarch to give "no more consideration to this voyage." Prince Arthur died before the nuptials, and Catharine afterwards became the unfortunate first wife of Henry the Eighth.

The discovery of North America, by young Cabot, then only twenty-one years of age, had conferred more immortal honor upon the English monarch and the English nation, than all the royal affiliations and the heaping up of gold. He was a native of England, and had opened a pathway for his countrymen to a new continent. But he was neglected by his king, and he finally went into the service of the Spanish sovereign whose daughter was then the wife of the monarch of England. On the death of Ferdinand, he was so annoyed by the jealousies of the Spanish nobles, that he returned to his native country, and not long afterward we find him on another voyage in search of a northwest passage to the Indian Seas. He penetrated to Hudson's Bay, and after fighting the ice-pack there, he returned to England discomfited, and never made another voyage to the coasts of North America. The successor of Ferdinand invited him back to Spain, and made him chief pilot of the realm. After several voyages, in one of which he made researches along the southeastern coast of South America, he, in his old age, resigned his office into the hands of the Spanish monarch, and returned to his native land. There he was highly honored and liberally pensioned by the "boy-king," Edward the Sixth. Queen Mary, whose husband was a son of the Spanish monarch whose third invitation to return to Spain was rejected by Cabot, neglected the eminent navigator, and he was allowed to die in comparative poverty, in the town of his birth (Bristol), when he was eighty years of age. His happy temperament, which made him always cheerful, was displayed the year before his death, when he danced at an assembly of young seamen with all the vivacity of youth.

The name of Americus Vespuccius or Amerigo Vespucci, as the Spaniards call him, appears prominent in history as one of the discoverers of America. He has no valid title to that distinction. Proofs accumulate as investigations proceed, which show conclusively that he was the author or abettor of a stupendous historical fraud by which Columbus was cheated out of the honor of having his name given to this continent.

Vespuccius first appears in history as a mercantile agent of the Medici family of Florence, first in Barcelona and soon afterward in Seville, in Spain. He was then about forty years of age, having been born in Florence in 1451. In Seville he was actively engaged in furnishing supplies for ships fitting out for exploring and mercantile expeditions. In that capacity he had much personal intercourse with Columbus, whilst the admiral was preparing the large fleet for his second voyage. The narratives of the great Genoese inspired Vespuccius with a strong desire to make a mercantile venture in a voyage to the new-found world, and he had ambitious dreams of becoming a discoverer likewise. He studied geography and the kindred sciences, to fit himself for such an expedition; and when, in May, 1499, Alonzo de Ojedo sailed from Port St. Mary, opposite Cadiz, with four ships, following the southern route of Columbus to South America, Vespuccius accompanied him simply as an adventurer and self-constituted geographer. They discovered mountains in South America, when off the coast of Surinam, and then ran along the continent to the island of Trinidad, which Columbus had named the year before. Thence they cruised along the coasts and islands of Venezuela, and crossing the Caribbean Sea, touched at Hispaniola. Proceeding towards Spain, they engaged in kidnapping the natives of the Antilles, and in June, 1500, entered the port of Cadiz, the four vessels crowded with captives who were sold as slaves to the Spanish grandees.

Vespuccius, who seems to have been a shrewd, audacious, and unscrupulous man, immediately sent an account of the discoveries, in a letter, to one of the Medici family, assuming for himself the credit of that discovery; and in order to establish his claim to first discoverer of the American continent, he antedated the time of the commencement of the voyage, making it in 1497, the year before Columbus and Cabot made their respective discoveries, and saying that the expedition was absent from Spain twenty-five months. To this statement, the learned and conscientious Charlevoix says: "Ojeda, when judicially interrogated, gave the lie direct." Herrera, an early Spanish historian, accuses Vespuccius of falsifying the dates of two voyages in which he was engaged, and of confounding the one with the other, "in order that he might arrogate to himself the glory of having discovered the continent."

Vespuccius in other letters, told of other voyages and great discoveries which he had made whilst in the service of the King of Portugal, but cotemporary navigators and chroniclers made no mention of them. They were probably fictions of the boastful Florentine who had become expert in the construction of charts, and was familiar with the details of the numerous exploring voyages made from Spain and Portugal in his day. Finally, when Columbus was dead and no voice of accusation or denial could escape his lips, these letters of Vespuccius, giving an account of his pretended voyages and discoveries, were published at St. Diey, in Lorraine, and dedicated to the reigning duke of that country, which was then, as now, a German province. In that publication the name of *America*, as applied to our continent, was used. For this Vespuccius is responsible. It is possible that the letters themselves were forgeries, and that Vespuccius was not blameable for their publication; but he became an abettor in the fraud by not repudiating them. They were published in 1507, the year after the death of Columbus and four years before that of the Florentine.

That Vespuccius is responsible for the fraud involved in giving his name to the newly-discovered continent, seems clear from other circumstances. He was in communication with a learned German schoolmaster and cosmographer, named Woldseemüler, who pedantically transformed his name (Wood-lake-miller) into the Greek one of Hylacomylus. He was a correspondent of the Academy of Cosmography which the Duke of Lorraine had established at Strasburg, and at the request or suggestion of Vespuccius he proposed to the members of that academy, under whose auspices the letters of Americus were published, the name of *America* for the western continent. At about the same time Hylacomylus issued at St. Diey a little work entitled "Cosmographie Rudimenta," in which it was proposed to name the continent *America*. He took an active part in the publication of the letters of his friend, and he may be regarded as the chief perpetrator of the fraud with Vespuccius as the accessory, at least, because he sanctioned it by his silence. "Considering the intimacy of the two parties," says the learned Viscount Santarem, "there is no doubt that the geographer was guided by the navigator in what he did." Referring to the honor so conferred on Americus Vespuccius, the late Dr. Francis Lieber wrote to the author of this history: "Ethically speaking, there has never been erected a monument so magnificent, enduring and cruelly unjust; as if the Madonna di Sisto were not called by Raphael's name but by that of the man who framed it first." It is probably too late now, after centuries of use, to correct the injustice by changing the name of America. Washington, with his usual clear conception of right, did justice to Columbus by giving to the territory in which the seat of our national government was permanently established, the name of the District of Columbia. Although Cabot probably discovered the continent a few days before Columbus touched the shores of South America, he is not entitled to the honor of giving his name to our continent. Voltaire justly declared: "The glory of having discovered the New World undoubtedly belongs to him who had the genius and courage to undertake the first voyage." Newton observed: "Those who follow are only disciples." Cabot was a noble disciple.

VESPUCCIUS. COLUMBUS. ISABELLA. CABOT.

Many other voyages in search of new lands and great treasures, which were made from Spain at the beginning of the sixteenth century, had no immediate relation to the history of our country, and we will pass them by unnoticed. Others had a direct or indirect connection with further discoveries and final settlements in this region of the world, and these we will consider.

When the discoveries of Columbus were made known, the King of Portugal felt a strong desire to send out a similar expedition at the expense of the crown. But the Spanish monarchs had, with wise sagacity, obtained from Pope Alexander the Sixth (the pontiff who, by accident, took a fatal draught from a poisoned bowl which he had prepared for another), the gift of all lands that lay three hundred leagues westward of the Azores; and the Portuguese sovereign dared not interfere with these rights of Spain. But when the news of Cabot's discovery of a continent in the northwest, reached Lisbon, King Emanuel the Great, immediately fitted out two caravels for a voyage toward that continent, and placed them under the command of Gaspar Cortereal. He was a gentleman of enterprising and determined character, who had been reared in the household of the Portuguese monarch, and ardently thirsted for glory. He first touched the northern extremity of Newfoundland, and, it is believed, discovered the Gulf of St. Lawrence. He went up the coast of Labrador almost to Hudson's Bay, discovering nothing of importance not already seen by Cabot. The natives appeared to him rugged and strong, and capital subjects for slaves; so he seized fifty-nine of them, carried them on board his vessels, and with this living treasure he returned to Portugal. There he made a profitable sale of his captives. "They are extremely fitted to endure labor," wrote the Venetian ambassador at the Portuguese court, "and will probably turn out the best slaves which have been discovered up to this time."

The profits of this voyage excited the cupidity of Cortereal and his king, and they determined to engage in an active slave-trade with Laborador (Labrador), so named because of the admirable qualities of the natives as laborers. Cortereal went on a second voyage in 1501, and was lost at sea. His brother Michael went in search of him and was never heard of afterward. The king sent a ship to search for the brothers, but no tidings of them were brought back. These disasters frustrated the cruel designs of the slave-traders, and the Portuguese monarch sought to win glory for his favorite and his crown, by claiming that Cortereal was not only the first discoverer of Newfoundland, but that he was the first to see the continent in that region. In a Portuguese map published in 1508, the coast of Labrador is called Terra Corterealis or Cortereal's Land; and in support of the claim that he was the first discoverer of it, maps were actually forged. But all efforts to deprive Cabot of that honor failed.

The new-found continent at once became an object of great interest and attraction to adventurers of every kind, and a thirst for gold occasioned the fitting out of expeditions for further discoveries on the coasts of the main north and west of Hispaniola. That island, where the first Spanish settlements were made, became the centre of operations in the seas around, and on the coasts of the adjacent main after its complete subjection to Castilian rule. Don Diego Columbus, the son and successor of the admiral, was appointed governor, and there, with pomp and ceremony, he and his "vice-queen" held a sort of court which spread a halo of romance around that West Indian empire. Diego had married a daughter of the renowned Duke of Alva, and in June, 1509, had sailed from San Lucar with his wife, his brother Don Fernando who had grown to manhood and was well educated, and his two uncles. They were accompanied by a numerous retinue of cavaliers with their wives, and young ladies of rank and family who were more distinguished for high blood than riches. The latter were adventurers also—sent out to find rich husbands among the settlers in Hispaniola. They were successful, for all of them were soon married to the wealthiest colonists, and refined the rude manners which prevailed among them.

Not long after Diego's arrival Juan Ponce, commonly known as Ponce de Leon, who had borne a conspicuous part in the subjugation of Hispaniola, as a military commander, was appointed by the king governor of Porto Rico, a large island east of Hayti. Distinguished in the wars with the Moors, and a companion of Columbus in his second voyage, Juan Ponce was regarded with reverence by many, for his locks were white with age, and he had a noble Castilian lineage. He was then an old man animated with the ambitions of youth; and he was still seeking renown and wealth. The enjoyment of life had ever been an exquisite pleasure to him, and his desire to prolong his earthly existence in vigor was intense. That desire made him readily believe the marvelous tales told by some of the natives, of crystal waters flowing from living springs among the Bahama Islands, or on the coast of a beautiful country near them, in which he who bathed would be instantly endowed with immortal youth and great beauty. They told him that these fountains of youth were among magnificent trees which bore golden fruit, where the air was perpetually laden with the most exquisite perfume of flowers, and that these fruits were gathered and given to strangers by beautiful maidens. Here was the old story of the Gardens of the Hesperides in another form, which Hesiod said lay "beyond the bright ocean." Ponce dreamed of these gardens, their fountains, their golden fruit and the beautiful maidens, until he could no longer repress his desire to go in search of them. So, at the beginning of spring in 1512—a month after Vespuccius expired at Seville—he sailed from Porto Rico for the Bahamas, with ships fitted out at his own expense. On reaching the group, he went from island to island tasting of and bathing in every stream and lake that met his vision. Finally, disappointed but not disheartened, he extended his researches in a northwesterly direction. A few days afterwards, west winds brought the delicious perfumes of flowers. The heart of the old cavalier leaped with joy and hope. Soon a long line of wooded shores were in view, and as he drew near, Ponce saw lofty trees (magnolias) whose marvelous blossoms were tinting the forest, and burdening the air with their delicate fragrance. He believed he was on the borders of the fabled paradise.

It was Easter morning when Ponce and his companions landed near the site of St. Augustine, on the southeastern borders of our Republic. After he and his followers had chanted a joyous hymn commemorative of the resurrection of Jesus, he took possession of the great island, as he supposed it to be, in the name of the sovereign of Castile. Because of its wealth of flowers, some say, or because he first saw the land on Palm Sunday (Pascua Florida), as others tell us, he gave to the country the name of Florida, now one of the States of our Union. Among its forests and savannahs he sought in vain for the miraculous Fountain of Youth and Beauty, exciting the suspicions of the natives. Then he cruised along its shores, doubled Cape Cañaveral, and struggling with the Gulf Stream, sailed southward until he became entangled in a group of small islands abounding with huge turtles. This group he called the Tortugas—the Turtles—their present name. On another group he discovered only a single inhabitant—an old Indian woman—who was not a realization of his dream of beautiful maidens in the gardens of the Hesperides. He took the wrinkled hermitess with him, hoping that she might tell him where among the Bahamas he should find the Bimini, the beautiful island with the miraculous fountain. After buffeting the elements for several days, Ponce transferred the old woman to the ship of Ortubia, one of his trusted captains, who was instructed to pursue the search. Then he returned to Porto Rico, an older if not a wiser man. He had not secured for himself immortal youth, but he had won the immortal honor of being the discoverer of Florida, a part of the North American continent before unknown.

Ortubia soon arrived at Porto Rico. The old woman had guided him to Bimini, where he found beautiful groves and sparkling springs and limpid streams, but not one of the waters could restore to an old man the vernal greenness of his youth. So Ponce turned his thoughts to more practical subjects. Returning to Spain a few months later, he told the sovereigns of the beautiful land he had discovered, and received the appointment of Governor of Florida on condition that he should plant a colony there. This was not attempted until several years afterward. He had been moping in disappointment at Porto Rico, after an unsuccessful expedition against the Caribs, until he was assured that Florida was not an island, but a part of the continent. Then ambitious desires moved his sluggish heart, and the brilliant achievements of Cortez in the west, aroused the slumbering energies of the old cavalier. With nearly all of his wealth in two ships, he sailed from Porto Rico in 1521, and landed on the shores of Florida, not far from where he had first discovered that land, to prepare for founding a colony there. He was met by a crowd of natives who had gathered near the beach with bows and arrows and long javelins, to defend their land from the intrusion of the pale faces, for they had lately been taught, by the bitter experience of their neighbors, to look upon them as children of the Evil Spirit. A sharp battle ensued. Several of the Spaniards were killed, and Ponce de Leon, badly wounded in his thigh, was carried on board his ship and conveyed to Cuba, where he died. Upon his tomb was written the following inscription, in Latin:

IN THIS SEPULCHRE REST THE BONES OF A MAN WHO WAS LION BY NAME AND STILL MORE BY NATURE.

Meanwhile, the avarice of the Spaniards in Hayti had been greatly excited by the reports of a mariner who had accidentally visited the coast

JUAN PONCE DE LEON CARRIED ON BOARD HIS SHIP.

near the entrance to the Savannah River, where the natives presented him with gold and pearls. He also represented the masculine natives as athletic and fine looking. A commercial company was soon formed in Hayti to visit that country to obtain gold and slaves. Luke Vasquez D'Allyon, a wealthy colonist who owned extensive mines in Hayti, was at the head of the company. His chief object in the movement was to obtain slaves to work in his mines, for cruelty had almost exterminated the native men of the island. With two ships he sailed in a northwesterly direction in the year 1520, and arrived on the coast of South Carolina through St. Helen's Sound. The natives, believing the ships were sea-monsters, crowded the shores in wonderment. When they saw clothed and bearded men come out of them, they fled to the woods in alarm. Two of them were caught and carried on board D'Allyon's ship, where they were feasted, dressed in Spanish costume, and sent back. Their appearance so pleased their sachem, that he sent fifty of his subjects to the vessels with fruits and provisions. When the Spaniards took long excursions through the forests, he sent men with them as guides and servants. In some of these excursions they were presented with gold and silver, and pearls; and they were everywhere entertained with the kindest hospitality. They were rudely feasted and were as rudely serenaded with the music of the pipe and drum. Dancing-girls afforded amusement for them, and they departed with pontifical blessings from the dwellings of chiefs and sachems.

Having fully "spied out the land" of this simple people, and being ready for departure, D'Allyon invited a large number of the native men to a feast on his ships, and to engage in traffic. Having finished the trade, they were invited below, where they were well fed, and filled with strong wine. When all were made stupid by intoxication, the hatches of the ships were closed and the deluded men were carried away captive. Many died from vexation and starvation, for they refused to take food. One of the ships was foundered at sea, and Spaniards and captives were all lost. The less fortunate captives were taken to Hayti, where D'Allyon, deaf to the voices of mercy, humanity and justice, made them slaves. The story of this perfidy and wickedness, spread rapidly from lip to lip along the coast, even so far as the region of St. Augustine, and it aroused the natives to those acts of defence and revenge, which resulted in the wounding of Juan Ponce de Leon, and the expulsion of his followers from the land, the next year.

Instead of being punished for his crime against mankind, D'Allyon was rewarded as a discoverer of new lands, when he visited the court of Spain soon afterwards. He was also appointed chief magistrate of the province of Chicora, as the native South Carolinians called their country; and he was vested with authority to plant a colony there. Under this commission he fitted out three ships at Hayti, and with the mariner Miruela, who first saw the coast near the mouth of the Savannah River, he sailed for Chicora, and passing through St. Helen's Sound reached the continent near the mouth of the Combahee. There he opened traffic with the natives, who seemed to be indifferent to his crime, and when he had finished trading he proceeded to plant his colony on an island in the waters of Port Royal Sound, near the site of the present town of Beaufort, South Carolina.

A part of D'Allyon's company had landed and prepared to lay the foundation of a town, when a deputation came from the sachem of the Combahee and invited the Spaniards to a great feast at his village at the mouth of that river. About two hundred of them went to the banquet, and were treated with the most friendly hospitalities. For three days and three nights the feast went on, and at the end of it, whilst the guests were soundly sleeping, the Indians fell upon and massacred the whole of them. They had fully matched the treachery of the pale-faces, but they were not satisfied. Hastening to the site of the projected town, they slew many there. Some of the Spaniards escaped to the ships. Among them was D'Allyon, who, badly wounded, died soon afterward. Retributive justice had overtaken him on the theatre of his great crime. So perished the first germ of a settlement of Europeans that was planted in the soil of our present domain.

In the meantime the Spaniards had been making explorations and conquests westward of Hispaniola or Hayti. In the year 1502, as we have already observed, Columbus had sailed from Cadiz with four ships, to search for a passage to the Indian Seas through the Gulf of Mexico, accompanied by his brother Bartholomew and his young son Fernando. He arrived in the Caribbean Sea in June and soon afterward he discovered the coast of Central America, which he explored from the Isthmus of Darien far up the shores of Nicaragua.

The region of Central America King Ferdinand divided into two provinces, in 1509, and prepared to plant colonies there. One of these provinces he placed under the command of the navigator Ojeda, and the other under Diego de Nicuesa. Late in the autumn Ojeda sailed from Hayti, accompanied by Pizarro, who afterward became the energetic and cruel conqueror of Peru. Hernando Cortez, who was afterward the savage conqueror of Mexico, would have sailed with Ojeda, had not a violently inflamed eye prevented. Ojeda was also accompanied by some friars whose chief business at the outset seems to have been the reading aloud to the natives, in the Latin language, a proclamation by the Spanish leader which had been prepared by learned divines in Spain. It declared that God who made them all, had given in charge of one man, named Saint Peter, who had his seat at Rome, all the nations of the earth with all the lands and seas on the globe; that his successors at Rome called Popes, were endowed in the same way by God; that one of them had given to the Spanish monarchs all the islands and continents in the Western Ocean; that all natives yet found had given cheerful submission to whatever the soldiers and priests required of them, and that the natives of the land before him were expected to do the same. In the event of their willing submission, he promised them many favors. "If you do not this," he said, "or wickedly and intentionally delay to do so, I certify to you, that, by the aid of God, I will powerfully invade and make war upon you in all parts and modes that I can, and will subdue you to the yoke and obedience of the Church and his majesty; and I will take your wives and children and make slaves of them, and sell them as such, and dispose of them as his majesty may command; and I will take your effects, and will do you all the harm and injury in my power, as vassals who will not obey or

OJEDA CUTTING HIS WAY THROUGH THE INDIAN RANKS.

receive their sovereign, and who resist and oppose him. And I protest that the deaths and disasters which may in this manner be occasioned, will be the fault of yourselves, and not of his majesty, nor of me, nor of these cavaliers who accompany me."

This infamous proclamation which justified murder and robbery under the sanction of that religion the chief attributes of which are justice, benevolence and mercy, was adopted as the formula, and indicated the spirit of the Spanish invaders of America afterwards. Although read aloud by the friars, the pagans could not understand a word of it. The Christians did not expect them to understand it. Their offices were fulfilled when the Latin words had gone into the ears of their dusky listeners. The consequences must be borne by the wondering heathen!

Delay in making a willing submission was speedily followed by violence. The natives were attacked by the intruders and some of them were killed. Some were sent captive to the ships. Ojeda, apprehending no danger, permitted his followers who were on shore to roam in quest of booty. He was mistaken. The outraged Indians gathered stealthily and attacked the Spaniards furiously with poisoned arrows. Ojeda and a few soldiers took refuge in a small cabin, where all but himself were slain. He was a small man and found shelter from a shower of arrows, under his buckler, for awhile, when he sprang from his covert like a tiger and cutting his way through the multitude uninjured, he found shelter and concealment among the matted roots of mango trees at the wooded base of a mountain. There he was found by his followers, almost dead with fatigue and hunger, and was carried to his ship.

NATIVE CUBANS WORSHIPPING A PICTURE.

At this juncture Nicuesa appeared with his squadron. The two governors soon agreed upon a plan of operations. Four hundred men and some horses were landed, and all started for the village of the Indians, which they desolated with fire and sword. No quarter was given to age or sex. Men, women and children were slain with weapons or perished in the burning cabins. Having gathered much spoil, the governors parted, Nicuesa for his prescribed province, and Ojeda for another part of his, for he would not attempt to plant a colony on the scene of his disaster.

The wants of his followers caused Ojeda to sail for Hayti for supplies. His crew rebelled and put him in irons, but when a great storm arose, they released him for the sake of mutual safety. The vessel stranded on the southern shores of Cuba which was then under native rule, and a place of refuge for the unhappy inhabitants of Hispaniola. The shipwrecked mariners suffered dreadfully in morasses, and more than half of them perished. They feared the natives and tried to avoid them; but hunger made the survivors bold, and a part of them, led by Ojeda, followed a path into an Indian village. The pagans there treated the suffering Christians with the most tender care and unstinted hospitality. The cacique sent men with provisions to hunt up survivors in the morasses; and when Ojeda departed, he sent guides and servants to conduct the Spaniard and his companions to a part of the island nearest Jamaica, on which his countrymen had lately settled. To that island Ojeda was taken, and thence to Hispaniola, where he died. At his own request his body was buried at the portal of the Cathedral of San Francisco. He chose that spot that every one who passed the portal might "tread upon his grave." So he sought to expiate his crimes by such post-mortem or after-death humiliation.

The natural kindness of the Cubans was requited the following year (1510) in the usual way. The Spaniards of Hayti, inflamed by Ojeda's account of the wealth of Cuba, conquered it, and there established the horrid social and political system which had made Hispaniola a land of mourning for its native inhabitants. The pious Ojeda had planted a germ of the Church in Cuba, and so gave the pagans there, as he believed, an equivalent for any disabilities which they might suffer under Spanish rule. In his distress he had made a vow to the Virgin, that if she should deliver him from the great peril, he would build a chapel in the first Indian village he might find, and over its altar place a precious little Flemish painting of the Sacred Mother, which he carried with him, and leave it there. He did so. The character and attributes of the Virgin, as the mother of God who rules the universe, he explained to the simple-minded cacique and his people, who, at the outset, were taught to revere the picture as a blessing from the skies. They kept the chapel swept clean; made votive offerings; composed couplets to the Virgin and sang them with accompaniments of instrumental music, as they danced in the groves around the sacred place; and in other similar ways they commended themselves to their pious conquerors as hopeful converts to Christianity. So it was that the Christian religion was introduced into Cuba more than three centuries and a half ago.

CHAPTER VII.

THE SPANIARDS ON THE ISTHMUS OF DARIEN—THEIR CRUEL TREATMENT OF THE NATIVES—STORY OF THE DISCOVERY OF THE PACIFIC OCEAN, BY VASCO NUNEZ DE BALBOA—HE TAKES POSSESSION OF IT IN THE NAME OF THE SPANISH MONARCHS—TIDINGS OF PERU—DEATH OF NUNEZ—CUBA CONQUERED—HERNANDO CORTEZ—STORY OF THE CONQUEST OF MEXICO—SUCCESS AND CRUELTIES OF THE SPANIARDS IN MEXICO—CAPTURE OF ITS CAPITAL—DESTRUCTION OF IDOLS—ATTEMPTED CONQUEST OF FLÓRIDA BY NARVAEZ—DREADFUL SUFFERINGS OF THAT LEADER AND HIS FOLLOWERS—THEIR DESTRUCTION.

THE Pacific Ocean, whose waters lave the western shores of our Republic along a distance, as a bird flies, of sixteen degrees of latitude, from San Diego on the south to Cape Flattery on the north, was discovered by one of the Spanish adventurers who accompanied the expedition under Nicuessa, to the coasts of Central America. That discoverer was Vasco Nuñez de Balboa, an active and energetic young man of noble lineage but of small fortune, who crossed the Atlantic to the West Indies in search of wealth, in the year 1501. On Hispaniola he had acquired a moderate competence, but having fallen in debt, he escaped his creditors by being carried in a cask (supposed to contain provisions) on board a ship commanded by the Bachelor Énciso, one of Nicuessa's lieutenants. When the vessel was fairly out at sea, Nuñez came from his cask. Enciso, astonished, and angry because of the deception, threatened to leave him on the first uninhabited island they should discover, but Nuñez succeeded in pacifying his commander and gaining his friendship.

At Carthagena, Enciso was joined by Pizarro, who had been left by Ojeda in charge of the remnant of his colony. With that remnant, much wasted by sickness, hunger, and the arrows of the natives, he was making his way back to Hispaniola, in a brigantine. He was persuaded by Enciso to remain and return with him to the place of Pizarro's departure. They were about to weigh anchor when they heard of a province called Zenu, lying at the westward, whose mountains they were told abounded with the precious metals, and where there was an ancient cemetery in which, for centuries, the Indians had been buried with all their golden ornaments. Enciso determined to hasten to that country, dig treasures from the mountains and sack the sepulchres, for he felt no compunction at the idea of rifling the graves of pagans. The whole expedition sailed for the coast of Zenu, where they were met by two caciques and many armed followers, who opposed the invasion of the Spaniards. Then Enciso caused the formula used by Ojeda to be read and interpreted to the caciques, expounding the nature of God, the supremacy of the Pope and the right of Roman Catholic sovereigns to all the lands by virtue of a grant from the occupant of the papal chair at Rome. The caciques courteously listened to the Spaniards, and then one of them said: "No doubt there is only one God, but the Pope must have been drunk to give away what was not his own, and the King of Spain must have been crazy to ask from him what belonged to others. We are lords of these lands and want no other sovereign, and if this king should come to take possession, we would cut off his head and put it on a pole."

Enciso attacked and defeated the Indians, but in rifling the tombs of their ancestors, he did not find sufficient treasure to assuage his grief at the loss of two of his men who had perished by poisoned arrows. He now proceeded to the seat of Ojeda's colony, where he found the fort and cabins erected there in ruins. Nuñez, who had been there before, with another adventurer guided Enciso to a village on the bank of a river which the natives called Darien, and there the seat of government was established, after expelling the natives. Discontents soon arose among the Spaniards, and Nuñez taking advantage of them, succeeded in having Enciso deposed and himself made chief magistrate. When Nicuessa came to assume chief command, the colonists, under the influence of Nuñez, refused their allegiance to him, and the usurper became governor. He expelled Nicuessa from the country, who, with a few followers, embarked in a crazy vessel for Hispaniola, and were never heard of afterwards. Enciso, seeing no chance for the recovery of his power whilst the energetic usurper lived, returned to Spain with feelings of revenge.

Nuñez was soon joined by two Spaniards who, to avoid punishment, had fled from Nicuessa's ship and found refuge and the kindest treatment with Careta, the cacique of Coyba. They requited this hospitality of the pagan chief by advising Nuñez to attack Careta in his dwelling, where he would find immense booty. The governor prepared to do so. One of the Spaniards returned to Careta to assist Nuñez in his betrayal, and the other acted as guide to the invaders. Nuñez was kindly received by the cacique and his people, and departed with presents. He halted a little way from the village, and when the Indians were all asleep, he led his men into the town at midnight and made Careta, his wives and children and many of his people captives. With them and a considerable booty, the treacherous Nuñez returned to Darien, when the good cacique, distressed at his situation, said: "What have I done to thee that thou shouldst treat me thus cruelly? None of thy people ever came to my land that were not fed, and sheltered, and treated with loving-kindness. When thou camest to my dwelling did I meet thee with a javelin in my hand? Did I not set meat and drink before thee, and welcome thee as a brother? Set me free, therefore, with my family and people, and we will remain thy friends. We will supply thee with provisions, and reveal to thee the riches of the land. Dost thou doubt my faith? Behold my daughter! I give her to thee as a pledge of my friendship. Take her for thy wife, and be assured of the fidelity of her family and her people."

Careta's daughter was young and beautiful. Nuñez was deeply impressed by her charms. He granted the prayer of Careta, took his daughter to be his wife according to the usages of her country, and becoming very fond of her, she soon acquired great influence over him. He assisted Careta in wars against his enemies, and they became fast friends. Whilst visiting a powerful cacique, a friendly neighbor of Careta, Nuñez was told by the son of that chief, that beyond the mountains toward which he pointed, was a mighty sea that could be discovered from the summits of the great hills; that the sea was navigated by vessels almost as large as the Spanish brigantines and equipped like them with sails and oars; that the rivers which flowed down from the southern slopes of the mountains abounded with gold, and that there was a country further southward, bordering on that great sea, where the kings ate and drank out of golden vessels, and that gold was as plentiful there as iron was among the Spaniards.

This information seemed like a revelation from heaven beaming into the mind of Nuñez. He felt a sudden impulse to abandon his wayward life, and an ambition to be ranked among the great discoverers of his age. If he could first see that mighty ocean and the precious rivers and the country where its kings ate and drank out of golden vessels, he would surely be elevated to fame and fortune. He eagerly inquired how the summits of the mountains and the borders of that sea might be reached. "You will have to fight your way to the top and down their slopes, and through the plains beyond, with powerful caciques and brave warriors," said the young man. "You will need at least a thousand men, armed like those who follow you."

Nuñez hastened back to Darien to make preparations for his journey. His thoughts were wholly occupied with plans for the discovery of the great sea beyond the mountains. He pondered the subject when awake and it gave color and shape to his night-dreams. With gold of the value of fifteen thousand crowns which he sent to Don Diego Columbus, in Hispaniola, to be forwarded to the king as the royal share of the winnings in Central America, he sent an appeal to that officer for aid in men and provisions, to enable Nuñez to fight his way across the isthmus. Whilst awaiting an answer he made several expeditions from Darien, and everywhere he heard the story of the great sea beyond the mountains. Finally, one hundred and fifty armed men, with ample supplies, arrived at Darien from Hispaniola, and Nuñez determined to march for the mountain summits. With one hundred and ninety men and a number of bloodhounds, he made his way to Coyba, where Careta furnished him with guides and Indian warriors; and on the 6th of September, 1513, the expedition set off for the great hills which loomed up in the southern horizon. They fought their way victoriously, spreading terror among the natives by their guns, which, to the Indians, seemed like demons vomiting lightning and thunder.

DISCOVERY OF THE PACIFIC.

At ten o'clock in the morning of the 26th of September, Nuñez and his followers emerged from a thick forest high up in the mountain range. Only sixty-seven of his Spanish soldiers now remained, who were able to climb that rugged height. The bald rocky summit alone remained to be ascended. Commanding his followers to halt, and not a man to stir from his place, he climbed to that summit, when the glorious apparition of a broad sea burst upon his vision. It seemed to him that a new and unknown world, separated from the known by the lofty mountain barrier on which he stood, had been unfolded to him. It was even so. Overcome by mingled feelings of awe and joy, he fell upon his knees and fervently poured out his thanks to God for permitting him to be the first of Europeans to discover that mighty sea. He then shouted to his followers to come up; and when they had gathered around him on that breezy height, and beheld the sea stretching out interminably, he exhorted them to be faithful to him and valorous in the conquests of rich heathen lands before them, and so give glory to God and their king and win riches for themselves. They embraced their leader and made vows of fidelity to him even unto death. Then they chanted the *Te Deum Laudamus.* So it was that the Pacific Ocean was discovered by Vasco Nuñez de Balboa. It was called by him the South Sea, but Magellan, who sailed into it through the straits which bear his name, a few years later, called it the Pacific Ocean, because its waters were far less turbulent than those of the Atlantic which he had just crossed.

Nuñez now called all of his followers to witness the fact that he took possession of that sea, with all its coasts and islands, in the name of the sovereigns of Spain; and the notary drew up a testimonial to that effect, which the leader and his sixty-seven warriors signed. Then a tree was cut down and wrought into a cross; and on the spot where Nuñez first saw the ocean, it was planted with solemn religious ceremonies, whilst the Indians looked on in wonder, not comprehending the meaning of the sacred symbol nor the significance of the act. It marked the subjugation of their land by an avaricious race.

Descending the mountains on their southern sides, Nuñez and his followers made their way to the sea. As the tide came flowing in upon the sandy beach, the leader took a banner on which the Virgin and Child were painted, and under them the arms of Castile and Leon. Then drawing his sword and throwing his buckler over his shoulder, he marched into the water until it covered his knees, and waving his banner he with a loud voice again proclaimed that he took possession of that sea and its islands, in the name of the sovereigns of Spain. A testimonial to that effect was again signed by all, and the conquest was regarded as complete. After that Nuñez made voyages along the coast of the Pacific, and heard tidings of the rich kingdom of Peru, where the Incas or monarchs ate and drank out of vessels of gold. That kingdom, then eminent for its civilization, was afterward conquered by Pizarro, with circumstances of great cruelty and wickedness. Vasco Nuñez de Balboa, falsely accused of traitorous intentions by his jealous rival and successor, Davila, was beheaded at Acla, in Central America, by order of that officer, in 1517, when he was in the forty-second year of his age.

At about the time when Central America was first colonized, Cuba was conquered by three hundred Spaniards under Diego Velasquez, who had been sent from Hispaniola for the purpose, by Don Diego Columbus, in 1511. Hernando Cortez, destined to make a conspicuous figure in history, accompanied the expedition, and was made the chief magistrate of Santiago, the Spanish capital of the island. He was a handsome, well educated, enterprising young man, then only twenty-six years of age, and had just married one of the young ladies who came from Spain with the Vice-Queen of Hispaniola. Cortez soon amassed a considerable fortune. He was a cruel worker of the natives in his mines. "How many of the Indians died in extracting gold for him," wrote Las Casas, "God will have kept a better account than I have."

Mexico had just been discovered by Juan de Grijalva. Cortez was sent with an expedition to conquer it. He set out from Cuba late in 1518, with five hundred and fifty Spaniards, nearly three hundred Indians, a few negroes, thirteen horses and ten brass cannon, in ten ships, and landed on the shore of Tabasco, on the 4th of March, 1519. There he had a battle with the natives, and so terrified them with his horses and great guns, that they fled in dismay. They gave him as a peace-offering, a beautiful Mexican slave girl, the daughter of a cacique, whom Cortez caused to be baptized with the name of Donna Marina. She was very intelligent, and bore a conspicuous part in the fortunes of Cortez. "Without her aid," says Arthur Helps, "his conquest of Mexico would never have been accomplished."

RAISING A MEMORIAL CROSS.

Pushing into the interior, Cortez was met by deputies of Montezuma, a native emperor and ruler of an empire which had existed full three hundred years. The emperor hearing of the approach of the Spaniards, sent to inquire what was their errand. "Has your king any gold?" asked Cortez. The deputies answered, "Yes." The invader replied: "Let him send it to me, for I and my companions have a complaint—a disease of the heart, which only gold can cure." This was the dreadful malady which afflicted all of the Spanish discoverers and conquerors; and the records of their search for the remedy have stained the pages of history with pictures of the most horrid crimes.

Cortez took possession of the country in the usual form, and planted the seeds of a colony on the site of Vera Cruz. He destroyed his ships to pre-

SPANIARDS DESTROYING MEXICAN IDOLS.

vent malcontents among his followers returning in them ; and, winning to his standard several native tribes who had suffered from Montezuma's tax-gatherers, and were ready to rebel, he marched toward the Mexican capital in the month of August, over the same route which was pursued by General Scott and his conquering army more than three hundred years afterward. He fought his way against overwhelming numbers who were terrified by the flashing of the armor of the Spaniards and the thunders of their cannon. The simple people regarded the invaders as divine personages and made human sacrifices to placate them; but the avarice and ambition of the Spaniards could not be appeased until they themselves had sacrificed thousands of human beings on the altar of their lust.

Discontented or alarmed, Mexicans continually flocked to the standard of Cortez. He fought and conquered the powerful Tlascalans and made them his allies; and early in November, after murdering a large number of Cholulans that fell into his hands, he appeared before the City of Mexico—Mexico the superb, sitting on the bosom of a beautiful lake and alive with more than three hundred thousand people. With him were six thousand native warriors and four hundred and fifty Spaniards. Montezuma and his nobles received the invaders with great pomp and kindness. A beautiful palace was assigned to Cortez for his quarters. Believing that a display of power would greatly increase his strength and influence, that leader made an attack of a few Mexicans upon some of his followers, a pretext for seizing the emperor in his own palace and confining him in chains in that of his guest, whilst seventeen of the offenders were burned alive before the gate of the imperial residence. Cortez also compelled his royal prisoner to acknowledge himself a vassal of Charles the Fifth, then Emperor of Spain, and to induce his nobles and tributary caciques to do likewise. He made that vassalage a pretext for exacting tribute, and in the name of his royal master, Cortez extorted from the fallen monarch gold to the amount of two hundred thousand dollars.

This audacious robber, from the time when he left Cuba, had been rebellious towards his superiors. Another adventurer, named Narvaez, was sent with nine hundred men, eighty horses and a dozen cannon for the field, to displace the rebel and send him back to Cuba. When Cortez heard of the landing of his appointed successor, he hastened with a part of his Spanish troops and native warriors toward the coast. He had guessed the errand of Narvaez, and at once attacked him in his camp. Cortez was victorious. The defeated troops joined the standard of the victor, and all marched for the City of Mexico, where the great leader had left a small garrison under the cruel Alvarado. The inhabitants there had risen in insurrection because

Alvarado, on suspicion of meditated rebellion, had caused to be murdered six hundred unarmed Mexican noblemen at the end of a solemn festival. The revolt had become formidable when Cortez returned, and in an attempt to appease his people, Montezuma had been slain. This event increased the horror and indignation of the Mexicans. The Spaniards were driven out of the city, and their rear-guard were cut in pieces. They fled before the

VASCO NUNEZ DE BALBOA TAKING POSSESSION OF THE PACIFIC OCEAN.

exasperated Mexicans, for the space of six days, dreadfully harassed by their pursuers. Finally, on the plain of Otamba, the fugitives turned upon the Mexicans, and on a hot day in July, 1520, a pitched battle was fought there. The Spaniards were victorious, and the fate of the dynasty of Montezuma was sealed.

Cortez now marched to Tlascala, where he was joined by an auxiliary native army. After subduing the neighboring provinces, he turned his forces toward the City of Mexico. The siege which ensued was one of the most remarkable recorded in history. It continued seventy-five days, when, on the 13th of August, 1521, the city was captured by the Spaniards with immense slaughter of the inhabitants. More human beings were that day offered upon the altar of ambition than had been slain in sacrifice before the Mexican gods in the space of ten years. The victory over the Mexicans was complete; the conquest of Mexico in less than two years, was a fact that had passed into history.

Impelled by his own religious zeal and prompted by the priests in his train, Cortez at once proceeded to further humiliate, horrify and exasperate the subdued people, by making a clean sweep, with the besom of destruction, over the idols and temples of the empire. In the great square in Mexico, the conqueror and his followers, with their garments stained with the blood of their fellow-creatures, devoutly sang the *Te Deum*, and prostrating themselves before the image of the Blessed Virgin which they had set up, they reverently thanked God for permitting them to be the humble instruments in annihilating image-worship and in staying the horrid rites of human sacrifice. Such was the spirit and temper of the age in which they lived. So was introduced Christianity into Mexico.

Pamphilio de Narvaez, who was sent to Mexico to supersede Cortez, had extraordinary adventures afterwards as a discoverer in Florida. He was a man of wealth, tall and muscular in form, commanding in appearance, with a red beard, a fine voice, and was an expert horseman. He went to Spain to complain of Cortez, where he remained several years, and finally, in June, 1527, he sailed from San Lucar, under the authority of the monarch, with six hundred men in five vessels, commissioned to conquer and govern Florida. After long detention in San Domingo and Cuba, he sailed from the latter island with four hundred men and eighty horses, accompanied by Cabeça de Vaca, as treasurer of the expedition and a sort of deputy governor. With less than four hundred men and only forty-two horses, he landed on the west side of the present Tampa Bay, on the 13th of April, 1528. The Indians fled from their wigwams or rude huts; and when all of his followers, with the horses, were on the shore, Narvaez raised the standard of Spain, and with the usual formula took possession of the country in the name of his monarch. His officers then took an oath of allegiance to him as their governor; and had he known how potent kind treatment would have been in securing the friendship of the Indians, he might have ruled the province in peace and good will and with abundant prosperity. Instead of pursuing this wise course, he relied upon force and cruelty to effect the subjugation of the natives. The consequences were disastrous to him and those who came after him. His cruel mutilation of a captive chief after his first hostile encounter with the natives, by causing his nose to be cut off; and his making Cuban bloodhounds tear in pieces the mother of the cacique in the presence of her children, created such intense horror and hatred among the people in all that Gulf region, that vengeance followed the footsteps of

THANKSGIVING BEFORE THE IMAGE OF THE VIRGIN.

the Spaniards closely and implacably, with the tenacity of their own savage dogs.

Narvaez marched with high hopes from Tampa, to explore the country, directing his ships to sail along the coasts for the same purpose. He had been told that not far off he would find Apalachee, a city and country of plenty. He crossed the Suwanee high up, and then the Ocktockonee. Every day he expected to come upon a city sparkling with wealth—filled with gold and food, like those of Mexico and Peru; and palaces of caciques with magnificent courts, and a country in which they might riot in luxury won by plunder as Cortez and Pizarro had done. Alas! it was an idle dream. All before him were but creations of imagination; all behind him were the dark realities of disappointment. The captives whom Narvaez forced to act as guides, led the invaders into dark forests, tangled morasses, and arid sands. Men and horses suffered dreadfully from the pangs of hunger. When a horse died from starvation, these cavaliers were compelled to eat it to avoid starvation themselves. At every rood they met hostility and treachery; and when they came to Apalachee, instead of a splendid city and fields and granaries burdened with food, they found a village of forty thatched huts in the midst of scattered fields of growing maize or Indian corn. There were no roads nor bridges, nor other evidences of civilization; and poverty was the common aspect of nature and people. The men had fled, but soon returned for their women and children with offers of friendship. These offers were accepted, and all might have been well had not Narvaez, in imitation of Cortez in Mexico, seized the principal cacique of the Apalacheeans, and held him as a hostage for the good behaviour of his people. Narvaez believed this spirited act would awe the inhabitants; but he had a more warlike people to deal with than the soft Aztecs of Mexico. They flew to arms to avenge the wrong; attacked the Spaniards with great fury; burned their own houses that they might not give shelter to their enemies, and then fled to their cornfields and the forests with their families.

Narvaez was now on the Appalachicola River. He learned from the captive cacique that he was in the richest region of that whole country; that forests and lakes and morasses everywhere abounded, and that he would be met at every step by expert and hostile bowmen. He told him that nine days journeying southward would bring him to the sea-coast and a better country, and assured him that gold had never been found in the region which he had penetrated. Misfortune made Narvaez listen patiently to these discouraging words, and he and his followers turned their faces toward the sea. Their sufferings on that march were dreadful. The country was broken into lakes, swamps, morasses and forests. They were compelled to wade through water sometimes waist deep and work their way through tangled vines and bristling brambles, every moment exposed to the arrows of expert bowmen who hung upon their flanks and rear. When they reached the sea—the Gulf of Mexico—at near the mouth of the Appalachicola, sickness was rapidly wasting Narvaez and nearly all his men. They had devoured for food all but one of their horses, and they were in the most pitiable plight. All thoughts of gold and dominion had left their minds, and they stood upon that shore, with no signs of their fleet visible, the victims of a cruel policy of their own. They had now no thought but the question, How shall we save our lives?

There was no other way of escape from death than by the sea. Surmounting the greatest difficulties, they built some frail boats, and provisioned them with Indian corn. With this, and some water in half-tanned horse-hides, they embarked, and coasted toward the Mississippi. Their food and water soon failed, and their sufferings were horrible. One by one they died, when a storm—a "norther"—struck and dispersed the flotilla. The boat that bore Treasurer de Vaca was stranded on an island, and he and his companions were kindly treated by the Indians. Narvaez was never heard of afterward. De Vaca seems to have been the only Spaniard who survived and returned to Spain. After eight years of captivity amongst the Indians, he made his way on foot, from tribe to tribe, until he had crossed the continent, and arrived at a port occupied by his countrymen on the Gulf of California. Thence he made his way to Spain, where he appeared at the court as one risen from the dead. His narrative was soon published, and it was read with an appetite such as the most marvelous romance creates. His revelations of the heroism of Narvaez made the deeds of that adventurer compare favorably with those of Cortez and Pizarro. Narvaez had not only fought hostile men with a handful of followers, but he had fought the climate and topography of Florida. Cortez had struggled in a salubrious climate seven thousand feet above the sea, and Pizarro had marched into the country of the Incas of Peru over a splendid highway built by that extraordinary people along the summits of the Andes. Narvaez was never, probably, one hundred feet above tide-water, in Florida, and much of the time he was breathing the deadly malaria of the Everglades.

CHAPTER VIII.

DE SOTO COMMISSIONED TO CONQUER AND GOVERN FLORIDA—HIS EXPERIENCE IN THE DOMINIONS OF A CREEK CHIEF—A FRIENDLY INDIAN QUEEN ON THE SAVANNAH RIVER—DE SOTO'S TREACHERY—HIS KIND RECEPTION IN THE COOSA COUNTRY—DE SOTO'S PERFIDY—HIS MARCH THROUGH ALABAMA—DE SOTO IS OUTGENERALLED BY THE EMPEROR TUSCALOOSA—TERRIBLE ENCOUNTER WITH THE ALABAMIANS AT THEIR CAPITAL—DE SOTO GOES FURTHER INTO THE INTERIOR—FATAL ENCOUNTERS WITH THE BARBARIANS—HE DISCOVERS THE MISSISSIPPI RIVER—HE CROSSES THAT STREAM AND MARCHES TOWARD THE ROCKY MOUNTAINS—DE SOTO RETURNS TO THE MISSISSIPPI AND DIES—HIS FOLLOWERS REACH MEXICO—DEATH OF HIS WIFE.

THE hideous story of the disastrous adventures of Narvaez and his companions in Florida seems sufficient to have deterred others from undertaking further enterprises among the fierce Apalachians, either for gold or dominion. But the effect was otherwise. Spanish chivalry had been stimulated, and thirst for glory had been intensified by the valorous exploits of the discoverers and conquerors in America, and the more hazardous the performance the greater was the renown. The very difficulties in the way seemed to sharpen desire; and when Hernando de Soto, who, as one of the conquerors of Peru under Pizarro, had returned to Spain with great wealth and reputation, proposed an expedition for the conquest of Florida, hundreds of young men, the flower of the Spanish and Portuguese nobility, flocked to his standard.

De Soto longed to rival Cortez and Pizarro in the brilliancy of his deeds. He had appeared at the court of Charles the Fifth in great splendor, as one of the richest men in Spain, and had been favorably received. He had lately married Isabella de Bobadilla, a scion of one of the most renowned of the Castilian families, and his influence at court was thereby strengthened; and when he offered to undertake the conquest of Florida at his own expense, the permission of his sovereign was readily given. Charles also commissioned him governor of Cuba, from which island he would sail for Florida, and made him captain-general of the provinces which he might secure by conquest on the main.

De Soto was of gentle birth; of known pre-eminence as a soldier; wise in council; prudent in action; brave to rashness in conflict, and his reputation was without blemish. In person, he was elegant; in deportment, courtly; as a horseman, expert; and in age, thirty-seven—the prime of young manhood. With these qualities and his generous offer to aid young cavaliers who needed assistance in equipping themselves in accordance with their rank and position, he soon gathered a band of six hundred brilliant adventurers. Some of the wealthier came in gorgeous suits of armor, rich dresses and trains of servants. Many of them had sold houses, lands and vineyards to enable them to embark in the enterprise, for De Soto believed there was more gold in Florida than in Mexico and Peru together, and had said so.

With this brilliant armament, and accompanied by his beautiful young wife and other noble ladies, De Soto embarked at San Lucar de Barrameda, at the mouth of the Guadalquiver, early in April, 1538, a little less than eleven years after Narvaez sailed on his unfortunate expedition from the same port. His armament consisted of seven large and three smaller vessels; and the flag-ship was the *San Christoval*, of eight hundred tons burthen. Their departure was cheered by the braying of trumpets and the shouts of a great multitude; and the fleet was followed by twenty-six merchant vessels bound for Mexico.

So bountifully had De Soto furnished his ships with stores, that every man was supplied with double rations; and in their enjoyment of plenty and wastefulness, they almost adored their munificent leader. Gayety and festivity—music, dancing and feasting—prevailed on board the *San Christoval* during that sunny voyage, in which richly-dressed ladies were conspicuous, with handsome young pages to do their bidding, especially on mild and brilliant moonlit evenings within the tropic of Cancer. All were joyous, for they thought they were on the way to an earthly paradise. At near the close of May the ships all entered Cuban waters. The bright sea-pageant vanished, for then the real business of the expedition was begun in earnest. There De Soto occupied a whole year in arranging affairs of government and preparing for the great enterprise in view.

Towards the middle of May, 1539, De Soto sailed from Havana with a fleet of nine vessels, large and small, and about a thousand followers with many horses, cattle, mules, and a herd of swine. He left public affairs in Cuba in the hands of his wife and the lieutenant-governor, where, for several days, he had given feasts and entertainments such as might be appropriate *after* a great conquest. A vessel had been sent to Florida to find a safe harbor and to kidnap some Indians to act as guides and interpreters. So prepared, De Soto bade Isabella de Bobadilla farewell, on board his ship, with the full expectation of returning speedily with the rich fruits of a glorious conquest. Alas! clouds soon gathered in the firmament of his hopes, and his brilliant dream was never realized. His voyage was pleasant; and when the armament anchored in Tampa Bay, near where Narvaez had landed, delicious perfumes came from the shores, for all Florida was in bloom. It was the 30th of May.

Had De Soto been wiser than the other conquerors, and conciliated the Indians by friendly acts, all might have been well. But he was no wiser than they. He sent armed men to capture natives, that he might obtain knowledge of the country, and so he imitated his predecessors. The savages had learned to be cautious from their contact with Narvaez, and they were too wily in their movements, and too expert with the bow and arrow, to be taken.

In one of their little excursions the Spaniards were startled as they were charging upon a band of Indians, by the voice of a man crying out in the Castilian tongue: "I am a Christian! I am a Christian! Slay me not!" The stout trooper stayed his lance, lifted the supplicant to his horse, and carried him to the main encampment. The Castilian in savage guise proved to be Jean Ortiz, a native of Seville, who had been a captive among the Indians for several years. He had heard of the landing of the Spaniards, and had hastened to meet them; and he was a godsend to De Soto because he was a valuable interpreter. The governor furnished Ortiz with clothes and a horse, and attached him to his personal staff.

De Soto was now ready to enter upon the conquest of Florida. His troops were clad in coats of steel to repel arrows, and bore breast-plates and helmets of the same metal. They had strong shields, swords, lances, arquebuses (a kind of rude short guns), cross-bows and one cannon. The cavaliers were mounted on one hundred and thirteen horses. Savage blood-hounds from Cuba were the allies of the Spaniards, and the Castilians were plentifully supplied with iron neck-collars, handcuffs and chains for their captives. With these instruments of cruelty, a drove of swine, many cattle and mules, and accompanied by mechanics, priests, inferior clergy and monks with sacerdotal robes, holy relics, images of the Virgin and sacramental bread and wine wherewith to make Christians of the conquered pagans, De Soto began his march in June, 1539. From the outset he was met by the most vigorous opposition. In narrow defiles and other exposed places, he and his followers were assailed by clouds of arrows from the hands of a multitude of natives who had been made intensely revengeful because of the cruelties of Narvaez and his men. They had resolved to fight the invaders until not one should be left upon the soil. Cruelty was met by cruelty. When a Spaniard was captured, he was mercilessly slaughtered. The captive Indians were loaded with chains and made beasts of burden, without regard to age or sex. The antagonism of the races was fearful. When De Soto, hoping to conciliate Acuera, a powerful Muscogee or Creek chief, whose territory he had entered, and invited the cacique to a friendly interview, he received this haughty reply:

THE CAPTIVE INDIANS.

"Others of your accursed race have, in years past, disturbed our peaceful shores. They have taught me what you are. What is your employment? To wander about like vagabonds from land to land; to rob the the poor; to betray the confiding; to murder the defenceless in cold blood. No! with such a people I want neither peace nor friendship. War — never-ending, exterminating war— is all I ask. You boast yourselves to be valiant — and so you may be; but my faithful warriors are not less brave; and of this you shall one day have proof, for I have sworn to maintain an unsparing conflict while one white man remains in my borders; not openly in the battle-field, though even thus we fear not to meet you, but by stratagem, ambush, and midnight surprisal."

In reply to a demand that he should yield obedience to the emperor, Acuera as haughtily said: "I am king in my own land, and will never become the vassal of a mortal like myself. Vile and pusillanimous is he who submits to the yoke of another when he may be free! As for me and my people we prefer death to the loss of liberty, and the subjugation of our country!" De Soto pressed his suit for a friendly interview, but was always answered by the cacique that he had given him all the reply he had to make.

De Soto remained twenty days in the dominions of Acuera, continually suffering from the enmity of that cacique. A Spaniard could not go a hundred paces from his camp without danger of being shot, and his severed head carried in triumph on a pike to the presence of the chief. In that way fourteen Castilians perished, and many were wounded. "Keep on! robbers and traitors!" said Acuera. "In my province and in Apalachee you will be treated as you deserve. We will quarter and hang up every captive on the highest tree!" And they did so. In open fight the Spaniards were always victors, but in ambush and skulking, the Indians were expert and fearfully dangerous.

Cutting his way through hostile tribes, De Soto reached the fertile region of Tallahassee, where he wintered. An expedition which sailed westward in his ships, to explore the coasts, returned in February with a report that the skeletons of the men and horses of Narvaez's party, who had perished at St. Marks, the place of that adventurer's last embarkation, had been discovered; also the sheltered bay of Pensacola. The commander of the vessels was ordered to return to Cuba immediately, and thence convey provisions and other supplies to Pensacola, whilst De Soto should march across the country to the same point. For this purpose the governor broke up his winter encampment in March, but being told that gold abounded in the north, he first went in that direction as far as Silver Bluff, on the Savannah River. On the opposite side of the stream (in Barnwell District, S. C.) lived an Indian "queen," young, beautiful and a maiden, who ruled over a large extent of country. In a richly wrought canoe filled with shawls and skins, and other presents, the dusky cacica glided across the river, and with kind words welcomed the governor and offered him her services. Presents were exchanged. A magnificent string of pearls was upon her neck. This she drew over her head and hung it around the neck of De Soto as a token of her regard. Then she invited him and his followers to cross over to her village. In canoes and on log-rafts they passed the stream, and encamping in the shadows of mulberry trees, they soon received a bountiful supply of turkeys and venison. There they remained until early in May, when they departed, De Soto requiting the hospitality of the royal maiden with treachery. He carried her away a prisoner, and kept her near his person as a hostage for the good behavior of her people towards the Spaniards. She finally escaped and returned to her home, a bitter enemy of the perfidious white people.

The Spaniards marched to the headwaters of the Savannah, in Habersham county, when they turned their faces westward, and crossing northern Georgia, through the picturesque Cherokee country, went over the Oostanaula near its confluence with the Etowah, and entered the large village of Chiaha, on the site of modern Rome. There they were received with the kindest hospitality by the young chief, who gave the intruders plenty of food and to their leader a string of pearls two yards in length, each pearl as large as a filbert. The streams in that region then abounded in the pearl-bearing mussel.

THE CHIEF OF THE COOSA INDIANS.

For thirty days the Spaniards remained at Chiaha. Then marching eastward, they entered northeastern Alabama, and were soon in the beautiful and fertile Coosa country. They were everywhere kindly received and bountifully fed by the inhabitants. Cultivated fields stretched out on every side, and granaries were filled with corn. Plum trees abounded, resembling those of Spain, and grapes hung in delicious clusters from vines that climbed the tall trees. It was now late in July, 1540. When the army came in sight of the capital of Coosa, the chief, a young man less than thirty years of age, borne upon a cushioned chair on the shoulders of four men, met him in the remote outskirts of the town, followed by a thousand warriors, tall, active and well-proportioned, with scanty garments and plumed heads. The cacique was clad in a mantle of marten skins thrown gracefully over his shoulder, and on his head was a diadem of brilliant feathers. Musicians attended him, singing songs and playing flutes; and the whole procession was almost as gorgeous as that of the Spaniards in their glittering armor.

The cacique received De Soto with joy, set apart the royal house for his accommodation, and dined with the governor every day. Finally, he besought De Soto to found a Spanish colony anywhere in his dominions. The governor, charmed with the delicious climate, would have done so but for the avaricious desire to find the great gold region which, he believed, was not far off. He declined the generous offer, with polite thanks, at the same time holding the chief as a hostage for the double purpose of securing the friendly offices of his people and extorting provisions and slaves. The natives were enraged at the indignity offered their sovereign, and fleeing to the woods prepared for war. The Spaniards pursued them, and returned with men and women in chains, many of whom they carried off as slaves when they departed in August. So, at every step, hospitality was repaid by injustice and cruelty. The Spaniards by their conduct justly earned the fate which finally overtook them.

De Soto continued his march through the beautiful regions of Alabama, taking with him the cacique of Coosa, as far as the great town of Tallase, where he was dismissed. Pushing southward, the Spaniards approached the temporary residence of Tuscaloosa, the renowned chief known as the Black Warrior, who was gigantic in stature, and the head of the Mobilian Indians. They found him seated on a commanding eminence upon a cushioned seat with beautiful mats under his feet and surrounded by numerous attendants. He was forty years of age, a head taller than any of his warriors, with a handsome face of grave and severe aspect. Lord of many tribes, he was feared by his neighbors and subjects; and his influence was widely spread over the region of the Alabama River to that of the Mississippi. He received De Soto with haughty courtesy; and when the governor ordered one of his largest pack-horses to be brought for the use of the giant chieftain, the latter mounted with sullenness and evident reluctance. He and De Soto rode side by side, and it was soon evident to Tuscaloosa that he was a prisoner of the Spaniards after the manner of other caciques who had been held as hostages. They crossed the Alabama a short distance below Selma, and passed down the right bank of that stream in the direction of the sea. De Soto now discovered signs which made him uneasy. The deference which had been paid to him since he left the Apalachee country had assured him that the conquest of Florida would be an easy matter. Indeed, he had regarded it as already accomplished. But the demeanor of Tuscaloosa caused him to doubt. The chief was in close and continual consultation with his principal followers, and was constantly sending runners to his capital, with messages, telling the Spaniards that he was preparing for their honorable reception. De Soto did not believe him, and took precautions against treachery. Side by side he and Tuscaloosa rode into the Mobilian capital, a large palisaded and walled town on a high plain by the side of a broad river, and called Manbila. The most acute students of the Spanish narratives believe that Choctaw Bluff, in Clarke county, about twenty-five miles above the confluence of the Alabama and Tombigby rivers, was its site.

It was at about eight o'clock on a bright October morning, when De Soto and Tuscaloosa rode into Manbila together, and were received in the great square with songs, the music of flutes, and the dancing of Indian girls. They alighted, and were seated under a canopy of state, when Tuscaloosa requested not to be held as a hostage any longer. The governor hesitated. The angered cacique sprang to his feet and with a proud and haughty step walked into a house close by. Ortiz, the interpreter, followed, and invited him to breakfast with De Soto. Tuscaloosa refused to return, saying: "If your chief knows what is best for him, he will immediately take his troops out of my country." The suspicions of the Spanish leader were confirmed, and he had scarcely recovered from his surprise when one of his spies came with information that ten thousand warriors, followers of Tuscaloosa and neighboring chiefs, were in the houses; that a vast amount of weapons and missiles, such as bows and arrows, javelins, clubs and stones, had been gathered in the town; that the old women and children had been sent to the forests, and that the Indians were then debating as to the proper hour to fall upon the Spaniards. It was a startling announcement for De Soto, for a greater part of his army was then lagging behind in fancied security, many of them scattered and hunting in the woods. The governor, anxious to postpone an attack until his army should come up, by regaining the person of Tuscaloosa, approached the cacique with smiles and gracious words. The haughty chief turned scornfully away, and mingled with his warriors. At that moment a chief rushed out, and with a loud voice denounced the Spaniards as robbers, thieves and assassins who should no longer impose upon their leader by depriving him of his liberty. Balthazar Gallegos, the greatest soldier of the expedition next to De Soto, angered by this insolence, cleft the chief, with his sword, from his head to his loins. That act let loose the fury of the people. Like bees from a hive the savages swarmed out of the houses by hundreds and thousands, and gradually pushed the invaders out of the ponderous gates into the plain. The Manbilans seized the Indian slaves of De Soto, together with all his baggage. The latter was stored within the walls, and the former, having their manacles knocked off, were armed and made to fight their late masters. In that first encounter, five Spaniards were killed and many were wounded, among them De Soto.

Unmindful of his wound, the governor, at the head of his cavalry, charged upon the mass of savages, and drove them back into the town with fearful slaughter. The Indians rushed to their wall-towers and loop-holes, and from these sent clouds of arrows and tempests of stones which drove the Spaniards back. As they receded, the Indians dropped from the walls and rushed out of the gates with huge clubs, beating the intruders and seizing their keen swords and deadly spears. The hand-to-hand conflicts were fierce and fatal, especially to the savages. For three hours the battle lasted, victory surging from side to side like the ebbing and flowing of the tides of the sea. The lagging army hearing the noise of battle had hastened forward, and were now coming up to the aid of their comrades. The daring of De Soto, who was everywhere in the battle, had already compelled the savages to take a permanent position within the walls of Manbila; and the priests, who on their knees had uttered copious prayers for victory for the Castilians, now sang the joyous *Te Deum*.

Having all of his forces in hand, De Soto now formed the foot soldiers in four divisions, who, armed with bucklers and battle-axes, charged upon the walls and portals. The Indians had closed and barricaded the gates and again fought from the towers and loop-holes. But the siege was not a long one. The gates were forced, and through these and over the walls the assailants made their way into the town. A dreadful carnage ensued. The cavalry remained outside to catch and slay any who might attempt to escape whilst the butchery was going on within. The Indians fought with all the gallantry and desperation of patriots defending their country. Although the ground was covered with the dead, not one of the survivors asked for quarter. Young women, in large numbers, fought side by side with the warriors, with equal bravery and skill, and their blood flowed as freely. At length De Soto, at the head of his cavalry, made a furious charge into the town, with a shout of "Our Lady and Santiago!" and made fearful lanes through the ranks of fighting men and women. As he arose to hurl his lance at a powerful Indian warrior, a heavy arrow pierced deeply into his thigh. Unable to pull it out or sit in his saddle, he continued to fight, standing in his stirrups. At length the houses were fired and the combatants were shrouded in the blinding smoke. As the sun went down, the sights and sounds of slaughter and groans of the dying were awful. When the twilight deepened into night, the contest was over. It had lasted nine hours. Manbila was a smoking ruin, and its inhabitants had perished.

That conflict was disastrous to both races. Eighty-two Europeans perished, among whom were some of the brightest flowers of Spanish chivalry. It was estimated that eleven thousand native Alabamians fell in the battle or were burned in the houses. It is believed that Tuscaloosa remained in his house and perished in the flames. Forty-five horses were slain. All the camp equipage and baggage were consumed in the place where the Indians had stored them; all the clothes, medicines, books, pearls, relics and robes of the priests with their flour and wine used in the eucharist or sacrament of the Lord's Supper; instruments, and much of the armor with many other things which could not be obtained in the wilderness, were utterly destroyed. Among the ghastly ruins and piles of the dead, the Spaniards passed the night after the battle. Many of them were wounded and dying. Only one surgeon was left. Seventeen hundred severe wounds called for his care, but his instruments had perished in the flames. De Soto, though badly wounded, bestowed all his care upon his suffering companions. For eight days they remained in the town, and then went out to the Indian huts on the plain. Foraging parties were sent out who found villages abounding in provisions. They brought in beautiful captive maidens from whom they learned that Tuscaloosa had formed a plan for the destruction of the Spaniards weeks before. When the Talases complained to him that their chief had given their people to De Soto for slaves, he said: "Fear nothing; I shall shortly send the Spaniards back from my country to Talase in chains, led by your people, whom they have enslaved. The whole land will be rid of the robbers." De Soto also learned from these captive maidens that his squadron was in the bay of Pensacola.

The fire at Manbila deprived the Spaniards of two widely differing sources of consolation, namely, wheat flour and wine for the eucharist, and playing-cards. Gambling was the besetting sin and most exciting pleasure of all; and they often staked their money, horses, jewels and even feminine slaves, at play. The priests went through all the religious forms excepting consecration, and the unusual ceremony was called Dry Mass. Cards were made of parchment and lent from one company to another, and deep gambling was resumed.

The news of his ships that were doubtless laden with clothing and provisions gave De Soto joy; but his spirits were soon clouded by a conspiracy which had been formed among some of his followers, to abandon him and sail in the ships from Pensacola to Spain or Peru. This discovery changed his plans. He resolved to turn his back upon his ships and go deeper into the wilderness. This determination was announced on the 18th of November, 1540. The order to march northward fell upon the ears of the discontented ones like a clap of thunder. It was made potential by a threat to put to death the first man who should speak of the ships.

Northward the Spaniards marched, and on reaching the waters of the

Black Warrior River, they were met by a large force of Indians in battle array, who longed to avenge the destruction of their friends at Manbila. The news of that tragedy had spread over a vast region, and kindled the fiercest hatred of the Spaniards in the hearts of the natives. Hundreds of opposing warriors were swelled to thousands, and De Soto was compelled to fight his way inch by inch through the land of the Choctaws. At length, after passing over the uplands of Mississippi—a beautiful, fertile and populous region—he reached the upper tributaries of the Yazoo River in Yalobusha county, and encamped in front of the town of Chickasa, the capital

THE SPANIARDS GAMBLING.

of the Chickasa nation. It was now December. Ice and even snow appeared and chilled the troops, and De Soto resolved to pass the winter there in a sheltered camp. The chief of the Chickasas feigned friendship for the Spaniards. It might have been real had the latter been wise and just. But they were not. Cruelty and wrong, as before, marked their dealings with the natives. When March came and De Soto thought of marching forward, he demanded of the Chickasa chief two hundred men as burden-bearers. The cacique answered the demand by a furious attack upon the Spanish camp on a dark night, during a wild gale from the north. The assailants came in four columns, with horrid yells and the hideous sounds of wooden drums and blasts on conch-shells. Before the sleeping Spaniards were fairly roused from their slumbers, their huts, made of cane and straw, were in flames, fired by arrows bearing torches. Blinded by the smoke, they ran out of the houses half-dressed, some leaving their weapons behind them. Horses in stables perished, and many swine, in roofed pens, were burned to death. The conflict that ensued was terrible. The Spaniards fought valiantly as best they might, and finally drove their dusky assailants into the forests. But the disaster to the Europeans was greater than that which befel them at Manbila. They had lost forty of their diminished number. The only Spanish woman in the camp—the wife of a soldier—was burned to ashes. Fifty horses had perished, and most of the men saved nothing excepting what they had on their backs or in their hands.

The remainder of the inclement season was passed by the Spaniards in great wretchedness. Cold and hunger, and grievous wounds tortured them; and the Indians fell upon them night after night like fierce tigers. At length, the warm sun of April alleviated their sufferings, and De Soto moved on in a northwesterly direction, in search of the land of gold about which he had dreamed so long. The exasperated savages assailed him everywhere, and at a town called Alibamo, he had another desperate encounter with them. Then he moved on, and in May he stood upon the banks of the Mississippi River, in Tunica county, near the lower Chickasa Bluffs, above the mouth of the St. Francis River. The mighty Mississippi, then full to the brim, filled De Soto with admiration. He had not found gold, but he was the first European who found the great river upon whose bosom floats, annually, wealth a thousandfold greater than the mines of Mexico or Peru ever yielded. He was not the conqueror of a country teeming with a weak people; but he had achieved a conquest far more glorious than Cortez or Pizarro had done, and had secured immortality for his name and deeds.

Still thirsting for gold, and expecting to find the Pacific Ocean not far off, De Soto crossed the Mississippi River; traversed the lagoons of Arkansas; climbed over the great Ozark hills, and penetrated the country westward almost to the eastern slopes of the Rocky Mountains. For a year he wandered in those wild regions; wintered far up the Arkansas River, and in the month of May, 1542, returned to the Mississippi at a point a little north of the mouth of the Arkansas. He now gave up gold-seeking; and on the eastern bank of the great river, in Bolivar county, Mississippi, he selected a site for a colony among a tribe of savage sun-worshippers. They showed intense hostility to the Spaniards; and when De Soto, in an address to them demanding their submission to his arms, called himself a child of the Sun, they ridiculed him. "If you are a child of the Sun," they haughtily replied, "return to him, dry up the Mississippi, and we will submit to you."

De Soto was now utterly discouraged, and he began the construction of two brigantines wherewith to communicate with Cuba. Exhausted in body and mind, he was soon prostrated by a malignant fever. Satisfied that he could not live, he ordered his attendants to carry him out of his hut into the balmy air under a wide-spreading live-oak, where he received the holy ministrations of the priests. Then he appointed Moscoso, his lieutenant, to be his successor in office and commander of the ragged remnant of his troops who gathered around him in silent grief. One bore a broken helmet, another a battered cuirass, a third a splintered lance, and a fourth a jagged sword. Some were dressed in skins, and some were half-naked. All, in person and equipment, were only shadows of the brilliant retinue who had gathered under his banner at San Lucar about five years before. He exhorted them to keep together, bade them farewell, and then died! To conceal the fact of his death, and to protect his body from desecration by the savages, his followers placed it in a trough made of live-oak; and at midnight, when darkness was intense, they sunk it to the bottom of the river. So perished the discoverer of the Mississippi, in the beautiful month of May, 1542, at the early age of forty-two years.

But little more need be said about this wonderful expedition. Moscoso led the Spaniards into the wilderness west of the Mississippi again, hoping to find Mexico. For a year they wandered there and then returned to the Mississippi, where they built brigantines and floated in them upon its bosom toward the sea. The once splendid army of one thousand men was now reduced to three hundred and twenty. Taking with them the beautiful young women whom they had captured at Manbila, and several of the best horses that survived, they sailed out into the Gulf of Mexico, crossed it, and after enduring untold miseries, they reached Panuco, a Spanish settlement on the coast of Mexico, in September. They went to the City of Mexico, where they were entertained by the viceroy; and the elegant Castilian ladies at that petty court were enraptured by the beauty of the dusky Mobilian girls, whom they caressed, and feasted, and dressed in Spanish costume.

Maldinado, the commander of De Soto's ships, had waited long for him at Pensacola. He had made several voyages in search of him, and finally, in the spring of 1543, while he was at Vera Cruz, he had heard of De Soto's death on the Mississippi, and that only three hundred of his followers lived to reach Mexico. This sad news cast a gloom over Havana; and poor Doña Isabel, the wife of the great leader, who had so long anxiously awaited his return, died of a broken heart.

CHAPTER IX.

VOYAGE OF VERAZZANI—HE EXPLORES THE COASTS FROM NORTH CAROLINA TO NEWFOUNDLAND—KIDNAPS AN INDIAN BOY—CARTIER DISCOVERS THE GULF OF ST. LAWRENCE—ON A SECOND VOYAGE HE DISCOVERS THE RIVER ST. LAWRENCE AND NAMES BOTH—HE EXPLORES THE RIVER TO THE SITE OF MONTREAL—TAKES A DAUGHTER OF A HURON CHIEF TO FRANCE—HE WINTERS AT THE SITE OF QUEBEC—CARTIER KIDNAPS THE "KING OF CANADA" AND SOME OF HIS CHIEFS, AND TAKES THEM TO FRANCE—ENGLISH EXPLORERS—THEIR SUFFERINGS IN NEWFOUNDLAND—CARTIER'S THIRD VOYAGE TO THE ST. LAWRENCE—HOSTILITIES OF THE NATIVES—THE LORD OF ROBERTVILLE ON THE ST. LAWRENCE.

WE will now leave the Spanish discoverers, and turn our attention to others who made voyages to the coasts of North America on similar errands.

Francis the First, one of the most energetic as well as enlightened sovereigns of France down to the sixteenth century, becoming jealous of the glory acquired by his rival of Spain, by discoveries and conquests on this continent, fitted out four ships late in the year 1523 for explorations on the North American coasts. They were placed under the command of John Verazzani, a Florentine, of whose career very little is known. He appears to have been a somewhat eminent navigator, but the narrative of his voyage to our country is so obscure in many parts that it is difficult to discover the truth. The account of that voyage on which historians have most relied, is given in a letter which, it is alleged, the navigator wrote to King Francis after his return, by which it seems he sailed for the Madeiras in December, 1523, and left them on the 27th of January, 1524, proceeding due west. Three of his ships were soon disabled by a tempest that swept over the Atlantic, and put back; and he went on with only one vessel. In that he reached the American coast in north latitude 34°, or not far from Cape Fear in southern North Carolina. That was in the month of March. He speaks of the climate as salubrious; of the coast as abounding with lakes and ponds—the numerous bays and inlets there; of the people as black-skinned, "not much differing from Ethiopians," with thick black hair worn tied back upon the head in the form of a little tail; and going entirely naked excepting at the loins, from which depended from a girdle of braided grass, a marten skin. These people gathered on the beach in considerable heads were uncovered. They lived in huts made of saplings and shrubbery, and navigated canoes dug out of a single log without any iron instrument whatever. In the tall reedy grass, the mariners found concealed "a very old woman and a young girl eighteen or twenty years of age. The old woman carried two infants on her shoulders, and behind her neck a little boy eight years of age." The women shrieked and made signs to the men, who had fled, to come to their rescue. "We took the little boy from the old woman," says the Florentine, "to carry with us to France, and would have taken the girl, who was very beautiful and very tall, but it was impossible because of the loud shrieks she uttered as we attempted to lead her away; so we determined to leave her, and take the boy only." The story of this kidnapping was soon spread over all that region, and planted the seeds of intense hatred of the white man in the bosoms of the natives. Their products were the bane of Raleigh's settlement on Roanoke Island on that coast, sixty years later.

Verazzani coasted further northward, and it is evident, from his topographical description, that he entered the harbor of New York and discovered the mouth of the Hudson River. He made a very brief tarriance there. The land seemed full of people, who received the mariners kindly. They did not differ much in appearance from the inhabitants further south, and were dressed in cloaks made of the beautiful plumage of birds. Weighing anchor after a very brief intercourse with these people, he sailed eastward, as the coast lay, discovered Block Island, off the Connecticut shore, and came to a beautiful hilly country in latitude forty-one degrees and forty minutes. He was then, evidently, in Narragansett Bay, and beheld the shores of Rhode Island, where the Northmen had settled more than five hundred years before. There he found the "finest looking tribe and the handsomest in their costume" of any he had seen on the voyage; larger in persons than the average European. "Among them," Verazzani said, "were two kings more beautiful in form and stature than can possibly be described;" the oldest, about forty years of age, wearing "a deer's skin around his body, artificially wrought in damask figures; his head without covering; his hair tied back in various knots, and around his neck he wore a large chain ornamented with many stones of different colors. "Their women," he said, "are of the same form and beauty, very graceful, of fine countenances and pleasing appearance in manners and modesty; wearing no clothing except a deerskin, ornamented like those worn by the men; some wear very rich lynx skins upon their arms, and various ornaments on their heads composed of braids of hair which also hang down upon their breasts on each side. Others wear different ornaments, such as the women of Egypt and Syria use."

heads were uncovered. They lived in huts made of saplings and shrubbery, and navigated canoes dug out of a single log without any iron instrument whatever. In the tall reedy grass, the mariners found concealed "a very old woman and a young girl eighteen or twenty years of age. The old woman carried two infants on her shoulders, and behind her neck a little boy eight years of age." The women shrieked and made signs to the men, who had fled, to come to their rescue. "We took the little boy from the old woman," says the Florentine, "to carry with us to France, and would have taken the girl, who was very beautiful and very tall, but it was impossible because of the loud shrieks she uttered as we attempted to lead her away; so we determined to leave her, and take the boy only." The story of this kidnapping was soon spread over all that region, and planted the seeds of intense hatred of the white man in the bosoms of the natives. Their products were the bane of Raleigh's settlement on Roanoke Island on that coast, sixty years later.

Verazzani coasted further northward, and it is evident, from his topographical description, that he entered the harbor of New York and discovered the mouth of the Hudson River. He made a very brief tarriance there. The land seemed full of people, who received the mariners kindly. They did not differ much in appearance from the inhabitants further south, and were dressed in cloaks made of the beautiful plumage of birds. Weighing anchor after a very brief intercourse with these people, he sailed eastward, as the coast lay, discovered Block Island, off the Connecticut shore, and came to a beautiful hilly country in latitude forty-one degrees and forty minutes. He was then, evidently, in Narragansett Bay, and beheld the shores of Rhode Island, where the Northmen had settled more than five hundred years before. There he found the "finest looking tribe and the handsomest in their costume" of any he had seen on the voyage; larger in persons than the average European. "Among them," Verazzani said, "were two kings more beautiful in form and stature than can possibly be described;" the oldest, about forty years of age, wearing "a deer's skin around his body, artificially wrought in damask figures; his head without covering; his hair tied back in various knots, and around his neck he wore a large chain ornamented with many stones of different colors. "Their women," he said, "are of the same form and beauty, very graceful, of fine countenances and pleasing appearance in manners and modesty; wearing no clothing except a deerskin, ornamented like those worn by the men; some wear very rich lynx skins upon their arms, and various ornaments on their heads composed of braids of hair which also hang down upon their breasts on each side. Others wear different ornaments, such as the women of Egypt and Syria use."

The inhabitants were kind, but shy. The men could never be persuaded to take their wives on board the ship of the Florentine. "One of the two kings," he said, "often came with his queen and many attendants to see the vessel," but the women were kept at a distance. The country seemed to be very fertile, and abounded in their season with apples, plums, filberts and other kinds of fruit and nuts; and in the forests were great numbers of deers, lynxes and other wild animals. The dwellings of the people were generally circular in form, and built of split logs; and sometimes they were large enough to accommodate a family of twenty-five or thirty persons.

From Narragansett Bay, Verazzani sailed eastward early in May, passing among the numerous islands off the coast of Massachusetts, and touching somewhere, probably, on the coast of Maine. There he found the people coarser in appearance, less friendly, and more fierce and warlike. They were clad in the skins of the bear, the lynx, the deer and the seal. No signs of cultivation appeared, and the inhabitants seemed to live almost wholly on the products of the forest and the waters. The hills were covered with vast woods; and far in the interior he saw lofty mountains. The voyagers had very little intercourse with these savages, and sailing eastward and northward, came to Newfoundland. Thence they turned their prow toward Europe and sailed to France. Verazzani had traversed the borders of the North American continent, as his ship sailed, about two thousand miles, and he named the vast country *New France*.

Verazzani's object was to find Cathay, in the extreme eastern limit of Asia, hoping there to discover a passage into the Indian Ocean, for which Columbus and Cabot had sought. What became of him after this marvelous voyage is not certainly known. He appears to have left the service of the French king, who was then warring desperately with Charles the Fifth of Spain and Germany. Early in 1525, Francis was defeated before Pavia, wounded, made a prisoner and carried captive to Madrid, where he was detained almost a year. His projects for foreign discoveries were, of course, abandoned for a time, and it was several years before they were resumed. Meanwhile, Verazzani, it seems probable, made two other voyages to America, but not as a commander. He appears to have had some communication with Henry the Eighth of England, and possibly was in his service, for an old chronicler says that he presented to that monarch a map of America, after he had made three voyages to this continent. It is certain that Henry sent out two exploring ships in 1527—the *Samson* and the *Mary of Guilford*—and it is asserted that Verazzani sailed in the first mentioned vessel. We have a record of another expedition having been sent to America by Henry, in 1536, for discovery or settlement.

For several years voyages for discovery from Europe to America ceased. Meanwhile, the brave Admiral de Brien (Chabot, Compte de Charni), who was a favorite at the French court, had urged his king to attempt making a settlement somewhere in New France, and so secure its possession for his crown. But it was not until ten years after Verazzani's voyage, that Francis yielded to the importunities of Chabot. Then a plan for making settlements in America was arranged under the direction of Chabot, and two ships, of sixty tons each, were fitted out at St. Malo, a fortified seaport of France, for that purpose, and placed in charge of Jacques Cartier (James Carter), a native of that port and then in the service of the French monarch.

After appropriate religious ceremonies in the cathedral of St. Malo, in which Chabot participated, Cartier sailed for America. He left St. Malo on a bright afternoon (April 20, 1534), with a crew of one hundred and twenty men in each of his vessels. The voyage was prosperous, and with generally fair winds he reached the eastern coast of Newfoundland in twenty days. Then he sailed northward, entered the Straits of Belle Isle, and touching the coast of Labrador, he formally took possession of the country in the name of his king by planting a cross and hanging upon it the arms of France. The natives, who had been fishing near, gathered around the Frenchmen in considerable numbers, with their chief, and looked with wonder as the mariners raised that symbol of the atonement made of the trunk of a tree, and thirty feet in height. The shield they hung upon it bore the lilies of France—the royal insignia—and over it they carved, in antique letters, *Vive le Roi de France!*—"Live the King of France." Then the mariners all knelt, and with hands stretched toward the skies, they thanked God for his mercies. The savage chief faintly comprehending the significance of the shield with the Gallic arms as a token of claimed sovereignty, told Cartier, by signs, that he could not allow a cross to be set up without his consent, whereupon the mariner satisfied him by the assurance that it was only as a beacon to guide other voyagers in those waters.

After spending some weeks in exploring the great gulf west and southwest of Newfoundland, discovering the Magdalen Islands, the northern coasts of Cape Breton and the bays of Chaleurs and Gaspé, now at the eastern extremity of Canada, Cartier landed and held friendly intercourse with the Indians. There he set up a huge wooden cross, as before, with a shield and the French lilies, and took possession in the name of King Francis. His kindness inspired the natives with such confidence, that one of the chiefs offered to Cartier two of his sons to accompany him to France, on the condition that he should return them to their home the next year.

From Gaspé Bay Cartier sailed northeast, and doubling the east end of great Anticosti Island, he went up that branch of the St. Lawrence some distance, without suspecting that he was in the mouth of a great river whose chief sources were immense inland seas of fresh water. As the season of autumn storms was approaching, he turned back, passed through the Straits of Belle Isle, and sailed away for France, reaching St. Malo early in September. His voyage was considered successful. Chabot was delighted, and Francis was encouraged to make new efforts on a larger scale, in the same direction. Three ships were fitted out late in the following spring—*La Grand Hermione*, *La Petite Hermione*, *L'Emerillon*. The first was a vessel of one hundred and twenty tons burthen; the second was sixty tons, and the third was smaller. Cartier was commissioned "Captain and Pilot of the King." He gathered his companions and seamen in the cathedral at St. Malo, at the middle of May, where the whole company received absolution—pardon of their sins—from the Bishop, and also his blessing. It was Whit-Sunday — a festival when all newly-baptized persons appear in the church in white garments. Beautiful and picturesque was the scene, and joyous was the occasion; and impressions of the pageant remained on the memory of each mariner long after he left the holy fane that day, and embarked for his voyage.

CROSS ON THE COAST OF LABRADOR

Cartier sailed from St. Malo on his second voyage to New France, with several French noblemen, on the 19th of May, 1535—*Le Grande Hermione* was his flagship. Storms soon separated the vessels, but they met at an appointed rendezvous in the Straits of Belle Isle, on the 26th of July. Going westward, they entered the gulf on which Cartier had sailed the previous year; and on the day dedicated to St. Lawrence, they passed into the waters between Anticosti and the main, on the north, to which Cartier gave the name of St. Lawrence. This title was afterward given to the gulf and to the great river at whose mouth Anticosti lies. That island, Cartier named L'Assumption. Its

Indian name was Natiscotec, the sound of which from the lips of the natives was, to English ears, Anticosti, and so they called it.

Voyaging on, Cartier found himself in a broad but narrowing and freshening river; and on the first of September, he was at the mouth of the dark and mysterious Saguenay River, where the St. Lawrence is ten miles in width. Proceeding more than a hundred miles further up the great stream, with high mountains a little way from its shores on his right and gentle slopes from the water's edge on his left, Cartier came to a large island which he called The Isle of Bacchus. It is now the Island of Orleans, in sight of Quebec. He went on shore with the two young men whom he had taken to France the year before, and the next day a handsome Algonquin chief, named Donnacona, who was "Lord of Canada," came to *La Grande Hermione* in a beautifully wrought canoe to confer with Cartier. The conference was easy, for the two young men were interpreters. "We have been to France," they said, "and have been well-treated. The whole country is full of riches. Great castles, great armies, great ships, great cities are there, and our master is a great man in his country." Donnacona was pleased. He asked Cartier to stretch out his bare arm. The king kissed it, and laid it about his own neck in token of affection. "Go to my village of Stadacona yonder," said the dusky prince. "You will find a safe harbor there and a welcome." Then entering his canoe he glided swiftly over the waters toward a bold, rocky promontory in sight, around which came sweeping into the St. Lawrence, from the West, a gentle stream. Cartier followed. Passing a high waterfall on his right, he was soon in the safe harbor, with scenery around him whose beauty and grandeur were enchanting. He was in the harbor of Quebec. The little stream which he called the St. Croix (Holy Cross) was the present St. Charles, and the lofty cascade was the famous Fall of Montmorenci. Stadacona, the capital of the "Lord of Canada," was, it is believed, on the site of the present suburb St. Roque in the city of Quebec, on the border of the St. Charles.

Cartier left his larger vessels at Quebec, and in the smaller one he ascended the St. Lawrence as far as Lake St. Peter, an expansion of the river. The two young men refused to go any further with him, because he had broken his promise to leave them at their home on Gaspé Bay. So Cartier had no interpreter on his voyage up the St. Lawrence. Obstructions in the stream near Lake St. Peter caused him to leave his ship and in a small boat, with three volunteers, make his way against the currents. They rowed up as far as the Indian town of Hochelaga, which, Cartier said, contained fifty houses, "about fifty paces long and twelve or fifteen broad, covered over with the bark of the wood as broad as any board, very finely and cunningly joined together," and having many rooms. On their tops were garrets, wherein they kept their corn. The town was circular in form, stockaded, and environed by three courses of ramparts made of timber and about thirty feet in height. There was only one gate or sally-port, which was closed with heavy timbers, stakes and bars. On the ramparts were magazines of stone for the defence of the city.

Dressed in his most brilliant attire, Cartier visited the town on the day following his arrival, where he was kindly received by the Huron king. With that monarch he climbed to the top of the lofty mountain back of the town, from which he beheld, with great admiration, a vast extent of level wooded country and the course of the mighty river for many miles. He called the great hill, Mont Real (royal mountain); and the city which lies upon the site of the Huron capital, bears the same name — Montreal. Such, also, is the name of the island containing the city and the mountain.

CARTIER AND DONNACONA.

After enjoying the hospitalities of the Hurons two or three days, Cartier departed, carrying with him the pretty daughter of one of the chiefs, about eight years of age, whom her father lent to him to take to France. He joined his little vessel, returned to Stadacona, and as the season was far advanced, it being near the middle of October, he resolved to winter there. His vessels were moored in the

St. Croix (St. Charles), and there the Frenchmen endured the terrible cold of a Canadian winter from November until late in March. Their sufferings were grievous. The scurvy which prevailed among the natives at Quebec, extended to the Frenchmen, and of the one hundred and ten Europeans there, eight died, and nearly all of the others were sick.

The ice remained so long in the St. Lawrence that Cartier could not depart until May. On the third of that month he erected a huge cross, thirty-five feet in height, on the site of Dalhousie Bastion, the highest point of Cape Diamond, the promontory at Quebec, and upon it he hung the arms of France with a Latin inscription: "*Francis First, by the grace of God King of France, reigns.*" On the same day, Donnacona, whose unstinted kindness Cartier had enjoyed, was invited with nine of his chiefs to a feast on the French flag-ship, where they were treacherously detained, and were borne away captives three days afterward. Cartier sailed out of the St. Lawrence on the southern side of Anticosti. He reached the open sea from the gulf, between Cape Breton and Newfoundland, and reached St. Malo on the 6th of July, 1536. The *Petite Hermione* was found to be so unseaworthy that she was left in the St. Charles, where her remains were found in the year 1848, imbedded in the mud.

At about the time when Cartier sailed from Quebec, two English vessels, the *Trinity* and the *Minion*, sailed from Gravesend, with the good wishes of Henry the Eighth, bearing "thirty gentlemen and ninety seamen," to explore the region of the St. Lawrence, and to plant a colony in Newfoundland. The expedition was organized by "Master How, of London, a man of goodly stature, and of great courage, and given to the study of cosmography." His companions were young men of rank and fortune. The ships were two months on the voyage to Cape Breton, where they first touched and then sailed to Newfoundland. There the company came very near starving to death. The famine was so great that some of the stouter sailors killed weaker ones in the woods, and ate them. The "gentlemen" were about to cast lots to determine which of their number should become food for the rest, when a French fishing-vessel, amply provisioned, came into the port. The Englishmen seized her, and with that vessel and their own they returned to England. The Frenchmen laid their case before Henry, who, when he learned how great had been the necessities of his countrymen when they took possession of the vessel, did not punish them, but paid the foreigners the value of their property out of his private purse.

Cartier's report of his second voyage was not cheering. The rigors of the climate on the St. Lawrence in winter; the ice-bound condition of that stream for several months, and the barrenness of the land in precious stones and metals, were so discouraging that more than four years passed away before another like expedition from a French port was planned. The king was then fighting Charles with more intense hatred than ever under the impression that the emperor had caused the death of the eldest son of Francis, who died from the effects of poison. For two years the father could think of nothing but revenge, when through the intervention of the Pope and the Queen of Hungary, the two monarchs whose mutual exasperation was intense, became reconciled and embraced and kissed each other as friends. But the French treasury was drained by long wars, and Francis would not listen to propositions for colonization in America, until late in 1540. Then Francis de la Roque, Lord of Robertval, in Picardy, importuned the king for permission to make further discoveries and plant a colony in New France. The monarch had, meanwhile, talked with Donnacona and learned much about Canada which Cartier could not know. He told him of the large numbers of fur-bearing animals in its woods and waters; the delicious salmon in its rivers, and the richness of its soil and value of its pine timber. Francis was willing to make another trial, and he gave his consent to the fitting out of ships according to the plan of De la Roque. He commissioned that gentleman Viceroy and Lieutenant-General of "Canada, Hochelaga, Saguenay, Newfoundland, Belle Isle, Cape Breton and Labrador;" and as the services of Cartier were indispensable, he was recommissioned "Captain and Pilot of the King," and appointed chief mariner of the expedition, in which six or seven ships were to be employed. De la Roque was authorized to make conquests in the name of France and to plant a colony. To obtain men for the latter purpose—for the founders of a State—the prisons of France were ransacked, and many desperate characters were mingled with good men in making up the required number. The work of preparation went vigorously on, and the harbor of St. Malo was alive with busy men in the spring of 1541. Every thing and every body were in readiness late in May excepting De la Roque.

Cartier was not pleased with being made subservient to the Lord of Robertval, in the enterprise before him, and when five vessels were ready, he was glad to find De la Roque dilatory. He gathered the whole company that were to go in them, in the cathedral, where all received absolution and blessings, and on the 23d of May they sailed from St. Malo for the St. Lawrence, leaving De la Roque to follow when he pleased. Storms arose when they approached the tracks of the polar icebergs as they were voyaging toward the tropics, and chilling fogs lay along their paths. It was late in August when the squadron entered the harbor of Stadacona or Quebec. The people there, led by King Agona, the successor of Donnacona, pressed eagerly to the ships to welcome their old monarch, for Cartier had assured them that he would bring him back. Alas! Donnacona was no more. He and his eight chiefs had been baptized in France, but had grieved themselves to death in slavery. All of them had died before Cartier's departure on his third voyage. The mariner dared not tell the whole truth to the people for fear of their resentment; he only acknowledged that Donnacona was dead, and then told them that the other chiefs had all become great lords in France, had remained there, and would never return. In token of his good faith he showed them the pretty little daughter of the Huron chief at Hochelaga, whom he had brought back. The people had grave doubts. They were sullen and unfriendly. The kidnapping—the inexcusable treachery—had left a bitter sting of wrong in their hearts. Their sullenness grew more cloudy, and very soon signs of absolute hostility were manifested.

Cartier sailed up the river a few leagues above Quebec, where he found a better anchorage; and at the beginning of September he sent two of his vessels back to France with an account of his doings, and to communicate the fact that De la Roque had not arrived. He again visited Hochelaga to ascertain whether there were serious obstructions to navigation above that town, and to give back to her father the little Indian princess. He gave to the chief a "cloak of Paris red, which cloak was set with yellow and white buttons of tin, and small bells." These acts made a favorable impression upon the Hurons, and they loaded him with favors. After visiting the rapids between Montreal and La Chine, he returned to Quebec, when the temper of the natives was so manifestly hostile that he was admonished to provide for the safety of himself and his followers. He accordingly built a fort on the island of Orleans, and made his winter quarters there, mooring his vessels in a cove. He waited patiently for the coming of the Viceroy, but he had not appeared when the St. Lawrence was bound with ice.

The winter was long, cold and gloomy. The Frenchmen were almost buried in the snow-drifts, and suffered much; and when the spring opened, the natives were evidently preparing to attack them. Their provisions being almost exhausted, and no tidings of De la Roque reaching him, Cartier left the St. Lawrence toward the end of May, 1542, and sailed for France. Running into the harbor of St. John near the southeastern extremity of Newfoundland, he there found De la Roque, Lord of Robertval, with three ships and two hundred men, and about twenty French fishing-vessels. De la Roque had left Rochelle in France on the 16th of April, and reached the harbor he was in on the 8th of June. He had been there several days when Cartier arrived. They held a conference, when the Pilot told the Viceroy that he had left the St. Lawrence because he could not withstand the natives, who were becoming very hostile. The country, he said, did not seem very fertile, and there were no mines of precious stones and valuable minerals. A few "diamonds"—quartz crystals—which he had gathered, and a small quantity of gold, were all that he had to show of mineral wealth, and he advised De la Roque to go no further, for he could never make a colony on the St. Lawrence profitable to himself or his king. The Viceroy regarded this advice as selfish, believing Cartier's object to be to bear all the honor of his discoveries, and the glory of founding a new empire, himself. De la Roque therefore determined to go on, and ordered Cartier to go with him to the St. Lawrence, not doubting that their united forces might overawe the Indians and secure peace and prosperity. But the Pilot resolved not to submit to the Viceroy. With apparent compliance with the commands of his superior, he returned to his ship. At twilight he secretly conferred with the captains of his two other vessels, and at midnight, when the heavens were cloudy and moonless and the darkness was intense, he escaped from the harbor with his little squadron and sailed for St. Malo. Cartier was then about fifty years of age, and seems to have abandoned the sea, for he afterward lived quietly at St. Malo and at a little village near, alternately. When and where he died is not known. It is believed that he lived in comparative poverty, and died soon after his return from his third voyage to Canada.

Toward the end of June, De la Roque left Newfoundland for the St. Lawrence, passing through the straits of Belle Isle. He did not stop at Quebec, for he found the natives very hostile, as Cartier had told him they were. He went further up the river, probably to the place where the Pilot's vessels were anchored when he sent the two ships back to France the previous year. There De la Roque built a fort, but there is no record of what else he did in Canada, excepting that he and his companions suffered severely during the following winter, and early in June, 1543, made an exploring voyage to the Saguenay, where one of his vessels was lost. In the autumn of that year he returned to France. Finding his king again warring fiercely with his old enemy Charles, against whose empire he had hurled five different armies at as many points, the Viceroy abandoned all projects of foreign colonization and re-entered the military service in which he had often before distinguished himself. Six years later, when Francis was dead (having perished because of his personal excesses at the age of fifty-three years), and Henry the Second, who had married Catharine de Medici, was on the throne of France, the Lord of Robertval again sailed for the St. Lawrence, and was never heard of afterward.

CHAPTER X.

THE PROTESTANT REFORMATION—THE HUGUENOTS OR FRENCH PROTESTANTS—COLIGNI AND CATHARINE DE MEDICI—PERMISSION GRANTED FOR A FRENCH PROTESTANT SETTLEMENT IN AMERICA—A SETTLEMENT PLANTED ON THE COAST OF SOUTH CAROLINA—THE COLONY NEGLECTED—HELPED BY THE NATIVES—A HUGUENOT COLONY IN FLORIDA—FRIENDSHIP OF THE NATIVES—THEY BUILD A FORT ON THE ST. JOHN'S RIVER—APPEARANCE THERE OF A SPANISH FLEET—THE COLONISTS WARNED CONCERNING IT—THE SPANIARDS LAND AT THE SITE OF ST. AUGUSTINE—FRUITLESS EXPEDITION AGAINST THEM.

NOW was the period of those earnest theological discussions and intense theological antagonisms in Europe, known as the Era of the Reformation. There had been a revolt in Germany, led by Luther and Melancthon, against the Italian hierarchy or rulers in the Christian Church whose head was the Bishop or Pope of Rome. A similar revolt had broken out in Switzerland, led by Zuingliss. It was a movement in favor of intellectual liberty—the perfect equality of *all* men, in Church and State, in the exercise of the inalienable rights of private judgment in matters of religion and politics. When, at a Diet or Congress held at Spires, in 1529 (at which Luther and several princes who were in sympathy with him appeared), the Church, by a decree, was made master in both spiritual and temporal affairs, the reformers entered a solemn *protest*. So they acquired for their party the name of pro*test*-ants, or PROTESTANTS. They found the Church so strong that they soon afterward formed a league for mutual defence, and so first *organized* the Reformation as an aggressive moral power. This led to theological and political combinations which resulted, twenty-five years later, in the freedom of the Germans from the domination of the Italian Church. So popular were the doctrines of the reformers, in Germany, that as early as 1558 not more than one-tenth of the people there were adherents of the Church of Rome.

But that Church was not disposed to yield its supremacy without a struggle, and it put forth all its energies for the maintenance of its power. By the mighty agencies of its traditions, its vantage-ground of possession, the Order of Jesuits which it had just created, and the Inquisition which it had re-established with new powers, its warfare was keen and terrible, and its victories were many. Those of its enemies were postponed. In the heat of that conflict, which has continued ever since, have been evolved the representative government, the free institutions, and the liberty, equality and fraternity which are the birth-rights of every American citizen of whatever hue or creed.

In France the Reformation met enemies in the court, the Church and a majority of the people, and its progress was slow and fitful. John Calvin was the chief reformer, and was banished. He took refuge in Switzerland, where he died in 1564. But he left devoted followers in France. Among these, Admiral Coligni, a favorite of Catharine de Medici when she was acting regent, was one of the most conspicuous leaders of the Huguenots, as the French Protestants were called. All parties admired him for his valor and his virtues and his eminent deeds in the service of his country. He persuaded Catharine to attempt to reconcile, by a conference, the contending religious factions. He failed When the peace conference ended in a quarrel, war ensued. The Duke of Guise, a descendant of Charlemagne, and claimant of the French throne, whom Catherine feared and hated, led the Roman Catholics. The Prince of Condé led the Protestants. The latter being greatly in the minority suffered much. Grieved because of their forlorn condition, Coligni resolved to procure an asylum for them in the milder regions of North America, far removed from civilized men, where they might enjoy perfect religious and civil freedom, unmolested by foreign powers or hostile factions.

MARTIN LUTHER.

Coligni sought an audience with Catharine. It was readily granted. That proud and unprincipled daughter of Lorenzo de Medici, was then a little more than forty years of age, stout and fair, and was wielding power with a prodigal hand. Coligni found her seated on a rich divan covered with blue damask satin. On her head was a coronet sparkling with a single large diamond. Around her plump neck glittered a circlet of gold and pearls, emeralds and rubies. She wore a skirt of gold embroidered white silk, and over this a rich robe of royal purple velvet, trimmed with a narrow band of ermine at the front and bottom, and with a close-fitting bodice edged at the top with rich lace. Her full puffed sleeves were of the finest linen and lace, with brilliant gems at the wrists. A gold chain fastened at her bosom with a diamond brooch extended to her feet and terminated in a golden cross studded with seed pearls. Near her, and playing with a fawn-colored Italian greyhound, was her royal son, who had lately ascended the throne of France as Charles the Ninth. The king's hair hung in ringlets about his shoulders, for he was a boy only ten or twelve years of age, and his fair complexion was heightened by his rich suit of royal purple velvet, with slashed sleeves, revealing white linen beneath. Only a single minister of state was present, and he and a young woman, a court favorite and cousin of the King of Navarre, who sat by a vine-trailed window embroidering, were the only companions of royalty when the Admiral entered the room.

Coligni was tall, elegant in figure and deportment, grave in aspect, with flowing hair and beard slightly streaked with gray, for he was about forty-five years of age. He was dressed in the uniform of his rank, and carried in his hand a rich green velvet cap, bearing a long ostrich plume. His doublet of crimson velvet with short skirt was sprinkled with golden lilies, and encircled with a belt from which depended a straight sword. The sleeves terminated at the elbows, and the rest of the arm to the wrist was covered with embroidered linen. His trunk-hose of velvet extended to the middle of the thighs, and was slashed and elegantly embroidered with gold thread. Up to this, tight-fitting stockings wrought of fine white wool, extended, and on his feet were buskins of polished russet leather, sparkling with diamond buttons that fastened silk rosettes to the insteps. From his shoulders hung an open short Spanish cloak of blue velvet, and around his neck was a modest ruff. A massive gold chain, bearing the Order of St. Louis, was seen upon his breast. Such was the group who appeared in the audience-chamber of the Regent of France, late in the year 1561, to confer upon the subject of discoveries, and the planting of a Protestant colony in America.

That conference was short. In few words Coligni set forth the happiness which the carrying out of his scheme would confer upon his suffering countrymen; and he dwelt specially upon the fact that it might redound to the glory of France. Catharine, who was a pauper in moral and religious convictions, and had espoused the cause of the Protestants only as a measure of state policy, was then the friend of Coligni. She readily granted all that he desired, in the name of the little king then playing with the greyhound; and the child's signature, hardly legible, was afterward placed to the charter given to the admiral, by which he was authorized to send an expedition to Florida and establish a colony there.

Coligni lost no time in making use of his privilege. He quickly fitted out two vessels of the character of Spanish caravels, chiefly for a voyage of discovery, and placed them under the command of John Ribault, an experienced mariner of Dieppe, who was an earnest Protestant. Ribault sailed from Havre de Grace on the 18th of February, 1562, with sailors and soldiers, and a few gentlemen of fortune who were prompted by curiosity, the love of adventure, or the prospect of gain, to accompany him. They arrived off the coast of Anastacia Island (it is supposed) below the site of St. Augustine, at the close of April. Sailing along the "sweet-smelling coast" northward, the two vessels entered the broad mouth of the River St. John, where the company landed and were most kindly received by the natives. The Frenchmen were delighted with everything—the soft climate; the sweetest blossoms; the magnificent trees festooned from root to top with grape-vines; birds of gay plumage and sweetest notes; and mulberry trees, on "the boughs of which were silkworms in marvelous numbers," and with people of finest forms and kindliest natures. They seemed to have entered a paradise. "It is a thing unspeakable," wrote Captain Ribault, "to consider the things that be seen there, and shall be found more and more in this incomparable land, which, never yet broken with plough irons, bringeth forth all things according to its first nature, wherewith the eternal God endowed it."

DUKE OF GUISE.

Under the shadow of a wide-spreading magnolia tree laden with blossoms at the edge of a green savannah, with half-naked men, women and children, painted and decorated with gold and pearls—wondering sun-worshippers—

standing a little way off, the Christians knelt upon the soft sward and poured forth thanksgiving to God for his mercy in giving them a safe voyage to such a delightful land. It was a bright May-day. At twilight they returned to their ships, and early the next morning the whole company went ashore again, in small boats, carrying a column of hard stone upon which was carved the arms of the French king. They set it up on a broad grassy knoll surrounded by tall cypress and spreading palmetto trees and sweet flowering shrubs; and with the usual ceremonies, they took possession of the country in the name of Charles the Ninth. They were probably not far from the lowest point to which Verazzani had sailed almost forty years before.

On the 3d of May the Huguenots went northward, visiting numerous islands and inlets, and toward the end of the month they entered the fine harbor of Port Royal on the coast of South Carolina, passing the high shore of Hilton Head on the left and the low grounds of St. Helena Island on the right. They anchored off Port Royal Island and went in small boats up the Broad River, and into the Coosaw and the Combahee. They were in the land where D'Allyon had committed his atrocities and met retributive justice about half a century before, yet they were kindly received by the natives and secured the friendship of the Indians by giving them kindness in return. Charmed with everything, Ribault, after exploring the surrounding country several days, called his people together on Port Royal Island near the site of the present town of Beaufort. He told them that he thought they were at the best place for a colony he had yet seen. He spoke of the advantages of a settlement there, and the glory they might acquire for themselves and France by planting in that beautiful and fertile land the seed of a great empire. Who will undertake the glorious work? he asked. The result was marvelous even to that hopeful man. So many were anxious to remain, that if all of them had stayed, Ribault would not have had sufficient men to navigate the ship back to France. A colony of thirty persons was organized by the choice of Captain Albert De la Pierria as governor. At the request of the volunteers, Ribault built them a fort and provisioned it before his departure, and named it Fort Charles (Fort Carolus or Carolina) in honor of his king. It was constructed on the eastern bank of Port Royal Island, about a mile and a half from Beaufort, where its remains were yet visible when I visited the spot in the spring of 1866. Near it were magnificent live-oaks draped with the trailing Spanish moss, which were there, probably, when Ribault built the fort.

After completing the little fortress, Ribault said to the men who were to remain: "Be kind to each other, and prudent with your provisions. Let each love God and his neighbor. Your interests are mutual. Let no jealousies grow, nor disputes make you live apart, but cultivate brotherly love and you will prosper. Farewell!" Then he went on board of his vessel and both ships sailed out of the harbor after exchanging salutes with the fort by firing guns. It was then near the middle of June, and Ribault attempted to explore the coasts northward, but foul weather opposed him and he sailed for France, whence he expected to return immediately with supplies for the colony.

Coligni was delighted with Ribault's report, but he was then unable to do anything for his colony. A civil war was raging in France between the theological factions—Roman Catholics and Huguenots—with unrelenting violence. The monarch, the court and Coligni were so involved in the strife that Ribault pleaded in vain for help for the colony in Florida. As soon as

CARTIER. CORTEZ. COLIGNI. DE SOTO. VERAZZANI.

it subsided, the admiral renewed his efforts in its behalf. The regent and her son provided him with money and three armed ships—the *Elizabeth of Honfleur*, Captain John Lucas; the *Petite Britain*, Captain Vasseur, and the *Falcon*, Captain Marchant. The little squadron was placed under the general command of Renè Laudonnière, who accompanied Ribault in the preceding voyage. With him went many young men of family and fortune; mechanics and laborers; Jacob Le Moyne as artist and geographer to the expedition, and two skillful pilots, the brothers Vasseur, of Dieppe. Laudonnière left Havre de Grace on the 22d of April, 1564, and at the end of two months he saw the coast of Florida; but he did not go to the relief of the colony at Port Royal Island. Why?

The colonists at Port Royal cultivated the friendship of the Indians, and were very happy for awhile, but when the provisions began to fail and Ribault did not return, they lamented their folly in not exercising forethought. They had not cultivated a rood of land nor made any other provisions for sustenance, and they were soon compelled to look to their Indian neighbors for their daily food. That was then scanty; and being informed of a rich country and a munificent king further south, a part of the company went thither in a little pinnace which they had constructed, and returned with it loaded with corn and beans. They had evidently been to the banks of the Savannah River, and there they had beheld a marvelous vision in the capital of King Ouadé. His house was adorned with tapestry formed of richly-colored feathers; white couches finely embroidered and fringed with scarlet; handsome mats made of woven split cane; and the monarch and his young queen richly adorned with golden chains and strings of great pearls. Better than these were his large granaries of food, from which their pinnace was so bountifully supplied; but their treasure was destined to suddenly disappear. Soon after their return to Fort Charles, their house, in which everything was stored, was burned, and they were left desolate. Their savage neighbors did all in their power to relieve their distress, and the munificent Ouadé furnished them with another pinnace full of corn and beans.

Dissension, the child of idleness, now appeared among the colonists. Governor Pierria applied the rules of discipline so harshly, that the people were exasperated, rose in mutiny and put him to death. They chose Nicolas Barré to be their leader, but their forlorn condition produced intense discontent. Gaunt famine was before them, and a growing distrust of the Frenchmen which appeared among the Indians menaced them with starvation. They determined to desert Port Royal and return to France. With the assistance of their neighbors they constructed a frail brigantine and sailed for home. She was scantily provisioned; and calms and headwinds kept them so long upon the ocean, that their food was almost exhausted. Then a furious tempest beat upon their frail barque and nearly engulfed her. A tremendous wave turned her upon her side, and so she floated. Starvation came. The sufferers tried to subsist upon their shoes and leather doublets, but one after another died and fell into the sea. The living had concluded to make the next victim their food, when another wave righted the crazy vessel, with some of the provisions uninjured. Half filled with water, she nevertheless floated. Again starvation came, and lots were about to be cast to determine who should be made food for the rest, when there was a feeble cry of "Land!" from one of them. They were, indeed, in sight of a green shore. Very soon a small English vessel came to their relief. One of her seamen was a Frenchman who had sailed with Ribault, and recognized the famished men. He gave them food and drink, and told them of home and friends. Upon what shore they were landed, it is not known, but it is certain that a part of these French adventurers were taken into the presence of Queen Elizabeth of England, and that their account of the beauties of Florida created an intense desire on the part of the English to colonize that region.

LIVE-OAK GROVE NEAR FORT CHARLES.

Laudonnière and his companions resolved to make the banks of the St. John's River, in Florida, their abiding place. At a council, he said: "If we should pass further north to go in search of Port Royal, this step would be neither very advantageous nor convenient, at least if we may rely on the report of those who have dwelt there a long time." He evidently had heard the report of those who had abandoned Fort Charles, before he left France. This answers the question, Why did he not go to Port Royal?

Laudonnière anchored his ships in the St. John's where Ribault had rested his, and he was received with marked kindness by the chief who dwelt near. He came to the captain with several of his noblemen gayly plumed and wearing short cloaks of marten skins or feathers, and besought him to go with them to the column which Ribault had set up. When they came to the grassy knoll they found the pillar surrounded with palm leaf baskets of corn and garlanded with fresh sweet flowers. Savages then kissed the stone with much reverence, extending their arms toward the skies as they assumed their erect position. They requested the Frenchmen also to kiss the stone, which they did. The attendants of the chief then brought spring-water to their guests in ornamented earthen jars, and presented to Laudonnière two live eagles. It was a ceremonial token of friendship, which pleased the captain, and with the permission of the cacique he proceeded to erect a fort on the south bank of the river. In this work the Indians gave him great assistance, for they were very expert palmetto-leaf thatchers, and covered the barracks with excellent roofs. When the work was finished, it was called Fort Carolina, in honor of King Charles.

Very soon rumors came to the willing ears of the Frenchmen of mines of gold and silver in the interior, and such a thirst for the precious metals was created, that an expedition went far up the river, in small boats, in search of them. Everywhere they had heard of gold and precious stones "further on," and they returned with such extravagant stories of their abundance somewhere far inland in the hands of dusky kings, that the colonists were made half crazy. The fever was at its height when, in July, the ships were sent back to France for supplies. Every man seemed anxious to seek treasure on his own account, and Laudonnière was compelled to threaten severe penalties against any person who should traffic for gold or precious stones, excepting for the benefit of the whole company. The delusion soon vanished. When it was known that the stories of the savages about the abundance of precious metals and stones in the interior were sheer fictions, the gold fever instantly subsided, and was followed by indolence and disappointment, with their attendant evils. The bane of the Port Royal colony was seen in this. There were too many idle and improvident persons among them—too many "gentlemen" who would not soil their hands with labor. Discontent soon created a mutinous spirit, and plots against the life of Laudonnière were planned and discovered. At length, some of the soldiers and seamen seized two small vessels, and sailing toward Cuba, engaged in piracy in the West Indian Seas. On their return, three months afterward, the ringleaders were shot. Great excitement ensued, and the colonists were kept from open mutiny only by being engaged in explorations of the country, or in wars with the enemies of friendly chiefs around them. They neglected the rich soil, and famine threatened them. Discontent became more rampant, and the captain determined to return to France with the whole company. They were delayed for want of sufficient vessels. Meanwhile, Sir John Hawkins, of England, sailed into the St. John's with several ships. Laudonnière bought one of them, and was about to embark for Europe in her, with his whole company, when Ribault appeared with a squadron of

STARVING HUGUENOTS ON THE SEA.

seven ships from France, bringing a fresh company of colonists. Amongst them were several women and children. He had sailed from Dieppe late in May, with a commission as governor of all the French on that coast, and arrived at the St. John's at near the close of August, 1565.

A few days after Ribault's arrival, five ships were seen coming in from the sea. They anchored within speaking distance of the French ships at the bar, and after a long silence the commander of the intruding squadron hailed the nearest vessel. He was answered, "France." "And what are you doing in the territories of King Philip?" he asked. "Begone!" The questioner was a Spaniard, and the Spanish monarch claimed all Florida by right of pre-discovery. The Spanish officer then asked: "Are you Catholics or Lutherans?" and was answered, "Lutherans of the new religion." The French officer then inquired who the Spaniard was and what was his errand, when (according to Barcia, the Spanish historian) he replied: "I am Pedro Menendez, commander of this armament, which belongs to the king of Spain, Don Philip the Second. I have come hither to hang and destroy all the Lutherans whom I shall find either on land or sea, according to my orders received from the king, which are so precise as to deprive me of the power of saving any one whatsoever; and these orders I shall execute to the letter; but if I should meet with any Catholic on board your vessels, he shall receive good treatment. As for the heretics, they shall die."

Ribault was not taken altogether by surprise, for just as he was about to sail from Dieppe, he was handed a letter from Coligni, in which the admiral wrote in postscript: "While closing this letter, I have received certain advice that Don Pedro Menendez is about to depart from Spain to the coast of Florida. You will take care not to suffer him to encroach upon us, any more than he would that we should encroach upon him."

The threat of Menendez and the hostile attitude of his ships caused the captains of the French vessels to cut their cables and put to sea. The Spanish vessels followed, firing the contents of heavy bow-guns after the fugitives. They chased them far, but in vain. "These enraged devils," wrote Mendoza, the chaplain of Menendez' squadron, "are such adroit seamen, and manœuvred so well, that we could not take one of them." The Spaniards finally turned back toward the coast, followed by the Frenchmen, who saw the smaller Spanish vessels enter a river several leagues south of the St. John's, and the larger ones, with the galleon of Menendez, anchor at its mouth. They also saw Spanish soldiers and provisions landed not far above that anchorage. With this important news the Frenchmen hastened back to the St. John's and reported to Ribault all they had seen. He immediately prepared to go in search of his enemies and attack them with his ships and his whole land force.

Whilst Ribault was holding a council in which Laudonnière opposed the measure suggested by the governor, an Indian came with tidings that the Spaniards were fortifying themselves on the bank of the river where they had landed. Ribault believed that they were preparing to march overland and attack Fort Carolina, and he hastened his preparations for seizing their ships, attacking them in their quarters, and so spoiling their scheme and possibly destroying them totally or driving them from the coast. Was he sure that he could seize their ships? The more cautious Laudonnière thought not, and still opposed the perilous expedition. The more fiery Ribault persisted in his resolution, and gathering as many soldiers on three ships (his larger one, the *Trinity*, being yet at sea) as they could conveniently carry, he sailed out of the river and down the straight coast, in full expectation of gaining a complete victory. He was sorely disappointed. A dead calm and a very low tide, when he first approached the enemy, prevented his attacking the Spanish ships, and whilst he was waiting for a favoring breeze and a flood-tide, there arose a very sudden and violent storm which drove the French vessels far out to sea, and exposed both ships and men to a sad fate, as we shall observe hereafter.

Meanwhile, Menendez dispatched one of his small vessels to Spain, and the galleon to Cuba, the latter for the purpose of bringing to Florida a reinforcement of Spanish troops known to be at Havana. But the galleon *St. Pelayo*—a large three-deck ship—did not reach its destination. There were several French prisoners on board of her whom Menendez had ordered to be sent to the Inquisition in Spain by way of St. Domingo. Soon after the great ship put to sea, these prisoners joined the sailors in a mutiny, and taking the command from the officers, they sailed for Europe and entered a port in Denmark.

CHAPTER XI.

MENENDEZ—HIS LANDING ON THE COAST OF FLORIDA—THE FRENCH ON THE ST. JOHN'S MASSACRED BY THE SPANIARDS—COMPLAINTS OF THE OUTRAGE UNHEEDED BY THE FRENCH MONARCH—THE CHEVALIER DE GOURGES AVENGES THE CRIME BY RETALIATION—THE FRENCH COURT FAVORS THE ROMAN CATHOLICS—WICKEDNESS OF CATHARINE DE MEDICI—THE MURDER OF COLIGNI—QUEEN ELIZABETH ESPOUSES COLIGNI'S PLAN FOR SETTLEMENT IN AMERICA—REPORTS CONCERNING THE WARMER REGIONS OF AMERICA RECEIVED FROM WALTER RALEIGH—FROBISHER'S VOYAGE IN SEARCH OF A NORTHWEST PASSAGE TO INDIA, AND FOR GOLD—HIS DISCOVERIES—THE GLOBE CIRCUMNAVIGATED BY DRAKE—HIS EXPLOITS AGAINST THE SPANIARDS.

MENENDEZ (or Melendez) seems to have been rather too harshly treated by historians, for his career in Florida was not wholly voluntary. He was a native of Avila, in Spain, and at the period under consideration, he was about forty-six years of age. He had already risen to the highest rank in the Spanish navy, and was a man of large fortune. In 1554, he commanded the vessel which bore his king to England to marry Queen Mary; and in 1561, he commanded the great treasure-fleet of galleons on their voyage from Mexico to Spain. One of the vessels containing his son and several relatives and friends disappeared, and was never heard of afterward. When he had delivered the fleet in Spain, he asked permission to go back in search of the lost vessel, but was then refused. Finally, after two or three years delay, his request was granted, but on condition that he should explore and colonize Florida. He fitted out an expedition for the purpose at his own expense, but when he was about to sail, orders came to him from Philip to exterminate all Protestants he might find there, or in whatever corner of the world he should discover them, on land or sea, in forests or marshes.

Philip had heard that the Huguenots who had fled from persecution in France were hiding in the forests beyond the Atlantic, and his zeal was so kindled for the domination of his church, that he gave the order to Menendez to extirpate the heretics. The mariner had no alternative but to obey or lose the opportunity of searching for his son. He was not even allowed to choose the alternative, for disobedience would have led him to the dungeons of the Inquisition. So he obeyed. The king, regarding it as a holy enterprise, added ships and treasure. Soldiers and seamen flocked to the standard of Menendez in great numbers, and he sailed with a fleet of eleven ships (one of them a galleon of nine hundred tons) with over twenty-six hundred persons, consisting, besides the soldiers and sailors, of adventurers and priests. This was the armament, the sailing of which Ribault had been apprised by Coligni. Storms and other disasters in the West Indies scattered it, and when it arrived on the coast of Florida, it was reduced to a squadron of only five vessels (one of them the great ship), bearing about a thousand persons of all descriptions.

When Menendez landed from the galleon, on the coast of Florida, he made the event an occasion for a pompous ceremonial. As he left the great ship in a boat with six oarsmen, accompanied by Mendoza, his chaplain, and followed by other boats filled with gentlemen and ecclesiastics, loud trumpets sounded, drums beat, cannon thundered, and flags were displayed on the ship and on the shore, where his soldiers had already begun the construction of a fort. As they touched the beach, the chaplain walked before, bearing a large cross and chanting a hymn. Menendez followed with his train, carrying aloft, with his own hand, the royal standard of Spain unfurled. He and his followers reverently knelt before the priest, who was arrayed in rich sacerdotal robes, and kissed the sacred symbol of the atonement which Mendoza held in his hand. It was firmly planted in the sand by the side of the flagstaff from which fluttered the royal banner in a gentle breeze; and a shield bearing the arms of Spain was leaned against the cross. Then Menendez drew his sword and formally took possession of the whole country in the name of King Philip of Spain. On that spot, and with such consecration, were laid the foundations of the city of St. Augustine, in Florida, forty years earlier than those of any other town in America, north of Mexico.

Menendez soon marched upon Fort Carolina, on the St. Johns, to execute his dreadful mission. His journey was in incessant rain over oozy ground, but zeal gave strength to his four hundred soldiers. The feeble Huguenot fort was in command of Laudonnière, who had only a handful of soldiers (for a greater portion had gone with Ribault), and he was burdened with civilians, men, women and children. With the ferocity of tigers, the Spaniards fell upon them. They were close to the fort before their presence was suspected. No person was spared on whom the assailants could lay hands. In their beds, in prayers for mercy, in flight, they were slaughtered. A few escaped to the woods without food and with scanty clothing. Many perished for want of food, and a few made their way to two small French ships, in which they sailed for Europe. Among them was Laudonnière. According to the chaplain, Mendoza, one hundred and forty-two of the Huguenots were slain, whilst the Spaniards did not lose a man. The women and children were butchered. A few men were hanged upon trees, and over them was placed the inscription:

Not as Frenchmen, but as Lutherans.

Leaving a garrison of three hundred men in Fort Carolina, and naming it Fort Matheo, Menendez returned in triumph to St. Augustine. His chaplain has left a glowing account of his reception there, and bestows unstinted praise on that leader as one of the most zealous of Christians. He was supported, he says, in his great fatigue by a "burning desire to serve our Lord and destroy this Lutheran sect, the enemy of our holy Catholic religion."

Ribault's vessels, meanwhile, had all been wrecked near Cape Canaveral, on the Florida coast. All of his people were saved from the sea, but perished at the hands of the less merciful Spaniards. They tried to make their way to Fort Carolina, ignorant of its sad fate. Ribault, with one hundred and fifty men, was betrayed by one of the sailors who had deserted Laudonnière and turned pirate, and under a promise of mercy he cast himself upon the clemency of Menendez. That leader proceeded to put to death the brave captain and his companions. "Seeing that they were Lutherans," says Mendoza, "the General condemned them all to death; but as I was a priest, and had the bowels of a man, I besought him to accord to me the favor, that he would not put to death those whom we should discover to be Christians. He granted my request. I made inquiry, and found ten or twelve, whom we selected from the number. All the others were executed because they were Lutherans, enemies of our holy Catholic faith." They were led out in parcels of ten, and with their hands tied behind them and at a line drawn in the sand with a cane, by Menendez, they were butchered. So, also, says Barcia, the Spanish historian, who regarded Menendez as the chosen instrument of the Almighty to vindicate his cause. Mendoza tells us, when writing of the massacre at Fort Carolina, that "the Holy Spirit enlightened the understanding" of the commander "to enable him to gain so great a victory."

A knowledge of these horrid crimes in Florida and the avowed cause of their commission, excited the greatest indignation throughout Europe, and the unchristian spirit of revenge glowed in many a manly bosom. The French Roman Catholics were greatly moved by this outrage upon their countrymen by the hated Spaniards. The relatives of the victims appealed to the French king to vindicate the wrongs of the emigrants who had been sent out under his sanction and authority. Coligni joined in the appeal; but the king and court, ruled by Catharine, whose theological views were then in a transition state, were profoundly indifferent. No remonstrances or complaint was sent to the Spanish court. No doubt information of the expedition of Ribault had been sent from the French court to Philip and caused the issuing of his bloody commission to Menendez. The courtiers of Charles the Ninth, who feared and hated Coligni because he was a Huguenot and a patriot, rejoiced at the failure of his scheme, and he was utterly unable to do more for his colony.

At this juncture a fiery avenger appeared. It was the Chevalier Dominic de Gourges, a gentleman of Gascony, member of an eminent family and a devoted Roman Catholic. In the military service of his country he had been made a prisoner by the Spaniards, who compelled him to do slave's work in Spanish galleys. His hatred of the Spanish blood thereby engendered was undying. When he heard of the treatment of his countrymen in Florida, at their hands, he was in retirement. Filled with indignation because of the crime and the criminal indifference of his king, he determined to fit out an expedition at his own expense, to punish the offenders. That was in 1567. He sold his property, borrowed money of his friends, and fitted out three small vessels, manned by one hundred soldiers (many of them gentlemen volunteers), and eighty mariners prepared with cross-bows and picks to act as soldiers. His vessels were so flat-bottomed that they might pass over the sand-bars of rivers.

De Gourges kept his destination a secret, and sailed from Bordeaux late in August for the coast of Benin, in Africa, as he publicly pretended. After various vicissitudes and delays, his little squadron left the extreme western end of Cuba for Florida, when, for the first time, he revealed to all his followers, his destination and designs. In a speech glowing with enthusiasm, he so warmed their hearts for the work that was before them, that they were impatient to reach the coast. Their eyes were gratified with a sight of Florida in the spring of 1568, when the squadron entered the mouth of a small river north of the St. John's. The Indians, supposing the new comers to be Spaniards, showed much hostility. De Gourges' trumpeter, who had been with Laudonnière, and understood a little of the Indian tongue, volunteered to go ashore. There he was delighted, not only by the discovery that the cacique was an old friend of Laudonnière, but that he was accompanied by a young Frenchman who had escaped the massacre of Fort Carolina. The cacique received the trumpeter kindly, and sent an invitation to De Gourges to come on shore and hold a conference. He did so, and his young countryman acted as interpreter. The cacique, painted and bedecked, was seated on a log in a beautiful grove, with several allied chiefs sitting in a semicircle around him. He placed De Gourges on another log, and then opened the conference with bitter complaints against the Spaniards, because of their cruelties. They had driven the Indians from their homes, murdered their children, and desolated their fields because they had treated the Frenchmen kindly. The Chevalier was pleased with this discourse, but was cautious. He told the cacique that the Spaniards should be punished for their crimes. "Do you intend to make war upon them?" quickly asked the cacique. "I do," as quickly answered De Gourges. "We will join you!" said the cacique with vehemence as he sprang to his feet; and the same words came from the lips of the other chiefs with equal vehemence as they seized their arms which they had laid upon the grass, and brandished their javelins in great excitement. An alliance against the Spaniards was made on the spot between the French and Indians, and steps were immediately taken to attack the common enemy. Other alliances were made between the French and Indians, many generations afterward, which were instruments of dire distress to the English settlers in America, as we shall observe as our story goes on.

The allies met at an appointed place not far from the St. Johns, on which the Spaniards had built two forts below Fort Carolina, on opposite banks of the river. Moving cautiously, they crossed a little stream behind a wood, arm-pit deep, the soldiers carrying their powder flasks on their helmets, an arquebuse in one hand and a sword in the other. Gathering in battle array near the little fort, the allies rushed forward with shouts and yells, and took it by surprise. The entire garrison, sixty in number, were slain, excepting a few who were reserved for another fate.

De Gourges now hastened across the river, with eighty men in boats, to attack the fort on the opposite side, followed by the Indians, who were so eager for the fray that they could not wait for the return of the little vessels. They plunged into the water, each holding a bow, javelin and quiver of arrows in one hand, and swimming with the other. Appalled by the number of pale and dusky enemies that threatened them, the garrison of sixty men fled in the direction of Fort Carolina (or Matheo), three miles above. They were overtaken by the French and Indians in the woods, and the whole company were slain, excepting a few who were held as prisoners. From these prisoners and from a spy who was discovered in the camp, the French commander learned that Fort Carolina was not very strong; that its garrison consisted of two hundred and sixty men, and that they were greatly alarmed by a report that the allies were two thousand in number. Encouraged by this information, De Gourges, after two days' preparation, marched with his whole force against the doomed fortress. After some severe fighting, the

FRENCHMEN PROCEEDING TO ATTACK THE SPANISH FORT ON THE ST. JOHNS.

fort was captured. The flower of the garrison had already been slain in a *sortie* or sallying out to attack the assailants, and many of the remainder had fled to the woods, where they were met by the Indians and slaughtered. There was an indiscriminate massacre as before, a few only being reserved as prisoners. Now these, with others who had been so reserved, were placed in a row under the very trees whereon the Huguenots had been hung, *not as Frenchmen, but as Lutherans.* De Gourges addressed them, and then suspended them all by their necks. Over them he placed the inscription, burned into wood with a hot iron:

NOT AS SPANIARDS AND MARINERS, BUT AS TRAITORS, ROBBERS, AND MURDERERS.

So was concluded the savage and unchristian work of retaliating upon the innocent the crimes of the guilty. Could the blow have fallen upon King Philip of Spain, or Menendez his executioner, or Mendoza his apologist and coadjutor, and not upon the mere machines of government—the common soldiers—retributive justice would have been more divinely vindicated. But we must judge Philip, and Menendez, Mendoza and De Gourges, leniently, in the light of the spirit of the age in which they lived. No Spanish monarch now; no military chief, no truly Christian minister in any Christian country, to-day, would do such horrid work for such a cause. The seminal idea of the protest at Spires has worked beneficent wonders in making men less savage and more divine, since it was projected into human society.

Too weak to brave the wrath of Menendez, who was at St. Augustine, De Gourges, with the assistance of the Indians, utterly destroyed the forts on the St. John's, and then sailed for France, where he arrived just in time to avoid vessels which Philip had sent out to intercept him. He was received with coldness at court. Philip had demanded of the weak Charles the head of De Gourges, and the Queen-mother, Catharine, had espoused the cause of the opponents of the Huguenots. In poverty De Gourges concealed himself for some years, declining an invitation of the Queen of England (Elizabeth) to enter her service. At length he died, whilst on his way to a seaport to take command of a fleet that was about to wage war on Philip.

Menendez firmly planted a colony at St. Augustine, and sent an expedition, with Jesuit missionaries, to explore the waters of Chesapeake Bay, plant a settlement there, and scatter the seeds of Christianity among the pagans. But his death in 1574, when he was High Admiral of the Spanish navy, arrested this enterprise, and no further attempts seem to have been made by the Spaniards to plant settlements within the domain of our Republic.

Coligni was deserted by his sovereign and his inhuman mother, and became a martyr. Catharine, with a strange perversion of a mother's natural instincts, after she became regent, plunged all of her children, in the flower of their youth, into a whirl of sensual pleasure, that soon weakened their minds and bodies beyond recovery, as she intended they should be. Her royal son, when he reached his majority, seemed incapable of resisting any temptation put in his way by his mother, and he was easily persuaded by her to order the destruction of the Protestants throughout France, on the eve of St. Bartholomew, in August, 1572. She had failed in a plot to bring the Duke of Guise to the scaffold, and now she had joined the league against the Huguenots, of which he was a leader. Coligni was selected as one of the first victims for sacrifice on that fatal night. Behme, a German assassin in the employ of the Duke of Guise, led a band of murderers to the room of Coligni, with concealed weapons excepting a boar-spear which he held in his hand. When he entered, the majestic presence of the Admiral and the serenity and dignity of his deportment so abashed the leader, that he was about to retire, when one of his followers whispered in his ear, "Coward!" Behme instantly recovered his self-possession and plunged the spear into the heart of Coligni, who fell dead at the feet of his murderers. His body was thrown out of the window into a court, where the Duke of Guise was waiting for the consummation of the crime. The Admiral's head was severed from his body and carried to Catharine, who had it embalmed and sent as a present to Pope Gregory the Thirteenth, at Rome. The Admiral's body was dragged through the streets of Paris amidst the execration of an infuriated mob, and then was hanged on a gibbet where Charles the Ninth and his courtiers viewed it.

We have observed that a remnant of Ribault's company who abandoned Port Royal were picked up at sea by an English vessel, and taken to the presence of Queen Elizabeth. She was the daughter of Henry the Eighth and the beautiful Anne Boleyn, and had succeeded her half-sister Mary as sovereign of Great Britain in 1558, when she was twenty-five years of age. She had not been long on the throne when these Huguenots were brought into her audience-chamber. They were treated kindly, for Elizabeth was in theological sympathy with them. She had always been a Protestant at heart, but to avoid many personal perils and even death during the reign of her half-sister, who was wife of Philip of Spain, she had so deported herself with singularly adroit hypocrisy, that she was only *suspected* of heresy. So completely did she deceive everybody, that only the day before she ascended the throne as queen, the Spanish ambassador at the British court wrote to his royal master: "She is a true Catholic; she declares that she prays to the Virgin and acknowledges the real presence [of the real body and blood of Christ] in the sacrament." That was at the middle of November. On Christmas she placed herself at the head of the Protestant world, by refusing to hear mass in the Royal Chapel; and yet, only three weeks later, when

THE ASSASSINATION OF COLIGNI.

she was crowned in Westminster Abbey, the religious ceremonials were all in accordance with the liturgy of the Church of Rome, and she partook of the sacrament at the hands of a Romish Archbishop. She was simply an adroit politician, and was moved altogether by political motives. For years she endeavored to gain the favor of *all* her subjects, Romanists and Protestants, by favoring both ; and there was a ludicrous mixture of the two ceremonials in the public worship of the realm.

At the time the distressed Huguenots were brought into the presence of Elizabeth, she was on the point of affording aid to their co-religionists in France and the Netherlands. She favored Coligni's scheme for colonization in America, and she listened with delight to the accounts given by these castaways of the beauty of the country, the amenities of the climate, and the fertility of the soil of the mysterious land peopled by a mysterious people, which they had been compelled to abandon. The enlightened and sagacious queen readily perceived the glory and advantages she might win for her country, by carrying forward Coligni's plan, with her own countrymen and the French Huguenots as the materials for a powerful colony. She felt a strong desire to do so, but she was then too deeply engaged in more important state work, and her desires did not ripen into action until several years afterward, although they grew in intensity. From her subjects who went over to France in considerable numbers to fight under the Prince of Condé and Coligni, she continually heard more and more of the grandeur and richness of the warmer regions of North America. From none of them came more vivid pictures than from Walter Raleigh, a young Devonshire gentleman who came from an ancient family, was well educated, and who was one of a small body of troops sent by his queen to assist the Huguenots in France. He served five years under Coligni, and then proceeded to the Netherlands to fight the Spaniards, under the banner of the Prince of Orange. He was in that service abroad when De Gourges returned from his foray in Florida, and Raleigh heard much of that region from the lips of the Chevalier. To his friends at home and to his court, he wrote letters filled with accounts of the wonders of the West, and when he returned to England he found the minds of many of the leading men of the realm, as well as that of his queen, filled with projects for making settlements in the warmer regions of North America.

Meanwhile, English navigators had been again trying to solve the question which Cabot had failed to do more than half a century before, namely, the existence of a northwest passage to Asia from the British Isles. Among them was Martin Frobisher, a Yorkshireman, whose zeal and patience were remarkable. He spent fifteen years in fruitless endeavors to get up an expedition to accomplish that object, when he was fortunate enough to secure the patronage of Ambrose Dudley, Earl of Warwick. The queen and her government took a lively interest in the undertaking, and early in June, 1576, Frobisher sailed from Deptford, on the Thames, with two barks of only twenty-five tons each and a pinnace of ten tons, with the avowed purpose of making the discovery or to die in the attempt. When the little flotilla passed by the palace at Greenwich, the queen, who was watching its movements from an open window, leaned out and waved her hand toward the commander in token of her good-will and a farewell.

Frobisher touched at Greenland, coasted up the shores of Labrador and entered a strait or inlet above the entrance to Hudson's Bay, which bears his name. There he landed and formally took possession of the country in the name of Elizabeth. Impenetrable pack-ice, the loss of some of his men and the growing discontent of others, caused him to return to England in the autumn, at the twilight of the polar night, taking with him some of the products of the new region which he had added to the British Empire. Among other things was a heavy dark stone, a fragment of which the wife of a man to whom Frobisher had given it threw into the fire, in a passion. Her husband snatched it out and quenched the glowing mineral in vinegar, when it glittered like burnished gold. On fusing it, a small quantity of the precious metal was found in it. The fact was soon noised abroad and produced a gold-fever. Many persons eagerly offered money to enable Frobisher to make another voyage to those high latitudes, and in May, 1577, he sailed from Harwich in a vessel of the royal navy, which the queen placed at his disposal, accompanied by two barks of thirty tons each.

SIR WALTER RALEIGH.

Only for gold were these adventurers ordered to search. They were not to seek the mysterious passage to India. Indeed Frobisher had demonstrated the impossibility of passing the polar ice-fields. On the shores of Frobisher's Inlet, the whole company landed, freighted the ships with the black stone, and returned to England. A commission was appointed by the queen to determine the value of the discoveries made. Very little gold, if any, was procured from the cargoes of stone, but the commission, for reasons not made clear, deemed it expedient to send out another expedition. Frobisher was now placed in command of a fleet, for he had twelve ships in addition to the three with which he made his second voyage. With these he sailed from Harwich on the last day of May, 1558, instructed to make search for genuine gold-ore, or for a northwest passage. Storms and currents scattered the fleet, and not more than half of the ships reached their destination. Some turned back, and two of them went to the bottom of the North Atlantic Ocean. No effort was made to force the vessels that reached Frobisher's Inlet to penetrate the ice-pack northward. They were laden with the dark stones (out of which not a particle of gold was obtained), and returned to England.

The three expeditions under Frobisher were unsuccessful, excepting in the discovery of several bays, inlets and islands on the northern coasts of America, before unknown. The brave leader, however, won the honors of a discoverer and the fame of having been the first European who had penetrated so far toward the Arctic Circle, for Frobisher's Inlet is under the sixty-third degree of north latitude. For these exploits and other brave deeds, especially as one of the chief captains in the British fleet that confronted the "Invincible Armada" of Spain, he received the honors of knighthood.

Whilst these expeditions were in progress, Francis Drake, another Devonshire man, was circumnavigating the globe; a feat performed by the Portuguese navigator, Magellan, half a century before. Drake had suffered much in person and property from the Spaniards, and had vowed vengeance and retribution. His friends fitted out five vessels for him to go on a voyage of discovery and plunder. Promising the queen gold and conquest, he sailed under her sanction at the middle of November, 1577, from the harbor of Plymouth, making the *Pelican*, of a hundred tons burthen—the largest vessel in his squadron—his flag-ship. After touching at Brazil, and other places down the east coast of South America, he passed through the Straits of Magellan at the southern extremity of the continent, early in September, 1578. Then he ran up the western coast, plundering the Spanish settlements in Chili and Peru, capturing a royal Spanish galleon heavily loaded with treasure, and taking possession of California in the name of his sovereign. Burdened with gold and silver, and with his revenge fully satisfied, Drake determined to return home. Fearing to meet a superior Spanish force in the ocean, he resolved to seek a passage around the northern shores of America. Repelled by severe cold, he sailed across the Pacific and Indian Oceans, doubled the Cape of Good Hope, and arrived at Plymouth late in September, 1579, having discovered points on the western coasts of our country as far north as Washington Territory, above the Columbia River. The queen partook of a banquet given by Drake on board the

Pelican in Plymouth harbor, that was spread under a rich canopy of silk and tapestry that covered the clean deck, on which lay beautiful Turkish mats. The queen was attended by several ladies and gentlemen of her court. The food was served on silver dishes, and the wine in golden goblets. All the fruit of plunder. When the banquet was ended, the queen conferred upon Drake the honor of knighthood. He was then between thirty and forty years of age. Richly dressed in the uniform of his rank, he knelt before his sovereign, at her command, in the presence of the goodly company, and

DRAKE KNIGHTED BY THE QUEEN.

with his own sword she smote him gently over the shoulders, three times, and then bade him stand, a knight of her realm.

After that the exploits of Drake on the sea were marvellous. They were against the Spaniards, whom he hated intensely. Within the space of a single year he captured and plundered Carthagena in South America, and several other towns in that region; burned Forts Antonio and St. Augustine, ravaged places in the West Indies, and running up the coasts of Florida,

Georgia, and the Carolinas, he visited Roanoke Island, and bore away from it, to England, a famishing colony which Raleigh had planted there. On another occasion he "singed the beard of the King of Spain," as he said, by burning one hundred Spanish vessels in the harbor of Cadiz. He was a terror to the Spaniards everywhere; and long after his death, in 1595, Spanish nurses used the name of Drake as a bugaboo to frighten children, representing him as a devouring dragon. Although he is honored for his enterprise and the glory he won for England, and is regarded as the founder of the Royal Navy, Sir Francis Drake was only a daring pirate on a large and legalized scale. Camden says: "Nothing troubled him more than that some of the chief men at court refused to accept the gold which he offered them as gotten by piracy."

In 1594, the Spanish king threatened England, with a great show of power. Drake entered the service of his sovereign, and with Admiral Hawkins he sailed for America in 1595, with twenty-six vessels. A divided command worked mischievously. Hawkins died at Porto Rico, partly from the effects of a wound, and partly from chagrin because of reverses. Drake soon afterwards achieved great triumphs. He destroyed several Spanish towns; but a fatal fever seized him late in the year. It was aggravated by mental agitation caused by a defeat of his forces, and he died in December. The gallant sailor was honored with a sailor's funeral. He was buried at sea in sight of Puerto Bello.

CHAPTER XII.

SIR HUMPHREY GILBERT'S PATENT—CHARACTER OF WALTER RALEIGH—ILLUSTRATION OF HIS GALLANTRY—A FAVORITE OF QUEEN ELIZABETH—GILBERT AT NEWFOUNDLAND—IS LOST AT SEA—RALEIGH RECEIVES A CHARTER FROM THE QUEEN—SENDS AN EXPLORING EXPEDITION TO AMERICA—ITS CHEERING RESULTS—THE QUEEN NAMES THE REGION EXPLORED VIRGINIA—RALEIGH SENDS A COLONY TO VIRGINIA—BAD LEADERS PRODUCE GREAT DISASTERS—A COLONY OF WORKING PEOPLE SENT—FIRST ENGLISH CHILD BORN IN AMERICA—THE COLONY LOST—RALEIGH'S DEEDS, AND HIS SUFFERINGS AT THE HANDS OF A BAD KING—HIS DEATH ON THE SCAFFOLD.

WHILST Drake was plundering Spanish settlements in South America and circumnavigating the globe to avoid his enemies, the minds of the British queen and many of her leading subjects were powerfully directed to the more beneficent object of founding colonies in the region of North America discovered by Cabot three-fourths of a century before. With these better desires were mingled a thirst for gold which they believed existed in abundance somewhere in those regions. There were yearnings, also, for planting settlements and searching for treasures on the borders of the beautiful lands whose marvellous imagery had been portrayed by the shipwrecked Huguenots and the letters of Raleigh from France. These desires had assumed a more tangible shape than the day-dreams which had floated in the minds of England's monarch and people. They had been stimulated into action by Raleigh, on his return from the continent; and his half-brother, Sir Humphrey Gilbert—a kindred spirit—through the intervention of the young pupil of Coligni, obtained a patent from Elizabeth, which authorized him to explore and appropriate remote and barbarous lands unoccupied by Christian powers, and to hold them as fiefs or estates of the crown of England. That was in the year 1578. Gilbert did not believe there could be profit in searching for gold in the higher latitudes. A more comprehensive view of the fisheries off Newfoundland, to which four hundred vessels from Europe repaired annually, turned his thoughts now to a project of planting a colony on that island; and in this scheme Raleigh acquiesced.

Walter Raleigh was one of the most illustrious of the English adventurers of his time. When, through his influence at court, Gilbert obtained his patent, he was only twenty-six years of age. Endowed with brilliant genius, unbounded ambition and extraordinary activity, his mind grasped the boldest projects, and his versatility, enthusiasm and credulity, led him to the immediate execution of any scheme which he might conceive. "Framed in the prodigality of nature," says an English author, "he was at once the most industrious scholar and the most accomplished courtier of his age; as a projector, profound, ingenious, and indefatigable; as a soldier, prompt, daring, and heroic; 'so contemplative (says an old writer), that he might have been judged unfit for action; so active, that he seemed to have no leisure for contemplation.' The chief defect of his mental temperament was the absence of moderation and regulation of thought and aim. Smitten with a love of glorious achievement, he had unfortunately embraced the

DRAKE. ELIZABETH. RALEIGH.

maxim that 'whatever is not extraordinary is nothing;' and his mind (till the last scene of his life) was not sufficiently pervaded by religion to recognize that nobility of purpose which ennobles the commonest actions, and elevates circumstances instead of borrowing dignity from them. Uncontrolled by steady principle and sober calculation, the fancy and the passions of Raleigh transported him, in some instances, beyond the bounds of rectitude, honor and propriety; and, seconded by the malevolence of his fortune, entailed reproaches on his character and discomfiture on his undertakings. But though adversity might cloud his path, it would never depress his spirit, or quench a single ray of his genius. He subscribed to his fortune with a noble grace, and by the universal consent of mankind his errors and infirmities have been deemed within the protection of his glory."

Raleigh became a favorite of his queen by a single act of gallantry. He had lately returned from Ireland, where he had distinguished himself in putting down the rebellion of the Desmonds. Meeting the queen one day whilst she was walking with two of her maids of honor, he took from his shoulders his rich velvet mantle, and bowing gracefully, spread it over a wet spot in her path for her to walk upon. Because of this delicate gallantry, Raleigh was immediately admitted to court, where he and the accomplished Essex became powerful rivals for the queen's special favor. Their intrigues were ceaseless and often romantic, and filled a large space in the gossip of court circles. Raleigh soon tired of such a fruitless life, and leaving the business of a courtier, engaged again in the graver thoughts and duties pertaining to American colonization.

Gilbert's patent, which bound him to pay to the crown one-fifth part of all gold and silver which the countries he might discover and colonize should produce, invested him with the powers of a civil and criminal legislator over the inhabitants of any territory which he might occupy, provided the laws should be in accordance with the statutes and policy of England, and not in derogation of supreme allegiance to the crown. It also guaranteed to his followers the civil rights of Englishmen. The patent, so far as it related to the appropriation of territory, extended six years, during which time no other persons should be permitted to establish a settlement within two hundred leagues of any spot which these adventurers might occupy.

Armed with these arbitrary powers and aided by Raleigh's friendship and money, Gilbert, at the expense of much of his own fortune, fitted out a small squadron and sailed for America late in 1579. He had been distinguished for gallant military service in Ireland, and in 1570 had received the honor of knighthood. Six years afterwards, he had published a book entitled "A Discourse of a Discovery for a New Passage to Cathay," which attracted a good deal of attention toward him. His reputation was so high that the sons of many of the nobility and gentry of England embarked with him as adventurers. They were utterly unfit to be the founders of a state (and were not permitted to become so), for most of them were idlers and some were dissolute.

It is said by some that Raleigh sailed with his half-brother. Heavy storms or Spanish war vessels destroyed one of the ships, and compelled the remainder to turn back, and for the space of four years afterwards the enterprise was held in abeyance. Gilbert was too much impoverished to undertake another expedition; but Raleigh and his friends, at the end of that time, fitted out another small squadron. It sailed from Plymouth in June, 1583, under the command of Gilbert, who bore as a present from the queen and as a token of her good-will, a golden anchor guided by a woman; and he was accompanied by a learned Hungarian. The little flotilla reached Newfoundland in August, and entered the harbor of St. John's, wherein the Lord of Robertval and Cartier had met almost fifty years before. There, on the firm earth, Gilbert set up a column with the arms of England carved on it; and in the presence of hundreds of fishermen from Western Europe, whom he summoned to the spot, he formally took possession of the country in the name of Queen Elizabeth.

RALEIGH SPREADING HIS MANTLE FOR THE FEET OF THE QUEEN.

Gilbert's vessels had suffered much from storms on the voyage; but the intrepid mariners, after making slight repairs, proceeded to explore the coasts southward. Off the shores of Cape Breton, heavy tempests beat upon his ships, and not long afterwards his larger one, in which he sailed, was dashed upon the rocks and lost with about one hundred men. The commander was saved and took refuge in the *Squirrel*, a little vessel of ten tons. Buffeting the waves until his flotilla was dispersed and hope failed, he turned the prow of his little vessel homeward, with another named the *Hind*. On a September day when a gale was rising, the two vessels were within speaking distance of each other. Gilbert was sitting abaft with a book in his hand, and in reply to a shout from the commander of the *Hind* that they were in great peril, he cried: "We are as near Heaven on the sea as on the land." The gale increased: night fell; the darkness became intense, and at midnight the lights of the *Squirrel* went out suddenly. The little bark had plunged beneath the waves and all on board perished. The *Hind* was the only vessel of the squadron that escaped the tempests and returned to England with tidings of the disaster.

Misfortune seemed to stimulate Raleigh to more energetic action. He was then paying court to the queen, with whom he was a great favorite. He asked her for a charter in all respects the same as that she had given to Gilbert, but covering lands further south. It was given in April, 1584. It constituted Raleigh Lord Proprietor of all countries between Delaware Bay and the mouth of the Santee River in South Carolina. Quick in the execution of his projects, two ships were made ready for sea before June, well equipped with men and provisions. Arthur Barlow, a skillful mariner, was placed in chief command, assisted by Philip Amidas, of French descent but a native of England. They were directed to explore the coasts within the parallels named, and choose a place for settlement. Instead of following the northerly path across the Atlantic, in which so many disasters had occurred, they went by the way of the Canary Isles, were wafted by the trade-winds to the West Indies, and approached the American coast in the latitude of Florida. Turning northward, they ran up the coast along the line of the Gulf Stream, and entering Ocracock Inlet, anchored off Wocoken Island, in July. There they landed, and were kindly received by the gentle natives who were as kindly treated in return. There Barlow set up a small column with the British arms rudely carved upon it, and waving over it the banner of England, in the presence of the wondering natives, took possession of the whole region—islands and main, inlets and sounds—in the name of the queen. They spent several weeks in explorations of Roanoke Island and Pamlico and Albemarle Sounds, and in trafficking with the natives. "The people," wrote the mariners, "were most gentle, loving and faithful, void of all guile and treason, and such as lived after the manner of the golden age."

On Roanoke Island the Englishmen were entertained, with a refined hospitality, by the mother of King Wingina (who was absent); and wherever they went, friendship was the rule. To the feelings of the strangers, everything on the islands and on the main was charming. Nature was then garnished in all her summer wealth, and to the eyes of the Englishmen her beauties there were marvellous. Magnificent trees were draped with luxuriant vines clustered with growing grapes, and the forest swarmed with birds of sweetest songs and beautiful plumage. After gathering what information they could about the neighboring country, Barlow and Amidas departed for England, with their company, attended by Manteo and Wanchese, two dusky lords of the woods and waters.

The glowing accounts of this newly-discovered region given by the mariners, and the pictures of the simple lives and gentle manners of the inhabitants which they drew, delighted Raleigh and his sovereign; and Elizabeth, as a memorial that the splendid domain had been added to the British realm during the reign of a virgin queen, named the country VIRGINIA. So say some. Others say that the name was given because the land retained the virgin beauty, purity and fertility of its first creation. The queen declared that such acquisition was one of the most glorious events of her reign; and she bestowed the honors of knighthood upon Raleigh. The parliament or congress confirmed his charter, and the queen, in order to enrich him, gave him the monopoly of the sale of sweet wines. His popularity was unbounded, and by an almost unanimous vote he was elected to represent the county of Devon in parliament.

Satisfied that his charter was a key that would unlock the coveted treasures of wealth, honor and power, Raleigh now took measures for sending out a colony to people his American domain. Friends in abundance stood ready to assist him, and on the 9th of April, 1585, he saw a fleet of seven ships sail out of Plymouth harbor, with one hundred and eighty colonists and a full complement of seamen, for the coast of Virginia. Sir Richard Grenville, one of the most gallant men of his times, was in command of the squadron, and Ralph Lane, a soldier and civilian of distinction, who had been an equerry in the royal court, was sent as the governor of the colony, with Amidas as his assistant. They were accompanied by Thomas Cavendish, who, the next year, followed the path of Drake around the world; by a competent painter to delineate men and things in America, and by Thomas Harriot, an eminent mathematician and astronomer, who went as historian and naturalist of the expedition.

The choice of Grenville as commander of the squadron was unfortunate. He was more intent upon plunder than colonization. Sailing over the southern route, he cruised among the West India Islands, capturing Spanish vessels, and so infusing the colonists with a spirit quite the reverse of that of peaceful settlers. They did not reach the American coast until late in June, when the vessels came near being wrecked upon a point of land which, from that circumstance, they named Cape Fear. Sailing up the coast they entered Ocracock Inlet and finally landed on Roanoke Island, with Manteo, who returned with them.

We learn all that we know about this colony in Virginia, from Harriot's narrative. He remained there a year, making observations and obtaining drawings of everything of interest. He had been Raleigh's tutor in mathematics, and took great interest in the expedition; and he labored hard to restrain the cupidity of the colonists, who were more intent upon winning gold and plunder, than in tilling the soil.

The example of Grenville led to infinite mischief. He sent Manteo to the mainland to announce their arrival, and soon followed him with Lane, Cavendish, Harriot and others. For eight days they explored the country, and were hospitably entertained everywhere. How was that hospitality requited? At an Indian village a silver cup was stolen from the English and was not immediately restored on demand. Grenville ordered the whole town to be burned, and the standing corn around it destroyed. A flame of indignation, furious and destructive, was enkindled in the savage mind, which could not be quenched. Unsuspicious of the consequences of his act, the commander left the colonists and returned to England with his ships. These all became pirates on the sea; and Grenville was warmly welcomed when he entered the harbor of Plymouth with his vessels laden with plunder from Spanish galleons and other vessels.

Lane was delighted with the country, and in a letter which he sent home by Grenville, he wrote: "It is the goodliest soil under the cope of Heaven; the most pleasing territory of the world; the continent is of a huge and unknown greatness, and very well peopled and towned, though savagely. The climate is so wholesome, that we have not one sick since we have touched the land. If Virginia had but horses and kine, and were inhabited by English, no realm in Christendom were comparable to it."

Harriot was a man of keen observation, and looked upon everything with the eye of a Christian philosopher. He perceived that the way to have the country permanently "inhabited by English," and supplied with "horses and kine," was to treat the natives kindly as friends and neighbors. He deprecated the conduct of Grenville, and tried to quench the fires of revenge which the leader's cruelty had enkindled. The Indians were curious and credulous. Many of them regarded the persons of the English with reverence and awe. Their fire-arms, burning-glasses, mathematical instruments, clocks, watches, and books seemed to the savage mind like the work of the gods. The colonists were never sick and had no women with them, and so the natives imagined that they were not born of woman and were therefore immortal—men of ancient days who had risen to immortality. Taking advantage of this feeling, Harriot displayed the Bible everywhere, told them of its grand and precious truths, and inspired them with such a love for it, that they often pressed it affectionately to their bosoms. King Wingina became very ill. He sent for Harriot, who found him in his bough-covered cabin on a couch of soft moss, with a priest making mysterious movements over the invalid, a "medicine man" offering him a decoction from a calabash, and a dancing juggler contorting his body and grimacing fearfully to drive away the Evil Spirit. Wingina dismissed all of these attendants, placed himself under the care of Harriot, and asked the prayers of the English. He recovered, and his example was followed by many of his subjects.

Had the other colonists been as wise and good as Harriot, all might have been well. But they were greedy for gold. Governor Lane had the fever, and all trusted more to their fire-arms than to friendship for the good-will of the Indians. The natives were treated with scorn and sometimes with cruelty, which kept alive the flame of vengeance. Seeing the Englishmen's greed for gold, they told them marvellous stories of a land at the headwaters of the Roanoke which was filled with the precious metals, and where the houses were lined with pearls. They told them that the source of the Roanoke was in a rock so near the Pacific Ocean, that sometimes the salt waves dashed over into the fountain. All this was told that the English might go in search of that land, and so divided and weakened, the Indians might fall upon and destroy them. The red men guessed shrewdly, for Lane believed their stories, and with a large number of followers went up the swift stream of the Roanoke, until he was satisfied that he had been deceived by pure fictions. He turned back, and his sudden reappearance discomfited the Indians, who had planned an attack upon the divided settlers. Their wrath was only checked, but not subdued. They regarded the fire-arms of the English as demons, and that the great sickness which then prevailed as the effects of wounds given by invisible bullets that came from unseen agents in the air. Believing that more Englishmen were coming to take their lands, they so yearned to exterminate the intruders that they could not conceal their enmity.

Lane, impressed with the belief that there was a wide-spread conspiracy to destroy his colony, prepared to strike the first blow. He invited Wingina and his principal chiefs to a friendly conference. They showed their confidence in the strangers by appearing without weapons. At a preconcerted signal, Lane and his followers fell upon the Indians and murdered the king and all of his companions. Thenceforth each party stood on the defensive, and very soon the condition of the English became desperate. Their provisions were exhausted; no ships came from England with supplies, and no food could be obtained from the Indians. Only the woods and waters offered them a precarious subsistence, and they were on the verge of despair, when they saw, one day, the joyful apparition of white sails coming in from the sea. It was the fleet of Sir Francis Drake, who was returning from his raid upon Spanish towns and settlements, and looked in upon the colonists that he might report their condition to his friend Raleigh. He offered them aid and encouragement, but they were so thoroughly despondent that they begged and received permission to return to England in the baronet's ships.

Whilst they were in Virginia, Lane and his associates had acquired a taste for smoking tobacco, a habit which prevailed among the natives; and they were the first persons who carried the plant into England. The Spaniards and Portuguese had introduced it on the continent. Raleigh adopted and encouraged its use in England, and very soon the habit became so widespread that the demand exceeded the supply. It became the staple product of Virginia and a bond of union between England and some of her American colonies, as well as a source of much revenue. It is said that Queen Elizabeth became Raleigh's apt pupil in the art of smoking tobacco. One

THE WAGER DECIDED.

day whilst she and the courtier and two or three others were indulging in the habit, Raleigh offered a wager that he would ascertain the weight of smoke that should issue from her lips in a given time. Elizabeth accepted the challenge. Raleigh weighed the tobacco that was put in her pipe, and then weighed the ashes that remained in it; the difference in the weight he assigned as the weight of the smoke. The queen, laughing, acknowledged that he had won the wager, and said he was the first alchemist she had ever heard of who had succeeded in turning smoke into gold.

Drake's ships had scarcely left the coast when a vessel appeared with supplies for the fugitive colonists. Finding the post abandoned, the ship returned to England; and a fortnight after it left Roanoke, Sir Richard Grenville arrived with three well-furnished ships, and searched in vain for the settlers. Unwilling to give up the possession of the country, he left fifteen men there to protect the rights of England, and then he, too, returned home.

Raleigh was not dismayed by these mishaps. Lane, whose failure as a leader was conspicuous, gave a gloomy account of the country, but the report of the learned Harriot was so encouraging, that Raleigh found very little difficulty in gathering another colony, and of better materials. They were not gold-seekers, but agriculturists and artisans, with their wives and children, who consented to become permanent settlers in America. John White was appointed governor of the colony, with eleven assistants, and late in April, 1587, a squadron of three ships, fitted out at Raleigh's expense, sailed for the Chesapeake Bay, where the proprietor intended to plant his farming settlement. White went first to Roanoke, and proceeded no further. He arrived there in July, when he found the little fort built by Lane broken down; the huts of the former colonists overgrown by rank weeds and inhabited by wild deer, and a heap of human bones that told the sad fate of Grenville's "protectors of the rights of England."

The new colonists wisely resolved to cultivate the friendship of the Indians, but some of the latter appeared hostile and killed one of the assistants. Manteo, who lived on Croatan Island, came with his mother and relatives, and invited them to make their abode on his domain, when White took the opportunity to have the chief receive the rite of Christian baptism, and to bestow upon him the order of a feudal baron as "Lord of Roanoke," by the command of Raleigh. This was the first and last peerage ever created on the soil of our Republic.

For a time matters went on smoothly, when an unlucky mistake of the English in attacking friendly Indians produced bad blood. At about the same time it became necessary for the ships to return to England for supplies. White was persuaded to go with them that he might hasten their return. He left behind him eighty-nine men, seventeen women and two children. Among these was his daughter, Eleanor Dare, wife of one of his assistants, who had given birth to a daughter since her arrival, to whom they gave the name of Virginia—Virginia Dare. On his way, White touched Ireland, where he left some potato plants, the first ever seen in Europe.

When White returned home, he found his countrymen in commotion on account of a threatened invasion from Spain, and all the great naval captains, as well as Raleigh, were engaged in plans for averting the evil. But the latter, by great exertions, sent White back with supplies in two ships in April, 1588. The greed of the governor made him neglect his first duty.

Instead of going directly to Virginia, he chased Spanish ships in search of plunder. Both of his vessels were so much injured that he was compelled to take them back to England, and it was not until 1590, a year after the defeat of the "Invincible Armada" of Spain in the British Channel, that White was permitted to go in search of the colony and his daughter. He sailed with two ships, and found Roanoke desolate. Had the colonists perished, or were they somewhere in the wilderness?

This question has never been answered. An inscription on the bark of a tree seemed to indicate that they had gone to Croatan. It was late in the season, and fearing the fearful storms which he knew prevailed on the coast at that period, White searched no further but hastened back to England with the sad tidings of the uncertain fate of the colonists. It was conjectured that the faithful Lord of Roanoke had saved their lives, and when they seemed to be abandoned by their countrymen, they had been incorporated with a native tribe and amalgamated with them. This conjecture finds plausibility in a tradition of the Hatteras Indians at a later period, which averred that such was the fate of the colony; and some find confirmation of the tradition in the fact that when European settlements were finally made in that region, individuals of the Hatteras family bore the mingled physical characteristics of the Indian and the Englishman. Perhaps when Jamestown was founded on the river of Powhatan, when Virginia Dare was twenty years of age, she was a beautiful young Indian queen on the banks of the Roanoke. Who knows?

Raleigh's means were now exhausted. He had spent about two hundred thousand dollars in vain attempts to colonize Virginia and in assisting other kindred enterprises; and he was compelled to abandon, in a degree, his magnificent scheme. He formed a company of merchants and adventurers under his charter, to whom he assigned a portion of his rights. Lacking his spirit and enthusiasm, they did nothing more than carry on a petty trade with Virginia for awhile, and at the time of Queen Elizabeth's death, in 1603, there was not a single Englishman settled in all America. Raleigh did not, for a long time, abandon the hope of finding the lost colonists of Roanoke; and it is said that he sent persons five different times, at his own expense, to search for them, but no traces could be found. The failure of Raleigh's colonization scheme was caused chiefly by the incompetence of his agents.

Among the statesmen and adventurers of England who directed the earliest efforts of subjects of that realm for the colonization of America, the name of Raleigh will ever stand brightest. In courage, perseverance, comprehensive views, lavish expenditure and ever-buoyant hopefulness, he had no peer. He was not only a soldier and statesman, but he was a historian, poet and philosopher—a scholar in most departments of learning. When, at the age of about thirty-seven years, he abandoned the scheme for colonizing Virginia, he proceeded to perform other services which, alone, would have made his name immortal. He did much toward the destruction of the Spanish Armada; accompanied Drake in his expedition to seat Don Antonio on the throne of Portugal; brought Edmund Spenser from Ireland and introduced him to the queen; discovered the "large, rich and beautiful empire of Guiana," in South America; assisted in the capture of Cadiz; was ambassador to the Netherlands, and governor of the island of Jersey. Immoralities stained his fair fame, and when Elizabeth died in 1603, the sun of his glory went down among clouds, yet none the brighter in itself because obscured to the visions of men. When King James of Scotland came to the throne of England, he stripped Raleigh of all his preferments. The great man was then a paralytic, but his lofty spirit bore him above repining.

Raleigh was soon afterward arrested on a false charge of conspiring to place Arabella Stuart on the English throne, and on conviction without proof he was condemned to death. Reprieved, he was sent to the Tower, where he was confined many years, accompanied much of the time by his faithful wife, who had been one of Elizabeth's maids of honor. There he was in 1615, when the base and avaricious king, wanting his services to search for gold in Guiana, released him from prison, on condition that he would go there, but did not pardon him. Raleigh was then sixty-three years of age and an invalid; but he went to South America with fourteen ships, in the fitting out of which he embarked the whole of his wife's fortune and his own. The expedition was a failure, and he returned to Plymouth in the summer of 1618 a wreck in fortune, health, reputation and spirits. The king, disappointed in his expectations of wealth as the fruits of the expedition, and jealous of Raleigh even in his almost helplessness, recommitted the old man to the Tower, and soon afterward caused him to be beheaded, in execution of the unjust sentence pronounced fifteen years before. "This is a sharp medicine, but it is a cure for all diseases," said the white-haired patriot, on the scaffold, as he felt the keen edge of the axe and handed it to the executioner.

That murderous act of King James was one of the foulest of all the foul performances of the detested monarch. Upon the altar of his lust he sacrificed one of the noblest patriots, far-seeing statesmen and brilliant scholars of the British realm. Raleigh's very existence, even in the obscurity of the Tower, wherein he wrote his "History of the World," was a perpetual honor to the reign of the bad king.

Raleigh had lived to see his scheme for colonizing Virginia carried out by other Englishmen. Ten years before his death, when he was in the Tower, Jamestown was founded; and when the axe finished his earthly course, a congregation of English Puritans were contemplating that emigration to America which occurred two years later, and which resulted in the founding of the commonwealths of New England. The French navigator,

RALEIGH ON THE SCAFFOLD.

Champlain, had laid the foundations of a permanent settlement on the St. Lawrence River; and whilst Raleigh was in Guiana, the Dutch were laying plans for a colony in New Netherland, which Hudson had discovered a few years before. George Calvert had just received the honors of knighthood, taken a seat in the Privy Council, and gained that special friendship of King James which finally led to his elevation to the peerage as Lord Baltimore, his attempts to colonize Newfoundland, and the possession of the fine domain of Maryland by his family. And after a lapse of almost two centuries, the inhabitants of North Carolina, on the shores of whose State the great adventurer had made his attempts at settlement, showed their sense of justice by giving to their capital the name of *Raleigh*.

CHAPTER XIII.

EXPLORATIONS OF THE NEW ENGLAND COASTS BY ENGLISH NAVIGATORS—GRAND SCHEME FOR COLONIZING VIRGINIA PATRONIZED BY THE BRITISH MONARCH—CHARTERS GRANTED—ATTEMPTS OF THE FRENCH TO PLANT SETTLEMENTS IN AMERICA—SAMUEL CHAMPLAIN FOUNDS QUEBEC AND MONTREAL—HE DISCOVERS AND NAMES LAKE CHAMPLAIN—WITH THE HELP OF THE JESUITS HE ESTABLISHES THE FRENCH DOMINION IN AMERICA—THE STORY OF THE VOYAGES AND DISCOVERIES OF HENRY HUDSON—HIS SAD FATE—THE DISCOVERERS.

THE enthusiasm which Raleigh had created in England in favor of American discovery and colonization did not die out in consequence of his conspicuous failures. Some of his associates continued to believe in the rich promises which such colonization held out. Among these believers was Bartholomew Gosnold, who had made a voyage to America, and who, like Raleigh, had not lost faith. They were much together; and when the Earl of Southampton offered to fit out a bark for the purpose of attempting to plant a small settlement in America if Gosnold would command the vessel, that navigator's illustrious friend advised him to do so. They had talked much about the northern and southern tracks across the Atlantic, which were then followed by ships from England, and they believed that a more direct route might be taken a thousand leagues shorter than by way of the Canaries and the West Indies. On the 26th of April, 1602, Gosnold sailed from Falmouth in a small vessel, with twenty colonists and eight mariners on the proposed direct track, and touched the American continent at near Nahant, in Massachusetts Bay, it is supposed, just eighteen days after his departure from England. Finding no good harbor there, he sailed southward, discovered a great sandy point which he named Cape Cod, because of the profusion of codfishes seen near its shores, and landed there with four of his men. Never before had the present route of ships from Europe to New England and New York been traversed; never before had the soil of New England been pressed by the foot of an Englishman.

Doubling the Cape, Gosnold passed around the promontory of Gayhead, which he named Dover Cliff, and entered Buzzard's Bay, where he found a group of attractive islands. He named the westernmost Elizabeth, in honor of his queen, and the whole group now bear that name. On Elizabeth, Gosnold and his followers landed. They were charmed with the aspects of nature there. Vegetation was luxuriant, and small fruits, such as strawberries, raspberries, and growing grapes were abundant. There the navigator resolved to plant his little colony, and on a small rocky island, in the bosom of a great pond, they built a rude stone-house and a fort.

Elizabeth Island now bears its original Indian name of Cattyhunk. Had the courage of the adventurers held out, they would there have won the honor of making the first permanent English settlement in America. But it did not hold out. They thought the Indians scowled upon them ; they were not sure of food in the future ; they could not agree upon a method for dividing profits ; what may the winter be? was a serious question, and a wilting home-sickness came upon them. So, when Gosnold had laden his vessel with sassafras root, then much esteemed in Europe for its medical properties ; also with furs gathered by traffic with the natives, and sweet cedar-wood and other products, and was ready to sail for home, the colonists resolved to go with him. They abandoned their little paradise of beauty, and in less than four months after their departure from home, they were back on the soil of England. They spoke in glowing terms of the serenity of the climate, and the beauty and fertility of the land they had visited ; of the shortness and safety of the voyage to it, and of the riches of the adjacent continent which might be gathered by traffic with the Indians. Raleigh strongly advised further efforts toward planting a colony in that part of America ; so also did Richard Hakluyt, prebendary of Westminster—a man learned in naval and commercial science, the counsellor of many who had engaged in the expeditions to America, and who became the historian of those voyages. Under the advice of such men, Bristol merchants fitted out two ships for traffic and discovery on the coast of what was afterward called New England.

Early in April (1603, about a fortnight after the death of the queen), the *Speedwell*, of fifty tons, and the *Discoverer*, a bark of twenty-six tons, sailed from Milford Haven under the command of Martin Pring, a friend of Raleigh and Gosnold. Pring commanded the *Speedwell* in person, which was manned by thirty men and boys. William Browne was master of the *Discoverer*, and was accompanied by Robert Galterns as a supercargo or general agent of the expedition. Galterns had accompanied Gosnold to America. They were furnished with clothing, axes, and trinkets for the natives ; and early in June the vessels entered Penobscot Bay. They went up the Penobscot River some distance, and then sailing along the coast, they entered the mouths of the Saco, Kennebunk, and Piscataqua rivers on the coast of

Maine. Gorges says Pring "made a perfect discovery of all these eastern rivers and harbors." That, however, was done three years later, when Pring was on another voyage.

Sailing southward, Pring and his companions went to the region where Gosnold and his handful of adventurers had tarried for awhile, and landed on a large island abounding with grapes, which they named Martin's Vineyard, now Martha's Vineyard. Thence they returned to England, after an absence of six months. Pring made a report confirming everything that Gosnold had told about the country. This confirmation led to other expeditions, and in 1605 the Earl of Southampton and Lord Arundel, of Wardour, fitted out a vessel, placed it under the command of George Weymouth, another friend of the now imprisoned Raleigh, and dispatched it to the eastern coasts of New England. Weymouth had already explored the coast of Labrador in an attempt to discover a northwest passage to India. He sailed from England in March, taking the shorter track, but storms delayed him on the way, and it was six weeks before he saw America, at Nantucket. Turning northward, he entered Penobscot Bay, where he opened a traffic with the natives. It was carried on for awhile in mutual confidence until signs of treachery appeared on the part of the Indians, when Weymouth determined to resent the affront. He invited some of the leading savages to a feast on board of his vessel, but only three of the cautious natives accepted the invitation. There he fed them and plied them with intoxicating drink, until they were half insensible, when he confined them in the hold of his ship. Then he went on shore with some of his men to entice others on board. They opened boxes and showed the natives trinkets, but they could not induce the savages to go to the vessel; so Weymouth and his men seized two of them. "It was as much as five or six of us could do to get them into the light horseman" [the boat], wrote Weymouth, "for they were strong, and so naked as our best hold was by their long hair on their heads." The Englishmen took with the captives two handsome birch-bark canoes, when the anchor was taken up and the ship sailed away for England with the five dusky prisoners. The canoes, like one carried home by Pring, attracted much attention as the work of savages. Three of the captives were given to Sir Fernando Gorges, then Governor of Plymouth, (who was a fast friend of Raleigh), and remained in his family three years, during which time they acquired considerable knowledge of the English language. This kidnapping left on the shores of New England the seeds of much future trouble.

All doubts respecting the commercial value of every part of the American coast from Florida to Newfoundland had now vanished from the English mind, and the voyage of Weymouth was immediately followed by the immediate execution of a vast plan for colonizing the shores of this Western World. King James was petitioned to sanction by his authority an organization for the purpose. He not only did so willingly, but he warmly commended the enterprise. He had seen the good effects of introducing industrious artisans and traders from the lowlands among the wilder Highlanders of his native country; and as war with France had lately ceased, there was a large number of restless, unoccupied soldiers in England for whom he would gladly open a new field of enterprise. Moved by these considerations, he issued letters-patent, on the 20th of April, 1606, to Sir Thomas Gates, Sir George Somers, Richard Hakluyt and others, granting to them those territories in America lying on the sea-coast between the thirty-fourth and forty-fifth degree of north latitude, together with all the islands situated within a hundred miles of their shores; that is to say, from Cape Fear to Nova Scotia. The design of this patent was declared to be "to make habitation and plantation, and to deduce a colony of sundry of our people into that part of America commonly called Virginia." The charter proclaimed that "so noble a work may, by the Providence of Almighty God, hereafter tend to the glory of his Divine Majesty, in propagating of Christian religion to such people as yet live in darkness and miserable ignorance of the true knowledge and worship of God, and may, in time, bring the infidels and savages living in those parts to human civility, and to a settled and quiet government."

The patentees were principally merchants and adventurers of London, Plymouth and Bristol, and by their charter they were required to form two companies, each under a distinct title; the one consisting of London adventurers to be called the "London Company," and the one composed of "knights, gentlemen and merchants" of the West of England, the "Plymouth Company." The vast domain was divided into two districts, called respectively North and South Virginia, the line of separation being about on the parallel of New York City.

Now dawned the bright era when English colonies were permanently planted in America. The story of their marvellous growth will be told hereafter. Raleigh, poor and in prison, was not allowed to share, personally, in the glory of any of that fruitful seed-time, the result of his genius, generosity and enterprise. When Richard Hakluyt, Bartholomew Gosnold, and Sir Fernando Gorges, three of his firm friends, were permitted by the king to visit the illustrious prisoner in the Tower, and tell him of the new enterprise, the interview was a touching one. They found Raleigh seated at a little table near an open window in the massive wall, tall and narrow, writing. Around him lay huge folios. On the walls hung maps, and on the deep window-sill was a mariner's compass. Near him sat his faithful wife, almost twenty years younger than he, who had just come to share his imprisonment. At her feet lay a sleeping spaniel belonging to the keeper of the Tower; and a picture of their son who was killed in Guiana leaned against a small cabinet at her side. When the three friends entered, Raleigh quickly arose and embraced them affectionately. When they told him of the great enterprise and the king's sanction, he sat down in his chair, and with clasped hands and eyes turned heavenward exclaimed: "God be praised for his goodness! Prison walls cannot defeat his justice. The English *nation* love truth and will defend the good name of her disciples. God save the king!" The final invocation was for the ears of the jailor who stood at the door. It had a double meaning on Raleigh's lips —a meaning of political loyalty, or an earnest prayer for the salvation of the monarch from the consequences of his bad life. It could not be interpreted to Raleigh's hurt.

RALEIGH'S JOY IN PRISON.

A Protestant sovereign, the great Henry of Navarre, was now on the throne of France, the first and best of her Bourbon kings. His heart was set on promoting the prosperity and true greatness of his kingdom. He had given it peace at home by the edict of Nantes, granting toleration to his Protestant subjects, proclaimed on the fifteenth of April, 1598, and cessation from war abroad by the treaty of Verviers with Spain, signed seventeen days afterward. Agriculture, manufactures, mining, internal improvements, and settlements in New France (America), which had not been attempted since the disappearance of Robertval more than fifty years before, were encouraged. In these labors of statesmanship he was led and assisted by Maximilien de Bethune, the great Duke of Sully, whose name shines with splendor in the annals of France.

Among the earliest of the new French adventurers was the Marquis de la Roche, a wealthy nobleman, who gathered a company from the prisons of France wherewith to found a colony in America. He sailed with a single ship in the spring of 1598, and landed on Sable Island, in the Atlantic Ocean, ninety miles southeast of Nova Scotia, where he left forty men and returned to France for supplies. Before he was ready to go back, he sickened and died, and the poor emigrants had no tidings from home or the rest of the world for seven years. Then a vessel was sent for them, but only twelve survived. These were pardoned on their return, because of their sufferings abroad, and their immediate wants were supplied by the king.

Whilst these men were on Sable Island, another expedition was sent from France on a similar errand. M. de Chastes, Governor of Dieppe, obtained from the king a charter for founding settlements in New France. He engaged Samuel Champlain of the French navy, a man of noble lineage and a favorite of the sovereign, to act as his delegate. The king commissioned Champlain lieutenant-general of Canada, and with this authority he embarked at Honfleur on the 15th of March, 1603, with a single vessel, commanded by Pont-Grevé, a skillful mariner of St. Malo, whose father had been an intimate friend of Cartier. They reached the St. Lawrence in May, and anchored near the site of Quebec, when Pont-Grevé, with five men, went up that stream in a canoe to the rapids of La Chine, above Montreal, where Cartier found an impassable barrier to his upward voyage. Then he turned back, carefully examining the shores of the river, and on reaching the ship he gave Champlain a minute account of all they had observed. Meanwhile, Champlain had held intercourse with the savages, whose memories and traditions ran back to Cartier's kidnapping, but they were placable, and the lieutenant-general was pleased with all he saw. They returned to France in the early autumn, when Champlain published an account of the country.

When the voyagers returned, they found M. Chastes dead and the concessions transferred by the king to Pierre de Gast, the Sieur de Monts, a wealthy Huguenot, who had received the commission of viceroy, with full power for settlement and rule over six degrees of latitude in America, extending from that of Cape May to the parallel of Quebec. That region was named, in the charter, L'Acadié, a corruption of the Greek Arcadia. The charter was published in all the maritime towns of France, and soon afterward De Monts and his associates were vested with the monopoly of the fur and peltry trade of his domain, and around the Gulf of St. Lawrence. A new arrangement was made with Champlain, and early in March, 1604,

De Monts, with his bosom friend Poutrincourt and Pont-Grevé as his lieutenants, and Champlain as the pilot, sailed from France with four vessels well manned, and a goodly company of Protestant and Roman Catholic emigrants. Among the latter were several Jesuits. They reached the St. Lawrence in April, when they found the river ice-bound and the weather so cold that the viceroy determined to plant his settlement further to the southward. They passed around Cape Breton and Nova Scotia into the Bay of Fundy, and on the northern shore of the Peninsula they anchored in a fine harbor environed by hills and meadows, early in May. Poutrincourt was so charmed by the appearance of the country, that De Monts allowed him to remain there with some of the emigrants. He gave him a grant of the region, which was confirmed by the king, and Poutrincourt named the place where he landed Port Royal. It is now Annapolis, in Nova Scotia. De Monts and the rest of the company, seventy in number, crossed over to Passamaquoddy Bay, and on an island not far from the mouth of the St. Croix River, the eastern boundary of Maine, they landed, built a fort with a chapel in it and cannon mounted on it, and there passed a severe winter. Half of them were dead in the spring, when the survivors explored the country westward as far as Cape Cod, and returned to Port Royal, where they joined Poutrincourt's colony. Early in the autumn, De Monts and Poutrincourt returned to France, leaving Champlain and Pont-Grevé to make further explorations of the region. They went to the southwest as far as Cape Cod, where they attempted to land and erect a cross, but were driven to their vessel by the Indians. In 1607, Champlain returned to France.

For a few years there was a struggle for existence and growth on the part of the colonists in Acadié. The Jesuit priests who accompanied Poutrincourt back to that land claimed the right to supreme rule by virtue of their holy office. He stoutly resisted their claim, and told them boldly: "It is my part to *rule* you on the earth; it is your part to *guide* me to heaven." When Poutrincourt had returned to France they made the same claim upon his son, whom he left in charge of the colony. The fiery young man threatened them with corporeal punishment, when they withdrew and settled on the island of Mount Desert, now so famous as a summer resort, and there set up a cross in token of sovereignty. They were there in 1613, when Samuel Argall, a freebooter of the seas, went, under the sanction of the governor of Virginia, to expel the French from Acadié as intruders upon the domain of the North and South Virginia Company. The Jesuits on Mount Desert, it is said, willing to use such an opportunity for revenge, piloted the Englishmen to Port Royal, which Argall plundered and laid in ashes, driving the colonists to the woods and breaking up the settlement. Acadié was again settled by the French, who suffered many vicissitudes and became the subject of romance and song.

De Monts was not disposed to contend with the powerful English company. He obtained a new charter with ample provisions, and proceeded to plant a colony on the St. Lawrence. Two vessels were fitted out in the spring of 1608, freighted with colonists and supplies, and were navigated under the direction of Pont-Grevé, with Champlain as governor. They were directed to form a settlement at Tadousac on the St. Lawrence, near the mouth of the Saguenay River. They arrived at that point on the 3d of June. Champlain perceived that it was not a good place for a colony, so he directed Pont-Grevé to sail further up the river. They entered the St. Charles, where Cartier had left one of his vessels, and on its banks at the foot of a rocky promontory he chose as the place for a settlement, and there he laid the foundations of the City of Quebec. That name is an Indian word, signifying "the narrows," and is pronounced *Kebec.* That was the first permanent French settlement planted in America. It grew, for the little colony took firm root under the culture of Champlain. He opened a profitable fur trade with the Indians, and planted a small settlement at Montreal. The colonists were induced to build houses and plant seeds; yet there were malcontents among them, who conspired to murder the governor. The plot was discovered; the ringleader was hanged, and order and obedience were secured.

Champlain, regarding the Iroquois in northern New York as inimical to his colony because it was in the bosom of the Huron nation who were their enemies, allied himself to the Hurons and went out with them upon the warpath. In the summer of 1609, he, with a boat's crew, went with the Indian warriors up the Sorel or Richelieu River to the Falls of Chambly, where he left his boat and the crew, and with only two men pushed on in a canoe until he discovered a great lake between two distant mountain ranges—the Green Mountains and the Adirondacks. He gave his name to the sheet of water, which is a beautiful, appropriate, and eternal monument to the memory of the mariner. On its shores he and his Indian allies had a fight with their enemies, and then returned to Quebec with fifty scalps as trophies of war. In September of that year Champlain returned to France, when he published an account of Canada and of his adventures.

The following spring Champlain returned, stopping at Tadousac, where he borrowed fifty warriors from a chief, with whom he penetrated the country to Lake Champlain to fight the enemies of the Hurons. He was defeated and wounded. So bad was his hurt that when he reached Quebec he found it necessary to return to France to have medical treatment. The aspect of affairs there was changed. The dagger of the fanatic François Ravaillac had killed his king; the fortune of De Monts was so much diminished that he could not continue the settlement at Montreal nor foster that at Quebec, and it appeared as if there were to be another ending of French settlements in America. At that moment the queen-regent, by a judicious act, saved the colony. She appointed Charles of Bourbon nominal governor of Canada, and the prince commissioned Champlain his lieutenant with large powers. So strengthened, the latter returned in 1612, and engaged vigorously in wars and explorations. Three years later he invited some Jesuit Fathers to the St. Lawrence, who accompanied him in expeditions of discovery extending up the Ottawa River and westward to Lake Huron. Turning eastward, they traversed the wilderness to Lake Ontario, and exploring that magnificent sheet of water its whole length, and the St. Lawrence to a point below Montreal, they returned to Quebec.

THE JESUIT TEACHER.

With the vision of a statesman, Champlain saw that the country with which he had made himself acquainted was fitted to become the seat of a magnificent colonial empire of Frenchmen, and he resolved to do all in his power to lay the solid foundations of such an empire. He went home, and in 1620—the same year when the London Company planted a permanent settlement in New England—he returned to Canada vested with the authority of governor, and taking with him his family and other emigrants with their families. He had seen the amazing influence of the Jesuit fathers over the Indian mind. He had also perceived that an alliance with the red men would be essential in building up and making permanent his future empire. To make them good allies, it would be necessary to Christianize the savages; so he invited more Jesuits to come. He had, very soon, as coadjutors, fifteen Jesuit priests and a considerable number of laymen. A college was established at Quebec for the instruction of the children of the Hurons in civilized modes of living, the French language, and the theology of the Roman Catholic Church. These Jesuits were peculiarly the men for the work;—sagacious, far-seeing, politic, zealous, obedient, devoted, industrious, persevering, long-suffering and self-sacrificing—men of the world who could adapt themselves to every condition and plane of life, from the pitiful suppliant as a beggar to the haughty bearing of a king. They worked with untiring energy and signal success for religion and the state.

So was wisely laid, by Samuel Champlain, the foundation-stone of the French empire in America; a political structure which always displayed as its chief source of strength a firm alliance with the Indians cemented by the religious teachings of the Jesuits, which made the dusky tribes and the pale-faces, to a remarkable extent, one in the Christian faith. So were secured those alliances in emergencies, between the French and Indians in America, already alluded to, which frequently gave the English colonists much and serious trouble.

Whilst the other Western nations of Europe were acquiring glory and solid territorial possessions by discoveries in America, Holland, then the greatest maritime nation on the earth, was quietly winning the gains of profitable commerce by sending her uncouth commercial marine over beaten ocean tracks, quite indifferent to the exciting day-dreams of fabulous wealth concealed in the bosom of the western continent, which so dazzled other people. But Holland, too, at this period of commercial activity, became a partner with others in making discoveries and settlements in America, in spite of her indifference. The story with its preface runs thus:

Upon the walls of the governor's room in the City Hall, New York, hangs a dingy canvas bearing the portrait of a man apparently about forty years of age, with short-cut hair and beard, and a broad ruff, such as were worn by the English gentry late in the reign of Queen Elizabeth. It is the portrait of Henry Hudson, "the bold Englishman, the expert pilot, and the famous navigator;" a pupil, probably of Drake, or Frobisher, or Grenville. Thoroughly imbued with the spirit of adventure then rife, he sought opportunities for winning renown in his profession; therefore it was a happy day for Hudson, early in the year 1607, when in its morning he received a summons to the parlor of Sir Thomas Gresham, a wealthy London merchant, who built the Royal Exchange. There he met a number of "certain worshipful merchants of London" who yet believed in the existence of a polar sea passage to India, and had conceived a plan for another search for it. They had sent for Hudson to join them in consultation. He found Sir Thomas and a number of friends sitting at a table covered with maps and charts, with just space enough besides for a rich silver salver holding bottles of wine and glasses to drink it. He was received graciously. The interview was not long, and it ended in a bargain between Hudson and the merchants for the navigator to command a small expedition for the discovery of a polar sea passage, not in the usual track in the northwestern waters, but around the north of Europe.

HUDSON. FROBISHER.

Hudson sailed from Gravesend on the first of May, 1607, a few days after an English colony had arrived in Virginia to plant the seeds of a great commonwealth there. The vessel in which Hudson sailed was a small one manned by only ten men and a boy. He went up the eastern coast of Greenland to the eighteenth degree, where a solid ice barrier compelled him to turn back. He had discovered the island of Spitzbergen, nothing more. Baffled but not discouraged, he returned to England at the middle of September. Neither were his employers disheartened. They fitted out another vessel in which Hudson sailed late in April, 1608, with full expectation that he should make the coveted passage between Spitzbergen and Nova Zembla. Again the impenetrable ice-pack compelled him to turn back, and he again returned to England. He was not yet disheartened, but his employers were, and gave up the enterprise. Hudson went over to Holland to seek similar employment in the service of the Dutch East India Company, a wealthy corporation of merchants at Amsterdam, which had been in existence about seven years. Hudson inspired them with a belief that a much shorter passage to their possessions in the East Indies might be found around the North of Europe, and they fitted out a small vessel of ninety tons, to go in search of it. Hudson was placed in command of her, with a choice crew of English and Dutch seamen. She was a staunch new vessel named *De Halve-Maen*—the *Half-Moon*—and in her he left the Texel early in April, 1609, and sailed for Nova Zembla.

After manfully fighting the ice-pack on the parallel of Spitzbergen, and its allies—the polar fogs and tempests—until all hope of conquests vanished, Hudson was compelled, a third time, to turn back. He determined not to go without fruit to the Texel, so he sailed around the southern shores of Greenland into the track of searchers after a northwest passage. Again the ice-pack foiled him, and he sailed southward until, at the middle of July, he discovered the American continent off the coast of Maine. It is supposed that he passed several days in Casco Bay, repairing his storm-shattered vessel, when the natives, among whom he found French trinkets, treated him kindly. Their hospitality was requited by plundering their property and driving them from their houses. They resented this treatment so fiercely that he was compelled to put to sea.

Hudson now sailed southward as far as the Capes of Virginia, touching at Cape Cod on the way. Then he sailed up the coast, discovered Delaware Bay, and entered the harbor of New York early in September, after spending several days in visiting the beautiful shores of Raritan Bay, where he held friendly intercourse with the natives, although he was ever watchful for expected treachery. The inhabitants showed a disposition to traffic, but Hudson was so suspicious that he repelled them in an offensive manner and kindled their enmity. One night, whilst a boat load of his crew were returning from an exploration in the neighborhood of the Narrows (between Long and Staten Islands), they were attacked by Indians, in canoes, and one of the seamen was killed. Sadly his comrades carried his body ashore the next day and buried it near the beach, while savage men, women and children looked on in wonder from a neighboring hill.

Northward from his anchorage after his vessel had entered New York Bay, Hudson saw a broad stream rising and falling with the tide, which the Indians told him came from beyond the pale blue mountain ranges in the distance. He believed it was a strait through which he might pass into the Indian Ocean; so he sailed up the stream a few miles, and anchored. Natives came to him in canoes from the shores with fruits and vegetables, and friendly gestures. The men were athletic; the women were graceful and the young ones often beautiful. All were half-clad in mantles made of skins or feathers depending from one shoulder and the waist, or in colored hempen tunics; and some of the women who came in the canoes, whose hair, long and black, hung loosely over their shoulders and bosoms, wore fillets ornamented with shells and the quills of the porcupine. They seemed anxious for friendly intercourse, but Hudson repelled and offended them.

The *Half-Moon* went leisurely up the river, anchoring here and there, whilst her commander held intercourse with the natives, sometimes friendly, sometimes hostile. When he passed the great mountains which he had seen in the distance, and found the water freshening, he was satisfied that he was not in a passage to India. It was only a beautiful river flowing down from more lofty hills three hundred miles from the sea, and called *Mahicannituck* by the natives. The Dutch afterwards called it the Mauritius, and the English gave it the name of Hudson's River.

THE HALF-MOON.

Hudson went up the stream with the *Half-Moon* and his small boats as far as Albany, and perhaps to the mouth of the Mohawk, and looked upon the foaming falls of Cohoes. Then he sailed leisurely back, everywhere charmed with the beauty and grandeur of the scenery and apparent fertility of the soil. He had discovered one of the richest portions of America. From New York Bay he sailed for England, after formally taking possession of the whole domain which he had discovered in the name of the States-General of Holland. Landing at Dartmouth in November, he hastened to London and told the story of his discoveries. The unworthy monarch on England's throne, jealous of the advantages which the Dutch might derive from these discoveries, would not let Hudson, an English subject, leave the realm. The navigator had outwitted the sovereign. Knowing his mean character, he had sent to his Amsterdam employers, by a trusty hand, all of his log-books, maps, charts, and a full account of his voyage and discoveries. These led to the commercial ventures between the Texel and the Hudson rivers which immediately followed, and which resulted in the planting of the City of New Amsterdam (now New York) at the mouth of the latter, and of New Orange (now Albany) at near the head of its navigable waters. These were the germs of the commonwealth of New Netherland, the domain of which is now known as the State of New York.

The fate of Hudson, the last of the discoverers who revealed the Atlantic coast of the American continent to Europe, may be told in a few words. He sailed from England in the spring of 1610 on his fourth voyage in search of a polar ocean passage, this time in the northwest. He discovered, far up North America, the Bay that bears his name, and intended to winter there, but a majority of his crew became mutinous and compelled him to sail homeward. On the way he, his son and seven of his men who had remained faithful to him were seized, pinioned, placed in an open shallop and abandoned on the icy sea, where, of course, they soon perished. Abacuck Pricket, one of Hudson's crew, who was confined to the cabin with lameness at the time, in his published account of the circumstances, after relating how he opposed the cruel proceedings, says: "Now were all the poore men in the shallop, whose names are as followeth: *Henrie Hudson, John Hudson, Arnold Lodlo, Sidrack Faner, Phillip Staffe, Thomas Woodhouse* or *Wydhouse, Adam Moore, Henrie King, Michael Bute.* The carpenter got of them a Peece, and Powder, and Shot, and some Pikes, an Iron Pot, with some meale and other things. They stood out of the Ice, the Shallop being fast to the Sterne of the Ship, and so (when they were nigh out, for I cannot say they were cleane out) they cut her head fast from the Sterne of our Ship, then out with there Top-sayles, and toward the East they stood, in a cleare Sea."

END OF BOOK I.

BOOK II.

SETTLEMENTS

FROM 1606 TO 1733.

CHAPTER I.

ENGLAND AT THE BEGINNING OF THE SEVENTEENTH CENTURY—HENRY THE EIGHTH AND THE CHURCH—DAWN OF THE AGE OF REASON—RURAL POPULATION OF ENGLAND—FURNITURE, COSTUME, METHODS OF AGRICULTURE, LEARNING AND FINE ARTS IN ENGLAND—LONDON AND PLYMOUTH COMPANIES—SETTLEMENTS ATTEMPTED IN NEW ENGLAND—ENGLISH SETTLERS ON THE JAMES RIVER—CAPTAIN JOHN SMITH—SETTLEMENT AT JAMESTOWN.

AT the beginning of the seventeenth century, when permanent English settlements were begun in America, the people of Great Britain had just passed from the reign of an age of Faith into that of an age of Reason. In the realm of the former, there was such absolute intellectual laziness, and indifference to the exercise of reason in speculative matters, that men accepted tenets in religion and politics, however absurd, as truths, and bestowed no thought upon them.

Theology was like a cast-iron machine, utterly inflexible. It fashioned social life in its most minute details. The people were simply passive portions of that machine obedient to its ecclesiastic movers. The monastery governed the throne and its subjects as a rigid master, and for centuries there had been very little improvement in the condition of the inhabitants. At length the glare of the moral volcano which had suddenly burst out in Germany shot across Western Europe and the English Channel and awoke the British mind from its sluggish repose. Faith gave way to Reason. A secular revolt assumed formidable proportions, and at the close of the same year, when the right of private judgment was proclaimed at Spires, the English House of Commons—the representatives of the people—presented a petition to King Henry the Eighth, which contained the germs of the English reformation. It accused the clergy of disloyalty and immorality, and attributed the disorders which affected the realm to the malign influence of the ecclesiastics. The king presented this petition to the bishops for an answer. That answer was arrogant, and offensive to the House of Commons. The latter stood firm in the position of accuser and champion for the laity, and waged a bitter war with the clergy. Henry, stimulated by his love for Anne Boleyn and angered by the opposition of the church to his unholy scheme of divorcement from his queen, united with the Commons, and employed the resolute Thomas Cromwell to lead a movement for the disseverance of the civil government of England from the controlling spiritual power of Rome. Cromwell did so, with a high hand, sanctioned and assisted by the Parliament, for already the rule of the people through representatives was recognized. That body, by law, suppressed all the monasteries in the kingdom, confiscated their property, and compelled the ecclesiastics to work for their own sustenance. "Go spin, jades; go spin!" was the unfeeling remark of Cromwell to some aged nuns. By law, Henry was made the supreme head of the church in England—a pontiff of a church in rebellion—and so was established the principle that canon or ecclesiastical laws must be subservient to the civil laws. It was a new thing under the sun.

England was now partially freed from a long political bondage, and the age of Reason dawned. The English mind was thoroughly aroused to action. Wonderful social changes followed; and during the reign of the adroit trimmer Queen Elizabeth, all classes had more freedom than ever before. Yet the laity were not wholly free. Henry had not specially changed the theology or the rituals of the church in England, and there appeared three powerful and antagonistic parties in the realm. These were the English party, or Churchmen, who adhered to and enforced the doctrines and rituals of the Church of Rome, but who gave their allegiance to the

English monarch, and not to the Pope; the papal party or supporters of the authority of the Roman hierarchy, and the doctrinal Protestants who were disliked by the others. When Parliament established a liturgy for the Church of England, the latter refused conformity to it, for they acknowledged no authority but the Bible in matters of religion. They were more austere in manners, more simple in their worship, and demanded greater purity of life, and so they acquired the name of *Puritans*. It was given in derision, but soon became an honorable title. Each class was intolerant, and for more than a century and a half, there was a chronic triangular contest between the English Churchmen, the Roman Catholics, and the Puritans, which caused many of each class to seek peace in the forests of America. But Reason swayed the age with a potent sceptre, and stamped its insignia of authority upon the movements of society. Individuals and associations found new and promising fields of action, the most attractive of which was the virgin soil of America. As we have seen, its worth was known and fairly estimated at the beginning of the seventeenth century; and then dawned the Era of Settlements within the domain of our Republic, now at the noon-tide of success, and turning the wilderness, everywhere, into a blooming garden.

The condition of the rural population of England had greatly improved under the new order of things. Down to the time of Henry the Eighth, there had been very little improvement since the Romans left the island. There was not much tillage, and that little was unskillfully done. Vast forests and fens covered the land, and malaria (unwholesome exhalations) was a perpetual scourge. The population was sparse and increased very slowly. It did not exceed five million in the whole island of Great Britain, when Henry the Eighth ascended the throne. The food of the common people was not equal in its nutrition and variety, nor their clothing in comfort, to that of our Indians when Europeans first came to America. Our savages lived in better habitations than did their British cotemporaries. Pestilence and famine kept the rural population sparse. The ecclesiastics rioted in coarse luxuries, and the morals of the towns were beastly in the extreme.

At the beginning of the seventeenth century, or a hundred years later, all this had materially changed. The methods of agriculture had been greatly improved, and its bounds immensely enlarged. Implements were better and tillage was far more productive. The farmers, generally, had an abundance of good food; lived in better houses; pewter dishes had taken the place of wooden ones; feather beds, those of straw and coarse wool, and the yeoman was fond of entertaining his neighbors. Clover had been introduced from the Netherlands, and increased the food for sheep and cattle. Gardens had begun to be cultivated. From the Netherlands had come the hop; also the cabbage, lettuce, apricot, gooseberry, musk-melon and apple. Cherries had come from France; currants from Greece, and plums from Italy; and from Flanders the Flemmings had brought the rose and other fragrant plants, natives of the East. Rural feasts were common among the yeomanry, and the materials for good cheer are enumerated in the following lines:

> "Good bread and good drink, a good fire in the hall;
> Braun, pudding and sauce, and good mustard withal;
> Beef, mutton and pork, shred pies of the best;
> Pig, veal, goose and capon, and turkey well drest;
> Cheese, apples and nuts; jolly carols to hear;
> All these in the country are counted good cheer."

In cities and among the nobility rapidly increasing wealth had fostered a taste for luxuries. Dwellings, furniture, and dress, felt its influence. Elegant and substantial houses were built. Furniture was elaborately carved and inlaid; glass mirrors had been introduced from France early in the reign of Elizabeth, and carpets from Turkey, which English weavers soon imitated, took the place on floors of rushes and mats on which royalty had before trodden. Chairs were cushioned with velvet coverings, and costly beds and bedsteads were seen. In many houses were ornamental French clocks, and knives were seen on English dinner-tables; but forks were not used whilst Elizabeth lived.

An old chronicler tells us of a merry scene in the palace of Henry the Eighth. On the morning after the supple-kneed Archbishop Cranmer pronounced the marriage of his king with Anne Boleyn lawful, the new queen received visits of congratulation from the whole court and the archbishop and several prelates in full canonicals. Henry was delighted with the honors paid to his beautiful wife, and whilst they were pressing about her, and both ladies and gentlemen were giving her tokens of their regard, the king went to a small cabinet, unlocked it, and taking from it a French clock which he had bought in France while he was there with Anne when she was a marchioness, he brought it and put it in her hands as a public pledge of his love and constancy whilst *time* should endure. It was of "silver gilt, richly chased, engraved and ornamented with fleur-de-lys, little heads, etc. On the top sits a lion holding the arms of England, which are also on their sides." It was about sixteen inches in height.

The costume of this period we are considering was a little less extravagant in mode and richness of materials than it had been when Elizabeth was in her prime, for Puritan simplicity better suited good taste. Crimson and blue velvets embroidered with gold were still worn by the rich and noble; and the ruff was yet seen around the necks of both men and women, but somewhat diminished in volume. Jewelry was yet used to excess, and perfumed gloves bordered with silver were common among the rich. Head-dresses were of every variety of pattern, but generally were not offensive to good taste. The pastimes of the common people were ball-playing, bowling, archery and rude theatrical exhibitions, whilst the gentry engaged in bull-baiting and horse-racing out of doors, and chess and backgammon amused them in hall and castle. Learning, until late in Elizabeth's reign, had been much neglected. Nobles and clergy were ignorant; but now a

JAMES THE FIRST. HENRY THE EIGHTH.

mighty impulse had been given to literature in England, for it was the age of Spenser and Shakespeare. Yet not one in ten of the gentry could write his or her name. The father of Shakespeare could only make his mark with a pen. The fine arts were very little encouraged. Henry the Eighth, who possessed good taste, caused some very fine buildings to be erected, and invited to his court painters and sculptors from abroad. Holbein the painter came from Switzerland, and Torregiano the sculptor came from Florence. But Elizabeth had no artistic taste, and we find only one eminent English painter during her reign—Nicolas Hilliard—to whom she sat for her miniature several times. She encouraged art so far as it ministered to the gratification of her vanity.

Such, in brief outline, is a picture of the social condition of England when the inhabitants of that realm began to make permanent settlements in America, at the beginning of the seventeenth century. The Tudor dynasty had ended with Elizabeth, and that of the Stuarts had begun. James the Sixth of Scotland, the only son of Mary Queen of Scots, had ascended the throne as James the First of England in 1603. He was in private and public an unwashed, ill-mannered, vulgar and contemptible man; fond of gross shows on which he wasted the treasures of the kingdom; and so great was his egotism that he considered himself more wise and learned than any man in his realm in church or state. He was a bigoted believer in the royal prerogative or exclusive privileges exercised by divine right; and he was a fickle tyrant who gave continual uneasiness to his subjects. This was the monarch who granted charters to the London and Plymouth Companies, authorizing them to make settlements in America.

The Plymouth Company, who were to control North Virginia, were first in the field of adventure. Circumstances seemed to be favorable. England was then burdened with two classes of men who would be willing to engage in any enterprise which might promise improvement in their condition. These were restless soldiers unemployed since war with France ceased, and who might soon become dangerous to the state; and impoverished spendthrifts, idle and often vicious, who had wasted their estates in riotous living. Such men stood ready to brave ocean perils and the uncertainties of life in a distant hemisphere; and when the corporators asked for emigrants, there was no lack of candidates.

The charter of each company was the same. The defined boundaries of each domain was as follows: that of the London Company, between the thirty-fourth and thirty-eighth degrees of north latitude, and that of the Plymouth Company, between the forty-first and forty-fifth degrees, leaving three degrees of space between North and South Virginia, on a breadth of one hundred miles of which, in the centre, neither party should be allowed to make settlements.

The mind of the king was visible in the grant. The idea of the royal prerogative was everywhere conspicuous. He gave to the colonists nothing but the bare territory and the privilege of peopling and defending it. Absolute legislative authority was reserved to the monarch, and he had control over all appointments. Supreme jurisdiction, under the monarch, was given to a small body of men residing in England, known as "The Council of Virginia," and local administration was entrusted to a council in the colony appointed by the one at home, the term of office of the members of both councils depending upon the caprice of the king. The only political privilege accorded to the emigrants was that of perpetual English citizenship for themselves and their children. Homage and rent were the prime conditions of the charter,—rent in the form of one-fifth of the net produce of the precious metals. The charter had not the slightest feature of a free government; for to the emigrants not a single elective franchise, or a right to self-government, was conceded. They were subject to the ordinances of a commercial corporation of which they were not allowed to be members; and even in matters of religion, they had no choice. The doctrine and rituals of the Church of England were to be the established theology and mode of worship in the American colonies, and no dissent was allowed.

The principal members of the Plymouth Company were Sir John Popham (then Lord Chief-Justice of England, who had condemned Raleigh to death), his brother George, Sir Fernando Gorges, Sir John and Raleigh Gilbert, sons of Sir Humphrey Gilbert who perished in the *Squirrel*, William Parker and Thomas Hanham. In 1606 they sent an agent in a small vessel to inspect the American domain. The Spaniards seized her. Popham fitted out another at his own expense, made the navigator Martin Pring her commander, and sent her to America on the same errand. Pring explored the New England coasts, and confirmed all that Gosnold and others had said about the beauty of the country and the fertility of the soil. This report stimulated Popham (who was the chief manager of the Plymouth Company) to energetic efforts towards founding a settlement, and at the beginning of the summer of 1607, a hundred emigrants sailed for America in three small vessels, with George Popham as their governor. They landed on a rather sterile spot on the coast of Maine, near the mouth of the Kennebec River, late in August, where they dug a well and built a store-house, a few log huts and a stockade fort. It was too late in the season to raise food from the soil. There was small promise of receiving any from the Indians, who, angered by the kidnapping by Weymouth, were sullen and hostile. With this prospect before them, all but forty-five of the emigrants returned home in the ships.

The ensuing winter was a fearful one. Frost closed the rivers against fishermen, and deep snows blocked the forests against hunters. The settlers had nothing to depend upon excepting the stores brought from England. At one time their huts were nearly buried in the snow-drifts. Of two of them only the chimneys were seen above the snow for a month, out of which rolled the blue smoke along the surface of the white drifts. It was difficult to get fuel to feed the hut fires, and they were about to make the store-house their general home, when, at midnight in January, it took fire and was consumed, with a part of their provisions, which they could not save. That fire produced a wild, weird scene, its red glare spreading a crimson glow far over the snow and through the dark forests. Distress followed. Confinement, hardship and scarcity gendered disease, and when the spring of 1608 opened, Governor Popham was dead.

The settlers were on the verge of despair when a ship came with supplies and brought the sad intelligence that the chief-justice and Sir John Gilbert were dead. These men were the stronger props of the enterprise. This news, with the terrible scenes of the past winter fresh in their memories, discouraged the emigrants, and they abandoned the country and returned home, taking with them a little vessel which they had built, and some furs

SETTLERS' HUTS BURIED IN THE SNOW.

and other products of the country. They were not fit men to found a state. They were compulsory emigrants sent hither by their personal necessities, and had left their country for their country's good. Happily for New England they were not allowed to be the founders of a commonwealth on its soil. They gave such discouraging accounts of the country that no one seemed willing to follow their example; and for a number of years afterward the Plymouth Company only kept up a little traffic with the natives of their domain, and fished in the neighboring waters.

The king, with commendable vanity, had prepared a code of laws for the colonies, really more liberal in their provisions than the intentions of the patentees, who desired immediate profitable return in money rather than the ultimate blessings of colonization. These laws enjoined the regular preaching of the gospel, kindness to the Indians and the communication of religious instruction to them, and other provisions for the well-ordering of a civil community. Under the charter and this code of laws, the London Company prepared to make a settlement in South Virginia. Sir Thomas Gates, Sir

George Somers, Richard Hakluyt, and Edward Maria Wingfield were its most active members, and in December, 1606, they sent Captain Christopher Newport with three small vessels and one hundred and five emigrants, with orders to land on Roanoke Island, where Raleigh's colony had perished twenty years before. It was a company of men no better fitted for the founding of a prosperous state than were those who wintered on the coast of Maine. No *family*, the true nucleus of a colony, accompanied either. Of the whole number who sailed for Virginia, there were only twelve laborers and a few mechanics. The remainder were "gentlemen," a word denoting persons who were not engaged in any industrial employments—drones in society, whose numbers are, happily, small in our country at this day. Many of these were idle and dissolute, whilst a few of those who were classed with the colonists, like Bartholomew Gosnold, the projector of the scheme, Captain John Smith, George Percy brother of the Duke of Northumberland, and Edward Maria Wingfield, were men of energy and steady habits.

The silly king, with his love for concealment, trickery and surprises, had placed the names of the councillors for the Virginia government in a sealed box, with orders not to open it until the emigrants should be landed and were prepared to form a settlement. This foolish order deprived the colonists of a head whilst on the sea, and there was no competent authority to decide questions or to quell disputes, if any should arise, during the long voyage of four months, for Newport took the old southern route by way of the Canary Islands and the West Indies.

Disputes, hot and fierce, did arise on that voyage. Before reaching the Canaries there were daily quarrels, chiefly owing to the brusque and imperious manner and outspoken opinions of Captain John Smith, who possessed more energy and wisdom than any man among them. Although he was then only twenty-nine years of age, he had acquired vast renown and experience by military exploits, and his fame filled his companions with envy. He had been a wild, rollicking lad, whose friends gave him ten shillings, he said, "to get rid of him," and he went to France as a servant to an English nobleman. He was soon dismissed by his new master, and then engaged in the wars in the Low Countries. At the end of a long campaign, when he was nineteen years of age, he returned to England, built himself a hut in a dark forest, turned hermit, and devoted much of his time to the study of military history and tactics, and practising horsemanship. The hermit became the theme of many a wild tale, when he suddenly disappeared. Rudolph, Emperor of Germany, was then waging war against the Turks, who were pressing westward through Hungary. Smith resolved to join the Christian army against them. After various vicissitudes he reached Marseilles, where he embarked for Italy in a ship filled with Roman Catholic pilgrims. A terrible storm arose. The superstitious pilgrims believed the howling tempest to be a token of God's anger because they were voyaging with a heretic; so they cast the young Englishman overboard. He swam to an island not far off, from which he was taken in a French vessel to Alexandria, and afterward on a voyage in the Levant, where they fell in with a Venetian vessel richly laden, and captured her. Soon after that, Smith joined the German army then fighting the Turks in Transylvania, where his skill and prowess won for him great renown. On one occasion, whilst besieging a town, a famous leader of the Mussulmans challenged any Christian to single combat for the amusement of the ladies of the city. Smith was the chosen champion.

CAPTAIN SMITH'S FIGHT WITH A TURK.

The Turkish lord appeared in the arena outside the walls in a suit of glittering mail. On his shoulders were large wings made of eagle's feathers, garnished with gold and precious stones. Smith appeared in a plain suit of steel. Both were on horseback, and their weapons were the lances of the old knights. From the walls, covered with ladies and soldiers, and from the Christian camp, went up loud shouts as the combatants approached each other. The tilt was fierce. By a skillful movement, Smith thrust his spear-point into the helmet of his antagonist, and pierced his brain. The Turk fell dead, when his head was cut off and sent to the Christian camp. Two other champions, who fought Smith to avenge the death of their leader, shared the same fate. The Prince of Transylvania gave him a patent of nobility and a coat-of-arms composed of a shield bearing three Turks' heads in two of the quarterings.

A little later Smith was made a prisoner and sold to a Pacha, who sent him to Constantinople as a slave for his mistress, whom that officer wished to marry. The gallant Christian, then in the bloom of young manhood, won the heart of the Turkish maiden, to whom, like the Moor, he told the story of his adventures. She tried to release him by sending him to her brother in the Crimea, but he there experienced the most grinding slavery. At length he escaped in the garb of his master whom he slew in anger, and after many stirring adventures on the continent he returned to England in 1604. Gosnold easily persuaded him to go to Virginia, where he became the real founder of that State.

After sharp quarrels on shipboard, Wingfield, who was a member of the London Company, accused Smith of a conspiracy to murder the council, whoever they might be, usurp the government, and make himself king of Virginia. This absurd charge was believed by some, and the brave soldier was imprisoned during the remainder of the voyage, which was very tedious. Whilst running up the American coast from the West Indies, they encountered a fierce storm which drove them far beyond Roanoke Island into Chesapeake Bay, the headlands of which they named in honor of the Prince of Wales and his next oldest brother, Cape Henry and Cape Charles.

A part of the voyagers landed on Cape Henry, and had a slight skirmish with the Indians; and that night the sealed box was opened, when the company were astonished to find the name of Captain Smith amongst those of the seven councillors. Yet he was not then released. They sailed across the deep waters at the mouth of the Chesapeake the next day, and landed upon a point grandly wooded and fragrant with the perfumes of flowers. Delicious was the comfort and rest of the wearied company in this paradise of beauty and repose, and with gratitude therefor they named it Point Comfort. There Fortress Monroe now stands. After resting a day or two, they entered the mouth of a broad river which the Indians called Powhatan, and sailing up that yellow stream for forty or fifty miles, they chose a place for a settlement on an island close by the northern shore of the river. There they organized government at the middle of May, by choosing Wingfield to preside over the council. In honor of their king they named the great river James, and resolved to call the island and the seat of government *James-*

town. The Rev. Robert Hunt, who was their chaplain, preached a sermon and invoked the blessings of God upon the undertaking. In that beautiful month of May, warm and sunny as in England at that season, the air laden with the perfume of wild flowers, and the children of the forest, friendly and kind, looking on in wonder, the sound of the metal axe was first heard in Virginia. The first tree was felled and the first foundation was laid for a dwelling on that charming spot where the first permanent English settlement in America was planted.

The English were told that far up the river lived Powhatan, the emperor of several confederated tribes; so, whilst the carpenters were hewing the timbers for the cabins, Newport, Smith, and twenty others went up the stream in boats to discover its head and to visit the dusky monarch. They followed its winding course to the Falls, where Richmond now stands; and on a hill, a mile below, they found Powhatan at one of his imperial residences, a large structure made of saplings and boughs and covered with skins. It was surrounded by a dozen wigwams of his chief counsellors, and fields of Indian corn almost ready to burst into bloom. The emperor received them kindly, but his chiefs murmured because of the intrusion of the English. Powhatan, who was afraid, said: "They hurt you not; they only take a little waste land."

Meanwhile, matters had not gone smoothly at Jamestown. The jealous and suspicious Wingfield restrained exercise with fire-arms and discouraged the building of a fort which Smith had recommended, for the latter knew that the idle and dissolute men of the company would soon make the Indians their enemies. When he returned his fears had been realized. The Indians had made a sharp attack upon the settlers, wounding several and killing a boy. Then the president consented to the building of a stockade, but daily and nightly watchings were necessary to avoid another surprise.

Newport now prepared to return to England with the ships. Smith had not been allowed to take his seat in the council, for he had not been tried nor had the charges against him been withdrawn. The jealous Wingfield, wishing to get rid of him, proposed that he should return with Newport and so avoid the disgrace of a trial. The indignant soldier rejected the proposal with scorn, and demanded an immediate trial. Smith's innocence was so plain to the comprehension of hi companions, and his services were so much needed, that they demanded his release. Wingfield withdrew his charges and Smith took his seat in the council, when it was adjudged by that body that the president should pay him £200 damages for false imprisonment. All of the property Wingfield had with him was seized to satisfy this award, when Smith generously "returned it to the store for the general use of the colony." From that time Captain Smith was the ruling spirit in Virginia.

At the middle of June, Newport departed for England for more emigrants and supplies, leaving a pinnace for the use of the settlers. Already the prudent thinkers had discovered impending perils. Much of their food had been spoiled during the long voyage, and the hostile Indians withheld supplies. "Our drink," wrote one of them, "was unwholesome water; our lodgings, castles in the air; had we been as free from all sins as from gluttony and drunkenness, we might have been canonized for saints." Most of the emigrants were too idle or too ignorant to make efforts to till the soil. The heat soon became intense and brought deadly malaria from the dank swamps all around them, that prostrated them with fevers and dysentery. Within a fortnight after Newport left hardly ten of them were able to stand, and before the beginning of autumn one-half of the emigrants were underground. Among the victims was the good Gosnold, a man of great worth, to whose example and the precepts of Parson Hunt the settlers were indebted for the little order that prevailed among them. Despair clouded the minds of the survivors, and in the midst of their distress, they discovered that the avaricious and unscrupulous Wingfield was living on choice stores and was preparing to abandon the settlement and escape to the West Indies in the pinnace. He was deprived of his office, and Captain John Ratcliffe, a man much weaker in mind and equally wicked, was put in his place. The settlers soon perceived their mistake, and taking the reins of government out of Ratcliffe's hands, they placed them in those of Captain Smith. It was an event that saved the colony from ruin. Hopeful, cheerful, energetic, honest, full of invention and equal to any emergency, Smith's words and example diffused light amid the general gloom and revived the spirits of the most desponding. He soon brought order out of confusion; inspired the Indians with awe and compelled them to bring him food. And so the settlers lived until the wild-fowl, returning from the northern waters, swarmed upon the bosom of the James in October, and at the beginning of November an abundant crop of Indian corn had been gathered by the savages, who shared it with their dependent white neighbors.

CHAPTER II.

ENERGY AND WISDOM OF CAPTAIN SMITH—HIS ENCOUNTER WITH INDIANS—SAVED FROM DEATH BY POCAHONTAS—HIS INFLUENCE AT JAMESTOWN, AND HIS EXPLORATIONS—DEMANDS OF THE COMPANY—SMITH'S RULE—CHANGE IN THE GOVERNMENT—PERILOUS PASSAGE OF A GOVERNOR AND COMMISSIONERS—VALUABLE EMIGRANTS—POCAHONTAS SAVES JAMESTOWN—THE "STARVING TIME"—ABANDONMENT OF AND RETURN TO JAMESTOWN—LORD DELAWARE'S ADMINISTRATION—A BETTER SOCIAL SYSTEM—POCAHONTAS KIDNAPPED—HER BAPTISM AND MARRIAGE—FRIENDSHIP OF THE INDIANS—THE STAPLE OF VIRGINIA—REPRESENTATIVE GOVERNMENT ESTABLISHED.

THE skill, prowess, and forethought of Captain Smith, had secured for the settlers an abundance of food and comfortable dwellings for the winter. The sickly season was over early in November, and nothing but fear of Indian treachery made the emigrants uneasy until their improvidence had again impoverished their stores. Smith had voyaged down the James River to Point Comfort and back, making observations of the people and country, and impressing the former with a sense of the wisdom and strength of the English; and he now proposed to explore the Chickahominy River, a broad stream at its mouth and flowing into the James from the northwest.

With singular ignorance of the progress of geographical discovery, and with intense greed for the wealth of India, the Company had given special instructions to the settlers to explore every considerable stream which they should find flowing from the northwest, hoping so to discover a passage to the Indian Ocean and coveted Cathay. Smith did not share the ignorance of his employers, but he gladly made their instructions his warrant for exploring the surrounding country; so, with half a dozen followers, he went up the Chickahominy in an open boat to its shallow waters among the swamps high upon the Virginia peninsula. There, with two others and two Indian guides, he penetrated the dark and tangled forests, leaving the remainder of his company in charge of the vessel with instructions not to go on shore. They disobeyed, and one of them was killed by prowling savages. Meanwhile, Smith had gone twenty-miles further in a canoe, when he left his two companions and with one guide he went into the woods in search of game. The savages, under Opechancanough, the king of Pamunkey, had watched the movements of the Englishmen. They slew the two men in charge of the canoe, and then sought their leader. Smith, seeing a large number of assailants, tied his Indian guide to his own body with his long garters, and making him a buckler he fought valiantly and slew several of the savages, as he moved backward toward his canoe. Falling into a quagmire, after being slightly wounded, he was made prisoner. Death would doubtless have been his immediate fate but for his presence of mind and

CAPTAIN SMITH'S ENCOUNTER WITH THE INDIANS.

quickness of thought. He drew from his pocket a compass, and explained to the king its wonderful nature as well as signs could convey the forms of thought. In the same way he told them of the shape of the earth; of the nature of the sun, moon and stars, and "how the sunne chased the night round about the world continually." The savages were at once impressed with the idea that he was a superior being, and they regarded him with wonder and awe.

The white captive was now conducted from village to village in great state, where the women and children stared at him in mute astonishment. In their march the king was just behind a file of warriors, and was followed by the prisoner whose arms were held by two huge savages, having six warriors, all painted and plumed in a gorgeous manner, on each side of them. At the capital of Opechancanough, who was an elder brother of Powhatan, they held incantations for three days to discover his character, for they were in doubts whether Smith was the embodiment of a good or an evil spirit. Then they conducted him to the presence of the Emperor Powhatan, at a place now known as Shelly, on the banks of the York River, in Gloucester county, Virginia, and asked him to decide the fate of the prisoner. There Smith obtained permission to send a letter to Jamestown, in which he informed the settlers of his condition, and directed them to impress the messengers with as much fear of the English as possible. The marvellous power of that letter perplexed the Indians. It had intelligent force, and more than ever they were in doubt concerning the real character of their captive, who was now feasted in a manner which made him think he was intended as food for a banquet when he should be well fatted.

Smith was finally brought before the emperor at a great council of full two hundred warriors. Powhatan, wearing a mantle of raccoon skins, and a head-dress of eagle's feathers, sat on a raised framework with a maiden on each side of him, before a fire. From this throne to the other end of the long house neatly made of boughs, the warriors stood in two rows, in their gayest attire, and back of them as many women with their necks and shoulders painted red, their heads covered with the white down of birds, and strings of white beads falling over their bosoms. When the captive was brought in, they all shouted. The Queen of Appomattox brought him water that he might wash his hands, and another woman brought him a bunch of feathers wherewith he might dry them. After this he was feasted, and then a solemn council was held. By that council he was doomed to die. Two huge stones were brought before the emperor, to which the prisoner was dragged and his head laid upon them, whilst two big savages stood by with clubs ready to beat out his brains. Matoa or Pocahontas, a young daughter of the emperor, begged for the life of the Captain, but in vain, when, just as the clubs were uplifted, she darted from her father's knee, clasped the prisoner's head with her arms and laid her own head upon his.

> "How could that stern old king deny
> The angel pleading in her eye?
> How mock the sweet, imploring grace
> That breathed in beauty from her face,
> And to her kneeling action gave
> A power to soothe and still subdue,
> Until, though humbled as a slave,
> To more than queenly sway she grew."—SIMMS.

The emperor yielded to the maid, and consented to spare the life of the captive that he might make hatchets for his majesty, and bells and rattles, beads and copper ornaments for his daughter, his favorite child. He did more; he released Captain Smith, sent him with an escort of a dozen men to Jamestown, and he and his people promised to be fast friends of the English. But for the energy and wisdom of Captain Smith and the tender compassion of an Indian maiden, the settlers at Jamestown would have all been murdered or dispersed. They had been reduced to forty persons, and when Smith returned he found the stronger ones on the point of abandoning the place and escaping in the pinnace. By his personal courage and moral force he compelled them to desist, and so, again, he saved the budding colony from ruin. These men, conscious of the purity of Captain Smith and of their own wickedness, now hated him with an intensity of feeling that impelled them to seek his destruction.

During Smith's absence among the Indians, the church at Jamestown had been burned, and the Rev. Mr. Hunt was laboring earnestly for the good of souls under the shadow of great trees. Of that first church edifice, Captain Smith has left us an interesting account. "When I first went to Virginia," he says, "I well remember we did hang an awning (which was an old sail) to three or four trees, to shadow us from the sun; our walls were rails of wood, our seats unhewed trees, till we cut planks; our pulpit a bar of wood nailed to two neighboring trees; in foul weather we shifted into an old rotten tent, for we had few better, and thus came by way of adventure for new. This was our church till we built a homely thing like a barn, set upon crotchetts, covered with rafts, sedge, and earth, so was also the walls. The best of our houses were of the like curiosity, but the most part far worse workmanship, that could neither well defend wind nor rain, yet we had daily Common Prayer, morning and evening, every Sunday two sermons, and every three months the Holy Communion till our minister died."

On his return, Smith found the settlers engaged in building a house for the President of the Council. When he was installed into that office not long afterward, he ordered the church edifice to be rebuilt. "Now the building of the palace was stayed as a thing needless," he said, "and the church was repaired;" and he assisted the minister in all ways in his power to make the people better.

When Newport returned to England he found the Council there increased in numbers and power, and he was employed to return immediately with new emigrants and supplies. He arrived at Jamestown early in 1608 with two vessels, and was received with joy. But he brought no better materials for a colony than before. Instead of needed mechanics and farm-

RELIGIOUS SERVICES AT JAMESTOWN.

ers with families, he brought chiefly idle "gentlemen," some of them vicious, whose friends, Smith said, had sent them away to "escape ill destinies at home"—the prison or something worse. There were one hundred and twenty of them, and there was scarcely a really useful man among them. There were several unskilled goldsmiths, whose ignorance caused a most destructive gold-fever to prevail in Virginia. They pronounced some glittering yellow earth near Jamestown to be a deposit of the precious metal, and in spite of the earnest remonstrances of Smith, the whole population turned gold-seekers. For awhile there was "no talk, no hope, no work, but dig gold, refine gold, load gold." On the recommendation of the goldsmiths, Newport loaded his vessel with the worthless earth, and returned to England with the impression that he was an immensely rich man. He was soon undeceived by a scientific test.

Captain Smith implored the settlers to plant and sow that they might have plenty and be happy, without the aid of the Indians, who, chiefly through the exertions of Pocahontas, were sending them supplies. But they would not listen to the wise man, and at length, in the early summer of that year, he turned from Jamestown in disgust, and with a few of the more sensible men he went in an open boat to explore the Chesapeake Bay and its numerous tributaries. In the space of three months, he made two voyages. During the first he went up the Potomac River to the Falls near Georgetown, and up the Rappahannock to the Falls near Fredericksburg, and then returned to Jamestown. During the second voyage he went up the Patapsco to the site of Baltimore and up the narrower part of Chesapeake Bay into the Susquehanna River, a short distance above Havre-de-Grace, where he heard of the powerful Iroquois Confederacy in the present State of New York. In these two voyages, Smith not only explored the shores of great waters, but penetrated into the country, made friendly alliances with several chiefs, and smoothed the way for the future planting of settlements on the borders of the noble Chesapeake. He had voyaged about three thousand miles in an open boat and made a map of the region explored, remarkable for its accuracy, which is preserved in London.

When Captain Smith returned to Jamestown early in September, he found the colony in confusion again. His advent was hailed with delight by the better sort of the settlers, and three days after his return he was chosen President of the Council. This wise measure soon produced some good fruit. The new president organized labor, and compelled the performance of the same; and when, a little later, Newport again came with two ships bearing supplies and seventy emigrants, he hoped to find among the latter better materials for a state. There were two women (the wife of Thomas Forrest, and her maid, Anne Burrows, who soon afterward married John Laydon, a carpenter), the first of European blood who had trodden the banks of the James; but the men were no better than the other emigrants. And yet the greedy corporation who had sent out such men for the founding of a state, disappointed and unreasonable, demanded impossibilities. They sent a message to the settlers by Newport, saying, in substance: "Unless you shall send us back in these ships sufficient commodities to pay the charges of the voyage [£2,000]; unless you shall also send us a lump of gold, the product of Virginia; assurances of having found a passage to the South Sea (Pacific Ocean), and also one of the lost colony sent to Roanoke by Raleigh, you shall be left in Virginia as banished men." To this threat Smith replied with spirit, showing them the absurdity of their demand, assuring them that it was as much as the settlers could do to sustain life with the assistance of the savages, and saying: "I entreat you rather send but thirty carpenters, husbandmen, gardeners, fishermen, blacksmiths, masons and diggers of trees' roots, well provided, than a thousand such as we have."

This threat assisted the president in enforcing rules for labor. He demanded six hours of work each day from every able-bodied man. "He who will not work shall not eat," he said. Very soon the "gentlemen" became expert in the use of the axe, and the little village showed signs of an orderly community; but so little attention had been given to agriculture that at the end of two years from the first arrival, and with two hundred emigrants in the settlement, not more than forty acres were under cultivation. They were compelled to depend upon the bounty of the red men for their sustenance during the winter of 1608–9.

With no respect for the rights of the settlers already in Virginia; with no desire to build up an industrious and prosperous colony on the banks of the James River, but with an intense longing for the speedy accumulation of wealth by the discovery of rich mines in America and a quick passage to India, the London Company sought to grasp all power and to abolish all freedom among the settlers, so making them little better than serfs. For this purpose they obtained wealthy and influential allies; and in the spring of 1609, the Company was composed of twenty-one peers, several bishops, ninety-eight knights, and a multitude of doctors, esquires, gentlemen, merchants and other citizens. They obtained a new charter in May under the title of "The Treasurer and Company of Adventurers of the City of London for the First Colony in Virginia," by which the boundaries of their domain were enlarged; the offices of president and council in Virginia were abolished, and all laws for the settlers were to be framed by the council in England and administered by officers appointed by that council. The rule of the governor was made absolute, and the lives, liberty and property of the settlers were placed at his disposal, whilst they were compelled to contribute a certain share of their net earnings to the proprietors. They were vassals, without any recognized power to cast off the yoke. Not a valuable civil privilege was conceded to them.

Nine ships were fitted out by the new Company, and freighted with stores and more than five hundred emigrants. These were placed under the general command of Captain Newport, and sailed for Virginia early in June, 1609. Sir Thomas West Lord De la Ware, had been appointed governor and captain-general of Virginia for life, with Sir Thomas Gates as his deputy. Sir George Somers was made admiral of Virginia, with Newport as vice-admiral; Sir Thomas Dale, high marshal, and Sir Fernando Wainman, general of cavalry. Gates, Newport and Somers were commissioned to administer the government until the arrival of Lord De la Ware, who was not then ready to go. As there had been no adjustment of precedence between these three men, and they could not settle that point, they agreed to go in the same vessel, the *Sea-Venture*, Newport's flag-ship. When she was near the coast of Virginia, a hurricane separated her from the rest of the fleet, and wrecked her on the shore of one of the Bermuda Islands. Another small vessel perished in the gale, but seven of the ships arrived at Jamestown, leaving a large company of emigrants composed of some of the worst classes of the population of England. These were licentious and profligate young men sent by their friends with a hope that amendment in their lives might follow, or to screen them from justice; tradesmen broken in fortune and spirits, and vagabonds of every grade, from idle "gentlemen" to dissolute criminals. The only things brought by the fleet that were valuable accessories to the settlement were horses, swine, goats and sheep, and domestic fowls. To these were added, two years later, one hundred cows and other cattle.

VALUABLE EMIGRANTS TO VIRGINIA.

Such emigrants were calculated to corrupt rather than improve the settlement, and mischief ensued. They had their leaders among the "gentlemen," who, on their arrival, proclaimed the new charter, and in the absence of the wrecked commissioners refused to obey the president. Anarchy menaced the colony, but Smith, with his usual energy, asserted his authority in the absence of legal agents of the Company, and now, as on other occasions, became the savior of the settlement from utter ruin. He devised new expeditions and new settlements that the vicious herd might be employed, and the libertines were kept in restraint until the autumn, when an accidental explosion of gunpowder so wounded Smith that he was compelled to go to England for surgical aid. He delegated his authority to George Percy, a brother of the Duke of Northumberland, a man of excellent character, but deficient in force. Smith never returned to Virginia.

It was more than six months after the departure of Captain Smith, when the three commissioners arrived from the Bermudas. Meanwhile, the

CAPTAIN SMITH AND POCAHONTAS.

settlers, left almost without restraint, had brought awful miseries upon themselves. They had indulged in every irregularity of life, and their ample store of provisions was soon exhausted. The new settlers, by injustice and cruelty, not only alienated the friendship of the Indians, but made them exasperated enemies. The red men, who had respect for Smith and feared his power, despised the new comers. They withheld food from the English, and killed those who came to their cabins in search of it. Finally, they devised a plan for exterminating the whole body of intruders. It was frustrated by Pocahontas, who proved to be the guardian angel of the settlers. When she heard of the plot, her soul was troubled. On a dark and stormy night she hastened to Jamestown, and revealing the conspiracy to Percy, put the English on their guard.

But death still brooded over the settlement. Famine came with its horrors and transformed civilized Englishmen into cannibals. They fed on Indians whom they slew, and sometimes upon their own companions who had perished of hunger. When the commissioners arrived in the spring of 1610, of the four hundred and ninety persons whom Smith had left in Virginia, only sixty remained alive. More than four hundred had perished within six months upon a soil out of whose generous bosom some moderate labor might have drawn ample sustenance for them all. Many a time during that winter and spring, which was ever afterward referred to as "the starving time," did those wretched men lament their folly and wickedness in not following the advice of Captain Smith, who was their true friend. His labors for their good had been disinterested. For his sacrifices he had received no reward but the approval of his conscience. Brave, honest and true, he won the imperishable honor of being the first planter of the Saxon race on the soil of the United States, and is entitled to the endearing name of *Father of Virginia.*

The commissioners and their fellow-passengers, who had been wrecked on a fertile but uninhabited island, found sufficient food in fruits there to sustain them whilst building two small vessels in which they embarked for Virginia. They hoped to find a happy and prosperous colony at Jamestown; but instead of the bright faces of contented people, they saw the horrid visages of sixty starving men in the depths of despair. They were perishing for want of food without a prospect of obtaining more. Gates, to whom the other commissioners had agreed to commit the administration of affairs in Virginia, saw no other way to save the lives of the starving men than to abandon the settlement, sail to Newfoundland, and distribute the settlers among the English fishermen there. So, embarking them in four pinnaces which were in the river, and giving them a share of his own stores, he sailed immediately for the far northeast. Some of the settlers desired Gates to set fire to the fort and dwellings at Jamestown, on their departure, but he would not consent. It was well he did not, for at the evening twilight the next day, the whole company, with others, were again at Jamestown offering thanksgiving to God for a great deliverance. At dawn that morning, the eyes of the disconsolate fugitives had been greeted by the apparition of white sails moving up the James River as Gates and his followers were approaching its mouth. They were the wings of Lord De la Ware's ships, which were filled with provisions and emigrants, accompanied by the governor, a pious, prudent, generous and humane man. Back to Jamestown they all sailed. The governor landed first. The emigrants followed, and when all were on shore, his lordship fell upon his knees and with bowed head engaged in a long silent prayer whilst the people stood reverently by. When he arose, he and the Rev. Mr. Bucke, who had come with him to supply the place of Mr. Hunt, led the people in procession to the unfinished church, where the new pastor preached a sermon, in the evening twilight, and a large portion of the congregation joined in singing anthems. After the religious services were ended, the governor presented his credentials and addressed the people. Some Indians were seen in the woods near by, listening in wonder to the songs of praise that went up from the lips of the grateful multitude on that warm June evening.

The dignity and amiable character of Lord De la Ware commanded the respect of the settlers, and the future seemed full of bright promises. He caused the church to be rebuilt, and to be dedicated with as much pomp and ceremony as circumstances would permit. It was daily garnished with white flowers; and there, every morning, a large number of the settlers were gathered to engage in common prayer, after which each man was required to work six hours during the day. The dwellings were improved and many more acres were cultivated. But the health of Lord De la Ware failed, and he returned to England in the spring of 1611, leaving the government in charge of Percy, Smith's successor. At the same time Sir Thomas Dale, a brave soldier, was out on the ocean in a ship with supplies, and on his arrival, which was hailed with delight, he assumed the reins of government and ruled by martial law both the church and state. He encouraged the Company to persevere in the dignified work which they had begun, and they sent Sir Thomas Gates with six well-furnished ships and three hundred emigrants. They arrived at the close of summer. These emigrants were a much better class than any who had yet appeared in Virginia. A greater portion of them were sober and industrious, and their influence upon the earlier settlers was salutary. Gates assumed the functions of governor, and Dale went up the river and planted settlements at the mouth of the Appomattox River (now Bermuda Hundred) and at the Falls (now Richmond). Over these the Rev. Mr. Whittaker was placed as pastor.

Another charter was now obtained for the Company, which allowed the powers of the association to be distributed in a democratic manner among all of the members, who met in mass for deliberation and legislation. The most important feature affecting the welfare of the settlement was that which allowed every man to cultivate a few acres of land for his own sole use and benefit. Before that time the land was tilled in common, and the industrious provided food for the lazy. There was no special incentive to industry in that system; but in the new arrangement there was such a stimulus to exertion that the privilege was enlarged, an ample supply of provisions for all was easily obtained, and the community system was abandoned. Although no political privileges were granted to the settlers by the new charter, they were contented.

And now a wicked act, which became a fortunate circumstance for the settlement, made a salutary change in the relations between the English and the Indians. Ever since the departure of Captain Smith, Powhatan had evinced hostility to the settlers, and the powerful Chickahominies, their nearest neighbors, sympathized with him, and allowed no food to be carried to Jamestown. Provisions there became scarce, and Captain Argall, the sort of buccaneer whom we met in Acadié, and who was then in Virginia, was sent with a vessel on a foraging expedition up the York and James Rivers. Being near the residence of Powhatan, he bribed an Indian with the gift of a copper kettle, to entice Pocahontas on board his vessel, where he detained her a prisoner, expecting to get a large quantity of corn from her father as a ransom for his daughter, and to recover some arms and implements of labor which had been stolen by the Indians. The emperor rejected the proposition of ransom with scorn, and refused to hold any intercourse with the pirate, but declaring to the authorities at Jamestown, that if his daughter should be released, he would forget the injury and be the friend of the English. They would not trust his word, and the maiden was taken to Jamestown and detained there several months, but was always treated with respectful consideration. The affair was assuming a very serious aspect, when Love, the powerful mediator, settled the difficulty. Among the young men of rank and education at Jamestown was John Rolfe, of an excellent English family, who became enamored of Pocahontas, and to him

> "She was a landscape of mild earth
> Where all was harmony and calm quiet,
> Luxuriant, budding."—BYRON.

Pocahontas reciprocated Rolfe's passion, and they agreed to be wedded. But one thing troubled the soul of the young Englishman. He was a Christian; she was a Pagan. "Is it not my duty," he said to himself, "to lead the blind into light?" Then came to his mind the Bible story of the visitation of the sons of Levi by God in his anger, because they sanctified strange women. But love conquered. He resolved to labor for her enlightenment and conversion. The young princess was an apt scholar, and very soon, in the little chapel at Jamestown, whose columns were rough pine trees from the forests, and its rude pews were of sweet-smelling cedar, and its rough communion-table and pulpit of black walnut, that dusky convert stood before a font "hewn hollow between like a canoe," and there received the rite of Christian baptism with the name of Rebecca, at the hands of Mr. Whittaker. She was the first Christian Indian in Virginia.

BAPTISM OF POCAHONTAS.

Very soon Pocahontas again stood before the chancel of the little chapel, now as a bride. It was a charming day in April, 1613. Her father's consent to her marriage had been easily obtained, and he had sent his brother Opachisco to give away his daughter according to the Christian ritual, for he would not trust himself wlth the English at Jamestown. Over the "fair, broad windows" hung festoons of evergreens bedecked with wild flowers, with the waxen leaves and scarlet berries of the holly. The communion table was covered with a "fair white linen cloth," and bore bread from the wheat fields around Jamestown, and wine from the luscious grapes from the adjacent woods. All the people at Jamestown were spectators of the nuptials. There were Sir Thomas Gates, and Master Sparks who had been co-embassador with Rolfe to the court of Powhatan. Young George Percy and Henry Spilman were there; and near them, an earnest watcher of the ceremony, was the elder brother of Pocahontas, with her younger brother and many youths and maidens from the forest. There, too, was Mistress John Rolfe, Mrs. Easton and child, and Mistress Horton and grand-child with her late maid-servant, Elizabeth Parsons, who, on Christmas Eve previously, had married Thomas Powell. These were all the English women then in Virginia, and all returned to Europe.

When all things were in readiness, the bride and groom entered the chapel. Pocahontas was dressed in a simple tunic of white muslin from the looms of Dacca. Her arms were bare even to her shoulders; and hanging loosely to her feet was a robe of rich stuff presented to her by Sir Thomas Dale, and fancifully embroidered by herself and her maidens. A gaudy fillet encircled her head, and held the gay plumage of birds and a veil of gauze, while her wrists and ankles were adorned with the simple jewelry of the native workshops. Rolfe was attired in the gay clothing of an English cavalier of that period, and upon his thigh he wore the short sword of a gentleman of distinction in society. He was a noble specimen of manly beauty and dignity in form and carriage, and she of womanly modesty and lovely simplicity. Upon the chancel steps, where no railing interfered, the good Whittaker stood in sacerdotal robes, and, with impressive voice, pronounced the marriage ritual of the Anglican Church, there first planted on the American continent. The governor, sitting on his right on a richly-carved chair of state, with his ever-attendant halberdiers with helmets, at his back, heartily said Amen! at the conclusion of the ceremony.

So were wedded the *Rose of England* and the *Totem* or Indian symbol of nationality, giving promise of a friendly union of races in Virginia. It brought present peace, and Powhatan was ever afterward the fast friend of the English. Rolfe and his spouse "lived civilly and lovingly together" until the departure of Governor Sir Thomas Dale for England in 1616, whither they, with several others of the settlement and all the English women there, accompanied him. There the "Lady Rebecca" received great attentions from the court and all below it. The Lord Bishop of London entertained her with "festival and pomp," and at court she was treated with the ceremonious respect due to the daughter of a monarch. The silly bigot on the British throne was angry because one of his *subjects* had dared to marry a *lady of royal blood;* and Captain Smith, for fear of the royal displeasure, would not allow her to call him "father" as she desired to do. Her simple, tender heart was grieved because of his seeming want of affection for her. The king, in his absurd dreams of the royal prerogative, imagined that Rolfe or his descendants might lay claim to the crown of Virginia, in behalf of his royal wife! And it was considered in council whether he had not committed treason!

Pocahontas remained in England about a year; and when she was about to embark for America with her husband and son, and Tomocome, her father's chief councillor, she sickened and died at Gravesend in June, 1617, when she was not quite twenty-two years of age. She left a son, Thomas Rolfe, who became a distinguished man in Virginia, and whose descendants have been numbered among the honorable citizens of that commonwealth.

Prosperity was now the destiny of the settlements in Virginia, although the prime element of a permanent state—the family—was yet wanting. Because of this want, the settlers continually indulged in dreams of returning home—to England. Dale, who had ruled with wisdom as well as energy, discouraged this feeling, and by engaging them in the cultivation of the tobacco plant, somewhat allayed it. His successors encouraged its production, and in spite of the silly efforts of King James to prevent its use in England, by forbidding its cultivation in the British islands, its growth and exportation to the mother country soon became the staple and very profitable business of the planters in Virginia. Its culture became a mania. The streets of Jamestown were planted with it, and food-producing products were so neglected, that while great cargoes of tobacco were preparing for England, the necessaries of life were wanting. It became the currency of the country, the money value of a pound of tobacco being fixed at about sixty-six cents.

Dale left Argall as deputy governor, but his petty tyranny and rank dishonesty disgusted the people. The story of his bad conduct told in England checked emigration, and his office was given to the excellent George Yeardley, a wise statesman and friend of man. On the death of Lord De la Ware while he was on a voyage to resume the reins of government there, Yeardley was appointed governor with broad discretionary powers. Abolishing martial law, releasing the planters from feudal service and confirming their titles to lands in their possession, and establishing a representative government on the banks of the James, he laid the foundations of a permanent colony. He had found the settlers yearning for the freedom enjoyed by their fellow-subjects in England under the British constitution. He could not reconcile that freedom with then existing disabilities, so, with the sanction of the Company, he introduced a new political system in Virginia. The settlements were divided into eleven boroughs, each having two representatives, called burgesses, who were chosen by the people. These, with the governor and council, constituted the colonial government. The burgesses were allowed to debate all questions pertaining to the colony, but their decisions were not law until confirmed by the Company in England. Because of these liberties, the settlers expressed their gratitude; and when in June, 1619, a representative assembly met at Jamestown, they felt that they had a *home* in Virginia. They "fell to building houses and planting corn," says an old chronicler; and these houses were soon made happy ones by domestic virtues. Within two years after the first meeting of the House of Burgesses—the first representative assembly in America—about two hundred and fifty reputable young women were sent over from England to become wives for the planters. These were received with gladness, and cherished with fondness. The tribe of gold-seekers had disappeared. Industry was the rule and not the exception in the settlements, and the COLONY of Virginia was firmly established.

CHAPTER III.

EXPLORATIONS IN NEW ENGLAND—KIDNAPPING INDIANS—RELIGIOUS PARTIES IN ENGLAND—PERSECUTIONS—A THEOLOGICAL CONFERENCE—BAD CONDUCT OF KING JAMES—PURITANS IN HOLLAND—LONGINGS FOR AMERICA—PREPARATIONS FOR EMIGRATION—"PILGRIMS" GO TO AMERICA—CONSTITUTION OF GOVERNMENT SIGNED—FOUNDING OF PLYMOUTH—SUFFERINGS OF THE EMIGRANTS—FIRST MARRIAGE IN PLYMOUTH COLONY.

WE have considered the failures of the Plymouth Company to plant settlements in America. We will now consider other attempts and failures, and the permanent establishment of a settlement in New England.

The restless Captain Smith did not long remain idle after his return from Virginia. In company with four London merchants, he fitted out two ships for the purpose of discovery and traffic in the northern regions of America. Captain Thomas Hunt commanded one of the vessels, and Smith sailed in the other. They left the Downs at the beginning of March, 1614, and first landed on the island of Mohegan, about twenty miles from the mouth of the Penobscot River, where they sought whales, but finding none Smith left the crews to engage in common fishing, while he and eight men, in a small boat, should explore the neighboring coasts and gather furs. They went up the several rivers far into the interior, and explored the whole coast from the Penobscot to Cape Cod. Smith constructed a map of the region; and after an absence of seven months, the vessels returned to England with cargoes of considerable value. He laid his map before Prince Charles, the heir apparent to the throne, and a man of considerable literary and artistic taste. The Prince procured from his father a confirmation of the title of *New England*, which Smith had given to the country, on his map; and so that region from twenty miles eastward of the Hudson River has ever since been called. As usual, crime dimmed the lustre of these achievements. Whilst Smith was exploring the coasts, Captain Hunt, an avaricious and profligate man, wishing, apparently, to impede settlements by inflaming the wrath of the Indians, so that he and a few others might enjoy the monopoly of traffic on that coast, kidnapped twenty-seven of the savages at Cape Cod, with Squanto their chief, and taking them to Spain sold them for slaves. Some of them were taken by benevolent friars, who educated them for missionaries among the tribes, but only Squanto returned to America. The effect of this crime satisfied the apparent wishes of Hunt. The next fishing vessels that came from New England brought word that the natives were greatly exasperated.

This news did not discourage Captain Smith. On his return he had an interview with the energetic and ever-hopeful Ferdinando Gorges, and inspired him with such desires to plant a settlement in New England, that the Plymouth Company asked Smith to lead a colony thither. He believed that he could allay the anger of the natives, as he had done in Virginia, and having accepted the invitation of the Company, he sailed with two ships and some emigrants in the spring of 1615. Smith's ship was shattered by a tempest and returned to port. On the 4th of July following he sailed again, in a bark of sixty tons, and was soon captured by a French squadron. While on board one of the Gallic vessels, he wrote an account of his voyage to New England, which was published the next year. After a brief captivity, he was released and returned home. Meanwhile, the Plymouth Company had made him admiral of New England; but, discouraged by ill luck, the association had again abandoned the project of planting a colony there. Smith now drops almost out of sight in history. He lived to see his friend, Prince Charles, seated on the throne of his father; and, not long afterwards (1631), the founder of the Virginia colony died at the age of fifty-one years.

Thus far English settlements in America had been attempted by private adventurers, or commercial associations, with no higher aim than the acquisition of wealth. That acquisition was denied, and full success was not obtained until better men, with more exalted motives, came to people the lands. These came to New England with families and were prepared to stay, not so much for the betterment of their temporal estates, as for the unmolested enjoyment of civil and religious freedom, which was denied them at home.

We have seen how three powerful religious parties—Roman Catholic, Anglican and Puritan—crystallized into distinct sects at about the beginning of Elizabeth's reign, all struggling for supremacy. The Puritans were fewer in numbers than either of their antagonists, but were stronger in the moral power which asserts and defends the rights of man. They boldly declared the right of private judgment in religious matters to be inalienable, and that every human being was endowed with the natural privilege of worshipping the Creator in accordance with the dictates of conscience. Upon the same platform of principles they asserted the rights of the people to the enjoyment of civil freedom. The Puritan pulpits became the tribunes of the common people, and sometimes the preachers were bold enough to promulgate the democratic doctrine, so dangerous to the royal prerogative, that *the sovereign was amenable to public opinion when fairly expressed.*

As the Romish ritual was retained in the Anglican Church, many of the leading clergymen of the latter opposed its use. Bishop Hooper made Puritanism conspicuous by refusing to be consecrated in the ecclesiastical vestments; and Bishop Coverdale, at a later period, and other high dignitaries, refused to subscribe to the Liturgy and ceremonials, and so led the great army of Nonconformists. The fears and jealousy of the queen were aroused, and after years of effort, the Thirty-nine Articles of Religion of the Anglican Church, were declared by an act of Parliament to be the rule of faith and practice for all subjects of the realm. Whitgift, Archbishop of Canterbury, was commanded to enforce discipline. He obeyed the royal voice with alacrity, and immediately issued instructions to the bishops to "forbid and prevent preaching, catechizing, and praying in any private family in the presence of persons not belonging to it, and to silence all preachers and catechists who had not received orders from Episcopal hands, or who refused or neglected to read the whole service, or to wear the prescribed clerical habits, or to subscribe to the queen's supremacy, the Thirty-nine Articles and the Book of Common Prayer." Under a provision of the Act of Supremacy, the queen now established a court of High Commission for the detection and punishment of Nonconformists, with powers almost as absolute as those of the Inquisition of the Italian Church. With that tremendous engine of despotism, the Primate worked with vigor in the suppression of heresy. Ministers were silenced; some persons were put to death, and there was petty persecution everywhere. Yet Puritanism flourished and grew more rank, especially in secret. Ministers and congregations withdrew from the Anglican Church, and so acquired the name of Separatists or Independents. They numbered, at the time of the death of Elizabeth, about twenty thousand in the British realm, and were the special objects for Whitgift's lash. Some of their ministers and

A PURITAN.

their congregations, unable to endure the pressure, withdrew to Holland, where there was religious freedom for all.

On the accession of James, a reputed "Presbyterian king," the Puritans indulged high hopes of toleration, perhaps of supremacy. They were doomed to wretched disappointment. Soon after James ascended the throne he called a conference at Hampton Court, in which he was the chief actor, playing the parts of brute and mountebank. The Puritan divines, some of them the most eminent scholars in the land, were annoyed by coarse browbeating by the Bishop of London, and the coarser jests of the king. Whitgift, venerable with age, was present, and when the "royal buffoon" said to the Puritan ministers: "You want to strip Christ again; away with your snivelling," and much more that was coarse and offensive, the Primate exclaimed, "Your Majesty speaks by the special assistance of God's Spirit;" and the Bishop of London fell upon his knees and said: "I protest my heart melteth for joy that Almighty God, of his singular mercy, has given us such a king as since Christ's time has not been." A brilliant modern English writer, expressing the verdict of history, says of that king: "He was cunning, covetous, wasteful, idle, drunken, greedy, dirty, cowardly, a great swearer, and the most conceited man on earth." The discussions at the Hampton Court conference, conducted with so much ill-breeding on the part of the king and some of the High Churchmen, led to the important result of the appointment of a commission of learned men to make that translation of the Bible now in use among Protestants.

The Puritans were humiliated and discouraged by this farce at Hampton Court; and when the king told them, "I will make you conform or I will harry ye out of the land," and silenced or imprisoned three hundred of their ministers, many of the thirty thousand Nonconformists in the kingdom felt like seeking refuge in a foreign country. And many of them did join their brethren already in Holland. Among them was Richard Clifton, pastor of a rural congregation in Nottinghamshire. In that congregation was John Robinson as teacher; and the most considerable private member was William Brewster, postmaster at Scrooby, and at one time a favorite of Secretary Davidson under Queen Elizabeth. The pastor and the congregation, after many trials, made their way to Amsterdam, in small companies, in 1608, where they were united. From that city, in the course of a few months, they went to Leyden, a city of seventy thousand inhabitants. Clifton was dead and Robinson was chosen to be their pastor, with William Brewster as the chief elder. After awhile they all found employment and were happy, with their families around them. The congregation became large and flourishing, for many of their persecuted brethren at home joined them.

English loyalty and patriotism asserted their power in the hearts of these exiles for conscience sake. Though driven from their native land by persecution, they had not lost their affection for it; and they yearned to live "under the protection of the state of England." They had heard of beautiful Virginia, and longed for the freedom of the forest. That band of noble men and women revealed a generous impulse when they said: "If God would be pleased to discover some place unto them, though in America, where they might live comfortably by themselves, and being freed from anti-Christian bondage, might keep their names and nature, and not only be a means to enlarge the dominions of the English state, but the Church also, if the Lord had a people among the natives, whither he would bring them; thereby they thought they might more glorify God, do more good to their country, better provide for their posterity and live to be more refreshed by their labors than ever they could do in Holland, where they were." Patriotism and Christian benevolence warmed their hearts.

"They sought not gold nor guilty ease,
Upon this rock-bound shore;
They left such prizeless toys as these
To minds that loved them more.
They sought to breathe a freer air,
To worship God unchain'd—
They welcomed pain and danger here,
When rights like these were gain'd."

The project of emigration to America caused much discussion. They looked every difficulty square in the face—the dangers of the sea and the savages; the burdens of fatigue that would be laid upon the weak and aged in so long a voyage; the cost of the enterprise, and the utter uncertainty that hovered around the whole project. These were all considered, and made dark shadings to the brighter pictures which faith and hope created. They pondered and prayed, and came to the conclusion to emigrate to America. The Dutch offered to send them to Hudson's River, free of charge, with their household goods and cattle, if they would settle there. They patriotically declined this generous proposal because they wished to live on "English land," somewhere within the bounds of the North Virginia domain, the proprietors whereof were then contemplating vast schemes of colonization under a new charter which they hoped to obtain from the king. That charter was granted late in 1620. It made the company absolute owners of a domain containing more than a million square miles. They superseded the original Plymouth Company, and assumed the corporate title of *The Council of Plymouth.*

Before the charter was granted, the congregation at Leyden sent two agents to England to ask leave of the Plymouth Company to settle within their domain, and to procure a guaranty from the king that they should enjoy religious freedom in their proposed new home. They obtained the permission of the Company, but the king would give them no written promise. Under the influence of Edward Sandys, he gave them an oral promise that they should not be disturbed so long as they should give no public offence. His word was considered no more stable than a rope of sand, and many were loth to unsettle themselves upon such a fickle tenure. But it was finally concluded to take the risk, and a deputation was again sent to England to make arrangements for the emigration. A joint-stock company with some London merchants and others was formed, by the terms of which the services of emigrants who could not contribute money were accepted as an equivalent for cash, the value of each share being fixed at £10. All profits were to be reserved for seven years, at the end of which time the lands, houses, and every product of their joint industry were to be valued, and an equal portion to be divided among the shareholders. Captain Smith, the founder of Virginia, offered to accompany them, but his aristocratic notions were a bar and his offer was declined.

It was agreed that only a portion of the congregation at Leyden—"the youngest and strongest"—should first go to America under the spiritual guidance of Elder Brewster, then a little more than fifty years of age, while the larger portion should remain with Mr. Robinson and follow the next year if the report of the pioneers should be favorable. Two small vessels were purchased for the voyage—the *Speedwell*, of sixty tons burthen, and the *May-Flower*, of one hundred and eighty tons. In the summer of 1620, a portion of the congregation at Leyden embarked in the former vessel at Delft Haven, for England, where she was joined, at Southampton, by the latter. These emigrants, like their brethren left behind, feeling that they had no home—no abiding place—but were pilgrims and strangers, assumed the name of Pilgrims, by which they are known in history—"The Pilgrim Fathers."

The embarkation at Delft Haven was a picturesque and interesting scene. A large portion of the congregation at Leyden followed the emigrants to the port, fourteen miles distant, after those who were to remain had feasted the pioneers at the house of the pastor. At the port, after another feast, they all engaged in religious exercises—prayers and psalm-singing—the voyagers on the deck of the *Speedwell* and the others on the quay. When the sails of the vessel were spread and she had left her moorings, the emigrants gave their brethren a parting salute with musketry and three small cannon.

The two ships sailed for America on the 6th of August. The *Speedwell* was soon reported to be too leaky to proceed, and both vessels went back to Dartmouth. She was repaired, and when again she was well out upon the Atlantic she was reported to be unseaworthy, and returned. It was believed that her captain and some of the company lost courage, and untruly reported her to be in a dangerous condition. She did not again sail for the Western world. The more courageous of her company joined those on the *May-Flower*, and on the 6th of September the latter sailed from Plymouth with forty-one men as settlers with their families, numbering in all one hundred-and-one souls. Among these were William Brewster and his numerous family, and William Bradford, of Scrooby; John Carver, a deacon in the Church at Leyden; young Edward Winslow and his bride, the richest couple of the flock; Miles Standish, a fiery little soldier, and his beautiful wife Rose; John Alden, the youngest of the Pilgrims, being only twenty-one years of age, and a favorite of Standish; John Allerton and Dr. Edward Fuller, all of whom were distinguished in the history of the colony.

After a boisterous voyage of sixty-three days, the *May-Flower* arrived off Cape Cod. Her destination was some "point near Hudson's River, but within the territory of the London Company"—somewhere on the shores of New Jersey. Turning southward, the ship encountered "perilous shoals," perhaps those off Nantucket, when she was made to retrace her line, double the headland, and come to anchor in the bay inclosed by the long peninsula of Cape Cod sixty miles in length, in what is now the roadstead of Provincetown. The weather was fine and the air was crisp, for it was early in November. To prevent anarchy when they should form a settlement, the following instrument was drawn up, and on a little table in the cabin of the *May-Flower* was signed by the entire company of forty-one adult masculine emigrants:

"In the name of God, Amen. We whose names are here underwritten, the loyal subjects of our dread sovereign lord, King James, by the grace of God, of Great Britain, France and Ireland, King, Defender of the Faith, etc., having undertaken for the glory of God, and advancement of the Christian Faith, and honor of our king and country, a voyage to plant the first colony in the northern parts of Virginia, do, by these presents, solemnly and mutually, in the presence of God and of one another, covenant and combine ourselves together into a civil body politic, for our better ordering and preservation, and furtherance of the ends aforesaid; and by virtue hereof to enact, constitute, and frame such just and equal laws, ordinances, acts, constitutions, and offices, from time to time, as shall be thought most meet and convenient for the general good of the colony; unto which we promise all

LANDING OF THE PILGRIMS

due submission and obedience. In witness whereof we have hereunto subscribed our names at Cape Cod, the 11th of November, in the year of the reign of our sovereign lord, King James, of England, France and Ireland, the eighteenth, and of Scotland the fifty-fourth, Anno Domini, 1620."

This was the first constitution of government ever signed by a *whole people.* More than a month passed after this act before the Pilgrims landed. Explorations of the coasts of the great Bay were made in search of a good place for a settlement. In a shallop and on foot the explorers wandered, often suffering much from the biting cold of winter, which came early with binding frost, and blinding, hindering snow. They saw few natives, and these were shy or hostile. They found some graves; some remains of human habitations; many deserted wigwams; some heaps of maize or Indian corn, and some tokens of civilized visitors here and there, when they touched the shores. They were assailed by a few savages who knew the English as kidnappers, for it was only a few years before that Hunt had carried away more than a score of their people. At length the explorers came to a snug harbor, and landed upon a rock on the site of Plymouth, almost due west across the water from where the *May-Flower* lay. It seemed a goodly place for a settlement, and they chose it as such. That landing took place on the 22d of December, 1620. It was an important event in the history of New England, and since the year 1767 its anniversary has been celebrated; and fragments of the rock—"Plymouth Rock," which has been called the "Blarney Stone of New England,"—are preserved on the spot with care.

The *May-Flower* was now immediately brought across and anchored in the harbor, when her precious cargo of human beings, men, women, and children—the seed of a nation—were landed. There had been an addition made to the number of the emigrants since the explorers departed, for the wife of William White had given birth to a boy, who was named Peregrine. The good ship that brought them safely across the stormy Atlantic was safely moored; and in grateful recollection of the hospitalities they had received at the port from which they had sailed from England, they named the spot *Plymouth.*

The first care of the Pilgrims was to build houses, after they had planted their five cannon on a platform and erected a store-house for their food. But with the labor began sickness. Exposure and poor food made dreadful ravages upon their vitality that could not be stayed. There were no delicacies, and very little wholesome food. The sailors unkindly refused to let them have a variety, by sharing with the suffering their abundance of coarse food on the ship, until sickness invaded their circle, and the kindness of the

Pilgrims taught them to be ashamed. Crowded in the cabin of the May-Flower, or exposed in half-finished huts, sometimes nearly buried with snow-drifts, the sufferers had little chance for recovery; and when, early in March, there came warm days and abundance of sunshine, forty-four of the passengers of the *May-Flower* were in their graves, doomed by quick consumption and lung fever. Governor Carver's son died soon after the landing. Six were buried in December, eight in January, seventeen in February, and thirteen in March. At one time there were only seven persons who had

BUILDING HOUSES AT PLYMOUTH.

strength enough to wait upon the sick and bury the dead. Early in April the governor died, and his heart-broken wife soon followed him to the grave. Yet with all the discouragements of that dreadful winter, the fidelity, faith, and fortitude of the Pilgrims never faltered; and when, in March, the sun shined warmly, and the birds came and sang pleasantly, and the sickness was stayed, the living chanted songs of thanksgiving to God for his manifold mercies.

There had been, earlier than this, a cheering voice from the savages whom the settlers so much dreaded. One day in February, when the sickness was at its height, an Indian passed through the hamlet and with plain Saxon words cried, "Welcome, Englishmen! welcome, Englishmen!" It was Samoset, a chief who had come from the island of Mohegan, where Captain Smith first landed, off the coast of Maine, and where he had learned a few English words from the sailors. He told them why they had seen so few Indians. It was because three or four years before a pestilence had almost depopulated the coast from Cape Cod to the Kennebec, as if clearing the way for Christians to plant the germs of civilization, unmolested. He came several days in succession, bringing with him other Indians, among them, at last, Squanto, whom Hunt had carried away and sold in Spain, but who had been sent back. That time Samoset came with a message from Massasoit, a neighboring king of the Wampanoags, of whom Squanto was a vassal, desiring an interview with the chief of the new comers.

Governor Carver gladly consented to hold a conference with the Indian monarch. Massasoit appeared on a neighboring hill, with sixty followers all painted and plumed. Winslow was sent with Squanto to meet him, bearing presents from the governor, whilst Captain Standish, who had been chosen military commander of the settlement, remained a little way off with several musketeers. Massasoit advanced slowly with twenty armed followers, leaving Winslow behind as a hostage or pledge, and met Standish at a dividing brook. Then the dusky men were conducted by the soldier to a building, where a rug and cushions were spread for the king and his courtiers. Sitting there in state, Massasoit received the governor, who came with the braying of a trumpet and the beating of a drum, followed by a few musketeers. After salutations and feastings, they entered into a treaty of peace and amity (Squanto acting as interpreter); and the sachem agreed to send messengers to neighboring tribes to invite them to come and make similar treaties, that they might all dwell lovingly with the pale-faces. Rising from the rug, the old chief, stretching forth his hand with dignity and pointing to the surrounding country, said, in substance: "Englishmen, take possession of the land, for there is no one left to occupy it. The Great Spirit came in his anger and swept the people from the face of the earth." That treaty was kept inviolate for forty-five years.

When the Indians had departed, the Pilgrims re-elected Carver governor of the colony, made some salutary laws, and sent the *May-Flower* home.

She was scarcely out of sight, when the governor died suddenly from the effects of a "sun-stroke," and William Bradford was chosen to fill his place. As the season advanced hope grew stronger. Game was found to be plentiful in the forest, and fish in the streams. The survivors cultivated the land industriously, and reaped abundantly. In a short time other emigrants joined them. The whole community was free as air; and the settlement, begun with so much suffering, bereavement and discouragement, was made permanent. Within a few months after the arrival of the *May-Flower*, the Christian men and women who survived that winter of terrible experience, planted strong and deep, on the principles of justice and the rights of man, the foundations of the colony and the commonwealth of *Massachusetts*.

RETURNING FROM THE WEDDING.

With the prose of suffering there was a little of the poetry of social romance at that tearful planting time. Among the victims of the famine and the fever was Rose Standish. Her husband laid her body tenderly in the earth, and feeling that it was "not good for man to be alone," almost immediately turned to Priscilla Mullins for consolation. She was a daughter of William Mullins, one of the *May-Flower* passengers. The captain was then thirty-seven years of age, and Priscilla had but lately bloomed into young womanhood. In Standish's family lived John Alden, a young cooper from Southampton, whom the Captain sent as an ambassador to Priscilla's father to ask his consent for the soldier to visit her with matrimonial intent. He performed the duties of his mission modestly and faithfully. The father readily gave his consent, adding, "But Priscilla must be consulted." She was summoned to the room. There sat John Alden, whom she knew well—a young man of graceful form, a handsome ruddy face and sparkling eyes, and of almost courtly manners.

ENGLISH SETTLERS IN AMERICA.

The embassador of love repeated his message from the soldier. The calendar tells us it was leap-year, when English maidens had the privilege of wooing. "Prithee, John," said Priscilla, as she fixed her mischievous eyes upon the face of the young diplomat, "why do you not speak for yourself?" John blushed, bowed and retired, for he was faithful to his trust. But his visit was soon repeated; and it was not long before the nuptials of the couple were celebrated by the whole community excepting Captain Standish, who could not readily forgive the weakness of his young friend in surrendering at the first assault from the eyes and lips of a maiden.

That was the first marriage in the colony, and the incidents were somewhat dramatic, for John Alden went to his nuptials seated on a young bull caparisoned with a piece of handsome broadcloth. Returning from the wedding, he led the bull by a ring in his nose, walking by his side, whilst his bride rode like a queen upon the animal. To the heart of Miles Standish, Priscilla upon Taurus was a repetition of the story of the carrying away of Europa, the Phœnician princess. Such is the story of tradition and poetry. History gravely tells us that there were no horned cattle in the colony until some time after this marriage.

From time to time the memory of that first marriage in New England has been revived by history and song. A vivid picture of it is given in Longfellow's "Courtship of Miles Standish;" and the notable wedding was brought to mind when, in April, 1874, Mrs. Phœbe C. Bailey died in Dover, New Hampshire, at the age of ninety-one years. She was the great-granddaughter of John Alden and Priscilla Mullins.

CHAPTER IV.

HUDSON'S VOYAGES AND DISCOVERIES—BLOCK'S EXPLORATIONS—CHARTER FOR NEW NETHERLAND GRANTED—DUTCH TRADERS ON THE HUDSON—TROUBLES WITH THE ENGLISH—DUTCH WEST INDIA COMPANY CHARTERED—PREPARATIONS FOR SETTLEMENT—AN ENGLISH INTRUDER—ARRIVAL OF WALLOONS AT MANHATTAN—SETTLEMENT ON THE DELAWARE—POLITICAL ORGANIZATION OF NEW NETHERLAND—NEW AMSTERDAM FOUNDED—FREEDOM THERE.

WE have already considered the incidents attending the discovery of the Hudson River and the country on its borders between its mouth and the site of Albany, in 1609. Let us now view the more prominent events connected with the establishment of a permanent settlement there.

In the year 1602, Dutch merchants in the India trade formed an association, with a capital of more than a million dollars, under the corporate title of "The Dutch East India Company." The government of Holland gave them the exclusive privilege of trading in the Eastern Seas between the Cape of Good Hope and the Straits of Magellan—that is to say, over all the Indian and South Pacific Oceans between Africa and America. The enterprise was so profitable that an application was made to the government, in 1607, for the incorporation of the Dutch West India Company to trade along the coast of Africa from the tropics to the Cape of Good Hope, and from Newfoundland to Cape Horn along the continent of America. But political considerations in connection with Spain deferred the issuing of a charter for such a company for several years. Meanwhile, the East India Company employed Hudson to make the voyage, which resulted in the discovery of a region in America far more valuable than any to which a northwestern passage to India would have led.

The report that the newly-discovered region abounded with bears, beavers, otters, and other fur-bearing animals, excited the keenest cupidity of the Dutch, for they had recently tasted the pleasures of a profitable fur trade which they had opened with Northern Russia. The *Half-Moon*, Hudson's discovery ship, had returned in the autumn of 1609. In the following spring she was fitted out with cheap trinkets and other articles suitable for traffic with the natives, and, with a part of her old crew, sailed from the Texel in the early summer for the "River of the Mountains." She was sent by private adventurers, some of them directors of the Dutch East India Company, to trade with the savages for peltries and furs. The island of Manhattan, at the mouth of the river, was so well adapted for commercial purposes that it was made the central point, where the treasures of the forests and the streams, gathered in the interior from the Delaware to the Housatonic and northward to the Mohawk, were collected for shipment to Holland.

Among the bold navigators who came from Holland to Manhattan was Adrien Block. His vessel was the *Tigress*. Late in the autumn of 1613, when she was laden with bear skins and was about to depart for Amsterdam, she accidentally took fire and was burned to a useless wreck. The Indians kindly offered the shelter of wigwams to the Dutchmen, but they, regarding

BURNING OF THE TIGRESS.

them too frail to keep out the winds and snows, built for themselves rude log huts where the warehouses of Beaver street now stand, and went cheerily at work to construct a new vessel. Before spring, the oaks that sheltered black bears on the wooded slopes where the "bulls" of Wall street now contend with bruins in financial warfare, were converted into a trim-built and staunch yacht of sixteen tons. They named her *Onrust*—"Restless"—a title that seems prophetic of that unresting activity which now marks the island of Manhattan. The little hamlet then built, and the vessel there constructed, were the fruitful seeds of the great commonwealth of New York.

Early in the spring of 1614, Block sailed from Manhattan in the *Onrust* through the narrow, turbulent and dangerous strait of Hell Gate into Long Island Sound. He discovered and explored the rivers now known as the Housatonic, Connecticut, and Thames; anchored in the bay at New Haven; touched at Montauk Point on the eastern end of Long Island, and landed upon a small island further eastward which Verazzani had discovered almost a century before, but which has ever since borne the name of Block, given to it by his countrymen. He then visited the shores of the main and the islands from Narragansett Bay around to Nahant beyond Boston Harbor. There he found the inhabitants numerous; for the plague, already mentioned, that swept along the coast three or four years later, had not yet appeared. They were "extremely well-looking, but timid and shy of Christians." There the *Onrust* fell in with the *Fortune*, commanded by Block's friend, Hendrick Christiansen, who was about to sail for Holland. Block left his own vessel in charge of another navigator and sailed for Amsterdam with his friend, to report to his employers.

Block's report further stimulated the commercial enterprise of Dutch merchants, and they hastened to avail themselves of an ordinance which the States-General or government of Holland had recently passed. It provided that whoever shall, from this time forward, discover any new passage, haven, lands, or places, shall have the exclusive right of navigating to the same for four voyages. The merchants concerned in Block's discoveries hastened to form an association, and took immediate steps to profit by the privileges offered by that ordinance. They employed an expert draughtsman, probably under the direction of Block, to construct a map of the newly-discovered regions, and appointed a deputation to go to the Hague, the seat of government, to obtain the special license to trade in these regions without interference.

At the Hague, the finest city of the Netherlands, and the residence of the Counts of Holland for four hundred years, may be seen a pile of buildings upon an artificial island irregular and quaint in appearance. They were erected at different periods, and inclose a vast quadrangle paved with small yellow bricks. There was the palace of those Counts. Its great hall, wherein hung trophies of Dutch valor and conquest, is now used as a repository of the archives of Holland. In a superbly-decorated room in the Binnenhof or inner court, the States-General held their meetings. To that sumptuous apartment went the deputies of the Amsterdam Company and gave, in a brief narrative of Block's discoveries, their reasons for asking for the special privilege. They were received by "twelve high and mighty lords" of the great council, who were sitting around an oval table. Among them was the incorruptible patriot John Van Olden Barneveldt, the grand-pensionary or chief magistrate of Holland, who, five years later, was beheaded in that court as a traitor, the victim of his jealous, malicious and unscrupulous prince. Block was probably one of the deputies. The map spoken of was spread upon the table; the countries were described, and their value as parts of the territories of the Dutch were fully set forth. The States-General gladly complied with the wishes of the Company, and on the 11th of October, 1614, a charter was given them, duly signed and sealed, by which the petitioners were granted the usual privileges of the ordinance. The territory included in the charter, and which was defined as lying between Virginia and New France—between the parallels of 40° and 45°—was called NEW NETHERLAND.

At the expiration of the charter at the beginning of 1618, the Amsterdam Company applied for its renewal. The privilege was denied, because the States-General contemplated the issuing of a more comprehensive and lasting patent to a West India Company. Meanwhile, the *Onrust*, which Block had left in charge of Cornelius Hendricksen, had entered and explored Delaware Bay and River, probably as far up as the Falls, near Trenton; and on the site of Philadelphia her commander had ransomed three Dutch traders, who had fallen into the hands of the Indians. Efforts were made to obtain a four years trading charter for that region also, but the States-General, considering the domain as a part of the province of Virginia, would not grant one. The directors of New Netherland then prosecuted their trading enterprise upon the borders of the Hudson with increased vigor. They had already built a fort on an island just below the site of Albany. They now enlarged their storehouse at Manhattan, and made the little hamlet a social village. The traders went over the pine-barrens into the Mohawk Valley and became acquainted with the powerful Iroquois league of Five Confederated Nations. They built a new fort on the main at the mouth of the Tawasentha, now Norman's Kill, a little below Albany, where a treaty of friendship was made with the Five Nations, and which was kept inviolate until New Netherland passed into the possession of the English, and long afterwards. It was a wise measure, for that confederacy was strong enough to have swept from the face of the earth all European intruders. Their power was felt, as we have observed, from the St. Lawrence to the Gulf of Mexico

"The fierce Adirondac had fled from their wrath,
The Hurons been swept from their merciless path,
Around, the Ottawas, like leaves had been strown,
And the Lake of the Eries struck silent and lone.

"The Lenapes, once lords of the valley and hill,
Made women, bend low at their conqueror's will;
By the far Mississippi the Illini shrank,
When the trail of the *Tortoise* was seen on the bank.

"On the hills of New England the Pequod turned pale,
When the howl of the *Wolf* swelled at night on the gale;
And the Cherokee shook, in his green smiling bowers,
When the foot of the *Bear* stampt his carpet of flowers."

Street's "Frontenac."

These Hollanders were so remote from the Jamestown settlement, and all New England being a wilderness untrodden by any European resident, that they were not disturbed. The Plymouth Company complained that they were intruders on their domain; and King James growled; and a word of warning was given by Captain Dermer of an English ship which, one fine morning in June, 1619, while on its way to Virginia, sailed through Long Island Sound, and lost an anchor in its encounter with the eddies of Hell Gate. That commander thought he was the first discoverer of that "most dangerous cataract" and the flowery islands between which he sailed, but when he was fairly out upon the Bay of New York, he saw the smoke of cottages on Manhattan, and was saluted by Hollanders. He did not stop then to talk to the intruders, but on his return he felt it to be his duty to go in and warn the traffickers to leave his majesty's domain as quickly as possible. "We found no Englishmen here, and hope we have not offended," replied the good-natured Dutchmen, and went on smoking their pipes, planting their gardens, and catching beavers and otters, as if they had never heard the voice of Captain Dermer, the

CATCHING AN OTTER.

"loving subject" of the king of England. The sounds of royal bluster that came occasionally from Great Britain did not deter the States-General from helping *their* "loyal subjects" in New Netherland, and they proceeded to charter the "Dutch West India Company," making it a great commercial monopoly by giving it almost regal powers to colonize, govern, and defend, not only that little domain on the Hudson, but the whole unoccupied coasts of America from Newfoundland to Cape Horn, and the western coasts of Africa from the Cape of Good Hope far northward.

That charter contained all the guarantees of freedom in social, political, and religious life necessary to the founding of a free state. Republicanism was recognized as the true system of government, and home, in its broadest and purest sense, as the prime element of political strength. No stranger was to be questioned concerning his nativity or his creed as matters which concerned the state. "Do you wish to build, to plant, and to become a citizen?" was the sum of their catechism when a new comer appeared. If the answer should be satisfactory, he was to be welcomed. That charter was granted on the 3d of June, 1620, at the time when the stricken Pilgrims at Plymouth, on the coast of Massachusetts, were cultivating their first fruit-gardens and cornfields.

The government of the West India Company was vested in five separate chambers of managers, composed of members in different parts of Holland. General executive powers were entrusted to a board of nineteen delegates, of whom about one-half were to reside in Amsterdam, and one was to represent the States-General. The government agreed to furnish the Company, in case of war, with sixteen armed ships, of three hundred tons burden each, to assist in maintaining their rights,—these, with an equal number of the Company's ships-of-war to be under the command of an admiral appointed by the States-General. Whilst the Company might make conquests of territories and treaties with native chiefs at their own risk, they were required to submit the instructions to their governors to the approval of the home government; and their officers were all required to take the oath of allegiance to the States-General.

It was two years after obtaining this charter before the Company was organized. It was an armed commercial monopoly, the chief object of which was traffic and the humbling of Spain and Portugal, and not colonization. Meanwhile, the Plymouth Company had obtained the coveted new charter already mentioned. By it their king conferred upon them almost regal powers. Without the consent of the Plymouth Company, no ships might enter any harbor on the American coast between Newfoundland and the latitude of Philadelphia; not a fish might be caught within three miles of the American coast; not a skin trafficked for in the forests, nor an emigrant live upon the soil. That extraordinary charter had been signed by the king a week before the arrival of the *May-Flower* off Cape Cod, with the Pilgrims; and that little colony who had braved the terrors of the Atlantic for the sake of freedom, were subjected, prospectively, to an almost irresponsible despotism. The House of Commons, alarmed because of this delegation of despotic power to a grasping company of traders, presented the patent as the first of "the public grievances of the kingdom." The French ambassador in London protested against it because Canada was included within the limits of the Plymouth Company's charter; and a little later the captain of a French vessel, anchored in the mouth of the Hudson River, attempted to set up the arms of France there, and take possession of the country in the name of his king. The Dutch, too, were concerned in the matter, for if the powers granted to the Plymouth Company might be exercised without hindrance, New Netherland would be useless to them.

In defiance of the House of Commons, King James upheld the monopoly. He scolded the representatives of the people, paid no attention to the Frenchman's protest, and reminded the States-General of Holland that Dutchmen were unlawfully seated upon the domain of a chartered English Company. The Hollanders at the Hague were as little moved by the covert threats of the British monarch as were those at Manhattan by Captain Dermer's warning. The complaint, however, had a useful result. It induced the West India Company, before its final organization, to take measures for securing the rights of eminent domain in New Netherland, in accordance with the principles of English policy which declared that first occupation gave those rights. So it was that the attention of that powerful Company was called from traffic to the founding of a permanent agricultural colony in America.

At that time there were thousands of refugees from persecution in the Netherlands. Among these were many of French extraction, who spoke the French language, called Walloons. They had inhabited the southern Belgic provinces of Hainault, Namur, Luxemburg, Limburg, and a part of the bishopric of Liege. When the northern provinces of the Netherlands formed their union more than forty years before, these southern provinces, whose inhabitants were mostly Roman Catholics, declined to join the confederation. There were many Protestants in those provinces, and they were made to feel, in all its rigor, the lash of persecution in the hands of the Spaniards. Thousands of them fled to Holland, where strangers of every race and creed were welcomed. There were the Walloons, a hardy, industrious, and skillful race of men and women, who introduced many useful arts into their adopted country. There they established their peculiar mode of public worship, and were soon ranked among the most thrifty, honest, and religious inhabitants. They were numerous in Amsterdam and Leyden, and were on friendly terms with the Puritan refugees from England. Like those Puritans they heard, from time to time, the enticing stories about the beauty and fertility of Virginia, and some of them desired to emigrate to America. They applied to the British ambassador at the Hague for permission and encouragement. He referred them to his king, and James submitted the matter to the London Company. The latter were not liberal enough in their proffered conditions to induce the Walloons to go. The States-General hearing of the movement commended them and their project to the West India Company. The latter perceived the great advantage which such emigrants would be to them in founding a permanent industrial colony in New Netherland, and took measures immediately to secure them. An agreement was made with several families, and in the spring of 1623, the emigrants were ready for departure for their new home.

The Company, anxious to commence their settlement with a sufficient number of willing hands, fitted out the *New Netherland*, a ship of two hundred and sixty tons burden, in which thirty families, consisting of one hundred and ten men, women and children, embarked. They were provided with agricultural implements, cows, horses, sheep and swine, and a sufficient quantity of household furniture to make them comfortable. The command of the ship was given to Cornelius Jacobsen May, of Hoorn, who was to remain in New Netherland as first director or governor. His lieutenant was Adrien Joris. The vessel sailed from the Texel early in March, and taking the long and tedious southern route by way of the Canaries and the West Indies, to avoid the storms of the northern Atlantic, they did not reach their destined haven until the beginning of May, where they found the French vessel above mentioned lying at anchor. The yacht *Mackerel* had just come down the Hudson. With two pieces of cannon taken from the fort at Manhattan, she compelled the Frenchman to desist, and convoyed his vessel out to sea. He went round to the Delaware on the same errand, and received similar treatment from the Dutch traders who were seated on its banks, when he sailed for France. With this ridiculous feat ended attempts of the French to assert jurisdiction below the forty-fifth parallel.

On a beautiful morning in May the Walloons landed from the *New Netherland*, in small boats, upon the rocky shore where Castle Garden now is. They made a picturesque appearance as they ascended the bank in their quaint costume, every man carrying some article of domestic use, and many women each carrying a babe or small child in her arms. They were cor-

LANDING OF THE WALLOONS.

dially welcomed by the resident traders and friendly Indians, and were feasted under a tent made of sails stretched between several trees. Under that tent a Christian teacher, who accompanied the settlers, offered up fervent thanksgivings to Almighty God for his preserving care during the long voyage, and implored His blessing upon the great undertaking before them. May then read his commission, which made him first director of New Netherland, and formally assumed the governorship of the colony and country.

Traditions have told us that these emigrants were immediately scattered to different points to form settlements, and so to secure a wide domain for the West India Company. Some, it is said, settled on Long Island and founded the City of Brooklyn; others went up the Connecticut River to a point near the site of Hartford, and built Fort Good Hope; others planted themselves in the present Ulster County in New York, and others founded Albany, where the Dutch had erected a military work and named it Fort Orange. Others, it is said, went to the Delaware and began a settlement at the mouth of Timber Creek, on the east side of the river, a few miles below the site of Philadelphia, and built a small fortification which they named Fort Nassau. The settlers engaged in this enterprise, it is said, were four young couples who were married on ship-board, and eight seamen who managed a little yacht that conveyed them to the South River, as the Delaware was called. This was to distinguish it from the North River, as the Hudson was then called, and which yet retains that name.

When May's lieutenant, Joris, returned to Amsterdam with a ship laden with furs worth over ten thousand dollars, and reported that the settlers were "getting bravely along," the Company were delighted, and sent out ships with cattle, horses, sheep, swine, farming implements and seeds for their use, and more emigrants. Political affairs in Europe were now favorable to the enterprise. King James of England, angered because of the failure of his son Charles to win the hand of a Spanish princess, had leagued with the Dutch against Spain. At his death, his son became King Charles the First, and he renewed the league with the States-General in a still stronger bond. This alliance with the British sovereign promising non-interference, on his part, in the growth of a permanent colony in New Netherland, the West India Company proceeded to lay the political foundations of a state. They commissioned Peter Minuit director-general or governor of the colony, with a council of seven men, a secretary of state, who was also keeper of the Company's accounts, and a *schout* or sheriff, who was also public prosecutor or manager of the revenue. The council was invested with all local legislative, judicial and executive powers, subject to the jurisdiction of the Amsterdam College or Chamber of Nineteen. The Council were empowered to administer justice in all criminal cases to the extent of imprisonment, but each capital offender "must be sent, with his sentence, to Holland."

Governor Minuit arrived at Manhattan in the ship *Sea-Mew*, at the beginning of May, 1626. So soon as he was installed in office, he opened negotiations with the Indians for the purchase of the island, so as to procure a more valid title to its possession than that of discovery and occupation. It was estimated that it contained about twenty-two thousand acres of land, and it was purchased for the West India Company for the sum of about twenty-four dollars. A fort was immediately staked out by the engineer Frederick, at the lower point of the island, where the "Battery" and its stately trees now are, the plan of which called for a work faced with stone and having four angles, by which the bay in front, and the East and Hudson Rivers on its flanks, might be commanded by cannon. Before the work was finished, it was named Fort Amsterdam, and afterward the city that grew up there was called New Amsterdam. It retained that name until the province was surrendered to the English, when it received the title of New York. The States-General constituted the province a county of Holland with an armorial distinction of a count. Its great seal bore the device of a shield, with an escutcheon enclosed in a chain, emblematic of union, and bearing the figure of a beaver. The crest was the coronet of a count.

While Fort Amsterdam was a-building an event occurred, the sad effects of which were felt long afterwards. Two adult Indians and a small boy, of a tribe in Westchester county, went from their homes to the Dutch settlement with beaver-skins to barter with the Hollanders at the fort. They followed the beaten trail along the East River to Kip's Bay (foot of Thirty-fourth street), where it diverged westward to the pond and marsh formerly known as *The Collect*, on the borders of which, on Centre street, New York, the Halls of Justice or the "Tombs" now stand. Near that pond, three farm-servants in the employ of Governor Minuit, robbed the Indians of their property and then murdered the men. The boy escaped. He vowed vengeance; and in after years, when he was a stalwart brave, he fearfully executed his vow. The murder was unknown to the Dutch authorities for a long time, and the guilty men probably escaped punishment.

When the stock of the Dutch West India Company was secured, and the several boards of direction were chosen, the College of XIX gave to the Amsterdam Chamber the exclusive management of the affairs of the province of New Netherland. Brodhead enumerates among the prominent members of that Chamber, Jonas Witsen, Hendrick Hamel, Samuel Godyn, John de Laet, the historian; Killian Van Rensselair, Michael Pauw, and Peter Evertsen Hulft. The names of these men were identified with the first European possession of the States of New York, New Jersey, Delaware, Pennsylvania, and Connecticut. The Company took measures immediately to secure their title to the domain by more extended actual occupation. They had taken possession of the country before their final organization, by virtue of their charter, because they knew how jealous were the English; and to give a show of actual occupation, they had sent trading vessels which bore instructions to the officers at Manhattan and on the North River, and, as we have seen, proceeded to build fortifications.

Within seventeen years after the discoveries of Hudson, the foundations of the great commonwealth of New York were laid by *families*, most of whom were voluntary exiles from their native land for the sake of freedom of thought and action. These were the first seeds of the state. To these were added, at the season of germination, noble plants from Holland, of genuine Hollanders, who brought with them those principles of toleration which lie at the foundations of a truly Christian state and give it sustenance. The community of their capital was very soon as cosmopolitan as their mother city of Amsterdam, of which Andrew Marvell quaintly wrote:

"Hence Amsterdam, Turk, Christian, Pagan, Jew,
Staple of sects and mint of schism grew;
That bank of conscience where not one so strange
Opinion, but finds credit and exchange;
In vain for Catholics ourselves we bear—
The *Universal Church* is only there."

New Amsterdam gave to the state and nation a race in whose veins courses the blood of Teuton, Saxon, Celt and Gaul. The colonists from Holland exhibited, from the beginning, a more enlarged vision of the rights of conscience and respect for the dignity of personal freedom, than any other of the early American settlers. Their passion for far-reaching commerce and adventurous enterprise has ever hovered over Manhattan Island like a tutelar deity, during all its social and political vicissitudes, and has made New York City the commercial emporium of the Western Continent.

SEAL OF NEW NETHERLAND.

CHAPTER V.

THE PLYMOUTH COMPANY IN PARLIAMENT—FIRST DEBATE IN PARLIAMENT ON AMERICAN AFFAIRS—GRANTS OF TERRITORY EAST OF MASSACHUSETTS—SIR WILLIAM ALEXANDER'S DOMAIN—EMIGRATION PLAN OF GORGES AND MASON—SETTLERS IN NEW HAMPSHIRE—DISSOLUTION OF THE PLYMOUTH COMPANY—GORGES GOVERNOR-GENERAL OF NEW ENGLAND—FOUNDING OF THE COLONY OF NEW HAMPSHIRE—GEORGE CALVERT (LORD BALTIMORE) SEEKS A CHARTER FOR MARYLAND—HIS SON RECEIVES IT—ITS CHARACTER—VOYAGE OF EMIGRANTS TO MARYLAND—FIRST SETTLEMENT IN MARYLAND, AND FOUNDING OF ITS CAPITAL.

WHILST French and English colonists from free Holland were planting settlements on the Delaware and Hudson Rivers and the borders of Cape Cod Bay, a seed-time had again begun on that portion of the soil of New England now covered by the States of New Hampshire and Maine. Sir Ferdinando Gorges was the chief promoter of this cultivation. He had been the controlling spirit in the Plymouth Company, from the beginning, and the chief instrument in procuring the despotic charter for the Plymouth Council. For its existence and powers he contended fearlessly before the hostile Parliament, standing firmly upon the king's prerogative. In that contest he had a powerful coadjutor in Sir George Calvert, a representative of Yorkshire, and who afterward became the founder of Maryland. Educated at Oxford; taught wisdom by travels; fostered in public life by Sir Robert Cecil, and through him advanced to the honors of knighthood; employed as one of the Secretaries of State when the Pilgrims were preparing to depart for America, and being possessed of a handsome person, winning manners and fluency of speech, he was very popular among all classes, and had been elected to a seat in the House of Commons by an immense majority. He had sought refuge from controversy (privately at first) in the bosom of the Roman Catholic Church. As that Church paid all due deference to the king as sovereign, it was not regarded with disfavor by James, and Sir George was an ever-welcome guest at the palace, for he was a thorough courtier.

It was a notable scene in the House of Commons, then convened for the first time in seven years, when Gorges appeared before that body to show cause why the charter should not be annulled, or its despotic powers abridged.

The king was present to defend his prerogative if it should be assailed. Gorges and Calvert were opposed by Sir Edwin Sandys, the wise statesman and friend of Virginia, and by the then venerable Sir Edward Coke, who had been Lord Chief-Justice of England. Coke was a member of Parliament and of the Privy Council, and he then began his famous contest with the king, which resulted in a curious exhibition of wrath and despotism on the part of James. Coke had procured the opposition of Parliament to the proposed marriage of the Prince of Wales to a Spanish princess, as dangerous to Protestantism in England. The angered king denounced the address which the House of Commons presented to him on the subject as an unlawful interference with his prerogative; mentioned the name of Coke, the author of it, as a culprit; and in a letter to the Speaker, declared his intention to "punish any man's misdemeanor in Parliament as well during the sitting as after." This threat was aimed at Coke, who immediately moved a protestation for the privilege of the House, setting forth the right of every member to freedom of speech, and like "freedom from all impeachment, imprisonment or molestation," on account of anything said or done in Parliament. It was carried and entered in the journals. On hearing of this act, the king immediately prorogued or dissolved Parliament, sent for the journals of the House, and with his own hand tore out the offensive record. Then he caused the arrest of Coke and others, in execution of his threat, and confined him in the Tower several months, when he was released on the petition of Prince Charles.

SIR EDWARD COKE.

In the matter of the charter, Sandys pleaded for the freedom in fishing and of general commerce, which was then becoming the staple of wealth for England. "The fishermen hinder the plantations," replied Calvert; "they choke the harbors with their ballast, and waste the forests by improvident use. America is not annexed to the realm nor within the jurisdiction of Parliament; you have therefore no right to interfere." "We make laws for Virginia," said another member; "a bill passed by the Commons and the Lords, if it receives the king's assent, will control the patent." Sir Edward Coke argued with numerous references to the statutes of the realm, that as the charter was granted without regard to pre-existing rights, it was necessarily void. This attack upon his prerogative aroused the angry monarch, who was sitting near the Speaker's chair, and he blurted out some silly words about the "divine right of kings," when the Commons, in defiance of his wrath, passed a bill giving freedom to commerce in spite of the charter. That bill had not gone through all the forms of legislation when the king broke up the Parliament for reasons just mentioned.

James, in the exercise of his prerogative, issued a proclamation forbidding any vessel to approach the shores of North Virginia without the special consent of the Plymouth Company. The Company commissioned Francis West admiral of New England, and sent him to protect their chartered rights. His police force was too feeble for so wide a domain, and the fishermen, in their fast-sailing shallops, eluded his grasp. The next Parliament proceeded to perfect what the former one had begun. The House was led by Coke, lately released from the Tower. "Your patent," he said to Gorges from the Speaker's chair, "contains many particulars contrary to the laws and privileges of the subject; it is a monopoly, and the ends of private gain are concealed under color of planting a colony." In debate, he said, "Shall none visit the sea-coast for fishing? This is to make a monopoly upon the seas, which want to be free. If you, alone, are to pack and dry fish, you attempt a monopoly of the wind and sun." The bill passed, but never received the signature of the king. The monopolists, discouraged by the opposition of the Commons, lowered their pretensions, and many of the patentees withdrew their interests in the Company. Those who remained, like Gorges, now did little more than issue grants of domain in the north-eastern parts of America.

This was the first debate on American affairs in the British Parliament; and it is a singular fact that in the course of it the supreme authority of the National Legislature over the American colonies was plainly asserted, the attempted exercise of which, in the matter of taxation, led to the old war for independence, one hundred and fifty years afterward, and the dismemberment of the British empire.

Before this disaster to the hopes of the Plymouth Company, grants of domain had been made. The first was to its secretary, Captain John Mason, who had been governor of Newfoundland. It embraced the country in Massachusetts between Salem and Newburyport, inland to the sources of the Merrimac River, and all the islands on its sea-front within three miles of the coasts. To forestall French settlements in the East, and to secure the country to Protestants, Gorges procured a grant to Sir William Alexander of the whole main eastward of the St. Croix River, excepting a small portion of Acadié. Sir William was Secretary of State from Scotland, and author of a hundred sonnets and some dull tragedies. The domain was named New Scotland. The charter being in Latin, it was written *Nova Scotia*, and has ever since retained that name. The baronet was invested with the regal privileges of a count-palatine, in 1630, and was created Earl of Stirling and Viscount of Canada. The domain was created a fief or dependence of the Scottish crown, and an attempt was made to establish a Scotch settlement there. It failed. Alexander lacked the energy necessary for such an undertaking.

When the suit of Charles for the hand of the Spanish princess was ended, he sought and obtained that of Henrietta Mary, sister of the King of France. Their marriage, in 1625, promised friendly relations between the two countries, notwithstanding she was a Roman Catholic; but the folly and baseness of the Duke of Buckingham, the court favorite, who had negotiated the union, soon plunged the two nations into war, the effects of which were seen in America. Sir David Kirk was sent with ships and soldiers to conquer Canada; and then occurred the surrender of Quebec to the English, mentioned in a previous chapter. It was a barren victory, for at almost the same time, Canada, Cape Breton, and undefined Acadié were restored to the French by treaty.

Meanwhile, Gorges and Mason had projected plans for a very extensive colonization. They obtained a patent for the country along the coast of New England between the Merrimac and Kennebec Rivers, and back to the St. Lawrence, under the title of the "Province of Laconia." It was represented to be a terrestrial paradise in beauty and fertility. Settlements at various points were projected and attempted, but none seem to have become permanent until about the year 1630. Mason and Gorges had agreed to divide their territory at the Piscataqua River, and in 1629 the former obtained a patent for the country between that river and the Merrimac, and gave it the name of New Hampshire. He built a house at the mouth of the Piscataqua, in 1631, and named the spot Portsmouth. He had been governor of Portsmouth, in Hampshire county, England, and these names he transferred to his new territory and first permanent settlement. Four years afterwards he died. His widow tried in vain to manage his large landed estate profitably. It passed into the possession of his retainers in payment for their services. These settlers were now left to themselves to fashion an independent state, but it was of slow growth. There was then only one agricultural settlement in all New England, excepting in Massachusetts, and scarcely the germ of a state had appeared. The colonists were mostly squatters, and moved frequently from place to place. They were chiefly hunters and fishermen, and cultivated the soil only for the production of a few vegetables and a little maize or Indian corn. Their huts were scattered along the harbors; and when some families came to Maine to establish a farming community, they were laughed at by the older residents as visionaries, and they went to the Plymouth colony. The whole enterprise was unprofitable to the proprietors. From the beginning the expenses had been greater than the receipts, and now the jealousy of different parties threatened the Company with utter ruin, whilst the French, resolved to maintain their hold upon New France, were building huts at the mouth of the Penobscot, and threatening to seize the territory between that river and the Kennebec. The Indians, too, were showing restlessness.

FISHERMEN ON THE COAST OF NEW ENGLAND.

In this unpromising state of the affairs of the Plymouth Company, Gorges was again summoned before the House of Commons to show cause why the charter should not be revoked. The merchants were restive under the restrictions of the monopoly; the Commons regarded it as a royal instrument; churchmen looked upon it as a foe to prelacy, because Puritans were sheltered on its domain; and the new king, Charles (whose father had died in 1625), suspected the New England colonists were enjoying liberties inconsistent with the royal prerogative. Charles was as bigoted a believer in the divine right of kings as his father, and that belief manifested in practice proved his ruin.

Gorges defended the Company against the various charges with vigor, but he and his associates perceived that further contention for its existence would be useless. Therefore they prepared for its dissolution by dividing North Virginia into twelve royal provinces, assigning each to persons named; and at their last meeting in April, 1635, they caused to be entered upon their minutes the following record: "We have been bereaved of friends; oppressed by losses, expenses and troubles; assailed before the Privy Council again and again with groundless charges; and weakened by the French and other foes without and within the realm, and what remains is only a breathless carcass. We, therefore, now resign the patent to the king, first reserving all grants by us made and all vested rights—a patent we have holden about fifteen years."

The king appointed eleven of his Privy Council a "Board of Lords Commissioners of all the American Plantations," and committed to them the general direction of colonial affairs. Gorges, then sixty years of age, and robust in mind and body, was appointed Governor-General over New England. A ship-of-war was in preparation to bring him to America, but was broken in the launching, and the baronet never crossed the Atlantic Ocean. His nephew, William Gorges, was sent over as his lieutenant, to administer the government. He made his headquarters at Saco, where he found about one hundred and fifty inhabitants governed by a voluntary social compact. There he established a regular government on the 28th of March, 1636, the first within the State of Maine. Soon afterward a royal charter made the elder Gorges lord proprietor of a large territory in that region, called the "Province or County of Maine." Gratified by this mark of royal favor, he began energetically in his old age to devise laws for his palatinate, such as a soldier and royalist would be likely to conceive, but they were little heeded in America. Gorges lived eight years in the enjoyment of his vice-regal honors, and soon after his death his province passed under the jurisdiction of Massachusetts.

Feeble and scattered settlements grew in New Hampshire, and in 1641 these formed a union with the flourishing Massachusetts colony, and remained a part of that province until 1680, when the king ordered their separation, and the more feeble partner became a royal province. Its first governor (John Cutts) was appointed by the Crown, who was assisted by a council also made by royal appointment; and there was a house of representatives elected by the people. Then was laid the foundation of the Commonwealth of *New Hampshire*.

Sir George Calvert has been alluded to as the founder of Maryland. He was a thorough courtier, and one of the most brilliant and able of the supporters of the royal prerogative. King James knighted him in 1617, and in

1619 he was commissioned one of the principal Secretaries of State. He was then thirty-seven years of age. For a few years afterward he was one of the most active of James's courtiers.

Calvert had taken great interest from early youth in the discovery and settlement of foreign countries. He was a member of the East India Company, and also of the London Company, by whom Virginia was colonized. The same year when the *May-Flower* came to America, he purchased a part of Newfoundland, and named his domain *Avalon*. He at once took vigorous measures for planting an English colony there, but failed. At about the same time his son Cecil married the beautiful Anne, daughter of the Earl of Arundel, who was a member of the Roman Catholic Church. This union brought him into more intimate relations with distinguished persons of that sect. Among them was Gondamar, the Spanish ambassador in London, and Tillières, the French ambassador at the same court. The influence of these men soon wrought a change in Calvert's religious thoughts. He became an advocate for the Spanish match, on the floor of the House of Commons; and he inflamed the resentment of King James against that body by giving him a highly-colored account of their proceedings in the matter. Finally, in the summer of 1624, his adherence to the Church of Rome became so palpable, that he was compelled to abandon the Secretaryship. Early the following March, James gave him an Irish peerage by creating him "Baron of Baltimore in the County of Longford." Sixteen days afterward the monarch died. When his successor came to White Hall and the oath of allegiance and supremacy was offered to Lord Baltimore as one of the Privy Council, he declined to take it, and retired to Ireland bearing a cordial letter of introduction and good-will from his king to the Lord Deputy of that country.

The Roman Catholics of England were suffering much persecution at that time from the Puritans on one side, who were daily increasing in strength, and from the Churchmen on the other; and Lord Baltimore desired to provide an asylum for them in America. In the summer of 1627 he visited Avalon to inspect it in person, with a view of planting a Roman Catholic colony there. He went in a ship armed with twenty cannon, as a protection against the French. A few friends and some priests accompanied him. After remaining a few months he returned to England, and the next spring he sailed again for Newfoundland with his second wife and all his children, excepting the married ones.

The following winter was a very severe one. In the spring he sent his children home; and at the beginning of autumn, with his wife and retainers, he sailed for Virginia, arriving at Jamestown in October. When he appeared before Governor Harvey and his council, and was asked what his purpose was, he answered: "To plant and dwell." "Will you take the oath which we all have taken?" asked the governor. "I cannot with a good conscience," his lordship answered. "Then you must leave with the first ship hence to England," said Harvey. He did so, leaving his wife and retainers to winter in Virginia. He returned for them in 1630, and brought with him a patent from King Charles for a territory south of the James River, for the rigors of the climate and the barrenness of the soil of Avalon, and the menaces of the French, had determined him to abandon his domain on Newfoundland. The Virginia Company made so much opposition to his new charter that he was induced to surrender it and accept one for territory north and east of the Potomac River, and embracing the Chesapeake Bay, which he had explored.

Lord Baltimore desired to call that chartered domain Crescentia; but in deference to the king, when the charter was drawn up, the space for the name was left blank that his Majesty might fill it as he pleased. When Baltimore appeared before Charles to receive his signature to the document, the monarch asked: "What will you call the country?" His lordship referred the matter to his Majesty. "Then let us name it after the queen," said Charles. "What do you think of Mariana?" The expert courtier dissented, because that was the name of the Spanish historian who taught the heresy that "the will of the people is higher than the law of tyrants." The king, still disposed to compliment his queen, said: "Let it be Terra Maria" —Mary Land. So it was that in the charter the province was named *Maryland*, in honor of Queen Henrietta Mary. Before the great seal of England was affixed to the patent, Lord Baltimore died in London. His son Cecil, the successor to his estates and titles, received the charter a few months afterward, dated June 20, 1632. The territory defined in the patent extended along each side of Chesapeake Bay from the fortieth degree to the mouth of the Potomac, and westward along the line of that river.

The Maryland charter, it is said, was drawn up by the hand of the first Lord Baltimore. It was evidently copied, substantially, from the one granted by Charles to his Attorney-General, Sir Robert Heath, for "Carolina," a territory south of the Roanoke River. It gave greater democratic privileges to the settlers under it than any yet issued by monopolist or monarch. It declared that the territory was "out of the plenitude of royal power;" the people were exempted from taxation by the crown except by their own consent; and other important political privileges were secured to them. It silently allowed religious toleration. While it directed the dedication and consecration of "churches, chapels, and places of worship" in accordance with the prescriptions of the ecclesiastical laws of England, the matter of a state theology was left entirely untouched, and within the legislative power of the colonists themselves. This toleration was a wise provision. It promoted the growth of the colony when it was established, for those who were persecuted by the Puritans of New England and the Churchmen of Virginia, went thither and found a refuge and peace. The charter also provided that the proprietary should have "free, full, and absolute power to enact all laws necessary for the common good, not, however, without the 'advice, consent, and approbation of the freemen of the province' or their representatives convoked in general assembly." This was the first instance of any provision having been made in an American patent for securing to the citizen a share in legislation.

CECIL, LORD BALTIMORE.

Armed with this charter, young Lord Baltimore set about the business of colonizing his domain, not for an asylum for his persecuted co-religionists, but chiefly for pecuniary gain. He appointed his half-brother, Leonard

Calvert, governor; and on the 22d of November, 1633, that kinsman and his brother, "with very near twenty other gentlemen of very good fashion, and three hundred laboring men" (so Lord Baltimore wrote to Wentworth, afterward Earl of Stafford), sailed from Cowes, in the Isle of Wight, in two ships, the *Ark* and *Dove*. The Calverts and the other "gentlemen" and some of the laborers were Roman Catholics, but a greater portion of the latter were Protestants, who took the oath of supremacy before leaving England. The emigrants were accompanied by two Jesuit priests, Fathers Andrew White and John Altham. They performed religious ceremonies at the point of departure, while a gentle east wind was blowing, "committing the principal parts of the ship to the protection of God especially, and of His most Holy Mother, and St. Ignatius, and all the guardian angels of Maryland."

The colonists took the tedious southern route by way of the Canaries and the West Indies. They had just escaped the perils of The Needles on the coast of the Isle of Wight, when the fear of the Turkish cruisers, then the terror of all Christian seamen, took possession of them. This fear was soon allayed by the appearance of a large English merchantman called *The Dragon*, well armed and bound for Angola, which would convoy them beyond the line of danger. When only two days out, they were overtaken by a furious gale. The *Dragon* turned back; the emigrant vessels went forward. The tempest increased when the night came on. The people of the *Dove*, the smaller vessel, notified the officers of the staunch *Ark* that in case of danger they would hang out a lighted lantern at the masthead. That signal of distress appeared at midnight for a few minutes, and then suddenly vanished. "All are lost!" thought the tenants of the *Ark*, and they grieved sorely. They had no doubt the *Dove*, with her precious freight of Christians, had gone to the bottom of the sea.

For three days the tempest swept the ocean, when suddenly the clouds gathered in fearful tumult, rain fell in torrents, and for a few minutes a dreadful hurricane threatened instant destruction to all in its path. It seemed as if "all the malicious spirits of the storm, and all the evil genii of Maryland had come forth to battle" against the good ship. Her mainsail was split from top to bottom; her rudder was unshipped, and she was left at the mercy of the winds and waves. In mortal terror the emigrants fell on their knees and prayed; and the Roman Catholics uttered vows in honor of "the Blessed Virgin Mary and her Immaculate Conception; of St. Ignatius, the patron saint of Maryland; St. Michael, and all the guardian angels of the same country." "I had betaken myself to prayer," says Father White, from whose narrative I have quoted, "when the sea was raging its worst, and (may this be to the glory of God) I had scarcely finished, when they observed that the storm was abating." After that the voyagers had delightful weather for three months, on the sea and on the land.

The *Ark* steered for Bonavista, one of the Cape de Verd islands, but altered her course and entered a harbor of the island of Barbadoes, on the eastern verge of the Antilles, where her people, all regarded as Roman Catholics, were coldly received, and charged extravagant prices for the provisions which they were compelled to purchase. The voyagers there learned that they had escaped a Spanish fleet lying at Bonavista, and also another peril in the port at which they had arrived. The slaves on the island had conspired to murder their masters, seize the first ship that should appear, and put to sea. The conspiracy had just been discovered, and its cruel purposes arrested. Their eyes were now greeted by the arrival there of the pinnace *Dove*, after a separation of six weeks. In the terrible gale she had put back while her lantern was at the masthead, and took refuge in the Scilly Isles, whence she sailed with a fair wind in search of her consort. After perilous wanderings over the waters, the *Dove* returned to the *Ark*.

The emigrants left Barbadoes after a short sojourn there, passed several islands of the Antilles, near one of which they encountered canoes full of naked and painted cannibals, and late in February they sailed in between the Capes of Virginia. They touched at Point Comfort and then went up to Jamestown, where royal letters borne by Calvert secured for them a friendly reception from Governor Harvey. Nine days they tarried pleasantly there, and then sailed for the Chesapeake and entered the broad mouth of the Potomac River. They were delighted with the great stream and the scenery on its banks, and gave to it the name of St. Gregory, in honor of the canonized Pope of that name. "Never have I beheld a larger or more beautiful river," wrote Father White. "The Thames seems a mere rivulet in comparison with it; it is not disfigured by any swamps, but has firm land on each side. Fine groves of trees appear, not choked with briers or bushes or undergrowth, but growing at intervals as if planted by the hand of man, so that you can drive a four-horse carriage, wherever you choose, through the midst of the trees. Just at the mouth of the river we saw the natives in arms. That night fires blazed throughout the whole country, and since they had never seen so large a ship, messengers were sent in all directions, who reported that a canoe, like an island, had come with as many men as there were trees in the woods."

The colonists sailed up the Potomac to the Heron Islands, and on Blackstone (which they named St. Clements) they landed at a little past the middle of March. The air was balmy, and sweet with opening spring flowers, and birds were filling the groves with rich melody. The shy natives came to them one after another, and were disarmed of all hostility by the kindness of the Britons. There, on the feast of the Annunciation (March 25th), the priests, in full canonicals, performed religious services, and administered the Lord's Supper for the first time in all that savage region. Then the whole company followed Governor Calvert and the priests in procession, bearing a huge cross which they had fashioned from a tree, and planted the symbol of Christianity and civilization at a chosen spot. The Roman Catholics, on bended knees, recited the "Litanies of the Sacred Cross" according to the Italian ritual. On the verge of the forest shadows, as wondering spectators of the strange scene, stood groups of savage men, women and children, clad in scanty and picturesque garments, with their emperor and his queen. He was at the head of a tribe called the Piscataways, and ruled over several small principalities, as did Powhatan, in Virginia.

Calvert proceeded at once to pay a visit of ceremony to the emperor to make a treaty of friendship and secure his influence over the surrounding tribes in favor of the colonists. In the *Dove* and another pinnace which they had procured at Jamestown, the governor, with Father Altham and a part of the emigrants, sailed up the river, leaving the *Ark* at anchor. Indians appeared here and there along the shores for a few minutes, and then disappeared in the woods, fleeing in alarm. They finally reached the village of Potomac, near Mount Vernon, whose king was a youth, and the people were ruled by his uncle as regent. Their fears were soon overcome, and Father Altham, through an interpreter from Jamestown, explained that their object in coming was to teach the Indians to lead better lives, and to live with them as brothers. The old sachem welcomed them, saying: "We will use one table—my people shall hunt for my pale-faced brother, and all things shall be in common between us."

The colonists, pleased with this peaceful conquest, went on to Piscataway, where they found five hundred warriors ready to dispute their landing. A parley ensued which ended in the emperor's venturing on board the *Dove*, where he was soon satisfied that his visitors were peaceful and powerful. He readily gave them permission to settle anywhere within his empire, near him or more distant. Calvert thought it better to settle nearer the mouth of the Potomac, and returned to St. Clements. There he found the natives very friendly and familiar, and watching with marvelling eyes the building of a brigantine, of timber brought over from England. They supposed the floating vessels had been each hollowed out of a single tree, as were their own canoes, and concluded England must be a mighty country where such big trees grew. They were awed by the flash and roar of the cannon, supposing them to be lightning and thunder under the control of the visitors.

The governor now explored the Wicomico River emptying into another (which they called St. George) twelve miles upward, and anchored at an Indian village of the same name, where he and his company were hospitably entertained that night, after holding a friendly conference with the reigning sachem, who gave up his own mat to Calvert to sleep on. The interpreter explained the object of the visit. The sachem said but little, but told them to examine the country. The governor did so the next day. Pleased

BUILDING OF A BRIGANTINE.

with the situation, the soil and the forest growth, he determined to plant his first settlement there, and make Wicomico the capital. He possessed delegated power to take possession of the country without leave or reward, in accordance with the custom of the strong mailed hand of Europeans at that time, whose creed ran—"We believe that Might makes Right," but *he* believed it to be more noble and wise to be just. He believed, too, that there was more worldly profit in honor than in dishonor—that "honesty" was "the best policy," and found it so. He entered into a treaty with the sachem for the *purchase* of a large portion of his domain. It was concluded; and Calvert gave the Indians some English cloth, axes, hoes, rakes, knives, and some trinkets for the women of little real value, for about thirty miles of territory, including the village; and he named the domain "Augusta Carolina." The Indians gave up to the colonists, for their immediate use, one-half of their village. Their houses were of "an oblong, oval shape," with a window in the roof which admitted light and also permitted the smoke to escape from the fire built in the centre of the room. They also agreed to give to the settlers one-half of their corn-grounds, which they were then planting, reserving the residue for their own use until the harvest should be gathered, when the whole of the purchased domain was to be given up to the Britons. They mutually agreed that if an injury should be done by one party, full satisfaction should be given by the other; and there was a tacit understanding that they should be allies in war. The king regarded this as essential; indeed it was the most cogent argument in favor of his making a treaty, for he wished a powerful ally, his territory having been desolated and his subjects driven from their homes, by the powerful "Susquehanocs" of the North.

On the 27th of March, 1634, Calvert took formal possession of the territory. The vessels came from St. Clements with the remainder of the emigrants, and when they landed, a cannon was fired to commemorate their arrival at the end of their weary wanderings. They built a store-house and a small battery and planted a portion of the soil. Then the governor, on a warm day in April, proceeded with a part of the company to a chosen spot fragrant with wild-flowers, about a mile from the river, where he laid out a capital city that was dedicated, with imposing religious ceremonies, to "the Blessed Virgin Mary," and was named St. Mary's. There the settlers immediately began to build, and were aided by the really gentle Indians. While they were so engaged, they were visited by Governor Harvey, of Virginia, who came in a pinnace with some of his councillors. Governor Calvert received him on board the *Ark* with great ceremony, and gave a banquet there to which several of the neighboring chiefs were invited. To the king of Patuxent, reigning eastward of St. Mary's, special attention was paid, for he was a conspicuous friend of the white people. He was seated at table between the two governors, when one of his followers seeing him there, and suspecting there was some evil design against his sovereign, would have leaped overboard, swam ashore, sped to his people and aroused them to arms with possible disastrous consequences, had he not been restrained by those near him, and assured by the king that all was right. When the warrior's suspicions were allayed and he was pacified, the monarch of the Patuxent addressed the other chiefs present, saying: "I love the English so well, that if they should go about to kill me, and I had so much breath as to speak, I would command the people not to avenge my death; for I know they do no such thing, except it were through mine own fault."

These settlers seem to have been exempted from the distresses which had befallen the earlier emigrants to other colonies. The surrounding native inhabitants were friendly; they had a genial climate; general good health prevailed; they had abundance of food, and the soil yielded to moderate tillage abundant fruit. They were vested with peculiar civil privileges; were not hampered by ecclesiastical restrictions; and a year after they had established their capital at St. Mary's, a legislative assembly, composed of the whole people—a purely democratic legislature—convened there. As their numbers increased by emigration, this method of legislation was found to be inconvenient, and in 1639 a representative government was established, the people being allowed to send as many delegates as they pleased. Then was founded the republican commonwealth of *Maryland.* It had been founded in justice, and by the exercise of kindness toward the native inhabitants; and, but for the wickedness of ambitious men, the white people and the Indians might have lived together in perfect harmony, for the savages were easily and powerfully impressed with a sense of gratitude for good treatment. This trait was exhibited by the king of the Piscataways, the most powerful tribe in Maryland. He was taken sick and forty conjurers tried to cure him by conjurations. He grew worse, when Father White asked and obtained permission to treat him. The priest gave him some medicine and bled him, when the king soon recovered his health. Grateful for the blessing, he begged the priest to baptize him, his queen, and their daughter, to prepare them to enter the Christian Church. In a chapel built of bark for the occasion, they and some chiefs were baptized; and in the afternoon the king and his queen were married according to Christian rites. Their daughter, as I have observed elsewhere, was sent to St. Mary's, to be educated.

CHAPTER VI.

CLAIMS OF THE DUTCH IN NEW ENGLAND—A DUTCH EMBASSY TO THE PILGRIMS—THE CAPITAL OF THE PILGRIMS—THE DUTCH AND ENGLISH IN THE VALLEY OF THE CONNECTICUT—FIRST ENGLISH SETTLEMENT THERE—THE DUTCH EXASPERATE THE INDIANS—EMIGRATION OF PURITANS TO THE CONNECTICUT VALLEY—CONFLICTING CLAIMS TO THE TERRITORY—HOOKER'S EMIGRATION—THE PEQUODS JEALOUS—WAR WITH THE PEQUODS—THEIR DESTRUCTION.

WE have observed that the Dutch who founded New Netherland and the city of New Amsterdam (now New York) extended their explorations and traffic east, west, north, and south. They even went as far as Narraganset and Cape Cod bays in search of the beaver and otter. As Captain Block had discovered the Connecticut River and named it the Fresh-Water, and had looked into Narraganset Bay, the Dutch felt that they had a legal claim upon those regions according to the English doctrine concerning the right of discovery. So early as 1623, the agent of the Dutch West India Company seems to have taken possession of the Connecticut River and the lands drained by its tributaries, in the name of the Company and of the States-General of Holland.

A peaceful and profitable trade might have been carried on with the natives of the Connecticut Valley, by the Dutch, had not the latter exasperated the Indians by the seizure of one of their chiefs and demanding a heavy ransom for his release. The savages threatened the intruders with violence, and the Dutch began to build a stockade fort for their own protection, at what is yet known as Dutch Point, near the City of Hartford. Wrath prevailed a long time. At length the Indians were pacified, and at their request the Dutch abandoned the fort.

A friendly intercourse was now opened between the Dutch on Manhattan and the English at New Plymouth. In the spring of 1627, Isaac de Rasieres, secretary of the colony of New Netherland, by order of Governor Minuit, wrote a letter to Governor Bradford, of Plymouth, officially informing him of the founding of a settlement and province on the Mauritius or Hudson's River, and assuring him that the Hollanders wished to cultivate friendly and commercial relations with the Pilgrims. Bradford reciprocated these friendly professions, but in his reply he warned the Dutch not to occupy or to trade in the country north of the fortieth degree of latitude, as that region was claimed by the Council of New England. He wished to maintain friendly relations with New Netherland, and proposed not to molest the Dutch provided they would refrain from trading with the natives on the waters at the very doors of the English. Minuit replied courteously, but firmly, that the Dutch had a right to traffic with the Narragansets as they had done for years. "As the English claim authority under the king of England," said Minuit, "so we derive ours from the States-General in Holland." Bradford was not disposed to contend, for obvious reasons. "For strength of men and fortification," he wrote to the Council for New England, "they [the Dutch] far excel us and all in this land."

Bradford made no reply to Minuit's letter. The latter finally sent a messenger to New Plymouth to invite the governor to send a deputy to Manhattan to confer orally with the authorities there. The messenger took with him a "rundlet of sugar and two Holland cheeses" as a present for Bradford, who entertained him generously in return. It was agreed that a commission should be sent to New Plymouth from Manhattan to confer upon all matters of intercourse. With De Rasieres at their head, such commissioners sailed in a bark laden with wampum and other things for traffic, and when they landed near one of the outposts of the Plymouth colony, the echoes of the forest and the attention of the Pilgrims were awakened by the braying of trumpets at the lips of sturdy Dutchmen. With the same noise the commissioners entered New Plymouth. They were hospitably entertained for several days at the table of the governor, whereat probably sat Elder Brewster, Miles Standish, Edward Winslow, Dr. Fuller and other passengers of the *May-Flower*. There the commissioners attended public worship on the Sabbath, of which De Rasieres gave a vivid account in a letter. "They assemble," he said, "by beat of drum, each with his musket or fire-lock in front of the captain's door. They have their cloaks on, and place themselves in order, three abreast, and are led by a sergeant without beat of drum. Behind comes the governor in a long robe. Beside him, on the right hand, comes the preacher, with his cloak on; on the left hand the captain, with his side-arms and his cloak on, and with a small cane in his hand. And so they march in good order, and each sets his arms down near him. Thus they are constantly on their guard, night and day," for they had excited the anger of the Indians.

The secretary also graphically described New Plymouth. "It lies on a slope," he said. "The houses are constructed of hewn planks, with gardens also inclosed behind and at the sides with hewn timber; so that their houses

PUBLIC WORSHIP AT PLYMOUTH BY THE PILGRIMS.

and court-yards are arranged in very good order, with a stockade against a sudden attack. At the ends of the streets are three wooden gates. In the centre, on the cross street, stands the governor's house, before which is a square inclosure, upon which four swivels are mounted, so as to flank along the streets. Upon the hill they have a large square house with a flat roof, made of thick sawn plank, stayed with oak beams; upon the tops of which they have six cannon, which shoot iron balls of four and five pounds weight, and command the surrounding country. The lower part they use for their church, where they preach on Sundays and the usual holidays." Such was the capital of the English colony six years after they had landed from the *May-Flower*, and at the time of the embassy of Secretary Rasieres. That

THE DUTCH ENTERING NEW PLYMOUTH.

mission opened a profitable trade between the two settlements, and led to the speedy planting of an English colony in the Valley of the Connecticut.

With a keen eye to self-interest, the Dutch advised the Pilgrims to leave their more sterile soil and make their home in the beautiful and fertile country on the banks of the Fresh-Water River, under the jurisdiction of New Netherland. The fertility of that region was set forth in glowing terms; and the stories of the Dutch were confirmed by native chiefs. One of these, of the Mohegan tribe, whose council fire was on the eastern bank of the Hudson, visited Governor Winthrop, of Massachusetts, in 1631, and with self-interest as strong as that of the Dutch, but rather more artfully concealed, he urged them to settle in the Connecticut Valley. He offered to give them lands, and an annual tribute of corn and beaver skins, if they would do so. The Mohegan chief's prime object was to so plant a barrier between his people and the powerful and warlike Pequods, whose seat was on the hills that stretch between New London and Stonington. The Puritans saw the selfish policy of both parties under the thin disguise of friendship, and declined to move in a body. They would not consent to become subjects of the Dutch nor to be made shields for the savages.

The stories of the "pleasant meadows" along the Connecticut River excited the attention of the English, and in 1632 Edward Winslow visited that region. He was delighted with the country, and confirmed all that Dutch embassadors and traders and savage chieftains had said about it. The fame of it had already reached Old England, and two years before Winslow's visit, the Council for New England had granted the soil of that region to the Earl of Warwick. That nobleman conveyed his chartered rights to the domain to other parties (Lords Say and Seal, Lord Brook, Mr. Saltonstall and others,) in 1632. In that conveyance the territory was defined as extending, "in a certain width throughout the main lands there, from the Western [Atlantic] Ocean to the South Sea" or the Pacific Ocean. These parties did not take immediate steps for colonizing the Connecticut Valley, and the ever-vigilant Dutch got there before them. The Dutch purchased the territory of the Indians, the rightful owners, and Commissioner Van Curler completed the redoubt already begun on Dutch Point, named it Fort Good Hope, and armed it with cannon.

Governor Bradford and Edward Winslow visited Governor Winthrop at Boston, and proposed an alliance for the purpose of taking immediate possession of the valley. Winthrop refused to join them in such an enterprise, but thought it necessary, in some formal way, to assert, promptly and firmly, the jurisdiction of the English over that now coveted region. He sent his bark the *Blessing of the Bay* on a trading voyage along Long Island Sound, her captain bearing a message to Manhattan, declaring that the "King of England had granted the river and country of Connecticut to his own subjects," and that the Dutch must "forbear to build there." The messenger and his companions were kindly treated by Governor Van Twiller, Minuit's successor, who, in a courteous letter to Winthrop, requested him to defer the "pretense or claim" to the Connecticut until their respective governments should agree upon the limit of the colonies. At the same time Van Twiller informed Winthrop that the Dutch had already purchased the soil and "set up a house with intent to plant."

These Dutchmen and initial "Yankees" were now playing a sharp game in diplomacy, with soft words. The Yankees outwitted the Dutchmen, and the Plymouth people outgeneraled those at Boston at first. At Plymouth was a company of "banished Indians"—families driven from the Connecticut Valley, with their chief, by the Pequods. From these the Plymouth settlers purchased a tract of land above Fort Good Hope. They prepared a house of wood, which they stowed in pieces on board of a bark commanded by Captain William Holmes. In this bark sailed the fugitive savages and some Englishmen, and went up the Connecticut River. When they approached Fort Good Hope, the commander of the fort hailed the little craft and demanded of Captain Holmes whither he was going, and for what purpose. "Up the river to trade!" answered the skipper. This little fib did not satisfy the suspicious Dutchmen, who rightly supposed that the intruders had orders to *settle* rather than *to trade*. "Heave to!" shouted the commander of the garrison standing by the side of a heavy gun, "or I'll shoot." "I must obey my commands," said the intrepid Holmes, and sailed by. The Dutchmen blustered, but did not shoot. The English landed above; hastily erected the house they had brought with them, and took possession of the country. They sent the bark back, palisaded their house, and prepared to maintain their position. This house was built on the site of Windsor, in Connecticut. So was begun the first English settlement in that region in the autumn of 1633.

WINTHROP AND VAN TWILLER'S LETTER.

When Van Twiller heard of this impertinent intrusion, he sent to Van Curler, at Good Hope, a protest to be delivered to Holmes, and a peremptory order for the latter to "depart forthwith with all his people and houses"—from that Dutch domain. "I am here," replied Holmes, "in the name of the King of England, whose servant I am, and here I will remain." Van Twiller stormed at this defiance, but prudently referred the matter to his superiors at Amsterdam. Before an answer could arrive, the subject became mixed with another of a serious nature. A Captain Stone had been on a trading voyage from Massachusetts to Virginia, and on his return ran into and up the Connecticut River to traffic with the Dutch garrison at Good Hope. He and his companions were treacherously seized and murdered by Pequods on the banks of the stream. This crime was soon followed by the massacre of some Indians friendly to the Dutch. Then Van Curler seized a guilty old sachem and some of his followers, and hanged them. This exasperated the Pequods. They flew to arms and declared war against the Dutch. They sought the friendship of the English, and for this purpose they sent four or five ambassadors to Boston to negotiate a treaty. These ambassadors appeared before the governor in all the barbaric splendor of paint and rich skins, gorgeous feathers and rude ornaments. A treaty was made which provided that the Pequods, in consideration of the passive friendship of the English, were to surrender to the latter the Connecticut Valley and the remaining two murderers of Captain Stone's party, and pay a large tribute of wampum and beaver-skins. So Winthrop gained a great advantage over Bradford in the accession of territory, and both parties won powerful allies, as they supposed, in the work of expelling the Dutch from the Connecticut Valley. At the same time, the position and security of the settlers at Windsor were strengthened.

At about this time, Van Twiller received instructions from Amsterdam, to maintain possession of the Connecticut at all hazards. He sent seventy men with arquebuses, swords, trumpets, and banners to dislodge the settlers at Windsor. The latter made a bold stand. After much blustering and a great deal of noise, there was a parley, when the Dutch withdrew and friendly relations were established. The region was opened for an influx of immigrants from Massachusetts Bay. Permission for such immigration was given by the authorities there, without any territorial restraints. The question to whom does the Valley of the Connecticut belong—to the Dutch, the Pilgrims at Plymouth, the Puritans at Boston, or to the savages? was not considered; and in the autumn of 1635, sixty men, women, and children from the Puritan settlements journeyed westward through the forests to join the colony planted by Holmes at Windsor. During the previous summer, a few pioneers had explored the country. They went from Dorchester and Watertown to the beautiful valley, and their report stimulated emigration.

The exodus from Massachusetts Bay began late in October, when frost and snow-flurries were prophesying of an early coming of winter. With oxen for tillage and beasts of burden, and cows for the production of food, these emigrants made their way on foot through the pathless woods a hundred miles or more, sometimes wading miry swamps, sometimes climbing rugged hills or fording swift streams, the men carrying the smaller children, and the larger ones with their mothers trudging after. At the end of a wearisome journey of a month's duration, they descended into the Connecticut Valley, then white with snow, and found the river so hard frozen that a vessel which had been sent with supplies could not ascend it. It never tried to navigate that stream, for it was wrecked on the rocks near Point Judith in a gale.

At Wethersfield, and on the site of Hartford, these immigrants built log huts in the snow, and there they passed a dreary, bitter winter in great privation, for a vessel in which had been sent clothing and household furniture,

EMIGRANTS ON THEIR WAY TO THE CONNECTICUT.

was kept back by the ice. Snow fell to a great depth. Many cattle suffered and perished from want of food, and the settlers were threatened with the horrors of famine. In the face of this impending peril many of them made their way to the mouth of the river in the vain expectation of finding their food-bearing vessel, which, alas! had been beaten into pieces on the rocks.

When almost despairing, another vessel appeared, in which they sailed to Boston. The settlers whom they left behind subsisted much of the time upon acorns, Indian corn and malt, until the spring opened and supplies were sent to them from Massachusetts, then rapidly filling with emigrants. Twenty vessels had brought three thousand colonists to its shores during the year 1635.

Governor Winthrop's son John, then twenty-nine years of age, arrived at Boston from England in October. He bore a commission as governor of the Connecticut territory, from the proprietors of the soil. With him came Hugh Peters, his senior by six years, and Henry Vane, only twenty-four years of age, who were joint commissioners with him, instructed to build a fort and plant a colony at the mouth of the Connecticut River. They were directed to gather the scattered settlers near the fort; but these were left where they had planted themselves. Other measures were taken to secure the possession of the territory and peace of the colony. Governor Bradford had denounced as "an unrighteous and injurious intrusion," the settling of Massachusetts people upon the lands on the Connecticut which the Plymouth people had purchased from the Indians, not considering that the "Plymothians," as the Dutch called them, were equally intruders upon the territory of New Netherland, according to English doctrine. And the Connecticut commissioners perfected their usurpation of the territorial authority of the Netherlands by driving away, by force of arms, a Dutch vessel which came into the river to protect the rights of the West India Company. "Might makes right," was the stern rule among the nations then; and the cannon at the mouth of the river gave a warrant for the more important emigration of the English to the Connecticut Valley, which occurred in the summer of 1636. The dispute with the Plymouth people was amicably settled.

Arrangements having been made for the accommodation of new settlers on the site of Hartford, the Rev. Thomas Hooker, a zealous non-conformist minister, who came to Boston from his refuge in Holland, in 1633, led a company of one hundred men, women, and children thither in the summer of 1636. He was accompanied by the Rev. Mr. Stone. Their followers consisted of their families and congregations. The emigrants drove before them one hundred and sixty head of cattle. The cows of the herd, pasturing in grassy savannas which they found on the way, gave them an ample supply of fresh milk. They had no pathway, and were guided only by a compass. Through thickets and morasses, and over streams they made their way, clearing away here with axes, making causeways and bridges there with felled trees, and resting in shady groves. The women and children were conveyed in wagons drawn by oxen, and Mrs. Hooker, who was an invalid, was carried on a horse litter.

The company had ample provisions and were regaled on the way by delicious strawberries growing in abundance in open places. The songs of birds and the fragrance of flowers afforded them exquisite delight in the midst of the weariness of travel. They made easy stages, consuming a fortnight in the journey of a hundred miles. It was ended when, on the fourth of July, they stood on the beautiful banks of the Connecticut, under the shadows of great trees and trailing vines, and sang hymns of praise to the Good Father. On the following Sabbath, Mr. Hooker preached and administered the Lord's Supper in the little chapel on the site of Hartford, which the first colonists there had erected. Some of the new comers settled at Wethersfield, and others went further up the river and founded Springfield. There were now five feeble settlements in the Connecticut Valley. One of these was near the fort at the mouth of the river, and in honor of two of the proprietors of the territory, Lords Say and Brook, it was called Say-Brook.

In the very morning of this colonial era of Connecticut, dark clouds gathered black and threatening, and for awhile a storm impended which seemed ready to sweep the little settlements from the face of the earth in a moment. The fiery Pequods had become jealous of the English because the latter appeared to be on friendly terms with the Mohegans on the west and the Narragansets on the east, the bitter enemies of this warlike tribe. Over the Pequods, a famous sachem and chief named Sassacus was ruler. He was cool, calculating, treacherous, haughty, fierce and malignant, and he was the terror of the neighboring tribes. He ruled over twenty-six sagamores or inferior princes, and his domain extended from Narraganset Bay to the Hudson River, and over Long Island. His bravery won the unbounded admiration of his warriors, of whom almost two thousand were always ready to follow him wheresoever he might lead. Seeing the power of the few English in garrison at Saybrook, and dreading the strength and influence of more who would undoubtedly join them, he resolved to exterminate the intruders. By every art of persuasion and menace, he tried to induce the Mohegans and Narragansets to become his allies. The united tribes could put four thousand men on the war-path at one time, while among all the English in the Connecticut Valley, there were not more than two hundred and fifty men capable of bearing arms. How easily might those fierce pagans have annihilated the pale-faced Christians!

The Pequods moved cautiously. At first they were sullen. Then they kidnapped children; and finally they murdered Englishmen found alone in the forests or on the waters, and destroyed or made captive families on the borders of the settlements. It was evident that they intended to exterminate the white people in detail, and terror prevailed throughout the valley. This was heightened by the capture of a Massachusetts trading vessel by the allies of the Pequods on Block Island, killing the commander and plundering the vessel.

The authorities at Boston determined to punish the Pequods and awe them into quietude. For this purpose they sent a small military force, in three vessels, into Long Island Sound. This force killed some Indians on

ATTACK ON THE INDIANS ON BLOCK ISLAND.

Block Island, burnt their wigwams, broke their canoes in pieces, and cut down their growing corn. Then they went over to the Pequod country on the main, where they made demands which they could not enforce, burnt some wigwams, destroyed crops, and killed a few people. The expedition, weak in numbers and injudiciously conducted, was looked upon with contempt by the savages, and intensified their hatred of the white intruders. They sent ambassadors to the monarch of the Narragansets urging him to join them at once in a war of extermination, declaring, as a powerful plea, that the two races could not live together in the same land, and that the Indians, who would soon be the weaker party, would be scattered and destroyed like leaves in autumn.

At this critical juncture, a deliverer appeared in the person of Roger Williams, a Puritan minister, who had been driven out of Massachusetts by persecution and had taken refuge in the land of the Narragansets, who soon learned to love and respect him. He heard of the proposed alliance and perceived the danger. Unmindful of the cruel wrongs he had suffered at the hands of his Puritan brethren, he hastened in an open boat on a stormy day, across Narraganset Bay, to the dwelling of Miantonomoh near the site of Newport, on Rhode Island. He was the acting chief sachem of the Narragansets (for his uncle, Canonicus, the chief, was very old), and was revered by them all. There Williams found fierce ambassadors from Sassacus, urging their suit, and at the peril of his life he opposed them with arguments. "Three days and nights," Williams wrote to Major Mason, "my business forced me to lodge and mix with the bloody Pequod ambassadors, whose hands and arms, methought, reeked with the blood of my countrymen, murdered and massacred by them on Connecticut River, and from whom I could not but nightly look for their bloody knives at my own throat, also." Williams prevailed. He not only prevented the alliance, but induced Narraganset chiefs to go to Boston, where they concluded a treaty of peace and alliance with the colonists. So the Pequods were not only compelled to carry on their proposed war alone, but to fight the Narragansets.

This failure did not dishearten the Pequods. They kept the settlements on the Connecticut in a state of constant fear, all the autumn and winter. They plundered and murdered whenever opportunities offered. Barns were fired and cattle were killed by them; and the murders were sometimes accompanied by the most horrid atrocities. Finally, a band of a hundred Pequods attacked Wethersfield, killed seven men, a woman and a child, and carried away two girls. They had now slain more than thirty of the English, and the settlers were compelled to choose between flight and destruction, or war and possible salvation. They resolved to fight, having promise of aid from the eastern colonies.

At this time there were in the colonies two brave soldiers who had served in the Netherlands. These were Captains John Mason and John Underhill. The former had taken an active part in military and civil affairs in Massachusetts, and was now in Connecticut. The latter was an eccentric character, and might have been mistaken at one time for a friar and at another for a buffoon. He had been brought to Massachusetts by Governor Winthrop to teach the young colonists military tactics, which it was evident they would need. Under him the authorities of that colony and Plymouth placed two hundred men to aid the Connecticut people in their war.

It was not safe for the settlers in the valley to wait for their allies on the sea-coast. They placed ninety men under Mason, who rendezvoused at Hartford. With twenty of them, the captain hastened to reinforce the garrison at Saybrook. There he found Underhill, who had just arrived with an equal number of men. Mason hurried back, assembled his whole force, and with these and seventy warriors of the Mohegans under Uncas, he marched down to the fort. Uncas was of the royal blood of the Pequods, and had been a petty chief under Sassacus, but was now in open rebellion against his prince, and a fugitive. He gladly joined the English against his enemy, and Captain Mason as gladly accepted his services. As the war was begun by the Connecticut people, Captain Mason was regarded and obeyed as the commander-in-chief of the expedition.

It was determined in council to go into the Narraganset country and march upon the rear of the Pequods, where they would least expect an attack. In three pinnaces the expedition sailed eastward. As they passed the Pequod country, those savages concluded that the English had abandoned the Connecticut Valley in despair. It was a fatal mistake; and the relaxation which that belief caused, ruined them. They had no spies out beyond the Mystic River; and when the expedition landed near Narraganset Bay, Sassacus was rejoicing in a sense of absolute security from harm. So he continued to rejoice while the white people, joined by two hundred Narragansets and as many Niantics—more than five hundred warriors in all, pale and dusky—were marching swiftly and stealthily toward the citadel of his power.

That chief stronghold of Sassacus was on a hill a few miles northward from both New London and Stonington, near the waters of the Mystic River. It was a fort built of palisades, the trunks of trees set firmly in the ground close together, and rising above it ten or twelve feet, with sharpened points. Within this inclosure, which was of circular form, were seventy wigwams covered with matting and thatch; and at two points were sally-ports or gates of weaker construction, through which Mason and Underhill were destined to force an entrance. When the invaders reached the foot of the hill on which this fort stood, quite undiscovered, and arranged their camp, the sentinels could hear the sounds of noisy revelry among the savages in the fortress, which ceased not before midnight. Then all was still, and the invaders slumbered soundly. At two hours before the dawn on a warm June morning, they were aroused from sleep and arranged in marching order so as to break into the fort at opposite points and take it by surprise. The Indian allies had grown weak in heart, all but the followers of Uncas. They regarded Sassacus as a sort of god, and supposed he was in the fort. So they lagged behind, but formed a cordon in the woods around the fortress to arrest any fugitives who might escape.

In the bright moonlight the little army crept stealthily up the wooded slope, and were on the point of rushing to the attack when the barking of a dog aroused a sentinel and he gave the alarm to the sound sleepers within. Before they were fairly awake, Mason and Underhill burst in the sallyports. The terrified Pequods rushed out of the wigwams, but were driven back by swords and musket-balls, when the tinder-like coverings of the huts were set on fire. Within an hour about seven hundred men, women and children perished in the flames, and by the weapons of the English. The strong, the beautiful, and the innocent were doomed to a common fate with the blood-thirsty and cruel. The door of mercy was shut. Not a dusky human being among the Pequods was allowed to live. When all was over, the pious Captain Mason, who had narrowly escaped death by the arrow of a young warrior, exultingly exclaimed: "God is over us! He laughs his enemies to scorn, making them as a fiery oven. Thus does the Lord judge among the heathen, filling the place with dead bodies." And the equally if not more pious Dr. Mather afterward wrote: "It was supposed that no less than 500 or 600 Pequod souls were brought down to hell that day." Happily a better Christian spirit now prevails.

Sassacus was not in the doomed fort, but was at another near Groton, on the Thames, to which point Mason had ordered his vessels to come. As the English were making their wearisome way to the river, three hundred warriors came from the presence of Sassacus to attack them. The savages were soon dispersed. Most of the victors then sailed for the Connecticut, making the air vocal with sacred song. The remainder, with friendly Indians, marched through the wilderness to Hartford to protect the settlements in that vicinity. There warriors and clergymen, Christians and pagans, women and children, gathered in a happy reunion after great peril.

Sassacus sate sullenly and stately in his embowered dwelling, when the remnant of his warriors, who escaped from the citadel, came to tell him of the great disaster. They charged the whole of the misfortunes of the day to his haughtiness and misconduct. Tearing their hair, stamping violently, and with fierce gestures, they threatened to destroy him, and doubtless they would have executed the menace had not the blast of a trumpet startled them. From the head-waters of the Mystic came almost two hundred armed settlers from Massachusetts and Plymouth to seal the doom of the Pequods. The question, Shall we fight or flee? was soon answered at the court of Sassacus, for there was little time for deliberation. After a strong and hot debate, it was determined to flee. They set fire to their wigwams and the fort, and with their women and children hurried across the Thames and fled swiftly westward, with the intention of seeking refuge with the Mohawks beyond the Hudson.

The English hotly pursued the Pequods, with despairing Sassacus at their head. As the chase was kept up across the beautiful country bordering on Long Island Sound, a track of desolation was left behind, for wigwams and cornfields were destroyed, and helpless men, women and children were put to the sword. At last the fugitives took refuge in Sasco Swamp, near Fairfield, where they all surrendered to the English excepting the sachem and a few followers, who escaped to the Mohawks. A blow had been struck which gave peace to New England forty years. A nation had been destroyed in a day. But few of the once-powerful Pequods survived the national disaster. The last representative of the pure blood of that race was, probably, Eunice Mauwee, who died at Kent, in Connecticut, about the year 1860, at the age of one hundred years. The proud Sassacus, haughty and insolent in his exile, fell by the hands of an assassin among the people who had opened their arms to receive him; and his scalp was sent to the English, whom he hated and despised. He was the last of his royal line in power excepting Uncas, who now returned to the land of his fathers and became a powerful sachem, renowned in war and peace. He remained a firm friend of the English, and was buried among the graves of his kindred near the falls of the Yantic, in the City of Norwich, where a granite monument, erected by the descendants of his white friends, marks the place of his sepulchre.

CHAPTER VII.

A SETTLEMENT BEGUN AT NEW HAVEN—A PECULIAR GOVERNMENT ESTABLISHED THERE—THE DUTCH AND ENGLISH AT VARIANCE IN THE CONNECTICUT VALLEY—A GOVERNMENT FORMED AT HARTFORD—ROGER WILLIAMS IN MASSACHUSETTS—HIS BANISHMENT—WILLIAMS AND OTHERS FOUND PROVIDENCE—RHODE ISLAND SETTLED—FORM OF GOVERNMENT THERE—ANNE HUTCHINSON AND OTHERS DRIVEN FROM MASSACHUSETTS—WILLIAMS OBTAINS A CHARTER FOR RHODE ISLAND—INTOLERANCE IN MASSACHUSETTS—RECEPTION OF WILLIAMS ON HIS RETURN FROM ENGLAND.

WHEN peace and security were established in the Connecticut region after the destruction of the Pequods in the summer of 1637, a desire for emigrating thither was revived. At about that time several gentlemen destined to occupy conspicuous places in history as founders of a state arrived at Boston. These were Rev. John Davenport, a popular Puritan preacher of London, who had been persecuted by Archbishop Laud and taken refuge in Rotterdam. Another was Theophilus Eaton, an opulent London merchant and member of Mr. Davenport's congregation; and a third was Edward Hopkins, another rich London merchant and member of the same society. They were much attached to Mr. Davenport, and gladly came to share his voluntary exile from his native land.

At the time of the arrival of these gentlemen, society in Massachusetts was violently agitated by bitter theological discussions, which will be noticed hereafter. Mr. Davenport and his friends belonged to a school who sought to carry out in practice the idea of finding in the Scriptures a special rule for everything in church and state. For the purpose of trying an experiment in government on the basis of that idea, they desired an unoccupied field. From some of those who pursued the fugitive Pequods along the country bordering on Long Island Sound, they heard of the beauty and fertility of that region, and early in the autumn Mr. Eaton and a small party visited the country. He was charmed with a harbor on the north side of the Sound; and on the banks of a stream, which the Indians called Quinnipiack, he erected a hut, where some of the party passed the winter to try the climate. That was on the site of New Haven, Connecticut. The place had been called by the Dutch navigator, Block, who had anchored in the harbor, "Roodenberg" or Red Hills, in allusion to the red cliffs a little inland.

NEW HAVEN IN 1637.

In the spring of 1638, Mr. Davenport and his friends sailed for Quinnipiack, where they arrived at the middle of April. They were accompanied by a number of followers, mostly persons from London who had been engaged in trade; and in proportion to their number, they formed the richest colony in America. They spent their first Sabbath there—a warm April day—mostly under the shadow of a great oak, where Mr. Davenport preached a sermon on the subject of Jesus being led into the wilderness. They purchased the land of the Indians and proceeded to plant the seeds of a new state by framing articles of association, which they called a "Plantation Covenant," according to their peculiar ideas. In it they resolved "that, as in matters that concern the gathering and ordering of a church, so likewise in all public offices which concern civil order, as choice of magistrates and officers, making and repealing of laws, dividing allotments of inheritance, and all things of like nature," they would "be ordered by the rules which the Scriptures held forth." So they began their settlement without any reference to any government or community on the face of the earth. The place where the first hut was built was on the present corner of Church and George Streets, New Haven, and the spot whereon stood the oak tree—their first temple for worship—was at the intersection of George and College Streets.

For about a year this little community endeavored to learn by experience, from reflection, and light from Heaven through the medium of prayer, what would be the best kind of social and political organization for the government of the colony. They talked together much, and early in the summer of 1639 they were nearly or quite all of one mind. Then they assembled in a barn—all the "free planters"—to compare views and settle upon a plan of civil government according to the word of God. Mr. Davenport prayed earnestly, and preached from the text: "Wisdom hath builded her house; she hath hewn out her seven pillars." In his discourse, he showed the fitness of choosing seven competent men to construct the government; and he then proposed for their adoption four fundamental articles: (1) That the Scriptures contain a perfect rule for the government of men in the family, in the church, and in the commonwealth; (2) That they would be ordered by the rules which the Scriptures held forth; (3) That their purpose was to be admitted into church-fellowship, according to Christ, as soon as God should fit them thereunto; and (4) That they held themselves bound to establish such civil order, according to God, as would be likely to secure the greatest good to themselves and their posterity.

These articles were unanimously adopted, when Mr. Davenport presented two other articles designed to put into practical operation the theories of the other four. These were (1) That church membership only should be free-burgesses or freemen endowed with political franchises, and that they only should choose magistrates, and transact civil public business of every kind; (2) That twelve or more men should be chosen from the company and tried for their fitness, and these twelve should choose seven of their number as the seven pillars of the church. These articles were subscribed by sixty-three persons present, and soon afterward by fifty others.

The twelve men were chosen, and after due deliberation they selected the "seven pillars." After another pause, these "pillars" proceeded to organize a church. Their assistants, nine in number, were regarded as freemen or "free burgesses," and the sixteen elected Theophilus Eaton as magistrate for one year. Four other persons were chosen to be deputies, and these constituted the executive and legislative departments of the new-born state of Quinnipiack. To these Mr. Davenport gave a "charge," grounded upon Deuteronomy i. 16, 17. A secretary and sheriff were appointed. The "Freeman's Charge," which was a substitute for an oath, gave no pledge of allegiance to king or Parliament, nor any other authority on the face of the earth, excepting that of the civil government here established. "It was a state independent of all others. It was resolved that there should be an annual General Court or meeting of the whole body, in the month of October, and that "the word of God [the Bible] should be the only rule to be attended unto in ordering the affairs of government." Then orders were issued for building a meeting-house; for the distribution of house-lots and pasturage; for regulating the prices of labor and commodities, and for taking measures to resist the attacks of savages. They resolved, also, to choose their own company, and it was ordained that "none should come to dwell as planters without their consent and allowance, whether they came in by purchase or otherwise." In 1640 they named the settlement *New Haven*.

In the meantime, the planters in the Connecticut Valley had been perfecting a system of government, and preparing to possess the land westward as far as the Hudson River. People from Quinnipiack and the valley planted themselves at Fairfield, Norwalk, Guilford, and Stratford and Milford on the Housatonic. Captain Patrick, the commander of a part of the forces sent from Massachusetts against the Pequods, and who had married a Dutch wife, settled as far westward as Greenwich, with a son-in-law of the elder Governor Winthrop. At that time there were no Dutch settlers east of the Harlem River excepting Bronck and his lessees or tenants. The Dutch, however, continued in possession of their lands at Fort Good Hope, and a small garrison was kept up there under Commissary Guysbert op Dyck. But the English, when they became strong in numbers, paid little respect to the rights of the Netherlanders. They ploughed up their lands, excusing themselves for the intrusion with the plea that the soil was lying idle and ought to be cultivated by *somebody*. When the Commissary attempted to resist these encroachments, his soldiers were cudgelled by the planters, who said they (the English) were Israelites, while the Dutch in New Netherland and the English in Virginia were Egyptians.

The troubles with their neighbors, pale and dusky, and the necessity which called for fundamental laws, induced the planters of the valley to meet in convention at Hartford at the middle of January, 1639, to form a constitution of government. Like that of the New Haven colony, it was framed without the slightest reference to any other government. It provided that all persons in the commonwealth should be freemen, and should take an oath of allegiance to the general government; that the governor, to be elected at each spring meeting of the freemen, should be a member of some church; that there should be as many magistrates (not less than six) and other officers as should be found necessary; that there should be a house of deputies, composed of four from each of the then existing towns, and as many as the General Court or legislature should determine from towns that might be created; and that the governor, four magistrates, and a majority of the deputies, should be competent to make all laws and deal generally for the good of the commonwealth. In the absence of special laws, "the rule of the word of God" was to be followed.

"This instrument which has been spoken of as the "first example in history of a written constitution—a distinct organic law, constituting a government and defining its powers," and which recognized no authority outside of its own inherent potency, continued in force as the fundamental law of Connecticut one hundred and eighty years. It secured for that commonwealth a degree of social order and general prosperity rarely equalled in the life of nations. The political organization under it was called the *Connecticut Colony*, and the domain acquired the title of "the land of steady habits." Notwithstanding the two colonies were not united until twenty-six years afterward, now, in the year 1639, was laid the foundations of the commonwealth of *Connecticut*.

While the framework of the colony of Connecticut was in process of construction, that of its little neighbor on the east, Rhode Island, was likewise in a formative state. Persecution by brethren had driven into the forests on the borders of Narraganset Bay, good men who became the founders of a state. That bay had been discovered and thoroughly explored by Block, the Dutch navigator, as early as 1614, when he gave the name of Roode Eylandt or Red Island to the insular domain on its eastern side, now known as Rhode Island. Eight or ten years afterward the Dutch on Manhattan carried on a profitable fur trade with the natives there, and a few years later they had the monopoly of that trade as far east as Buzzard's Bay. The Pilgrims at Plymouth were annoyed by this commercial intrusion, as we have seen, and especially when the New Netherlanders claimed territorial jurisdiction as far east as Narraganset Bay, and westward from a line of longitude from that bay to Canada. That claim was made at about the time when Roger Williams, the founder of the commonwealth of Rhode Island, sought refuge from persecution in the forests on the borders of the Narraganset. The claim was not relinquished until many years afterwards, but was never pressed with injurious vehemence.

Mr. Williams was a Welch Puritan educated in England by Sir Edward Coke, who found him in London, a mere youth, reporting sermons and Star-chamber speeches in shorthand. At the age of thirty-two years he fled from persecution to New England, where he arrived in 1631 with his beautiful bride Mary, a charming young English woman. He was soon appointed assistant minister in the church at Salem, where his broad and enlightened views respecting the freedom of conscience and the injurious character of a wedded church and state offended the dignitaries in both, at Boston, and he withdrew to Plymouth. There he was an assistant minister, acceptable to the people, for about two years, when he returned to Salem and became pastor of the congregation to whom he had ministered as assistant.

Bolder than ever, his convictions having become more firmly rooted by opposition and controversy, Mr. Williams now put forth his views in sometimes intemperate language, for in support of toleration he became intolerant. He boldly questioned the authority of magistrates in respect to the right of the king to appropriate and grant the lands of the Indians without purchase, and the right of the civil power to impose faith and worship. This denial of the right of magistrates to intermeddle, even to restrain a church from heresy or apostacy, was regarded as so monstrous and dangerous an error and innovation that the banishment of Williams from the colony was decreed unless he should recant, or take back what he had said. He would not recant. He maintained with vehemence his opinion that there was an absolute and eternal distinction between the spheres of the civil government and the Christian church. He also appealed in writing to the charter against the decision of magistrates; and he wrote a long letter to his own congregation in favor of the rigid separation of church and state. These writings were among his enumerated offences, and were called "letters of defamation" in the preface of his sentence of banishment which was now put in force, and which ran thus:

"It is therefore ordered that the said Mr. Williams shall depart out of this jurisdiction within six weeks now next ensuing, which, if he neglect to perform, it shall be lawful for the governor and two of the magistrates to send him to some place out of this jurisdiction, not to return any more without license from the court."

This sentence was pronounced late in 1635. The friends of Williams were indignant. The enlightened Edward Winslow, who was then governor of Plymouth, sympathized with him; and twenty leading men in the two colonies determined to go with him to the wilderness and share his privations of exile. Salem was in an uproar, and the magistrates began to suspect that they had made a mistake in passing the sentence. A rumor spread that he intended to found a colony among the Narragansets, with whom he had become familiar while he was at Plymouth and gained the friendship of their sachems and learned their language.

A colony founded upon the liberal principles advocated by Williams was not a pleasant subject for the contemplation of Massachusetts magistrates and clergymen at that period, and the time for his departure was extended until spring. Williams regarded this as a concession. No doubt he had formed a plan for founding a new colony, and was now glad of an excuse to leave Massachusetts; so he taught his doctrines with more fervor, and boldly proclaimed himself to be an Anabaptist—one who denies the validity of infant baptism—a Baptist of our day. This was too much for his people and the authorities in church and state, and it was resolved by Governor Haynes to send the "troubler" back to England. He had refused to obey a summons to appear before the magistrates at Boston, and they sent a pinnace to Salem, with a warrant to Captain Underhill to arrest him, take him on board the little vessel, and convey him to a ship then ready to sail for England.

Williams had been informed of this order. Ex-Governor Winthrop had kindly but secretly advised him to "steer his canoe to the Narraganset Bay and Indians;" and when Underhill and his men went to his house to arrest him, they found only his sorrowing wife and two babes. Williams had been gone three days. On a cold winter's night, the moon on the wane, he had kissed his wife and children and departed in the gloom to seek a refuge with the dusky pagans, who were more tolerant than his pale-faced Christian brethren. He went forth alone with a long staff and a scrip thrown over his shoulders. The snow was deep. Wild beasts were in his path. Behind him were the treasures of wife and children; before him, as radiant and enticing as the "star in the east," glowed the brilliant luminary of Christian ethics, which was his pole-star and guide. He made his way to the house of Massasoit, the venerable sachem of the Wampanoags, where he was warmly welcomed. The sachem gave him a tract of land on the Seekonk River, eastward of the site of Providence, at which place he and some friends who joined him seated themselves in the spring of 1636. Some distance above them, on the Seekonk or Pawtucket River, was a solitary settler named William Blackstone. He was a non-conformist minister, who disliked the "lords brethren" of Massachusetts as much as

WILLIAMS GOING INTO EXILE.

the "lords bishops" of England. He had withdrawn to the wilderness, and there lived the life of a hermit at a place which he named Rehoboth—room. He was the first *settler* but not the *founder* of Rhode Island, for he refused to join Williams and his friends.

Just as the new colony had begun to build and plant near the present Manton's cove, a friendly letter came from Governor Winslow saying they were within the jurisdiction of the Plymouth Colony, and as he did not wish to offend "the Bay," and desired the undisturbed repose of the exiles, he advised Williams and his little party to pass to the other side of the Seekonk, where he would have a large country before him beyond the jurisdiction of both colonies on the coast.

The settlers heeded this kind and wise advice. The six exiles left the Seekonk in a large canoe, with all the worldly goods which they had brought into the wilderness, and rounding the headlands known as Fox and India Points, they went up to the mouth of the Mooshansic River and landed. It was a warm day late in June. Near by, upon a grassy slope shaded by sycamore trees, they saw a gushing spring. It was a joyful sight to the thirsty pilgrims. Around it they gathered, and after partaking of its clear waters, they fell on their knees and offered fervid supplications and thanksgiving to God for his goodness. At that spring, now surrounded by a populous city and yet shaded by sycamores, these devout men resolved there to lay the foundations of a free state. In commemoration of "God's merciful providence to him in his distress," Williams named the spot *Providence*, and dedicated it as "a shelter for persons distressed for conscience."

The freedom enjoyed at Providence was spoken of at Boston, and persecuted men flocked to the new settlement with their families. Williams had purchased the land from the aged Canonicus and the younger Miantonomoh, who had learned to love him. These men, naturally shy and suspicious, had perfect confidence in Williams, and willingly took him and his friends into their bosoms. "It was not thousands nor tens of thousands of money," Williams wrote, "that could have bought of them an English entrance into the bay." It was the personal influence of the men who there established a pure democracy, under the following simple article of agreement:

"We, whose names are hereunder written, being desirous to inhabit in the town of Providence, do promise to submit ourselves, in active or passive obedience, to all such orders or agreements as shall be made for public good by the body in an orderly way, by the major consent of the inhabitants, masters of families, incorporated together into a township, and such others as they shall admit into the same, only in civil things."

Every man was required to sign this compact, which left him free in all but "civil things." The conscience was left absolutely free. The founder reserved no political power to himself, and the leader and follower had equal dignity and privileges. Under the sunny skies of such freedom, the settlers fell to work cheerfully. The summer was too far advanced to allow them to procure much food from the soil; and when Governor Winslow visited Providence in the autumn, the planters were much pinched. This fact is made evident by the touching manner in which the founder gratefully alludes to the kindness of the governor. "He put a piece of gold into the

WILLIAMS AND HIS FELLOW-EXILES AT THE SPRING.

hands of my wife for our supply," he wrote;—that sweet, loving wife who shared with her husband the privations as well as the comforts and honors which were his lot.

Now came the war with the Pequods. Persecution and slander had not embittered the feelings of Williams toward the authorities of Massachusetts. Seeing the danger, he warned them of it early. He sent to Governor Winthrop a rude map of the country along the coast from the Narraganset to the Connecticut, which he had drawn from descriptions by the Indians, with a plan for a campaign, and perilled his life for the good of his enemies. He saved his persecutors from destruction, yet the rulers in church and state in Massachusetts had not the Christian manliness to show gratitude by expunging from their records his sentence of banishment and receiving him to their bosoms as a brother. They proclaimed a solemn thanksgiving at the close of the war, and received the leaders of their troops in triumph with feasting and rejoicing; but they passed no vote of thanks to one who had achieved more for the life of that commonwealth than any soldier or statesman. Winthrop tried to procure a vote of thanks and Williams's recall from banishment, but bigotry prevailed. The following couplet, written by Governor Dudley, expresses the prevailing sentiment of magistrates and clergy then in Boston:

> "Let men of God, in court and churches, watch
> O'er such as do a toleration hatch."

The theological disputes already referred to as agitating the people of Massachusetts divided them and sent many into exile. A brilliant woman, named Anne Hutchinson, of powerful intellect and beautiful person, came to Boston. She was a sister of Rev. John Wheelwright, a popular preacher there. She agreed, generally, in theological views, with Roger Williams, and very soon boldly proclaimed the doctrine that conscience, the indwelling Holy Spirit in every believer, and the conscientious judgment of the mind, are of paramount authority. She denounced the prevailing spiritual despotism, and startled and charmed the best thinkers with the loftiness of her ideas concerning the spiritual freedom of the individual. She soon drew many leading men after her. Among these was the young Henry Vane, then governor of the commonwealth, and a few of the clergy, but only her brother among the ministers ventured to openly advocate her doctrines. He was censured by the civil authorities, when he threatened to appeal to the king. This threat a synod of clergy and lay delegates, called to act upon the subject, construed into a menace of rebellion, and gave them a pretext for recommending the civil authorities to disarm the "Hutchinsonians."

The war of words was waged more fiercely. The civil authorities arraigned Mrs. Hutchinson, her brother, and another leader in the movement, on a charge of heresy. The result was a decree for the banishment of these three persons, and the disarming of sixty citizens of Boston. They were forbidden, upon the penalty of a fine, to buy or borrow any other arms or ammunition, until permitted by the General Court or legislature. Unwilling to endure this indignity, a large portion of them, under the leadership of John Clarke and William Coddington, left Boston with their families, accompanied by Mrs. Hutchinson and her brother, with the intention of settling on the Delaware Bay. They were so "lovingly entertained" by Roger Williams at Providence, and so kindly invited to settle in the land of the Narragansets, that they paused. Through the influence of Williams they were enabled to purchase from the Indians the beautiful island of Aquetneck, now Rhode Island; and at the close of March, 1638, they began a settlement at Portsmouth, near its northern extremity. The colonists were charmed with the salubrity of the climate, and thankfully exchanged their home on Shawmut (the Boston peninsula) for one on Rhode Island. They all immediately adopted and all signed a written agreement similar to that of the Providence colony, in these words:

"We, whose names are underwritten, do swear solemnly, in the presence of Jehovah, to incorporate ourselves into a body politic, and, as He shall help us, will submit our persons, lives, and estates, unto our Lord Jesus Christ, the King of kings and Lord of Hosts, and to all those most perfect and absolute laws of His, given us in his Holy Word of Truth, to be guided and judged thereby."

In imitation of the Jewish form of government, under the judges, Mr. Coddington was chosen judge or chief ruler of the Rhode Island colony. Both settlements flourished. They were separate governments, but one in aims and sentiment. The persecuted came to them and population rapidly increased. Liberty of conscience was there absolute; and upon the seal which the Rhode Island colony adopted was the motto: *Amor Vincit Omnia*—"Love is all-powerful." The jealousy of the Massachusetts authorities was frequently conspicuous, and stood in the way of a friendly intercourse and a profitable trade between the two colonies. Because a refugee from Boston, writing from Providence, spoke harshly of Massachusetts magistrates, the latter passed an ordinance forbidding citizens of Providence, of like views, coming into that colony.

Unwilling to yield allegiance to either of the other colonies, the Rhode Island and Providence settlements sought an independent charter which should unite them in one commonwealth. At about that time, a confederacy of the New England colonies, for mutual defence, was formed, but the stern bigotry which banished Mr. Williams and Mrs. Hutchinson, excluded these settlements on the Narraganset from the Union. That isolation, in case of trouble with the savages, would be both perilous and inconvenient,

18

and Williams was sent to England to obtain a royal charter. He sailed from New Amsterdam in the summer of 1643, and arrived in Great Britain at the time when the civil war was raging violently. Circumstances favored his mission. The king was powerless; the Parliament was supreme. That body had entrusted the management of colonial affairs to a commission of which the Earl of Warwick, the original grantee of Connecticut, was the head as "Governor-General and Lord High Admiral of the colonies in America." He was assisted by a council composed of five peers and ten commons. Henry Vane, who had returned to England and had been created a baronet, was one of that Council. He received Mr. Williams cordially,

ROGER WILLIAMS. OLIVER CROMWELL. JAMES II.

and introduced him to his associates. That body listened to Mr. Williams's statements with great attention, and granted his prayer. On the 14th of March, 1644, they issued a charter in the name of the king, which connected the towns of Providence, Portsmouth, and Newport under the title of "the Incorporation of Providence Plantations in the Narragansett Bay in New England."

Mr. Williams left England for his home in the summer of 1644, bearing the charter. He also bore a letter signed by several members of Parliament, addressed to the authorities of Massachusetts, in favor of the exile, and with this he landed in Boston. The letter did not weaken the asperities of the magistrates toward him, excepting sufficient to allow him to pass to Providence unmolested. That heretical colony, now that it had received a charter and been applauded by high authority in England, was more than ever an object of distrust and suspicion on the part of the Massachusetts authorities. But Mr. Williams bore himself meekly under their frowns. As he approached Providence he was cheered by a gratifying spectacle. The people had heard of his coming, and all turned out to meet him and welcome him home. The Seekonk was covered with well-filled canoes gaily decked with flowers and evergreens, and the shore was alive with men, women and children in holiday attire, who greeted him with loud huzzas, the waving of handkerchiefs, and the singing of psalms. The charter which he bore to the people on the banks of the Narraganset was the corner-stone of a state. Then was founded the commonwealth of *Rhode Island*.

CHAPTER VIII.

SOCIAL CONDITION OF HOLLAND IN THE SEVENTEENTH CENTURY—INDUCEMENTS TO SETTLE IN NEW NETHERLAND—THE PATROONS, THEIR PRIVILEGES AND DEPENDANTS—A SETTLEMENT IN DELAWARE AND ITS FATE—THE SWEDES ON THE DELAWARE—THE DUTCH AND SWEDES AT VARIANCE—THE SWEDES MAINTAIN THEIR POSITION—NEW JERSEY GRANTED TO ROYAL FAVORITES—INDUCEMENTS TO SETTLE THERE—GOVERNOR CARTERET AND SETTLERS AT ELIZABETHTOWN—TROUBLE WITH THE SETTLERS—A REPUBLICAN PROPHET.

WHEN industry was made honorable in Holland, the feudal system began to decay. It was a system embracing large landowners, whose tenants were military men who controlled all labor and bore allegiance to the lordly proprietor. In the new era which had gradually dawned in Holland, the owner of the soil was no longer the head of a band of armed depredators who were his dependants, but the careful proprietor of broad acres, and devoted to industry and thrift. The nobles who composed the landlord class gradually came down from the stilts of exclusiveness, and in habits and even costume imitated the working people. The latter became elevated in the social scale. Their rights were respected, and their value in the state was duly estimated. Ceaseless toil in Holland was necessary to preserve the hollow land from the invasion of the sea, and the common needs assimilated all classes in a country where all must work or drown.

It was this state of society in Holland which stimulated agricultural interests in New Netherland, and changed trading into farming communities. This impulse was much accelerated by a charter of "Privileges and Exemptions" given by the Dutch West India Company in 1629, for the purpose of encouraging agricultural settlements on their American domain. They reserved the lands on and around the island of Manhattan, which they called the commercial emporium of the province, and required that all products for exportation should first be brought there. To persons who were disposed to settle in any other part of the province, the Company offered as much land as each emigrant might be able to improve, with "free liberty of hunting and fowling," under the direction of the provincial governor. They also offered to every person who should "discover any shores, bays, or other fit places for erecting fisheries, or the making of salt-ponds," an absolute property in such discovery.

The rural tenantry of Holland were not rich enough to avail themselves of this privilege, so the Company offered inducements for wealthy citizens to promote emigration, by transplanting into America the modified feudal system of the Netherlands. They offered to grant lands and manorial privileges and exemptions to any member of the Company who should, within four years, plant a colony of fifty adults in any part of New Netherland outside of Manhattan Island; such proprietor being constituted feudal chief of the domain which he might thus colonize. The lands of each colony were limited to sixteen miles along one shore of a navigable stream, or to eight miles if they occupied both shores, but they might extend into the interior indefinitely. It was also provided that if any proportionably greater number of emigrants should be settled by a proprietor, the area of his domain should be extended in the same ratio. He was to be absolutely lord of the manor, political and otherwise. He might hold inferior courts for the adjudication of petty civil cases; and if cities should grow up on his domain he was to have power to appoint the magistrates and other officers of such municipalities, and have a deputy to confer with the governor.

The settlers under the "patroons," as these manorial proprietors were called, were to be exempted from all taxation and tribute for the support of the provincial government for ten years; and for the same period every man, woman and child was bound not to leave the service of the patroon without his written consent. The colonists were forbidden to manufacture cloth of any kind, on pain of banishment; and the Company agreed to furnish them with as many African slaves "as they conveniently could;" also to protect them against foes. Each colony was bound to support a minister of the Gospel and a schoolmaster, and so provide a comforter for the sick and a teacher of the illiterate. It was also provided that every colonist, whether patroon or an independent settler, should first make a satisfactory arrangement with the Indians for the lands they should occupy.

Such is a brief outline of the charter of "Privileges and Exemptions" under which several large manorial estates were acquired in New Netherland, one of which (the Van Rensselaer Manor on the Hudson) existed, with some of its privileges, until late in the present century. It recognized the right of the Indians to the soil; invited independent farmers to whom a homestead should be secured; promised protection to all in case of war, and encouraged religion and learning. Yet this system of colonization was not so favorable to the development and growth of popular liberty as was that in New England.

While this charter was under consideration in the meetings of the Company at Amsterdam, two of the directors (Samuel Godyn and Samuel Bloemmaert) purchased of the Indians a tract of land on Delaware Bay, extending from Cape Henlopen (the southern boundary of New Netherland) northward, full thirty miles, and two miles in the interior. This purchase was ratified by the Company when the charter was issued. Very soon afterward Killian Van Rensselaer purchased a large tract of the natives on the upper navigable waters of the Hudson River; and Michael Pauw, another director, secured by the same means a large tract in New Jersey at the mouth of the river, opposite Manhattan, and all of Staten Island. This adroit management of wide-awake directors, in securing the best lands in the province, as to situation—who "helped themselves by the cunning trick of merchants"—provoked jealousy and ill-will among their fellow-directors, which was finally allayed by admitting others into partnership with them.

Immediate steps were taken for colonizing these manors. Under the direction of Captain de Vries, an eminent navigator and friend of Godyn, who had made him a partner in the purchase, two ships sailed with colonists, cattle, seeds and agricultural implements, for Delaware Bay. They left the Texel under the command of Peter Heyes on the 12th of December, 1630, and took the long southern route by way of the Canaries and the West Indies. One of the vessels was captured; the other, carrying eighteen cannon, did not reach the Delaware until April following. Near the site of the village of Lewiston, thirty emigrants, with their cattle and implements, seated themselves. There Heyes set up a wooden column, and on it placed a piece of tin emblazoned with the arms of Holland in token of taking possession of the country in the name of the States-General. The place was named Swaanendael. They built a house and stockaded it; and then Captain Heyes went over to the New Jersey shore and purchased from the Indians, in the name of Godyn, a tract of land along the coast from Cape May, twelve miles. In the autumn, Heyes returned to Holland, leaving the colony in charge of Gillis Hossett.

In the spring of 1632, De Vries went with two vessels to the Delaware. There a sad sight greeted him. The house which the settlers had built was in ruins; the palisades had been burned; and the bones of the settlers strewed the ground. They had all been murdered by the Indians. One of the savages told De Vries all about it. A chief thoughtlessly took down the piece of tin which bore the arms of Holland, to make a tobacco-pipe of it. Hossett made such ado about it, that the Indians, to allay the feeling, slew the offending chief, and sent his scalp to the Dutch commander. When the bearer presented it, Hossett told him the Indians had done wrong; that had the offender been brought to him he would only have cautioned him not to repeat the offence. The friends of the victim burned with vengeful desires, and determined to destroy the white people as a retribution. A party of warriors visited the settlement under the guise of friendship, and massacred the whole of them in their houses and in the fields. This crime was forgiven, and the Indians and Hollanders remained friends.

A competition with the English and Dutch for American possessions now appeared in the North. The enlightened Gustavus Adolphus, King of Sweden, had looked with longing eyes westward as he heard from time to time of the rich countries beyond the British isles. At length he was excited to action by William Usselincx, the projector of the Dutch West India Company, who, dissatisfied with his associates in that corporation, visited Sweden, and laid before its monarch well-arranged plans for colonization on the Delaware. The king was delighted. He entered warmly into the projects of Usselincx, and was preparing for the execution of a scheme for planting a colony in America that should be an open asylum for all Christians, when the danger which threatened Protestantism in Germany called him to the field to contend for the principles of the Reformation. While leading victorious armies against the Imperial hosts marshalled under the banner of the Pope on the fields of Germany, he did not forget the scheme for American colonization. At Nuremburg he drew up a paper for his great chancellor, the Count Oxenstierna, in which he recommended the enterprise as "the jewel of his kingdom." A few days afterwards he was face to face with his enemy at Lutzen, in battle array. On their knees he and the brave Swedes sang Luther's glorious hymn, *Eine feste Burg ist unser Gott*—"A tower of strength is our God." Then they sang a hymn composed by the king himself, and springing to their feet, they made a furious charge upon the Imperialists, Gustavus leading the right wing. He fell covered with mortal wounds.

But the words of Gustavus did not die. Oxensteirna, at the head of a regency, administered the government for the heir to the throne, Christina, who was then only six years of age. "A colony in America would, indeed, be a precious jewel in the crown of Sweden," said the wise Chancellor. He had favored the project from the beginning; and in 1634, he issued a charter for a Swedish West India Company.

Governor Minuit, who had been recalled from New Netherland because he had favored the grasping patroons too much, it was thought, hastened to Stockholm and offered the fruits of his experience in America and his personal services to the new company. They were gladly accepted; and at near the close of 1637, he sailed from Gottenburg with fifty emigrants in two vessels, bearing a commission to plant a colony on the west side of Delaware Bay, within the manor of Godyn and Blommaert, where he knew no settlement then existed. He landed at the site of Newcastle in April 1638, and purchased from the Indians the whole territory from Cape Henlopen to the falls of the Delaware River at Trenton without the slightest regard to

GUSTAVUS ADOLPHUS AT THE HEAD OF HIS TROOPS.

the claims of the Dutch. Then he sailed into the mouth of the river, and anchored in a creek at the site of Wilmington. They built a fort and then a church, and named the place Christina, in honor of their young queen. The territory they had purchased they called New Sweden.

When the Dutch at Fort Nassau, fifteen miles further up the river, heard of this intrusion, they went down to inquire what it meant. Minuit gave them evasive answers at first, but finally told them that he intended to plant a settlement in the country, and build a fort there. "The Queen of Sweden," he said, "has as good a right to build a fort here as the Dutch West India

Company." A messenger to tell the news was at once sent to Manhattan. Kieft, the newly-arrived governor, sent an officer to Minuit at Christina to protest against the movement. The warning was unheeded. Then Kieft issued a proclamation saying that he was persuaded that the Queen of Sweden had not authorized the building of forts within the domain of New Netherland, and that while he would not be responsible "for any mishap, bloodshed, trouble and disaster" which Minuit and his people might suffer thereafter, he was resolved to defend the rights of the West India Company as he should deem proper.

Minuit paid no attention to this proclamation, but built Fort Christina on the site of Wilmington, and erected posts with the royal initials and the crown of Sweden carved on them. Well acquainted with the Indian traffic, from long experience at Manhattan, he soon drew to Christina a profitable fur-trade; and at midsummer he sent the vessels back to Sweden with cargoes of peltry and other products of the land. The fort was well garrisoned and provisioned, and the settlers there planted and reaped. So was established the first permanent settlement on that soil, and there and then was planted the fruitful seed of the commonwealth of *Delaware*.

Eastward of the Delaware Bay and River (so called in honor of Lord De la Warr, Governor of Virginia,) lies New Jersey. Its domain was included in the New Netherland charter. So early as 1622, transient trading settlements were made on its soil at Bergen and on the banks of the Delaware. The following year, as we have observed, Director May, moved by the attempt of a French sea-captain to set up the arms of France on the Delaware, built a redoubt called Fort Nassau at the mouth of Timmer Kill or Timber Creek, a few miles below Camden, and settled some young Walloons near it. The most southern headland of New Jersey and now popular summer resort, Cape May, received its name from the first director-general of New Netherland, who gave it, also, to several other places.

The Walloons—young couples who had been married on shipboard—settled on the site of Gloucester. This was the first settlement on the soil of New Jersey that lived long; but it, too, withered away in time. It was seven years later when Michael Pauw made his purchase of the Indians extending from Hoboken to the Raritan River, and latinizing his name, called it Pavonia. In this purchase was included the settlement of some Dutch at Bergen. Other settlements were attempted, but none became permanent until about forty years afterward. Cape May, which Captain Heyes bought of the Indians—a territory sixteen miles square—remained an uncultivated wilderness all that time yielding the products of its salt meadows to the browsing deer.

We must now run ahead of our story, as we have, a little, at other times, in coming to the period when the foundations of a colony were actually laid, and glance at an important event in the political history of New Netherland. Charles the Second, King of England, granted a greater portion of the claimed territory of New Netherland to his brother, the Duke of York, then Lord High Admiral of the realm. The duke sent a fleet and army to take possession of his domain. This armament, stronger than any in New Nether-

THE SWEDES ON THE DELAWARE.

land, found the task an easy one, and early in the autumn of 1664, the province passed into the hands of the English. Soon after that armament sailed, and while it was yet on the bosom of the Atlantic, the duke conveyed to two of his favorites all the territory between the Hudson and Delaware rivers from Cape May north to the latitude of forty degrees and forty minutes. These favorites were Lord Berkeley, brother of the governor of Virginia and the duke's own governor in his youth, and Sir George Carteret, then the treasurer of the Admiralty, who had been governor of the island of Jersey, which he had gallantly defended against the forces of Cromwell. In the charter this province was named "Nova Cæsarea or New Jersey," in commemoration of Carteret's loyalty and gallant deeds while he was governor of the island of Jersey. Colonel Richard Nicolls, the commander of the expedition to seize New Netherland, and deputy-governor of the province, changed the name to *New York;* and, ignorant of the charter given to Berkeley and Carteret, he called the territory west of the Hudson *Albania*, so honoring his employer, who bore the title of Duke of York and Albany.

Berkeley and Carteret hastened to make use of their patent. They framed a constitution of government for the new domain under the title of "The Concessions and Agreement of the Lords Proprietors of the Province of

Nova Cæsarea or New Jersey, to and with all and every of the new adventurers and all such as shall Settle and Plant there." It was a fair and liberal constitution. It provided for a governor and council appointed by the proprietors, and deputies or representatives chosen by the people, who should meet annually, and with the governor and his council form a General Assembly for the government of the colony. It provided for the choice of a president by the representatives when in session, in case of the absence of the governor and deputy governor. All legislative power was vested in the Assembly of Deputies, who were to make all laws for the province—these to be consistent with the laws and customs of Great Britain, and not repugnant to the interests of the proprietors. Provision was also made for the encouragement of emigration to New Jersey. To every freeman who should go to that province with the first governor, furnished with a good musket and plenty of ammunition, with provisions for six months, was offered a free gift of one hundred and fifty acres of land; and for every able man-servant that such emigrant should take with him, so armed and provisioned, a like quantity of land. Any person sending such servants should be likewise rewarded; and for every weaker servant or slave, of either sex, over fourteen years of age, which any person might take or send, at that time, should be given seventy-five acres of land each, "Christian servants" being entitled, at the expiration of the term of service, to the land so granted for their own use and benefit. To all who should settle in the province before the beginning of 1665, other than those who should go with the governor, were offered one hundred and twenty acres of land, on like conditions.

These offers were certainly attractive, and the proprietors expected to see their country rapidly peopled with industrious settlers. They appointed Philip Carteret, a cousin of Sir George, governor, and with about thirty emigrants, several of whom were Frenchmen skilled in the art of salt-making, he sailed for New York, where he arrived in July, 1665. The vessel had been driven into Chesapeake Bay in June and anchored at the mouth of the James River, whence the governor sent despatches to New York. Among them was a copy of the duke's grant of New Jersey. Governor Nicolls was astounded by the folly of the duke in parting with so much of his valuable domain, for he regarded Albania as the "most improveable" part of the territory. He was mortified by this dismemberment of a state over which he had been ruling for many months with pride and satisfaction. But he kept his thoughts between his lips until the arrival of Carteret, whom Colonel Nicolls received at Fort James, late Fort Amsterdam, with all the honors due to his rank and station. That meeting in the governor's quarters in the fort was a notable one. Nicolls was tall, athletic, and about forty-five years of age; a soldier, haughty and sometimes very irritable, and brusque in speech when excited. Carteret was shorter and fat, good-natured and affable, with polished manners which he had learned by being much at court. He entered the governor's room with Bollen, the commissary of the fort, when the former arose, beckoned his secretary to withdraw, and received his distinguished visitor cordially. But when Carteret presented the outspread parchment, bearing the original of the duke's grant with his grace's seal and signature, Nicolls could not restrain his feelings. His temper flamed out in words of fierce anger at first. He stormed, and uttered denunciations in language as respectful as possible. He paced the floor backwards and forwards rapidly, his hands clenched behind his back, and finally calmed down and begged his visitor's pardon for his uncontrollable outburst of passion.

Nicolls yielded gracefully but sorrowfully to circumstances, and contented himself with addressing a manly remonstrance to the duke, in which he urged an arrangement for the grantees to give up their domain in exchange for "a hundred thousand acres all along the sea-coast." It was too late. In pursuance of the duke's orders, Nicolls formally surrendered Albania into the quiet possession of Carteret, and thenceforth that region appeared as New Jersey on the maps. Its governor crossed over to his domain early in August, and landed, at the head of a few followers, with a hoe on his shoulder in token of his intention to become a planter among them. He chose for his seat of government a beautifully shaded spot not far from the strait between Staten Island and the main, called The Kills, where he found four English families living in as many neatly-built log cabins, with gardens around them. In compliment to the wife of Sir George Carteret, the governor gave to the place the name of Elizabethtown, which it yet retains. There he built a house for himself near the bank of the little creek, and there he organized a civil government. So was laid the foundations of the colony and commonwealth of *New Jersey*.

The land on which Governor Carteret found the four families had been bought of some Indians on Long Island, who claimed it as their own. They gave a deed of it to John Bailey, Daniel Denton, and Luke Watson of Jamaica, Long Island, and Governor Nicolls granted a patent for it to seventy-four associates, whose descendants are numerous in East Jersey. This patent was given before Nicolls had heard of the extraordinary grant of the Duke of York; and when the governor's grantees were informed of that transaction, they resolved to assert their rights, as against the claims of the duke's friends. Some of the company went to Elizabethtown to confer with Carteret on the subject. At the head of the embassy was John Ogden, of Long Island, who had left England on the accession of Charles the Second to the throne, for he was a republican. The governor received them under the shadow of a great tulip tree on the borders of the creek, and there the conference was held. Ogden showed the Indian deed and the Nicolls grant. Carteret showed the duke's grant with his seal and signature attached. Ogden declared that Indian titles were more valid than royal titles, because

GOVERNOR CARTERET ENTERING NEW JERSEY.

the grantors were the original owners of the soil. This point was conceded, when the governor pointed to the lion in the British arms impressed upon the seal, as an emblem of competent power, intimating that *might* makes *right*. By this intimation the spirit of Ogden was powerfully stirred. Pointing to the sun as the visible presence of the Great Spirit whom all the Indians worshipped, he said: "As far above petty kings and their powers as is the sun in the heaven, now making the earth teem with abundance and beauty, above all below, so far is justice, the prime attribute of God, above might—the mere brute force that gives kingship to the lion and the eagle among beasts and birds. The Dutch acquired possession of this soil by the divine right of a just purchase from the Indians; King Charles had no right to this domain but that of a strong-armed robber. The British lion on that seal is, in this case, only an emblem of oppression and wrong, whose only warrant for injustice is his strength to conquer. In this land monarchs will yet be taught that they have no divine rights not the common property of their subjects, and that there is more strength in justice than in the sword."

John Ogden was a prophet. Under that tree on the soil of New Jersey, that sturdy republican caught luminous visions of the struggles of a people with royalty for the rights of man, which, more than a hundred years afterwards, led to the dismemberment of the British empire and the founding of our free Republic. Carteret admired his spirit, but his words sounded too much like the voices of the followers of Cromwell, and he refused to hold further conference with him. "Very well," said Ogden. "We shall maintain our rights as best we may;" and he and his friends were about to depart, when the courteous governor invited them into his house to partake of refreshments. He then accompanied them to their boat at the Kills, and gave them a cordial invitation to come again as friends, but not as ambassadors.

The Long Islanders liked the good-natured governor personally, and to show their kind feeling toward him and his family, they gave the name of "Elizabethtown Associates" to their company, and to their territory the "Elizabethtown Grant." They adhered to their determination to defend their rights; and during the seven years that Philip Carteret governed New Jersey, there were frequent and severe conflicts between the "Associates" and the grantees of the Duke of York.

CHAPTER IX.

THE "FRIENDS" OR "QUAKERS"—WILLIAM PENN OBTAINS A CHARTER FOR PENNSYLVANIA—EMIGRATION TO PENNSYLVANIA—PENN VISITS AMERICA—THE SWEDES ON THE DELAWARE—TREATY WITH THE INDIANS—PENN VISITS NEW YORK—MEETS THE FIRST PENNSYLVANIA ASSEMBLY—VISITS LORD BALTIMORE—FOUNDS PHILADELPHIA—SETTLERS IN NORTH CAROLINA—THE CAROLINAS GRANTED TO ROYAL FAVORITES—SETTLEMENTS ON THE CAPE FEAR—CHARLESTON FOUNDED—GOVERNMENT FOR THE CAROLINAS FRAMED.

LATER in the seventeenth century than the period of settlement in Delaware and New Jersey, was the domain called Pennsylvania colonized, chiefly by a sect called Quakers in derision. That sect appeared in England at about the time when Roger Williams was there to procure a charter for Rhode Island. Their founder and preachers were among the boldest and yet the meekest of the non-conformists. Their morality was so strict that the world called them ascetics—persons who devote their lives to religion only. They carried this strictness into all departments of life and personal habits. Fashionable dress, extravagance in expenditure, dancing, attendance at theatres, games of chance and other amusements were forbidden; and music was discouraged as a seductive vanity. Taking part in war, slavery, lawsuits, intemperance and profanity of speech, was a sufficient reason, if persisted in, for the expulsion of a member from the Society; and the whole body was bound to keep a watch upon the actions of each other. Their practices so generally agreed with their principles that society was compelled to admit that the profession of a Quaker or "Friend," as they styled themselves, was a guaranty of a morality above the level of the world.

George Fox, a shoemaker of Leicestershire, England, was the founder of this sect. At the age of nineteen years, conceiving himself to be called by God to preach the gospel of Jesus, he went from place to place exhorting his hearers to repentance and newness of life. He complained of the coldness and spiritual deadness of all the modes and forms of religious worship around him, and thereby he soon excited a persecuting spirit by which his ministerial life of about forty years was marked as a pilgrimage from one prison to another. When, in 1650, he was called before Justice Bennet, of

Derby, he admonished that magistrate to repent, and "tremble and *quake* before the word of the Lord," at the same time his own body was violently agitated by emotion. Then and there the sect received the name of Quakers.

Among the multitude of converts to the moral and religious doctrines of George Fox was young William Penn, a son of the distinguished admiral of that name. He embraced the doctrines and adopted the mode of life of George Fox and his followers, while he was yet in college. Then he had a long and severe struggle with his father, a worldly and ambitious man, for the privilege of following the directions of his conscience. He was beaten and turned out of doors by the angry admiral; he was sent to France to be lured with gayety; and he was dazzled with promises of wealth and distinction. He suffered with his sect. On one occasion he was tried, with another, on a charge of preaching in the streets. The jury, after being kept without fire, food or water two days and nights, brought in a verdict of "not guilty," when they were each heavily fined by the court and committed to Newgate; and Penn and his companion were also fined and imprisoned for contempt of court in wearing their hats in the presence of that body. The young Quaker was then only about twenty-four years of age.

PENN AS UMPIRE.

Many "Friends" had emigrated to America, and two had become proprietors of New Jersey. Penn acted as umpire between them, in a dispute that arose, and so his particular attention was drawn toward this country. He looked with longing eyes across the Atlantic for a home for himself and his sectarian friends, out of the reach of persecution. From the crown he obtained a charter for a vast territory beyond the Delaware, in payment of a debt of eighty thousand dollars due to his father from the government, with perpetual proprietaryship given to him and his heirs, in the fealty of an annual payment of two beaver skins. Penn proposed to call the domain "New Wales," in honor of the land of his ancestors, but the Welch secretary of state objected. Then he suggested "Sylvania" as appropriate for such a woody country. The secretary who drew up the charter prefixed the name of Penn to Sylvania, in the document. The proprietor offered him a hundred dollars if he would leave it off. On his refusal to do so, Penn complained to the king—the "merrie King Charlie"—who insisted that the province should be called "Pennsylvania," in honor of his dead friend the admiral. And so it was. The domain extended north from New Castle in Delaware three degrees of latitude, and five degrees of longitude west from the Delaware River. To Penn was given power to ordain all laws with the consent of the freemen, subject to the approval of the king. No taxes were to be raised except by the Provincial Assembly; and clergymen of the Anglican Church were to be allowed to reside in the province without molestation.

Penn's charter was granted on the 14th of March, 1681. In May he sent his kinsman, William Markham, to take possession of his province and to act as deputy governor. A large company of emigrants went with him. They were employed by the "Company of Free Traders," who had purchased lands in Pennsylvania of the proprietor. They seated themselves near the Delaware and "builded and planted." With the help of Algernon Sidney, the sturdy republican martyr who perished on the scaffold soon afterward, Penn drew up a code of wise, liberal and benevolent regulations for the government of the colony, and sent them to the settlers the next year for their approval. It was not a formal constitution, but a body of wholesome laws for the benefit of all concerned.

Penn found that the want of a seaboard for his province would be a serious bar to its future prosperity. He coveted Delaware for that purpose, and resolved to have it if possible. It was claimed by Lord Baltimore as a part of Maryland, and had been a matter of dispute between him and the Duke of York. The latter, for the sake of peace, offered to buy the territory of Baltimore. The baron would not sell. Penn then assured the duke that Lord Baltimore's claim was "against law, civil or common." The duke gladly assented to the opinion, and the worldly-wise Quaker obtained from his grace a quit-claim deed for the territory comprising the whole State of Delaware, then, as now, divided into the counties of Newcastle, Kent, and Sussex; also for all of his interest in the soil of Pennsylvania.

When Penn had gained these coveted possessions, he made immediate preparations for going to America; and within a week after the bargain was officially settled, he set sail in the ship *Welcome* with about one hundred emigrants, many of whom died of small-pox on the voyage. That was at the close of August, 1682. On his arrival at New Castle early in November, he found almost a thousand new emigrants there. These, with the three thousand old settlers—Swedes, Dutch, Huguenots, Germans and English—composed materials for the solid foundation of a state. There, in the presence of the people, he received from the agents of the Duke of York a formal surrender into his hands of that fine domain. The Dutch had, long before, conquered and absorbed the Swedes on the Delaware; and by virtue of his charter, giving him a title to *all* New Netherland, the duke claimed this territory as his own. By this transfer, Penn inherited for himself and descendants a dispute with the proprietors of Maryland. In honor of the duke, the courteous Quaker called Cape Henlopen Cape James, but the two capes of the Delaware—Henlopen and May—have preserved their original name given to them by the Dutch.

Having secured his domain, Penn went many miles up the Delaware River, to the present Kensington district of Philadelphia, and there, under a

PENN'S VOYAGE UP THE DELAWARE.

wide-spreading elm, just shedding its foliage, he concluded a treaty with Indian chiefs, not for the purchase of lands, but to confirm what Markham had promised them for him, and to make an everlasting covenant of peace and friendship with them. "We meet," Penn said, "in the broad pathway of good faith and good will; no advantage shall be taken on either side, but all shall be openness and love. I will not call you children; for parents sometimes chide their children too severely; nor brothers, only; for brothers differ. The friendship between me and you, I will not compare to a chain;

PENN'S TREATY WITH THE INDIANS.

for that the rains might rust, or a falling tree might break. We are the same as if one man's body was to be divided into two parts; we are all one flesh and blood." Then he gave them presents, and they in turn handed him a belt of wampum as a pledge of their fidelity. They were delighted with his divine words, and believed in his noble promises. "We will live in love with William Penn and his children," they said, "as long as the sun and moon shall endure." And they did. Not a drop of the blood of a Quaker was ever shed by an Indian.

William Penn had achieved a marvellous victory over the savage arm and the savage spirit. While in other colonies the might of the sword and musket, of the arrow and the hatchet, were making fearfully red records of crime; while the savages were in fierce array, secretly and openly, against the pale-faced intruders, Penn had conquered and subdued those of Pennsylvania by *love*. There were not even contentions between the races there. "We have done better," said the Friends, in their Plantation Speech, in 1684, "than if, with the proud Spaniards, we had gained the mines of Potosi. We may make the ambitious heroes whom the world admires, blush for their shameful victories. To the poor, dark souls round about us, we teach their rights as MEN." Significant is the question of the historian: "Was there not progress from Melendez to Roger Williams? from Cortez and Pizarro to William Penn?"

There is no written record of that treaty made in the open air on the banks of the Delaware. We have accounts of the personal character of the council. Penn was then a graceful man, strong built and of fair complexion, and thirty-eight years of age. Most of his companions were younger than himself, and all were dressed in the garb of the Quakers—the fashion of the more simple Puritans during the Protectorate of Cromwell. The Indians were clad in the skins of beasts, for it was on the verge of winter—their harvest time was over. Frost and expanding buds were stripping the trees of their foliage, and every aspect of the scene was becoming dreary excepting the bright council-fire under the great elm around which the high contracting parties were gathered. Penn was accompanied by the deputy governor and a few others; and the Indian sachems brought their wives and children, who sat upon the ground modestly back.

From that treaty place, Penn journeyed through New Jersey to New York and Long Island, visiting Friends and preaching with fervor. Then he returned to the Delaware, and on the seventh of November he went to Uplands (now Chester), where he met the first Provincial Assembly of his province. There he made known his benevolent designs toward all men, civilized and savage, and excited the love and reverence of his hearers. The

Assembly tendered their grateful acknowledgments to him, and the Swedes authorized one of their number to say to him in their name that they would "live, serve and obey him with all they had," declaring that it "was the best day they ever saw." He informed the Assembly of the union of the "territories" (as Delaware was called) with his province, and received their congratulations. Then was laid the foundations of the commonwealth of *Pennsylvania*.

From Chester, Penn went to Maryland to confer with the third Lord Baltimore concerning their boundary lines, but did not make a satisfactory arrangement. On his return, he went up the Delaware in an open boat to Wicaco, to attend the founding of a city, to which allusion had been made in his "Concessions, &c.," in 1681. Before his arrival in this country he had determined to give to the future city the name of *Philadelphia*—a Greek word signifying *brotherly love*—as a token of the principles in which he intended to govern his province. Near a block-house which the Swedes had built, and which they had changed into a church, he purchased lands extending from the high banks of the Delaware fringed with pines to those of the Schuylkill. There his surveyors laid out the city of Philadelphia upon a plan which would embrace twelve square miles.

A PLEDGE OF FRIENDSHIP.

Although the efforts of Raleigh and Coligny to make settlements in the warmer portions of North America had utterly failed, and the country south of the James River was untrodden by the foot of the white man unless by the few survivors of the lost colony of Roanoke Island or around the Spanish fort at St. Augustine, the desire to plant colonies there remained strong, and finally led to the wished-for result. From time to time restless, discontented, adventurous or greedy persons went there to find homes for themselves and their children, or to acquire fortunes, but no permanent settlement was planted until past the middle of the seventeenth century.

So early as 1609, some colonists under the direction of Captain John Smith left Jamestown and seated themselves on the Nansemond River, near the Dismal Swamp. In 1622, the ambitious Porey, Secretary of the Virginia colony, penetrated the country southward to the tide-waters of the Chowan River. He told, in earnest words, of the beauty and richness of the country, but did not induce settlers to go there. Eight years later, as we have observed, Sir Robert Heath, the Attorney General of Charles the First, obtained from his king a charter for a domain south of Virginia, six degrees of latitude in width, and extending westward to the Pacific Ocean. This included the region between Albemarle Sound and the St. John's River in Florida. That patent was declared void in 1663, because neither the proprietor nor his assigns had fulfilled their agreements.

Sufferers from the oppression of the State Church in Virginia looked to the wilderness for freedom, as the Huguenots and the Pilgrims had done. In 1653, a few Presbyterians from Jamestown settled on the Chowan River near the present village of Edenton. Other non-conformists followed, and the settlement flourished. Already the New England colonies had begun to swarm. The Massachusetts hive had become too small; and in 1661, some adventurous New Englanders appeared in a small vessel, in the Cape Fear River, in search of a home in a more genial climate. They purchased lands of the Indians, and were making the experiment of establishing a colony of farmers and herdsmen there, when news came that the whole region had been given by Charles the Second to some of his favorites. The New Englanders had partners in their enterprise, in London. These pleaded, in behalf of the claims of the colonists, their prior purchase of the soil, and also their right to self-government. A compromise was offered by the patentees, yielding to every claim of the settlers excepting the ownership of the soil; and that they offered at a yearly rent of a half-penny an acre. The soil was not inviting enough for those who might choose a dwelling-place from almost an entire continent. Most of the New Englanders returned home and "spread a reproach on the harbor and the soil" at Cape Fear.

The grant alluded to was made to several of the rapacious courtiers of Charles the Second, the most of them men past middle-life in age, and possessed of the easy virtue which distinguished the reign of that monarch. They begged the domain of the king under the pretence of "a pious zeal for the propagation of the gospel" among the heathen. Their real object was to rob the "heathen" of their lands, and to accumulate riches and honor for themselves. These grantees were the covetous and time-serving Earl of Clarendon, the historian and the Prime Minister; Monk, who, for his conspicuous and treacherous services in the restoration of Charles to the throne of his father, had been created Duke of Albemarle; Lord Craven, who is supposed to have been the husband of the Queen of Bohemia; Sir Anthony Ashley Cooper, afterward Earl of Shaftesbury; Sir John Colleton, a corrupt loyalist who had played false to Cromwell; Lord John Berkeley and his younger brother, Sir William, who was then governor of Virginia; and the "passionate, ignorant and not too honest" Sir George Carteret, proprietor of New Jersey. It is said that when these petitioners appeared before Charles in the garden at Hampton Court and presented their memorial so full of pious pretensions, the monarch, after looking each in the face for a moment, with a merry twinkle of his eye, burst into loud laughter, in which his audience joined involuntarily. Then taking up a little shaggy spaniel, with large, meek eyes, and holding it at arms length before them, he said: "Good friends, here is a model of piety and sincerity which might be wholesome for you to copy." Then tossing the little pet to Clarendon, he said: "There, Hyde, is a worthy prelate; make him archbishop of the domain which I shall give you." He granted the prayer of the petitioners, and in March, 1663, he gave them a charter for the territory which had been given to Sir Robert Heath. By the terms of that charter, the proprietors were made absolute sovereigns of the domain, returning to their king only a bare allegiance. Charles, with grim satire, introduced into the preamble of the charter the statement that the petitioners, "excited with a laudable and pious zeal for the propagation of the Gospel, have begged a certain country in the parts of America not yet cultivated and planted, and only inhabited by some barbarous people who have no knowledge of God." The title of "Carolina," in honor of the king, was given to this vast domain.

We have observed that some non-conformists from Virginia were settled on the banks of the Chowan ten years before the charter was granted. How extensive was the settlement at the latter period, we do not know. The plantations were mostly on the northern bank of the Chowan, and had become so conspicuous that in the autumn of 1663 the new proprietors authorized Governor Berkeley, of Virginia, to extend his jurisdiction over them. He organized a separate government instead, under the title of the *Albemarle County* Colony, so named in honor of Monk. He appointed William Drummond, a Presbyterian emigrant from Scotland to Virginia, and a republican at heart, governor, and gave to the colonists every freedom which they could reasonably desire. Here was presented the anomaly of a colony founded under the direction and control of rigid churchmen and royalists who were filling the prisons of England with men like John Bunyan, composed of non-conformists as rigid as these, and republicans as staunch as Sidney. And they were left to grow into an independent state with very little hindrance.

Two years later some English emigrants came from Barbadoes, purchased from the Indians a tract of land on the Cape Fear River, thirty-two miles square, including the domain abandoned by the New Englanders, and near the site of Wilmington founded a settlement. They treated the few New Englanders who had remained very kindly, and harmony prevailed. This settlement was soon organized into a political community under the title of the *Clarendon County Colony*, in honor of the historian. Sir John Yeamans, an impoverished baronet who had settled in Barbadoes to improve his fortune, was appointed governor of the new colony, with a jurisdiction extending from Cape Fear to the St. John's River. The poverty of the soil prevented a rapid growth of the settlement, yet the industry of the inhabitants made them prosperous. Finding themselves in the bosom of a vast pine forest, the settlers turned their labor into the manufacture of boards, shingles and staves, and the gathering of turpentine, for all of which they found a ready and profitable sale in the West Indies. The settlement became permanent; and so, with the organization of the two colonies, the foundation of the commonwealth of *North Carolina* was laid.

The avaricious courtiers now sought the acquisition of more territory, and in June, 1665, they readily obtained from the king another charter which confirmed the former one, and gave renewed assurance and commendation of the "pious and noble purpose" under which these men thought it decent to cloak their ambition and rapacity. It granted to them the territory from the now southern boundary of Virginia to the peninsula of Florida, and westward to the Pacific Ocean, comprising all of our States excepting the lower part of Florida south of the thirty-sixth degree, and a part of Mexico, the whole under the name of *Carolina*. The terms of the charter give evidence that the founding of a great empire was contemplated. Provision was made for the appointment of legislators and magistrates; for levying troops and erecting fortifications; waging war by sea and land; erecting cities; establishing manors and baronies, and creating titles; levying impost duties; and other features coincident with those of the existing British government. "Every favor was extended to the proprietors," says an eminent historian; "nothing was neglected but the interests of the English sovereign and the rights of the colonists." It was the duty of Clarendon, as Prime Minister of the realm, to affix the great seal of the kingdom to this charter that conferred such extraordinary privileges upon himself and his seven associates.

In the year 1670, the proprietors sent three ships with emigrants to settle the more southern portions of Carolina. These were under the directions of William Sayle and Joseph West. Sayle had already explored the coasts; and twenty years before, he had endeavored to plant in the Bahama Isles a Puritan colony from Virginia, and to establish an "Eleutheria"—a place dedicated to liberty—among the islands near the coast of Florida. The three ships entered Port Royal harbor, and the emigrants landed at Beaufort Island, near the place where the Huguenots built Fort Carolina a hundred years before. There Sayle died early in the following year, and was buried under a broad live-oak tree draped with Spanish moss. The emigrants

SETTLERS IN SOUTH CAROLINA.

abandoned Beaufort soon afterward, and sailing northward entered Charleston harbor. On the banks of a stream a few miles above the site of Charleston, they landed, built houses and cultivated the soil. There they planted the first seeds of the colony of South Carolina at a spot known as Old Town.

The settlers found the Indians unfriendly, for tradition had taught them to believe that the white man was a cruel robber. The planters were compelled to labor in the fields and on the waters, well-armed, yet they prospered; and they soon conquered the savages by kindness. West exercised the authority of magistrate until the arrival of Sir John Yeamans from Barbadoes with the commission of governor late in 1661. He brought with him fifty families and many negro slaves. This was the introduction of slave-labor into South Carolina, which has always been pre-eminently a planting state.

The settlement at Old Town was organized under the title of the *Carteret County Colony*, and representative government was established there in 1672. So was founded the commonwealth of *South Carolina*. It was known as a place where freedom was enjoyed, and emigrants flocked to it from England, Holland, and New York. They spread over the peninsula between the Ashley and another stream which they called the Cooper River, both so named in honor of Ashley Cooper, one of the proprietors. At Oyster Point, at the junction of three streams, on the verge of a fine harbor and in sight of the sea, they laid the foundations of a capital city for the province eight or ten years later, and named it Charles Town (Charleston) in compliment to the king. Old Town was abandoned, and the new village flourished. Very soon thriving settlements were seen along the Santee and Edisto Rivers; and the region between the Ashley and Cooper—the Ke-a-wah and E-ti-wan of the Indians—became quite populous with industrious inhabitants.

We have observed that it was designed to establish a great empire in the region of the Carolinas. It was deemed proper to devise a scheme of government commensurate with that grand idea. To Sir Ashley Cooper, and the philosopher John Locke, was entrusted the task of framing a constitution. Cooper was then about forty-seven years of age, and in the full maturity of his genius and power. He was of an old and wealthy family, and was connected with some of the most distinguished members of the English aristocracy. He was now a royalist of the strictest pattern. A few years later (1672), he was elevated to the peerage as Earl of Shaftesbury, and made Lord High Chancellor of England. Locke was much younger—only thirty-four—but was a more profound thinker than Cooper, and was already famous as a philosopher. He was a tutor of Cooper's son. His views of government were consonant with those of his friend, the statesman and courtier. Neither of these men was fitted for the task of framing an acceptable constitution for the government of a free people, and the magnificent scheme which they prepared, with the title of "Fundamental Constitutions," was entirely inconsistent with the condition and circumstances of the American colonists. It was the production chiefly of the brain and hand of Locke, it is believed, and was perfected in 1669.

For purposes of settlement, the proposed constitution provided for dividing the vast domain into counties, each to contain four hundred and eighty thousand acres. These lands were to be distributed in five equal parts, one-fifth to remain the inalienable property of the proprietors; another fifth the inalienable property of two orders of nobility, namely, landgraves or earls, and caciques or barons, one of the former and two of the latter belonging to each county; and the remaining three-fifths to belong to "the peoples," that is to say, farmers and lords of manors, the latter having no prescriptive legislative powers, but exercising judicial functions on their respective domains, in baronial courts. The number of the nobility was not to be increased nor diminished, the places of those who should not leave heirs, to be supplied by election. It gave to every freeman of Carolina absolute power over his negro slaves; and tenants, cultivating small quantities of land, were not only to be denied political franchises of any kind, but were serfs of the soil, and under the jurisdiction of their lord, without appeal; and all their children were to endure the same social degradation "to all generations."

When that elaborate constitution, which provided for titles, and classes, and aristocratic distinctions in America, was submitted to the people of the Carolinas, they rejected it as absurd in its details. They had made judicious laws for their own government, were satisfied with their workings, and resolved to have nothing to do with the scheme of the proprietors. Under their own laws they built up flourishing colonies, inseparable in interests and aims, and so they remained over sixty years, when they were dismembered and formed the separate colonies of *North and South Carolina.*

CHAPTER X.

THE ENGLISH AND SPANIARDS—SLAVES IN SOUTH CAROLINA—PRISONERS FOR DEBT IN ENGLAND —REVELATIONS OF THE PRISONS—MEASURES FOR THE RELIEF OF THE PRISONERS—CHARTER FOR GEORGIA GRANTED—GENERAL OGLETHORPE ACCOMPANIES EMIGRANTS TO THE SAVANNAH RIVER—JOY OF THE CAROLINIANS—FRIENDSHIP OF THE INDIANS—TO-MO-CHI-CHI—A TREATY —INDIANS ACCOMPANY OGLETHORPE TO ENGLAND—THEIR RECEPTION THERE—OGLETHORPE RETURNS TO GEORGIA WITH THE WESLEYS—AN UNWISE CODE FOR GEORGIA.

SELFISHNESS and philanthropy went hand in hand in promoting English settlements in the country south of the Savannah River. There seemed to be an unconquerable antagonism between the Spaniards and the English, in both hemispheres. The Spaniards viewed with jealousy the rapid increase of English settlements in America, especially in the region bordering on Florida, which the Castilians held by right of undoubted first discovery. They saw the English rapidly gaining the monopoly of the trade with the Indians and exercising a wide influence over the native inhabitants in the Gulf region, who had been taught by past sad experience to look upon the Spaniards as their abiding enemies. Therefore the Castilians in Florida were disposed to cast obstacles in the way of an extension of the English colonies southward.

Early in the eighteenth century, South Carolina was well stocked with slaves from Africa, especially in the rice-planting districts, where negroes performed nearly all of the manual labor. They had become essential to the prosperity of the colony. The Spaniards believed that the most effectual way to discourage the English planters and to prevent their making settlements below the Savannah River, would be to entice away their slaves by promises of the freedom and the privileges of the Spanish subjects. This measure was successfully employed. A complete regiment was formed at St. Augustine of runaway slaves from South Carolina; and they were taught to hate the English as their enemies. This was an alarming state of things for the South Carolinians, and they anxiously sought a remedy for the evil.

Between the Savannah and Alatamaha rivers, there was a region wholly unoccupied by white inhabitants at the end of the first quarter of the eighteenth century. The South Carolinians proposed to erect a barrier between themselves and the Spaniards in Florida, by the planting of an English colony in that region. They asked the British government to do so. There were great obstacles in the way. Voluntary emigrants preferred a settled country away from immediate danger from foes; and a penal colony for British convicts was not desirable.

At that juncture, the subject of the condition of prisoners for debt in Great Britain, was attracting general attention. These men, unconvicted of any crime, were crowding the jails of the kingdom, and enduring sufferings more horrible than those inflicted upon negro slaves in the West Indies. Disease and moral degradation were making sad havoc among them. The hearts of the benevolent yearned to relieve them. A humane and wealthy citizen of London bequeathed his fortune to the government to be employed in liberating the most deserving insolvent debtors from the jails, where they were doomed to hopeless indigence and misery by the cruel laws oftentimes more cruelly administered.

This act caused the appointment of a committee by Parliament to inquire into the condition of prisoners for debt. It was done at the suggestion of Colonel James Edward Oglethorpe, a graduate of Oxford, a brave soldier, and then a member of Parliament. That was in the year 1728. Colonel Oglethorpe was made chairman of the committee, and they entered upon their duties with vigor. The revelations of the prisons were horrible and sickening. The writings of the afterwards illustrious Howard give us vivid pen-pictures of the scenes. The pencil of Hogarth has left us actual delineations of them. The English merchant, unfortunate in his business, was often suddenly plunged from a sphere of affluence and usefulness, to the dreadful dens called prisons, there to herd with the ignorant and vile in hopeless poverty and degradation.

Oglethorpe stood before one of these men who had been a distinguished alderman, in London, when he was a boy, and had been highly esteemed for his many virtues and practical benevolence. He had also been a "merchant prince," but had been ruined by great losses. His creditors sent him to prison. In an instant he was compelled to exchange a happy home and delightful society for a loathsome prison cell and the company of the debased. One by one his friends, who could aid him in keeping famine from his wretched abode, disappeared, and he was forgotten by the outside world. Twenty-three years he had been in jail. Gray-headed, haggard, ragged and perishing with hunger, he lay upon a heap of filthy straw in a dark, damp, unventilated room. His devoted wife, who had shared his misery eighteen years, had just starved to death, and lay in rags by his side, silent and cold. An hour before he had begged his jailor, with outstretched arms of supplication, to remove her body to the prison burying-ground. The inhuman wretch, who knew his history, refused with an oath, saying, with horrid irony: "Send for your alderman's coach to take her to the Abbey!"

The man expired when he had finished his sad story. There and then, inspired by God, Oglethorpe conceived a scheme of providing an asylum for such as these beyond the sea, where they might enjoy comfort and happiness. He also resolved to bring such jailors to punishment. The records of some of the English state trials show how earnestly he pursued these felons.

THE PRISONER FOR DEBT.

Oglethorpe proposed to plant the colony of unfortunates in the unoccupied country below the Savannah. His colleagues readily assented, and in his report to the House of Commons, he laid a scheme for the colony before that body. It promised the advantages of securing that domain to the British Crown, relieving the South Carolinians from danger, and doing good to a large class of worthy British subjects. The king and Parliament approved the project. An appropriation of money for the object was made, and on the 9th of June, 1732, the king granted a charter for founding a colony with the title of *Georgia*. That name was given in compliment to King George the Second, then the ruling monarch of England.

The management of the new settlement was entrusted to twenty-one "noblemen and gentlemen," who were constituted "Trustees for Settling and Establishing the Colony of Georgia." Colonel Oglethorpe was one of them. They were vested with legislative powers for the government of the colony for the space of twenty-one years, at the expiration of which time a permanent government was to be established by the king or his successors in accordance with British law and usage.

Oglethorpe generously offered to accompany the emigrants and assist them in making their first settlement. Every feature of the project commended itself to the hearts of the British people. Donations from all ranks and classes were freely given to assist the emigrants in planting comfortable homes in the wilderness. The Bank of England made a generous gift; and the House of Commons, from time to time, voted money, amounting in the aggregate, in the course of two years, to one hundred and sixty thousand dollars. Lord Viscount Percival was chosen president of the trustees, and a code of regulations for the colony, with agreements and stipulations, was speedily prepared.

All things being in readiness, thirty-five families—one hundred and twenty emigrants, men, women, and children—sailed from Gravesend for Georgia in the ship *Anne*, of two hundred tons burden, on the 6th of November, 1732. They were accompanied by Colonel Oglethorpe as governor, the Rev. Mr. Shubert, of the Church of England, as a spiritual guide, and a few Piedmontese silk-workers; for one of the projects of the trustees was the growing of silk in Georgia.

The *Anne* arrived at Charleston harbor at the middle of January, 1733, where the emigrants were received with joy by the inhabitants. The Assembly of South Carolina voted them a large supply of cattle and other provisions, for they were regarded as valuable auxiliaries. Their mutual aid was foreshadowed by the following lines which appeared in the *Gentleman's Magazine:*

"To Carolina be a Georgia joined!
Then shall both colonies sure progress make,
Endeared to either for the other's sake;
Georgia shall Carolina's protection move,
And Carolina bloom by Georgia's love."

The *Anne* was piloted from Charleston into Port Royal Sound, near Beaufort Island, whence the emigrants were to be conveyed to the Savannah River in small boats. From that point, Oglethorpe, accompanied by a guide furnished by the council of South Carolina, went forward to select a suitable place for a settlement. He chose Yamacraw Bluff, on the Savannah River, about ten miles from the sea, where Governor Moore, of South Carolina, had planted a small tribe of Creek Indians thirty years before, as owners of the soil. It was a high plain, its river front forty feet above the stream, and gently sloping to the swamps in the rear. There he laid out a town and returned to Beaufort, where the emigrants had landed, to conduct them to their final destination. They all arrived there on the first of February, and slept in tents that night.

The South Carolinians had sent boats with the additional provisions, and a body of rangers for the protection of the colonists while the latter should build cabins and a fort for their defence. The town projected by the governor was named Savannah, and there the emigrants soon had comfortable dwellings and a formidable military work armed with cannons. Concerning this spot, Oglethorpe wrote to the trustees:

"Upon the river side, at the centre of this plain, I have laid out a town, opposite to which is an island [Hutchinson's Island] of very rich pasturage, which I think should be kept for the trustees' cattle. The river is pretty wide, the water fresh, and from the key of the town you see its whole course to the sea, with the island of Tybee, which forms the mouth of the river. For about six miles up into the country the landscape is very agreeable, the stream being wide and bordered with high woods on both sides."

Before their departure from England, the colonists had received some military training from the sergeants of the guards, in London. Oglethorpe now formed them into a company of militia with officers; and he frequently exercised them that the Indians might be impressed with their military skill. The fort was soon completed and cannon mounted upon it. Then the governor turned his earnest attention to the important business of establishing friendly relations with the Indians. He was within territory claimed by the powerful Creek Confederacy, and not far from the seat of a tribe composed partly of Yamacraws and partly of Yamasees or Savannahs, over whom presided To-mo-chi-chi, a venerable chief. He had suffered banishment at the hands of his people, the Lower Creeks, but for what cause is unknown. He was then ninety-one years of age, of commanding person and grave demeanor. His power over his immediate followers was supreme, and his name had great weight throughout the Confederacy as a renowned warrior and wise sachem. Oglethorpe therefore sought an early interview with To-mo-chi-chi. It was held under the tall pines and wide-spreading live-oaks that covered Yamacraw Bluff, with Mary Musgrove, the half-breed Creek wife of a South Carolina trader, then at Savannah, as interpreter.

That interview was very satisfactory. To-mo-chi-chi pledged his unwavering friendship for the English, and assisted Oglethorpe in making arrangements for a general convention of the heads of the Confederacy. That convention assembled in one of the large houses at Savannah, late in May, 1733, and was attended by fifty chiefs representing eight tribes of the Creek Nation.

Oglethorpe addressed the assembled chiefs. He told them of the great power, wealth and wisdom of the English people, and of the advantages the Indians might derive by the cultivation of friendly relations between the two races. He expressed a hope that as the Indians had a superabundance

OGLETHORPE'S MILITIA.

of land, they would freely resign a portion of it to those who had come over the sea for their instruction and benefit. When the governor ceased speaking, the venerable To-mo-chi-chi arose and, in behalf of the Creek warriors present, he gave their cordial assent to Oglethorpe's proposition. "I was a banished man," he said. "I came here, poor and helpless, to look for good lands near the tombs of my ancestors, and the trustees sent people here. I feared you would drive us away, for we were weak and wanted corn; but you confirmed our land to us, gave us food and instructed our children." After further declaring the goodness of the English and expressing thanks, To-mo-chi-chi said, as he gave a buffalo-skin to the governor, on the inside of which were delineated the head and feathers of an eagle: "Here is a little present. I give you the skin of a buffalo adorned with the head and feathers of an eagle, which I desire you to accept, because the eagle is an emblem of speed and the buffalo of strength. The English are as swift as the bird and as strong as the beast; since like the former, they flew over vast seas to the uttermost parts of the earth; and like the latter, they are so strong that nothing can withstand them. The feathers of the eagle are soft, and signify love; the buffalo's skin is warm, and signifies protection; therefore I hope the English will love and protect our little families."

A satisfactory treaty was made by which all unoccupied lands within defined boundaries were assigned to the English. This treaty was ratified by the trustees on the 18th of October, 1733, when the English obtained sovereignty over the domain between the Savannah and Alatamaha rivers, westward from the Atlantic to the extent of tide-water, and all the islands but three from Tybee to St. Simons. Unfortunately the Indians were allowed to reserve for their use in hunting, bathing and fishing the islands of Ossabaw, Sapela and St. Catharines, which were within the limits of the English domain. This reservation was a source of trouble afterwards.

At the conclusion of the treaty, To-mo-chi-chi invited the members of the convention to his own town near by, where they spent the night in feasting and dancing. The treaty was signed on the 21st, when the governor distributed the following presents among the Indians: A laced coat and a laced hat and shirt to each of the chiefs; to each of the warriors, a gun and a mantle of duffils (a coarse woolen cloth with nap and fringe), and to all their attendants coarse cloth for clothing; a barrel of gunpowder; four kegs of bullets; a piece of broadcloth; a piece of Irish linen; a cask of tobacco pipes; eight belts and cutlasses with gilt handles; tape, and of all colors; eight kegs of rum to be carried home to their towns; one pound of powder, one pound of bullets, and as much provision for each one as they pleased to take for their journey home. Rum appears to have been freely used at first in Georgia. In the minutes of the trustees, under date of August 11, 1733, is the following record: "Read a letter from Mr. Oglethorpe with an account of the death of several persons in Georgia, which he imputed to the *drinking of rum*. Resolved, That the drinking of rum in Georgia be absolutely prohibited, and that all which be brought there be staved." This was a short but pretty effectual prohibitory law.

In the spring of 1734, Oglethorpe went to England, leaving the colony in the care of others. Believing that a sight of England, its inhabitants and evidences of its power, by some of the Indians, would increase the reverence of the savages for Englishmen and add strength and permanence to the colony, he invited To-mo-chi-chi and some of his friends to go with

20

him. The invitation was accepted, and the old Creek monarch with his queen, See-naw-ki; their adopted son and nephew, Too-na-ho-wi and five chiefs, went on the voyage. The vessel reached England in June, when Oglethorpe sent a letter to his friend, Sir John Phillips, in which he spoke of To-mo-chi-chi as an aged chief, "the mico or king of Yamacraw, a man of an excellent understanding, so desirous of hearing the young people taught the English language and religion, that, notwithstanding his advanced age, he has come over with me to obtain means and assistant teachers. He has brought with him a young man whom he calls his nephew and next heir, and who has already learned the Lord's prayer in the English and the Indian language." The reception of the governor and his dusky friends was cordial. The Indians were objects of great curiosity, none having been seen in England since Schuyler took some Mohawk kings to the court of Queen Anne. To-mo-chi-chi was made the subject of an ode of eleven stanzas of ten lines each, the first of which was as follows:

A GEORGIA CHIEFTAIN.

"What stranger this? and from what region far?
This wondrous form, majestic to behold?
Uncloath'd but arm'd offensive for the war,
In hoary age and wise experience old?
His limbs inured to hardiness and toil,
His strong large limbs what mighty sinews brace!
Whilst truth sincere and artless virtue smile
In the expressive features of his face,
His bold, free aspect speaks the inward mind,
Arm'd by no slavish fear, from no vile passion blind."

On the first of August the Indians were conveyed in three of the royal coaches, each drawn by six horses, to Kensington palace, to have an interview with the king. They had been dressed at the office of the trustees in

English costume. To-mo-chi-chi and his queen in scarlet and gold. The chiefs, less gorgeously attired, had their faces painted according to their home-custom. They were received at the door of the palace by the royal body-guard and conducted to the presence of the king and queen, who were seated on thrones. Then To-mo-chi-chi presented some eagle's feathers to the monarch, and said:

"This day I see the majesty of your face, the greatness of your house, and the number of your people. I am come for the good of the whole nation called the Creeks, to renew the peace which was long ago had with the English. I am come over in my old days, although I cannot live to see any advantage to myself. I am come for the good of the children of all the nations of the Upper and Lower Creeks, that they may be instructed in the knowledge of the English.

"These are the feathers of the eagle which is the swiftest of birds, and who flieth all around our nations. These feathers are a sign of peace in our land, and have been carried from town to town there; and we have brought them over to leave with you, O great king! as a sign of everlasting peace. O great king! whatsoever words you shall say to me, I will tell them faithfully to all the kings of the Creek nations."

The sovereign gave a gracious answer to this speech, assuring the old chief that he and his people might rely upon the friendship of the English. Then they withdrew. A cloud was upon their spirits. One of the chiefs, a brother of queen See-naw-ki, was very sick with the small-pox. He soon died, and was buried with the custom of his country as nearly as possible. Then Oglethorpe took the whole party to his estate, where they bewailed their loss for several days. After remaining four months in England, and becoming deeply impressed with the greatness of the English people, To-mo-chi-chi and his company returned to Georgia, in the company of a considerable number of new emigrants. The Indians were conveyed to the ship at Gravesend, in the royal coaches, bearing with them presents valued at two thousand dollars. The Prince of Wales had given to To-mo-chi-chi's heir a gold watch, with an injunction to call upon Jesus Christ every morning, when he looked on it. They reached Savannah late in December, 1734. Among the emigrants was an English baronet (Francis Parkhurst) and his family, and fifty-six Saltzburghers newly arrived from Rotterdam.

Oglethorpe did not return to Georgia until the beginning of 1736, when he was received with joy by the colonists and the Indians. He took with him several cannon and about one hundred and fifty Scotch Highlanders, well skilled in the military art, who constituted the first army in Georgia during its early struggles. With him also came the Rev. John Wesley, the founder of the Methodist Church, and his brother Charles, who came to preach the gospel to the heathen. To Mr. Wesley, To-mo-chi-chi remarked: "I am glad you are come. When I was in England, I desired that some one would speak the *great word* to me. I will go up and speak to the wise men of my nation, and hope they will hear. But we would not be made Christians as the Spaniards make Christians; we would be taught before we are baptized."

With a population of more than five hundred souls; with a military force, and with means for religious instruction, the foundations of the colony of Georgia were now firmly laid. And had the wisdom of the trustees been equal to their benevolence, immediate and great prosperity would have been visible. But they bound the colonists by such unwise rules and regulations that their energies were cramped, and it seemed, at one time, as if the grand object of the trustees, and the hopes of Englishmen, would be frustrated.

We have now considered the more prominent events in the history of the planting of settlements in America, and the development of many of them into permanent colonies. The ingredients of the story are highly picturesque. The simple outline picture, when drawn from nature with fidelity, possesses marvellous interest to the student of human nature. The imagination may not conceive incidents more romantic than those which sober truth reveals in the career of men and women who came from Europe to explore and make homes in the wilds of America. Nearly all of them were impelled to the undertaking by those powerful motives of human action,—avarice, ambition or the love of liberty. In all of the earlier adventurers and settlers, we see these passions dominating all others. The discoverers stand out on the page of history as grand heroes, worthy of a representation on the shield of Achilles. In the delineation of their deeds and of those of their followers who occupied what they discovered, faith, hope, courage, hardihood, fortitude, indomitable perseverance and untiring energy, are prominent features in the picture. These were the necessary elements of success in the wide and wild fields of adventure, and were ever present in great abundance when required in laying the foundations of our Republic.

We will now consider the processes by which small settlements grew into great commonwealths in the form of British-American colonies.

END OF BOOK II.

BOOK III.

COLONIES

FROM 1733 TO 1763.

CHAPTER I.

THE VIRGINIA COLONISTS—INTRODUCTION OF SLAVES FROM AFRICA—YOUNG WOMEN SENT TO VIRGINIA—FAMILIES AND SCHOOLS ESTABLISHED THERE—CONSTITUTION OF VIRGINIA—BETTER PROSPECTS—MASSACRE BY INDIANS—RETALIATION—PESTILENCE—THE NEW BRITISH MONARCH—AN UNPOPULAR GOVERNMENT DEPOSED—SIR WILLIAM BERKELEY—ANOTHER MASSACRE BY THE INDIANS—DEATH OF THE INDIAN EMPEROR—END OF THE CONFEDERACY—BERKELEY AND ROYALTY—THE "OLD DOMINION."

WE have observed that in Virginia was first established a permanent English colony in our country, when, in 1619, Governor Yeardley organized representative government there, and so laid the foundations of a commonwealth. The tribe of gold-seekers had disappeared forever; but the unwholesome influences of a tribe of felons from the prisons of England, which the king had ordered to be sent to Virginia—a hundred in number—was yet felt in the scandal it had brought upon the colony, and in their demoralizing example. Captain Smith declared that they gave

Virginia such a bad reputation, "that some did choose to be hanged ere they would go thither, and *were*."

Another element was introduced into Virginia society in 1619, which had a powerful influence over the destinies, not only of that colony, but of the nation of which it afterward formed a part. Just at sunset, on a hot evening in August, a Dutch trading vessel arrived from the coast of Guinea with a strange cargo of living creatures for sale. They were black men and women who had been stolen from their homes on that coast and destined for slaves. The planters had heard of the capacity of Africans for enduring labor in warm regions, and they purchased twenty of them—fourteen men and six women. They found them to be good workers and very docile. Others were imported; and so was begun the system of negro slavery in our country—a stain which was washed out with blood almost two centuries and a half afterwards, when the servile race numbered about four million.

At about the same time another element was introduced into Virginia society, which exerted a most healthful and beneficent influence over the colony. The wise Sir Edwin Sandys, who had lately been appointed treasurer of the London Company, had, for the purpose of effecting a reform, entered upon a thorough and fearless investigation of the abuses which had attended the colonization of Virginia, and retarded its progress. It was then twelve years since the first emigrants landed at Jamestown. A large amount of money had been spent in sending persons to people the region, and yet there were only about six hundred Europeans there when Sandys entered upon his duties. He pursued his purpose with zeal, and very soon he purged Virginia of its bad name. His reputation for candor and other virtues were so well known, that within the space of one year he persuaded more than twelve hundred emigrants to go to the James River. He had patriotic colleagues in the Board, and they effected a wonderful change in the fortunes of the colony.

The English settlers, more delicate in their tastes and habits than the French and Portuguese, would not marry the Indian women, and very few English women had ventured to cross the Atlantic. Therefore the planters of Virginia had not the comforts and sacred connections of married life. Few of them expected to remain in the colony. Most of them looked for a return to England when they should acquire a competency. They were unsettled, and unfitted for patient industry. The sagacious Sandys clearly perceived their needs and the remedy. He proposed to send over to Virginia one hundred virtuous and attractive young English women from the middle class in society, to become wives for the planters, the cost of the transportation of each to be paid by the husband who should choose her.

The scheme involved a half-social, half-commercial speculation. It was tried and succeeded. Ninety young women of the class named were induced to go to Virginia early in 1620. When they arrived at Jamestown, they were landed from the ship in small boats. The shore was covered by young planters who came to see the disembarkation of the novel and precious cargo. Led by the rector of the parish, these maidens walked in procession to the church, where thanksgivings were offered to their Maker for their preservation from the perils of the sea. The church was crowded; and within

INTRODUCTION OF NEGRO SLAVERY INTO VIRGINIA.

the space of a few days, every maiden was wooed and won by the young planters. "Love at first sight" was the rule. Several nuptials occurred in the church at the same time. According to cotemporary witnesses, the seeming indelicacy of the transaction was qualified by the true affection which prevailed among the married couples, most of them being happily mated. The young matrons sent word home for other maidens to come, and sixty more, "young and handsome," arrived at Jamestown the next year. Others followed.

The price of a wife was at first fixed at one hundred and twenty pounds of tobacco, then the currency of the colony. The money value was about ninety dollars. It finally arose to one hundred and fifty dollars. A debt incurred for a wife was regarded as a "confidential" one. It took precedence of all others. To encourage wedding, the Company gave preference to married men in conferring employments. The salutary effects of the scheme and of this policy were soon visible in the colony. HOMES—firesides—family altars—the purest and strongest elements in the foundations of a virtuous and prosperous state, were established. Domestic ties so created, promoted personal virtue and habits of thrift. Men no longer talked of returning to England, but called Virginia their home. Emigration rapidly swelled the population, and before the close of 1621, fifty patents had been granted for land, and there were three thousand five hundred inhabitants of European blood in Virginia. Settlements had been already made so remote from the capital as the Falls of the James River, where Richmond now stands. Below there, at what is known as Dutch Gap (so called because Germans were employed to cut a new channel for the river across a narrow isthmus there), a town had been founded which was named Henricopolis, and there a church had been built and a grammar-school established for the education of Indian children. When the school was endowed with money and thousands of acres of land, the dignified title of The University of Henrico was given to it. The church, the college and the town have long ago crumbled into ruins, which no longer attract the eye of the curious or the scrutiny of the antiquary.

The blessings of marriage created the necessity for making provision for the education of children. English Bishops and other philanthropists collected money for the purpose. The colonists bore a share of the burden. Other schools beside that of Henrico were established in which Indian children were also taught. Finally, in the reign of William and Mary, more than seventy years after the emigration of the maidens, a college was established at Williamsburg, the new capital of Virginia, which still flourishes, and yet bears the names of those sovereigns.

In the year 1621, the London Company granted a written constitution to the Virginia colonists, modelled after that of England, but exceedingly simple; the Pilgrims in the *May-Flower*, more democratic, gave to themselves a written constitution at about the same time, fashioned to meet the circumstances of their case, and still more simple. A century and a half afterward, as we shall discover, the inhabitants of these two colonies, then founded, were leaders in the great struggle for that political independence which these early constitutions foreshadowed. The Virginia constitution provided for a governor and council to be appointed by the Company, and a popular legislative body to be chosen by the people, and called the House of Burgesses. Each settlement was allowed two burgesses, and these, with the governor and council, composed the General Assembly. That Assembly exercised full legislative power, but none of its acts were valid until they received the sanction of the Company in London. With unexampled justice, it was also provided that no orders from the Company should be binding on the colonists, unless they should be, in like manner, ratified by the General Assembly. This was the work of the Earl of Southampton (the bosom friend of Shakespeare), Sir Edwin Sandys and the patriotic party in England, who were careful to imbue public life in Virginia with the principles of popular freedom. It was at the dawn of that eventful day of political disputes in England which resulted in the beheading of her king and the abolition of monarchy for a season.

When Sir Francis Wyatt came to Virginia, bringing with him the new constitution, he was pleased with the aspect of everything around him; and the colonists rejoiced in the prospect of long years of peace and prosperity before them. The atmosphere of their daily life appeared perfectly serene. There was no cloud in the firmament. But at that moment a fearful tempest was brooding, in restraint, in the forests around them. Powhatan, the friend of the English, was dead, and his younger brother, the subtle, treacherous and truly savage Opechancanough (the captor of Smith in the forest), was then wielding the sceptre of his empire. He could command fifteen hundred warriors to do his bidding. He hated the English intensely, and inspired his followers with the same passion; yet he feigned the warmest friendship for them, and deceived them with Satanic smiles. He believed that the English intended to seize the lands of his empire and exterminate his race, and his patriotism impelled him to strike a blow for his country and countrymen.

Opechancanough used various arts to inflame the anger of the Indians against the English. He had a rival in the admiration of his people, who had shown himself to be a bitter enemy of the colonists. For the double purpose of ridding himself of this rival and exciting the anger of his nation against the English, the emperor sent word to Governor Wyatt that he gave him liberty to cut that man's throat. Such an act would surely have aroused the savages into furious war. It was not done; but, unfortunately, in an affray with a settler, the man was shot. The wily emperor pretended to bewail his loss, and so he fired the resentment of the Indians against the

English. Then he went secretly to the governor, half-clad in skins, his head plumed with eagle's feathers, and bearing in his belt a finely-wrought hatchet. After making warm professions of friendship, he demanded in a haughty tone, some concessions to his incensed people. His demand was refused, and forgetting himself for a moment, he snatched the hatchet from his belt and struck its keen blade into a log of the cabin, uttering a curse

THE ANGER OF OPECHANCANOUGH.

upon the English. His words fell like a fearful revelation upon the mind of the governor. Instantly recovering himself, the savage smiled, and said blandly: "Pardon me, governor; I was thinking of that wicked Englishman [Argall] who stole my niece [Pocahontas], and struck me with his sword. I love the English who are the friends of the family of Powhatan. Sooner will the skies fall than my bond of friendship with the English shall be dissolved."

Sir Francis warned his people that there was treachery abroad. They were slow to believe it. There had never been a war with the Indians. Their settlements were scattered—some of them in solitary places—and yet no one had ever been disturbed by the savages since the happy marriage of Pocahontas. So secure had they felt, that they had broken a law which forbade the teaching of the use of fire-arms to the Indians, and had employed them to hunt with the musket. In the midst of this calm of confidence, the tempest suddenly burst upon the colony. At mid-day, on the 1st of April [the 22d March, old style], 1622, the Indians rushed from the forests upon all of the remote settlements at a pre-concerted time, and in the space of an hour three hundred and fifty men, women and children were slain. Even the devoted missionary at Henrico, who had instructed the children of the savages and tenderly nursed the young and old in sickness, was not spared. Among the victims were six members of the council and several of the wealthier inhabitants. On the very morning of the massacre, the treacherous savages were in the houses and at the tables of those whom they intended to murder at noon.

The people at Jamestown were saved by Chanco, a Christian Indian, who heard of the conspiracy in the evening before the massacre. He hastened to Jamestown to warn a friend of impending danger. The alarm spread, but it was too late to reach the more remote settlements. The people at Jamestown were prepared to meet the assassins, and so averted the blow which might have extinguished the colony. Those at a distance, who survived the carnage, beat back the savages and then fled to Jamestown. In the course of a few days, eighty inhabited plantations were reduced to eight. But a large part of the colony was saved.

The people thus gathered at Jamestown by a terrible necessity prepared for vengeance. A vindictive and exterminating war was immediately waged. Every man capable of bearing arms appeared in the field, and fearful retaliating blows were given. The English spread death and desolation over the peninsula between the York and James rivers. The Indians were slaughtered by scores, or driven far back into the wilderness. Opechancanough fled for his life to the land of the Pamunkeys, and lost much of his influence by a show of cowardice. His power was broken, and the strength of his people had departed. Before the war, there were about six thousand Indians within sixty miles of Jamestown, occupying a domain eight thousand square miles in extent; at the close of the war, there were probably not a thousand within that territory.

The blight of war, pestilence and famine fell upon the colony. Sickness prevailed among the people, who were gathered into a narrow space for mutual protection. Large areas of land were left uncultivated; and many of the settlers, discouraged and terrified, returned to England. The colony of almost four thousand souls was soon reduced to twenty-five hundred; and these never retired at night with an assurance that they would not hear the savage war-whoop before the dawn.

The sufferings of the colonists excited the liveliest sympathy in England. Ships were sent with supplies. The mean king made it the occasion for a false show of generosity. He sent to the colonists a number of guns from the Tower of London, which had been cast aside as useless in Europe. "They may serve the people," said the king, "against ignorant and naked heathen salvages." The generous Captain Smith, deeply interested in the fate of the colony he had helped to found, offered his services to the Company to lead an expedition to overawe the Indians and to protect the people. Some of the Company, moved by inordinate greed more than by compassion for the colonists, offered to give Smith permission to lead an expedition at his own expense, provided he would give the Company one-half the plunder.

The meddlesome King James, finding a majority of the London Company surely drifting toward republicanism, and disliking the freedom of debate in the General Assembly of Virginia, resolved to control the Company and the colony. "The Virginia House of Burgesses," said Gondamar, the Spanish envoy at the English court, "is but a seminary to a seditious Parliament." The king believed it; and at the election of officers for the Company in 1622, he tried to control the choice of candidates. He failed. Then he determined to deprive the Company of their charter, and, by taking control of the affairs of the corporation, regain what he had lost by granting them the liberal third charter. He sent a commission to Virginia, composed of his pliable instruments, to inquire into the affairs of the colony. They tried to coax and frighten the House of Burgesses into a relinquishment of the rights guaranteed to them by the terms of the charter. Finding these representatives of the people firm in support of their liberties, the commissioners recommended a dissolution of the charter. A pliant judiciary assisted the king in the measure, and in July, 1624, the patent was cancelled and Virginia became a royal province again. No material change was made in the domestic affairs of the colony. The monarch appointed Sir Francis Wyatt governor, with twelve councillors of state, but wisely refrained from interfering with the House of Burgesses. He boasted that he would make the colony more prosperous than ever, but he died soon afterward, and was succeeded by his son, Charles the First, on the 6th of April, 1625.

King Charles was a thorough disciple of his father in the science of what James was pleased to call kingcraft, the prime elements of which, as he exhibited it, were lying and deception. He was also as bigoted as his father in his belief in the doctrine of the divine right of kings to govern the people absolutely, and the sacredness of the royal prerogative or the enjoyment of special privileges not accorded to the people. He was only twenty-five years of age when he ascended the throne; and he was a pliant tool in the hands of the Duke of Buckingham, his father's base court favorite, who assisted in bringing to England as the queen of the young king, a Roman Catholic French princess, sister of the monarch of France. Three months after he became king, Charles received the princess at Dover and married her at Canterbury; but they did not enter London for some time because of the ravages of an epidemic there, by which over thirty-five thousand persons perished.

The queen brought with her a retinue of priests and other Roman Catholic attendants. The Protestant sentiment of a majority of the English people was alarmed. This fact, combined with the character of the king, which was uniformly marked by insincerity, deception, falsehood and treachery—the fruits of the favorite's training—made him feared, hated and despised by the honest portion of his friends, as well as his foes, and brought swift trouble upon himself and his country. There were causes which nourished opposition to monarchy, and cherished discontents. These soon led to a civil war, the beheading of the king and the abolition of monarchy in England for a season. Such was the sovereign with whom the American colonists had to deal for many years, while England was in a state of transition from absolutism or the unbridled rule of the monarch, to constitutional liberty or the enjoyment of rights guaranteed to the people by a constitution respected by the sovereign because his subjects have the power to enforce it. It was a state which Charles would not comprehend; and his stupid obstinacy plunged his country into war with itself, and also with France and Spain.

CHARLES THE FIRST.

Charles did not materially change the political situation of the Virginians. His appointment of Sir George Yeardly, the magistrate who had established representative government in Virginia, was a guaranty that no such change would take place. But the king, who was selfish as well as weak, sought to enlarge his private fortune out of the profits of the industry of the Virginia planters of tobacco. He gave them the monopoly of production for the market of England, saying: "It may be well said that the plantation is built wholly on *smoke* which will easily turn into *air*, if either English tobacco be permitted to be planted or Spanish be imported." At the same time, he forbade the tobacco-growers selling their products to any persons excepting such as the king had appointed his agents. Among these agents was Sir John Harvey, who had been one of the governor's council, and who has been represented as a rapacious, unscrupulous, avaricious and cruel royalist.

These arrangements did not disturb the Virginians, and the colony prospered until Harvey was made governor in 1629, two years after the death of Yeardly. In 1628, not less than a thousand English people emigrated to Virginia. But the advent of Harvey in 1630 was the beginning of confusion. He was represented by his political foes as an enemy of the people, and he made himself unpopular because he advocated and promoted a system of land grants which would tend to place the soil of the province into the possession of a few landed aristocracy—and so be injurious to the prosperity of the colony. In various ways he offended the Republicans. Violent disputes arose, and after a war of words for several years, the House of Burgesses deposed Harvey and sent commissioners to England with an impeachment. The governor went with the commissioners. The king refused to hear any complaints against his agent, and sent him back clothed with power to rule the state independently of the people.

Harvey was succeeded in 1639 by Sir Francis Wyatt, whose administration was an uneventful one. It ended in February, 1642, when Sir William Berkeley, brother of Lord Berkeley (one of the earliest English proprietors of New Jersey), arrived at Jamestown with the commission of chief magistrate of Virginia. He was a fine specimen of a young English courtier, only thirty-two years of age. Handsome in person, educated at Oxford, polished by extensive travel on the continent and possessing exquisite taste in dress, he was one of the most elegant of the cavaliers of his time. Some salutary measures which he adopted at the beginning of his administration for the benefit of the people made him popular in Virginia; and his natural suavity of manners, and the generous hospitality dispensed at his mansion at Green Spring, not far from Jamestown, sustained that popularity for many years. He was a staunch loyalist, but not a bigoted one; and so prudent was the method of his adhesion to the cause of the king during the civil war from 1641 to 1649, that a greater part of the Virginians were in sympathy with him. There was a party for the Parliament, in Virginia, but it was not sufficiently strong to show any serious opposition to royal rule. The colonists were warmly attached to the Church of England, yet there were many Puritans there, for toleration had been the rule—Puritans had even been invited to come, with their ministers, when the peculiar character of the revolution, then going on in England, brought religious sects into political prominence. The Puritans in England were identified with the Republicans in their struggle with royalty. Governor Berkeley was of the cavalier class, and despised the non-conformists. He perceived that a great majority of the inhabitants of Virginia were warmly attached to the Church of England, and he conceived that to tolerate Puritanism in Virginia was to nurture a Republican party there. So he decreed that no Puritan minister should preach or teach publicly, except in accordance with the constitution of the Church of England. This was soon followed by the banishment of non-conformists from the colony. It was a calamity; but a heavier one soon fell upon the Virginians.

Ever since the massacre by the Indians in 1622, there had remained a deadly hostility between the two races. In 1643, the Virginia Assembly decreed that no terms of peace should be entertained with the Indians. Opechancanough was yet living and past ninety years of age. He had been on the Pamunkey, nursing his wrath for twenty years. Prudence only had restrained his nature, and now he was too old and feeble to make war, on his feet. But his malice was as keen and his will as strong as they had ever been in the days of his prime.

When, at length, Thomas Rolf, the son of Pocahontas, and then nearly thirty years of age, came from England by consent of the Virginia Assembly to visit his uncle, the aged emperor, and Cleopatra the sister of his mother, Opechancanough heard from his lips about the war between the English factions. The old emperor concluded that the time for him to strike a vengeful blow had arrived. He sent runners throughout his empire, and very soon a confederacy was formed over an area many hundred square miles in extent for the extermination of the Europeans. A day was fixed for the execution of the scheme. The confederates were to begin at the frontiers and sweep the country to the sea. Opechancanough was carried at the head of his warriors, on a litter, when early in April, 1644, the savages began their horrid work. In the space of two days they slew more than three hundred of the settlers, sparing none who fell in their way. So they almost depopulated the region of the Pamunkey and York rivers. Governor

Berkeley met the murderers with an armed force, and drove them back with great slaughter. Their old monarch was taken prisoner, and carried in triumph to Jamestown. He was so much exhausted that he could not raise his eyelids, and in that forlorn condition he was mortally wounded by a bullet from the gun of an English soldier who guarded him, and who was impelled by the remembrance of the bereavements he had suffered at the hands of the Indians, and of the agency of the old chief in the matter. The people out of curiosity gathered around the dying emperor. Just before he expired, hearing the hum of a multitude, he asked one of his attendants to raise his eyelids. When he observed the crowd, he raised himself from the ground, and in a haughty tone commanded an officer near him to summon the governor before him. When the magistrate came, the old monarch said, as fiery indignation gave strength to his voice: "Had it been my fortune to have taken Sir William Berkeley prisoner, I would not meanly have exposed him as a show to my people." He then stretched himself upon the earth and died.

With Opechancanough expired the Powhatan confederacy. After ceding large tracts of land to the Virginians, the chiefs acknowledged allegiance to the authorities of the province, and so passed away the political life of that once powerful empire. The colonists then had peace and prosperity. In 1648, there were twenty thousand Europeans in Virginia. "The cottages were filled with children, as the ports with ships and emigrants." The people were loyal to Charles because he left them in the enjoyment of liberty. They felt none of the oppressions, nor were they distracted by the disputes which afflicted their kindred at home. They exercised the freedom of an independent government; and when the king was beheaded, they opened wide their hospitable arms to the cavaliers who fled in horror from England. Many of these fugitives were of the gentry, nobility and clergy. They were valuable additions to the refined society of Virginia, and strengthened the royal cause in that province. When the king was slain, the Virginians acknowledged his exiled son as their sovereign; and Sir William Berkeley conducted the affairs of the colony as governor, under a commission sent to him by that prince, from Breda, in Flanders. Virginia was the last country belonging to England that submitted to the government of the rulers of the commonwealth which succeeded the monarchy.

The Republican Parliament was offended by this persistent attachment to royalty, and in the early spring of 1652, sent Sir George Ayscue with a powerful fleet to reduce the Virginians to submission. It bore commissioners of the Parliament, who were clothed with power to exercise conciliatory or harsh measures—to compromise, or to proclaim freedom to the slaves and to put arms in their hands to make slaves of their masters. Berkeley met the commissioners with firmness. They were astonished at the boldness of the Virginians, and deemed it more prudent to compromise than to coerce. They made satisfactory arrangements, by which the political freedom of the colonists was guaranteed. Berkeley disdained to make any stipulation for himself with those whom he regarded as usurpers, and he withdrew to his plantation at Green Spring, where he lived in retirement as a private person. The Virginians then elected Richard Bennet, governor. When news of the preparation of an armament for the subjugation of the colony reached Virginia, Berkeley and the cavalier party resolved not to submit, and they sent a messenger to Breda to invite Prince Charles to come over and be their king. He was preparing to come, with his mother and some others of his family, when affairs took a turn in England which foreshadowed a speedy restoration of the monarchy there. That event occurred in 1660, when the prince ascended the throne of his father, as Charles the Second, at the age of thirty years. The monarch did not forget the loyalty of the Virginians. He caused the arms of that province to be quartered with those of England, Scotland and Ireland, as an independent member of his empire. From this circumstance the title of the "Old Dominion" was given to Virginia. Coins, with these quarterings, were struck as late as 1773.

CHAPTER II.

BERKELEY AN OPPRESSOR—REPUBLICANISM IN VIRGINIA—ROYAL FAVORITES ENRICHED—CONDITION OF THE VIRGINIANS—WAR WITH THE INDIANS—BERKELEY'S BAD CONDUCT—BACON'S REBELLION—BERKELEY'S CRUELTIES—A BREACH OF PRIVILEGE—A PROFLIGATE GOVERNOR—VIRGINIANS IMPOVERISHED AND DEGRADED BY MISRULE—POLITICAL TROUBLES IN ENGLAND—WHITE SLAVES IN VIRGINIA—GROWTH OF REPUBLICANISM THERE—THE REVOLUTION OF 1688.

THE Virginians soon felt the deep significance of the injunction: "Put not your trust in princes." When Matthews died (1660), whom Cromwell had appointed Governor of Virginia, the people elected Berkeley. He refused to serve, excepting under royal appointment; and he went to England to congratulate Charles on his accession to the throne, when he was graciously received by the sovereign. The king spoke very kindly of the Virginians, because of their loyalty, and praised them as the "best of his distant children." These manifestations of love were the velvet coverings of the iron hand which soon afterwards signed those decrees of a pliant Parliament which deeply oppressed the Virginians by restrictions upon their commerce, their political franchises and their religious liberty.

Charles gave Berkeley a new commission, and he returned to Virginia prepared to execute his master's will in full. At an election of members for a new House of Burgesses, the candidates of the cavaliers and land-owners were chosen, and Berkeley had as pliant an assembly of royalists as his king possessed in the Parliament. Navigation laws, oppressive to the commerce of the colony, were passed, and Berkeley executed them. Marriage laws, the freedom of elections and almost every other franchise possessed by the people were modified, abridged or abolished. The Church of England was made supreme, and persecution with its fiery broom attempted to sweep Baptists, Friends and other Puritans out of Virginia. When Owen, the bold Quaker preacher, stood with his head covered with his hat before the court at whose bar he had been summoned, and said meekly but firmly, "Tender consciences obey the laws of God however they suffer," the angry reply of the court, in the spirit of the age, was: "There is no toleration for wicked consciences." Berkeley enforced the laws; and Friends and Puritans sought peace and a refuge in the wilds of upper North Carolina, where they formed settlements.

Less tolerant and just than when he was younger and weaker, Berkeley, in the later years of his administration, drifted, in thought and action, with the cavaliers, who hated everything that marked the character of the Puritans. They despised the popular education and consequent elevation of the "common people" of New England; and Berkeley wrote, some years after the restoration of monarchy, "I thank God there are no free schools nor printing in Virginia, and I hope we shall not have them these hundred years. For learning has brought heresy and disobedience and sects into the world, and printing has divulged them, and libels against the best government; God keep us from both!"

Stimulated by oppression, republicanism grew vigorously in Virginia. The men of toil, and righteous ones of the aristocracy, soon formed a powerful republican party. Their strength was increased by the rank injustice of the king, who seems not to have had a clear perception of right and wrong. He gave to profligate favorites large tracts of land in Virginia, some of them under cultivation; and in 1673, he actually gave to Lord Culpepper, a cunning and covetous member of the Commission for Trade and Plantations, and the Earl of Arlington, a heartless spendthrift, "all the dominion of land and water, called Virginia," for the term of thirty-one years.

This act excited the alarm of the more thoughtful men of the aristocratic assembly, and a committee was appointed to carry a remonstrance to the king. Its mission was unfruitful. The republicans were inflamed with just indignation, and rebellious murmurs were heard everywhere. The toiling people were made to regard the aristocracy as their natural enemies. The latter had the power to promote the welfare of the people at large, but omitted to do so. Everything of a public character was neglected. There were no roads or bridges in Virginia. In boats and along bridle-paths the people were compelled to travel, and to ford or swim the streams. There were no schools. Every planter was compelled to be his own mechanic. Most of the houses of the toilers were mean log-huts with unglazed windows. Villages nowhere existed, for the inhabitants were scattered over a wide domain. Even the capital of the colony consisted only of a church, state-house and eighteen dwellings at the time we are considering, and the Assembly had, until lately, met in the hall of an alehouse.

Meanwhile, the large land-owners were living in luxury in fine mansions in sight of some beautiful rivers. They were surrounded by slaves or indentured servants, and were engaged in a sort of patriarchal life. At the same time Governor Berkeley was clamoring for an increase of salary, while in his stables and his fields he had seventy horses; and large flocks of sheep whitened the broad acres of the Green Spring plantation. The "common people" saw clearly that the tendency of circumstances in Virginia was toward a rich landed aristocracy and an impoverished peasantry, and they longed for a pretext and an opportunity to assert their natural rights. That pretext and opportunity soon appeared.

In the summer of 1675, the Indians, in despair, invaded Virginia from the north. When they were sweeping through Maryland, John Washington,

LAND TRAVELERS IN VIRGINIA.

the great-grandfather of our Beloved Patriot, met them with a force of Virginians. A fierce border war ensued. Governor Berkeley, who had the monopoly of the beaver trade with the Indians, and was willing to be just, treated them leniently. When he heard that six of their chiefs who came to treat for peace had been treacherously murdered by Englishmen, he exclaimed with warmth: "Had they killed all of my nearest relations, yet if they had come to treat of peace they ought to have gone in peace."

Fired by this treachery, the savages swept over the country between the

VIRGINIANS DEFENDING THEMSELVES AGAINST INDIANS.

Rappahannock and the James rivers, strewing their pathway with death and desolation. They ceased not to kill until their wrath was appeased by the slaughter of at least ten Englishmen for each of their chiefs slain. Insecurity was everywhere felt, and dread filled every cabin. The apparent supineness of the governor in the presence of the great peril, aroused the people to vigorous action. Led by the young and wealthy Nathaniel Bacon, a planter and lawyer on the James, who was fluent in speech and bold in action, and who was very popular, they petitioned the governor for leave to arm and protect themselves. The governor had reason to suspect Bacon of ambitious rather than patriotic motives, for he had been concerned in a partial insurrection the previous year, suffered imprisonment and had been generously pardoned by the executive. So Berkeley refused their petition.

The impetuous Bacon took fire at this refusal. He knew the hidden cause. He at once proclaimed that he was ready to lead the people against the dusky invaders, without permission, if another white person should be murdered. Very soon the news came that some on his own plantation, near Richmond, had been slain. The people gathered under the shadows of a great tulip tree to consult. Bacon was among them. He mounted a stump, and with impassioned eloquence stirred their hearts as if with electric fire. He denounced the governor as neglectful or imbecile, and advised his hearers to take up arms in their own defence.

The excited colonists followed Bacon's advice. The multitude were soon embodied in military form, and chose Bacon to be their general. He asked the governor to give him a commission in confirmation of the expressed will of the people. Berkeley refused, and Bacon marched against the Indians. He had not yet crossed the York River, when the governor, yielding to the bad advice of an aristocratic faction in the Assembly, proclaimed him to be a rebel and ordered his followers to disperse. A few weak-kneed Peters obeyed, but a large portion clung to Bacon's standard. He led the expedition forward. At the same time the lower settlements arose in insurrection, and demanded the immediate dissolution of the aristocratic Assembly.

Bacon drove the Indians back toward the Rappahannock. A new Assembly was chosen, and he was elected to a seat in the House of Burgesses, from Henrico county.

The new Assembly represented popular opinion in Virginia, and in their legislation they proceeded upon the principles of freedom, justice and humanity, and the governor and his fellow cavaliers were compelled to yield at all points. The Assembly voted to give the required commission to

Bacon, but Berkeley refused to sign it. Some of the members were disposed to support him in the refusal. Bacon, fearing treachery, retired to the Middle Plantation (now Williamsburg), where he was soon surrounded by about five hundred followers who proclaimed him commander-in-chief of the Virginia forces. With these he marched to Jamestown and demanded his commission. The governor, regarding the movement as rebellious, again refused to sign it. In an angry moment the old cavalier went out and confronted the insurgents. Baring his bosom to their weapons, he cried out: "Shoot! shoot! it is a fair mark!" Bacon said respectfully: "Not a hair of your head shall be hurt; we have come for our commissions to save our lives from the Indians."

The passion of the governor soon yielded to his judgment or his fears, and he not only signed the commission but joined his council in commending Bacon to the king as a zealous, loyal, and patriotic citizen. That was done on the 4th of July, 1676, just one hundred years to a day before the representatives of English-American colonies signed the famous document written by a Virginia "rebel," which declared these colonies to be free and independent States.

On receiving his commission, Bacon marched against the savages beyond the York River. Berkeley appears to have learned lessons of faithlessness from his immoral king, in his old age, for as soon as Bacon had departed, the governor went over the York into Gloucester county, called a convention of the inhabitants, and proposed to proclaim Bacon a traitor. The convention, though loyal, spurned the proposition, when the proud and obstinate baron issued such a proclamation in spite of their remonstrances. When the news of this perfidy reached Bacon, in his camp on the Pamunkey River, he said: "It vexes me to the heart, that while I am hunting the wolves and tigers that destroy our lands, I should, myself, be pursued as a savage. Shall persons wholly devoted to their king and country—men hazarding their lives against the public enemy—deserve the appellation of rebels and traitors? The whole country is witness to our peaceable behavior. But those in authority, how have they obtained their estates? Have they not devoured the common treasury? What arts, what sciences, what learning have they promoted? I appeal to the king and Parliament, where the cause of the people will be heard impartially."

Bacon felt compelled, by the action of the governor, to lead in a revolution. He invited the Virginians to meet in convention at the Middle Plantation, to devise means for saving the colony from the grasp of tyranny. The best men in the colony hastened to the gathering. From noon until midnight on a warm August day, that convention debated and deliberated.

Bacon's eloquence and logic led them to vigorous action, and the whole assemblage took an oath to support their leader in subduing the Indians and preventing civil war.

In the strength of these popular pledges, Bacon proceeded against the savages. The governor, alarmed by the demonstration at the Middle Plantation, fled, with some of his council, to the eastern shore of the Chesapeake, where, by promises of booty, he tried to raise an army among the inhabitants and the seamen of English ships in the ports. This movement demanded prompt action on the part of Bacon. With this leader was the brave William Drummond, who had been the first governor of North Carolina. He was accompanied by his wife Sarah, who was as brave as he. She did much to inspire the Virginians—civilians and soldiers—with courage to go on in revolution; and she was denounced as a "notorious and wicked rebel." When her husband proposed to declare Berkeley's flight from Jamestown to be an abdication of government, and the appointment of another in his place, and it was suggested that a power would then come from England that would ruin the republicans of the colony, Sarah Drummond, who knew that the realm was then distracted by factions, snatched up a small stick from the ground, and exclaimed: "I fear the power of England no more than a broken straw. The child that is unborn," she said, "shall have cause to rejoice for the good that will come by the rising of the country."

Drummond's proposition was agreed to. Government in the colony was declared to be abdicated by Berkeley, and that he was fomenting civil war; and Bacon and four of his colleagues issued writs for a representative convention of the people. Meanwhile Berkeley had gathered a motley host of followers on the eastern shore, many of them allured by hopes of plunder. He had proclaimed freedom to the slaves of "rebels" who should join his standard. The English vessels on that coast were placed at his service, and some Indians joined him. With this army under the command of Major Beverly, in five ships and ten sloops, the governor sailed for Jamestown, and landed there early in September. After offering thanksgiving for his safe arrival, he again proclaimed Nathaniel Bacon a traitor.

The republican leader was taken by surprise. He had but a few followers in arms; but the news spread swiftly through the forests and over the plantations, and very soon Bacon was at the head of brave Virginians marching toward their capital. On their way, they seized as hostages or pledges of honor on the part of their husbands the wives of royalists who were with Berkeley.

On a moonlit evening the republicans appeared before Jamestown, and cast up an intrenchment. In vain the governor urged his troops to go out and attack them. His men were not made of stuff for soldiers. Only the seamen showed pluck, and they were too few to do much. At length the royalists stole away in their ships by night and compelled the indignant governor to follow them. Then Bacon entered Jamestown—the only village in all Virginia—and assumed the reins of civil power. He was startled by a rumor that the royalists of the upper counties were coming down upon him. In a council of war it was resolved to burn the capital, that no shelter might remain for an enemy. At twilight the torch was applied, and the blaze of the conflagration was seen by the royalists on the ships, far down the James River. Drummond set fire to his own house—one of the best in the village—as a sacrifice to freedom. So perished the first town founded in America by Englishmen. It was never rebuilt. No vestige of it remains but the ruins of the church tower and a few monuments in the graveyard near it.

RUINS OF THE OLD CHURCH TOWER.

Bacon now hastened to meet the royalists from the north. These were not disposed to fight, and in a body they deserted their leader and joined the patriots. The royalists of Gloucester yielded their allegiance to Bacon, and he resolved to cross the Chesapeake and drive the cavaliers and their adherents out of Virginia. But a deadlier foe than these now attacked the republican leader. The malaria from the marshes around Jamestown poisoned his blood, and he died of a malignant fever on the 11th of October, 1676. There was no man to receive his mantle of authority and influence, and his departure paralyzed the cause he had espoused. His followers made but a feeble resistance thereafter, and before the first of November Governor Berkeley returned to the Middle Plantation and resumed the functions of govern-

EDMUND CHEESEMAN'S WIFE BEFORE GOVERNOR BERKELEY.

ment. Nathaniel Bacon failed, and he is embalmed in history as a *rebel.* Had he succeeded, he would have been immortalized as a *patriot.*

The vexations and fatigues which Berkeley had endured in his contest with the republicans soured his haughty temper and made him very miserable. He signalized his return to power by acts of wanton cruelty. His king had proclaimed Bacon to be a traitor, and sent an armament under Sir John Berry to assist in crushing the rebellion in Virginia. These were the first royal troops sent to America to suppress the aspirations of the people for freedom. The incident was repeated a hundred years later when Howe, Clinton, Cornwallis and Burgoyne were here, like Sir John Berry, leading British troops to suppress a more formidable and successful uprising of Americans in favor of the rights of man.

Feeling strong, Berkeley, with strange stony-heartedness, pursued the accomplices of Bacon with malignant severity, until twenty-two of them were hanged. Even King Charles was disgusted with his cruelty, and said: "The old fool has taken more lives in that naked country than I have taken for the murder of my father." The first martyr was Thomas Hansford, a gallant young native of Virginia. When he was brought before Berkeley, he boldly avowed his attachment to the republican cause; and when he was sentenced to be hanged, he said: "I ask no favor but that I may be shot like a soldier and not hanged like a dog." The governor replied: "You die, not as a soldier, but as a rebel." When he came to the gallows, he said: "Take notice, I die a loyal subject and a lover of my country."

When Edmund Cheesman was arraigned before the governor, and he was asked why he engaged in Bacon's wicked scheme, before he could answer, his young wife stepped forward and said: "My provocations made my husband join in the cause for which Bacon contended; but for me, he had never done what he has done. Since what is done," she said, as she fell upon her knees in an attitude of supplication, with her head bowed and covered with her hands, "was done by my means, I am most guilty; let me bear the punishment; let me be hanged, but let my husband be pardoned." The governor angrily cried out: "Away with you!" and added a brutal insinuation against her virtue. The poor young wife fainted, and her husband was led to the gallows.

So fearful, at first, was the cruel old baron that some of his intended victims might escape through a verdict of acquittal by a jury, that men were taken from the tribunal of a court-martial directly to the gallows without the forms of civil law. When the brave Drummond, who had been captured, was brought before him, the governor with wicked satire made a low bow and exultingly cried: "You are very welcome; I am more glad to see you than any man in Virginia; you shall be hanged in half an hour." "I expect no mercy from you," Drummond replied. "I have followed the lead of my conscience, and done what I might to free my countrymen from oppression." He was condemned at one o'clock, and was hanged at four o'clock. By a decree, his brave wife Sarah was denounced as a traitor and banished, with her children, to the wilderness, there to subsist by the charity of sympathizing friends. And after these judicial murders had been publicly condemned by the king as contrary to his commands and offensive to his clemency, Berkeley continued to fine, imprison and confiscate the property of all those who, in any way, were accomplices of Bacon, until he was recalled in the spring of 1677, and went to England with the returning fleet of Sir John Berry. So glad were the colonists at the departure of the governor that they fired great guns and lighted bonfires. In England his cruelties were severely censured; and Sir William Berkeley died of grief and mortified pride before he was permitted to stand before his king. Circumstances had transformed a wise, prudent and benevolent magistrate in the days of his young manhood, into an unwise and cruel oppressor in his old age.

With the troops under Sir John Berry came Colonel Jeffreys, appointed to recall Berkeley and succeed him as governor. With him were associated Sir John and Colonel Moryson as commissioners to inquire into and report the causes of "Bacon's Rebellion." They found the Virginia Assembly pretty thoroughly winnowed of its aristocratic elements, and in sympathy with the people. The Burgesses would yield nothing repugnant to liberty because of the presence of troops quartered in Virginia; and when Jeffreys and his associates demanded that all the books and journals of the Assembly should be submitted to their inspection, they hesitated. Those papers were seized; and when the Assembly demanded reparation for the insult, and Jeffreys appealed to the Great Seal of England in defence of the act, the Burgesses firmly replied to him that "such a breach of privilege could not be commanded under the Great Seal, because they could not find that any king of England had ever done so in former times." When the king was informed of this reply, with foolish arrogance worthy of his grandfather, he commanded the governor to "signify his majesty's indignation at language so seditious, and to give the leaders marks of the royal displeasure." The Burgesses were quite indifferent to the royal frowns or to the royal favors.

Soon after Berkeley's departure from Virginia, the king appointed Lord Culpepper, one of his favorites to whom he had leased the province for the term of a generation, governor of the domain for life, with a salary double in amount that received by the late magistrate, because he was a peer. It now became a proprietary colony. Culpepper went there reluctantly, in 1680, with instructions to bury all animosities growing out of Bacon's "rebellion." But the profligate governor began his administration by disfranchising all of the willing followers of Bacon. He despoiled the colonists of privilege after privilege, and exercised measures which impoverished them. By a proclamation forbidding, under severest penalties, all disrespectful words concerning the governor and his administration, he closed the royal ear against all complaints of his tyranny; and having accumulated, by a system of pillage, a considerable sum of money, he returned to England to spend it in dissipation.

THE SEIZURE OF THE VIRGINIA RECORDS ORDERED.

Culpepper returned to Virginia in 1682. His profligacy and rapacity so disgusted the people and fostered discontents, that, unable to endure him longer, they broke out into insurrection. His false reports of the matter induced the king to issue an order for the hanging of several of the most influential leaders; but at length the true state of the case was laid before Charles, and he recalled the grant made to Culpepper and Arlington, and constituted Virginia a royal province again. Lord Howard of Effingham was sent over as governor in Culpepper's place. His greed was excessive, and was not controlled by moral principles. He was instructed by the king not to allow a printing-press to be set up in Virginia, and he was left free to sway the judiciary for his own benefit. With him was sent a frigate to cruise on the coast and enforce the navigation laws. His rapacity was so shameless in the methods of its gratification, that the colonists were on the point of rising in a general insurrection, when news came of the death of King Charles and the accession to the throne of his brother James, Duke of York. The Virginians rejoiced, for they felt that any change must better their condition—it could not well be made worse.

Virginia was so impoverished and really degraded by misrule, that voluntary emigration to its shores had almost ceased at the time of the accession of James, in 1685. Another and strong tide of emigration now began to flow thitherward.

Charles the Second had a son born out of wedlock, whom he had created Duke of Monmouth. He had participated in a movement for making himself the successor of his father instead of the Duke of York, and had fled to Holland. On the accession of James, this young man engaged with others to carry out the project. He sailed from Holland with eighty men, and landed on the west of England, where he was joined by about six thousand partisans, many of them men of good families and education. Monmouth was defeated, captured and beheaded, and his partisans were most severely treated. Sir George Jeffries was then Lord Chief Justice of England. He was sent into the insurgent district, where he held what are known in history as the "Bloody Assizes." The partisans of Monmouth were brought before him by scores. He seemed to delight in convicting and punishing them. The king wrote: "Lord Chief Justice is making his campaign in the west. He has already condemned several hundreds—some of whom are already executed, more are to be, and the others sent to the plantations." He caused three hundred and twenty to be hanged or beheaded, and more than eight hundred to be sold as slaves in the West Indies or Virginia. Many of them were given to court favorites that they might sell them on speculation, or extort money for the pardon of those who had any to give.

In this nefarious business Effingham engaged. So, also, were some of his friends; and many men of culture, as well as good mechanics, were sent to Virginia to be sold as slaves, and so added good social materials to the population. "Take all care," wrote the malignant monarch to Effingham, by the hand of Sunderland, "that they continue to serve for ten years at least, and that they be not permitted in any manner to redeem themselves by money or otherwise, until that term be fully expired. Prepare a bill for the Assembly of our colony, with such clauses as shall be requisite for this purpose." This malice was not countenanced by the Assembly. The Burgesses showed, on all occasions, a manly spirit of resistance to wrong; and when a new government in England pardoned these exiles in December, 1689, the Virginians received them with open arms as brethren and citizens.

A new Assembly convened in 1688. It was "more turbulent," the governor and council said, "than any which had preceded." They paid very little attention to the unlawful requirements of the chief magistrates, and boldly discussed the rights of citizens. To check this stimulant to republicanism, the governor and council determined to dissolve the Assembly. The people resented the attempt to interfere with the privileges of their representatives, and flew to arms. They were on the verge of open insurrection, when the news came over the sea that King James had been driven from the throne, and it was occupied by his daughter Mary and her husband William of Orange.

The revolution in England which placed William and Mary on the throne had such an important bearing upon the colonial history of our country, that a brief outline of its principal events is necessary for a clear understanding of that bearing. That revolution had been gathering head ever since, soon after James's accession to the throne, it became evident that he contemplated the overthrow of the constitutional system of England, and the restoration of the Roman Catholic religion and polity there as they existed at the accession of Henry the Eighth. By a series of crimes and blunders, the king, in less than three years, had arrayed all of his subjects against him excepting the Roman Catholics and a few pliant dissenters. The foreign policy of the government was made subservient to France, then ruled by Louis the Fourteenth, a kinsman of James.

In the summer of 1688, a crisis occurred. The king had ordered a declaration of indulgence to be read in all the churches. The order shocked the Protestant sentiment of England, and met with strenuous opposition. The Archbishop of Canterbury and six bishops were sent to the Tower on a charge of libel, because they ventured to petition the king against the order. This outrage shook English society to its foundations, with the most intense excitement. The prelates were acquitted, yet the excitement continued; and in obedience to what was undoubtedly the common wish of Protestant England, some of the leading peers and prelates of the realm invited Prince William of Orange to invade England and dethrone the Stuart. William was the husband of Princess Mary, the eldest daughter of King James, and both were Protestants.

William accepted the invitation, and on the 5th of November, 1688, he landed at Torbay, with fifteen thousand troops. The friends of James all deserted him—even his daughter Anne, the wife of Prince George of Denmark. James fled to France, and William called a convention of the notables of England to settle the momentous questions of the future monarchy. In February, 1689, William and Mary were proclaimed joint monarchs of England, and their effigies, or profiles of their faces, were placed together on the coins of England. To this the couplet refers in speaking of lovers

> "—— cooing and billing,
> Like William and Mary on a shilling."

The detested and detestable Stuart dynasty now disappeared forever. Higher political principles were diffused through English society. A declaration of the rights and liberties of the subject was made by the British Parliament at the accession of the new sovereigns; and from that time the people of the realm had a more direct and controlling participation in the administration of the public affairs of the realm, than even in the time of the Commonwealth and Cromwell. The salutary influence of that great change in the English government and policy upon the destinies of the English-American colonies was remarkable. From the period of that revolution, to the beginning of the French and Indian War at the middle of the eighteenth century, the history of Virginia is the story of the steady, quiet progress of an industrious people, who were ready in "the fullness of time" to join with other colonies in the establishment of a great republic.

CHAPTER III.

EXECUTIVE GOVERNMENT OF NEW NETHERLAND—TROUBLES WITH INDIANS—DUTCH INDIA COMPANIES—ADMIRAL HEYN AND HIS MOTHER—A NEW SCHEME OF COLONIZATION—GOVERNOR VAN TWILLER—INTERCOURSE WITH VIRGINIA—DE VRIES IN VIRGINIA AND AT NEW AMSTERDAM—VAN TWILLER'S FOLLY—PLAIN TALK BY A PARSON AND SHERIFF—GOVERNOR KIEFT AND HIS ADMINISTRATION — COVETOUSNESS OF THE PATROONS — MONOPOLY REBUKED — FARMERS IN NEW NETHERLAND—NEW ENGLAND INTRUDERS—TROUBLES WITH THE INDIANS—FIRST POPULAR ASSEMBLY—MASSACRE OF INDIANS AT HOBOKEN—RETALIATION.

WHILE the English were laying the foundations of a flourishing commonwealth in Virginia on the broad basis of republicanism, the Dutch were busy fashioning a state upon the still broader foundations of justice, liberty, equality and fraternity, with its capital on the site of the city of New York.

We have seen how refugees from persecution in France, and native Hollanders, first made settlements on Manhattan Island and elsewhere, and so established the colony of New Netherland, and founded a city which they called New Amsterdam, with Peter Minuit as director-general or governor. Minuit was an energetic man from Wesel, in Rhenish Prussia, where he had been a deacon in the Walloon or French Refugee Church, and had good family connections. He was assisted, we have observed in Chapter IV of the Second Book, by a council appointed by the Dutch West India Company. Also by a secretary who was the bookkeeper of the Company, and a sheriff who was also the manager of the revenues of the province. These several officers composed the executive government of New Netherland; its laws derived their life from Holland, and were subservient to the supposed interests of the Company. The first commissary or chief secretary was Isaac de Rasieres, already mentioned as a correspondent with the Pilgrim and Puritan authorities in New England.

The intercourse between the Dutch and Indians was friendly for some time. The Hollanders had extended their traffic as far north as the upper waters of the Hudson, and built a military work on the site of Albany which they called Fort Orange. Eight families had settled there and begun to cultivate the land, when the Mohawk Indians on one side of the river and the Mohegans on the other, both friendly with the Dutch, quarreled and went to war. The commander of the fort foolishly joined the Mohegans in an expedition against the Mohawks in violation of the treaty made at Tawasentha. They were met by the fierce Iroquois, and in a battle with them, the Dutch commander and three of his men were slain, with many of the Mohegans. The settlers at Fort Orange were terrified, and were about to flee to Manhattan in their boats, when Barentsten, a very popular trader, arrived, and received a deputation of Mohawks, who came to justify their deed. "We have done nothing against the white people," they said; "why did they meddle with us? Had it been otherwise, this would not have happened from us." The position was considered unsafe, and the eight families, with every woman in the garrison, were removed to New Amsterdam. That was in the year 1626.

Now followed the correspondence and personal intercourse between the Dutch on Manhattan and the Puritans in New England mentioned in Chapter VI of the Second Book. During that time, and until 1628, wars between the Indians on the upper Hudson caused Fort Orange to remain only a military and trading post, for settlers would not venture much beyond the bounds of Manhattan Island. But while the extension of settlements in New Netherland was thus checked by the hostilities of two savage nations, and the general prosperity of the colony was somewhat depressed, the Dutch West India Company were reaping a rich harvest of wealth and honors from the circumstances of war between Christian nations—Holland, Spain and Portugal. Its battle-ships depredated fiercely and successfully upon the floating commerce of those kingdoms of the Peninsula. The fleets of the two India companies were then the right arm of Dutch power and controlled the state.

Peter Petersen Heyn, who had risen from the position of a peasant boy to that of a distinguished naval commander, captured for the Company, in 1629, the Spanish "Silver Fleet" while on its way from Yucatan with the spoils of the mines of Mexico and Peru. He put about five million dollars of treasure into their coffers. The joy of the people of Holland was unbounded when the news reached Amsterdam. The reception of the victor there was princely in its display. He was conducted into the Assembly Chamber of the States-General at the Hague, and there received the thanks of the nation publicly. He asked for no share of the booty he had won; and when the commission of Admiral was offered him, he refused it, saying: "It is too great a dignity for one of so mean birth and unpolished manners to possess." It was forced upon him, and he went forth to win other victories. The next year, while fighting two Dunkirk pirates, with his ship between them, he was killed on the deck of his vessel. His body was conveyed in regal pomp to the old church at Delft, wherein the Pilgrim fathers had worshipped on the shores of Holland; and he was buried by the side of Prince William of Orange. His grateful government erected over his remains under the great aisle a superb marble monument. When the States-General sent a letter of condolence to his peasant mother by the hand of a high officer, she said: "Aye, I thought that would be the end of him. He was always a vagabond; but I did my best to correct him. He has got no more than he deserved."

Compared with other sources of wealth, the profits derived from New Netherland now seemed insignificant to the Company, and they devised new schemes for increasing the value of the province. Nothing seemed wiser than an increase in the population; so they adopted the plan of making separate and independent colonies on the Hudson and Delaware rivers, in the form of manorial estates not more than sixteen miles in length if lying on one side of a river, or eight miles if on both sides, as we have observed on page 267. They were to be fashioned after then existing manors in Holland and England. In order to enlist private capital in this undertaking, the College of XIX proposed to give a charter which should confer those "patroon" privileges and exemptions mentioned on the page above referred to. This proposition was approved by the States-General in 1630; and so the feudal system displayed by the manorial estates in Holland and England was transferred to America.

Governor Minuit returned to Amsterdam in 1632, leaving the province in a state of increasing prosperity. The fur trade was enlarging. Comfortable homes and commodious warehouses were seen clustered around Fort Amsterdam, and gardens were blooming around many dwellings. He was succeeded the following year by Walter Van Twiller, a narrow-minded and inexperienced clerk in the Company's warehouse at Amsterdam, who had married the niece of the rich pearl-merchant Killian Van Rensselaer, one of the directors. Van Twiller seems to have had very little fitness for the position of governor of the colony, excepting the alacrity with which he would be likely to serve the interests of his wife's rich kinsman, who had become a "patroon" and whose estate lay on each side of the upper Hudson, at the site of Albany and its surroundings. He had been employed by the "patroon" in shipping cattle to his colony, and was pretty well versed in the mysteries of traffic. But he was entirely ignorant of public affairs, and had not a single quality of a statesman. He was one of those sleek, rotund, bullet-headed Dutchmen who had ease of mind and body; dull of intellect, yet shrewd and cunning; courageous when there was no danger; always undecided and wavering, and was a capital butt for the jokes of the wiser men of New Amsterdam. Irving has left us a spirited caricature of his person, as a "model of majesty and lordly grandeur." The chronicler says:

"He was exactly five feet six inches in height, and six feet five inches in circumference. His head was a perfect sphere, and of such stupendous dimensions that dame Nature, with all her sex's ingenuity, would have been puzzled to construct a neck capable of supporting it; wherefore she wisely declined the attempt, and settled it firmly on the top of his backbone just between his shoulders. His legs were very short, but sturdy in proportion to the weight they had to sustain; so that, when erect, he had not a little the appearance of a beer-barrel on skids. His face, that infallible index of the mind, presented a vast expanse unfurrowed by any of those lines and angles which disfigure the human countenance with what is termed expression. Two small grey eyes twinkled feebly in the midst, like two stars of lesser magnitude in a hazy firmament; and his full-fed cheeks, which seemed to have taken toll of everything that went into his mouth, were curiously mottled and streaked with dusky red, like a Spitzenberg apple. His habits were as regular as his person. He daily took his four stated meals, appropriating exactly an hour to each; he smoked and doubted eight hours, and he slept the remaining twelve of the four-and-twenty."

GOVERNOR VAN TWILLER.

Van Twiller's administration lasted about four years, and the colony flourished in spite of him. Just before his advent, a pleasant intercourse was opened with Virginia by Captain de Vries, one of the "patroons," who had an estate on the South or Delaware River, where he and others attempted to establish a whale fishery. It did not succeed; but De Vries made valuable explorations up the river and formed salutary relations with the natives. He finally sailed for Virginia for supplies, rightfully supposing that he would find corn more abundant there than at New Amsterdam. He was anxious, too, to be the first Hollander from New Netherland to enter the James River. As his vessel neared the shore at Jamestown, and displayed the flag of Holland, Sir John Harvey, then Governor of Virginia, came down to the beach with some halberdiers, and in a friendly tone demanded where he was from. "From the South Bay in New Netherlands," said Captain De Vries. The governor invited him to his house, presented him with a glass of "Venice sack," and then taking an English chart, pointed out South Bay as named Delaware in honor of Lord De La Ware (a former governor of Virginia), who, some years before, had been driven into that bay. Finding it full of shoals and supposing it to be unnavigable, the English, Harvey said, had "not looked after it since. Yet it is our king's land," he continued, "and not New Netherland."

De Vries then gave the governor a glowing account of the beauty of the Delaware Bay and river, only a hundred miles north from Jamestown, and a history of what the Dutch had been doing there. Harvey was astonished. He had heard that the Dutch had built a fort upon "Hudson's River, as the English call it;" but, being uncertain whether there was a Delaware Bay or river, had sent a small vessel, with several seamen, the previous autumn to search for them. These men had not returned, and he supposed they had gone to the bottom of the sea in a storm. De Vries told him that he had seen Indians with English jackets on, and had no doubt his seamen had been murdered by them.

No dispute arose about the territory. "There are lands enough," said the knight; "we shall be friends and good neighbors with each other. You will have no trouble from us Englishmen, if only those of New England do not approach too near you, and dwell at a distance from you." So began a pleasant intercourse between New Netherland and Virginia. Sir John's half-formed warning was prophetic, for from New England came encroachments and annoyances to the Dutch.

De Vries sailed for the Delaware with an ample supply of provisions and some goats as a present from Sir John to the governor of New Netherland. He found his affairs on the Delaware far from prosperous; so he abandoned the country to the Indians and sailed into the harbor of New Amsterdam, where lay the ship which had just brought over Governor Van Twiller. It was well for the Company that a man of pluck like De Vries was at New Amsterdam at that time, for a former commissary at Fort Orange, Jacob Elkens, came a few days after De Vries's arrival, in the English ship *William*, with the intention of going up the Hudson to trade with the Indians.

Elkens knew Van Twiller at Amsterdam, and counted on his impotence. When the governor demanded his papers, he refused, saying: "The country belongs to England, for it was discovered by an Englishman. I command an English ship and will go where I please." Van Twiller ordered the Orange flag to be run up over Fort Amsterdam, and a salute of three guns to be fired in honor of Prince Maurice. Elkens displayed the British flag on the *William*, and fired a salute of three guns in honor of King Charles. "I will go up the river if it costs me my life," said Elkens, and weighing anchor he boldly sailed up the Hudson.

This audacious act aroused the wrath of Van Twiller. He opened a cask of wine at the gate of the fort, assembled the people there, drank a full glass himself and called upon those who loved him and their prince to follow his example and assist in protecting him from the violence which the Englishman had committed. The people drank his wine but laughed in his face, for the *William* was out of sight. De Vries dined with the governor the same day, and told him plainly that he had played the fool. He advised Van Twiller to send an expedition after the intruder, which the stupid governor did, and very soon Elkens was sent to sea with an injunction not to attempt any further interference with the Dutch on the Hudson.

The province yet lacked a prime element of permanent prosperity. There were no independent farmers in New Netherland cultivating their own land. The wealthy monopolists owned the land; the tiller might own the house he lived in—no more. A great incentive to industry was wanting. Large tracts of land, accessible and fertile, were left uncultivated. There were continued disputes between the grasping patroons and the agents of the Company concerning the monopoly of the fur-trade, which each was seeking to secure. The governor had lost the respect of all parties, and was simply a clog to progress. Parson Bogardus, who came over with him from Holland, called him a "child of the devil" to his face; and he also told him, on one occasion, that if he did not behave himself he would give him such a "shake from the pulpit" the next Sabbath as would make him tremble like a bowl of jelly. Lubbertus Van Dincklagen, his sheriff, and one of the most learned men in the colony, spoke contemptuously of him to his face, when the governor, unfortunately for himself, summoned courage sufficient to resent it, and sent the offender to Holland in disgrace, without paying him three years' salary which was due him. Dincklagen was expert with his tongue and pen, and he made such representations of the character of Van Twiller in a memorial to the States-General of Holland, that he was finally recalled. It was a sad interruption of Van Twiller's sweet dream of peace. He had bought Nutten and other islands near Manhattan, with the expectation of vegetating in riches and dying there. He has left no memorial of his name upon anything. There is a simple reminder of him in the present Nutten Island, lying nearest the "Battery" in New York Bay, which is known as the Governor's Island.

In 1637, Van Twiller was succeeded by William Kieft, whose portrait had been hanged on a gallows at Rochelle at one time. De Vries recorded him among the great rogues. Spiteful, rapacious, energetic; fond of quarrels and never happy excepting when in trouble with some one; unscrupulous in the use of means to promote his own interest, and a petty tyrant, he was, nevertheless, a better man for the Company than Van Twiller. He was an agitator, and agitation is healthier than stagnation.

Kieft's administration was stormy, and therefore a delightful one for him. He had regarded Minuit as a model governor, and Minuit, for a long time, was the bane of Kieft's official peace and quiet. The next governor had hardly become seated in the executive chair, when tidings reached him that Minuit had led a colony of Swedes to the Delaware. Then news came that the impertinent Swedes, having built a house between two trees, claimed the whole country west of the Delaware from its falls at Trenton to Cape Henlopen and as far inland as they pleased. Kieft stormed at first, and then issued a proclamation, as we have observed, protesting against this invasion of the territory of New Netherland.

Kieft began his administration by concentrating all executive power in his own hands; and he and his council had such dignity, in their own estimation, that it became a high crime to appeal from their decision. While shaking his official fist at the Swedes and threatening war, he was not unmindful of the wants of the growing capital of the colony. He found public affairs in a wretched condition, and needing the strong hand of an autocrat to bring order out of confusion. Abuses everywhere abounded, and he set about reforming them with a vigor that very soon almost stripped the citizen of privileges. He caused Fort Amsterdam to be repaired, and new warehouses to be erected. By example and command he made fruit-trees to bud and blossom in gardens where brambles had flourished. Police ordinances were framed and thoroughly enforced. Religion and morality were fostered for a time, and ordained ministers conducted public worship. A spacious stone church was built within the fort; and it was a gala day in New Amsterdam when the Connecticut architect hung the Spanish bells captured at Porto Rico in the little tower, and the governor gave a supper to the builders and the city magistrates. It was a proud day for Parson Bogardus when he ascended the new pulpit and preached in the presence of Englishmen from Puritan New England and Cavalier Virginia. When, after long absence, De Vries returned to Manhattan, he saw much to praise in the management of the new governor. These are some of the brighter tints in the picture of Kieft's career.

A change for the better was wrought by the States-General in 1638. The Company had pursued the unwise policy of peopling the province with its own dependants. The States-General and some of the wise directors saw that this was a capital error. A proposition was made to the Company to place the control of New Netherland in the care of the States-General, making it a colony of Holland instead of the possession of a commercial monopoly. It would have been a salutary measure for the colony, but the Company were not disposed to surrender their control. Meanwhile the grasping patroons had asked the States-General to enlarge their privileges and exemptions, by allowing them to monopolize more territory; have a longer time to settle colonists; enjoy free trade throughout and around New Netherland; be invested with greater feudal powers so as to be independent of the Company in their control of the government of their respective manors; have a vote in the council of the governor and to be supplied with convicts from Holland as servile laborers, and with negro slaves. They actually asked that all "private persons" and poor emigrants should be forbidden to purchase lands from the Indians, and should be required to settle themselves within the manors and under the jurisdiction of the great manorial lords.

This scheme for monopolizing all the lands of the province by a few wealthy men, and making the "common people" mere serfs on the manorial estates, was so offensive to the States-General that they were disposed to abridge the privileges enjoyed by the patroons. They compelled the Company to throw open the internal trade of the province to free competition for all inhabitants of Holland, under restrictions; and the governor of New Netherland was instructed to accommodate every emigrant with as much land as he and his family might properly cultivate, such grantee paying a quit-rent to the Company of one-tenth of all produce.

This more liberal policy stimulated emigration from Holland and gave a powerful impulse to the prosperity of the colony. Private enterprise and industry were left free for development and expansion. Emigrants pressed into Amsterdam to seek opportunities to go to New Netherland. The Company, enamored of the new policy, wisely offered a free passage and other inducements to respectable farmers. A good class of citizens soon sought homes in New Netherland—men of culture and fortune. Among them came De Vries, with emigrants, and planted a colony on Staten Island. Strangers came from New England and Virginia, for there was freedom of conscience in the Dutch dominions. The only obligation required from strangers was an oath of fidelity and allegiance to their High Mightinesses the States-General of Holland.

In view of the increasing demand for homesteads, Governor Kieft purchased from the Indians nearly the whole of the present Queens county on Long Island, and the lower part of Westchester county. Meanwhile the New Englanders had become as troublesome in their territorial encroachments, as the Swedes on the Delaware. Like busy ants they were spreading over the fertile country westward of the Housatonic River. At the mouth of that stream they had planted the flourishing village of Stratford, and they had made settlements at Norwalk and Greenwich. It being evident that the New Englanders intended to push their settlements to the Hudson River, Kieft, in 1640, purchased of the Indians all the islands near Norwalk and the domain westward, which comprised nearly the whole of Westchester county, and raised thereon, at Cow Bay, the arms of the States-General. For awhile the New Englanders disregarded Indian title-deeds and Dutch proclamations; and fillibusters from Connecticut cut down the arms of Holland and mocked the officials at New Amsterdam. But they soon learned that Kieft was a more energetic man than Van Twiller, who had excited their contempt. The new governor soon put a stop to these encroachments, and compelled the settlers on the newly-purchased domain to take an oath of allegiance to the States-General.

Had Kieft's policy and conduct been as wise and just as it was firm and energetic, his administration might have been marked by peace and great prosperity. But he pursued a policy toward the Indians which inflamed whole tribes with resentment against the Dutch. His partiality for the Mohawks, with whom the Dutch came in immediate contact at Fort Orange, excited the jealousy of the River Indians. Their anger was also kindled by the bad conduct of dishonest traders, who sold them rum and cheated them in traffic while they were intoxicated. Kieft's avarice having obtained the mastery of his justice, he winked at these offences and shared in the plunder. He also exacted tribute of furs, corn and wampum from the tribes around Manhattan; but when they came with the costly offerings and cast them at the feet of the oppressor, they turned away with a bitter curse against the Hollanders.

Kieft saw that a cloud of vengeance was gathering, and his fears awakened his cruelty. With the instinct of a bad nature, he sought to further injure those whom he had wronged. Some swine had been stolen by white people from De Vries's plantation on Staten Island. The governor charged the innocent Raritans of New Jersey with the crime and sent an armed force to chastise them, with a belief that a show of power would disarm the vengeance of the savages. Several Indians were killed. The event was the foreshadowing of the fate of others; and all the neighboring tribes were aroused, and prepared for war. The River Indians refused to pay tribute any longer. The Raritans murdered Hollanders whenever they met them in the forests of New Jersey, and the innocent settlement on Staten Island was ruined by them. The Raritans were outlawed, and a bounty was offered for the head of every member of the tribe.

Fifteen or twenty years before, some of Minuit's men had murdered an Indian belonging to a tribe seated beyond the Harlem River. His nephew, then a boy, who saw the outrage and made a vow of vengeance, had now grown to be a lusty man. He proceeded to execute his vow by murdering an unoffending Dutchman in his wheelwright shop high upon Manhattan

MURDER OF THE DUTCH WHEELWRIGHT.

Island. While the mechanic was stooping over his chest of tools, the young Indian seized an axe and almost severed his head from his body. With his scalp and the plunder of his dwelling, the savage returned in triumph to his tribe. Kieft demanded the murderer, but his chief would not give him up, saying he had been revenged according to the customs of his race.

The governor determined to chastise that tribe as he had the Raritans.

He called upon the people to shoulder their muskets for the fray. They saw the danger to which the rashness of Kieft was leading them, and refused. They had been witnesses of his rapacity and greed, and they now charged him with seeking war that he might "make a wrong reckoning with the Company." They also reproached him with a selfish cowardice. "It is all well for you," they said, "who have not slept out of the fort a single night since you came, to endanger our lives and our homes in undefended places."

This bold attitude of the people transformed the autocrat. He invited all the heads of families in New Amsterdam to meet him in convention to consult upon public affairs. They assembled at Fort Amsterdam, and promptly chose twelve select men to act as their representatives. So appeared the first popular assembly, and so was chosen the first representative congress for political purposes, in New Netherland. So were planted the seeds of a representative democracy, in the year 1641, almost on the very spot where, a century and a half later, our Republic, founded upon similar principles, was inaugurated, when Washington took the oath of office as first President of the United States.

De Vries was chosen president of the Twelve. To that body Kieft submitted the question whether the murderer of the wheelwright ought to be demanded of his chief, and whether, in case of the chief's refusal, the Dutch ought to make war upon his tribe and burn the village wherein he dwelt. The Twelve counselled peace, and proceeded to consider the propriety of establishing in New Netherland a government similar to that of the Fatherland. The governor was alarmed by this proposed blow at his absolute rule in the colony, and he cunningly offered a compromise. He agreed to make popular concessions if the Twelve would authorize him to make war on the offending tribe at a proper time. They foolishly trusted his honor and agreed to his proposition. Then the wily governor dissolved them, saying he had no further use for them, and forbade any popular assemblage thereafter.

Kieft sent an expedition against the offending tribe early in the spring of 1642. His thirst for blood was disappointed by a treaty. It was soon gratified, however. The River Indians were tributary to the Mohawks, and in midwinter, 1643, a large party of these Iroquois came down to collect, by force of arms, tribute which had not been paid. The native dwellers along the lower Hudson, five hundred in number, fled before the invaders. They took refuge with the Hackensacks at Hoboken, and craved the protection of the Dutch. At the same time many of the offending Westchester tribe and others fled to Manhattan and took refuge with the Hollanders. The humane De Vries proposed to make this an occasion for establishing a permanent peace with the savages, but the wicked governor and some leading citizens, who pretended to speak for the people, overruled his wisdom and mercy, and it was made the occasion for treacherously spilling innocent blood.

On a cold night late in February, 1643, the fugitives at Hoboken, and those at "Corlaer's Hook," Manhattan, were slumbering in fancied security. Without provocation—without the shadow of an excuse, Kieft sent eighty Hollanders to murder those at Hoboken, and a less number to slay those at Corlaer's Hook. Forty of those at the Hook were massacred, while the

MASSACRE OF INDIANS AT HOBOKEN.

Hollanders, who had stealthily crossed the river among floating ice, were making the snows at Hoboken crimson with the blood of confiding Indians, and lighting up the heavens with the blaze of their wigwams. They spared neither age nor sex. "Warrior and squaw, sachem and child, mother and babe," says Brodhead, "were alike massacred. Daybreak scarcely ended the furious slaughter. Mangled victims, seeking safety in the thickets, were driven into the river; and parents rushing to save their children, whom the soldiery had thrown into the stream, were driven back into the waters and drowned before the eyes of their unrelenting murderers." Almost a hundred of the dusky people perished there.

De Vries watched the butchery by the light of the burning wigwams from the ramparts of Fort Amsterdam. He told the blood-thirsty and cowardly governor, who was careful to remain within the walls of the fortress, that he had now commenced the ruin of the colony. Kieft ridiculed the clemency of De Vries; and when the soldiers returned to the fort next morning, with thirty prisoners and the heads of several Indians upon pikes, the governor shook their blood-smeared hands with delight, praised them for their bravery, and made each of them a present.

This treachery aroused the fiery hatred of the savages far and near, and a fierce war was kindled. The mutual animosities of tribes disappeared, and zeal for a common cause everywhere prevailed. Farms, hamlets, and villages were swept away by the broom of devastation. The white people were butchered wherever they were found by the incensed Indians. The Long Island tribes, hitherto friendly, joined their kindred in race, and, for awhile, the very existence of the Dutch settlements was in jeopardy. For two years the war continued, and the colony was on the verge of ruin.

Kieft was frightened by the fury of the tempest which his wickedness and folly had raised, and he humbly asked the people to choose a few men, again, to act as his counsellors. Eight were chosen. The colonists had lost all confidence in the governor, and relied wholly upon these eight citizens to relieve them from the fearful web of difficulties in which they were involved. The Council of Eight possessed no legal executive power, and their plans for a pacification of the Indians were often frustrated by the faithless Kieft. Disorder everywhere prevailed, and there appeared no hope of relief so long as Kieft was governor. In obedience to the wishes of the people, the Eight sent an energetic and respectful letter to the States-General, setting forth the critical condition of the province, and asking them to recall Kieft. Their prayer was granted; and there was much rejoicing throughout New Netherland when the despised governor sailed for Europe in the spring of 1647. The vessel in which Kieft departed was richly laden, and bore much of his ill-gotten wealth. It was wrecked on the coast of Wales, and there the governor and his treasure perished.

CHAPTER IV.

THE GOVERNMENT OF NEW NETHERLAND—PETER STUYVESANT APPOINTED GOVERNOR—RECEPTION OF STUYVESANT—HE DEFINES HIS POLICY BY WORDS AND DEEDS—A REPRESENTATIVE GOVERNMENT—STUYVESANT'S VIGOROUS ADMINISTRATION—SETTLES DISPUTES WITH CONNECTICUT—SPIRIT OF FREEDOM COMBATTED BY STUYVESANT—THE DUTCH SIGH FOR THE FREEDOM OF THE ENGLISH—REVOLUTIONARY PROCEEDINGS—POPULAR REPRESENTATIVES—STUYVESANT'S PLUCK—THE SWEDES SUBDUED—TROUBLES WITH THE INDIANS—NEW NETHERLAND SURRENDERED TO THE ENGLISH—THE ENGLISH RULE—THE DUTCH RE POSSESS AND RE-SURRENDER THE PROVINCE.

THE College of XIX changed the mode of government in New Netherland in the spring of 1645. All power for the management of the public concerns of the colony was vested in a Supreme Council, consisting of the director-general or governor, a lieutenant-governor, and fiscal or treasurer. At that time Peter Stuyvesant, a brave Dutch soldier, who had served gallantly in the West Indies and lost a leg in an attack upon the Portuguese island of St. Martin, was at Amsterdam. He had been governor of Curaçoa, in which capacity he had shown great vigor and wisdom. The loss of his leg compelled him to return to Holland for surgical aid, and the College appointed him to succeed Kieft as governor of New Netherland. He was then forty-four years of age; strong in physical constitution; fond of official show; admiring the arbitrary nature of military rule; a thorough disciplinarian, and a stern, inflexible, just and honest man. Owing to disagreements concerning some of the details of policy in the proposed management of New Netherland, Stuyvesant did not arrive at Manhattan until late in May, 1647. Meanwhile the inhabitants, who had been informed early of his appointment, openly showed their dislike of Governor Kieft. Dominie Bogardus, whom the governor had charged with drunkenness and sedition, denounced Kieft and some of his official companions from the pulpit as men who thought of "nothing but to plunder the property of others, to dismiss, to banish, to transport to Holland." To avoid these severe censures, they absented themselves from church, and the governor encouraged all sorts of noisy amusements near the place of public worship on Sundays. Drums were beaten and cannon were fired in the fort in which the church was situated, while the people were worshipping; and the communicants were insulted. The quarrel ended only when Kieft and Bogardus left for Holland in the same ship and were lost on the coast of Wales.

Stuyvesant came with the commission of director-general over New Netherland and the adjoining places, and also over the islands of Curaçoa, Buenaire, Aruba, and their dependencies. He was accompanied by Lubbertus Van Dincklagen, who had caused the recall of Kieft, as vice-director or lieutenant-governor. They landed on a fine morning in the presence of all the people, who came out with guns and received them with shouts. So vehement was their welcome that nearly all the breath and powder of the city was exhausted. Stuyvesant marched to the fort in great pomp, dis-

RECEPTION OF STUYVESANT AT NEW AMSTERDAM.

playing a silver-mounted wooden leg of fine workmanship. After keeping the principal inhabitants who went to welcome him waiting for several hours bareheaded, while he remained covered, "as if he were the Czar of Muscovy," he told the people that he should govern them "as a father his children, for the advantage of the chartered West India Company, and these burghers and this land." He assured them that justice should rule; at the same time, he asserted the exclusive privileges of the directorship, and frowned upon every expression of republican sentiment. He declared it to be treason to "petition against one's magistrates, whether there be cause or not;" and he defended Kieft's conduct in rejecting the interference of the Twelve, saying: "If any one during my administration shall appeal, I will make him a foot shorter, and send the pieces to Holland, and let him appeal in that way." These sentiments made the people suspect that the new governor would be an inflexible despot instead of an indulgent father.

Stuyvesant *was* despotic, yet honesty and wisdom marked all his acts. He set about needed reforms with great vigor. The morals of the people, the sale of liquors to the Indians, the support of religion and the regulation of trade, commanded his attention; and it was not long before he infused much of his own energy into the community, and enterprise took the place of sluggishness. His foreign policy was as decided, and its execution was energetic. He sent a protest southward to the offending governor of the Swedes, and an invitation eastward to commissioners of New England to meet him for the adjustment of mutual rights. His kindness toward the Indians soon won their confidence and friendship; and so affectionate was their bearing toward him, that the foolish story went abroad that he was forming an alliance with the savages to exterminate the English.

The grand principle announced by the founders of our Republic, that taxation without representation is tyranny, had prevailed in Holland for two centuries. The principle was favorable to the growth of republicanism in New Netherland, for Stuyvesant was compelled to respect it. He found the finances of the colony in such a low state that taxation was a necessity. He dared not tax the people without their consent, for fear of offending the States-General; so he called a convention of citizens, and directed them to choose eighteen of their best men, of whom he might select nine as representatives of the tax-payers, who should form a co-ordinate branch of the local government.

Stuyvesant was careful to hedge around this germ of representative government as closely as possible, with restrictions. The first Nine were to select their successors, so that the people should not be choosers after that; and the governor was careful to hold nearly all the power in his own hands. But the Nine were far more potent than the Twelve, under Kieft. They nourished the prolific seed of democracy which burst into vigorous life in the time of Jacob Leisler, fifty years afterward.

By prudent and adroit management, Stuyvesant soon swept away annoyances in the shape of territorial claims. When the Plymouth Company, at the time of its dissolution, mentioned in the Fifth Chapter of the Second Book, assigned their American domain to twelve persons, they conveyed to Lord Stirling, the proprietor of Nova Scotia, "a part of New England and an island adjacent called Long Island." Stirling had tried to take possession of Long Island, but failed. At his death, in 1647, his widow sent a Scotchman to assert the claim, and act as governor. He proclaimed himself as such, at Hempstead. Stuyvesant had him arrested, and put on board a ship bound for Holland. She touched at an English port, where the "governor" escaped, and no further trouble with the family of Lord Stirling ensued.

In 1650, Stuyvesant went to Hartford, and, by treaty, settled all disputes with the New Englanders which had annoyed his predecessors. Then he turned his attention to the suppression of the expanding power and influence of the Swedes on the Delaware. The accession of a new queen to the throne of Sweden made it necessary to make a satisfactory adjustment of the long-pending dispute about the territory. Stuyvesant was instructed to act firmly but discreetly. Accompanied by his suite of officers, he went to Fort Nassau, on the New Jersey side of the Delaware, whence he sent to Printz, the governor of New Sweden, an abstract of the title of the Dutch to the domain, and called a council of the Indian chiefs in the neighborhood. These chiefs declared the Swedes to be usurpers, and by solemn treaty gave all the land to the Dutch. Then Stuyvesant crossed over, and near the site of New Castle in Delaware he built a military work, which he called Fort Cassimer. Governor Printz protested in vain. The two magistrates held friendly personal intercourse, and they mutually promised to "keep neighborly friendship and correspondence together." That was in the year 1651.

An important concession was made to the inhabitants of New Amsterdam the following year. There was continual antagonism between Stuyvesant and the Nine. The governor tried to repress the spirit of popular freedom; the Nine fostered it. They wished to have a municipal government for their growing capital, and made direct application to the States-General for the privilege. It was granted. To the people of New Amsterdam was allowed a government like the free cities of Holland, the officers to be appointed by the governor. Under the new arrangement, New Amsterdam (afterward New York) was organized as a city, early in 1653. The soul of Stuyvesant was troubled by this "imprudent entrusting of power with the people."

Stuyvesant had scarcely recovered from his chagrin, when a new danger appeared. For several years English families had come to New Netherland from the East, to escape the intolerance of the authorities of New England, excepting in Rhode Island, and to enjoy liberty of conscience in church and state. They had been encouraged by the Dutch. Land was freely granted to them, and an English secretary for the colony had been appointed. They intermarried with the Dutch, and readily embraced the republican doctrines of the Hollanders. These formed strong allies of the friends of the Nine, and bore a conspicuous part in the democratic movements which gave Stuyvesant so much trouble during the latter years of his administration.

Republicanism, like any other truth, has remarkable vitality. Persecution promotes its growth. The more Stuyvesant attempted to stifle it, the more widely and vigorously it spread. His methods of rule were so arbitrary that all classes of citizens became discontented. He made his own will the supreme law. His councillors had to be his obedient servants or the subjects of his animosity. The powerful patroons of Rensselaerwyck and the poorest laborer were alike regarded as his subjects, and were required to submit to his tyrannous rule. He was an honest despot—it was his nature to be so—and opposition to his commands as governor he regarded as rank rebellion. The Dutch sighed for the freedom enjoyed in Holland, and the English settlers determined to exercise the liberty which English subjects then enjoyed under the rule of Cromwell. Stuyvesant saw the tidal wave of popular feeling rising, but like Canute he sat still, firm in his integrity and convictions of his righteousness, until he was compelled to yield or perish.

That popular feeling had expression when, late in the autumn of 1653, a convention of nineteen delegates, who represented eight villages or communities, assembled at the town-hall, in New Amsterdam, ostensibly to take measures to secure themselves against the depredations of savages and pirates. The governor tried to control their action, but they paid very little attention to his wishes and none to his commands. When they adjourned, they gave a parting collation, to which Stuyvesant was invited. Of course he would not sanction their proceedings by his presence; and the delegates told him bluntly that there would be another convention soon, and that he might do as he pleased and prevent it if he could.

The ire of the governor was fiercely kindled by the revolutionary movement in his capital. He stormed and threatened, but prudently yielded to the demands of the people that he should issue a call for another convention, and so give legal sanction for the election of delegates thereto. These met in New Amsterdam on the 10th of December, 1653. Of the eight districts represented, four were Dutch and four were English. Of the nineteen delegates, ten were of Dutch and nine were of English nativity. As this was the first real representative assembly in the great State of New York in its infancy—now an empire containing about five million souls—it seems proper to give here the names of the delegates, and the districts they represented. They were as follows:

From the capital (New Amsterdam), Van Hattem, Kregier, and Van de Grist; from Breucklen (Brooklyn), Lubbertsen, Van der Beeck, and Beeckman; from Flushing, Hicks and Flake; from Newtown, Coe and Hazard;

from Heemstede (Hempstead), Washburne and Somers; from Amersfoort, (Flatlands), Wolfertsen, Strycker, and Swartwout; from Midwout (Flatbush), Elbertsen and Spicer; and from Gravesend, Baxter and Hubbard. Baxter was the English secretary of the colony, and led the English delegates.

The object of the Convention was to form and adopt a remonstrance against the tyrannous rule of the governor. It was drawn by Baxter. After expressions of loyalty to the States-General, it proceeded with a statement, under six heads, of the grievances endured by the colonists. It was a severe indictment of Stuyvesant for mal-administration or bad management of public affairs. The paper was signed by all the delegates and sent to the governor, with a demand for a "categorical answer" to each of its heads.

Stuyvesant met this severe document with his usual pluck. He denied the right of some of the delegates to seats in the Convention. He denounced the whole thing as the wicked work of the English, and doubted whether "George Baxter, the author, understood what he was about." He wanted to know if there was no one among the Dutch in New Netherland "sagacious and expert enough to draw up a remonstrance to the director and council," and severely reprimanded the city government of New Amsterdam for seizing "this dangerous opportunity for conspiring with the English [with whom Holland was then at war], who were ever hatching mischief but never performing their promises, and who might to-morrow ally themselves with the North," meaning Sweden and Denmark.

The Convention was not to be silenced by bluster or threats. They told the governor by the mouth of Beeckman, of Brooklyn, that if he refused to consider the several points of the remonstrance, they would appeal to the States-General. At this threat the governor took fire, and, seizing his cane, ordered Beeckman to leave his presence. The plucky ambassador folded his arms and silently defied the magistrate. When Stuyvesant's wrath had subsided, he politely begged the representative to excuse his sudden ebullition of passion and receive assurances of his personal regard. But he was not so complaisant with the Convention as a body. He ordered them to disperse on pain of his "high displeasure." He said, "We derive our authority from God and the Company, not from a few ignorant subjects; and we, alone, can call the inhabitants together." The Convention executed their threat by sending an advocate to Holland, with papers, to ask the reforms which their enumerated grievances demanded.

In the midst of these domestic troubles, the tranquillity of Stuyvesant's foreign relations was disturbed. Governor Printz had returned to Sweden, and in his place was John Risingh, a more warlike magistrate, who came to the Delaware with some soldiers under the bold Swen Schute. They soon appeared before Fort Cassimer and demanded its surrender. "I have no powder; what can I do?" said Bikker, the commander, to the Dutch residents, who fled to the fort for protection. Bikker went out an hour afterward, leaving the gate of the fort wide open, and shook hands with Schute and his men, welcoming them as friends. The Swedes fired two shots over the fort in token of its capture, and then blotting out its Dutch garrison and its name, called it Fort Trinity. The surrender occurred on Trinity Sunday, 1654.

STUYVESANT AND BEECKMAN.

When news of this event reached Stuyvesant, he was enraged and perplexed. He was expecting an attack from the English. They did not come, and the governor prepared to wipe out the stain on Belgic prowess by that "infamous surrender." After a day of fasting and prayer, and after a sermon on the first Sunday in September, the following year (1655), seven vessels, carrying more than six hundred soldiers, sailed from New Amsterdam for the Delaware, under the immediate command of Stuyvesant. His flagship was *The Balance*. Some of his civil officers, and the pastor of the church, were with him. They landed on the beach between Fort Cassimer and Fort Christina near Wilmington. An ensign with a drum was sent to demand the surrender of the former. Schute complied the next day, and in the presence of Stuyvesant and his suite, he drank the health of the governor in a glass of Rhenish wine. So ended the bloodless expedition against Fort Cassimer; and before the end of the month, the conquest of New Sweden was accomplished. Like Alfred of England, Stuyvesant wisely made citizens of the conquered, and they became loyal friends of the Dutch.

When Stuyvesant returned to Manhattan, he found the wildest confusion there. Van Dyck, a former civil officer, detected a squaw stealing peaches from his garden, and killed her. The fury of her tribe was kindled. The long peace with the savages for ten years was suddenly broken. Before daybreak one morning almost two thousand of the River Indians appeared before New Amsterdam in sixty canoes, landed, distributed themselves through the town, and under pretence of looking for Northern Indians, they broke into several dwellings in search of Van Dyck. A council of the inhabitants was immediately held at the fort, and the sachems of the invaders were summoned before them. The Indian leaders agreed to leave the city and pass over to Nutten (now The Governor's) Island before sunset. They broke their promise, and in the evening they shot Van Dyck and menaced others. The people flew to arms and drove the savages to their canoes. The Indians crossed the Hudson, and ravaged New Jersey and Staten Island. Within three days a hundred inhabitants were killed, one hundred and fifty were made captives, and the estates of three hundred were utterly desolated by the dusky foe. Stuyvesant returned at the height of the excitement, and soon brought order out of confusion. Yet distant settlements were broken up, the inhabitants, in fear, flying to Manhattan for safety. To prevent a like calamity in the future, the governor issued a proclamation ordering all who lived in secluded places in the country to gather themselves into villages "after the fashion of our New England neighbors."

Excepting difficulties between the governor and the citizens, growing out of his arbitrary rule, New Netherland prospered in quiet for almost ten years after the Indian invasions, when a crisis in its political affairs approached. The people were generally industrious, and happy homes abounded. In them were many uncultured minds but affectionate hearts, and life was enjoyed in a dreamy, quiet blissfulness, unknown in these bustling days

The city people arose at dawn, dined at eleven o'clock, and went to bed at sunset in the summer. Fashionable parties began at three o'clock in the afternoon in winter and ended at six, so that all the members of a family might be ready for evening devotions and bed at seven. Very little attention was paid to political questions by the "commonalty" or the mass of the people; but there were many wide-awake men and women who were restive under the sharp administration of Stuyvesant. Some declared that they would be willing to endure English rule for the sake of enjoying English liberty. They very soon had an opportunity to try both.

Charles the Second assigned to his brother James, Duke of York, the whole territory of New Netherland, with Long Island and a part of Connecticut. Charles had no more right to that domain than the Prince of Darkness had to the "kingdoms of the world" which he offered to the Redeemer if he would worship the Evil One. But the brutal argument that "might makes right" justified the royal brothers, in their own estimation, in sending ships, men and cannon, the "last argument of kings," to take possession of and hold the territory. Four ships-of-war, bearing four hundred and fifty soldiers commanded by Colonel Richard Nicolls, a court favorite, arrived before New Amsterdam at near the close of August, 1664. Stuyvesant had been warned of their approach, and tried to strengthen the fort; but money, men, and will were wanting. English influence and the governor's temper had alienated the people, and they were indifferent. Some of them regarded the invaders as welcome friends. Stuyvesant began to make concessions to the popular wishes. It was too late; and New Amsterdam became an easy prey to English conquerors—freebooters in the eye of justice.

Revolutionary movements had taken place among the English on Long Island, early in this year, which the governor could not suppress, and the province was rent by internal discord for several months. A war with the Indians above the Hudson highlands had also given the governor much trouble, but his energy and wisdom had brought it to a close. The anthems of a thanksgiving day had died away, and the governor, assured of peace, had gone to Fort Orange (Albany), when news reached him of the coming English armament. He hastened back to his capital, and on Saturday, the 30th day of August, Nicolls sent to the governor a formal summons to surrender the fort and city. He also sent a proclamation to the citizens, promising perfect security of person and property to all who should quietly submit to English rule.

Stuyvesant assembled his council and the burghers or magistrates, at the fort, to consider public affairs. They favored submission without resistance.

The governor, true to his superiors and to his own convictions of duty, would not listen to such a proposition, nor allow the inhabitants to see the proclamation. The Sabbath passed without any answer to the summons. It was a day of great excitement and anxiety in New Amsterdam, and the people became impatient. On Monday the magistrates explained to them the situation of affairs, and they demanded a sight of the proclamation. It was refused; and they were on the verge of open insurrection, when a new turn in events took place.

STUYVESANT AND GOVERNOR WINTHROP.

Governor Winthrop, of Connecticut, with whom Stuyvesant was on friendly terms, had joined the English squadron. Nicolls sent him to Stuyvesant as an ambassador, with a letter in which was repeated the demand for a surrender. The two governors met at the gate of the fort. When Stuyvesant read the letter, he promptly refused to comply. Closing the gate, he retired to the council chamber and laid the letter before his cabinet and the magistrates. They said, "Read the letter to the people and so get their mind." The governor stoutly refused. The council and magistrates as stoutly insisted that he should do so, when the enraged governor, who had fairly earned the title of "Peter the Headstrong," unable to control his passion, tore the letter into pieces. The people at work on the palisades, hearing of this, hastened to the State-House, where a large number of citizens were soon gathered. They sent a deputation to the fort to demand the letter. Stuyvesant stormed. The deputies were inflexible, and a fair copy of the letter was made from the pieces, taken to the State-House and read to the inhabitants. At that time the population of New Amsterdam did not exceed fifteen hundred souls. There were not more than two hundred men, excepting the little garrison, capable of bearing arms.

The impatient Nicolls sent a message to the silent governor, saying: "I shall come for your answer to-morrow with ships and soldiers," and anchored two war-vessels between the fort and the Governor's Island. Stuyvesant's proud will would not bend to circumstances, and from the ramparts of the fort he saw their preparation for attack, unmoved. And when men, women and children, and even his beloved son, Balthazzar, entreated him to surrender that the lives and property of the citizens might be spared, he replied: "I had much rather be carried out dead." At length, when the magistrates, the clergy and many of the principal citizens entreated him, the proud old governor, who had "a heart as big as an ox and a head that would have set adamant to scorn," consented to capitulate. He had held out for a week. On Monday morning, the 8th of September, 1664, he led his troops from the fort to a ship on which they were embarked for Holland, and an hour afterward the red cross of St. George, as the flag of England (whose most conspicuous figure is a red cross) is sometimes poetically called, was floating over Fort Amsterdam, the name of which was changed to Fort James, in compliment to the duke.

The remainder of New Netherland soon passed into the possession of the English, and the city and province were named New York, also in compliment to the duke. Colonel Nicolls, whom the duke had appointed his deputy-governor, was so proclaimed by the magistrates of the city; and all officers within the domain of New Netherland were required to take an oath of allegiance to the British crown.

In the curious fort the new governor made his abode. It must have appeared ludicrous as a fortification, to the eyes of an experienced European soldier like Nicolls. It contained besides the governor's house and barracks, a steep gambrel-roofed church with a high tower, a wind-mill, gallows, pillory, whipping-post, prison, and tall flag-staff. There was, generally, a cheerful submission to the conquerors on the part of the inhabitants, and profound quiet reigned in New York after the turmoil of the surrender.

So passed into the domain of perfected history the Dutch dominion in America, after an existence of half a century. By that unrighteous seizure of a territory which had been discovered and settled by the Dutch, England became the mistress of all the domain stretching along the coast of the Atlantic Ocean from Florida to Acadié, and westward across the entire continent. But upon New Netherland the Dutch, in that brief space of time, had made so deep an impression of their institutions, their social and religious habits, their modes of thought and peculiarities of character, that,

GOV. STUYVESANT DESTROYING THE SUMMONS TO SURRENDER.

From the original painting by Powell in the possession of the publishers.

Johnson & Miles, Publishers, New York.

like the Greeks when overcome by the brute force of the Romans, they remained unconquered in the loftier aspect of the case. The best characteristics of the Dutch of New Netherland are now, after the lapse of more than two centuries, marked features in the society of New York.

In 1665, Stuyvesant went to Holland to report to his superiors. They wished to shift the responsibility of the disaster from their shoulders to that of their last director. They declared that the governor had not done his duty, and asked the States-General to disapprove of "the scandalous surrender" of New Netherland. Stuyvesant made a similar counter-charge and begged the States-General to come to a speedy decision of his case, that he might return to America for his family. Their High Mightinesses, as the representatives of Holland were called, required him to answer the charges of the West India Company. He sent to New York for sworn testimony, and at the end of six months he made an able report, its allegations sustained by unimpeachable witnesses. Among other affidavits was that of Van Ruyven, the then agent of the Company at New York and former secretary of the province, in which it was distinctly charged that the disaster was owing to the neglect of the Company. The latter made a petulant rejoinder, when circumstances put an end to the dispute. War between England and Holland, then raging, was ended by the peace concluded at Breda in 1667, when the latter relinquished to the former its claim to New Netherland. This finished the controversy between Stuyvesant and the West India Company.

GOVERNOR STUYVESANT.

Stuyvesant now departed for New York by way of England, where he obtained from King Charles the concession of the privilege for three Dutch vessels to have free commerce with New York for the space of seven years. Then he sailed for America, with the determination of spending the remainder of his life in New York. He was cordially welcomed by his old friends; and he was kindly received by his political enemies, who had learned by experience that he was not a worse governor than the duke had sent them. Stuyvesant retired to his *bowerie* or farm on the East River, and in the quiet of domestic life he enjoyed the respect of his fellow-citizens. There he died in 1682, at the age of eighty years; and under the venerable St. Mark's Church, in the city of New York, his remains repose. With all his faults magnified by prejudice, Peter Stuyvesant stands out conspicuous in our annals as a grand historic character.

The dreams of freedom under English rule were never realized. The inhabitants of New York soon found that a change of masters did not increase their prosperity or happiness. "Fresh names and laws, they found," says Brodhead, "did not secure fresh liberties. Amsterdam was changed to York, and Orange to Albany. But these changes only commemorated the titles of a conqueror. It was nearly twenty years before that conqueror allowed, for a brief period, to the people of New York, even that partial degree of representative government which they had enjoyed when the three-colored ensign of Holland was hauled down from the flag-staff of Fort Amsterdam. New Netherland exchanged Stuyvesant, and the West India Company, and a republican sovereignty, for Nicolls, and a royal proprietor, and a hereditary king. The province was not represented in Parliament, nor could the voice of its people reach the Chapel of St. Stephen at Westminster as readily as it had reached the Chambers of the Binnenhof at the Hague."

Nicolls ruled wisely, and Francis Lovelace, his successor in 1667, ruled mildly. The latter was a quiet man, unfitted to encounter great storms, yet he showed considerable energy in dealing with the hostile Indians and French on the northern frontier of New York during his administration. He held friendly intercourse with the people of New England; and in the summer of 1672, when a hostile squadron of Dutch vessels of war appeared before his capital, he was on a friendly visit to Governor Winthrop, of Connecticut. There was war, again, between England and Holland, at that time, and the Dutch inhabitants of New York had shown signs of discontent because of the abridgment of their political privileges, and a heavy increase in their taxes, without their consent. Personally they liked Lovelace, but they were bound to consider him as the representative of a petty tyrant. When, in menacing attitude, they demanded more liberty and less taxation, the governor, in a passion, unwisely declared that they should "have liberty for no thought but how to pay their taxes." This was resented, and when the Dutch squadron came, nearly all the Hollanders regarded their countrymen in the ships as liberators. When Colonel Manning, who commanded the fort, called for volunteers, few came, and these not as friends but as enemies, for they spiked the cannon in front of the State-House.

Manning sent an express for Lovelace, and seemed to do what he might to defend the fort. When the ships came up and fired their broadsides upon it, he returned their fire and shot the Dutch flag-ship "through and through." Then six hundred Holland soldiers landed on the bank of the Hudson above the town, where they were joined by four hundred Dutch citizens in arms, who encouraged them to storm the fort. They were marching down Broadway for the purpose, when they were met by a messenger from Manning with a proposition to surrender the fort, if his troops might be allowed to march out with the honors of war. The proposition was accepted. The English garrison marched out with their colors flying and drums beating, and laid down their arms. The Dutch soldiers marched in, followed by the English troops, who were made prisoners of war and confined in the church.

On that hot summer day, the 9th of August, 1672, the flag of the Dutch republic waved over recovered Fort Amsterdam, and the name of the city of New York was changed to that of New Orange, in compliment to William Prince of Orange, the stadtholder or chief magistrate of Holland. The rest of the province soon submitted to the conquerors, and British sovereignty over it was extinguished. Stuyvesant, a quiet but exultant spectator of these momentous events, was avenged. *The Dutch had taken New York!*

CHAPTER V.

NEW NETHERLAND RESTORED TO THE BRITISH—ANDROS AND THE DUKE OF YORK—GOVERNOR DONGAN AND THE FIRST GENERAL ASSEMBLY IN NEW YORK—JAMES II AND THE COLONIES—A NEW HEIR TO THE THRONE—JACOB LEISLER AND HIS CAREER—REPUBLICANISM IN NEW YORK—GOVERNOR FLETCHER AND HIS DISCOMFITURE AT HARTFORD—INDIANS INVADE NEW YORK—GOVERNOR BELLAMONT—CAPTAIN KIDD, HIS ASSOCIATES AND CAREER—GOVERNOR HYDE AND HIS ADMINISTRATION—OTHER GOVERNORS OF NEW YORK—POLITICAL PARTIES—FREEDOM OF THE PRESS VINDICATED—NEGRO PLOT.

THE swift conquest of New York by the Dutch was speedily supplemented by the submission of the settlers on the Delaware within the domain of New Netherland. The other English colonists were amazed by the unlooked-for event, and some of them prepared for war. Connecticut foolishly talked of an offensive war; others prepared to stand on the defensive. Anthony Colve, the governor of re-conquered New Amsterdam, was wide-awake. He kept his eye on the movements of the savages and Frenchmen on the North; watched every hostile indication in the East, and sent proclamations and commissions to towns on Long Island and in Westchester to compel hesitating boroughs to take the oath of allegiance to Prince William of Orange. He had strengthened his fortifications; and upon the fort and around the city of New Orange he had planted one hundred and ninety cannon. But all anxiety was ended by a treaty of peace between the Dutch and English, made at London early in 1674, by which New Netherland was restored to the British crown. Some doubts arising about the validity of the duke's title after these changes, the king gave him a new grant of territory in June, 1674, within the boundary of which was included all the domain west of the Connecticut River, to the eastern shores of the Delaware; also Long Island and a territory in Maine. King Charles had commissioned Major Edmund Andros to receive the surrender of the province from the Dutch governor. He was now appointed governor of New York. The surrender took place, in a formal manner, at Fort James, in October.

Andros, who was destined to play an important part in American affairs, was then thirty-seven years of age. He had been brought up in the royal household, and accompanied the exiled family to Holland, where he began his military career. As major of Prince Rupert's regiment of dragoons, he performed gallant service, and being a favorite of the king and the duke, a good Dutch and French scholar, a thorough royalist and an obedient servant of his superiors, he was well fitted to perform the part which his masters appointed him to play. His private character was without blemish, and the

FINAL SURRENDER BY THE DUTCH TO THE ENGLISH.

evil things spoken of him relate to his public career. The duke's instructions favored the constitution of the province of New York, and Andros enforced them with ever-increasing vigor. In his zeal he even exceeded his instructions; and in a short time he acquired the just title of "tyrant." The duke, his master, was a strange compound of wickedness and goodness;

slow to perceive right from wrong and seldom seeing the truth in its purity. Bancroft says of him—"A libertine without love, a devotee without spirituality, an advocate of toleration without a sense of the natural right to freedom of conscience,—in him the muscular force prevailed over the intellectual. He was not blood-thirsty; but to a narrow mind fear seems the most powerful instrument of government, and he propped his throne with the block and the gallows. He floated between the sensuality of indulgence and the sensuality of superstition, hazarding heaven for an ugly mistress, and, to the great delight of abbots and nuns, winning it back again by pricking his flesh with sharp points of iron, and eating no meat on Saturdays." Of the two brothers, the Duke of Buckingham said well, that "Charles would not, and James could not see." The fact that he was the destined successor of Charles on the throne of England—a king whose irregularities of life were rapidly hurrying him to the grave—made James an object of intense interest to the Protestants of the realm, and the subject of intrigues to prevent him ascending to the seat of his brother.

With all their political disabilities under Andros, the people of New York were prosperous and therefore comparatively happy. Luxury had not corrupted their tastes, and wants were few. A man worth three thousand dollars was rich; the possessor of five thousand dollars was opulent. There was an almost dead level of equality in society. Beggars were unknown. "Ministers were few, but religions many;" and out of matters of faith grew many controversies. There seemed little reason for the twenty thousand inhabitants of the domain to be unhappy; but the divine instinct of freedom, which demanded a free exercise of the rights of self-government, made many of them discontented and in some places mutinous.

It was then a stormy time in England. Theological disputes culminated in bloodshed and universal disorder, and thousands were *sent* to America, and other thousands *fled* to the colonies. Of the former, women were often burnt in the cheek, and men marked by cutting off their ears. These fugitives, many of them people of good families and education, inoculated all the provinces with healthful republican aspirations.

At about this time the duke's daughter Mary married her cousin Prince William of Orange. These nuptials were distasteful to the duke, who was becoming more and more a confirmed Roman Catholic; for William was recognized as the leader of the Protestants of Europe. "I predict," said the French ambassador in London to James, "that such a son-in-law will inevitably be your ruin." The prediction was soon fulfilled, as we shall observe presently. The nuptials of those cousins led to very important events in the history of England and America.

The career of Andros outside of New York was more striking—more dramatic—than within that domain. This career we shall have occasion to notice hereafter. It is sufficient to say here, that after an administration of about nine years, he was succeeded in 1683 by Thomas Dongan, a mild-mannered and enlightened Irishman of the Roman Catholic faith, who reached New York in August. Andros had ruled with vigor, keeping peace with the powerful Iroquois Confederacy; curbing religious enthusiasts; frowning upon every sign of republicanism, and asserting with great tenacity the powers of the duke within the chartered limits of his territory. Meanwhile the duke had listened to the appeals of the inhabitants of New York and heeded the judicious advice of William Penn, to give the people liberty; and Dongan was clothed with authority to call an assembly of representatives of the people. Dongan's sympathies were with the popular desires, and performing the duty with alacrity, he saw a Legislative Assembly in session in Fort James at New York, on the 17th of October, 1683—about thirty years after the Dutch, in the same city, made a demand for a popular convention. It is a memorable day in the history of the State of New York. Then was established the first General Assembly of the Province of New York, composed of seventeen representatives, who sat three weeks, and passed fourteen acts, all of which were assented to by the governor and his council. The first of these was entitled "The Charter of Liberties and Privileges, granted by his Royal Highness, to the inhabitants of New York and its Dependencies." It declared that supreme legislative power should forever be and reside in the governor, council and people, met in general assembly; that every freeholder and freeman should be allowed to vote for representatives without restraint; that no freeman should suffer but by judgment of his peers; that all trials should be by a jury of twelve men; that no tax should be assessed, on any pretence whatever, but by the consent of the Assembly; that no seaman or soldier should be quartered on the inhabitants against their will; that no martial-law should exist; and that no person, professing faith in God, by Jesus Christ, should, at any time, be any wise disquieted or questioned for any difference of opinion. Not a feature of the intolerance and bigotry of New England charters appeared in this first "Charter of Liberties" for the province of New York.

The hopes raised by the ratification of this Charter of Liberties were doomed to early disappointment. When, at the beginning of 1685, James ascended the throne, on the death of Charles, he refused to confirm as king what he had solemnly promised as duke. He immediately began to demolish the fair fabric of civil and religious liberty which had been reared in New York. A direct tax was ordered; the printing-press—the right arm of knowledge and of freedom—was forbidden a place in the colony; and as he had determined to establish the Roman Catholic faith as the state religion throughout his realm, the provincial offices were filled by adherents of the Italian Church. The liberal-minded Dongan lamented these proceedings; and when the stupid king instructed the governor to introduce French priests among the *Five Nations*, Dongan resisted the measure as dangerous to the English power on the continent. Fortunately the Iroquois Confederacy remained firm in their friendship for the English, in after years, and stood as a powerful barrier against the French, when the latter twice attempted to reach the white settlements at Albany.

The clear-headed and right-minded Dongan stood by the people and the interests of England with a firmness that finally offended the monarch. He knew that James had a great love for the French, and when he saw the advantages which he gave them in America by unwise acts, he could not but regard the sovereign's conduct as treason to his country. For his faithfulness, he was rewarded with the gratitude of the people of New York, and with dismissal from the office of governor by the king. In the spring of 1688, he received a letter from James, ordering him to surrender the government into the hands of Andros, who had a vice-regal commission to rule New York and all New England.

The viceroy journeyed from Boston to New York early in August, where he was received by Colonel Bayard's regiment of foot and horse, and was entertained by the loyal aristocracy. In the midst of the rejoicings, the news came that the queen, the second wife of James, had been blessed with a son, who became heir to the throne. The event was celebrated the same evening by bonfires in the streets and a feast at the City Hall. At the latter, Mayor Van Cortlandt became so hilarious, that he made a burnt sacrifice to his loyalty of his hat and periwig, waving the burning victims over the banquet table on the point of his straight sword.

The Dutch inhabitants of New York, as well as the Protestant republicans, were disappointed by the royal birth, for they had looked forward with hope for the accession of Mary, the wife of their own Prince of Orange, to the throne of England. This event intensified the general discontent because of the consolidation of New York with New England and the abridgment of their rights, and the people were on the verge of open rebellion when a revolution in England changed the whole aspect of affairs there and in America, and satisfied the aspirations of the Dutch at New York by seating William and Mary on the throne. The general result of that revolution has been recorded at near the close of the Second Chapter of the Third Book.

The effect of the accession of William and Mary, in New England, will be noticed hereafter. Andros and his political associates were seized at Boston, and sent to England. This act was followed in New York by the seizure of Fort James. In this movement Jacob Leisler, an influential merchant and commander of militia, took a leading part. He was a German colonist; a Presbyterian in church-fellowship; an enthusiastic admirer of William of Orange, but with democratic tendencies. About five hundred men in arms rallied around him at the fort, whence he issued this declaration: "As soon as the bearer of orders from the Prince of Orange shall have let us see his power, then, without delay, we do intend to obey, not the orders only, but also the bearer thereof."

THE MAYOR'S BURNT-OFFERING.

Leisler refused to proclaim the accession of William and Mary, until he should be officially certified of the fact. At his request, delegates from a few towns assembled in convention, formed a Committee of Safety of ten, and proceeded to organize a provisional government. They commissioned Leisler commander of the province, when Nicholson, whose time-serving policy had alienated from himself the confidence of the people, fearing the populace, fled on board a vessel and sailed for London. This flight gave Leisler and his adherents an unexpected advantage. The people consented that he should act as governor in the absence of regularly constituted authority. The aristocracy were offended because an "insolent foreigner and plebeian" was in the high seat of power. They bitterly opposed him, but he managed public affairs so well that his enemies were compelled to praise him. Van Cortlandt, Bayard and other leaders of the aristocracy retired to Albany, where a convention of the people acknowledged allegiance to William and Mary, defied the power of Leisler, and denounced him as a treasonable usurper. Their influence in the province was great, and the communities on the Hudson generally disapproved of the mutinous proceedings in New York.

When, late in the year (1689), royal letters were received addressed to the governor, or, in his absence, to "such as, for the time being, take care for preserving the public peace and administering the law in New York," Leisler considered that his own authority had received the royal sanction. He now, with clouded judgment and inconsiderate rashness, determined to bring into obedience the aristocratic party, whose focus of strength was at Albany under the lead of Peter Schuyler, the mayor of that city. He sent his son-in-law, Jacob Milborne, with a few troops to enforce that obedience. He was resisted by argument and physical force until the awful destruction of Schenectady by the Indians in February, 1690, spread universal alarm and pointed to the necessity for uniting for the common defence. The authority of Leisler was acknowledged, for the people of the north sorely needed his help.

Another year passed by. Meanwhile the ears of the monarchs had been filled with reports of Leisler's usurpation and disloyalty, and they appointed Henry Sloughter governor of New York, who sent forward his lieutenant, Ingoldsby, to take possession of the province. When that officer arrived early in 1691, he haughtily demanded of Leisler the surrender of the fort. He did not deign to show his credentials, and Leisler properly refused compliance with his demands, at the same time treating Ingoldsby, and the few soldiers whom he brought with him, with respect. The aristocratic party were enraged by Leisler's refusal, and for several weeks the city was fearfully excited by the violence of factions. And when, in March, Governor Sloughter arrived, and Leisler sent him a letter loyally tendering to him the fort and province, that functionary, under the influence of the aristocratic leaders, answered it by sending an officer to arrest the "usurper" and Milborne, and six of the "inferior insurgents," on a charge of high treason. They were taken to prison, and when they were arraigned, the two principal offenders, denying the authority of the court, refused to plead, and appealed to the king. They were condemned, and sentenced to death (as were, also, the other six); but Sloughter, who, in his sober moments, was just and honest, refused to sign the death-warrant until he should hear from the king. The implacable enemies of the "usurper," determined on causing his destruction, invited the governor to a dinner party on Staten Island on a bright day in May. One of them carried to the banquet a legally drawn death-warrant, and when the governor had been made stupid by liquor, he was induced to sign the fatal paper. It was sent to the city that evening, and on the following morning Leisler and Milborne were summoned to prepare for execution. Leisler sent for his wife, Alice, and their older children, and after a sorrowful parting with them, he and his son-in-law were led to the gallows in a drenching rain. They confessed their errors of judgment, but denied all intentional wrong-doing. The blamelessness of their lives confirmed their declarations of innocence. Before Sloughter was permitted to recover from his debauch, they were hanged. It was a foul murder. The governor was tortured with remorse for his act, and died of *delirium tremens* three months afterward.

Leisler's appeal to the king was not sent. His son repeated it. The result was the return to the families of Leisler and Milborne of their confiscated estates, and before four years had passed, the British Parliament declared them innocent of treason, by reversing the attainder. Their death created a deep feeling of sympathy for the cause of popular sovereignty, of which they were representatives and proto-martyrs. From that hour republicanism had a very vigorous growth in the province of New York, and gave future royal governors a great deal of trouble.

Benjamin Fletcher succeeded Sloughter as governor of New York. He was a man of violent passions, weak judgment, greedy, dishonest and cowardly, and as dissolute as his predecessor. How he came to be intrusted with the governorship at all, and especially with the large powers of commander of the militia of Connecticut, New York and New Jersey with which he was invested, is a problem not easily solved. He soon disgusted all parties; and the recklessness of his administration caused more decided resistance to imperial power than ever before. Among his acts of petty tyranny, which displayed his folly and weakness, was his visit to Hartford, with Colonel Bayard and others, late in the autumn of 1693, to assert his disputed military authority there, by ordering out the Connecticut militia at a season when parades had ceased. The charter of the colony denied Fletcher's jurisdiction, and the Assembly, then in session, promptly gave utterance to that denial on this occasion. "I will not set my foot out of this colony, till I have seen his majesty's commission obeyed," said Fletcher to the governor of Connecticut. The latter yielded so much as to allow Captain Wadsworth to call out the train-bands of Hartford.

When the troops were assembled, Fletcher stepped forward to take the command, and ordered Bayard to read his excellency's commission. At that moment Captain Wadsworth ordered the drums to be beaten. "Silence!" angrily cried the petulant governor, and Bayard began to read again. "Drum! drum! I say," shouted Wadsworth; and the sonorous roll drowned the voice of Bayard. Fletcher, in a rage, stamped his foot and cried

"Silence!" and threatened the captain with punishment for insubordination. Whereupon Wadsworth stepped boldly in front of the governor and said, while his hand rested on the handle of his sword: "If my drummers are interrupted again, I'll make the sunlight shine through you. We deny and defy your authority." The cowardly governor sullenly folded up his commission, pocketed it and the affront, and with his retinue returned to New York in a very angry mood. He complained to the king. The matter was compromised by making Fletcher commander of the Connecticut militia only in time of war.

GOVERNOR FLETCHER AND CAPTAIN WADSWORTH.

During the whole of Fletcher's administration of seven years, party rancor, kindled by the death of Leisler, burned intensely, and, at one time, menaced the province with civil war. At the same time it was threatened with a destructive invasion by the French and Indians from Canada, under the guidance of the venerable Count Frontenac, the energetic governor of that province. These foes were then traversing the wilderness in northern

New York, seeking for a passage through the country of the Five Nations to the English settlements below. Fortunately the governor listened to the wise advice of Mayor Schuyler, of Albany, who had a marvellous influence over the Iroquois Confederacy; and under his leadership, about three hundred English and as many Mohawk warriors beat back the foe to the St. Lawrence. They so desolated the French settlements in the vicinity of Lake Champlain, slaying about three hundred French and Indians at the north end of the lake, that Frontenac was glad to remain quiet at Montreal.

Although the New York Assembly was filled with the bitter enemies of Leisler, they, as boldly as he, asserted the supremacy of the people, and would suffer no encroachments on colonial rights and privileges. They rebuked the interference of the governor in legislation, by insisting upon amendments to bills, and drew from him, on one occasion, the reproachful words which tell of their independence and firmness: "There never was an amendment desired by the Council Board, but what was rejected. It is a sign of a stubborn ill-temper." With that "stubborn ill-temper" of the Assembly, Fletcher was almost continually in conflict; and when, in 1698, he was superseded by the Earl of Bellamont, he seemed as glad to leave the province as the people were to get rid of him.

Bellamont was an honest and energetic Irish peer. He had been on the Committee of Parliament appointed to make inquiry concerning the trial and death of Leisler, and was well acquainted with the questions which divided the factions. He rebuked the little aristocratic oligarchy who had hovered around Fletcher; and his wise and liberal course strengthened the republican cause. It opened the way to just legislation, and the ascendency of liberal men in the Assembly. That body, in the year 1700, on receiving a letter from the king, asking them to indemnify the family of Leisler from a "gracious sense of the father's services and sufferings," confirmed the verdict of Parliament in favor of the innocence of the martyr by granting the request.

Bellamont labored earnestly to reform existing abuses in the management of public affairs. It was a sharp commentary on the character of his predecessor, when he uttered the promise: "I will pocket none of the public money myself, nor shall there be any embezzlement by others." Such confidence had the Assembly in his integrity, that they voted a revenue for six years and placed it at the disposition of the governor. Notwithstanding his character was above reproach, it passed under a cloud because of his unfortunate connection with the famous pirate, Captain William Kidd. The story may be briefly told:

English commerce suffered greatly from the depredations of pirates and

French privateers. The English government could not suppress the evil. A company was formed to do that work. It was composed of several English noblemen and the king, and Robert Livingston, the first "Lord of the Manor," and Governor Bellamont, in America. They fitted out a galley called the *Adventure*, as a privateer. Livingston, then in England, recommended Captain Kidd, of New York, to be her commander, and he was duly commissioned as such by the king. In the *Adventure*, Kidd did noble service in protecting the commerce in American waters from the sea-robbers. He recruited from time to time, until his crew numbered one hundred and fifty men. Then he resolved to measure strength with the pirates of the Indian Ocean. Arming his men with pistols, cutlasses and pikes, and the *Adventure* with a swivel gun at her stem and stern, he sailed for Madagascar, where he turned pirate. He respected no flag, no nationality, no circumstance; but swept the seas for booty alone, roving over the vast expanse of ocean from Farther India westward to the coasts of South America. Thence he sailed up among the West India Islands and along the shores of North America, to the vicinity of his home; and on Gardiner's Island, eastward of Long Island, he buried much treasure, consisting of gold, silver, and precious stones.

The piracies of Kidd were long known in England before the Company noticed them. At length the matter became so scandalous that they felt it necessary to vindicate their character. The belief was general that the king, the earl, the "lord of the manor," and their associates had shared the plunder with Kidd, and the odium of complicity in piracy rested heavily upon them. They needed a scape-goat, and Kidd was made the victim. He appeared openly in the streets of Boston, unsuspicious of real danger, for he had his king's commission in his pocket, and Bellamont was his business partner. But the governor, expressing horror at his crimes, ordered his arrest, and very soon the pirate appeared before the earl a prisoner in irons.

Kidd now saw that he was to be sacrificed, and he sought to win the earl's favor and aid, by telling Bellamont where he had hidden the treasure. In immovable firmness at that critical moment lay the governor's safety; and he turned a deaf ear to the prayers of the prisoner with bowed head, and the entreaties of his wife who begged for mercy, human and divine, for her erring husband. There was a struggle between the pride and fear, and the better nature of Bellamont. The former triumphed. Kidd was sent to England and tried for murder and piracy. Convicted of the former, he was hanged. So the penalty of the sins of omission, at least, of the monarch and nobles and rich civilians, were borne by the commoner on the scaffold.

The earl received the buried treasure, and at his coffers its history ends in impenetrable mystery.

The king and the earl died soon after Kidd perished, and Sir Edward Hyde, uncle of Queen Anne, who was then monarch of England, became governor of New York. He was a libertine and a knave, who cursed the province with misrule for about seven years. He was a bigot, too, and persecuted all denominations of Christians outside of the Church of England. He embezzled the public money, involved himself heavily in debt, and on all occasions was the persistent enemy of popular freedom. "I know no right which you have as an assembly," he said to the representatives of the people, "but such as the queen is pleased to allow you." That was in 1705, the year when that Assembly won the first substantial victory for democracy over absolutism or despotic rule. They obtained from the queen permission to make specific appropriations of incidental grants of money, and to appoint their own treasurer to take charge of extraordinary supplies. That was a bold and important step in the direction of popular independence and sovereignty.

So the very vices of the governor disciplined the people to resistance of oppression, and secured to them the recognition of rights which might have been postponed for many years. The governor, who was weak-minded, mean-spirited and vacillating, was so overpowered by the indomitable will of the people—a hardy, mixed race—that he meekly submitted to reproof, and in his poverty of soul and purse humbly thanked the Assembly for simple justice. In 1708, the queen, yielding to the wishes of the people, recalled him. When he left the chair of state his creditors cast him into prison, where he remained until the death of his father made him Lord Cornbury. Then he was released by the unjust law of England yet in force, which will not permit a peer of the realm, and consequently a member of the House of Lords, to be arrested for debt.

Lord Lovelace was Hyde's successor. With his brief administration began those contests between democracy and absolutism in the province of New York which ended only with the victory of the former at the close of the old war for independence. Already the political friends of Leisler had achieved a signal triumph over his enemies. Colonel Bayard and others, who had published libels on the royal lieutenant-governor (Nanfan) before Hyde's arrival, had been arrested by that energetic officer and tried for and convicted of treason under a law which these men had made in 1691 to meet Leisler's case. Bayard was sentenced to be "hanged, drawn and quartered," but was reprieved until the pleasure of the monarch should be known. When Hyde arrived, soon afterward, he reversed the attainder, and the offender was set at liberty. The power of the self-constituted aristocracy was broken, and their controlling influence disappeared. When Lovelace came, and the crown demanded a permanent revenue without appropriation, the legislature of New York, in the exercise of popular sovereignty or rule of the people, and taking the ground that "taxation without representation is tyranny," would raise only an annual revenue for specific purposes. From that time, until 1732, the royal representatives, unable to resist the will of the people, as expressed by the Assembly, allowed democratic principles to grow, flourish, and bear fruit.

From Lovelace to Cosby, there were three governors—Robert Hunter, William Burnet and John Montgomery—and three acting governors. The first was a literary man, fond of good cheer, but unfitted by temperament to be governor of New York at that crisis. He brought with him three thousand German Lutherans from the Palatinate of the Rhine, who had been driven from their homes by the persecution of Louis the Fourteenth. These settled in different parts of the province of New York, and in Pennsylvania. They were chiefly the ancestors of the German population of the latter State.

Hunter and his council, under instructions, insisted that the popular Assembly, like themselves, existed only by the mere grace of the crown. The Assembly as vehemently insisted that they possessed an inherent right to legislate, that was derived not from any commission or grant from the crown, but "from the free choice and election of the people who ought not, nor justly can be, divested of their property without their consent." The governor could not assent to this doctrine. The Assembly were inflexible; and Hunter's administration was marked by violent political contests between the chief magistrate and the representatives of the people. "I have spent three years," he wrote at one time, "in such torture and vexation that nothing in life can make amends for it." He loved his ease, and sighed for quiet. Failing health compelled him to return to England in 1719, when he left the government in the hands of Peter Schuyler, the oldest member of the council. That accomplished gentleman completely restored the friendship between the English and the Five Nations, which had been disturbed.

Hunter was succeeded by William Burnet, son of the celebrated Bishop Burnet. For awhile he was very popular, but at length he incurred the displeasure of a powerful party of merchants who controlled the Assembly, and his position was made so very uncomfortable that he was transferred to the government of Massachusetts. It was during his administration, that William Bradford, in the autumn of 1725, established the first public newspaper in New York. He had set up the first printing-house in the province, in 1693, when Fletcher was governor. His paper was entitled "The New York Weekly Gazette." John Montgomery succeeded Burnet in 1728. Death closed his uneventful administration, in the summer of 1731, when Rip Van Dam, the senior member of the council, took charge of public affairs until the arrival of William Cosby as governor, in 1732.

Cosby was avaricious and arbitrary by nature, and opportunity made him exercise his passions almost without stint. His first act was to demand of Van Dam an equal share of that councillor's salary received by him while acting as governor. "Give me half the perquisites of your office from the time of your appointment until your arrival," said Van Dam, "and I will agree to your proposition." This fair proposal was rejected, and Van Dam refused compliance with the governor's requisition. Cosby sued him in the Supreme Court. A majority of the judges were the governor's personal friends, and gave judgment against Van Dam. Chief-Justice Morris decided against the governor. The latter removed the chief justice without consulting his council, and put James De Lancey in his place.

BURNING OF ZENGER'S PAPERS.

The sympathies of the people were with Van Dam, and the governor's high-handed proceedings aroused their indignation to an intense pitch. They induced John Peter Zenger, who had been an apprentice and business partner with Bradford, to establish a newspaper to be the organ of the democratic party. He did so in November, 1733, calling it the "New York Weekly Journal," with Van Dam behind him as financial supporter. Bradford's paper was then controlled by the government.

The "Journal" made vigorous warfare upon the governor and his political friends. It kept up a continual fire of squibs, lampoons and satires, and finally charged them with violating the rights of the people, the assumption of tyrannical power, and the perversion of their official stations for selfish purposes.

The officials endured these attacks tor a year. In the autumn of 1734, the governor and council ordered Zenger's papers, containing his offensive articles, to be burned publicly by the common hangman, and he was arrested and thrown into prison on a charge of libelling the government. The Grand Jury refused to find a bill of indictment for this offence, but he was held by another process, and was kept in jail until early in the next August, when he was brought to trial in the City Hall, New York. The case excited intense interest throughout the whole country, for it involved the great question of liberty of speech and of the press.

Meanwhile an association called the "Sons of Liberty", had worked diligently for Zenger. The venerable Andrew Hamilton, of Philadelphia, then eighty years of age and the foremost lawyer in the country, was engaged as the prisoner's counsel. On the hot morning when the trial commenced, the court-room was densely crowded. Chief-Justice De Lancey presided. A jury was empaneled. The prisoner pleaded "Not Guilty," but boldly admitted the publication of the alleged libel, and offered full proof of its justification. The attorney-general had just risen to oppose the introduction of such proof, when the venerable Hamilton unexpectedly entered the room, his long white hair flowing over his shoulders, instead of being queued in the fashion of the day. The excited audience, most of them in sympathy with the prisoner, arose to their feet, and in spite of the voice and frowns of the chief-justice, waved their hats and shouted loud huzzas. When silence prevailed, the attorney-general took the ground that facts in justification of an alleged libel were not admissible in evidence. The court sustained him.

When Hamilton arose, a murmur of applause ran through the crowd. In a few eloquent sentences he scattered to the winds the sophistries which supported the pernicious doctrine that "the greater the truth the greater is the libel." He declared that the jury were themselves judges of the facts and the law; that they were competent to judge of the guilt or innocence of the accused, and reminded them that they were the sworn protectors of the rights, liberties and privileges of their fellow-citizens, which, in this instance, had been violated by a most outrageous and vindictive series of persecutions. He conjured them to remember that it was for them to interpose between the tyrannical and arbitrary violators of the law and their intended victim, and to assert, by their verdict, in the fullest manner, the freedom of speech and of the press, and the supremacy of the people over their wanton and powerful oppressors.

Notwithstanding the charge of the chief-justice was wholly adverse to the doctrines of the great advocate, the jury, after brief deliberation, returned a unanimous verdict of "Not Guilty." Then a shout of triumph went up from the multitude, and Hamilton was borne out of the court-room upon the shoulders of the people to a grand entertainment which had been prepared for him. On the following day a public dinner was given him by the citizens. At the close of September following, the corporation of the city of New York presented to Mr. Hamilton the Freedom of the City and their

A POPULAR TRIUMPH CELEBRATED.

thanks, in a gold box weighing five-and-a-half ounces, made for the occasion. In this document they cordially thanked him for his "learned and generous defence of the rights of mankind, and the liberty of the press," and for his signal service which "he cheerfully undertook, under great indisposition of body, and generously performed, refusing any fee or reward."

This triumph of the popular cause—this vindication of the freedom of the press—this evidence of the determination of the people to protect their champions, and this success of an organization in its infancy which appeared in power thirty years later under the same name of "Sons of Liberty," was a sure prophecy of that political independence of the colonies which was so speedily fulfilled. Yet the stupid governor, staggered by the blow, could not understand the meaning of the prophecy; and only his death, a few months after the trial, put an end to his vindictive proceedings.

From the arrival of Cosby until the beginning of the French and Indian war at the middle of the century, the history of the province of New York is composed chiefly of the records of party strife. Only one episode in that history demands special attention here. It is known in our annals as the "Negro Plot;" as unsubstantial in fact as was the "Salem Witchcraft." Several incendiary fires had occurred in quick succession in the city of New York, in 1741. The idea suddenly took possession of the minds of the inhabitants that it was the work of negroes, who had conspired to burn and plunder the city, murder the white inhabitants and set up a government under a man of their own color. A fearful panic ensued. Suspected negroes of both sexes, and some white men and women, were arrested and tried; and before the excitement was over, four white people were hanged, and eleven negroes were burned. Eighteen of the latter were hanged, and fifty were sent to the West Indies and sold as slaves. On the site of the present City Hall, three negroes were burnt at the stake at one time. Two of them were men and one was a woman. All who suffered at that time were, undoubtedly, innocent victims of terror created by imaginary danger.

CHAPTER VI.

GOVERNOR BRADFORD—THE FIRST PUBLIC THANKSGIVING IN NEW ENGLAND—FRIENDSHIP WITH THE INDIANS—CANONICUS AND HIS CHALLENGE—WESTON'S COLONY AND ITS CAREER—SOCIAL CHANGES—ENTERPRISE OF THE PILGRIMS—RELIGIOUS MATTERS—COLONY AT CAPE ANN—ENDICOTT AT SALEM—HIS AUSTERITY—MASSACHUSETTS BAY COLONY—GOVERNOR WINTHROP AND THE INDIANS—REPUBLICAN AND REPRESENTATIVE GOVERNMENTS ESTABLISHED—INTERCOURSE WITH OTHER COLONIES—PERSECUTION IN ENGLAND AND INTOLERANCE IN MASSACHUSETTS—PREPARATION TO RESIST TYRANNY.

WILLIAM BRADFORD, the first historian of Massachusetts, was the official successor of John Carver, the earliest governor of the Plymouth colony. He entered upon his duties as chief-magistrate a few weeks before the States-General of Holland chartered the Dutch West India Company, under whose auspices the province of New Netherland, as we have observed, was first settled by Europeans.

Bradford was a native of Ansterfield, Yorkshire, in the north of England, where he was born in the year 1588. His pecuniary circumstances were easy, when he followed persecuted Puritans to Holland and became fully identified with them in exile. From early life he had been accustomed to their teachings; and at the age of seventeen years, he attempted to fly to the Netherlands, with some others, whither their harassed brethren had gone. Betrayed, he was seized and imprisoned at Boston, in Lincolnshire, for awhile, but finally escaped and joined the fugitives at Amsterdam, where he learned the silk weaver's art and pursued it. On receiving his patrimony, he entered into unsuccessful commercial operations, and lost a greater portion of it. When the establishment of a free colony in America was projected at Leyden, he was one of the most zealous promoters of the measure; and he and his young wife were among the earliest emigrants to that land of promise. Before a site was selected for a settlement, and while the *May-Flower* was yet riding at anchor in Cape Cod Bay, Mrs. Bradford fell into the sea and was drowned. That was the first death among the Pilgrims after their arrival on the coast of America. Shrewd, wise, active, humane and generous, Bradford was very popular; and he was in the chair of state almost continually from 1621 until his death in 1657, a period of thirty-six years.

We have observed toward the close of Chapter III of the Second Book, that the Pilgrims at Plymouth rejoiced in an abundance of food in the autumn of 1621, the first year of their settlement. Thereby their hearts were filled with gratitude, and after the fruits of their labors had all been gathered, the governor sent out huntsmen to bring in supplies for a general and common thanksgiving. That was the first celebration of the great New England festival of Thanksgiving, now annually held in almost every State and Territory of the Union in the month of November. Great quantities of wild turkeys and deer were gathered at Plymouth, and for three days the Pilgrims indulged in rejoicing, firing of guns and feasting—entertaining, at the same time, King Massasoit and ninety of his dusky followers, who contributed five deer to the banquets. Seven substantial houses had been built during the summer; the inhabitants were in good health; a few emigrants from England had come in a second ship, and there were happy homes in the wilderness the ensuing winter. Among the new comers was

AN INDIAN CHALLENGE.

the Rev. Robert Cushman, one of the founders of the colony, who, in December, 1621, preached the first sermon in New England.

Governor Bradford's chief anxiety, at first, was for the establishment of friendly relations between the English and the Indians. That was already secured with Massasoit and his people; but Canonicus, the haughty chief of the Narragansets, living on Canonicut Island opposite the site of Newport, was loth to be friendly at first. To show his contempt for and defiance of the English, he sent a messenger to Governor Bradford with a bundle of arrows in a rattlesnake's skin. That was at the dead of winter, 1622. It was a challenge to engage in war in the spring. Like the venomous serpent that wore the skin, the symbols of hostility gave warning before striking—a virtue seldom exercised by the Indians. Bradford acted wisely on the occasion. He accepted the challenge to fight the multitude of savages, by sending the significant quiver back, filled with gunpowder and shot. "What

PURITANS BARRICADING THEIR HOUSE AGAINST INDIANS.

can these things be?" inquired the ignorant and curious savage mind, as they were carried from village to village in superstitious awe as objects of evil omen. They had heard of the great guns at the seaside, and they dared not keep the mysterious symbols of the governor's anger, but sent them back to Plymouth in token of peace. The pride, if not the hatred, of Canonicus was subdued, and he and other chiefs humbly begged the English for friendship. But the alarmed colony spent the remainder of the winter and spring in fear, for Canonicus could send five thousand warriors to the field, it was said. The English, with much labor, built the fort mentioned in Chapter III of the Second Book, which served, also, for a meeting-house. And when tidings came of the massacre by the Indians in Virginia, in April (see Chapter I, Book III), every man worked diligently. Their houses were all barricaded, and "watch and ward were constantly kept."

Not long after this, the first war between the English and savages broke out. Weston, a wealthy and dissatisfied member of the Plymouth Company, sent over a colony of sixty unmarried men to plant a settlement on his own account, somewhere on the shores of Massachusetts Bay. He boasted of the superior strength of such a settlement by bachelors to that of Plymouth, which was "weakened by women and children." They were mostly idle and disorderly young men like those who went early to Virginia. Many of them were very dissolute. After living several weeks upon the scanty means of the Plymouth families, they went to the site of Weymouth, where they began a settlement. Idle and wasteful, they were soon compelled to confront gaunt Famine; and beggary and starvation were the alternatives presented to them. They exasperated the Indians by plundering their cornfields and other sources of supplies. The savages, failing to discriminate between the righteous and the unrighteous, or fearing the vengeance of the other white people if they should destroy the young men at Weymouth, formed a plot for the extermination of all the English in their land. The peril was great, and was discovered only a few days before the fatal blow was to be struck. Massasoit, who had been nursed into health after a deadly sickness, by the brave hands of Edward Winslow, revealed the plot to his benefactor. The Plymouth people immediately sent Captain Standish, with a few soldiers, to protect the offending Englishmen, and in a contest that ensued an Indian chief and several of his followers were killed. The victor carried the chief's head upon a pole, in triumph, into Plymouth, and placed it on the palisades of the fort. When the good Robinson, at Leyden, heard of this, he wrote: "O, how happy a thing it would have been, had you converted some, before you killed any." If they were not "converted," the savages were very much frightened, and sued for peace. So the settlement of strong unmarried men was saved by the Plymouth people, who were "weakened by many women and children." The childless Lord Bacon, in one of his essays, says: "Certainly the best works and of greatest merit for the public have proceeded from the unmarried or childless men." Weston's experience was the reverse. His colony, too weak to endure, was broken up within a year after it was planted, and the most worthless of its members, happily for the Plymouth people, returned to England.

TRIUMPHAL MARCH INTO PLYMOUTH.

We have observed (Chapter III, Book II) that the Pilgrims and London merchants and others, formed a partnership in making the settlement of the Plymouth colony. The speculation, as such, was a failure. Ill-feeling arose between the two classes of proprietors. The merchants and others wished to dissolve the league, whose prescribed term of existence was seven years.

It continued to the end of that time, when the colonists purchased the interest of their partners in England. Then the community system, or the common sharing of labor and its products, was abandoned, and the whole property was divided among the inhabitants. New incentives to industry were thereby created; and very soon the blessings of plenty drawn from the unfruitful soil of New England, rewarded labor there. The cultivators of the soil became free-holders, and general prosperity was soon manifested.

The restless enterprise of the children of the Pilgrims of our day marked the "Fathers." While their number was few and their strength feeble, they stretched forth their hands to grasp other landed possessions. At an early day they acquired rights of domain on Cape Anne and on the borders of the Kennebec. Nothing but the interfering spasms of the dying Plymouth Company, of whom the veteran Gorges was the latest survivor, prevented their extending the jurisdiction of Plymouth over all New England. His efforts to sustain the claims and existence of the Company, and his ambitious aspirations in his old age as governor-general of New England and lord proprietor of Maine, have been already considered in the Fifth Chapter of the Second Book.

The colony had been spared the affliction of a governor sent by Gorges, and from the beginning had enjoyed self-government without the royal sanction. That government was simple. At first the only officers were a governor and one assistant magistrate. In 1624, five assistants were chosen, and in 1630, when the colony numbered about five hundred souls, seven assistants were chosen by the whole people. This pure democracy existed at Plymouth until 1639, a period of nineteen years, when a representative government was established and a pastor was chosen as a spiritual guide.

From the beginning the Pilgrims had cause for uneasiness concerning religious matters. They greatly desired to have their pastor, Mr. Robinson, come over from Leyden, but the greed of their speculating partners in England prevented his transportation to America. He was regarded as the head of the English Non-conformists or Puritans, though away in Holland. To please the Crown and the Church of England, for purposes of gain, these partners persistently opposed his emigration to America in any English vessel, and he never saw his beloved church that was planted in the wilderness. Meanwhile efforts were made, through the deception of false pretences, to bring the Pilgrims under the control of the Church of England, but failed. A hypocrite named Lyford was sent there to preach, and he and a confederate (John Oldham) conspired to overthrow both the political and religious system at Plymouth. Their wickedness was discovered, and on being arraigned before Governor Bradford, Lyford "burst into tears and confessed that he was afraid that he was a reprobate." His confederate was banished, but Lyford was pardoned on making loud professions of penitence. They were insincere; and being caught in seditious tricks again, he was deposed from the ministry and banished from Plymouth.

The Pilgrims regarded Mr. Robinson as their pastor until his death in 1625. Religious services at Plymouth had been conducted, from the beginning, by Elder Brewster, in the form of prayer and exhortation, and were kept up until a regular pastor was provided. Some of their exercises were conducted in a democratic manner. On Sunday afternoons, a question would be propounded by the elder, to which all had a right to speak. In the exercise of private judgment these religious meetings sometimes became the arena of intemperate debates; and after a pastor was called, it was difficult to retain one there, because of the restiveness of the people under even moderate discipline.

The independent colony of Weston failed, but another was attempted at Cape Ann, where Gloucester now stands, by the Rev. John White, rector of Trinity Church, Dorchester, England, and several influential persons whom he persuaded to join him. They expected to found there a flourishing fishing colony, but the enterprise failed and was abandoned. White was not disheartened. He infused his own spirit into other powerful citizens, whose names afterward appeared conspicuous in the annals of New England. They formed a Company in 1628, and purchased a tract of land extending from three miles north of the Merrimac River to three miles south of the Charles River, and westward to the South Sea or Pacific Ocean.

In the summer of that year, the Company sent John Endicott, one of their number (including his wife and children), with emigrants, to settle on the domain. Endicott was commissioned governor or general manager of the colony; and then he began his long and eventful career in New England. He was then forty years of age; possessed of an imperious and unyielding will; was a most rigid Puritan in thought and manner; benevolent though austere, and was intolerant of all dissenting opinions.

Endicott conducted the little colony to Naumkeag, where some of White's men from Cape Ann were seated. After settling some disputes about the right of occupation and control, he named the place *Salem*, the Hebrew word for "peaceful." There he soon displayed his stern opposition to all "vain amusements," by causing a May-pole to be cut down, which the Dorchester people had set up. He lectured them on the folly of amusements, and warned them to "look there should be better walking."

Several persons of wealth and influence in Boston, Lincolnshire, and elsewhere, joined the company early in 1629, and in March a royal charter was granted creating them a corporation under the name of "The Governor and Company of the Massachusetts Bay, in New England." The administration of public affairs was intrusted to a governor, deputy, and eighteen assistants or magistrates, who were to be elected annually by the stockholders of the Company. A general assembly of the freemen of the colony was to be held at least four times a year to legislate for the colony. The king claimed no jurisdiction, for he regarded the whole affair as a trading

CUTTING DOWN THE MAY-POLE.

operation, and not as the founding of an empire. He could not comprehend the moral and religious movements going on around him, and was lavish of privileges which he could not easily recall. The charter conferred upon the colonists of Massachusetts Bay all the rights of English subjects without exacting many corresponding duties; and it was afterward used as a text for many powerful discourses against the usurpations of royalty.

The Company were careful to make "plentiful provision of godly ministers" for the colony, and in the summer after Endicott's departure, three of these—Skelton, Higginson and Bright—were sent to Salem, with about two hundred additional settlers. Soon after their arrival a church was organized by the choice of Samuel Skelton as pastor, and Francis Higginson as teacher or assistant. They were ordained by a simple ceremonial. Mr. Higginson and three or four of the gravest men laid their hands on Mr. Skelton's head, while he knelt, and then prayed. Mr. Higginson was consecrated by Mr. Skelton in the same way. Mr. Higginson then drew up a confession of faith and plan of church government, and an invitation was sent to the Plymouth people to be present at a formal organization of the society. On a warm day, the 6th of August, the people were gathered in the shade of great elms at Salem, when the two ministers preached, and thirty persons signed the covenant and associated themselves as a church. Governor Bradford and others, who came from Plymouth by sea, did not reach Salem until the ceremony was ended, when they "came into the assembly and gave them the right hand of fellowship." So was founded the first church in New England. They claimed that they were not Separatists—that is, separated from the Church of England—but a better part of it, discarding its corruptions and trying to reform it. Yet in all outward things they *were* Separatists. Endicott and his friends punished two brothers named Browne for worshipping in accordance with the prescriptions and rituals of the Book of Common Prayer, the governor declaring the liturgy and ceremonials to be "sinful corruptions of the worship of God." The offenders persisted and Endicott sent them back over the ocean, telling them that New England was no place for such as they. The Company did not disclaim the act, but simply asked Endicott to be discreet, for fear of offending the home government.

This high-handed act unreproved, established the fact that the authorities of Massachusetts might, at their discretion, exclude all persons from the colony who did not conform to the pattern of morals and religion prescribed by the governor and ministers. This was the beginning of that blind intolerance of the Puritans of Massachusetts, which appears as a dark stain upon the annals of New England. We must judge those early settlers leniently by the standard of ethics which prevailed in civilized society at that time.

Toward the close of the summer of 1629, an important measure was adopted by the Company, which gave a mighty impulse to emigration to Massachusetts. It was the transferring of the government of the colony from the Company to the people there, and so establishing a democracy like that at Plymouth. That was done on the 29th of August. The old officers in the colony resigned, and John Winthrop, one of the many wealthy and influential heads of families who had determined to emigrate to Massachusetts in the event of such a change in its political affairs, was chosen governor. John Humphrey, brother-in-law to the Earl of Lincoln, was chosen deputy-governor, but, on the eve of embarkation, his place was filled by Thomas Dudley, a veteran soldier and then the manager of the estates of the earl. Eighteen assistants were also chosen.

Winthrop was then forty-two years of age. He was a native of Groton, Suffolk county, where he had considerable landed property. A lawyer by profession, he had moved in the higher circles of society among eminent men in church and state, by which means he became learned in statesmanship and polished in manners. Dudley had served as a soldier under Henry the Fourth of France thirty years before and "was old enough," Palfrey says, "to have lent a shrill voice to the huzzas at the defeat of the Armada." Of the assistants, Johnson, Saltonstall, Eaton, Bradstreet and Vassall were the most conspicuous. Isaac Johnson was the richest of the emigrants, and son-in-law of the Earl of Lincoln. Sir Robert Saltonstall, of Halifax, Yorkshire, was an opulent supporter of the enterprise. Theophilus Eaton was an eminent merchant of London, and a polished courtier who had been the earliest minister of Charles the First, in Denmark. Simon Bradstreet was the son of a Puritan minister in Lincolnshire and college graduate, and William Vassall was an opulent West India merchant.

Winthrop and his companions, consisting of about three hundred families, sailed from Yarmouth in the spring of 1630. The governor was in the *Arabella*, a ship carrying twenty-eight guns, and so named in compliment to Arabella Johnson, wife of one of the assistants. Before leaving the port, the governor, in behalf of his company, sent an address, drawn by the Rev. Mr. White, to "the rest of the brethren in and of the Church of England," saying that they esteemed it a favor to call that church their "dear mother;" that they wished her prosperity, and that they left her and their native land with "much sadness of heart and many tears." They declared that they went to establish an *independent* church, but not a *separate* one.

The *Arabella* arrived at Salem in June. They found there neither a church nor town. A rather stately house, in which the governor lived, and a few hovels, constituted the shelter of the settlers, among cornfields. Death had been busy, during the previous winter and spring, with the older settlers, and many of the survivors were weak and sick. Provisions were scarce. Disease attacked the new comers, and before the close of autumn, of a thousand emigrants who had arrived that year, two hundred were in their graves. The charming Arabella Johnson—the "queen of the colony"—

who came from a home of luxury, died within a month after her arrival; and grief for her loss consigned her husband to the grave a few weeks afterward.

Winthrop sought a more attractive place than Salem for the seating of his colony. Endicott's people had built some huts at Charlestown, whither some of Winthrop's people went. Others seated themselves at Dorchester, Roxbury, Watertown, and Cambridge. It was proposed to found the capital of the colony at Charlestown, and there the first court of the assistants was held late in August. But an epidemic disease, caused, it was supposed, by unwholesome water at Charlestown, induced the governor and magistrates, and others of the settlers, to remove to the peninsula of Shawmut, the site of Boston, where they found an abundance of pure spring water. There they built cottages and founded the capital of New England. The peninsula was composed of three considerable hills, and was called Tri-mountain for some time. The capital was named Boston, in commemoration of the native place of some of the emigrants from Lincolnshire. At the close of 1630, a large number of new emigrants had arrived, and the settlement on Shawmut was greatly increased. During the season, seventeen ships had brought almost fifteen hundred emigrants from England.

From the beginning the people were jealous of the power of the magistrates and ministers. They well knew the tendency toward tyranny of men exercising unrestrained control, and they thought it wise to assert popular rights—the rights of the people—at the outset. At a general court of the magistrates or assistants, in May, 1631, it was agreed that thenceforth all the officers of the government should be chosen annually by the freemen of the colony. These consisted of only men who were members in good standing of some church. This was an attempt to establish a sort of religious aristocracy for the control of the state, for, of the whole population, only one hundred and eighteen persons were qualified to be freemen, according to the prescription. This intimate relation between church and state gave rise to many disorders, and it was dissolved in 1665.

There was another change in 1634, when a representative government was established, the second in America. There were now eight distinct settlements in Massachusetts, and the growth of the colony was more rapid and sturdy than that of Plymouth. Winthrop, whom the people re-elected, ruled wisely. Like Bradford, he courted the friendship of the surrounding Indians, and chiefs and sachems dined at his table. There might have been seen a sagamore from the Mohegans on the distant Hudson River to tell him of the beautiful Connecticut Valley, and invite him to send settlers there. There, also, might have been seen the son of the aged Canonicus;

his nephew Miantonomoh, the brilliant young chief of the Narragansets, and the representatives of the Nipmucs and Wampanoags with Massasoit, the good chief of the latter nation. Winthrop also cultivated friendly relations with the neighboring settlements and distant colonies. He journeyed on foot from Shawmut to Plymouth, to exchange courtesies with Governor Bradford; and he sent messengers to New Netherland to have a friendly talk there with the authorities about the occupation of a part of the Connecticut Valley. His policy was peace and good-fellowship. A ship, trafficking with corn, that came from Virginia, met a friendly greeting when she sailed into Boston harbor.

For awhile after the arrival of Winthrop and his company, the flow of emigration to Massachusetts almost ceased. Men wished to see the experiment there fully tried before venturing. The intolerance of the authorities in church and state, in Massachusetts, was another cause for hesitation. The narrow views of civil and religious freedom entertained by those authorities and practically enforced, did not suit the more liberal-minded of the English Non-conformists, who were disposed to emigrate. There were too many shades of opinion among them to expect harmony before such an inexorable censor as they would meet in the half-ecclesiastical or church government of Massachusetts. But political and religious events in England soon gave an amazing impetus to emigration to America. Laud, the primate or head of the church, in England, who hated Puritans intensely, was then carrying forward persecution with a high hand. He was an implacable inquisitor, and sent men to prison without mercy, because they did not conform to his requirements in their method of worshipping Almighty God. At the same time there was a violent struggle for power between the monarch and the people. The king had, in effect, abolished the Parliament, and was ruling England at the bidding of his uncontrolled will. Civil war was evidently brewing in the hearts and minds of the people, and those who loved quiet and foresaw the coming storm fled to America to avoid its consequences. During the year 1635, full three thousand new settlers went to Massachusetts, among whom were men of wealth, influence, and distinction. Among these were the fiery Hugh Peters, an eloquent Puritan preacher, and Henry Vane, an enthusiastic young man twenty-five years of age, who took a conspicuous part in the affairs of the colony. Meanwhile the harsh proceedings of Endicott and others toward those who did not conform to their rigid discipline, and the intemperate zeal which characterized the authorities in Massachusetts, in their opposition to the church and crown, aroused the jealousy and resentment of both. These feelings were intensified by the intimations of the enemies of the colonists, that they "aimed not at new discipline, but sovereignty," and action was taken to bring them into subjection. Much had been made of the fact that Endicott had caused a part of the red-cross of St. George to be cut out of the English flag at Salem, and that many of the citizens refused to follow it before it was so mutilated. These things were cited as evidence of disloyalty to the crown. On the contrary, it was loyalty to bigotry. Endicott regarded the cross in the flag as a "relic of Anti-Christ," because the Pope had given it to the King of England as an ensign of victory. The whole aspect of the act was theological, not political; but the royalists chose to interpret it otherwise, and it was one of the reasons for tyrannical action toward the colony, when orders were issued to the authorities of Massachusetts to produce their charter before the Privy Council in England. This was followed, in the spring of 1634, by the appointment of an arbitrary special commission for the colonies, with Laud, the primate, at their head. He and his associates received full power over the American colonies to organize new governments and dictate laws; to regulate public worship, and to inflict punishments and revoke charters.

When the news of these proceedings reached New England, with a rumor that a governor-general or viceroy was on his way, the authorities of Massachusetts took the boldest measures. Fortifications were ordered, and three thousand dollars—then a large sum for the poor colonists—were raised to pay for them; and it was resolved not to receive a governor appointed by the crown. They determined to resist as long as possible. It was at that juncture that the great emigration just spoken of took place.

CHAPTER VII.

THEOLOGICAL DISPUTES—HENRY VANE MADE GOVERNOR OF MASSACHUSETTS—MRS. HUTCHINSON AND HER FATE—ENGLISH POWER RESPECTED BY THE SAVAGES—THE NEW ENGLAND CONFEDERACY—FIRST COINAGE IN AMERICA—THE PURITAN AND HIS WAYS—PURITAN MAGISTRATES OUTWITTED—DEALINGS WITH A THIEF—APOLOGY FOR INTOLERANCE—PERSECUTION OF FRIENDS OR QUAKERS—CHARLES I. BEHEADED—CROMWELL—MONARCHY RESTORED—FATE OF THE KING'S JUDGES—GOFFE AND WHALLEY—MASSACHUSETTS AND CHARLES II.

WHEN the fiery Hugh Peters and the gentler Henry Vane arrived at Boston in 1635, the colony was somewhat excited by theological disputes. The new-comers engaged in the controversy, and it soon took the form of a bitter quarrel. Peters was a rigid Puritan preacher just from a six years' exile in Holland, and he was made pastor of the church vacated by Roger Williams when he was banished, whose doctrines the new preacher denounced, and whose adherents he expelled from the congregation.

Vane was only twenty-three years of age. He was a son of one of the king's high officers of state, and a young man of purest morals. Forsaking the preferments which awaited him at court, he fled to New England to enjoy the freedom of simple worship among those whose cause he had espoused. In after years Milton praised him for his goodness, and Clarendon regarded him as equal to Hampden in statesmanship.

The colonists regarded the advent of Vane as a token of the speedy emigration to Massachusetts of leading men of the realm. They received him with open arms, and in the delirium of their joy they seemed to forget their veterans, and elected him governor of the colony. With broad and generous views, he defended the tenets of Mr. Williams and Mrs. Hutchinson in the controversy—the leading points of which have been defined in the Seventh Chapter of the Second Book. This gave intensity to the partisan feeling, both in politics and theology, and a strong opposition to Vane was organized. After a tempestuous year Vane was defeated at the next annual election, when he returned to England.

Soon after Vane's departure Mrs. Hutchinson was banished, and she settled in Rhode Island. There she became a widow. Dreading the persecutions of bigots which menaced her, she left New England and took up her abode within the domain of New Netherland, among the sons of the forest. Her cabin was near the present village of New Rochelle, in Westchester county, and with her dwelt all her family, in peace, until the wickedness of Governor Kieft excited the wrath of the Indians. With blind fury they swept through the forest destroying every white settler and settlement. Mrs. Hutchinson did not escape. She and all her family, excepting a granddaughter, fair and curly-haired, eight years of age, were murdered. Her house and barns were burned; her cattle were butchered, and her grandchild was carried away captive. The young warrior who spared her life took her tenderly in his arms and soothed her with caresses, while an attendant bore upon a pole the scalps of some of her kinsfolk. When, four years afterward, little Anna Collins was delivered to the Dutch governor at New Amsterdam to be sent to her friends at Boston in accordance with the terms of a treaty, she had forgotten her own language and was unwilling to leave her Indian friends.

THE LITTLE CAPTIVE.

The good results of the war with the Pequods promised future security to the New England colonists against dangers from the wrath of the savages. The power of the English manifested in that war made the Indians peacefully inclined for a whole generation of time. Emigration, stimulated by persecution, began to flow into New England in a copious stream. The exodus of Puritans from British shores, and the amazing development of a republican state in America, soon excited the jealousy and the fears of the church and the government. They put forth their strength to stay the tide, as we have observed, in vain. Other causes effected what royal decrees and armed men could not do.

Troubles in England which threatened the overthow of the monarchy and the hierarchy or church establishment withdrew the attention of both from the distant colonies; and when the civil war that ensued promised better times for the lovers of freedom at home, emigration to America almost ceased.

Meanwhile the ties of interest and common sympathy united the struggling colonists in New England. They were natives of the same country, and were the social and political products of persecution—alike exposed to the weapons of hostile Indians and the greed for territory and power of the French and Dutch on their eastern and western borders. They were equally menaced with punishment by the parent government for non-conformity in matters of state and religion. They were, in fact, one people, bound by interwoven interests. Therefore when the civil war in Old England broke out in 1641, and the New England colonists, numbering more than twenty thousand, with fifty villages, almost forty churches, and their commerce expanding and manufactures of cotton from Barbadoes making them independent of the mother country so far, the aspect of the present and future made them seriously contemplate the establishment of a new nation. No tie of gratitude exacted their allegiance to the British government. On the contrary, their happiness in freedom was the result of neglect and oppression, rather than of care and protection. In 1643, the British Parliament acknowledged that "the plantations in New England had, by the blessing of the Almighty, had good and prosperous success without any public charge to the parent state."

A confederation of New England colonies for mutual defence had been proposed by Connecticut immediately after the war with the Pequods. When the crown threatened to deprive Massachusetts of her charter, in 1638, the other colonies counselled resistance, and the people of the Bay threatened secession from the British realm. Now, relieved of the pressure of royal rule under royal displeasure, the inhabitants of New England resolved to unite in a political league. In May, 1643, deputies from the colonies of Plymouth, Connecticut and New Haven met those of Massachusetts in Boston. They very soon agreed upon twelve articles of Confederation, and constituted a confederacy under the title of "The United Colonies of New England." That written agreement was signed on the 20th of August following. Rhode Island and the settlements in New Hampshire and Maine asked to be admitted to the Union, but were denied, chiefly, as Winthrop said, "because they ran a different course from us, both in their ministry and civil administration." They would not bend to the dictates of Massachusetts in matters which concerned the conscience.

Whereupon, as we have observed, Rhode Island, which refused required allegiance to Plymouth, took immediate and successful steps to procure an independent charter. See Chapter VII, Book II.

The New England Confederacy—the harbinger of the United States of America—was simply a league of independent provinces, as were our thirteen States under the "Articles of Confederation," as we shall observe hereafter, each jealously guarding its own privileges and rights against any encroachments of the "general government." That central body was really no government at all. It was composed of a Board of Commissioners consisting of two church members from each colony, who were to meet annually or oftener if required. Their duty was to consider circumstances and recommend measures for the general good. They had no executive nor independent legislative powers, their recommendations becoming laws only after the separate colonies had acted upon and approved them. The doctrine of State supremacy was controlling.

That famous league, of which Massachusetts assumed the control because of its greater population and its being a "perfect republic," remained in existence more than forty years, during which period the government of England was changed three times. Unlike the Virginians, the New Englanders sympathized with the English republicans, and found in Oliver Cromwell, the ruler of England next to the beheaded Charles the First, a sincere friend and protector. The colony of Massachusetts, in particular, prospered. A profitable commerce between that colony and the West India Islands was created. That trade brought bullion, or uncoined gold and silver, into the colony, which led, in 1652, to the exercise of an act of sovereignty on the part of the authorities of Massachusetts by the establishment of a mint. It was authorized by the General Assembly, in 1651, and the following year silver coins of the denominations of three-pence, six-pence, and twelve-pence, or shilling, were struck. This was the first coinage within the territory of the United States.

The Puritan of Massachusetts, at this time, was the straitest of his sect—an unflinching egotist who regarded himself as eminently his "brother's keeper," whose constant business was to save his fellow-men from sin and error; sitting in judgment upon their belief and actions with the authority of a God-chosen high-priest. His laws, found on the statute-books of the colony or divulged in the records of court proceedings, exhibit the salient points in his stern and inflexible character as a self-constituted censor, and a conservator of the moral and spiritual destiny of his fellow-mortals. He imposed a fine upon every woman who should cut her hair like that of a man. He forbade all gaming for amusement or gain, and would not allow cards or dice to be introduced into the colony. He fined families whose young women did not spin as much flax or wool daily as the selectmen had required of them. He would not allow a Jesuit or Roman Catholic priest to live in the colony. He forbade all persons to run or even walk "except reverently to and from church" on Sunday; and he doomed a burglar, because he committed his crime on that sacred day, to have one of his ears cut off. He commanded John Wedgewood to be put in the stocks for being in the company of drunkards; Thomas Petit, for "suspicion of slander,

PURITAN MORALITY ENFORCED.

idleness and stubbornness," he caused to be "severely whipped;" Captain Lovell he admonished to "take heed of light carriage;" Josias Plaistowe, for stealing four baskets of corn from the Indians, was ordered by him to return to them eight baskets, to be fined five pounds, and thereafter to "be called by the name of Josias, and not Mr. Plaistowe, as formerly. He directed his grand jurors to admonish those who wore apparel too costly for their income, and if they did not heed the warning to fine them; and in

1646, he placed on the statute-book of Massachusetts a law which imposed the penalty of flogging for kissing a woman in the street, even in the way of honest salute.

Almost a hundred years after that law was passed, its penalty was inflicted upon the commander of a British man-of-war. She arrived at Boston after a long cruise. As her commander was going toward his home in that city, he met his wife in the street hastening to greet him, when he gave her an affectionate kiss. A stern old magistrate in a cocked-hat and powdered hair in a queue, who was "learned in the law," seeing the act, caused his immediate arrest. The next morning, after due trial, the captain was convicted and the punishment of flogging was administered in a very mild way, but in a public place, causing much merriment. When the victim was about to sail on another cruise, he invited that magistrate and others whom, he understood, had approved of his punishment, to a complimentary dinner on board of his vessel, as a token of his forgiveness and submission. They accepted it, and when they were all merry with good cheer, and were on deck ready to depart, he ordered his boatswain and mate to give the magistrates a sound flogging. Each officer was armed with a knotted cat-o'-nine-tails, and they drove the astonished guests pell-mell over the side of the vessel into the boat waiting to receive them. The captain sailed away, and the law was soon afterward repealed. Governor Winthrop tempered these laws with merciful mildness in their execution. On one occasion it was reported to him that a man had been stealing from his store of winter's firewood, and he was urged to punish him. "I will soon put a stop to that bad practice," said the governor sternly. He sent for the offender. "You have a large family," he said to the offending culprit, "and I have a large magazine of wood; come as often as you please, and take as much of it as you need to make your dwelling comfortable." Then turning to his accusers, he said: "Now I defy him to steal any more of my firewood."

The bigotry and austerity of the Puritans in Massachusetts were vehemently condemned at the time of their iron rule in New England, and have been ever since. But there are peculiar considerations in their case, which the eye of justice cannot overlook. Their theology and their ideas of church government were founded upon the deepest heart-convictions of a people not broadly educated. They had encountered and subdued a savage wilderness for the purpose of planting therein a church and a commonwealth fashioned in all their parts after a narrow but cherished pattern. They felt that the domain which they had conquered with so much peril and toil was their own, and that they had as good a right to regulate its internal affairs according to their own notions, and exclude all obnoxious persons, as had a householder the affairs of his family and the avoidance of an unwelcome visitor. They had boldly proclaimed the right to the exercise of private judgment in matters of conscience, and so they tacitly invited the persecuted of all lands to come to them. Therefore, "unsettled persons," libertines in unrestrained opinions, came to Massachusetts from abroad to disseminate their peculiar views. In that dissemination the Puritans saw clear prophecies of a disorganization of their church. They took the alarm early, and with a mistaken policy they resisted such encroachments upon their domain and into their society with fiery penal laws implacably executed. But it was only in respect to religion that the Puritan laws were specially harsh as compared with the general jurisprudence or science of law of that day. "God forbid," said Governor Dudley in his old age, "our love for the truth should be grown so cold that we should tolerate errors—I die no libertine." "Better tolerate hypocrites and tares than thorns and briers," exclaimed that "famous man of God," as Norton called Parson John Cotton. "To say that men ought to have liberty of conscience is impious ignorance," said Parson Ward of Ipswich, author of "The Simple Cobbler of Agawam." "Religion admits of no eccentric notions," said Parson Norton, the colleague of Ward, biographer of Cotton, and persecutor of the Friends or Quakers.

Friends or Quakers. The peculiarities of this sect, we have considered in Chapter Ninth of the Second Book. Among the earlier disciples of George Fox were many enthusiasts whose zeal led their judgment. They were absolute fanatics, and sometimes became lunatics in their religious views and actions, and were utterly unlike the sober, mild-mannered members of that society to-day. They ran into the wildest extravagancies in the exercise of the liberty of speech; openly reviling magistrates and ministers with intemperate language; overriding the rights of all others in maintaining their own, and scorning all respect for human laws. They made the most exalted pretensions to the exclusive possession of the gifts of the Holy Spirit and the power of persuasion with which they were endowed. Some, in the pride of their egotism, went to Rome to convert the Pope; others went to the East to convince the Grand Turk and his people of their errors; and some came to America to proselyte the Puritans in New England, the Roman Catholics in Maryland, and the Cavaliers and Churchmen in Virginia. Some of them behaved so wildly and disorderly in Boston that they suffered intensely from the indignation of the magistrates and clergy there; and they so disgusted the tolerant Roger Williams, that he tried to root them out of Rhode Island.

The first of the sect who appeared conspicuous in New England were Mary Fisher and Anna Austin, who arrived at Boston in the summer of

1656, when John Endicott was governor. There was then no special law against them, but under a general act against heretics, they were arrested; their persons were examined to find marks of witchcraft, with which they were suspected; their trunks were searched, and their books were burned publicly by the common hangman. These innocent and well-behaved women were so treated because of the stories of the disorderly acts of some of the sect in England who had come over the sea. After keeping them in prison several weeks, the authorities of Massachusetts sent them back to

FRIENDS OR QUAKERS GOING TO EXECUTION.

England. Mary Fisher afterward visited the Sultan of Turkey, passing everywhere unharmed because his people reverenced a crazy person, for such they took her to be.

This harsh treatment of the first comers fired the zeal of the more enthusiastic of the sect in England. They sought martyrdom as an honor. They flocked to New England and fearfully vexed the souls of the Puritan magistrates and ministers. One woman came all the way from London to warn the authorities against persecutions. Others came for the purpose of reviling and denouncing—vehemently scolding—the powers in church and state. They would rail at magistrates and ministers from windows, as these functionaries passed by. They mocked the institutions of the country; and some fanatical young women appeared without clothing in the churches and in the streets, as emblems "of the unclothed souls of the people," while others, with loud voices, proclaimed that the wrath of the Almighty was about to fall like destructive lightning upon Boston and Salem. Horrified by their blasphemies and indecencies, the authorities of Massachusetts passed some very cruel laws. At first they forbade all persons "harboring Quakers," imposing severe penalties for each offence. Then they imposed mild punishments upon the Friends themselves. These statutes were ineffectual; and finally, driven by resentment and mistaken judgment, they passed laws which authorized the cropping of the ears, boring of the tongues with hot irons, and hanging on a gibbet, of offending Quakers. Yet these terrible laws did not keep them away. They were fined, imprisoned, whipped and hanged during the administration of the rigid Endicott, who was implacable. On a bright October day in 1659, two young men named William Robinson and Marmaduke Stevenson, with Mary Dyer, wife of the secretary of state of Rhode Island, were led from the Boston jail, with ropes around their necks, and guarded by soldiers, to be hanged on Boston Common. Mary walked between her companions hand in hand to the gallows, where, in the presence of Governor Endicott, the two young men were executed. Mary was unmoved by the spectacle. She was given into the care of her son who came from Rhode Island to plead for her life, and went away with him. But she returned the next spring, defied the laws, and was executed on Boston Common.

The severity of these laws caused a revulsion in public sentiment. The Friends stoutly maintained their course with decency, and were regarded by the more thoughtful as real martyrs for conscience sake. The people, at length, demanded a repeal of the bloody enactments, and by that repeal, in 1661, the Friends achieved a triumph. The fanaticism of both parties subsided. A more Christian spirit prevailed; and the attention of the more sober-minded Friends was turned to the task of converting the Indians. They nobly assisted the Apostle Eliot and others in propagating the gospel among the pagans of the forests for whom that Apostle had labored for years. He had established a Christian church among them at Natic, and at the time of the repeal of the cruel laws, there were no less than ten villages of converted Indians in Massachusetts.

The reign of republicanism in England, under Oliver Cromwell and his son, was short. King Charles the First, after contending with the people for the royal prerogative and the throne for several years, was beheaded on a cold winter's morning in January, 1649, in front of his own palace of Whitehall. Royalty was then abolished. Late in May, 1660, the son of King Charles, who had been proclaimed monarch of England under the title of Charles the Second, rode into London on horseback between his brothers the Dukes of York and Gloucester, and took up his abode in the palace of Whitehall, while flags waved, bells rang, cannon roared, trumpets brayed, shouts rent the air and fountains poured out costly libations of wine as tokens of the public joy. After a struggle for about twenty years between royalists and republicans, the monarchy was restored, and the English people again became subjects of the head of the Scottish house of Stuart.

ENTRANCE OF CHARLES THE SECOND INTO LONDON.

The members of the House of Commons had constituted a High Court of Justice for the trial of Charles the First, and many of them signed his death-warrant. These were hunted by the royal vengeance. Some perished on the scaffold. Among these were Hugh Peters and Henry Vane, who had figured conspicuously in New England more than twenty years before. Many fled and so escaped the fatal block. Among these were Edward Whalley and William Goffe, who went to New England and gave the first news of the restoration of monarchy. The former was a cousin of Cromwell and of Hampden, and a distinguished cavalry officer. He had been intrusted with the custody of the royal prisoner, and was one of the signers of his death-warrant. Cromwell appointed him one of the major-generals who assisted in the government of the commonwealth, and was one of his most active lieutenants. Goffe, a son of a Puritan clergyman, was Whalley's son-in-law, a colonel of infantry and member of the High Court who signed the death-warrant of the king. He, also, was one of Cromwell's ten major-generals.

Orders speedily followed the fugitives to New England for their arrest, and officers came from Old England for the same purpose. The "regicides," or king-killers, as they were called, were, after awhile, closely hunted, but the authorities and people of New England effectually concealed them from their enemies for years. When danger lowered, they fled from Boston to New Haven, and for a long time occupied a cave not far from that place. Finally they made their abode in the remote town of Hadley, where they were joined by Colonel Dixwell, another "regicide," who finally settled in New Haven. In Hadley, Whalley died. Goffe survived him until after King Phillip's war, which we shall notice presently; but from the time when they took up their abode there, in disguise, they disappeared from public view. During that period, so terrible to New England settlers, Hadley was surrounded by hostile Indians. The people were in the meeting-house observing a fast day. They were armed, as usual, and sallied out to drive off the savages. At that moment a tall, venerable personage, with a white, flowing beard, clad in a white robe and carrying a glittering sword, suddenly appeared among the people, took the lead of the armed men, caused them to observe strict military discipline, and led them to victory. The people believed the stranger (who as suddenly disappeared) to be an angel sent by the Lord for their deliverance. The "angel" was General Goffe, who was stout in body and valiant in spirit. It is related that soon after his arrival in Boston, a fencing-master erected a stage on the Common, on which he walked several days, defying any man to fight him with swords. Goffe accepted the challenge. He wrapped a huge cheese in a linen cloth as a shield, and arming himself with a mop filled with muddy water from the gutter, he appeared on the platform. The fencing-master made a thrust at him, which Goffe received in the cheese in which he held the sword until he had smeared his antagonist with mud. The enraged fencing-master caught up a broad-sword, when Goffe exclaimed: "Stop, sir; hitherto, you see, I have only played with you, and not attempted to harm you; but if you come at me now with the broad-sword, know that I will certainly take your life." The alarmed fencing-master cried out, as he dropped his sword, "Who can you be? You must be either Goffe, or Whalley, or the Devil, for there were no other men in England who could beat me."

The New England colonies, and especially that of Massachusetts, expected very little favor from the new monarch, for their republicanism was decided and conspicuous. In the course of a few months after the restoration, the General Court of Massachusetts sent addresses to the King and Parliament, chiefly because enemies of New England evidently possessed the confidence of the monarch and his ministers. In those addresses, general loyalty was expressed, and they prayed for a "continuance of civil and religious liberties" which they had long enjoyed, and promised for the crown, in return for its protection of their freedom, the "blessings of a people whose trust is in God."

The king returned a gracious answer in the form of general expressions of good-will, but his smiles were not propitious. He resolved not to show

GOFFE AND THE FENCING-MASTER.

these distant political enemies of his father any favors. The stringent provisions of the navigation laws and commercial restrictions from which Cromwell had exempted the New Englanders were now renewed and rigorously enforced. Expecting collisions with the Crown, the latter, in Massachusetts, issued a declaration of natural and chartered rights, in which they claimed the liberty to choose their own executive officers and representatives; to admit freemen on their own prescribed terms; to appoint all officers and define their powers and duties; to exercise, by annually elected magistrates and deputies, any function of human government; to defend themselves by force of arms, if necessary, against every aggression, and to reject, as an infringement of their right, "any parliamentary or royal imposition prejudicial to the country and contrary to any just act of colonial legislation."

Massachusetts now sent agents to London to persuade the king of their loyalty, at the same time to secure their independence in local affairs, as a self-governing people. It was a difficult task, but John Newton and Simon Bradstreet successfully performed it. In the autumn of 1662, the king confirmed the Massachusetts charter, and granted a conditional amnesty or general pardon for all past offences during the late civil war; at the same time the king asserted his right to interfere with the domestic concerns of the colony.

The people of Massachusetts did not concede this royal right, and in 1664, commissioners were sent over, in a royal fleet, destined to take possession of New Netherland (see page 350), commanded by Colonel Nicolls, one of the commissioners, to "settle the peace and security of the country on a solid foundation"—in other words, to rule New England as deputies of the monarch. The people of Massachusetts were greatly irritated by this measure, and spoke out freely. False stories were carried to the ears of the king respecting the rebellion of the colonies, and for awhile there was a general belief in London that Whalley and Goffe were at the head of a New England army, and that the New England Confederacy had been formed for the express purpose of casting off all dependence on the mother country and establishing a republic in America. At the same time the colonists regarded the commissioners as royal instruments of oppression who would destroy their liberties. Massachusetts boldly protested against the exercise of their authority within its domain. So did the other New England colonies excepting Rhode Island. The acts and orders of the commissioners were generally disregarded, and after producing much ill-feeling and stimulating a democratic spirit throughout New England, they departed in 1666, leaving the colonies triumphant. Massachusetts ever afterwards held a front rank in the sturdy battle for independence which was waged for more than a hundred years. Yet she had a fierce struggle, at times, with royalty abroad, royal agents in her bosom, and pale and dusky enemies on her borders. At about the time when she triumphed over the efforts of the Crown to enslave her, she was involved in a most disastrous war with Metacomet, or King Philip, a son of the then dead Massasoit. That contest is known in our history as KING PHILIP'S WAR.

CHAPTER VIII.

KING PHILIP—HIS PATRIOTISM—ANGER OF HIS PEOPLE—HE DECLARES WAR—TERRIBLE EVENTS OF THAT WAR—DEATH OF PHILIP AND FATE OF HIS SON—DEATH OF CHARLES II AND ACCESSION OF JAMES II—ANDROS MADE GOVERNOR-GENERAL—REVOLUTION IN ENGLAND—ANDROS DRIVEN FROM BOSTON—FRENCH JESUITS IN AMERICA—THE FRENCH AND INDIANS—A CONGRESS OF DELEGATES IN NEW YORK—CANADA INVADED—THE ENGLISH REPULSED—NEW CHARTER FOR MASSACHUSETTS.

MASSASOIT, as we have observed, kept his treaty with the English inviolate so long as he lived. He died in 1661, at the age of about eighty years, leaving two sons whom the English called, respectively, Alexander and Philip. The former did not long survive his father, when Philip became chief sachem and warrior of the Wampanoags, with his royal residence on Mount Hope, not far from Bristol, Rhode Island. He was called *King Philip*. He resumed the covenants with the English made by his father, and observed them faithfully for a dozen years.

It had become painfully evident to Massasoit before his death that the spreading colonies would soon deprive his people of their land and nationality, and that the Indians would become vassals of the pale race. The more warlike Philip pondered these possibilities with deep bitterness of feeling, until he resolved to strike an exterminating blow against the English in defence of his country and his race. His resolution was natural and patriotic. His unaided warriors would be inadequate to the work; so, in the primeval forest at Mount Hope, surrounded by seven hundred fighting men, he planned a confederacy of the New England tribes, which might have numbered about twenty-five thousand souls. It was a difficult task, the power of so many being overshadowed by that of the English, weakening and dividing them. Before any actual conspiracy was effected, Philip found himself compelled to declare war and lift the hatchet.

At that time there were many Christian converts among the Indians, who were firmly attached to the English. The Wampanoags had always discouraged the spread of Christianity among themselves, but there were many "praying Indians" there. One of these—John Sassamon, who had been educated at Cambridge, where John Harvard had established a college—was a sort of secretary to Philip. Becoming acquainted with the plans of the sachem, he revealed them to the authorities at Plymouth. For this treachery he was murdered, and three Wampanoags, who were convicted of the crime on very slender testimony, were hanged. The anger of the tribe was fiercely kindled by the event, and they were clamorous for war. The cautious Philip hesitated, for he knew his weakness. His young warriors would not listen to reason. They taunted him with causing the wrongs which his people endured because of his unwillingness to fight. Then they pointed to the humiliation and disgrace of his people when, a few years before, their firearms were taken from them by the jealous white men. His eyes kindled with rage. He had never forgotten nor forgiven that injury. The reminder excited his fiercest wrath. Springing from his seat he snatched up a bow and quiver, a gleaming hatchet and a keen knife, and vowed that none of these weapons should sleep whilst a pale-face remained in New England. He sent his women and children to the Narragansets for protection; and yielding his judgment to passion, he trampled upon solemn treaties and kindled the flames of war. Swift runners were dispatched to other tribes to arouse them to co-operation, and he required all of his followers to curse the white man and to swear eternal hostility to his race. It was but a foolish rushing to destruction. It has been well said: "Frenzy prompted their rising. It was but the storm in which the ancient inhabitants of the land were to vanish away. They rose without hope, and therefore they fought without mercy. To them, as a nation, there was no to-morrow."

Philip struck the first blow at Swanzey, twenty-five miles southwest from Plymouth. It was on the 4th of July, 1675. Expecting hostilities, the people had been to the house of worship to engage in fasting and prayer. As they were returning—men, women and children—the savages fell upon them furiously, slaying and capturing many, while others fled to the surrounding settlements. The country was aroused. Armed men from Plymouth, Boston, and other places near, joined, and making a forced march toward Mount Hope, besieged the Wampanoags in a swamp several days. Philip escaped with most of his followers, and took refuge with the Nipmucs in the interior of Massachusetts, who espoused his cause. At the head of fifteen hundred warriors he pressed through the forests to the beautiful valley of the Connecticut to lay waste the settlements there.

Meanwhile the armed white men entered the country of the Narragansets, and compelled Canonchet, son of Miantonomah, then chief sachem of that people, to make a treaty of friendship with the English. When Philip heard of this he was amazed. His stout heart almost failed. But reflecting upon the perilous nature of his enterprise and his position, and that everything depended upon vigorous action, he aroused other tribes to join him in exterminating the pale-faces by the methods of treachery, ambush, and surprise. The scourge that now appeared was terrible. Men in the fields, families in their beds at midnight, and congregations in houses of worship, were murdered. The English settlements east of the Hudson then numbered about fifty thousand souls, and, at one time, it seemed probable that

AN INDIAN RAID.

few of them would escape the fury of the savages, who hung upon and enveloped the parties like a consuming fire.

The Wampanoag chief entered the Connecticut Valley at Springfield, and swept northward almost to the present line between Massachusetts and Vermont like a destructive tornado, leaving desolation in his track. Near

Brookfield, a party of twenty Englishmen, while on their way, at near the middle of August, to treat with the Nipmucs, fell into an ambush and were treacherously murdered. Almost every house in Brookfield was set on fire—excepting a stone one—into which the people had gathered for safety. There they were besieged two days, when the Indians set the house on fire. Just at that moment a shower of rain came like a providence and put out the flames, and at the same time a relief party of white people, under Major Willard, arrived, and drove away the savages. Early in September a hot battle was fought at Deerfield, where seven hundred Indians were defeated by one hundred and eighty Englishmen; but a week later, prowling savages laid the town in ashes. On the same day—the Sabbath—Hadley was attacked, and, as we have seen, was saved by the bravery of Goffe the regicide.

For a moment the scourge was stayed at Hadley, but it soon swept mercilessly over other settlements. The blood of many valiant young men, under Captain Beers, flowed freely in the paths of Northfield, late in September. A few days afterward a company of young men of highest character—"the flower of Essex"—under Captain Lathrop, were murdered by many hundred Indians on the banks of a little stream near Deerfield, which is yet known as Bloody Brook, when the savages were beaten off by others who came to the rescue. Springfield was burned, and Hadley was again assailed.

The Indians were masters of the situation, and Philip, encouraged by his successes, now resolved to attack Hatfield, the chief settlement above Springfield. He was joined by the natives there who, until then, had been friendly to the English. They showed much zeal, and at near the close of October, Philip gathered his warriors around a huge fire, when the braves engaged in the wild scalp-dance, chanting heroic songs. Upon long poles they exhibited trophies of their horrid work—the long shining tresses of women and even the bright curls of little maidens whom they had slain—as they whirled around the flames with fearful contortions of limbs and body. Then, with almost a thousand warriors, the Wampanoags fell upon the settlement. The people were prepared for the onslaught. They had palisaded their houses with heavy timber standing upright in the ground bound close together with green withes, and the upper ends sharpened. Behind these stood armed men and resolute women waiting for the approach of the Indians, and when they came they were repulsed with such slaughter that Philip left the Connecticut Valley, with his shattered forces, and fled to Rhode Island. The Narragansets, in violation of their recent treaty with the English, received him with open arms, became his allies, and, late in the year, went out upon the war-path with him.

This perfidy of Canonchet and his people was terribly punished by the English at the close of the year. Fifteen hundred armed men from Massachusetts, Plymouth and Connecticut, under Captain Josiah Winslow, marched into the Narraganset country. The Indians, three thousand strong, had gathered in their wigwams within a large fort in the bosom of a dark swamp near the present village of Kingston, Washington county, Rhode Island, with their store of winter provisions. Snow had fallen to a great depth, and the savages felt secure for the season. Suddenly, at near the end of December, Winslow and his little army appeared before the fort in the frozen swamp. They soon beat down the feeble palisades, and in the course of a few hours hundreds of men, women and children, with all the provisions, perished in the fire. About a thousand warriors were killed or wounded, and several hundreds were made prisoners. Among the latter was Canonchet, who was put to death. Philip, and a remnant of the Narragansets, escaped, and took refuge with the Nipmucs. Eighty Englishmen were killed, and one hundred and fifty were wounded. The surviving savages suffered fearfully. Hiding in a cedar swamp, with no shelter but evergreen boughs, no food but nuts and roots which they might find beneath the deep snow, many of them perished. So disappeared the dominion of the Narragansets.

Philip was not idle during the winter. He tried in vain to induce the Mohawks to join him. Some of the exasperated Indians eastward of Massachusetts flocked to his standard, and early in the spring of 1676 the work of destruction began. In the course of a few weeks, the war spread over an area of almost three hundred miles. Villages and isolated dwellings were burned, and their inmates were destroyed. Weymouth, Groton, Medford, Lancaster and Marlborough, in Massachusetts, were laid in ashes; and Warwick and Providence, in Rhode Island, were given to the flames.

A terrible scene occurred at Lancaster. Forty-two persons took shelter in the house of Mary Rowlandson. It was set on fire by the Indians. "Quickly," wrote Mrs. Rowlandson in her narrative, "it was the dolefullest day that ever mine eyes saw. Now the dreadful hour is come. Some in our house were fighting for their lives; others wallowing in blood; the house on fire over our heads, and the bloody heathen ready to knock us on the head if we stirred out. I took my children to go forth; but the Indians shot so thick that the bullets rattled against the house as if one had thrown a handful of stones. We had six stout dogs, but none of them would stir." A bullet went through Mrs. Rowlandson's side, and another through a child in her arms, and she was made captive, having of her family only one poor wounded babe left. "Down I must sit in the snow," she continued, "with my sick child, the picture of death, in my lap. Not the least crumb of refreshing came within our mouths from Wednesday night until Saturday night, except a little cold water."

Quarrels among themselves soon weakened the power of the Indians. The Nipmucs and the Narragansets charged their misfortunes to the ambition of Philip. The alliance was dissolved. The eastern Indians hastened to their mountain fastnesses. Many who had been in arms surrendered to avoid starvation. Others marched off to Canada and joined some of the tribes there; and Captain Benjamin Church, the most famous

THE CAPTIVE MOTHER AND BABE.

Indian fighter of his day, hunted and slew all the hostile red-men he could find. Between two and three thousand of them perished or submitted in the course of the year 1676, and the proud Narragansets, to whom other tribes had paid homage, were reduced to a hundred bowmen. Like the Pequods, they were utterly ruined.

Philip eluded his pursuers for several months, hiding in many places, with a resolution to never surrender. He had a handful of faithful followers, but he cleaved the head of one of these friends with his hatchet, because he counselled submission. At last circumstances conquered his pride and his will. He returned secretly to Mount Hope. His wife and son were soon afterward made captive, when the "last of the Wampanoags" bowed beneath this crushing misfortune, and said: "Now my heart breaks; I am ready to die." Captain Church was then close upon his track; and a few days afterward, a faithless Indian shot him in a swamp. Church cut off the dead king's head with his sword, and it was borne upon a pole into Plymouth while hymns of thanksgiving were sung by the people. The ghastly trophy was placed upon the palisades; and the people slept that night with a sense of security which they had not felt for years.

The disposition of Philip's little son—the heir to the throne of Massasoit—was a subject of grave debate. Some of the elders proposed putting him to death. Others suggested selling him as a slave. The most profitable measure appeared to be the most merciful, and the boy was sold to be a bond-slave in Bermuda. So perished the dynasty of the good Massasoit, and so ended the famous *King Philip's War*. The Mohegans, who held sway in Connecticut, were firm friends of the English, and not a drop of blood was shed in that colony during the war. The other colonies had suffered dreadfully. More than six hundred men, chiefly young, had fallen in the struggle. Thirteen villages had been destroyed. A large number of women and children had been murdered or carried into captivity. Full six hundred houses were burned, and the cost of the expenditures and the losses equalled in value half a million dollars. The war was carried on a little longer by the Eastern Indians, for they drew supplies from the French in Acadié. Finally, in 1678, hostilities were ended by a treaty.

While Massachusetts was feeling the heavy losses of her sons and treasure, the English government attempted to carry out a long-cherished desire of the king to resume the control of the colony. The Privy Council sent Edward Randolph, a greedy adventurer and faithful servant of his royal master, to collect the customs at Boston, to exercise other authority as the agent of the crown, and to spy out the strength and weakness of the people. Randolph excited the cupidity, fears and jealousy of the king and his court, by exaggerating the number of the population, wealth, power and independence of the colony; and, being rejected by the authorities of Massachusetts, his wrath gave vehemence to his assertions. The governor (Leverett) was firm in his opposition to Randolph's pretensions. "The king," he said, "can in reason do no less than let us enjoy our liberties and trade, for we have made this large plantation in the wilderness at our own charge, without any contribution from the crown." Because of this spirit of independence, the people were reproached. "You are poor," said the Earl of Anglesey, "and yet proud."

They were justly "proud." They had established a free and flourishing state, and were resolved to maintain their natural and chartered rights at all hazards. When Randolph, by royal authority, declared the charter of Massachusetts to be void, and attempted to govern, the people spurned him. Then the king resolved to make the colony a "more palpable dependence," and issued a writ of *quo warranto*—a command for the authorities to appear before the monarch and his council and show by what warrant they held jurisdiction in Massachusetts. It was his intention to exercise the arbitrary power of his grandfather, James the First, if necessary, by taking possession of the domain without forms of law; but a pliant High Court of Chancery decided in the king's favor. Before the monarch could effect his object he died. That was early in 1685.

Charles's brother, the Duke of York, now ascended the throne as James the Second. More tyrannical than his predecessor, he declared, without the formalities of law, the charter of Massachusetts to be void, and appointed Joseph Dudley president of the country from Rhode Island to Nova Scotia. All England, misinformed by the rulers, approved the measure, and the tone of society there was one of contempt for the "plantations." Dryden, whose muse was then subservient to the crown, wrote in a dramatic prologue:

"Since faction ebbs, and rogues go out of fashion,
Their penny scribes take care to inform the nation,
How well men thrive in this or that plantation.

"How Pennsylvania's air agrees with Quakers,
And Carolina's, with Associators;
Both e'en too good for madmen and for traitors.

"Truth is, our land with saints is so run o'er,
And every age produces such a store,
That now there's need of two New Englands more."

Dudley was succeeded by Edmund Andros, who arrived in Boston late in 1686, bearing the commission of viceroy or governor-general of all New England. His character and purpose have already been considered on page 355. The rigid executor of his master's will, he soon made the rod of oppression keenly felt. He abridged the freedom of the press; interfered with marriage contracts, and frequently extorted money—levied "black-mail"—advanced the fees of all officers of government, and threatened to make the Church of England the established religion in all America.

The people of Massachusetts resented his conduct, and, in compliance with the doctrine of Cromwell's motto, "*resistance to tyrants is obedience to God*," they were about to drive him out of the colony by force of arms, when the news came from England that James had been driven from the throne. That news reached Boston in April, 1689, with the welcome tidings that Protestant William and Mary were on that throne.

This intelligence, like an electric spark, kindled an insurrection which burst out spontaneously in Boston, and in a few hours the revolt became universal. Andros sent soldiers to arrest the venerable Simon Bradstreet, then ninety years of age, as the most obnoxious republican in the city. He was governor when the king struck down the liberties of Massachusetts by taking away its charter. The people immediately reinstated him. From the balcony of the State-House, the vigorous old man, with long white hair and beard flowing over his shoulders and breast, addressed the populace with eloquent words. They seized Andros and fifty of his most obnoxious associates, and cast them into prison. A Committee of Safety was appointed. An assembly of representatives were soon convened. That body, by unanimous vote, declared their ancient charter to be resumed. In May, William and Mary were proclaimed in the colony; and from their sovereigns the provisional government of Massachusetts received a letter sanctioning their late proceedings, and directing them to send Andros to England to answer the charges preferred against him.

Another storm of disaster was now brooding over Massachusetts. King James (who was a Roman Catholic) had fled to the court of Louis the Fourteenth, a co-religionist and kinsman, who espoused his cause. William, as Prince of Orange, was then at the head of a coalition of several powers in a Protestant league against Louis; and soon after his accession, England became a member of that league and declared war against France. Hostilities between the two nations began the same year (1689); and the quarrel soon extended to their respective colonies in America. Here it became a strife chiefly for a monopoly of the fur-trade and the fisheries. The conflict then opened, and which continued more than seven years, is known in our history as King William's War.

There was a powerful and controlling religious element in that contest, and in others which occurred between the French and English in America. In fact the power of France had been carried into the heart of the American continent more by the zeal and patience of religious enthusiasts, than by the ambition of monarchs, the wisdom of statesmen, or the greed of commoner.

Coeval with the rise of Protestantism in Germany, was the foundation of a society designed to counteract its influence. It was established by

Ignatius Loyola, a Spanish enthusiast, and was called the *Society of Jesus*. It is better known in later times as the *Order of Jesuits*. Their organization was as perfect as any which human wisdom has yet devised for a special object. They are not a society of priests, but of Roman Catholics of every degree, bound by a solemn oath to extend the sway of the Church of Rome, and to fight Protestantism wherever it may be found. Their missionaries were soon found proselyting in every quarter of the globe. They regarded as a brother every man, without respect to skin or lineage; and the French Jesuits, who were the pioneers of French dominion in America, regarded every convert to Christianity among the savages an enfranchised citizen of France. Whole tribes came under their spiritual sway, and many of the votaries of commerce, who followed them into the wilds of America to traffic with the Indians, made wives of the native maidens, and so established strong social ties between the French and the savages. When, therefore, the former quarrelled with the English, they could rely upon the latter as faithful allies; and this barbarian element in the contest made border wars tenfold more distressing to the English colonists, especially to those of New England. The border settlers in New York had the powerful Iroquois Confederacy, like a strong wall, between themselves and the Indians in Canada.

MAJOR WALDRON SEIZED BY INDIANS.

The eastern Indians were easily excited into hostility by those white allies. Dover, a frontier town of New Hampshire, was the first to feel the violent hands of the mongrel foe. There three hundred Indians had been treacherously doomed to slavery years before. Revenge had slumbered; now it was awakened and was gratified. The venerable Major Waldron, then eighty years of age, and a local magistrate, had been a party to the treachery. On a warm evening in July, 1689, two squaws craved lodging at his house. They lay upon the floor, and in the night they unbarred the doors and let in several painted warriors. The aroused old man seized his sword and fought valiantly, until he was overpowered, when, with bitter taunts, they tortured him to death in his own hall. Then they laid his house in ashes, killed twenty of the garrison, and carried away nearly thirty persons and sold them as slaves to the French in Canada.

In August, a party came from Penobscot, after being purified by confession by Thury a Jesuit priest, and captured the garrison at Pemaquid, which Andros had established there. In February following, Governor Frontenac sent three hundred French and Indians from Montreal to destroy Albany. Through deep snows they made their way as far as Schenectady, a frontier town on the Mohawk, and at midnight burned the dwellings and murdered more than sixty of the inhabitants there. Seventeen of the slain were children. Early the next spring several eastern villages shared the same fate, and scores of women and children were carried away captives and suffered untold cruelties.

These atrocities—murders in cold blood—aroused all the colonies to a sense of danger, and on the suggestion of Massachusetts, a congress of delegates from several colonies met at New York on the first of May, 1690, to devise measures for the general security. Already the colony of Massachusetts had fitted out an expedition against Acadié, under Sir William Phipps, of Pemaquid, consisting of eight vessels with eight hundred men. He seized Port Royal, and obtained plunder sufficient to pay the expenses of the expedition. The town was again plundered by English privateers from the West Indies, in June; so retaliation went on. The Congress at New York resolved to invade Canada by land and sea, with an army that should march from the Hudson River by way of Lake Champlain to Montreal; and, at the same time, a strong naval armament was to ascend the St. Lawrence and attack Quebec. The army was placed under the command of a son of Governor Winthrop, of Connecticut, the cost of the expedition being borne jointly by that colony and New York; and Milborne, son-in-law of Leisler [see Chapter V of this Book], undertook to furnish the supplies. The command of the fleet, which was composed of thirty-four vessels manned by two thousand New Englanders, was given to Phipps.

The army moved from Albany early in July, at a snail's pace. At the beginning of September the bulk of them had only reached the head of Lake Champlain, where they remained, while some troops, and Indians of the *Five Nations*, under Colonel Peter Schuyler, pushed on toward the St. Lawrence. Old Frontenac was in Montreal when an Indian runner told him of the approach of the invaders. He called out his Indian allies. Taking a tomahawk in his hand, he danced the war-dance and chanted the war-song, in their presence, and then led them against the foe. Schuyler was repulsed, and the whole army returned to Albany. Leisler charged Winthrop with treachery, and Winthrop, in turn, charged the failure of the expedition to the inefficiency of Milborne in furnishing supplies.

Meanwhile Phipps, without charts or pilots, had crawled cautiously around Acadié and up the St. Lawrence for nine weeks, giving a swift Indian runner an opportunity to go from Pemaquid to Canada with the news of Phipps' departure, in time to allow Frontenac to reach Quebec before the arrival of the hostile fleet. The fortifications of the ancient town were strengthened; and when Phipps arrived before it, and sent a summons for its surrender, his message was treated with derision. It was then the middle of October. Hearing of the failure of the land expedition, Phipps weighed anchor and crawled cautiously back to New England before the winter storms set in. The French and Indians in Canada and Acadié were greatly elated, and the repulse was considered so important by Louis that he ordered a commemorative medal to be struck, with the legend: FRANCE VICTORIOUS IN THE NEW WORLD. These military operations exhausted the treasury of Massachusetts, and the government emitted bills of credit to the amount of about one hundred and thirty-four thousand dollars. This was the first paper-money ever issued on the American continent.

Soon after his return from the St. Lawrence, Sir William Phipps went to England to solicit aid for the colonies in their further warfare with the French and Indians, and to assist in efforts there to procure a restoration of the charter of Massachusetts which King James had annulled. Aid was refused; and instead of restoring the old charter, William gave a new one, by which Massachusetts, Plymouth, Maine and Nova Scotia were united under the name of "Massachusetts Bay Colony," and was made a royal province, with Phipps as governor. The baronet was a man of dull intellect, rudely educated, utterly lacking in qualities of statesmanship, headstrong, egotistical, superstitious, patriotic, and every way unfitted as a leader in civil and military affairs. He had gained distinction in his native colony only by his wealth and title, both of which were acquired by his successful raising of treasure from a Spanish ship with a diving-bell. He returned to Massachusetts in 1692, bringing the new charter with him.

The people of Massachusetts were not only dissatisfied with the new charter, but offended by it, for it greatly abridged their liberties. Wise and enlightened statesmen and churchmen in England advised William and his

Parliament not to make the liberties of the colonists less. Tillotson, the Archbishop of Canterbury, charged the king "not to take away from the people of New England any of the privileges which Charles the First had granted them." Others did likewise; but the government refused to listen to wise advice. The king reserved the right, in the new charter, to appoint the governor, his deputy and the secretary of the colony, and of repealing all the laws within three years after their passage. This robbery of their liberties alienated the affections of the people from the mother country. It was one of the series of blunders made by the crown and ministers which fostered discontent in the colonies and tended to the final dismemberment of the empire in 1776.

Yet in some respects the new charter was an improvement upon the old. While the rights of citizens were abridged in some things, they were enlarged in others. Toleration was granted to every form of the Christian religion excepting, unfortunately, the Roman Catholic; and the right of suffrage—to vote—was no longer restricted to members of Congregational churches, but was made almost universal. Bigotry and intolerance were, so far, disarmed; and they never afterward held controlling sway in the policy of the State.

Here let us pause a moment in our narrative of political transactions and of the horrid war then raging, to consider a strange social feature in the history of Massachusetts, known as SALEM WITCHCRAFT.

CHAPTER IX.

WITCHCRAFT—THE SAD STORY OF "SALEM WITCHCRAFT"—SUPERSTITION AND WICKEDNESS HAND-IN-HAND—RESULT OF THE DELUSION—KING WILLIAM'S WAR—NEW ENGLAND'S SUFFERINGS—CAPTURE OF PEMAQUID—THE BARON DE CASTIN—FRENCH AND INDIANS MAKE WAR TOGETHER—THE EXPLOIT OF HANNAH DUSTIN AND HER COMPANIONS—TREATY AT RYSWICK—THE PRETENDER—QUEEN ANNE—NEW ENGLAND MORE TOLERANT.

IN the seventeenth century, a belief in witches and witchcraft was almost universal. The Church of Rome, more than three hundred years ago, sanctioned punishments for the exercise of witchcraft; and after that, thousands of suspected persons were burned alive, drowned or hanged. During the sixteenth century, more than one hundred thousand accused and convicted persons perished in the flames, in Germany alone. In England, enlightened men embraced the belief. The eminent Sir Matthew Hale, who flourished during the civil war, the commonwealth and the period of the restoration of monarchy, repeatedly sentenced persons to death accused of witchcraft. The Puritans brought the belief with them to America. They established laws for the punishment of witches; and before 1648, four persons had suffered death for the alleged offence, in the vicinity of Boston. The ministers of the gospel there were shadowed by the delusion; and, because of their powerful social influence, they did more to foster the wild excitement and produce the distressing results of what is known in history as "Salem witchcraft," than all others.

In 1688, a wayward daughter of John Goodwin, of Boston, about thirteen years of age, accused a servant girl of stealing some of the family linen. The servant's mother, a "wild Irish woman" and a Roman Catholic, vehemently rebuked the accuser as a false witness. The young girl, in revenge, pretended to be bewitched by the Irishwoman. Some others of her family followed her example. They would alternately become deaf, dumb and blind; bark like dogs and purr like cats, but none of them lost their appetites nor sleep. The Rev. Cotton Mather, a credulous and egotistical clergyman (who seems to have believed, with Hubbard, the Puritan historian, that "America was originally peopled with a crew of witches transported thither by the devil"), hastened to Goodwin's house to allay the witchery by prayer. Wonderful were the alleged effects of his supplications. The devil was controlled by them for the time. Then four other ministers of Boston and one of Salem, as superstitious as himself, joined Mather, and they spent a whole day in the house of the "afflicted" in fasting and prayer, the result of which was the "delivery" of one of the family from

DELIVERANCE FROM WITCHCRAFT BY PRAYER.

the power of the witch. This was sufficient proof for the minds of the ministers that there must be a witch in the case, and these deluded clergymen prosecuted the ignorant Irish woman as such. She was bewildered before the court, and spoke sometimes in her native Irish language, which nobody could understand, and which her accusers and judges construed into involuntary confession. Mather and his clerical associates had the satisfaction of seeing the poor old Irish woman hanged as a witch, "for the glory of God."

Skeptics ridiculed Mather. He defended his cause by the assertion of alleged facts. He called the "afflicted" daughter of Goodwin to his study, when the artful girl thoroughly deceived him. The devil would allow her to read "Quaker books, the Common Prayer and Popish books," but a prayer from the lips of Mather, or the reading of a chapter of the Bible, threw her into convulsions. The credulous parson believed all he saw and heard, and cried from his pulpit, with outstretched arms and loud voice, "Witchcraft is the most nefarious high-treason against the Majesty on High. A witch is not to be endured in heaven or on earth." Mather's discourse on the subject was scattered broadcast among the people by means of the printing-press; and with it went out his narrative of the events in the Goodwin family, which led to greater tragedies in the spring and summer of 1692, when an epidemic disease resembling epilepsy broke out in Danvers (then a part of Salem), and spread rapidly. The physicians could neither control nor cure it; and with the sermon and statements of Mather before them, they readily ascribed the malady to the work of witches.

A niece and daughter of the parish minister at Danvers were first afflicted. Their strange and unaccountable actions frightened other young women, who soon exhibited the same symptoms, such as convulsions and spasmodic swellings in the throat, undoubtedly produced by hysterics. A belief quickly spread over Salem and throughout the province that evil spirits having ministering servants on earth had been permitted to overshadow the land with an awful visitation. Terror took possession of the minds of nearly all the people, and the dread made the malady spread widely.

Other old and ill-favored women now shared with the Irish woman in the suspicion of being witches, and several of them were publicly accused and imprisoned. The "afflicted," under the influence of the witchery, professed to see the forms of their tormentors with their "inner vision," and would forthwith accuse some individual seen. At length the "afflicted" and the accused became so numerous that no person was safe from suspicion and its consequences. Even those who were active in the prosecutions became objects of suspicion. A magistrate who had presided at the condemnation of several persons, becoming convinced of the wrongfulness of the proceedings and protesting against it, was himself accused and suffered much. A constable, who had arrested many and refused to arrest any more, was accused, condemned and hanged. Neither age, sex nor condition were considered. Sir William Phipps, the governor of Massachusetts, his lieutenant-governor, the near relations of the Mathers, and learned and distinguished men who had promoted the dreadful delusion by acquiescing in the proceedings against accused persons, became objects of suspicion.

The governor's wife, Lady Phipps, one of the purest and best of women, was accused of being a witch. The sons of Governor Bradstreet were compelled to fly to avoid the perils of false accusations; and near relatives of the Mathers were imprisoned on similar charges. Malice, revenge and rapacity often impelled persons to accuse others who were innocent; and when some statement of the accused would move the court and audience in favor of the prisoner, the accuser would solemnly declare that he saw the devil standing beside the victim whispering the touching words in his or her ear. And the absurd statement would be believed by the judges on the bench. Some, terrified and with the hope of saving their lives or avoiding the horrors of imprisonment, would falsely accuse their friends and kinsfolk; while others, moved by the same instinct and hopes, would falsely confess themselves to be witches.

When the magnates in church and state found themselves in danger, they thought of the golden rule, and suspected they had been acting unrighteously toward others. They cautiously expressed their doubts of the policy and justice of further proceedings against accused persons. A citizen of Andover, who was accused, wiser and more bold than governor and clergy, immediately caused the arrest of his accuser on a charge of defamation of character, and laid his damages at five thousand dollars. The effect of this act was wonderful. The public mind was in sympathy with it. The spell was instantly broken, and witchcraft was no more heard of in Andover. The impression then made quickly spread over the province, and deluded and wicked persons hastened to make amends for their errors and crimes.

The abashed clergy were compelled to take action because of the unexpected change in public opinion. At a convention held in June, 1693, they declared that it was not inconsistent with Scripture to believe that the devil might assume the shape of a good man, and that he may so have deceived the "afflicted." So his Satanic majesty as usual was conveniently made the scapegoat for the sins and follies of magistrates, clergy, and people. Many of the accusers and witnesses came forward and published solemn recantations or denials of the truth of their testimony, which had been given, they said, to save their own lives. Governor Phipps, after his wife was accused and the Andover citizen had killed the monster delusion, gave orders for the release of all persons under arrest for witchcraft. The Legislature of Massachusetts appointed a day for a general fast and solemn supplication "that God would pardon all the errors of his servants and people in a late tragedy raised among us by Satan and his instruments." And Judge Sewall, who had presided at many trials in Salem, stood up in his place in church on that fast day, and implored the prayers of the people that the errors which he had committed "might not be visited by the judgments of an avenging God on his country, his family, or himself." Mr. Paris, the parish minister in Danvers, in whose family the delusion had its rise, and who, throughout the "reign of terror," was one of the most earnest prosecutors of alleged witches, was compelled to resign his charge and leave the country.

These recantations, acknowledgments of error and pleadings for mercy, could not restore to the bereaved the spirits of those who had been hanged, nor make amends for the pains others had suffered. The delusion had prevailed in greatest vehemence more than six months, and it was not allayed for more than a year. During that time nineteen persons had been hanged, and one had been killed by the horrid process of pressing to death; fifty-five had been tortured or frightened into a confession of guilt; one hundred and fifty had been imprisoned, and full two hundred had been named as worthy of arrest. Amongst those hanged was the Rev. Mr. Burroughs, an exemplary clergyman, whose purity of character was conspicuous. Others, whose innocence and good name should have shielded them from harm, were coarsely assailed at the scaffold. One aged citizen, as was afterward proven, was falsely accused by a malignant enemy. While declaring his innocence to the multitudes, smoke from the executioner's pipe choked his utterances, when his accuser and his associates brutally shouted: "See how the devil wraps him in smoke!" A moment afterward he was hanged.

During the prevalence of this terror, all mutual confidence was suspended, and the noblest sentiments of human nature were trampled under-foot. The nearest blood relations became each other's accusers. One man was hanged on the testimony of his wife and daughter, who impeached him merely for the purpose of saving themselves. But this dreadful delusion was not an unmixed evil. "It is likely," wrote a contemporary, "that this frenzy contributed to work off the ill humors of the New England people—to dissipate their bigotry, and to bring them to a more free use of their reason."

The belief in witches did not end with the strange excitement. Cotton Mather and his clerical associates and others wrote in its defence. Mather's account of the delusion is unprofitable reading, because it deals in the absurd fancies of a man deluded by bigotry, superstition, and childish credulity. This may be seen in scores of sentences similar to the following:

"It is known that these wicked spectres [ghosts] did proceed so far as to steal several quantities of money from divers people, part of which individual money dropt sometimes out of the air, before sufficient spectators, into the hands of the afflicted, while the spectres were urging them to subscribe their covenant with death. Moreover poisons, to the standers-by wholly invisible, were sometimes forced upon the afflicted, which, when they have with much reluctancy swallowed, they have swollen presently, so that the common medicines for poison have been found necessary to relieve them; yea, sometimes the spectres, in their troubles, have so dropt the poisons that the standers-by have smelt them and viewed them, and beheld the pillows of the miserable stained with them. Yet more, the miserable have complained

AN AGED VICTIM OF SUPERSTITION.

bitterly of burning rags run into their forcibly distended mouths; and though nobody could see any such cloths, or indeed any fires in the chambers, yet presently the scalds were seen plainly by everybody on the mouths of the complainers, and not only the smell, but the smoke of the burning, filled the chambers."

"Once more, the miserable exclaimed extremely of branding-irons, heating at the fire on the hearth to mark them; now the standers-by could see no irons, yet they could see distinctly the print of them in the ashes, and smell them too, as they were carried by the not seen furies unto the poor creatures for whom they were intended; and these poor creatures were thereupon so stigmatized with them that they will bear the marks of them to their dying day. Nor are these [he had related many others] a tenth part of the prodigies that fell out among the inhabitants of New England.

"Flashy people may burlesque these things, but when hundreds of the most sober people, in a country where they have as much mother-wit certainly as the rest of mankind, know them to be true, nothing but the absurd and froward spirit of sadducism [disbelief in spirits] can question them."

They *were* burlesqued. Robert Calef, a merchant of Boston, in a series of letters which he wrote and published, exposed Mather's credulity, and greatly irritated the really good man. Mather retorted by calling Calef a "weaver turned minister." Calef tormented him the more by letter after letter, when Mather, wearied with the fight, called his opponent "a coal from hell," and prosecuted him for slander. When these letters were published in book form, Mather's kinsman, then president of Harvard College, caused copies of the work to be publicly burned on the college grounds.

This strange episode in the history of Massachusetts astonished the civilized world, and made an unfavorable impression on the surrounding Indians, who despised a people that cherished a religion which sanctioned such cruelties toward their countrymen. It gave a large advantage to the French, whose Jesuit missionaries, then laboring among the savage tribes on the frontier, contrasted their own mild and beneficent system of religion as exhibited there with that of the Puritans, whose ministers had been so prominent in the fearful tragedy. It had a serious effect upon the future destiny of New England, for the barbarians on the frontiers were, henceforth, strongly wedded to the fortunes of the French.

We paused to consider "Salem Witchcraft." Let us resume the narrative of general events.

"King William's War" continued in Europe and in America until it was closed by a treaty at Ryswick in 1697. Meanwhile the New England people had suffered much from the incursions of the French and Indians. Governor Phipps visited some of the tribes with whom he had made a treaty at Pemaquid, on Bristol Bay in Maine, and endeavored to secure their friendship and alliance with the English. They were willing to abide by the terms of their treaty, but, more attached to the French than ever, they refused to listen to any proposition for an English alliance, for Jesuits had told them that Protestants were enemies to the true religion of Christ. "The French," they said, "have driven witchcraft from among us, and we do not care to associate with a people who cherish it." Phipps returned disappointed, and soon afterward sailed to England, leaving the government in the hands of Stoughton, his deputy, who exercised the authority of chief magistrate about three years.

During Stoughton's administration, internal feuds disturbed, and border wars distressed the province continually. The French and Indians now prosecuted their peculiar warfare with relentless vigor. They spread death and desolation over the frontier. The French, by conquest, extended their colonial dominion. Nova Scotia submitted to the rule of France again; and in the summer of 1696, a strong force of French and Indians, under Colonel Iberville, attacked and captured Fort William Henry, at Pemaquid. They were accompanied by the Baron de Castin, a colonel of the French army, who came to America with his regiment, remained, and in 1687, set up a trading-post at the mouth of the Penobscot River, which spot yet bears his name. There he married a daughter of a powerful Indian chief, and exercised great influence over the dusky tribes. With two hundred of such followers, he joined Iberville, assisted in the capture of the fort and with his own hands helped to level it with the ground. So Castin was avenged for the burning of his house by the English.

This severe blow mortified and alarmed the New Englanders and excited the victors to a more distressing warfare. The French and Indians penetrated New England further than they had ever done before, destroying villages, and dispersing settlements, and carrying away people into captivity. Among the places that felt the severest blasts of the storm was Haverhill, within thirty miles of Boston, which was attacked by Indians in March, 1697, when forty persons were killed or made captives. Among the latter was a part of the family of Thomas Dustin, who was in his field when the savages suddenly appeared with horrid yells and gleaming knives and tomahawks. Seizing his gun and mounting his horse, he hastened to his house to bear away his wife, eight young children and a nurse to a place of safety. His youngest child was only a week old. He ordered the other seven to fly in a direction opposite to the approach of the savages, and was lifting his wife from the bed when the Indians attacked his house. "Leave me," cried the mother, "and fly to the protection of the other children." Seeing no chance to save his wife, Dustin again mounted his horse and soon overtook his precious flock, who were filled with joy when they saw their father. The Indians had pursued. Placing himself between the savages and his precious charge, he defended his children so valiantly as the foe pressed him back, that the savages gave up the pursuit, and the children were saved in an unoccupied house.

Meanwhile the scenes at Mr. Dustin's house were most distressing. The savages found Mrs. Dustin in bed, and the nurse attempting to fly with the infant. They ordered the feeble mother to rise instantly, while one of the savages, taking the infant out of doors, dashed out its brains against an apple-tree. Then they plundered and set fire to the house; and before the terrified mother was dressed, they compelled her to follow them in a hasty retreat. She was forced to walk twelve miles the first day, in the March

THOMAS DUSTIN HASTENING FROM THE FIELD.

slush of snow and mud, without shoes, encounter the chilling winds half-clad, and lie upon the ground, when resting, with no covering but the cold gray sky. This was repeated day after day until, by a circuitous route, they reached the island in the Merrimac River, at the mouth of the Contotook Creek, six miles above Concord, New Hampshire, now known as Dustin's Island. There was the home of the chief, who claimed Mrs. Dustin and her nurse as his captives. They were lodged with his family, which consisted of two men, three women, seven children and a captive English lad, who had been with them more than a year. The savage pretended to be a Christian. "When I prayed the English way," he said, "I thought it was good; but I think the French way better."

A few days after their arrival at the island, the prisoners were told that they were soon to start for a distant Indian village, when they would be compelled to "run the gauntlet"—that is, to be stripped naked and run for their lives between two files of Indian men, women and children, who would have the privilege of scoffing at them, beating them, and wounding them with sharp hatchets. The two women resolved not to endure the indignity and danger, preferring death. Mrs. Dustin planned a means for escape, and her nurse and the lad leagued with her in the execution of it. The Indians believed the lad to be faithful to them, and did not suppose the women would have courage to attempt to escape. So they did not keep watch.

On the day before the plan was to be carried out, Mrs. Dustin ascertained, through inquiries made by the lad, how to kill a man instantly, and how to take off his scalp. "Strike him here," said the Indian inquired of, placing his finger on his temple, "and take off his scalp so," showing the lad how. With this information, the plot was ripe. Before daylight the next morning, when the whole family were in deep slumber, Mrs. Dustin arose, awakened her nurse and the lad, and with their assistance instantly killed ten of the twelve sleepers, she slaying her captor and the lad killing the man who told him how to do it. A squaw and a child fled to the woods; and the prisoners, after scuttling all the boats there but one, to prevent pursuit, started in that one down the river, with provisions from the wigwam. They had not proceeded far when Mrs. Dustin, reflecting that they had not scalped their victims, and that her friends might demand ocular proof of the truth of her thrilling story, went back with her companions, took off the scalps, and carried them away in a bag.

With strong hearts the three voyaged down the Merrimac to their homes, every moment in peril from savages or the elements, and were received as persons risen from the dead. Mrs. Dustin found her husband and children saved. Soon afterward she went to Boston, carrying with her a gun and tomahawk which she had brought from the wigwam, and her ten trophies; and the General Court of Massachusetts gave these brave sufferers fifty pounds as a reward for their heroism. Ex-Governor Nicholson, of Maryland, sent a metal tankard to Mrs. Dustin and Mrs. Neff, as a token of his admiration. That tankard is now (1875) in the possession of Mr. Emery Coffin, of Newburyport, Massachusetts. During the summer of 1874, one hundred and seventy-seven years after the event, citizens of Massachusetts and New Hampshire erected on the highest point of Dustin's Island an elegant monument commemorative of the heroic deed. It displays a figure of Mrs. Dustin, holding in her right hand, raised in the attitude of striking, a tomahawk, and a bunch of scalps in the other. On it are inscribed the names of HANNAH DUSTIN, MARY NEFF, and SAMUEL LEONARDSON, the English lad.

Other places suffered dreadfully during the summer of 1697. Haverhill was again attacked and desolated. The treaty at Ryswick (a small village near the Hague, in Holland), soon afterward stayed the flow of blood in Europe and America. There a peace was agreed upon between Louis the Fourteenth of France, and England, Spain, Holland and the German Empire, which ended a war of more than seven years duration. Louis was compelled to acknowledge William of Orange to be the sovereign of England. That war cost Great Britain one hundred and fifty million dollars in cash, besides a hundred million dollars loaned. The latter laid the foundations of the enormous national debt of Great Britain, now amounting to about four thousand million dollars.

A little before the treaty at Ryswick a *Board of Trade* and *Plantations* was established in England, whose duty it was to have a general oversight of the affairs of the American colonies. It was a permanent commission, the members of which were called "Lords of Trade and Plantations." It consisted of seven members, with a president, and was always a ready instrument of oppression in the hands of the sovereign. It became, as we shall see, a powerful promoter of those discontents in the colonies which finally broke out into a flame of rebellion in 1775.

The lull in the storm of war, caused by the treaty at Ryswick, was of short duration. Aspirants for power again tormented the people with the evils of war. King James the Second died in France in September, 1701. He had been shielded by Louis after his flight from his throne to France and now the French monarch acknowledged James's son, James Francis Edward (who is known in history as The Pretender), to be the lawful king of England. This act offended the English because the crown had been settled upon Anne, James's second and Protestant daughter. Louis likewise offended the English by placing his grandson, Philip of Anjou, on the throne of Spain, so increasing French influence among the dynasties of Europe. William was enraged, and was preparing for war, when a fall from his horse, while hunting, caused his death. He was succeeded by Anne, and the causes already mentioned, with others of less importance, impelled her to declare war against France after her accession to the throne. Hostilities began in 1702, and, as before, the colonies of the two governments in America became involved in the conflict. In the war that ensued, and which lasted almost a dozen years, the New Englanders again suffered dreadfully from incursions of the French and Indians. That contest is known in our annals as QUEEN ANNE'S WAR.

It may be observed that at this opening of a new era in the history of New England, when the liberal and enlightened reign of William was making a deep impression upon England and her American colonies, the people of our present Eastern States were more united, more enlightened, and less bigoted than they had ever been before. The Earl of Bellamont, whom we have mentioned as governor of New York, was made governor of Massachusetts and New Hampshire also. When he visited Boston in 1699, he found controversies allayed, passions cooled, and the prevalence of a general disposition to promote harmony and good-fellowship. Wisdom and moderation had taken the places of folly and vehemence in thought and action; and there was a happy toleration abroad. The printing-press was doing its beneficent work efficiently in scattering the seeds of knowledge, thereby creating a sentiment of brotherhood among separated religious communities. From the beginning, the New Englanders were distinguished for their appetite for knowledge and the ready reception, when untrammeled by arbitrary restraints, of truths of every kind. This disposition formed the springs of that love for liberty which has always distinguished the inhabitants of New England.

CHAPTER X.

BELLAMONT GOVERNOR OF MASSACHUSETTS—FRENCH CLAIMS IN NEW ENGLAND—QUEEN ANNE AND OTHERS DECLARE WAR AGAINST FRANCE—STRUGGLE WITH THE FRENCH AND INDIANS—INFLUENCE OF THE JESUITS—DEATH OF FATHER RALE—DESTRUCTION OF DEERFIELD—FATE OF THE WILLIAMS FAMILY—THE VILLAGE BELL—ACADIE INVADED—PROGRESS OF FRENCH DOMINION—INDIAN "KINGS" IN ENGLAND—EXPEDITION AGAINST CANADA—A LONG PEACE—CAPTURE OF LOUISBURG—FRENCH ATTEMPT TO RETAKE IT—TREATY OF AIX-LA-CHAPELLE.

WE have observed that the Earl of Bellamont found public affairs in pleasant shape in Massachusetts, on his arrival in Boston in 1699. He was the only English-born nobleman who ever governed a New England province. His conduct won for him the profound respect of the rigid Puritan republicans, for he fairly estimated the mutual dependence of ruler and people, and acted accordingly. One day at his table, at which sat many representatives of the people of the commonwealth, he said to his wife: "Dame, we should treat these gentlemen well: they give us our bread."

Nothing disturbed the serenity of Bellamont's administration excepting the encroachments of the French, who had outgeneraled the English in securing the control of the mouth of the Mississippi River, and were then preparing to extend their territorial jurisdiction in the East as far westward as the Kennebec River.

According to the interpretation of the English court, the St. Croix River, now the eastern boundary of the United States, was to be the western boundary of the French dominion in that quarter. The French king chose to interpret it otherwise; and his representatives in Nova Scotia gave notice to the authorities of Massachusetts that it was their intention to assert jurisdiction as far westward as the Kennebec. Bellamont informed the British ministry of the threatened invasion, but his communication received little notice. No doubt the invasion would have been successfully carried out had not the war between England and France began soon afterward.

In May, 1702, Queen Anne and her allies the Emperor of Germany and the States-General of Holland declared war against France and Spain. When hostilities began in Europe, they were the signal for the English colonists in America to prepare for another fierce struggle with the French and Indians. Governor Dudley and some magistrates of Massachusetts held a conference with the Eastern Indians at Casco, in June, 1703. The savages, with well-feigned friendship, readily renewed former treaties. They declared that the French had asked them to take up the hatchet against the English, but they had refused because the friendship for the people of Massachusetts was "as firm as the mountains, and as enduring as the sun and moon."

Some believed in the sincerity of the Indians. Wise men shook their heads in doubt, and others declared their belief that the savages, under the tutelage of the French, were playing a treacherous part. Circumstances soon settled the question. Only a few weeks after the conference these same Indians fell, with remorseless fury, upon the frontier settlers of Massachusetts and New Hampshire. The solemn treaties were scattered to the winds. The tribes from the Merrimac to the Penobscot desolated the border settlements, murdering the innocent, plundering the thrifty, and laying in ashes cabins, mansions, and villages. Not even the benefactors of the Indians, the Friends or Quakers, were spared. They respected "neither the milk-white brows of the grave ancient," nor "the mournful cries of tender infants."

This treachery greatly exasperated the English against the French Jesuits, to whose counsels they professed to trace the cause of the dire calamity. Already this Order had incurred the intense hatred of the New Englanders, because many circumstances pointed to Jesuit influence inciting the Indians to make war on the English. The revelation of Bomaseen, a sachem who visited Boston, intensified that hatred. He declared that the Jesuits had told the Indians that Jesus Christ was a Frenchman; that his mother, the Virgin Mary, was a French woman; that the English had murdered him; that he had gone up to heaven to plead for mankind, and that he who would receive his favor must espouse the cause of his countrymen, the French, in the pending quarrel. Bomaseen was a crafty Indian, and may have invented this story; but it was believed by the colonists. The Legislatures of both New York and Massachusetts had already passed laws for the expulsion of the Jesuits from their respective provinces; but nothing could diminish their secret influence over the Indians. Warriors from Canada joined those south of the St. Lawrence, and in their murderous forays they were often accompanied by French troops and ecclesiastics.

The white men and Indians all confessed their sins to the priests and received pardon for them, before engaging in their bloody work. A day was appointed for such confession and pardon. "I exhorted them," [the

Indians], says Father Rale, of Norridgewock, "to maintain the same interest in religion as if they were at home; to observe carefully the laws of war; to practice no cruelty; to kill no one except in the heat of battle; and to treat their prisoners humanely." What a ghastly commentary on their merciful instructions were the savage cruelties of these absolved men, as they swept along the frontier from Casco to Wells immediately after leaving the presence of the priest, staining the fields with the blood of the innocent, and lighting up the heavens at night with the flames of burning dwellings! Twenty years afterward, Rale fell a victim to the fiery indignation of the English against him and his fellow Jesuits for their alleged complicity in the atrocious acts of the Indians for more than a quarter of a century. Nor-

A SPIRITUAL LEADER.

ridgewock, where he had labored as a missionary more than thirty years, was attacked by the English in 1723. Rale was shot dead, it is said, at the foot of a cross, where his flock, with wild cries, bewailed his death. On that spot, in 1833, a monument was erected to his memory. With Rale, Bomaseen and some of his kindred also fell.

During the winter of 1703-4, the people along the New England frontier lived in perpetual dread of the foe. At length, late in February, a party of French and Indians, who had traveled with snow-shoes all the way from Canada, approached the pretty village of Deerfield on the Connecticut River, in Massachusetts. The snow lay four feet deep in that region, and was covered with a crust that bore the invaders. The drifts around the town were almost as high as its encircling palisades. Over these Major Hertel de Rouville, the commander of the motley party, and his followers, easily crept into the village while the inhabitants were slumbering before the dawn of the first day of March. The first intimation the villagers had of danger was the bursting open of their doors and the sound of the horrid war-whoop of the savages. The people were dragged from their beds and murdered or carried into captivity. The village was set on fire, and every building excepting the chapel and one dwelling-house was laid in ashes. Forty of the inhabitants were killed, and one hundred and twelve were borne to the wilderness an hour after sunrise.

Among the victims was the Rev. John Williams, the village pastor, and his family. Two of his children and a black servant were murdered at his door. With his wife and five children he began the toilsome journey. Mrs. Williams fainted with fatigue on the second day. The tomahawk of an Indian cleft her skull, and so they were relieved of the burden. Her husband and children were taken to Canada, and after a captivity among the Caughnawagas, near Montreal, for nearly two years, they were ransomed and returned home. Only a daughter, ten years old, was kept. The Indians would not part with her. She grew up to womanhood in Indian habits and tastes, became a Roman Catholic, married a young Mohawk brave and bore children; and when she visited her relations in Deerfield in after years, she could not be induced to abandon her Indian mode of life, nor leave the church to which she was attached.

The chief object of this expedition was to procure the little bell in the meeting-house in Deerfield. It had been bought in France for the church of St. Louis, at Caughnawaga. The vessel that bore it to America was captured by a New England privateer and taken into Boston. The bell was purchased by the congregation at Deerfield, and hung in the belfry of the meeting-house. The invaders carried it away, under the charge of Father Nicolas, of the church at Caughnawaga, who accompanied the expedition. It was borne in triumph to its original destination, and it now summons the people to worship from the belfry of the church of St. Louis at Caughnawaga.

For years these tales of horror were the true narratives of the experience of New Englanders on the border. Remote settlements were abandoned. The tillers of the soil gathered in palisaded villages and labored in the fields in groups, and well-armed. There was no semblance of civilized warfare in the methods of the French and Indians, and their cruelties inspired good men everywhere with horror. "I hold it to be my duty towards God and my neighbor," wrote the good Peter Schuyler, Mayor of Albany, to Vaudreuil, the French governor of Canada, "to prevent, if possible, these barbarous and heathen cruelties. My heart swells with indignation when I think that a war between Christian princes, bound to the exactest laws of honor and generosity, which their noble ancestors have illustrated by brilliant examples, is degenerated into savage and boundless butchery. These are not the methods for terminating the war. Would that all the world thought with me on this subject."

Such protests were uttered in vain. The savages were unrestrained by their Christian allies. The power of the church and state encouraged them

THE CAPTIVE WILLIAMS FAMILY.

in their bloody deeds. At length the New Englanders determined to make aggressive movements. In 1707, Massachusetts, New Hampshire and Rhode Island, resolved to carry war into the French domain on the East. Early in June a thousand men under Colonel Marsh sailed for Nantucket, under convoy of a British war-ship, to attempt the conquest of Acadié. The French at Port Royal were prepared for them, and the expedition was a failure.

In 1710, another expedition, fitted out at the joint expense of the New England colonies and New York and New Jersey, sailed from Boston, with a fleet from England under the command of Colonel Nicholson. There were thirty-six vessels in all. They sailed in September, and six days afterward the fleet was anchored before the fort at Port Royal. The place was surrendered to the English on the thirteenth of October, and the name and fortress of Port Royal were changed to Annapolis, in honor of Queen Anne. Acadié was annexed to the realm of Great Britain, under the title of Nova Scotia or New Scotland. The British flag has waved perpetually over that fortress from that day to this.

Nicholson carried the good news to England, and urged the conquest of Canada. The people of the province of New York, though shielded from invasion by the French and Indians from Canada by the neutral Five Nations who stood an impassable barrier, favored the project, because they looked with concern upon the progress of French dominion in the West, its arms reaching from the great lakes on the North toward others extending from the Gulf of Mexico on the South. The French then claimed all the region in the Valley of the Mississippi to "the South Sea;" named the country Louisiana in honor of their king, and were preparing to establish a great empire there.

The Legislature of New York sent a memorial to the queen on the subject of French encroachments, by the hand of Colonel Schuyler, just mentioned, who was accompanied to England by sachems of the Five Nations, as representatives of the Iroquois Confederacy.

In London these dusky "kings," as they were called, drew crowds of wondering gazers. Multitudes followed the sachems wherever they went, and the print-shops soon exhibited engravings of their portraits. They felt awkward in English small-clothes of black, and scarlet mantles trimmed with gold lace, in which they were clad, and preferred the scanty wardrobe of their forest homes. They were entertained at sumptuous banquets by the principal nobility of the realm, and shown the glory of the kingdom. They saw reviews of troops, and went on board some of the great ships of the Royal Navy; and at the London theatre they were amused by gorgeous displays. In the state carriage drawn by six horses, they were conveyed to the court and held an audience with the queen; and before their departure, they addressed to her Majesty, and to the Lords of the Privy Council, letters bearing their signatures in the form of rude pictures of the Wolf, the Bear, and the Tortoise—their respective *totems* or tribal arms—in which they promised perpetual friendship and alliance with the English, and confirmed them by presenting belts of wampum, their tokens of fidelity. With Schuyler, they returned to America in the ship *Dragon*, with Colonel Nicholson, and arrived in Boston early in the summer of 1711. They had seen evidences of the amazing strength, power and glory of Great Britain, which made a deep and abiding impression upon the ambassadors and their countrymen. They were ready to aid the English in the conquest of Canada.

An expedition for that conquest was planned by Henry St. John, afterward Lord Bolingbroke, the friend of Pope and Swift, the brilliant orator and conversationalist, and the popular and unscrupulous Secretary of War of Queen Anne. Fifteen ships-of-war, forty transports and six store-ships were placed under the command of Admiral Sir Hovenden Walker, and with marines and battalions of veteran soldiers, then sailed for America and arrived at Boston in June, 1711. New England colonies promptly raised a provincial force, and the ships sailed for Quebec on the 10th of August, bearing about seven thousand troops. At the same time other colonies had formed a provincial army for the capture of Montreal and the holding of the region of the upper St. Lawrence. These were under the command of Nicholson, who held a general's commission and marched from Albany, on the Hudson, on the same day when the fleet left Boston. They were four thousand in number, and were chiefly furnished by New York and Connecticut. Six hundred of them were warriors of the Five Nations.

News of these movements soon reached Governor Vaudreuil at Montreal. He sent out Jesuit missionaries and other agents to secure Indian allies, and hastened to Quebec to prepare for the invaders. The fortifications were strengthened; and so enthusiastic were the inhabitants in the cause of defensive war, that women worked on the forts. But there was no occasion to fight for Quebec, for the British armament on the sea did not get into the St. Lawrence. When the ships arrived at its mouth after loitering by the way, they were overtaken by a storm of wind and a thick fog. It was a perilous place among rocks and shoals. Haughtily rejecting the advice of the New England pilots, the admiral listened to that of French pilots, who had an interest in misleading him. His fleet was soon driving on the shore, on the night of the 2d of September. Just as he was going to bed the captain of his vessel came down to him and said, "Land is in sight; we are in great danger." Walker did not believe him. Presently a provincial captain rushed down and exclaimed: "For the Lord's sake come on deck, or we shall be lost; I see the breakers all around us." Leisurely putting on his gown and slippers, the admiral ascended to the deck and saw the imminent peril. His orders for salvation, immediately given, were too late. The vessels were driven on the iron-bound shore, and eight of them were lost. Almost a thousand men perished in the sea.

A few days afterward, a council of war concluded that it would be wise to abandon the expedition. The disheartened admiral returned to England with his ships, while the provincial troops were sent to Boston. Hearing of the calamity and the result, Nicholson unwillingly retraced his steps to Albany, and left Montreal unmolested. Walker actually claimed credit for himself in retreating after falsely charging the disaster to the incompetence of the New England pilots. "Had we arrived safe at Quebec, ten or twelve thousand men," he wrote, "must have been left to perish of cold and hunger; by the loss of a part, Providence saved all the rest." The admiral was disappointed in not receiving public honors for his exploits in assisting Providence.

THE SLAIN MISSIONARY.

In the spring of 1713, the war was ended by a treaty concluded at Utrecht, by which England obtained the privilege of being the chief trader of the world in African slaves, and received large accessions of territory from France. The eastern Indians, wearied with the war, sent delegates to Boston to sue for peace; and at Portsmouth, the governor of Massachusetts and New Hampshire made a solemn treaty of amity with the chiefs of those tribes on the 24th of July.

A long peace now ensued. For thirty years the colonists of New England enjoyed comparative repose. It was broken only by discontented Indians in the East—the powerful Abenakes. They disputed the claims of Massachusetts to their territory, which the French had surrendered. Their chief said, "I have my land where the Great Spirit has placed me; and while there remains one child of my tribe, I will fight to preserve it." Finally, the English seized the young Baron de Castin, the son of an Indian woman. Smarting under this indignity, the Indians resolved to retaliate. The torch was again lighted, and Brunswick was laid in ashes. The Jesuit missionary, Rale, clearly perceiving their comparative weakness, told them plainly that their country was lost. The exasperated New Englanders overran portions of it with small military expeditions, striking blows here and there. It was in one of these forays upon Norridgewock that Rale was killed. He was the last Jesuit missionary in New England, and with him perished French influence over the Indian tribes in the East.

For several years after the close of these contests with the Indians, the history of Massachusetts consists chiefly of the record of warm political disputes by which the growth of republican principles was greatly stimulated. Controversies, sometimes violent and sometimes conciliatory, were carried on between the governors and the representatives of the people, the former contending for prerogatives and salaries which the latter deemed inadmissible. These disputes were suddenly arrested when, late in the spring of 1744, news came that France had declared war against Great Britain. The colonists knew that the evident result would be hostilities between their respective colonies in America, and they prepared for the conflict which is known in our history as "King George's War." It was so called because King George the Second was then on the throne of England, and had espoused the cause of the Empress of Austria, the celebrated Maria Theresa, who fought for the crown of Austria against the Elector of Bavaria. The king of France espoused the cause of his opponent, and this led to war. In Europe it was known as "The War of the Austrian Succession."

This war was not marked by any very stirring events in America, excepting some military and naval operations in the East. Before war was declared, some French soldiers from the island of Cape Breton, surprised, captured and carried to Louisburg a small English garrison at Canseau. Then some Indians attacked the dilapidated fort at Annapolis, but were repulsed. These things compelled the English colonists to contemplate retaliation, and they resolved to attempt to capture the fortress at Louisburg, and so secure an important advantage. The men taken from Canseau had been sent to Boston on parole, and gave a minute account of that fortress. It had been built by the French after the treaty of Utrecht at a cost of five and a half million dollars, and because of its great strength it was called "The Gibraltar of America."

At that time, William Shirley, a good soldier and energetic statesman, was governor of Massachusetts. He asked England for aid in the expedition against Louisburg. He appealed to the other colonies. The Legislature of Massachusetts made provision for the expedition. New York sent some artillery, and Pennsylvania some food. The New England colonies raised men, Massachusetts alone furnishing more than three thousand. So the common danger was extending the idea of a necessity for a political union of the English-American colonies long before it assumed a practical shape in 1754, and especially in 1774.

The colonists had reason to expect the co-operation of a British fleet then in the West Indies, under Admiral Sir Peter Warren. They waited some time for its appearance, but in vain. Finally, at the beginning of

April, 1745, New England troops sailed from Boston for Canseau, under the general command of William Pepperell, a wealthy merchant of Maine, who was afterward made a baronet for his distinguished services. The ice was yet floating around Cape Breton in such huge masses that ships could not enter the harbor of Louisburg, and the expedition was detained at Canseau almost a month, when it was unexpectedly joined by five war-ships and soon afterward by others from England, under Admiral Warren. That officer had received instructions from home to give to Massachusetts all the aid in his power. On the day after Warren appeared, some vessels arrived from Connecticut with a considerable land force from that colony.

The New England vessels of all sorts now at Canseau numbered one hundred. Governor Shirley had instructed Pepperell to have all of these vessels arrive near Louisburg at the same hour, in the night; and no matter what might then be the condition of the surf, to land all the troops on the rocky shore before daylight, march at once through thickets and over morasses to the city and beyond it, and to take the fortress and town by surprise. Of course a strict compliance with these orders was impossible, but it was undertaken. The vessels all left Canseau, bearing about four thousand troops, and early in the morning of the 30th of April appeared in Gabarus Bay, eastward of Louisburg. The troops were disembarked on the same day, and most of the artillery, ammunition, and provisions were landed. The alarm bells of the city were rung, and cannon from the fortress were fired to warn the suburban inhabitants of danger.

The assailants had heavy work before them, with seemingly inadequate means for its execution. The walls of the fortress were forty feet thick at the bottom, of solid masonry, and from twenty to thirty feet in height. Around them was a ditch, filled with water, eighty feet wide. More than one hundred heavy cannon, and nearly eighty swivels and mortars, composed the armament of the fort. All the walls were swept by artillery from the bastions, and a garrison of sixteen hundred men defended these strong works. There were also batteries with many cannon outside the fort to defend the approaches to it. It seemed possible for two hundred men to defend it against five thousand. The heavy artillery of the assailants consisted of only eighteen cannon and three mortars.

The French sent out a force to oppose the landing, but they were soon put to flight. On the following morning, Lieutenant-Colonel Vaughan, of New Hampshire, a resolute volunteer, full of zeal and courage, conducted a small advance column through the woods within sight of Louisburg, and with three cheers greeted the first sight of the fortress. The same evening he marched to a part of the harbor where there were large warehouses containing a vast amount of naval stores, and set them on fire. The smoke, driven by a strong wind into the grand battery situated near, so terrified its garrison that they spiked their guns and fled into the city. Vaughan took possession of the battery, and held it until he was reinforced, in spite of a resolute effort of a French force to retake it. The guns of the battery were unspiked by Major Seth Pomeroy, a Massachusetts blacksmith, who afterward became a useful officer in the French and Indian war. "It looks as if our campaign would last long," the gallant Pomeroy wrote to his wife; "but I am willing to stay till God's time comes to deliver the city into our hands." "Suffer no anxious thought to rest on your mind about me," answered that patriotic New England woman. "The whole town is much engaged with concern for the expedition, how Providence will order the affair, for which religious meetings every week are maintained. I leave you in the hand of

NEW ENGLANDERS MARCHING FOR LOUISBURG.

God." Such was the spirit of the descendants of the Puritans. The New Hampshire troops bore on their banners the motto given them by the eminent Whitefield—"*Nil desperandum Christo subduce*"—Nothing is to be despaired of with Christ for the leader. It inspired many of them with the zeal of crusaders, for they regarded it as an efficacious benediction by a highly gifted and holy man; a true servant of heaven.

The English troops encamped in a semicircle around Louisburg. The heavy cannon and mortars, under the charge of Captain Richard Gridley (who was conspicuous in the siege of Boston thirty years afterward, as an engineer), were dragged on sledges across morasses; trenches were dug by the zealous soldiers; batteries were erected, and on the last day of May a regular siege was commenced. Meanwhile Warren had captured a French seventy-four gun ship, with five hundred men and a large quantity of military stores.

Finally, a combined attack of the fleet and army was made, and on the 17th of June, the city, the fort and garrison, and the batteries, were surrendered to the English, together with the Island of Cape Breton. The value of the stores and prizes then captured was a little less than five million dollars. On the day of surrender New England ministers preached in the chapel of the fortress; and in view of the amazing strength of the place, one of them said from the pulpit: "God has gone out of the way of his common providence, in a remarkable and almost miraculous manner, to incline the hearts of the French to give up, and deliver this strong city into our hands."

The pride of France was deeply mortified by the results of this daring and successful expedition. Her rulers determined to recover the lost city and fortress, and to desolate the colonies of the English in America. For that purpose a powerful fleet was sent to Cape Breton, under the command of the Duke d'Anville. His vessels were dispersed, and several of them were wrecked by violent storms; and disease wasted hundreds of his men. He was compelled to abandon the enterprise without striking a blow, and with two or three ships—the remnant of his fleet—he took shelter in the harbor of Chebucto (now Halifax) in Nova Scotia. There he died, it is believed, from the effects of self-administered poison; and his lieutenant who succeeded him, committed suicide because of mortified pride. As in the case of the capture of Louisburg, the New Englanders now regarded this delivery as the interposition of a special providence; and the bells of Boston and other towns rang out merry peals of joy, while thousands knelt in the meeting-houses and poured out thanksgivings to God for his evident favors.

Hostilities continued two years longer, but the Americans suffered very little from the war, excepting from incursions by the French and Indians, on their frontiers. In October, 1748, a treaty at Aix-la-Chapelle put an end to the war, when it was agreed that all prisoners taken by either party should be released, and all acquisitions of property or territory by either party should be restored. So Cape Breton and its fortress passed into the possession of the French by peaceful means, and the colonies were paid by the British government for their expenditures in capturing them, amounting to more than a million dollars. Both the principals in the contest were heavy losers. Nothing had been gained. Humanity had severely suffered.

National animosities, religious differences, and recent causes for irritation, had created the most intense hatred between the English and French colonists; and the acts of horrid cruelty by the Indians made the people on the frontiers regard them as almost as obnoxious as ravenous beasts of prey. Yet, firm in their allegiance to the crown of Great Britain, and loyal to the duty of obedience, the people of New England, and especially of Massachusetts, were impelled to a restraint of their resentment while England and France were at peace. But it was not long before disputes about territorial boundaries began which soon led to preparations for hostilities in America between the three races who occupied the country. At about the middle of the last century, they came to blows, and then began the fierce struggle of the English and French for dominion on this continent, known in history as "The French and Indian War." This we shall consider hereafter.

CHAPTER XI.

THE GOVERNMENT OF MARYLAND—DIFFICULTIES WITH CLAYBORNE—THE INDIANS UNEASY—A CIVIL WAR—TOLERATION ACT—DISTURBANCES IN MARYLAND—GEORGE FOX IN THE PROVINCE —RULE OF THE CALVERTS—INSURRECTIONS—REVOLUTION IN ENGLAND—COODE THE DISTURBER OF MARYLAND—ANNAPOLIS THE SEAT OF GOVERNMENT—LORD BALTIMORE AND WILLIAM PENN—TRANQUILLITY IN MARYLAND—THE FRENCH AND INDIAN WAR.

AT the close of Chapter V of the Second Book, we have observed that in the year 1639, a representative government was established in Maryland. It was crude in form, but possessed the prolific seeds of a sturdy republicanism. The freemen chose as many representatives as they pleased. So did the proprietor. These, with the governor appointed by the proprietor, and a secretary, composed the government of Maryland.

In that first representative assembly, the people boldly asserted their rights and dignity. The proprietor presented to the Legislature a system of laws which he had framed. The representatives of the people, feeling that the inherent right to make laws resided in their constituents, rejected the whole system. They adopted a Declaration of Rights, defining the powers and duties of each branch of the government, and set to work to pass bills for the security to the people of every privilege that belonged to a British subject. This popular sovereignty was briefly contested by Lord Baltimore, by a series of vetoes or refusals to sign such bills. After vetoing more than forty, and finding the people firm, the proprietor gave up the contest and yielded gracefully to the popular will.

The province now had an aspect of profound repose, for the Indians regarded the new settlers as friends. Everything social and political promised for Maryland a long career of peace and prosperity, when personal ambition and greed, as usual, disturbed the serenity of society. A restless adventurer, named William Clayborne, had received authority from the governor of Virginia, so early as 1627, to explore the headwaters of Chesapeake Bay north of the 34th degree of latitude. Four years later, King Charles gave to Clayborne the privilege of making discoveries in the same region, and trafficking with the natives. He established a trading-post on Kent Island, in Chesapeake Bay, not far from Annapolis. When Governor

Calvert visited Governor Harvey, while the colonists for Maryland were on their way to that province, Clayborne appeared and gave them ominous warnings of the hostilities of the Indians, to which they would be subjected. Not succeeding in frightening the emigrants, he insisted upon the exemption of Kent Island from the jurisdiction of the Maryland proprietor, because his grant was older than Lord Baltimore's thereto. The Virginia Assembly secretly supported his claim; and when Calvert insisted that Clayborne should either leave the island or take an oath of allegiance to the governor, he would do neither, but fitted out an armed vessel to protect his domain and cruise against the colonists. His vessel was captured by a Maryland force, and Clayborne, who was not in the expedition, prudently fled to Virginia, and there effectually excited the hostility of the Indians against Calvert's colony, telling the savages that they were Spaniards. The governor of Maryland demanded the body of Clayborne as a rebel and traitor, and he was saved from arrest only by fleeing to England. The Maryland Legislature, in 1638, deprived Clayborne of his civil rights and property, within their jurisdiction. He laid his case before the king, and it was decided against him. For a few years afterward he did not appear as an open enemy of the Maryland government.

During the lull in Clayborne's active hostility, he had secretly poisoned the minds of the Indians with suspicions of dark designs on the part of the settlers toward them. The king of the Patuxents showed much unfriendliness, and the colonists were disquieted. But the more powerful king of the Piscataways resolved to become a Christian. He had been very sick. His forty conjurors could not kill the malady and it was likely to kill him, when Father White, the Roman Catholic priest already mentioned, by the judicious use of medicines, cured the monarch. With a grateful heart the king asked to be baptized. He urged his chiefs to receive the rite. On a warm summer's day in 1640, in a chapel made of bark for the occasion, the king, his queen, and their little child, with several of his council, were baptized in the presence of the governor and other distinguished citizens. The king was named Charles in honor of the British sovereign; and in the afternoon he and his queen were married, in accordance with Christian rites. His daughter, an intelligent young woman, followed her father's example, and was sent to school at St. Mary's. His example was also followed by many other leading persons among the Indians; and they promised to be a shield for the colonists against outside barbarians. But the king soon afterward died, and his daughter at St. Mary's became queen. She could not protect the Christians against hostile pagans within their borders and beyond, with whom Clayborne and his emissaries had tampered.

The Indians, alarmed by the rapid increase of Englishmen in their country, and made suspicious by the false testimony of Clayborne, at length took a hostile position and made war on the intruders in 1642. The war was mild, but lasted between two and three years. It had just ended when Clayborne, assisted by Captain Richard Ingle, stirred up the people to rebellion. The insurrection flamed out with greater vehemence than the Indian war, but was not so long. Civil war was then raging in England, and the proprietor could not expect aid from the virtually dethroned monarch.

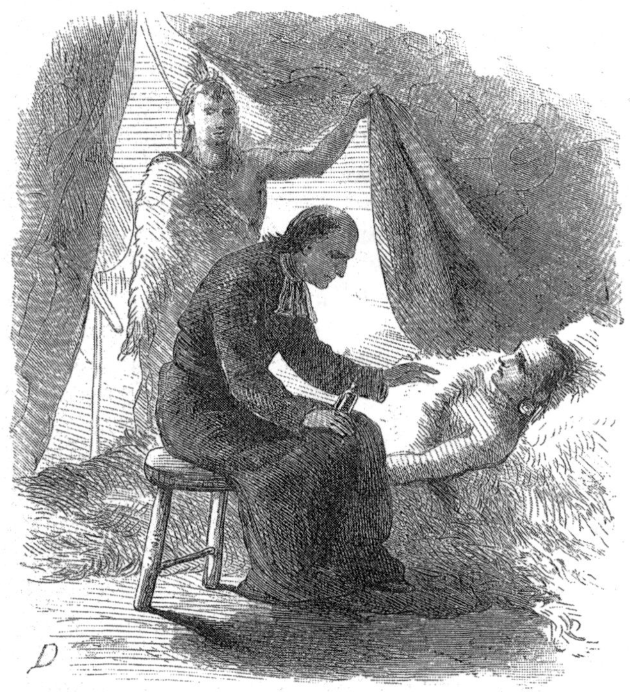

THE PRIEST AS A PHYSICIAN.

The rebels, assisted by disaffected Indians, instantly triumphed, and the governor and his council were compelled to fly into Virginia. For about a year and a half the insurgents held the reins of power, and the horrors of civil war brooded over fair and once happy Maryland. The rebellion was crushed in the summer of 1646, when the governor returned to his chair of state. During the turmoil many of the records of the province were destroyed, and a greater portion of them were carried into Virginia by

Captain Ingle and were lost. A wise clemency extended a general pardon to the rebels, excepting Ingle, and tranquillity was speedily restored.

Lord Baltimore displaced Green, a Roman Catholic, who had been acting-governor since the decease of Leonard Calvert, and commissioned William Stone of Virginia, a Protestant and warm friend of Parliament. Through his influence the Virginia Puritans came to the waters of the Chesapeake, insisting upon liberty of conscience. Soon after that the Maryland Assembly of 1649 met, says John Hammond (a friend of Lord Baltimore, in a pamphlet published in London in 1656), composed of Puritans, Church of England men, and a few Roman Catholics. It was this body of a majority of Protestants that passed the Toleration Act of which so much has been written. That act seems to have been an outgrowth of statutes passed by the British Parliament in 1645 and 1647, and adopted by the Maryland Legislature under the pressure of the strong Puritan influence then existing there. By that act, every believer in Jesus Christ and the Trinity, was allowed the free exercise of his or her religious opinions, but from this "toleration" Jews and Unitarians were alike excluded, and it was far from being a full "Toleration Act." No man was allowed to reproach another on account of his peculiar religious doctrines, excepting under the penalty of a fine to be paid to the person so insulted; and to Maryland the persecuted in other colonies now flocked to enjoy this broader freedom—Churchmen from New England, Puritans from Virginia, and Roman Catholics from all. That act is the pride and glory of Maryland's early legislation, yet it was not the first act of the kind (as has been often alleged) passed by a colonial assembly in America. In May, 1647—two years before—the General Assembly of Rhode Island adopted a code of laws which closed with the declaration that "all men may walk as their consciences persuaded them, without molestation—every one in the name of his God." This would include Jew or Mohammedan, Parsee or Pagan. It was absolute toleration.

For more than ten years republicanism prevailed in England. Lord Baltimore, whose politics and theology were easy-fitting garments, professed to be a republican when the king lost his head, but he had too lately been a decided royalist to secure the confidence of Parliament. They appointed a commission, of which Clayborne was a member, to govern Maryland. These commissioners entered upon their duties there with a high hand. They demanded a sight of Governor Stone's commission, and when he produced it, they snatched it from his hands, removed him and his subordinates from office, took possession of the records and abolished the authority of the proprietor of the province. A few months afterward they reinstated Governor Stone, put Kent and Polmer's islands into the possession of Clayborne, and so enabled the vigorous "outlaw" to trample over his enemy, Lord Baltimore.

When the Long Parliament was dissolved in 1653, Cromwell restored full power to Baltimore as proprietor. Stone proclaimed the movements of the commissioners to have been rebellious. He displaced all officers appointed by them, and in other ways acted very unwisely. The incensed commissioners returned to Maryland and compelled the governor to surrender his authority. Then they vested the government of the province in a board of ten commissioners.

Now the passions of the opposing political and religious parties were aroused into vehement action. The Protestants, who were still the majority in the General Assembly which convened in the fall of 1654, were imbued with the narrow bigotry of the early Puritans of Massachusetts, and, unmindful of the better principles of the Toleration Act of 1649, they wantonly disfranchised the Roman Catholics and members of the Church of England, by passing a law which declared that Papists and Churchmen were not entitled to the protection of the laws of Maryland. These zealots flogged and imprisoned Quakers; and their unworthy triumph was celebrated in a book published in London entitled "Babylon's Fall in Maryland."

When intelligence of these unrighteous proceedings reached London, Lord Baltimore obtained an audience with Cromwell, then Lord High Protector and real monarch of England. These eminent men met in the Council Chamber at Whitehall, in friendly conference. Cromwell in power was not like Cromwell fighting for power. He was tolerant. His Latin Secretary, the eminent John Milton (who was present at the interview), had assisted in making him so. When Baltimore courteously protested against the injustice of Puritan legislation in Maryland, the Protector said: "I would that all the sects, like the cedar and the myrtle and the oil-tree, should be planted in the wilderness together," and assured Lord Baltimore that he disapproved of the ungrateful decree. That assurance was followed by an order which Cromwell sent to the commissioners "not to busy themselves about religion, but to settle the civil government."

So encouraged, Lord Baltimore determined to vindicate the rights of his people. He upbraided Stone for his want of firmness, and ordered him to raise an army for the restoration of the authority of the proprietor. Stone, smarting under rebuke, acted vigorously. He raised a force, chiefly of Roman Catholics, seized the colonial records, resumed the office of governor, and inaugurated civil war. Skirmishes followed. Finally, a sharp battle was fought, early in April, 1655, near the site of Annapolis, in which Stone was defeated and made prisoner, and about fifty of his party were killed or wounded. The governor and others were tried for treason. His life was spared, but four of his colleagues were hanged.

For several months, anarchy reigned supreme in Maryland, when Lord Baltimore appointed Josias Fendall, a former insurgent, to be governor of the province. Suspected of favoring the Roman Catholics, the Protestant Assembly ordered his arrest as a disturber of the peace, and for two years longer there was bitter strife between the people and the agents of the proprietor. The latter finally made important popular concessions, and Fendall was permitted to act as the governor. By prudent conduct he secured the confidence of the people, and Lord Baltimore anticipated a lasting relief from trouble on account of his American possessions, when Cromwell died and there were disquieting presages of a change in the government of England. The people of Maryland did not wait upon movements at home, but boldly asserting their supreme authority, dissolved the proprietary portion of the General Assembly in the spring of 1660, and assumed the whole legislative power of the State. The popular representatives then gave Fendall a commission as governor.

Three months after this political revolution in Maryland, monarchy was restored in England, and the son of the beheaded sovereign ascended the throne as Charles the Second. This event was soon followed by the restoration of his proprietary authority to Lord Baltimore. Fendall was tried for and found guilty of treason, because he had accepted office from the "rebellious assembly." But Baltimore wisely proclaimed a general pardon for all political offenders, and for about thirty years afterward Maryland enjoyed comparative repose, while her neighbor, Virginia, was torn by civil war. Under the mild proprietary rule, the province prospered and the people were happy. Commerce flourished. The soil yielded rich rewards for labor. Industry was fostered by well-paid labor, and feminine hands found ample and profitable employment, as in peaceful Pennsylvania at the same time. A quaint writer of the period, discoursing on Pennsylvania, says in relation to the "price of women's labor:" "One reason why women's wages are so exorbitant is that they are not very numerous, which makes them stand upon high terms for their several services, and moreover, they are usually married before they are twenty years of age, and when once in that noose, are for the most part a little uneasie, and make their husbands so too, till they procure them a maid-servant to bear the burden of the work, as also, in some measure, to wait on them, too."

Emigrants came to Maryland from almost every part of Europe to enjoy the tolerant rule there; and the pleasant spectacle was seen of George Fox, the founder of the sect called "Friends," or "Quakers," preaching in the evening twilight on the shores of the Chesapeake to a multitude of people, comprising members of the Legislature and other distinguished men of the province, and a large group of Indian kings and chieftains, with their wives and children, led by their emperor. But the refusal of the Friends to perform military duty or take an oath, subjected them to fines and harsh imprisonments. This was a civil matter, and had nothing to do with their religious tenets.

When monarchy was restored, the people of Maryland were in full possession of the liberty founded upon popular sovereignty, and never parted with the precious treasure. The population of the province consisted of about ten thousand white people living together in comparative harmony, the fierceness of religious bigotry having been subdued by mutual concessions.

GEORGE FOX PREACHING IN MARYLAND.

Lord Baltimore died in 1675, after a rule in Maryland, with several interruptions, for forty-three years. He was crowned in his old age with the blessings and honors of a colony which he had planted in his youth. He had never trodden the soil of Maryland, but a grateful people cherished his memory as they would that of a beloved father known to them in person. The commercial capital of that State bears the name of his title. His son and successor, Charles, followed in the footsteps of his liberal father in fostering toleration and humanity; and he and his successors continued, with a few interruptions, to administer the government of the province until the storm of the revolution, which burst forth in 1775, swept away every vestige of proprietary and royal government in the English-American colonies. The title of Lord Baltimore became extinct in 1771, and the last of the family in England, of whom anything is known, was a prisoner for debt in the Queen's Bench prison in London, in 1860. In that, and the Fleet prison, he had then been confined, by the fiat of the barbarous law, twenty years.

Maryland, like the other colonies, was shaken by the revolution in England in 1688, and experienced deep sorrows for awhile. For several years before, the democratic ideas then rapidly spreading over the provinces, could not reconcile the rule of a lord proprietor with the principles of republicanism. Even so early as when Charles Calvert went to England after the death of his father, signs of political discontent were conspicuous in Maryland. In 1678, the General Assembly, influenced by the popular feeling, established the right of suffrage—casting of a vote for rulers—on a broad basis. When Charles returned in 1681, he annulled this act, and by an arbitrary ordinance restricted the right to freemen owning fifty acres of land or personal property of the value of forty pounds sterling. This produced great disquietude, and Ex-Governor Fendall planned an insurrection for the purpose of abolishing the proprietorship and establishing an independent Republican government. The king was induced to issue orders that all offices of government in Maryland should be filled by Protestants alone; and so, again, the Roman Catholics were deprived of their political rights.

In 1684, Lord Baltimore again went to England, leaving the government of his province in charge of several deputies under the nominal governorship of his infant son. There he found his rights in great peril; but before the matter was brought to a direct issue by the operation of a writ of *quo warranto*, King James was driven from the throne and Protestant William and Mary ascended it. Lord Baltimore immediately acquiesced in the political change. Because his instructions to his deputies to proclaim the new monarchs were delayed in their transmission, he was charged with hesitancy; and a restless spirit named Coode, an associate of Fendall in his insurrectionary movements—a man of loose morals and blasphemous speech—excited the people by the cry of "a Popish plot!" He circulated the false story that the local magistrates in Maryland, and the Roman Catholics there, had engaged with the Indians in a plot for the destruction of the Protestants in the province. An actual league at that time between the French and the Jesuit missionaries with the savages on the New England frontiers for the destruction of the English colonies in the East gave the coloring of truth to the story, which created great excitement. The old feud burned intensely. The Protestants formed an armed association. Led by Coode, they marched to the Maryland capital, took possession of the records and assumed the functions of a provisional government, in May, 1689. They met in convention in August following, when they prepared and sent to the new sovereigns a report of their proceedings and a series of absurd and false accusations against Lord Baltimore. In conclusion, they requested the monarchs to depose Lord Baltimore by making Maryland a royal province and taking it under the protection of the crown.

The sovereigns listened favorably to the representations of the convention and complied with their requests. Coode was ordered to administer the government in the name of the king, and so the people were punished for their folly in elevating him to leadership. He ruled with the spirit of a petty tyrant, until the people of every religious and political creed were heartily disgusted with him. He was displaced in 1692, when the king sent Sir Lionel Copley to be governor of Maryland.

The new governor arrived in the spring of that year and summoned a General Assembly to meet at St. Mary's in May. New laws were instituted. Religious toleration was abolished. The Church of England was made the state church for Maryland, to be supported by a tax on the whole people. "Thus," says McMahon, "was introduced, for the first time in Maryland, a church establishment sustained by law and fed by general taxation. Other laws oppressive in their bearings upon those opposed in religious views to the dominant party were enacted, some of which remained in force until the glorious emancipation day in the summer of 1776 gave freedom to our nation.

Partly because the whole people of Maryland might be better accommodated, but largely for the purpose of punishing the adherents of Lord Baltimore, who constituted a greater portion of the population of St. Mary's, the seat of government was moved from there to Anne Arundel town, on the shore of the Chesapeake, early in 1694, and there a General Assembly was convened in February. The following year the name of the place was changed by authority to Annapolis, and the naval station of the province was established there. Annapolis has continued to be the capital of Maryland until now. St. Mary's, dependent for its existence upon its being the capital of the province, speedily sunk into insignificance and fell into ruins.

Lord Baltimore never recovered his proprietary rights. Neither did he return to America, but died in England in 1714, at the age of eighty-five years. He was succeeded by his son Benedict Leonard Calvert. That son had abandoned the faith of his father and died in the spring of 1715, when his title to the province devolved upon his infant son Charles, who, with his brothers and sisters, had been educated as Protestants.

Charles Calvert Lord Baltimore and William Penn were cotemporaries, and were equally conspicuous for their beneficent disposition. They are regarded as the best of all the proprietaries who owned chartered domains in America. This sentiment is shadowed in the following lines by a minor English poet:

> "Laws formed to harmonize contrarious creeds,
> And heal the wounds through which a nation bleeds;
> Laws mild, impartial, tolerant and fixed,
> A bond of union for a people mixed;
> Such as good Calvert framed for Baltimore,
> And Penn the Numa of th' Atlantic shore."

WILLIAM PENN.

There being no longer any objection to the Baltimore family on account of religion, the British government restored to the young scion of that noble house, all the rights of proprietaryship in 1715. This restoration did not affect the republican sentiment of a great majority of the people of the province, except to stimulate its growth. The first legislature which met, after the Restoration, passed a body of laws based upon the broadest principles of civil and religious liberty, some of which yet remain in force in Maryland. There was a single blot on the legislation of that Assembly.

They introduced into Maryland all of the odious test-oaths and disabilities which were enforced in England against the consciences of men.

For almost forty years after the Restoration the colony enjoyed remarkable tranquillity. Only the natural disputes that arose between a lord proprietor and a people of strong republican tendencies in thought and action, and the flutter of excitement caused by the furnishing of men to aid the northern colonies in their struggles with the common foe on the frontiers, disturbed the general repose.

Charles Lord Baltimore died in 1751, after ruling the province in person and by deputies about thirty-six years. During that period the growth of the province in wealth and population was remarkable. The inhabitants then numbered more than one hundred and thirty-five thousand souls, of whom about forty thousand were black men and women, who were mostly slaves. The several provinces were then agitated by the encroachments of the French upon the territory of the Ohio and Mississippi valleys, toward which English adventurers were casting longing eyes. In the French and Indian war that broke out in 1755, Maryland became involved, at first, simply in the maintenance of an attitude of self-defence and a generous assistant of its sister colonies. Its legislature for awhile persistently stood aloof from aggressive warfare in spite of the commands of the king and the entreaties of Virginia. They consented to send delegates to the colonial convention which assembled at Albany in 1754, but the delegates offended their constituents by agreeing to a plan of union submitted by Dr. Franklin, by which the several colonies might act with national power in the prosecution of measures of defence against the common enemy. The Marylanders, ever jealous of their colonial rights and proud of their separate independence as a colony, and their inherent sovereignty, had always opposed every attempt to effect a fusion of the colonies into one government. When the plan agreed upon at Albany was submitted to the General Assembly of Maryland, it was unanimously disapproved as "tending to the destruction of the rights and liberties of his majesty's subjects in the province."

The time soon arrived when the Marylanders could no longer stand in the attitude of separatist and avoid taking an active aggressive part in the war, for its surges were beating upon the borders of their province. The Indians were plundering their frontier. The General Assembly, aroused by immediate danger, voted men and money for a vigorous prosecution of the war; and the command of all the forces engaged against the French on the Ohio was given, by a royal commission, to Governor Sharpe, of Maryland. The people of that province were forced by circumstances to consent to a union which was finally cemented by the blood of the Revolution.

CHAPTER XII.

THE CONNECTICUT COLONIES—AN ABSURD RUMOR ABOUT THE DUTCH—CHARTER FOR CONNECTICUT OBTAINED—TYRANNY OF GOVERNOR ANDROS—HIS ATTEMPT TO SEIZE THE CHARTER—THE CHARTER OAK—FREEDOM ENJOYED IN RHODE ISLAND—SOCIETY THERE—NEW CHARTER FOR RHODE ISLAND OBTAINED—ITS DURATION—ANDROS IN RHODE ISLAND—NEW JERSEY CONSIDERED—ITS SOCIAL AND POLITICAL CONDITION—THE PROVINCE DIVIDED—THE QUAKERS SETTLE THERE—ANDROS IN NEW JERSEY—IT BECOMES A ROYAL PROVINCE.

THE Connecticut colonists worked in harmony as brethren of the same nation and creed until their fusion into one commonwealth in 1665. They managed their private and public affairs prudently and were prosperous. Troubles with the Dutch, concerning territorial boundaries, were amicably settled with Stuyvesant when he visited Hartford in 1650; but the mutterings of dissatisfaction which fell from the lips of the neighboring Indian tribes gave them some disquietude, and made them heartily approve and join the New England Confederacy formed in 1643. The following year the little independent colony at Saybrook, at the mouth of the Connecticut River, which had been formed in 1639, was annexed to that of Connecticut at Hartford, and was the precursor of the final union of the three colonies about twenty years afterwards.

The repose of the colonists was broken in 1653, by a war between England and Holland. An alarming rumor had spread over New England that Ninigret, an "old, crafty and wily sachem" of the allied Niantics and Narragansets, who had spent part of a winter at New Amsterdam, had made a league with Stuyvesant for the destruction of the New England colonies. The majority of the commissioners of the New England Confederacy believed the absurd story, and decided to make war on the Dutch. The Connecticut people were specially eager for war, for they were more immediately exposed to the effects of such a plot than the other colonists. But Massachusetts refused to furnish men and arms for an aggressive war, before an investigation of the matter. Messengers were sent to Ninigret and his associate sachems for the latter purpose. These were questioned separately, and all concurred in the solemn assurance that they had no knowledge of such a plot. Ninigret, who went to New Amsterdam for medical treatment, said with emphasis, in his denial, "I found no such entertainment from the Dutch governor, when I was there, as to give me any encouragement to stir me up to such a league against the English, my friends. It was winter time, and I stood a great part of a winter day knocking at the governor's door, and he would neither open it, nor suffer others to open it, to let me in. I was not wont to find such carriage from the English, my friends."

The story of the Dutch-Indian plot appears to have been a pure invention of Uncas, the crafty sachem of the Mohegans, who was a foe of Ninigret, and was extremely jealous of the supposed friendship between that sachem and the English. It caused the frightened Connecticut colonists, when Massachusetts refused to join them in war upon the Dutch, to ask Cromwell for aid. The Protector sent four ships-of-war, but before their arrival a treaty of peace had ended the war between England and Holland, and blood and treasure were saved in America.

NINIGRET AT THE DOOR.

On the restoration of monarchy in England, in 1660, the Connecticut colonists had fears regarding their future. Their sturdy republicanism and independent action in the past might be mortally offensive to the new monarch. The General Assembly of Connecticut, therefore, resolved to make a formal acknowledgment of their allegiance to the crown and ask the king for a charter. A petition was accordingly framed and signed in May, 1651, and Governor John Winthrop bore it to England. He was a son of Winthrop of Massachusetts, and was a man of rare attainments and courtly manners, and then about forty-five years of age. He obtained an interview with the king, and was received with coolness. His name and the people over whom he was the chosen ruler were associated with radical republicanism, and the king received the prayer of the petitioners with disfavor. Winthrop left the royal presence, disappointed but not disheartened, and sought and obtained another interview.

The "merrie monarch" was now in more genial mood. He chatted freely with Winthrop about America—its soil, productions, the Indians and the settlers; yet he hesitated to promise a charter. Winthrop, it is said, finally drew from his pocket a gold ring of great value, which the king's father had given to the governor's grandfather, and presented it to his majesty with a request that he would accept it as a memorial of the unfortunate monarch, and a token of Winthrop's esteem for, and loyalty to King Charles, before whom he stood as a faithful and loving subject. The king's heart was touched. Turning to Lord Clarendon, who was present, the monarch said: "Do you advise me to grant a charter to this good gentleman and his people?" "I do, Sire," responded Clarendon. "It shall be done," said Charles, and he dismissed Winthrop with a hearty shake of his hand and a royal blessing.

The governor left Whitehall with a light heart. A charter was issued on the first of May, 1652. It confirmed the popular constitution of the colony, and contained more liberal provisions than any yet issued by royal hands. It defined the boundaries so as to include the New Haven colony and a part of Rhode Island on the East, and westward to the Pacific Ocean. The New Haven colony reluctantly gave its consent to the union, in 1665, and the boundary between Connecticut and Rhode Island remained a subject of dispute for more than sixty years. That old charter, engrossed on parchment, is among the archives in the Connecticut State Department. It bears the miniature portrait of Charles the Second, drawn in India ink by Samuel Cooper, it is supposed, who was an eminent London miniature painter of the time.

During King Philip's war, the colonists of Connecticut did not suffer much from hostile Indians, excepting some remote settlers high up the Connecticut River. They furnished their full measure of men and supplies, and their soldiers bore a conspicuous part in that contest between the races for supremacy. But while they were freed from dangers and distress of war with the Indians, they were disturbed by the petty tyranny of Governor Andros, whose advent in New England and New York has been noticed.

Seated at New York, Andros claimed jurisdiction as far east as the Connecticut River. To the mouth of that stream he went, with a small naval force, in the summer of 1675, to assert his authority. Captain Bull, the commander of a small fort at Saybrook, permitted him to land; but when the governor began to read his commission, Bull ordered him to be silent.

Andros was compelled to yield to the commander's bold spirit and his superior military power, and in a towering passion he returned to New York, flinging curses and threats behind him at the people of Connecticut in general, and Captain Bull in particular.

For more than a dozen years after this flare-up of ambition and passion, nothing materially disturbed the public repose of Connecticut. Then a most exciting scene occurred at Hartford, in the result of which the liberties of the colony were involved. Andros again appeared as a usurper of authority—the willing instrument of his master King James the Second, who had determined to hold absolute rule over all New England.

CHARLES THE SECOND.

On his arrival in New York, as we have seen, Andros demanded a surrender of all the colonial charters into his hands. The authorities of all the colonies complied, excepting those of Connecticut. The latter steadily refused to yield their charter voluntarily, for it was the guardian of their political rights. To subdue their stubbornness, the viceroy proceeded to Hartford with sixty armed men, to demand the surrender of the charter in person. On his arrival there on the 31st of October (O. S.), 1687, he found the General Assembly in session in the meeting-house. The members received him with the courtesy due to his rank. Before that body, with armed men at his back, he demanded a formal surrender of the precious document into his own hands.

It was now near sunset. A subject of some importance was under debate, and the discussion was purposely continued until some time after the candles were lighted. Then the charter, contained in a long mahogany box, was brought in and laid upon the table. A preconcerted plan to save it from the grasp of the usurper was now instantly executed. As Andros put forth his hand to take the charter, the candles were all snuffed out and the document was snatched by Captain Wadsworth, whose train-bands were near to protect the Assembly from any violence which the royal soldiers might offer. Wadsworth bore away the charter, the crowd opening as he passed out, and closing behind him, and hid it in the hollow of a venerable oak tree on the outskirts of the village. When the candles were re-lighted, the members were seated in perfect order, but the charter could not be found.* This was the same Captain Wadsworth who afterward silenced Governor Fletcher, as related on page 362.

So, again, the tyrannical purposes of Andros were foiled in Connecticut. Wisely restraining his passion at that time, he assumed the control of the government; declared the charter annulled, and Secretary Allyn wrote the word FINIS after the last record of the Journal of the Assembly. From that time until he was expelled from the country in 1689, he governed Connecticut as an autocrat—an absolute sovereign. Then the charter was brought out from its place of concealment, in May, 1689; a popular Assem-

* This is the form of the story as it has appeared in our histories. In April, 1775, Mr. Hoadley, keeper of the State records of Connecticut, called my attention to the manuscript journals of the Colonial Assembly at this period. I there found reasons for giving a modified version of the story. In the Journal for June 15, 1687, is the following entry:

"Sundry of the Court desiring that the Patent or Charter might be brought into the Court, the secretary sent for it, and informed the governor and Court that he had the charter, and shewed it to the Court, and the governor bid him put it into the box again, and lay it on the table, and leave the key in the box, which he did forthwith."

This was the original charter granted by Charles the Second to Governor Winthrop, and sent over in a neat mahogany box; and the above is the whole of the entry on the subject made at that time. The records reveal the fact that there was a duplicate of the charter written on parchment when Andros came, and seem to warrant the following explanatory suggestions concerning that mysterious act of the General Court of the colony:

Andros was doubtless expected to appear at Hartford at any time to demand the charter, and it was determined to save it if possible. The box was left on the table, with the key in it, for somebody to take the charter out without the knowledge or apparent connivance of the Connecticut authorities. It was done by somebody, who caused a duplicate of the charter to be made on parchment, and the original to be concealed in the hollow of the famous oak tree, several months before the arrival of the viceroy. The duplicate was placed in the mahogany box of the original; and it was that duplicate that was placed on the table, and carried away in the dark by Captain Wadsworth. So, if Andros had secured the box, he would not have secured the original charter, but a worthless duplicate. The original was lying in safety in the then venerable oak.

The fact that it was the *duplicate* that Wadsworth carried away at that time is attested by the same colonial records. There is an entry in the Journal in 1715, stating that the sum of "twenty shillings" was granted to Captain Wadsworth "out of the Colonial treasury" as a token of their grateful remembrance of "such faithful and good service" in "securing the duplicate charter of the colony in a very troublesome season." It is probable that Captain Wadsworth took the charter from the box, had a duplicate made of it, and put the original in the hollow oak, from which it was taken the next year. According to the colonial records, he had the duplicate in his possession in 1698.

bly was convened; Robert Treat was chosen governor, and Connecticut again assumed the position of an independent colony. The tree in which the document was hidden was ever afterward known as the "Charter Oak." It remained vigorous, bearing fruit every year until a little after midnight in August, 1856, when it was prostrated by a heavy storm of wind. It stood in a vacant lot on the south side of Charter street, a few rods from Main street, in the city of Hartford.

About six years after Andros was outgeneraled at Hartford, his successor

HIDING THE ORIGINAL CHARTER IN THE OAK.

in office, Benjamin Fletcher, was foiled, at the same place, in his attempts to exercise control over the militia of Connecticut. The exciting scene has been recorded in the Fifth Chapter of the Third Book. From that time, during the space of about three-fourths of a century, the history of Connecticut is intimately woven with that of the other colonies planted in America by English people. The inhabitants of Connecticut, by prudent habits and good government, steadily increased in numbers and wealth. They went hand in hand with those of other colonies in measures for the promotion of the welfare of all; and when, in the fullness of time, the provinces were ripe for union, rebellion and independence, the people of Connecticut were foremost in their eagerness to assert their rights as a free people.

We have seen that Rhode Island was favored with a charter from Parliament in 1644. Yet with this guaranty of strength, it was not free from the dangers which excessive liberty often creates. But Rhode Island passed that fiery ordeal almost unscathed. In the plenitude of freedom there enjoyed, each individual was, in a degree, "a law unto himself." In religion and politics the people were absolutely free. The General Assembly, in a code of laws adopted in 1647, declared, as we have observed, that "all men might walk as their consciences permitted them—every one in the name of his God." Almost every religious belief might have been encountered there; "so that if a man lost his religious opinions, he might have been sure to find them in some village in Rhode Island." Society was in a continual ferment, but the agitation was healthful. Town meetings, and other like gatherings of the people, were stormy; and the disputes of rivals were sometimes fierce, but never brutal. There was a remarkable propriety of conduct on all occasions; and out of the political agitations came to the surface the best men in the colony to administer public affairs. Throughout the whole community, so independent in thought and action, appeared a healthier religious sentiment than in Massachusetts, where the people were straight-laced by creeds and dogmas, and were constantly tempted to be hypocrites. There was a high-toned morality, based upon that religious sentiment, which preserved society from many dangers. "Our popularitie," says one of their records, "shall not, as some conjecture it will, prove an anarchie, and so a common tirannie; for we are exceeding desirous to preserve every man safe in his person, name, and estate."

A little danger menaced the commonwealth when, in 1651, the Executive Council of State in England granted to William Coddington a commission for governing the islands within the limits of the Rhode Island charter. This threatened a dismemberment of the little empire and its absorption by neighboring colonies. The people were alarmed. Roger Williams and John Clarke hastened to England, and with the assistance of Sir Henry Vane, the "sheet-anchor of Rhode Island"—the "noble and true friend to an outcast and despised people"—the commission was recalled and the charter given by Parliament was confirmed. That was in October, 1652. This act put an end to the persevering efforts of Massachusetts to absorb the little commonwealth.

While Roger Williams was in England, he partly supported himself by teaching. He then enjoyed the intimate friendship of Cromwell, Hampden, Milton, Sir Henry Vane, and other distinguished men. On his return, he was again hailed with joy as a benefactor; and in the autumn of 1654, he was chosen president of the colony. The following year, Cromwell, as ruler of England, confirmed the charter given by Parliament, and the colony prospered in peace. Religious disputes agitated the people; but reason, left free to combat error, allowed no persecution.

On the restoration of monarchy in 1660, the inhabitants of Rhode Island sent to Charles an address, in which they declared their loyalty and begged his protection. This was followed by a petition for a new charter. The prayer was granted; and in July, 1663, the king issued a patent highly democratic in its general features, and similar, in every respect, to the one granted to Connecticut. Benedict Arnold was chosen the first governor under the royal charter, and it continued to be the supreme law of the land for the period of about one hundred and eighty years. In 1842, the people of Rhode Island adopted a constitution, and the power of the old royal charter ceased.

JOHN MILTON.

When, in 1687, Andros demanded the surrender of the colonial charters, the inhabitants of Rhode Island instantly yielded. When the order for the seizure of these charters was first made known, the Assembly of Rhode Island had sent a most loyal address to the king, saying: "We humbly prostrate ourselves, our privileges, our all, at the gracious feet of your majesty, with an entire resolution to serve you with faithful hearts." Andros, therefore, found no opposition in the little colony. Within a month after his arrival at Boston, he proceeded to Rhode Island, where he was graciously received. He formally dissolved the Assembly; broke the seal of the colony, which bore the figure of an anchor and the word Hope; admitted five of the inhabitants into his legislative council, and assumed the functions of governor. But he did not take away the parchment on which the charter was written.

The people of Rhode Island were restive under the petty tyranny of

Andros; and when they heard of the imprisonment of the despot at Boston, in the spring of 1689, they assembled at Newport, resumed popular government under the old charter, and began a new and independent political career. From that time until the enforced union of the colonies for mutual defence at the breaking out of the French and Indian war, the inhabitants of Rhode Island always bore their fair share in defensive efforts, especially when the hostile savages hung along the frontiers of New England and New York like a dark and ill-omened cloud. The history of that commonwealth is identified with that of all New England, from the beginning of King William's war soon after the expulsion of Andros.

Let us now turn again to a consideration of the history of New Jersey as a *colony*. We have traced its progress from the period of its first settlements to that of its permanent political organization as a British colony, with a governor and council, and when a cluster of four houses at Elizabethtown were dignified with the title of a colonial capital. Agents were sent to New England to invite settlers, and a company from New Haven were soon seated on the banks of the Passaic. Others followed; and when, in 1668, the first legislative assembly met at Elizabethtown, it was largely made up of representatives of New England Puritanism. The fertility of the soil; the salubrity of the climate; the exemption from fear of Indian hostilities and other manifest advantages, caused a rapid increase in the population and prosperity of the province; and nothing disturbed the general serenity of society there until the year 1670, when specified quit-rents of a half-penny for each acre of land was demanded. The people murmured. Some of them had purchased their land of the Indians before the proprietary government was established, and refused to pay the rent, not on account of its amount, but because it was an unjust tax levied without their consent.

Disputes concerning rents continued almost two years, and the province was cast into confusion. The whole people combined in resistance to the payment of the tax. There was actual rebellion; and in May, 1672, the disaffected colonists sent deputies to a popular Assembly which met at Elizabethtown. That body chose a weak and dissolute illegitimate son of one of the proprietors to be their governor, and compelled Philip Carteret, the proprietary ruler, to vacate his chair and leave the province. He went to England for more authority; and while the proprietors were making preparations to recover the province by force of arms, New Jersey and all the rest of the territory in America claimed by the Duke of York fell into the hands of the Dutch, with whom the English were then at war. That was in August, 1673.

When, fifteen months afterward, these territories were restored to the

English, and the duke received a new charter from his brother the king, he appointed Andros governor of the whole domain. Carteret complained, and his authority was partly restored ; but sufficient was reserved to give Andros a pretext for asserting his authority and annoying the proprietors and the people.

Lord Berkeley was now so disgusted by the losses and annoyances which he had endured in connection with his ownership of New Jersey, that he sold his interest in the province to John Fenwick and Edward Byllinge, English Friends or Quakers, for the sum of five thousand dollars. The tract sold to these Friends was in the western part of the province. With some emigrants, mostly of the Society of Friends, Fenwick sailed for his new possessions. They settled at a spot not far from the Delaware River, which they named Salem, on account of the peaceful aspect of the country and the surrounding Indians. There, with the peculiar gravity of the sect, Fenwick and his two daughters, thirteen men (most of them heads of families) and one woman, the wife of one of the emigrants, sat in silent worship according to their custom, under the shadow of a great tree, with covered heads and quiet bodies, on the ensuing "First Day" after their arrival. Then they built log cabins for shelter, and so began a new life in the wilds of New Jersey.

Byllinge was the principal proprietor, but soon after the departure of Fenwick, heavy losses in trade made him a bankrupt, and his interest in New Jersey was first assigned to William Penn and others for the benefit of his creditors, and was afterward sold to them. These purchasers and others who became associated with them, unwilling to maintain a political union with other parties, bargained with Carteret for a division of the province. This was done in July, 1676. Carteret retained the eastern part of the province, and the new purchasers held the western part. From that time until they were united and became a royal province in 1702, these divisions were known as *East* and *West Jersey*. From this circumstance, the expression "The Jerseys," heard in our day, was derived.

The proprietors of West Jersey gave to the settlers, who were mostly Friends at first, a remarkably liberal constitution of government, entitled "The concessions and agreements of the proprietors, freeholders, and inhabitants of the province of West New Jersey in America." The following year (1677) more than four hundred Friends came from England and settled below the Raritan. Andros required them to acknowledge his authority as the representative of the Duke of York. They refused, and the matter was referred to the eminent crown-lawyer and oriental scholar, Sir William Jones, for adjudication. Sir William decided against the claims of the duke, who submitted to the decision, released both provinces from allegiance to him, and the Jerseys became independent of foreign control. The first popular Assembly in West Jersey met at Salem in November, 1681, and adopted a code of laws for the government of the people. One of these laws provided that in all criminal cases, excepting treason, murder and theft, the aggrieved party should have power to pardon the offender.

Carteret died late in 1679. The trustees of his American estates offered East Jersey for sale. It was bought in 1682, by William Penn and others, among them the Earl of Perth, the friend of Robert Barclay, whom the proprietors appointed governor of the domain for life. Barclay was an eminent young Friend, whose writings have ever been held in high estimation by his sect, especially his "Apology for the true Christian Divinity, as the same is held forth and practised by the people called in scorn Quakers," and his "Treatise on Christian Discipline." The purchase was made, not in the interest of religion or liberty, but as a land speculation. Barclay governed the province by deputies until his death in 1690, when he was only forty-two years of age.

QUEEN ANNE.

A large number of Friends went from England and Scotland to East Jersey, and other immigrants flocked in from Long Island, to find repose and peace. They soon found that repose was not to be enjoyed by lovers of freedom anywhere under royal rule. They were also impressed with the significance of the injunction: "Put not your trust in princes," for James the *king* failed to keep the promises of James the *duke*, and they were compelled to submit to the tyranny of Andros. When that detested viceroy was driven from the country in 1689, the Jerseys were left without a regular civil government, and so they remained several years.

Wearied with contentions with the people of the provinces and with the government in England, and annoyed by losses in unprofitable speculations, the proprietors of the Jerseys surrendered them to the crown in 1702, when Queen Anne was the reigning British monarch. The government of that domain was then confided to Sir Edward Hyde (Lord Cornbury), whose instructions constituted the supreme law of the land. He was then governor of New York, and possessed almost absolute legislative and executive control within the jurisdiction of his authority. In New Jersey the people had no voice in the judiciary or the making and executing of laws other than recommendatory. Liberty of conscience was granted to all but Roman Catholics, but the bigoted governor always showed conspicuous favors to the members of the Church of England. Under the rule of that dishonest libertine, the people of New Jersey were slaves. Printing was prohibited in the province except by royal permission, and the traffic in negro slaves was specially encouraged.

The province of New Jersey remained a dependency of New York, with a distinct legislative assembly of its own, until the year 1738, when, through the efforts of Lewis Morris, its chief justice, it was made an independent colony, and so continued until the war for independence. Mr. Morris was commissioned the first governor after the province had gained its freedom from New York. He was the son of an officer in Cromwell's army who, at about the year 1672, settled on a farm of three thousand acres on the Harlem River, New York, which was named Morrisania.

The last of the royal governors of New Jersey was William Franklin, son of Dr. Benjamin Franklin, who was appointed, in 1763, and closed his official career in the summer of 1776, when he was deposed by the Continental Congress, and sent under guard to Connecticut, where he was released on parole and sailed for England. He died there in 1813.

CHAPTER XIII.

WILLIAM PENN IN PENNSYLVANIA—GROWTH OF THAT PROVINCE—PENN GOES TO ENGLAND—HIS TROUBLES THERE—HE RETURNS TO AMERICA—GIVES A THIRD AND MORE LIBERAL CHARTER TO THE COLONISTS—HIS DEATH, AND THE FATE OF THE PROVINCE—ATTEMPTS TO FORCE THE "FUNDAMENTAL CONSTITUTIONS" ON THE CAROLINAS—EFFECTS OF NAVIGATION LAWS —REBELLION IN NORTH CAROLINA—ARCHDALE MADE GOVERNOR OF BOTH CAROLINAS—SOCIAL CONDITION OF NORTH CAROLINA—SETTLEMENTS AND POLITICAL TROUBLES IN SOUTH CAROLINA—GROWTH OF THE COLONY—THE HUGUENOTS AND THEIR HISTORY—REBELLION IN SOUTH CAROLINA—THE GOOD DEEDS OF JOHN ARCHDALE.

WHEN William Penn, with the help of Thomas Holme, the surveyor, laid out the city of Philadelphia at the close of 1682, he caused the boundaries of the streets to be marked on the trunks of the chestnut, walnut, locust, spruce, pine and other forest trees that covered the land. Several streets of that city yet bear the names of those trees, then given to them. The growth of the new town was rapid. Within a year after the surveyor had finished his task, almost a hundred houses were erected there, and the Indians came daily with the spoils of the forest as presents for "Father Penn," as they delighted to call the proprietor.

In March following, the new city was honored by the gathering there of the second Assembly of the province, when Penn offered to the people, through their representatives, a new charter. It was so liberal in all its provisions that when the question, "Shall we accept the new constitution or adhere to the old one?" came up in that body, there was a solid vote in favor of the new one. It constituted a representative republican government, with free religious toleration and having justice for its foundation; and the proprietor, unlike those of other provinces, surrendered to the people his chartered rights in the appointment of officers. From the beginning, the happiness and prosperity of his people appeared to be uppermost in the heart and mind of William Penn. It was this happy relation between the proprietor and the people, and security against Indian raids, that made Pennsylvania far outstrip her sister colonies in rapidity of settlement and permanent prosperity.

Late in 1682, a small house was erected on the site of Philadelphia for the use of Penn. It survived until our day, occupying a place in Letitia

Court, between Front and Second streets. There he assisted in fashioning those excellent laws which gave a high character to Pennsylvania from the beginning. Among other wise enactments, it was decreed that, to prevent lawsuits, three arbitrators, to be called peace-makers, should be appointed by the county courts, to hear and determine small differences between man and man; that children should be taught some useful trade; that factors wronging their employees should make satisfaction, and one-third over; that all causes for irreligion and vulgarity should be repressed; and that no man should be molested for his religious opinions. They also decreed that the days of the week and the months of the year "shall be called as in Scripture, and not by heathen names (as are vulgarly used), as y[e] First, Second and Third dais of y[e] week, and First, Second and Third months of y[e] year, beginning with y[e] day called Sunday, and y[e] month called March," so beginning the year, as of old, with the first spring month. At about the same time Pennsylvania was divided into three counties—Bucks, Chester and Philadelphia; and the annexed territory was also divided into three counties—New Castle, Kent and Sussex—known for a long time afterward as the "Three Lower Counties on the Delaware."

In the summer of 1684, Penn returned to England. He left the government of the province, during his absence, in the care of five members of the council and Thomas Lloyd as president, who held the Great Seal. His mission in America had been one of solid triumph over the hoary prejudices of feudalism and the selfish instincts of man. His wise and beneficent conduct had given wings to a report that William Penn had opened, in a beautiful land beyond the ocean, an asylum to the good and oppressed of every nation and creed. These and others came from Scandinavia, the borders of the Rhine, and from England, Wales, Scotland and Ireland, to plant quiet homes in the dominions of the "Quaker King." His "City of Brotherly Love" had, in the course of two years, grown more rapidly than had the city of New York in almost half a century. At the close of the year following his departure for England, it contained six hundred houses; schools were established, and William Bradford, who had landed where Philadelphia was afterward laid out, had set up a printing-press there. His "Almanack for the Year of the Christian's Account, 1687," was printed there on a broadside or single sheet, with twelve compartments, the year beginning with March. Looking upon the result of his work, Penn, with righteous exultation, wrote to Lord Halifax: "I must, without vanity, say I have led the greatest colony into America that ever any man did upon private credit, and the most prosperous beginnings that ever were in it are to be found among us." Penn bade the colonists farewell, with the most cheering forebodings for the future, saying: "My love and my life are to and with you, and no water can quench it, nor distance bring it to an end. I have been with you, cared over you, and served you with unfeigned love; and you are beloved of me and dear to me beyond utterance. I bless you in the name and power of the Lord, and may God bless you with his righteousness, peace and plenty all the land over." . . . . "And thou, Philadelphia, the virgin settlement of this province, my soul prays to God for thee, that thou mayest stand in the day of trial, and that thy children may be blessed." The blessings of the whole people rested upon the good man, when, on a bright day in August, the vessel that bore him to England weighed anchor at near the foot of Chestnut street.

Four months after Penn's return to England, Charles the Second died, and his brother James ascended the throne. Then began a period of great theological and political excitement in England, in the perils of which Penn became involved. He and the new king had long been personal friends; and through Penn's influence, twelve hundred persecuted Friends were released from prison, in 1686. When it was seen that James was under the powerful influence of the Jesuits, his Quaker friend was suspected of being one of them; and after the revolution that drove James from the throne, he was arrested three times, on a false charge of treason, and as often acquitted. The last time was in 1690. Meanwhile there had been great political and theological commotions in Pennsylvania, and in April, 1691, the Three Lower Counties on the Delaware, offended at the action of the council at Philadelphia, withdrew from the Union, and Penn yielded to the secessionists so far as to appoint a separate deputy governor over them.

In consequence of representations which came from Pennsylvania, the monarchs William and Mary deprived Penn of his rights as governor of his province, in 1692, and the control of the domain was placed in the hands of Governor Fletcher, of New York, who, in the spring of 1693, reunited the Delaware counties to the parent province. Fletcher appeared at the head of the council at Philadelphia on Monday, the 15th of May, with William Markham, Penn's deputy, as lieutenant-governor.

Powerful friends interceded with King William for the restoration of Penn's rights. He was called before the Privy Council to answer certain accusations, when his innocence was proven. A few months afterward his rights were all restored. That was in the summer of 1694. His fortune had been wasted, and he lingered in England, under the pressure of comparative poverty, until 1699, when, with his daughter, and his second wife, Hannah Callowhill, he sailed to Philadelphia. Meanwhile his colony under his old deputy, William Markham, had asserted their right to self-government, and made laws for themselves. Penn found them prosperous, but clamorous for political privileges guaranteed to them by law. Regarding their demands as reasonable, he gave them a new constitution or frame of government, in November, 1701, more liberal in its concessions than former ones, and perfectly satisfactory to all. Finding the people of the "Territories," or Three Lower Counties, restive under the forced union with Pennsylvania, he made provision for their permanent separation in legislation, in 1702; and the first independent legislature in Delaware was assembled at New Castle in 1703.

JOHN WINTHROP. WILLIAM III. JOHN LOCKE. EDWARD WINSLOW.

Although Pennsylvania and Delaware ever afterward continued to have separate legislatures, they were under the same governor until the Revolution in 1776.

While Penn was in America, tidings came that measures were pending before the Privy Council, for bringing all of the proprietary governments under the crown. Penn had come to Philadelphia to live and die there; and had built a fine brick house to reside in, which stood on the corner of

Second street and Norris alley, until a few years ago. But the news from England determined him to return to his native country to defend his rights. He did so late in 1701, and succeeded. He never returned to America. Harassed and wearied by business connected with his province, he was making arrangements in 1712 to sell it for sixty thousand dollars, when he was prostrated by paralysis. He survived the first shock six years, when he died, leaving his estates in America to his three sons. His family governed Pennsylvania, as proprietors, until the Revolution made it an independent State in 1776. Meanwhile the province had sustained its share of the burden of mutual defence with its sister colonies during the troubles with the French and Indians.

Let us now return to a consideration of the colonial history of the Carolinas from the formation of the "Fundamental Constitutions" by Locke and Cooper (afterward Lord Shaftesbury) for the government of the colonists of those regions, until the period of the old war for independence.

We have observed that the scheme for a splendid government was completed in 1669. The "constitutions" were signed in March, 1670, and were highly lauded in England as forming the wisest scheme for human government ever devised. Monk, duke of Albemarle, was created Palatine or viceroy for the new empire, who was to display the state parade of his office, with landgraves, barons, lords of manor, caciques, and courts of admiralty and heraldry, among the scattered settlers in the pine forests living in log-cabins with the Indians. The idea seems too ludicrous to have been seriously entertained. Yet it was entertained; and, so far as the proprietors were concerned, this splendid government was established. But the simple settlers had something to say; and when the governor of the Northern or Albemarle county colony attempted to introduce the new government, they said, "No," with peculiar emphasis, as the question was forced upon them, "Will you accept it?" They had a form of government of their own far better adapted to their social circumstances than the one sent from England, and they resolved to adhere to it.

The attempts to enforce obedience to the new form of government; the oppressive taxation imposed upon the people, and especially the commercial restrictions authorized by the English navigation laws, produced wide-spread discontent. This was fostered by refugees from Virginia, who had been implicated in "Bacon's Rebellion," and who sought personal safety among the people below the Roanoke. These refugees scattered broadcast over a generous soil the germinal ideas of popular freedom; and successful oppression was made difficult, if not impossible.

The whole State of North Carolina did not, at that time, contain quite four thousand inhabitants. They carried on a feeble trade in tobacco, maize and fat cattle, with the merchants of New England, whose little vessels brought in exchange those articles of foreign production which the settlers could not otherwise procure. English cupidity envied them their privileges, and the navigation laws of 1672 were put in force. An agent of the government appeared, who demanded a penny for every pound of tobacco sent to New England. The colonists resisted the levy. The tax-gatherer was rude, and had frequent personal collisions with the people. On one occasion he attempted to drive away a steer in satisfaction of a demand for the tax on

THE TAX-GATHERER BEATEN OFF.

the tobacco of a planter, which had just been shipped for Boston, when the sturdy wife of the yeoman beat him off with a mop-stick, and saved the animal from the tax-gatherer.

Finally, the exasperated people, led by John Culpepper, a refugee from the Southern or Carteret county colony, seized the governor and the public funds; imprisoned him and six of his councillors; called a new representative Assembly, and appointed a chief magistrate and judges. That was in December, 1677. For two years the colonists conducted the affairs of their government without any foreign control. Meanwhile Culpepper, whom the royalists denounced as an "ill man," one who merited "hanging for endeavoring to set the people to plunder the rich," conscious of his integrity, went boldly to England to plead the cause of the colonists. There he was arrested, just as he was re-embarking for America, on a charge of treason, for which he was tried and acquitted. Returning to North Carolina, he was appointed surveyor-general of the province; and in 1680 he was employed in laying out the city of Charleston in South Carolina.

The Northern colony now enjoyed repose for awhile, until the arrival of Seth Sothel as governor. He had purchased the share of Clarendon in the soil of the provinces, and was sent to administer government there. On his voyage he was captured by Algerine pirates, but escaped, and reached North Carolina in 1683. Avaricious, extortionate, cruel, without the abilities of a statesman and mean-spirited—"the dark shades of his character not relieved by a single virtue"—he sought the government with the hope of winning a fortune thereby. His advent disturbed the public tranquillity. He plundered the people, cheated the proprietors, and on all occasions seems to have prostituted his delegated power to purposes of private gain. After enduring his misrule for about six weeks, the people rose in rebellion, seized the governor, and were about to send him to England to answer their accusations before the proprietors, when he asked to be tried by the colonial Assembly. That body were evidently more merciful than his associates in England would have been, for they found him guilty and sentenced him to only one year's banishment and perpetual disqualification for the office of governor. Sothel then withdrew to the Southern colony, where we shall meet him presently.

Sothel's successor, Philip Ludwell, was an energetic and honest man. By the exercise of wisdom and justice, he soon restored order and good feeling in the colony. He was succeeded by other honorable men, among them the good John Archdale, a member of the Society of Friends, who came in 1695 as governor of the two colonies. His administration was a blessing. The people of North Carolina, over whom he ruled, were almost as free in their opinions and actions, as the air they breathed. There were few restraints of any kind, legal or moral, yet the people were generally enemies to violence, and gentle-tempered. They were widely scattered, with not a city or town, and scarcely a hamlet in their sylvan domain. There were no roads but bridle-paths from house to house, and these were indicated by notches cut in trees. There was no settled minister of the gospel among them until 1703. The first church erected in North Carolina appeared in 1705. No building for a court-house was constructed until 1722; and it was not until 1754—about a hundred years after the first permanent settlement was made in the region of the Chowan—that a printing-press was set up in the province.

The Southern or Carteret County colony was, meanwhile, steadily advancing in population and wealth. The settlers there, perceiving the fatal objections to the "Fundamental Constitutions" as a plan of government for their colony, did not attempt conforming thereto, but established a more simple government adapted to their condition. It was crude. Under it the first legislative assembly of South Carolina convened in the spring of 1672, at the place on the Ashley River where the colony was first seated. In that body, jarring political, social and theological interests and opinions produced passionate debates and violent discord. There was a Proprietary party and a People's party; a High Church party and a Dissenter's party, each bigoted and resolute. At times debates were so angrily carried on, that members almost came to blows; and it was a relief to the people when the Assembly adjourned, for it seemed to be a nest out of which might come the rapacious vulture of civil war, that would be perilous in the extreme, at that time, when surrounding savages were evidently hostile. The danger from these foes finally healed the dissensions among the settlers. Moved by the instinct of self-preservation, they joined in a successful warfare upon the Indians, who had begun to plunder the plantations of grain and cattle, and to menace the lives of the colonists. The savages were subdued in 1680, and those who were made captive were sent to the West Indies and sold for slaves. Then Old Town, as their first place of settlement was called, was abandoned, and on Oyster Point, as we have observed, was founded the city of Charleston, the future capital of the colony. It was settled chiefly by the English, for the Dutch and others spread over the country along the Edisto and Santee rivers. Immigrants from different parts of Europe rapidly swelled the population of Charleston and its vicinity, and aspirations for political independence were manifested there at that early day.

A second popular Assembly met at Charleston in 1682. It was more harmonious than the first. Wise laws were framed, and a more tolerant religious spirit prevailed. Immigrants flowed in with a full and continuous stream. Families came from Ireland, Scotland and Holland; and when the edict of Nantes, which secured toleration to Protestants in France, was revoked, a large number of Huguenots fled from their country, and many

INDIANS PLUNDERING SOUTH CAROLINA PLANTATIONS.

sought an asylum in the Carolinas. The traditionary hatred of the English for the French was shown at this time. For full ten years these French refugees were denied the privileges of citizenship in the land of their adoption.

Meanwhile a little colony of ten Scotch families who had fled from persecution in their native land, and led by the Presbyterian Lord Cardross, landed at Port Royal on the coast of South Carolina, and proceeded to plant a settlement there in 1682. The existence of that little colony was brief. The Spaniards claimed Port Royal as a dependency of St. Augustine; and in 1686, during the absence of Cardross in Britain, they attacked and dispersed his colony and laid waste their property. Some of them returned to Scotland, and others joined the colony between the Edisto and Santee rivers.

The Huguenots, who infused warm blood into the veins of the Southern colony, and carried the sunshine of their buoyant natures into other American provinces, deserve more than a passing notice here. We have already considered their forlorn condition in the time of Coligni, a hundred years earlier. The decree of Henry the Fourth, issued from Nantes in 1598, giving them free toleration within his dominions, secured them from severe persecution. They had prospered, and had become, as a body, the best citizens of France.

When the profligate Louis the Fourteenth approached old age, he became the slave of a fascinating woman, widow of the comic poet Scarron, who is better known in history as Madame de Maintenon. She was then fifty years of age, but was still beautiful, graceful and witty, and wise and discreet in all her ways. The king, then forty-eight, fascinated by the charms of her mind and person, married her secretly. From that time she fashioned his future life. She had been a Calvinist, but was now a devoted daughter of the Church of Rome. When remorse for past sins clouded the mind of the king, she shed the light of religious consolation into its darkened recesses. He would pass whole days with her alone in a library of the palace, listening to her charming conversation or her reading from books of devotion. As amends for past misconduct, she persuaded him to take measures for the conversion of the Huguenots and to win them back to the Church of Rome.

This work was begun in earnest, by every species of bribery, and every means of coercion excepting actual personal violence. These Huguenots were driven from all public employments, and were reinstated only upon the condition of entering the church as communicants. They were persecuted by being subjected to all kinds of disabilities, social and political, and finding relief only in a profession of the Romish faith. These measures operated powerfully, and, in a degree, successfully. It was perceived that the surest road to popular favor was by converting Huguenots, and Louvois, the Minister of War, determined to outdo Madame de Maintenon in this work, by the use of soldiers, whom he quartered on the Huguenots with orders to torment them in every possible way short of personal violence. These Protestants were forbidden to leave France, and so, like hunted deer driven to close quarters, they were dreadfully worried by the hounds. At length, following the advice of Madame de Maintenon, the king revoked the tolerant edict of Henry, and the Huguenots were exposed to the unbridled passions of the soldiery and the intolerance of religious bigots. So, Louis hoped he had gained the favor of Heaven and secured the salvation of his own soul.

LOUIS THE FOURTEENTH.

The sufferings of the Huguenots were now horrible. The most cruel torments were used to "convert" them. It is said that full ten thousand of them perished at the stake and other places of torture, for conscience sake. In the face of vigorous measures for preventing emigration, full five hundred thousand of these useful citizens, numbering multitudes of skilled mechanics, fled from their country, and so impoverished the kingdom. They created Huguenot villages in Germany. They swelled the army of William wherewith to win the throne of England. They filled a whole suburb of London, and introduced the art of silk-weaving into England. Some went to the Cape of Good Hope, and many of them sought peaceful homes among the American colonists. They were welcomed everywhere, and became blessings to every community among whom they settled. Many families were seated in New York and other colonies; but the warmer climate of the Carolinas was more congenial to these children of sunny France. They gave some of the best blood to the American colonies; and their descendants have borne a conspicuous part in building up our free Republic.

The South Carolinians resisted all attempts to make them submit to the authority of the "Fundamental Constitutions." Annoyed by persistent efforts to compel them to accept that form of government, they felt disposed to cast off all allegiance to the proprietors and the mother country. At that crisis, John Colleton, one of the owners, was appointed governor of the province, with full powers to bring the people into submission. That was in 1686. His administration of four years was a very turbulent one. Finally, his continual collisions with the people drove them into open rebellion. They seized the public records; imprisoned the secretary of the province; called a new Assembly, and defined the power of the governor. The latter, pleading the danger of an impending invasion of Indians or Spaniards, made it a pretext for calling out the militia, with whom he hoped to suppress the insurrection. He declared the province to be under martial-law, and proposed to rule by its vigorous code.

The militia were a part of the people, and no troops appeared at the call of the governor. His act greatly exasperated the colonists. He was impeached, and banished from the province by the Assembly, in 1690. The Revolution in England at the same time was initiated in miniature in South Carolina.

During the turbulence at near the close of Colleton's administration, Seth Sothel arrived from North Carolina, pursuant to his sentence of banishment. He espoused the cause of the people against the proprietors, and the former, in the moment of their anger, unwisely chose him to be their governor. Their poor judgment was rebuked, and the people were punished for this rash act by the conduct of the new governor. While he followed the popular will in opposing the claims of the proprietors to political domination, he plundered the people, trampled upon their dearest rights, and ruled them with insolence and undisguised tyranny. His misrule was endured for about two years, when the people heartily seconded the measures of his fellow-proprietors for his removal. When they heard of his usurpations, they sent him letters of recall, with an order from the king to appear in England to answer charges of disloyalty and other grave offences. Sothel was compelled to retire from the office in 1692, when he withdrew to North Carolina, where he died two years afterward. It was during the administration of Sothel that the Huguenots in South Carolina were as fully enfranchised, or granted the liberty of citizens, as if they had been born on the soil. This act of enfranchisement was repealed in 1697.

Colonel Philip Ludwell, of Virginia, and then governor of North Carolina, as we have seen—a man wholly unconnected with the interests of the province—was appointed the successor of Sothel. When the people found that a part of his mission was to restore the authority of the proprietors and impose upon them the absurd "Fundamental Constitutions," they were restive under the rule of even so good a man as he. He was authorized to inquire into grievances, but had no power to redress them; and after a brief and unhappy administration, he gladly retired from the chair of state.

The proprietors were now satisfied that they could never impose upon the people of the Carolinas the form of government framed by Locke and Cooper, and after a trial of about twenty years, the scheme was abandoned. They sent good John Archdale, as we have seen, to govern both provinces under more simple forms of government prepared by the people themselves. His administration was short, but highly beneficial. He healed dissensions; established equitable laws, and with the spirit of a true Christian he set a true Christian example of toleration and humanity. He made no distinction on account of religious creeds in the choice of his council. He cultivated friendly intercourse with the surrounding Indians, and ransomed Indian captives who were exposed for sale as slaves. Chiefs of tribes formerly hostile were sometimes seen at his table; and two Indian maidens were paid servants in his family. With the Spaniards at St. Augustine he cultivated friendly relations, for the liberal spirit of the Quaker could respect the faith of the Roman Catholic. With keen foresight he introduced and promoted the growth of rice on the seacoasts of the Carolinas, some seed having been given to him by the captain of a vessel from Madagascar. It was distributed among the planters; and so the cultivation of this valuable cereal was begun in our country. The name and deeds of John Archdale were kept green in the memory of the Carolinians for generations.

From the close of Archdale's administration, the history of the two Carolinas should be considered separate and distinct, although they were not politically disunited until 1729.

CHAPTER XIV.

THE CAROLINAS—DISAPPEARANCE OF THE INDIANS—INTERNAL COMMOTIONS—EMIGRANTS FROM FRANCE, SWITZERLAND AND GERMANY—AN INDIAN RAID AND MASSACRE OF WHITE PEOPLE—FURTHER TROUBLE WITH THE INDIANS—SOUTH CAROLINA—THE GOVERNOR MAKES WAR ON THE SPANIARDS IN FLORIDA—WAR WITH INDIANS—POLITICAL TROUBLES—SOUTH CAROLINA INVADED BY SPANIARDS AND FRENCHMEN—THE FOE EXPELLED—AN INDIAN LEAGUE—REVOLUTION IN SOUTH CAROLINA—THE TWO COLONIES BECOME ROYAL PROVINCES—GEORGIA—RELIGIOUS MISSIONARIES THERE—OGLETHORPE AND THE SPANIARDS IN FLORIDA—CONDITION OF THE GEORGIA COLONY—OGLETHORPE INVADES FLORIDA—THE SPANIARDS INVADE GEORGIA—PUNISHMENT OF A DESERTER—THE SPANIARDS DRIVEN OUT OF GEORGIA—OGLETHORPE IN ENGLAND—GEORGIA BECOMES A ROYAL PROVINCE.

WHEN the good Archdale had left the impress of his example and teachings upon the Carolinians, both provinces began their career of permanent prosperity. Although they were politically united, each acted independently of the other from the close of the seventeenth century. Both made a steady advance in population and wealth, and the arts of refined society.

The North Carolinians turned their attention to the richer lands away from the sea; and hunters trapped the beaver and otter in the waters far in the interior among the hills. The Indians along the sea-board had melted before the warmth of civilization like snow in the sunbeams of spring-time. The powerful Hatteras tribe, that numbered about three thousand when Harriot healed King Wingina, were reduced to fifteen bowmen in the year 1700. Another tribe on the Chowan had entirely disappeared; and the remainder of the savages in that region had been defrauded of their lands and driven back into the deep forests, when they and their brethren there perished by hundreds by the vices and diseases of the white man. The broad domain from the sea to the Yadkin and the Catawba then lay almost uninhabited, and invited to its bosom the skill of the husbandman with promises of wealth and comfort.

At about that time the freedom of the North Carolinians—"every one of whom," it was said, "did what was right in his own eyes, paying tribute to neither God nor Cæsar"—was disturbed by an attempt, in 1704, to establish there the ecclesiastical dominion of the Church of England.

Deputy-Governor Daniells had been sent for that purpose. He caused the first church in the province, already mentioned, to be built at the public expense. The people opposed the scheme. The Friends led in the opposition, and the turbulence that ensued soon bore the aspect of a political quarrel. Anarchy prevailed for awhile. On one side in the dispute were Churchmen and Loyalists; on the other side were Dissenters and Republicans, among whom the Friends, who were rapidly increasing in numbers, were the most active, and were ranked by the adherents of the proprietors as a "rabble of profligate persons." There were two governors and two legislatures for a time; but their dissensions were soon quieted. The people passively acquiesced in the ecclesiastical scheme of the deputy-governor, but they did not become Churchmen. Several years afterward, there was only one clergyman in the provinces, for no congregations could be gathered.

Meanwhile some excellent immigrants had enriched the colony. In 1607 some Huguenots came from their temporary settlement in Virginia, and seated themselves on the beautiful banks of the Trent, a tributary of the Neuse. They were followed two years afterward by emigrants from Switzerland, who founded New Berne at the head of the Neuse. At about the same time a hundred fugitive German families from the devastated Palatinates on the Rhine came to seek shelter and repose. They were led by Count Graffenreid, and founded settlements upon the headwaters of the Neuse and the banks of the Roanoke.

Soon after these inland settlements were fairly planted, and were spreading, a fearful calamity fell upon the Germans. The remnants of the exasperated tribes, who had been driven into the forests, had nursed their revenge until it became too strong for repression. Incited and led by the Tuscaroras, a fierce Algonquin tribe, they joined in an effort to re-possess their lost country. In this patriotic endeavor the Corees, a tribe near the seaboard further south, became their allies. They all fell with terrible force upon the scattered German settlers along the Roanoke and the borders of Pamlico Sound; and in a single October night in 1711, they slew one hundred and thirty men, women and children, and lighted up the country for scores of miles with the flames of burning dwellings. With the hatchet and torch they swept like fiends along the borders of Albemarle Sound, killing, plundering and burning, during the space of three days, until they were overcome with fatigue and drunkenness. On the eve of this murderous raid, John Lawson, surveyor-general of the province, and Count Graffenreid, were taken captive by the savages. They tortured Lawson to death by burning him at a sapling, but the Count saved his life and gained his liberty by adroitly persuading them that he was the sachem of a tribe of men who had lately come into the country, and were in no way connected with the English.

The wildest excitement spread over North Carolina. The people fled in affright toward the sea, and many left the province. Those who remained called upon their brethren of South Carolina for help. Colonel Barnwell hastened northward with some Carolinians and a body of friendly Indians composed of Creeks, Cherokees, Catawbas, and Yammasees. The savage tide was rolled back. The Tuscaroras were driven to their fortified town in the present Craven county, and there a solemn treaty of peace was made between the white men and the Indians. All might have been well but for the treachery of the South Carolinians, who, on their way homeward, violated the treaty by committing outrages upon the Indians. The latter were enraged, and speedily flew to arms. Terror everywhere prevailed. It seemed as if the purpose of the savages to annihilate the intruders would be accomplished. Back to the rescue of their brethren from destruction went the Carolinians. Colonel Moore, with a small number of white men and a large body of Indians, soon met and defeated the hostile savages. The Tuscaroras were driven to their fort in the present Greene county, where eight hundred of them were made prisoners. The remainder of the tribe fled to the north, and joined their kindred near the southern shores of Lake Ontario, when they became the sixth nation of the Iroquois Confederacy in the province of New York. A treaty of peace was made with the Corees afterward, and North Carolina never again suffered from the hostility of Indians. The war had cost the province a large sum of money, for the payment of which bills of credit

ON THE WAR-PATH.

31

were issued to the amount of forty thousand dollars. This was the first issue of paper money in North Carolina.

During the years when the people of the northern colony were suffering from civil commotions and Indian raids, the South Carolinians were excited by troubles with the Spaniards and the neighboring barbarians. The governor (James Moore) was more belligerent and aggressive than his predecessors. When he heard of Queen Anne's proclamation of war with France in May, 1702, and that Spain was involved in the quarrel, he proposed an expedition against the Spaniards at St. Augustine. The Assembly agreed with the governor and appropriated nearly ten thousand dollars for the enterprise. An army of twelve hundred men (one-half of them Indians) was raised, and in two divisions they proceeded, one by land and the other by sea, to make the attack. The governor commanded the forces on the ships, and Colonel Daniels the division that crossed the Savannah River, traversed Georgia along the coast, penetrated Florida, and made the first attack. The Spaniards retired within their fort, with provisions for four months, where they were quite safe from harm, for their enemies had no artillery.

Governor Moore arrived with his vessels and troops soon afterward, and blockaded the harbor of St. Augustine. When Daniels had plundered the town, he was sent to Jamaica for battering cannon, but before his return two Spanish war-vessels had frightened the blockaders away, and the colonel came very near being made captive. He reached Charleston in safety, and the ill-advised expedition was then at an end. It cost the colony a large sum of money, and to defray the expenses bills of credit were issued to the amount of twenty-six thousand dollars. This was the first issue of paper money in South Carolina.

Late in the following year, Governor Moore tried his skill again in making war. This time it was against hostile Indians who were in league with the Spaniards. These were the Appalachians, a Mobilian tribe, who occupied a region in Georgia between the Savannah and Alatamaha rivers. There their chief villages were situated, and there large gardens were cultivated. Against these the governor proceeded with a force competent to insure success. The villages were desolated; the gardens were laid waste; eight hundred men, women and children were carried into captivity, and the inhabitants of the whole region were made vassals or subjects of the English. By this movement a thorn of irritation was planted in the bosom of the surrounding Indians which rankled for years, and was one of the causes that spurred them into fierce hostility afterward.

Just as the province was becoming tranquil after the war with the savages, it was disquieted by turbulence in civil affairs in its own bosom. The proprietors resolved to establish the liturgy of the Church of England in South Carolina, as the standard order of public worship. Sir Nathaniel Johnson, who was the official successor of Governor Moore, found a majority of Churchmen in the Assembly, and easily executed the wishes of his masters. Dissenters were disfranchised—deprived of the rights of free citizens—and actually suffered persecutions. After a season of much turbulence, they appealed to the crown, and in the autumn of 1706, the Assembly, by order of Parliament, repealed the law of disfranchisement. But the Anglican Church maintained its supremacy in ecclesiastical affairs in the province until the war for independence.

The attack of the South Carolinians on St. Augustine excited the anger of the Spaniards. An expedition, consisting of five vessels-of-war under the command of the French admiral Le Feboure, and a large body of troops, was sent from Havana to attack Charleston, conquer the province and annex it to the Spanish territory in Florida. When, in May, 1706, the squadron crossed Charleston bar, and about eight hundred troops were landed at different points, the commander sent a flag to the city with a peremptory order for a surrender, and threatening to take it by storm in case of a refusal to submit. Governor Moore had been apprised of the expedition, and was prepared to meet it. When the flag arrived, he had so disposed the provincial militia and a host of Indian warriors, as to give an exaggerated idea of the strength of the Carolinians. Before the messenger could make any extended observations he was dismissed with the defiant reply that the people were ready to sustain the promised attack.

A FLAG OF TRUCE.

This was followed by a furious assault, just at dawn, upon the invaders on shore by a strong party of South Carolinians. They killed many, captured more, and drove the remnant back to their ships. At the same time the little provincial navy, lying in the harbor, prepared to attack the invading squadron. The French admiral, amazed and alarmed by the display of valor on shore, weighed anchor and fled to sea. A French war-ship, uninformed of these events, sailed into the harbor soon afterward, with troops, and was captured. The victory was complete. The dark storm-cloud, from which a destructive tempest was expected, suddenly dissolved, and the sunshine of peace and prosperity gladdened the colonists for a season.

At length a more frightful tempest was seen brooding over the colony. It had gathered with fearful celerity. A league had been formed among the surrounding Indian tribes to exterminate the English. It was the secret work of the Spaniards in Florida and the French in the Mississippi Valley. Within the space of forty days, a confederacy had been formed, including the whole Indian tribes from the Cape Fear on the north to the St. Mary's on the south, and back to the rivers beyond the mountains in the west. The warriors of the league were full six thousand strong. It comprised the Cherokees, Choctaws, Chickasaws, Catawbas and Congarees on the west, and the Creeks, Yammasees and Appalachians on the south. At the same time a thousand warriors broke forth from the forests of the Neuse region to avenge their misfortunes in the war two or three years before.

So secretly had the savages organized, that not a whisper of impending danger had reached the inhabitants of Charleston, before the news came that on the morning of Good Friday (April 13, 1715), the Yammasees had begun an indiscriminate massacre of the white people along the seaboard. The news had been carried from the scene of destruction by a swift-footed seaman who broke through the lines of the furious savages, ran ten miles and swam one, and told the dreadful tale to the settlers at Port Royal. These fled in canoes and in a ship, and carried the first intelligence of the sad event to Charleston. A stream of terror-stricken planters and their families began pouring into the city at the same time. The capital was in peril. The governor (Craven) acted promptly and efficiently in the emergency. He took measures to prevent men leaving the colony. He declared the province to be under martial-law; took measures to secure all arms and ammunition to be found, and called upon the citizens to prepare to fight valiantly for their lives and property. He put arms into the hands of faithful negro slaves; and with a motley army of white men, Indians and black men, twelve hundred strong, he marched to meet the savages, who were approaching from the interior with their knives and hatchets in fearful activity. After some severe encounters with them, the governor drove the Yammasees across the Savannah River and through Georgia, giving them no rest until they found it under the protection of the guns of St. Augustine. Meanwhile the warriors from the north had been driven back to the forests, and the Cherokees and their neighbors, who had not yet taken up the hatchet, had retired to their hunting-grounds, deeply impressed by the evidences of the strength and prowess of the white people. So, again, was sunshine brought to South Carolina, in the beautiful month of May, 1715.

Proprietary government in South Carolina was now drawing to a close. It had been a heavy burden upon the colonists from the beginning. The

THE ALARM.

governors appointed by the proprietors, being independent of the people, had often been haughty and exacting, and they irritated rather than conciliated the popular mind. While the colonists were laboring to build up a permanent and prosperous State, the proprietors refused to assist them in times of danger or to reimburse their expenses incurred in defending the domain from invasion. The people were not only compelled to bear the whole expense of the late war with the Indians, but the proprietors enforced their claims for quit-rents more remorselessly than ever.

The colonists saw no way to cast off their chains but by revolution, and no security for the future but in royal rule and protection. So they resolved to revolt. Their popular Assembly declared that they would have nothing further to do with the proprietors, and asked Governor Johnson to rule in the name of the king. He refused, when a Convention of the people prepared to choose a governor for themselves.

Johnson had appointed the first day of December as the time for a general review of the militia of the province. The Convention chose the same day as the time for the election of a popular governor. Johnson then countermanded the order for the review. But the militia assembled in large numbers in the public square at Charleston. They were a part of the people; and when the governor ordered their commander to disperse them, he said: "I obey the Convention." Then the people proceeded to the election of a chief magistrate, when James Moore was chosen. Soon afterward proprietary rule was dismissed from the soil of South Carolina. The royal ear listened favorably to a petition presented by an agent of the colony, in England. The charter of the proprietaries was abrogated, and in 1720, South Carolina became a royal province, with Francis Nicholson as royal governor.

North Carolina was relieved of proprietary rule without enduring the throes of actual revolution. From the time when its southern sister passed under royal rule and protection, the people of the northern colony became more and more restive. They seemed to be on the verge of revolution, when, in 1729, the proprietors, seeing the inevitable drift of public sentiment, made a virtue of necessity, and sold that domain to the king for about eighty thousand dollars. It then became a royal province. The two Carolinas were then separated. George Burrington was appointed governor of North Carolina, and Robert Johnson was made chief magistrate of South Carolina. The people of the provinces were soon convinced that they had gained nothing by a change of rulers; and from the time of the separation until the French and Indian war, their history is largely made up of the records of disputes between the people and the royal governors.

The latest planted of the English colonies in America was Georgia, the founding of which we have already considered. The settlers there had very little intercourse with or knowledge of the outside world, and thought of but little excepting the material interests of their new homes, until after Oglethorpe's return from England early in 1736. Then foreign politics threatened dangers from their neighbors, and religious teachings stirred the sluggish society into some activity.

With the great guns and the Highlanders skilled in military art, came with Oglethorpe many Germans to join their Moravian brethren who had settled in Georgia two or three years before. He was also accompanied by John and Charles Wesley, sons of an English poet and divine in the reigns of James, William, and Anne. They were religious enthusiasts, and were clergymen of the Church of England. The great guns and the Highlanders came to make war upon visible invaders of the domain; the Wesleys came to make war upon the invisible foes of righteousness. John was then thirty-three years of age, and came as a missionary of the gospel among the settlers and the surrounding pagans. Charles came as an assistant to his brother in this warfare, and as secretary to Governor Oglethorpe. They had lately begun that course of independent action in England, which caused the pulpits of their church to be closed against them and led to the founding of the Methodist denomination.

John Wesley was fervent in spirit and eloquent in speech. A large congregation attended his ministrations at Savannah, at first; but the austerity of his maxims, his fearless denunciations of vice and even foibles, and his rigid exercise of ecclesiastical authority, soon involved him in serious disputes with the settlers, who were a peculiarly mixed people. He became unpopular, and was sorely vexed and irritated by opponents on every side. At length he became involved in a difficulty with a woman whom he had refused to admit to the communion, and he left the province in disgust at the end of two years, and returned to England, "shaking the dust off his feet," as he expressed it. His mission in Georgia was a failure.

At that time there was a sturdy young preacher in England who was swaying multitudes by his fervid eloquence. He was a friend of the Wesleys, and obtained permission to join them in Georgia. He was not quite twenty-four years of age when he arrived at Savannah. The Wesleys had departed, but the young missionary, George Whitefield, entered upon his sacred duties with fervor. More practical than Wesley, he became a blessing not only to Georgia, but to other American colonies, where he labored much as an independent itinerant preacher. He established an asylum for orphans at Savannah, which was founded and supported several years by voluntary subscriptions which he procured in England and elsewhere. He worked lovingly with the Moravians in Georgia, who made a most salutary impression upon society there.

On his return, Oglethorpe discovered that the Spaniards at St. Augustine were very jealous of the rapid growth of the Georgia colony. He was not fairly prepared to resist an invasion by arms, and he sent a messenger to St. Augustine to invite the commander to a friendly conference. At about the same time he went, with a number of his martial Highlanders, on an exploring expedition among the islands and along the coasts of Georgia. On St. Simons' Island he founded Frederica and built a fort there. Sailing up Alatamaha Sound, he visited New Inverness (now Darien), where a few Scotch people had planted a settlement. He was dressed in Highland costume, and with his Gaelic followers he was warmly welcomed by the settlers, who came to the beach in their plaids, bearing various weapons, and expressing their delight with the sounds of the bagpipe in merry tunes. There, too, he marked out a small fortification.

It was now warm spring weather. Oglethorpe's messenger had not returned from St. Augustine, and he proceeded to manifest the intention of Great Britain to sustain its claims to the country as far south as the St.

OGLETHORPE RECEIVED AT DARIEN.

John's River. On Cumberland Island, to which he sailed on leaving Darien, he marked out a fort to be called St. Andrew's, which would command the mouth of the St. Mary's, the stream which finally became the southern boundary of Georgia. At the southern extremity of an island at the entrance of St. John's River, he also planned a small military work, which he called Fort St. George. He also founded Augusta far up the Savannah River, and erected a stockade there as a defence against Indians from the west who might be under the influence of French or Spanish traders.

These hostile preparations irritated the Spaniards at St. Augustine. They detained Oglethorpe's messengers as prisoners, and threatened war. The news spread among the friendly Indians. To-mo-chi-chi came with painted warriors to offer his aid. So, too, did other chiefs ; and the Chickasaws sent a delegation to bear assurances of friendship and alliance to the ears of the governor, and a crown of brilliant feathers, adorned with the polished horns of the buffalo, for the brow of Oglethorpe. With these tribes at his back as allies, Oglethorpe felt strong. The governor of St. Augustine, who had tampered with them, hearing of their alliance with the English, expressed a willingness to treat for a settlement of all disputes. An honorable treaty was made. The messengers were released, and the Georgians abandoned Fort St. George. But the home government of Spain did not approve the treaty, and Oglethorpe was notified that a commission from Cuba would meet him at Frederica. He appeared with his secretary, after leaving three regiments of Spanish infantry at St. Augustine, and peremptorily demanded the evacuation by the British of all Georgia and of South Carolina below the parallel of Port Royal, claiming all of that region as a part of the dominions of Spain. The conference ended without an agreement.

Oglethorpe now hastened to England to confer with the trustees and seek military strength for his colony, for he was satisfied that it was in peril from the increased number of soldiers thrown into Florida. He was commissioned a brigadier-general, and invested with authority over the military in Georgia and South Carolina. He was also authorized to raise troops in England to serve in America. He did so, and with these he arrived in Georgia in the autumn of 1738, when he found general discontent prevailing. The colony was not prosperous, owing partly to the unwise regulations of the trustees referred to at the close of Book II, and partly because many of the emigrants who came from England were men unaccustomed to manual labor and habits of industry. The use of slave labor, so productive in other colonies, was forbidden in Georgia, and tillage was neglected. Even the industrious Scotch, Swiss and German settlers in Georgia previous to the year 1740, when the colony contained twenty-five hundred souls, could not give that vitality to industrial pursuits which was necessary for the development of the resources of that virgin soil.

The greed of English merchants, who were growing rich by illicit trade on the coasts of Spanish-America at the expense of Spanish commerce, was fostered by the English ministry, who were blindly bent on destroying the Spanish colonial system in the so-called New World. Spain resented this interference with her rights, and for this—the real cause—England declared war against that kingdom late in 1739.

Oglethorpe had been apprised of this measure at an early date. He knew that St. Augustine had been strengthened by more troops, and he resolved to strike a blow there before his enemy should be well prepared. He had just put an end to a conspiracy in Georgia to assassinate him, and a negro insurrection in South Carolina—both incited by Spanish emissaries. He first penetrated Florida with a small force, and captured some outposts, early in 1740. In May he marched into Florida with six hundred of his regular troops, four hundred Carolina militia, and a large body of friendly Indians. He was before St. Augustine in June, after capturing two little forts, one within twenty miles of the city, and the other only two miles distant. A demand was made for the instant surrender of the fortress and garrison. It was defiantly refused. Oglethorpe determined to starve the garrison by a close investment. He surrounded the town, and with a little squadron blockaded the harbor. For awhile supplies for the fort were cut off, and the English were promised success, but very soon swift-sailing galleys ran the weak blockade and placed ample supplies in the fort. Oglethorpe had no cannon wherewith to batter and breach the fortress. Warned by the increasing heats of summer and the approach of the sickly season, whose malaria had already invaded his camp, the general raised the siege and returned to Savannah.

Hostilities were now suspended for almost two years, when the Spaniards determined to invade Georgia. With a fleet of thirty-six vessels from Cuba and a land force about three thousand strong, they entered the harbor of St. Simons in July, 1742. The vigilant Oglethorpe, who had been informed of the expedition, was there before them, but with less than a thousand men including Indians. The governor of South Carolina had failed to furnish men or supplies, and upon the Georgians devolved the task of defending both provinces from invasion. The intrepid general, when he saw the white sails of the Spanish ships in the distance, went on board one of his own little vessels, and addressing the seamen, said: "We must protect Carolina and the rest of the colonies from destruction, or die in the attempt. For myself, I am prepared for all dangers. I know the enemy are far more numerous than we; but I rely on the valor of our men, and by God's help, I believe we will be victorious."

When the fleet passed the English batteries at the southern end of the island, Oglethorpe saw that resistance would be vain. He ordered his vessels to run up to Frederica, while he spiked his guns at St. Simons and retreated to the same place with his troops. There he waited for reinforcements from Carolina, but they did not come. Spanish detachments annoyed him with frequent attacks, but he always repulsed them.

At length Oglethorpe resolved to act on the offensive, and make a stealthy night attack upon the Spanish encampment near St. Simons. He moved cautiously along a road which he had constructed, with a dense live-oak forest draped with Spanish moss on one side, and a deep morass on the other. When he was near the camp, a Frenchman in his little army ran ahead, fired his musket, and deserted to the enemy. The Spaniards were aroused, and Oglethorpe fell back to Frederica.

The general punished the deserter in a novel way. He employed a Spanish prisoner to carry a letter to him, secretly, in which Oglethorpe addressed him as a spy in the enemy's camp. He told him to represent the Georgians as very weak in numbers and arms, and advise the Spaniards to attack them at once; and if they would not do so, to try and persuade them to remain at St. Simons three days longer, for within that time a British fleet with two thousand land troops would arrive to attack St. Augustine.

OGLETHORPE. COTTON MATHER. GEORGE THE SECOND. JOHN WESLEY.

The bearer of the letter, as Oglethorpe expected and hoped he would, carried it to the Spanish commander. It produced a great commotion in camp. The Frenchman was arrested and put in irons, and afterward hanged as a spy. A council of war was called, and while it was in session some vessels from Carolina were seen at sea. They were mistaken for the British fleet alluded to, and the Spaniards determined to attack Oglethorpe immediately, and then hasten to the defence of St. Augustine.

An advanced division moved immediately on Frederica. On the narrow road flanked by the forest and the morass, within a mile of the fort, they were assailed by Oglethorpe and his Highlanders, who lay in ambush. Almost the whole party of the invaders were killed or captured. A second party pressing forward to their relief, met the fate of the first. The Spaniards retreated in confusion, leaving about two hundred of their companions dead on the field. They fled to their ships and hastened to St. Augustine, only to find that they had been outgeneraled by the governor of Georgia. The place of the battle has been called "The Bloody Marsh" to this day. The stratagem of Oglethorpe had worked such disaster to the Spanish expedition that its commander, Don Manuel de Monteano, was dismissed from the service. That stratagem probably saved Georgia and South Carolina from utter ruin.

Oglethorpe had settled, colonized and defended Georgia with rare courage, energy and skill, not for personal glory and worldly gain, but for a great and benevolent purpose. Having firmly established the colony, he returned to England in 1743, where, after performing good military service for his king against the "Young Pretender," he retired to his seat in Essex. When General Gage returned to England from America in 1775, he was offered the chief command of the British army in this country, though he was then almost eighty years of age. His benevolent ideas did not suit the temper of the British ministry then, and General William Howe received the appointment. When, at the close of the Revolution, John Adams went to England as American minister at the British court, Oglethorpe was among the first to congratulate him because of the independence of his country. The brave Founder of Georgia died the next year, at the age of almost ninety years, with all his mental faculties in full vigor.

Oglethorpe was a benefactor in the higher sense of that term. For the good of his fellow-men, he had renounced ease of body and mind and the enjoyment of fortune and friends in his native land. He had encountered dangers in many forms unknown in England, not for the glory that leads a soldier to brave the perils of a strange land. He was gentle and good; merciful toward offenders and enemies; a father to the emigrants whom he led to the banks of the Savannah River; the warm friend of the Wesleys and kind guardian of the Moravians, with a missionary spirit ever anxious for the spiritual welfare and mental culture of the pagans around him; and it always gave him pleasure to relieve the poor and the weak of their burdens. Oglethorpe outlived most of the companions of his youth; but he was so loving and lovable that he made "troops of friends" on his long journey of life, who were to him in his vigorous old age like green branches nourished by his abounding virtues. Even in that old age, his person was spoken of as "the finest figure that ever was seen." His prominent eyes retained their brightness undimmed, and his person, tall and straight, was like a vigorous pine until the close of his life.

After the departure of Oglethorpe, Georgia enjoyed repose from conflicts with hostile neighbors. He left the country in a state of tranquillity. The same year it passed from the control of a mild military government to that of a civil organization, managed by a president and five councillors or assistants, under the supreme authority of the trustees, in England. Yet the colony languished for reasons already mentioned, and general discontent prevailed. The restrictive laws were generally relaxed and were generally evaded, especially those relating to slave-labor. Slaves were brought across the Savannah from South Carolina, and hired to the Georgia planters for a hundred years, the sum paid for such life-service being the market value of the slave. The transaction was practically the introduction of the slave-labor system into Georgia. It was not interfered with; and very soon ships laden with negroes from Africa came to Savannah, and men, women and children were offered for sale, in a way somewhat evasive of law, in the open market, by the auctioneer. In the year 1750, Georgia was really a slave-labor province. Then agriculture flourished, and the colony took its place as a planting State in an equal position by the side of its sister across the Savannah.

In 1752, when the twenty-one years named in the charter had expired, the trustees gladly gave that instrument to the king, and Georgia became a royal province. So it remained until the old war for independence.

CHAPTER XV.

REVIEW OF THE HISTORY OF DISCOVERIES—SETTLEMENTS AND COLONIZATION IN AMERICA—PLANTING THE SEEDS OF FRENCH DOMINION IN AMERICA—THE LABORS, INFLUENCE AND SUCCESS OF THE JESUITS—ADVENTURES BEYOND THE GREAT LAKES—FATHER MARQUETTE AND HIS DISCOVERY OF THE MISSISSIPPI RIVER—HIS VOYAGE UPON THAT STREAM AND ITS RESULTS—LA SALLE—HIS EXPEDITION TO THE VALLEY OF THE MISSISSIPPI—HE VOYAGES ON THAT RIVER TO THE GULF OF MEXICO—HE DISCOVERS AND NAMES LOUISIANA—HIS ATTEMPTS TO COLONIZE THAT REGION—DISCOVERY OF TEXAS—DEATH OF LA SALLE—SUBSEQUENT COLONIZATION BY THE FRENCH.

WE have now traced the history of our country from its discovery at near the close of the fifteenth century, until the time when European colonies planted here, were forming that political union for mutual defence which speedily crystallized into the grand form of an independent nation late in the eighteenth century.

In the course of these investigations, we have noted how the allurements of science, human enterprise, a lust for dominion and power, and the greed of individuals, impelled men to spend fortunes and risk their lives in making voyages of discovery along the coasts of the American continent, from the regions of the frozen ocean to those under the equator; also among the islands that lie in American waters within the tropic of Cancer. We have seen how the monarchs and navigators of Spain, Portugal, France and England struggled for the honors and emoluments to be derived from such discoveries; how the Spaniards extended their dominions by force over the islands and coasts of the western world in the space of a few years, by the help of the Roman Pontiff, and obtained the mastery over vast and fertile regions in the warm zone, while the French, English and Dutch discovered and took possession of extensive domains in the temperate zone and far toward the verge of the Arctic Circle.

These great movements were made in the "fullness of time," as if in preparation for that expansion of the human intellect and those wonderful human achievements which had then begun in Europe. Geographical science was then a favorite study, and the cosmographers were enthusiasts in the field of speculative philosophy founded upon that science. Stimulated by the few revelations of the learning of the East which commerce had brought into Europe, men were impelled to make those great discoveries on the surface of our planet, which were soon succeeded by the marvels revealed by the newly-found telescope, by which astronomy was released from the dull chrysalis of astrology and allowed to soar into the higher regions of celestial truths.

Then followed the era of settlements. To this end, a desire for winning riches was the first powerful impulse given to men and women that led them to make the sacrifice. It was soon followed by the higher motives which were born of aspirations for personal, intellectual and spiritual liberty, at a time when the tocsin or alarm-bell of the Reformation had aroused the powers of church and state into the most active opposition to everything which seemed to endanger their absolute domination. These motives led to the plantation of devotees of freedom in isolated communities all along the Atlantic seaboard from Maine to Florida.

Then followed the gradual change of *settlements* into *colonies*. We have seen how many of these settlements seemed, at first, to be only temporary asylums from the grasp of oppression, or the abiding-place of men until they should get sufficient wealth to return to their native land and live in ease. But many of them, contrary to their early promise, became permanent colonies, whose members determined to make America their final earthly abode. We have traced the progress of these colonies, step by step, from their inception. We have seen how the spirit of liberty which pervaded these communities led them by cautious methods to assert their right to the exercise of self-government. New political ideas were then stirring the popular mind in Europe, and bold thinkers were expressing them audibly and through the new-born printing-press. These were the seeds of republicanism which, when wafted to America, found here a congenial soil. These ideas took vigorous root, as we have seen, in every community, and flourished even among the sour elements of theological controversy and the persecution of bigots. They were made vigorous by the peculiar circumstances of the colonists, among whom existed affinities of race, language, and Christian tenets of great strength, and they were accustomed to common political institutions and thought. These formed the groundwork in the structure of each colony for union, and composed the broad foundations of the nation that was finally developed.

We have traced, in rapid outline, the history of each of these colonies, showing their material and moral growth, their advance in political ideas and practices from feudalism to independence, and their general condition as great and flourishing commonwealths, animated by a national spirit, and coalescing in measures for the defence of the common domain on which they were destined to raise the strong and beautiful structure of our Republic. It now remains for us to take a brief survey of the history of the French dominion and influence among the savage tribes on and beyond the frontiers of the English settlements in America, and to view the social condition of the European colonists who, at the middle of the last century, occupied a selvedge of the continent along the Atlantic, averaging about a hundred miles in width and almost a thousand miles in length.

We have already observed that the French in America, through the influence of the Jesuits, made a powerful impression upon the minds of the savages of this country, and easily persuaded them to become the friends of Frenchmen in peace and their allies in war. We have seen how the seeds of French dominion in America were planted by Champlain at Quebec. He had selected for his companions and spiritual co-workers some of the mild and benevolent priests of the Franciscan Order, who, he said, were "free from ambition," except to be instrumental in the salvation of souls. But these priests were not sufficiently aggressive to suit the ambitious Gallican Church, nor worldly-wise enough to serve the state in carrying out its political designs for enlarging its dominions in America. They were withdrawn, and the task of converting the heathen of Canada and serving the church and state at the same time was entrusted to the Jesuits. With their help Champlain established an alliance with the Hurons on the St. Lawrence and in the country westward; and so began that wide-spread affiliation of the French and Indians that became so disquieting to the English colonists.

So early as 1636 there were fifteen Jesuit priests in Canada—a band of zealous, obedient, self-sacrificing men, ready to endure every privation and encounter every danger in the service of their church. At an assembly of Huron chiefs and sachems at Quebec, Champlain introduced three of these black-robed missionaries to his savage allies as men who were to teach good things for themselves and their children. These were Brebeuf, Daniel and Davost. With faith that never forsook them, these men followed the bare-footed Indians through the dreadful forests of the Huron dominions stretching along the northern borders of the St. Lawrence and Lake Ontario to the shores of Lake Huron, near which they established the first mission-house of the Jesuits among the dusky barbarians. It was a journey full of fatigue and peril. The priests shared in all the toil. They waded streams and swamps; climbed rocks; plied the oar when on the waters; assisted in carrying the canoes around almost forty waterfalls; slept on the bare earth with no covering but the sky, and for daily bread ate pounded Indian corn mixed with water. In the script of Brebeuf were materials for the administration of the Holy Communion; and around the neck of each was a cord that held a heavy breviary or order of the daily service in the Roman Catholic Church. The devotion of Brebeuf, in particular, was marvellous in the eyes of the wondering savages. Twice a day, often, he whipped his own bare back with hard cords; he wore a bristling hair-shirt next to his skin, and under it an iron girdle studded with sharp points; and while others slept, he "watched

PASSING WATERFALLS.

and prayed." The barbarians regarded him with reverence and awe, as the greatest "medicine man" they had ever known: and when he told them of visits he had received from the Mother of God, and how he had battled with foul fiends, they believed him; and it was not long before whole tribes bowed at altars in rude Jesuit chapels in the forest, and became nominal Christians.

They were taught to believe in Jesus as the guardian spirit of their lives; and that it was he, and not one of the many deities with which they had peopled earth, air and water, that had all along afforded them protection in great perils. So the Jesuits took a firm grasp of the savage minds, and held a controlling influence over the children of the forest far and near, from the Gulf of St. Lawrence to the Gulf of Mexico. The Church in France, and the Pope, took a deep interest in the work; and a year before Massachusetts provided for the establishment of a college in that province, one was founded in Canada for the education of Indian boys. And very soon afterward a young and rich widow of France established the Ursuline Convent at Quebec for the education and religious training of Indian girls. She came with three nuns. They were received on the shore at Quebec by the governor and garrison of the fort. As they touched the ground when stepping from the boat, these devoted women stooped and kissed the earth in token of their adoption of the country as their home. Then they were escorted to the church, followed by a crowd of Indian men, women and children, where the *Te Deum* was chanted in the midst of thanksgivings.

So began the expansion of the dominions of the French in America. In 1640 they took possession of Montreal, and a united prayer went up from the people of France that the Queen of Angels might take that region under her protection. Missionary after missionary followed; and in the space of thirteen years, forty-two of them had carried the Gospel and French power from the Niagara River to the remotest bounds of Lake Superior. They established mission-houses here and there, and encountered the greatest perils among the savages, who were continually at war. These Jesuits carried their lives in their hands, and often lost them. Upon those seemingly weak props rested the fabric of French colonization in America. At times these props seemed to be giving way, for whole villages of converted Indians would sometimes be destroyed in an hour by some hostile tribe, and the pitiful sight of women and children clinging to the knees of the priest for protection from the tomahawk would be presented.

In 1654, two young traders went from Quebec to the wilderness far westward toward the Mississippi River. Two years afterward they returned with fifty canoes and a retinue of Indians. Their tales of the magnificent countries which they had traversed excited great enthusiasm, and the church and state determined to possess that goodly land. Father Alloüez, a daring Jesuit, went boldly into that region. Among the Chippewas he proclaimed the King of France as their sovereign, and built mission-houses there. He preached to the fiery Sioux; and from them he heard of the magnificent Mississippi River, which the Indians called the Father of Waters. This intelligence was sent back to Quebec, and Fathers Marquette and Dablon, two energetic priests, set out to explore the mysterious land and plant the banner of the Cross in the very heart of the heathen world. Among the Chippewas they labored lovingly for their God and their king. And when Joliet, an agent of the French government of Canada, arrived there, Marquette gave him efficient aid in his political designs. He summoned a convention of all the surrounding tribes, at the Falls of St. Mary, between Lakes Superior and Huron, where he had erected a rude chapel and founded a mission. There, by the side of the cross, the national emblems of France were raised in token of the dominion of Louis the Fourteenth.

Marquette resolved to seek for the Mississippi River. He, an "ambassador of God," and Joliet, an "envoy to discover new countries," went up the Fox River to the water-shed between the Mississippi and the Lakes, in birch canoes, and crossing the portage went down the Wisconsin River until its waters were mingled with those of the great stream. Late in June, 1673, they were upon the bosom of that mighty river which De Soto had discovered, nearer the Gulf, a century and a quarter before. The Indians called it *Mississippi*, which, in their language, signified The Great Water. So it was that the seeds of civilization and Christianity were first planted in the Valley of the Mississippi.

Marquette and his companions spread light sails over their canoes and voyaged quite rapidly on the bosom of the Mississippi with winds and currents, past the inflowing waters of the Missouri and Ohio, and other less tributaries, stopping on the shores and holding friendly intercourse with the natives. At length they reached a point below the mouth of the Arkansas River, where they found a tribe of sun-worshippers who appeared hostile. The missionaries would, undoubtedly, have been destroyed had not a revered symbol been held by Marquette. On the borders of Iowa a chief had presented him with a beautifully wrought and richly ornamented calumet, or pipe of peace, which the good father held aloft. Its well-known form, and the rich plumage that adorned it, commanded the attention of the fierce savages, when their leader, a venerable man, with nine others in an immense log canoe, came toward those of Marquette and Joliet. The old man bore in his hand a calumet, and, singing as he approached, he offered it to Marquette as a token of friendship. These Indians had axes of steel, which implied intercourse with Europeans.

Having satisfied himself that the Mississippi did not flow into the Atlantic nor the Pacific Ocean, but at some intermediate receptacle, Marquette turned the prow of his canoe northward, and he and Joliet reached Green Bay before the frosts of October were seen there. Two years longer Marquette labored among the barbarians in the vicinity of Chicago, when he crossed to the eastern shore of Lake Michigan. Suffering from mortal sickness, and conscious that his death was near, he passed along that shore in his canoe, propelled by two men, until it entered a small stream which bore his name a long time afterward. They carried him tenderly ashore, and laid him upon the leaves in the shadows of the forest. He told

FATHER MARQUETTE AND HIS SYMBOL OF PEACE.

them, with joy, that he was about to die, but requested them to leave him alone while they should unload the canoe; and promising to call them when his end should be nigh. He did so very soon. Then he asked for some holy water which he had prepared, and taking a crucifix from his neck, placed it in the hands of one of his companions and desired him to hold it

DEATH OF FATHER MARQUETTE.

constantly before his eyes while he lived. With clasped hands he then pronounced aloud the profession of his faith, and soon afterward he died, as he had desired to do, in the bosom of the wilderness in the service of his Master, without human aid. Then his companions carried him to a grave they had dug, ringing his little chapel bell which he had brought with him and so wished them to do. Near his grave they erected a large cross as a mark for passers-by. So disappeared the mortal remains of a discoverer of the Mississippi and the founder of Michigan. "The people of the West," wrote Bancroft almost forty years ago, "will build his monument." Steps were taken late in 1873 for the fulfillment of the prophecy. Marquette's remains lie in the bosom of Michilimackinack or Mackinack.

At this time Robert Cavalier de la Salle, a young Frenchman who had been educated for the priesthood in a Jesuit seminary, but who preferred a secular life, was seated at the foot of Lake Ontario, and was enjoying a monopoly of the fur trade with the Five Nations south of the lake. He had built a fort on the site of modern Kingston and named it Frontenac, in honor of his patron. The mild Franciscans, who were now tolerated in Canada, were carrying on their religious work among the Indians under the favor of La Salle.

The enterprising young Frenchman had been stirred by accounts of the Spanish voyages to America, and especially by the adventures of De Soto, and the events attending his discovery of the Mississippi River in the warmer regions of the continent. His ambition was influenced by the story of Marquette's voyage on that stream so mighty in the higher latitudes, with a desire to become a pioneer in those far-off regions and perfect the explorations of the "Great Water." He had heard, also, of the Ohio River, and the beauty and wealth of the country through which it flowed; and he resolved to attempt the establishment of a widely-extended commerce with the natives there, and, if possible, plant colonies in the vast wilderness. With these aspirations he went to France, and there found favor with Colbert, the famous minister of Louis the Fourteenth.

The sagacity of Colbert comprehended the possibilities of La Salle's scheme, and he induced the king to extend La Salle's monopoly of the fur trade among the Indians, and to give him a commission to perfect the explorations of the Mississippi River. With some mechanics and others, and Tonti, an Italian, as his lieutenant, La Salle returned to Fort Frontenac late in 1678. With these, and Franciscan priests, in a great canoe, they crossed Lake Ontario and went up the Niagara River to the site of Lewiston. In that region a trading-house was established; and at near the site of Buffalo, above the cataract, they built a sailing vessel in which they crossed the lakes to Mackinack, and pushing forward, anchored in Green Bay, west of Lake Michigan. From Mackinack or Mackinaw, La Salle sent back his brig laden with a rich cargo of furs, and awaited her return. He tarried impatiently among the Miamies at Chicago, for some time, when with Tonti, Father Hennepin and two other Franciscans, and about thirty followers, he boldly penetrated the wilderness westward on foot and in canoes, until he reached Lake Peoria, in Illinois. There he built a fort, and sent Father Hennepin forward to explore the Upper Mississippi, while he returned to Frontenac to look after his property.

FATHER HENNEPIN AT ST ANTHONY'S FALLS.

Hennepin, with two oarsmen, went down the Illinois River to the "Great Water," which they reached late in March. When the floating ice in the Mississippi had passed by, he invoked the aid of St. Anthony of Padua, and ascended the stream to the great falls which bear the name of his patron saint. Hennepin was a man much given to romancing, and permitting the creations of imagination to be represented as realities. He claimed to have discovered the source of the Mississippi, when it is known that he never went above the Falls of St. Anthony. These he described with tolerable accuracy, and near them he carved a cross and the arms of France upon the forest trees. In the autumn of 1680 he returned to Green Bay by the way of the Wisconsin and Fox rivers. In the meantime Tonti had been driven out of Illinois by the savages, and had taken refuge among the barbarians on the western shore of Lake Michigan.

La Salle returned to the Illinois country with men and supplies for an exploration of the Mississippi. That enterprise was undertaken early in 1682. La Salle was accompanied by twenty-three Frenchmen, and eighteen

New England Indians with ten women and three children. They reached the Mississippi in February, and embarked upon its bosom in a strong and spacious barge which had been constructed, and his people followed in canoes. They descended the Mississippi to the Gulf of Mexico, everywhere observing the evidences of unbounded wealth in the bosom of the soil along its course. They stopped at many places and held intercourse with the natives, who came to the river banks in large numbers to meet them. At one place below the mouth of the Arkansas River, they found a powerful king over many tribes, to whom La Salle sent presents. His embassadors were received with great respect, and the monarch sent word by them that he should visit their chief in person. He came in great state. He was preceded by two horses, and by a master of ceremonies with six men, who cleared the ground over which his majesty was to pass, and erected a pavilion of mats to shield the king from the sun. The monarch was dressed in a white robe falling to his knee, that had been beautifully woven of the inner bark of trees. He was on foot, and was preceded by two men bearing immense feather fans as white as snow. A third carried plates of copper highly polished. With grave demeanor and gracious words, he held an interview with La Salle, and they parted with mutual assurances of friendship. The people over whom the king ruled were a part of those barbarians of the Gulf region who worshipped the sun. They were called Taenses.

La Salle proceeded southward, planted a cross and the arms of France on the borders of the Gulf of Mexico, and proclaimed that the whole Mississippi Valley was a part of the dominions of King Louis. He named the magnificent domain *Louisiana* in honor of that monarch, who was then at the height of his power. So was planted in the heart of our continent the germ of the French empire that grew up there early in the eighteenth century.

Having performed this great service, La Salle went back to Quebec, and thence hastened to France and laid a report of his great discovery before the delighted court. Colbert was dead, but his son was in power and inherited his father's genius and enterprise. He procured for La Salle the king's commission to colonize Louisiana. With four ships and almost three hundred emigrants, La Salle sailed from Rochelle late in July, 1684, for the Mississippi River by way of St. Domingo. His company was composed of one hundred soldiers, and the remainder (one hundred and eighty souls) were chiefly artisans and farmers, with a few young women. Unfortunately Beaujeu, the commander of the ships, was cold and proud. He could not comprehend the lofty purposes of La Salle, and often thwarted them in a degree. His pride would not allow him to listen to La Salle, and caused him to miss the mouths of the Mississippi while sailing westward over the Gulf of Mexico. They soon found themselves in Matagorda Bay, on the coasts of Texas, and there La Salle determined to disembark. His store-ship was wrecked at the entrance to the bay, and its precious cargo was scattered over the bosom of the sea by a gale that arose in the evening. Despondency seized a part of the company, and they returned to the vessels. The remainder adhered to La Salle. The ships with the timid ones sailed away to France, leaving two hundred and thirty emigrants on the beach. These, with La Salle for the architect, soon constructed a fort on a stream that flowed into the western part of Matagorda Bay, and called it Fort St. Louis. This was the beginning of the settlement of Texas, and so it was made a portion of Louisiana. France took possession of the domain, and caused the arms of the kingdom to be carved on the great trees of the forest there.

La Salle now proposed to seek the Mississippi. In December, 1685, he departed, with some of his men. They forded small streams, crossed the larger ones on rafts which they constructed, and encountered many fearful perils. One man was eaten up by alligators. The bite of a rattlesnake killed another. Some of the Indians were hostile. Discontent arose in the party and some of the men deserted. La Salle had penetrated almost to the Red River, when his necessities compelled him to retrace his steps. When he reached the fort he had a dozen men less than when he departed.

La Salle was now allured in another direction by stories concerning rich mines in New Mexico. With a few followers he started in search of the treasures. He found a country wealthy in fertile soils, but not in precious metals; and he returned to the fort disappointed. That was in the spring of 1686.

La Salle now determined to go to Canada for reinforcements and supplies for his colony in Louisiana. Leaving a garrison at Fort St. Louis, he departed with sixteen men and five wild horses which he had procured in New Mexico. They had crossed Texas to the uplands of Trinity River, when some of the men became mutinous. Two of them, who had embarked all their fortunes in the enterprise, and who blamed La Salle for their losses, conspired against his life. One of them, named Duhaut, invited one of La Salle's nephews (who was of the party) to go with him on a buffalo hunt. Duhaut quarrelled with the young man, and murdered him. The leader, ignorant of the cause of his nephew's absence, went in search of him, and found the two conspirators near the brink of the river. Duhaut hid in the grass, but his companion approached La Salle with apparent friendliness.

"Where is my nephew?" inquired the leader. He was answered by a musket-ball from the skulking Duhaut, and fell dead. Then the conspirators plundered his body, and left it to be devoured by eagles and wolves. Joutel (a friend of La Salle), and two of the great leader's kinsmen, escaped, made their way to the Mississippi, and returned to Canada with the sad tidings of the explorer's death.

The French had now traversed the interior of America from Newfoundland and Nova Scotia by way of the St. Lawrence, the chain of the great lakes and the Mississippi River, to the Gulf of Mexico, and asserted the authority of King Louis everywhere. Trading-posts, mission-stations, and colonies followed in the path of the explorers. New Orleans was founded early in the eighteenth century. Other places were settled on the Mississippi, the Illinois, and the lakes. At the middle of the last century, the French claimed dominion over the whole continent north of the Spanish possessions, excepting the narrow border of territory on the sea-coasts occupied by the English. They coveted the whole country, and resolved to possess it. Their alliance with the Indians, through the influence of the Jesuits, had that permanent object in view; and we have seen how fearfully those allies worked along the frontier settlements of New England, with torch and hatchet, to accomplish that end. Had they succeeded in their attempted conquest of New England, the Iroquois Confederacy, that stood like a wall of defence for the settlers in New York and Pennsylvania, might have been swept away, and the day-dreams of Louis the Fourteenth, that he was to become sole master of North America, been realized. The struggle for that mastery continued forty-five years after his death, and was ended only when the English had destroyed French dominion in America, by force of arms, and by conquest stripped France of a great portion of its claimed territory in our country.

CHAPTER XVI.

NATIONALITIES OF THE AMERICAN COLONISTS—THEIR SOCIAL CHARACTERISTICS—THEIR INDUSTRIES AND COMMERCIAL RESTRICTIONS—THEIR EDUCATIONAL INSTITUTIONS—NEWSPAPERS IN THE COLONIES—THE TENDENCY OF THE PEOPLE TO LOCAL SELF-GOVERNMENT AND UNION—PLANS FOR A NATIONAL UNION—CONGRESSES—DESIGNS OF THE ROYAL GOVERNORS—A CRISIS—LORDS OF TRADE AND PLANTATIONS—RESISTANCE TO THE ROYAL PREROGATIVE—COMPLAINTS BY ROYALISTS IN AMERICA—REVOLUTION PREVENTED BY THE FRENCH AND INDIAN WAR.

SEVERAL European nations, as we have seen, contributed materials for the English-American colonies. They were people of varied and opposite tastes, habits and theological views, but, as a rule, they commingled without asperity; and when the time came for a political union, no serious antagonisms were apparent. Churchmen and Dissenters, Roman Catholics, Puritans and Friends, finally settled down quietly together, and labored with a generous faith in each other for the public good. The Puritans of New England, the Friends of Pennsylvania, the Roman Catholics of Maryland and the Churchmen of Virginia, though often narrow in their theological views, manifested a common love of liberty, and acted upon the common rule that the majority should govern.

A great majority of the emigrants who settled the English domain in America were of Teutonic origin. The English, Lowland Scotch, Dutch and Swedes, were decidedly of German blood. The Irish and French were few at first. Denmark and the Baltic regions contributed a considerable number, and natives from Africa were soon scattered among the white population of all the colonies. With the exception of Georgia, the emigrants had founded settlements and colonies without the aid of the British government, and often in defiance of its expressed wishes and absolute decrees. Subjects of the same perils and hardships, there grew up among them, insensibly, a brotherhood of feeling that prepared the people of thirteen of the colonies, after uniting in resistance to the aggressions of the French during a war of more than seven years duration, to resist, almost as one man, every form of oppression, when the government to which they acknowledged their allegiance became an oppressor.

There was a great diversity of character seen among the inhabitants of the several colonies, owing, chiefly, to their origin, early habits, and the climate. Those of Virginia were from classes in English society wherein a lack of rigid moral discipline allowed free living and its attendant vices. This circumstance, combined with the influence of a mild climate, produced a tendency to voluptuousness and ease among the Virginians and their southern neighbors. They generally exhibited less moral restraint, more hospitality, and greater frankness and social refinement, than the people of New England. The latter were from the middling classes of society. They included a great many religious enthusiasts, possessing more zeal than knowledge. Very rigid in their manners, shy and jealous of strangers, they

CAVALIER. PURITAN. HOLLANDER. FRIEND.

COSTUMES OF THE SETTLERS IN AMERICA.

were extremely strict in their notions, and attempted to regulate the habits and tastes of society by formal standards. Their early legislation, as we have seen, recognizing as it did the right to control the most minute regulations of social life, often presents food for merriment for their descendants. The General Court of Massachusetts, on one occasion, required the proper officers to notice the "apparel" of the people, especially their "ribbands and great boots." Drinking of healths in public or private; wearing funeral badges; celebrating the Church festivals of Christmas and Easter, and many other things that seemed quite improper to magistrates and legislators, and especially to the Puritan clergy, were forbidden. At Hartford, the General Court kept an eye constantly upon the conduct of the people. Freemen were compelled to vote under a penalty of six-pence; the use of tobacco was prohibited to persons under twenty years of age, without the certificate of a physician; and no others were allowed to use it more than once a day, and then they must be more than ten miles from any house. The people of Hartford were compelled to rise in the morning when the watchman rang his bell. And so, in a great variety of enactments, the law-makers, with pure intentions, noble purposes and virtuous aims, tried to make the whole people Christians after their own pattern. If they did not accomplish these higher designs, they erected strong bulwarks against the smaller vices which compose, in a great degree, private and public evils. They dwelt upon a parsimonious soil. Possessing neither the means nor the inclination for sumptuous living indulged in by their southern brethren, the New Englanders lived in very plain houses and their habits were frugal.

The ideas, manners, customs and pursuits of the Dutch made a deep impression upon the colonists of New York and portions of New Jersey and Pennsylvania, which is not yet effaced, but appears conspicuous in many places. They were a race of industrious, frugal, plodding money-getters, loving personal ease and freedom from disturbance. They possessed very few of the elements of progress. They were constitutionally averse to change, and had very little faith in anything not known to their fathers. They were distinguished by many of the more substantial virtues that are necessary in giving health to society and stability to a State. The Swedes and Finns on the Delaware did not differ much from the Dutch in their general characteristics; but the habits of the Friends, whose influence predominated in West Jersey and Pennsylvania, were quite different. There was a refined simplicity in the manners and habits of the latter that won the esteem and confidence of virtuous and cultivated people, and the respect of every class. They made no ostentatious display in their dress or of their piety. They were governed in their daily life by a religious sentiment without fanaticism, which was a powerful safeguard against vice and immorality.

The Maryland settlers were greater formalists in religion and less restrained in their conduct than the New Englanders or the Dutch. They were generally more refined than the colonists of the East, and equally industrious, but they lacked the unwearied perseverance in pursuits of the latter. As in New England, so in Maryland, the peculiarities of the inhabitants had been greatly modified by inter-migration at the middle of the last century. Religious intolerance had been subdued; and when common danger called for common defenders of the soil and of the chartered rights of the colonists, they stood shoulder to shoulder in battle-array and in legislative halls.

The principal pursuit of the English-American colonists was agriculture. At the time we are considering, commerce and manufactures were struggling here against unwise and unjust laws for existence. With forced self-reliance, the people had been compelled, from the beginning, to make their own apparel, their simple furniture, and their implements for labor, which they could not buy from the looms and workshops of Old England; and manual labor was regarded as honorable and dignified, especially in New England and the immediately adjoining provinces. The evil example of an idle privileged class was never before the settlers in the forests of America.

The commerce of the English-American colonies had a feeble infancy, and was stunted in its growth by oppressive navigation laws. Indeed, their trade may not properly be dignified with the name of commerce before the Revolution. So early as 1636, a Massachusetts vessel of thirty tons made a voyage to the West Indies; and two years later another vessel went from Salem to New Providence, and returned with a cargo of cotton, salt, tobacco and negroes. This was the beginning of negro slavery in New England. It was recognized by law in Massachusetts, in 1641; in Connecticut and Rhode Island, about the year 1650; in New York, in 1656; in Maryland, in 1663; and in New Jersey, in 1665. There were but a few slaves in Pennsylvania. Some were there as early as 1690, and were chiefly in Philadelphia. At about the same time a few appeared in Delaware. In Virginia, as we have seen, they were introduced in 1619; and in the Carolinas, at the time of their settlement. By an evasion of law they were taken into Georgia about the year 1752.

The successful voyages of these vessels from Massachusetts were regarded with joy, as the harbingers of a flourishing American commerce; and the New England people, especially, looked forward with expectations of much wealth to be derived from the ocean, for they were then quite extensively engaged in fishing. But a navigation act passed by the republican parliament in 1651, gave them warning of English jealousy; and its restoration, with more stringent clauses, by the royal parliament in 1660, satisfied the colonists that their commerce was doomed, because it seemed to be regarded as a promising rival of that of Great Britain. After that the attention of parliament was called from time to time to the industries of the American colonies, and laws were made to regulate them. In 1719, the House of Commons declared that "erecting any manufactories in the colonies tended to lessen their dependence on Great Britain," and they were discouraged. A little earlier a British author had written: "There be fine iron works which cast no guns; no house in New England has above twenty rooms; not twenty in Boston have ten rooms each; a dancing-school was set up here, but put down; a fencing-school is allowed. There be no musicians by trade. All cordage, sail-cloth and mats, come from England; no cloth made there worth four shillings per yard; no alum, no salt made by their sun."

Later, woolen-goods, paper and hemp were manufactured in New England, and almost every family made coarse cloth for domestic use. A heavy duty had been laid on pig-iron sent from the colonies to England, and the Americans made successful attempts to manufacture it into bars for native blacksmiths, and to make steel. Hats, also, were manufactured and sold in different colonies; and small brigantines (square-rigged, two-masted vessels) were built in Massachusetts and Pennsylvania, and exchanged with West India merchants for rum, sugar, wines, and silks. Again the jealousy of the British government was awakened, and greater restrictions upon colonial manufactures were imposed, they being foolishly considered as detrimental to the interests of the English at home. It was ordained by a law that all manufacturers of iron and steel in the colonies should be considered "a nuisance" to be abated within thirty days after notice being given, under a penalty of one thousand dollars. A law was enacted in 1750 which prohibited the "erection or continuance of any mill or other engine for slitting or rolling-iron, or any plating-forge to work with a tilt-hammer, or any furnace for making steel in the colonies." The exportations of hats from one colony to another was prohibited; and no hatter was allowed to have more than two apprentices at one time. The importation of sugar, molasses and rum was burdened with exorbitant duties; and the Carolinians were actually forbidden to cut down a tree in their vast pine forests for the purpose of converting its wood into staves, or its juices into turpentine. The raising of sheep in the colonies was restrained, because wool was then the great staple of England. The interests of the landed aristocracy were consulted more than justice. In the preamble to a restraining act, it was avowed that the motive for its enactment was a conviction that colonial industry would "inevitably sink the value of lands in England." And so, for about a hundred years, the British government had attempted, by restrictive laws, to confine the commerce of the colonies to the interchange of their agricultural products for English manufactures only. The trade of the colonies was certainly worth preserving, for the exports from Great Britain to them averaged, in value, at that period, about three-and-a-quarter million dollars annually. But the unrighteous measures adopted to secure that trade produced (as unrighteousness generally does in the end) a great loss. These acts of oppression constituted the chief item in the "bill of particulars" presented by the Americans in the account with Great Britain when, on the fourth of July, 1776, they gave to the world their reasons for declaring themselves "free and independent" of the British crown.

Education had received special attention in most of the colonies, and particularly in New England, from the beginning. So early as 1621, schools were established in Virginia for the education of white and Indian children. This was the first provision for education made in the colonies. For reasons not clearly defined, these schools did not flourish, and the funds appropriated for their support were finally given to the trustees of William and Mary College, which was founded at Williamsburg, in Virginia, in 1692. Fifty-four years before, the Rev. John Harvard had given half his estate and three hundred of his books for the founding of the college at Cambridge, Massachusetts, which bears his name. And eight years after the establishment of William and Mary College, ten clergymen met at Saybrook, near the mouth of the Connecticut River, and each contributing some books, took measures for founding a college there. It was accomplished in 1701. The most generous patron of the institution in its infancy was Elihu Yale, then president of the English East India Company. He was born in New Haven, Connecticut. His name was given to the college, and in 1717 it was removed to the place of his nativity, where it still flourishes. King's (now Columbia) College was established in the city of New York in 1750; and these four seminaries com-

ELIHU YALE. SEAL OF HARVARD COLLEGE. GREAT SEAL OF WILLIAM AND MARY.

posed the chief seats of learning in the English-American colonies when the French and Indian war broke out.

While these higher institutions of learning were struggling even for existence, the common schools—the glory and pride of New England especially—were flourishing. At the beginning of the existence of the Connecticut colony, a law provided that every town—organized religious communities—containing one hundred householders, should maintain a grammar school. Similar provision was made for popular education throughout New England, and that region was soon conspicuous for the intelligence of its people. The school teacher in many places had a variety of duties, so that his time was wholly employed in and out of school. At Portsmouth, New Hampshire, an ordinance of the selectmen defined the duties of the schoolmaster, as follows: "To act as a court messenger; to serve summonses; to lead the choir on Sundays; to ring the bell for public worship; to dig the graves; to take charge of the school, and to perform other occasional duties."

Reading took the place of frivolous amusements, which were discouraged by law in New England. History and theology were the chief topics of most of the books then read in that region, and many volumes were sold. A traveler mentioned the fact that before the year 1686, several booksellers in Boston had "made fortunes by their business."

In time newspapers began to appear in the colonies, but were of little worth, as vehicles of general information, until the period of our Revolution. The first one issued in America was published in Boston in September, 1690. It was printed on three pages seven by eleven inches square, on a folded sheet, and was entitled "Public Occurrences both Foreign and Domestic." The editor said of it: "It is designed that the country shall be furnished once a month (or if any glut of occurrences happen, oftener) with an account of such considerable things as have arrived unto our notice." And he gave warning in his first number that his paper should be the vehicle for exposing slanderers and false reporters, saying: "It is supposed that none will dislike this proposal, but such as intend to be guilty of so villainous a crime." Only one number of this newspaper was published. The first permanent newspaper was "The Boston News-Letter," first issued in the spring of 1704. The first in Pennsylvania was "The American," published in Philadelphia in 1719. The first in New York was "The New York Gazette," in 1725; the first in Maryland was the "Maryland Gazette," issued at Annapolis in the summer of 1728. "The South Carolina Gazette," printed at Charleston at the beginning of 1732, was the first issued in that province; the first in Rhode Island was "The Rhode Island Gazette," printed at Newport in 1732; the first in Virginia was "The Virginia Gazette," printed at Williamsburg in 1736; the first in Connecticut was "The Connecticut Gazette," printed at New Haven in 1755; the first in North Carolina was "The North Carolina Gazette," printed at New Berne the same year; and the first in New Hampshire was "The New Hampshire Gazette," printed at Portsmouth in the summer of 1756. At the period of the French and Indian war newspapers were printed in all of the colonies excepting in New Jersey, Delaware and Georgia. The printing-machines on which all the colonial newspapers and books were printed were simple in form and rude in construction, as may be seen in the picture of the Ephrata printing-press here given.

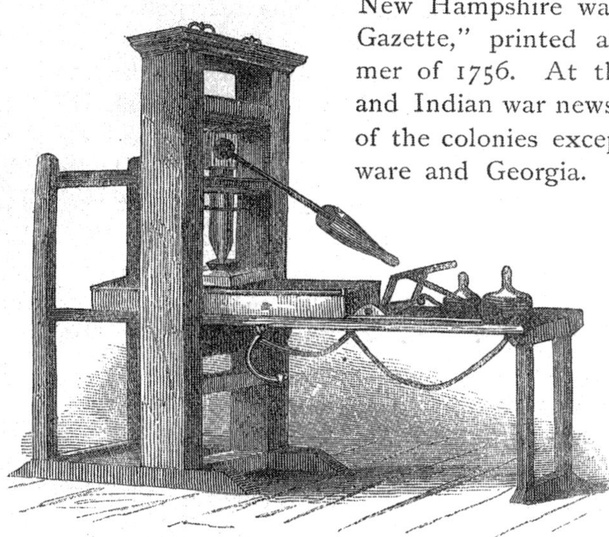

THE EPHRATA PRINTING-PRESS.

Of the number of the inhabitants of the colonies at that time, we have no exact enumeration. Mr. Bancroft, after a careful examination of many official returns and private computations, estimated the number of white inhabitants of all the colonies to be 1,165,000, and the blacks (who were mostly slaves) to be 260,000, distributed as follows:

	WHITE.	BLACK.		WHITE.	BLACK.
Massachusetts	207,000	3,000	Pennsylvania and Delaware	195,000	11,000
New Hampshire	50,000		Maryland	104,000	44,000
Connecticut	133,000	3,500	Virginia	168,000	116,000
Rhode Island	35,000	4,500	North Carolina	70,000	20,000
New York	85,000	11,000	South Carolina	40,000	40,000
New Jersey	73,000	5,000	Georgia	5,000	2,000

Since the English Revolution in 1688—a period of only sixty-six years—the growth of the colonies in population had been marvellous. New England had increased from 75,000 to 425,000; New York, from 20,000 to 85,000; New Jersey, Pennsylvania, Delaware and Maryland, from 47,000 to 372,000; Virginia, from 50,000 to 168,000; and the Carolinas and Georgia, from 8,000 to 135,000. The assertion of a letter of an "American Farmer" was almost literally true when he wrote: "We are all tillers of the earth

33

from Nova Scotia to West Florida. We are a people of cultivation, scattered over an immense territory; communicating with each other by means of good roads and navigable rivers; united by the silken bands of mild government; all respecting the laws, without dreading their power because they are equitable."

While the English-American colonists were treated by the mother country as minor children or as absolute subjects to be governed, without questionings, by her capricious will; and while every measure of the British ministry was calculated to trammel their advance toward local self-government, that lofty idea was working out in America the great problem of republicanism, whose demonstration by actual achievements the monarchs of Europe were dreading. It was an idea that had spontaneous birth in the minds of all the colonists when they first felt the stimulating air of the freedom of their forest homes; and it grew into a mighty force in the bosoms of individuals before any one dared to openly promulgate it. It was the early inspiration out of which grew the democracy that finally impelled the colonists to proclaim themselves independent and to establish a nation here.

The common danger, as we have seen, caused a confederation of New England colonies in 1643, but the national idea was lacking, and it was short-lived. A half a century later William Penn put forth a plan for a general union of all the colonies, for their mutual welfare, in which he proposed the appointment of persons in each colony, who should meet at specified times, in a general congress to mature plans for the common good, whose presiding officer should be a high commissioner appointed by the crown, and in time of war should command all of the colonial forces. Penn's plan was commended by many thoughtful persons, and it was likened to the Grecian Amphictyonic Council. After that, writers in England and the colonies publicly discussed the topic, not with any idea of the independence of the colonists as subjects of Great Britain, but with a feeling that a national union here would redound to the glory and happiness of Great Britain and her American citizens. When, early in the last century, public attention was called to the evident designs of the French to supplant the English in America, Daniel Coxe, who had been a prominent man in New Jersey, published a volume in London (1722), in which he proposed that all the British colonies here should be united by a national covenant, in a national government, over which a supreme viceroy or governor, appointed by the crown, should preside in some part of America, the governors of the several colonies to be subordinate to him; and also that there should be a general congress of deputies chosen by the several colonies to promote unity of action in times of danger. Men of all shades of political opinion made similar suggestions; and Dinwiddie, governor of Virginia, recommended, not only a union of the colonies for mutual defence, but a confederation of the Indians then friendly toward the English, with the tribes more in the interior and under the influence of the French.

Meanwhile there had been several congresses or conventions of leading men in the colonies, having for their object the union of the people of the several provinces for the public good, or to cultivate the friendship of the Indians. One of these was held at Albany in 1684, composed of the officers of the governments of Massachusetts, New York, Maryland and Virginia, and sachems of the Five Nations. In 1693, Governor Fletcher, of New York, in compliance with a letter of instructions from the king, called a congress of commissioners from New England and other colonies to consult about the quotas of men and money which the several provinces should raise for common defence against the French. The call was so feebly answered that nothing was done by the few present. This was followed the next year by a meeting of commissioners at Albany with sachems of the Iroquois Confederacy, the object being to prevent the Five Nations from making a peace with the French in Canada.

When it was resolved to invade Canada with a land and naval force, in 1711, a convention was held at New London, Connecticut, to consult upon the matter, at which the governors of several of the colonies appeared and agreed upon the quotas. The expedition that followed, under Colonel Nicholson on land and Sir Hovenden Walker on the water, proved disastrous, as we have seen. In 1722, a congress of colonial officials and Indian sachems was held at Albany for the promotion of a friendly feeling and the strengthening of the alliance then existing with the Iroquois Confederacy. And in 1744, a similar congress, for the same purpose, met at Lancaster, in Pennsylvania, whereat over two hundred and fifty representatives of the Six (late Five) Nations were in attendance.

The last of these colonial congresses, all exhibiting tendencies toward a national union, was held at Albany in the summer of 1748, soon after news had reached the colonies of a preliminary treaty of peace having been signed by the commissioners of England and France. The congress was called for a two-fold purpose. The antagonisms between the royal governors and the people were alarming to the crown officers in America, and the latter wished to secure a colonial revenue through British interference, and not be subjected, in the matter, to the will or caprice of colonial assemblies. Foremost among these crown officers who were willing to abridge the rights of the people, were Governor Clinton, of New York, and Governor Shirley, of Massachusetts. They had promoted the assembling of the congress with a hope that that body would favor their scheme, and they were both there with their political friends. Another purpose of the meeting was the strengthening of the bond of friendship between the Six Nations and their savage neighbors on the west, and the English. A vast concourse of barbarians were there. The royal governors gained nothing for themselves; but a satisfactory arrangement was made with the Indians. They agreed that no Frenchman should abide within their borders; also, not to send any delegation to Canada, and to have their warriors ready for the service of the English whenever they should be called for.

A crisis in political affairs in the colonies was now at hand. The royal governors perceived that something must speedily be done to curb the democratic spirit of the people, or local self-government would supersede royal authority. It was necessary to convince parliament of this truth. Only through the *Lords of Trade* and *Plantations* could this be done. This was a Board or Committee appointed by the crown in 1696, to whom was entrusted a general oversight of the affairs of the American colonies. It was originally composed of seven members and a president. To them the royal governors were requested to give frequent and full information of the condition of their respective governments concerning political and commercial affairs, and particularly of the proceedings of the assemblies; also of the appropriations for the public service, and how they were expended. To this Board the royal agents in the colonies addressed their letters. "It was the lion's mouth," says Frothingham in his *Rise of the Republic of the United States*, "into which the accusations and complaints against the colonies were indiscriminately cast."

To arouse the Lords of Trade and Plantations to action, some overt act of disobedience on the part of the colonies must be obtained. The bluff Admiral Clinton, then governor of New York, was chosen to bring on the crisis, and that province was to be the theatre of the collision. The royal governors were to aid him by representations to the Board of the turbulence of the people and their disloyalty. Governor Shirley took occasion, when the people of Boston had liberated some of their citizens from the grasp of a British admiral who had impressed them into the naval service, to represent the act as a rebellious insurrection. "The chief cause of the mobbish turn of a town inhabited by twenty thousand inhabitants," he continued, "is its constitution, by which the management of it devolves on the populace, assembled in their town meetings." Royalists in Pennsylvania wrote words of warning, saying that "the obstinate, wrong-headed Assembly of Quakers" in that colony, "pretended not to be accountable to his majesty or his government," and that "they may, in time, apply the public money to purposes injurious to the crown and the mother country." "Virginia," wrote its governor, "formerly an orderly province, has nothing more at heart than to lessen the influence of the crown." In a similar strain loyalists wrote from all the provinces; and the Earl of Halifax, a young man a little more than thirty years of age, who had been placed at the head of The Lords of Trade, was satisfied that royal authority in the colonies was in peril, and so informed the ministry. In a letter to Governor Glen, of South Carolina, he promised "a very serious consideration on the just prerogatives of the crown and those defects of the constitution which have spread themselves over many of the plantations, and are destructive to all order and government."

Governor Clinton sought, and soon found an occasion for a quarrel with the New York Assembly. He demanded of that body an appropriation for the support of the government, for five years next ensuing, with a view of making himself, as governor, independent of the assembly. As he expected, they refused their compliance. Then he warned them of the danger of incurring the displeasure of parliament, and dissolved the assembly. He at once wrote letters to the Lords of Trade, complaining of the rebellious tendencies of a greater portion of the assembly, charging them with claiming "all the powers and privileges of parliament;" that they had "set up the people as the high court of American appeal;" that they had "virtually assumed all of the public money into their own hands, and issued it without warrant from the governor," and, also, had assumed the right to nominate all officers of government; to reward all services by granting the salaries annually, "not to the office, but by name to the person in the office," and that the "system if not speedily remedied, would effect the dependency of the colonies on the crown." He besought the king to "make a good example for all America, by regulating the government of New York." He declared that until that should be done he could not "meet the assembly without danger of exposing the king's authority," and himself, "to contempt."

After violent quarrels with all political factions in the province, Clinton abandoned the government in disgust, and returned home. He was succeeded by Sir Danvers Osborne, who came with instructions to demand from the assembly a permanent revenue to be disbursed solely by himself. His council assured him that the assembly would refuse compliance with the demand. Foreseeing much trouble ahead, he became despondent. This state of mind was aggravated by grief because of the recent death of his wife, and he hanged himself with his pocket-handkerchief to the garden fence at his lodgings in New York.

The attitude of the New York Assembly was applauded by the leaders of popular opinion in the other colonies; and had measures for the maintenance of the royal prerogative and the supreme authority of parliament which Halifax proposed been pressed with vigor much longer, the revolution which broke out about twenty years later would doubtless have occurred then. But more urgent considerations occupied the attention of the British government and the American colonies at that time. Ever since the English captured Louisburg, in 1745, and D'Anville experienced his naval disasters, the French had put forth the most vigorous efforts for the extension and strengthening of their dominion in America. They were resolved on a persistent strife for power; and their aggressive movements about the year 1753, aroused the British government and the American colonial assemblies and people to the necessity of employing equally vigorous measures for opposing their common enemy. Then the colonists united among themselves and with the Home Government in defence of British dominion in America. Then began the conflict known in America as the *French and Indian War*, and in Europe as the *Seven Years War*, which we will now consider.

CHAPTER XVII.

THE TREATY OF AIX-LA-CHAPELLE—EFFORTS OF THE ENGLISH TO MAINTAIN THEIR DOMINION IN AMERICA—THE OHIO LAND COMPANY—EVENTS IN NOVA SCOTIA—SUFFERINGS OF THE FRENCH INHABITANTS THERE—ATTEMPTS TO ENSLAVE THE AMERICANS RESISTED—MAHEW'S PATRIOTIC SERMONS—MOVEMENTS OF THE FRENCH ALARM THE ENGLISH—THE OHIO COUNTRY EXPLORED—TREATY WITH THE INDIAN TRIBES—HOSTILE ATTITUDE OF THE FRENCH—MAJOR WASHINGTON'S EMBASSY TO THE FRENCH COMMANDER.

THE famous treaty at Aix-la-Chapelle in 1748 produced the pacification. of Europe, and a lull in warfare in America. It seemed to promise a long repose from war in both hemispheres. In that ancient city of Rhenish Prussia, where Charlemagne was born and where he died, and where fifty-five emperors have been crowned, the representatives of Great Britain, France, Holland, Germany, Spain and Genoa, signed a solemn treaty which ended a war begun in 1740. That was the consequence of the ascension of the throne of Austria by Maria Theresa in conformity to the "Pragmatic Sanction"—a royal ordinance—of her father, Charles the Sixth of Germany, made in 1713. That treaty confirmed six other treaties which had been made in the space of a century; and hopeful men looked for the peace of the millennium almost. But that treaty was made delusive by a further struggle between France and England for dominion in America.

The commissioners at Aix-la-Chapelle had hardly reached their homes before the rash and inexperienced Earl of Halifax, at the head of the Board of Trade and Plantations, observing the steady encroachments upon claimed English domain in America, and the menacing attitude of the French there, resolved to employ measures for securing to England the conquered territory on the east and the valley of the Ohio River on the west: the latter by settlements and colonization. The Indians there were friendly to the English, and the Six Nations held the passes from Canada to that rich valley.

Virginians and Marylanders had proposed the planting of an English colony beyond the Alleghany Mountains, where there was seen only here and there the solitary cabin of an English trader. Halifax regarded that region as "the centre of the British dominions," and he persuaded the king to instruct the governor of Virginia to grant to a company of speculators five hundred thousand acres of land on the north side of the Ohio, between the site of the present city of Pittsburgh and the mouth of the Kanawha River. This association was known as *The Ohio Land Company.* It was agreed that the company should not be called upon for quit-rent for the space of ten years. It was also agreed that within seven years at least one

THE ACADIANS FIRST DISTURBED.

hundred families should be settled on the tract, and the company, at their own expense, to build a fort there. Among the proprietors was Robert Dinwiddie of Scotland, then surveyor-general for the southern colonies, who was soon afterward made lieutenant-governor of Virginia.

At the same time cruel measures were adopted by the English government for securing dominion in Acadié, or Nova Scotia. The French government and French priests proceeded to coax the simple French inhabitants to leave their ancient settlements on the peninsula and take a position near the frontier, the object being to make them a barrier against the encroachments of the English. At about the same time Governor Shirley, of Massachusetts, proposed to remove the Acadians altogether, and distribute them among the English colonies, because they were French Roman Catholics, and to settle their country with Protestants. This atrocious proposal was opposed by the British ministry at first. A more humane policy was adopted. It was to settle so many Protestants among the Acadians that the obedience of the French inhabitants to British authority would be secured. Protestants in European countries were invited to settle there, under English protection, but responses were few. Finally, the British government induced disbanded British soldiers and marines to accept lands among the Acadians and to settle there. During the year 1749, about fourteen hundred of these, led by Colonel Cornwallis, went among the Acadians and planted the first English town east of the Penobscot, in a dreary place, and named it Halifax. This was in compliment to the energetic earl who had actively promoted the emigration.

Now the serious troubles of the simple-minded Acadians began. When, twenty years before, they bowed submissively to English rule, they had been promised freedom in religious matters, and exemption from bearing arms against the French and Indians. This gave them the name of French Neutrals. Now they were ordered to take an oath of allegiance to Great Britain, and the supremacy of the crown in religious matters, and be subjected to all the duties of English subjects. A thousand of the men signed a petition humbly asking permission to sell their lands and remove to some place to be provided by the French government. Their hearts bore allegiance to France and the ancient church, and they begged not to be compelled to take up arms against the one, nor to forswear the other. The haughty Cornwallis said to the ambassadors who brought the petition to him: "Take the oath or your property will be confiscated. It is for me to command: you to obey."

More cruel were the proceedings against the Indians on the peninsula, whom Jesuit priests had incited to furious raids along the New England frontiers. Cornwallis summoned a powerful Micmac chief to his presence. He came, feathered and painted, with two young warriors. Wrapped in his blanket, he stood erect and defiant before the English commander. Cornwallis demanded the instant submission of all the tribe to British authority. The chief haughtily replied: "The land on which you sleep, is ours; we sprung from it as do the trees, and the grass, and the flowers. It is ours forever, and we will not yield it to any man;" and turning on his heel went back to his people. Under the orders of his superiors, who declared that the Indians on the peninsula were "banditti, ruffians or rebels," Cornwallis offered ten guineas for every one of them "taken or killed," to be paid on producing the body or scalp of the savage. Such were the measures adopted by the English at the middle of the last century for checking the encroachments of the French on the east and west of their domain. At that time the English in America numbered almost a million and a half; the French were not more than a hundred thousand strong, but they controlled much of the Indian power of the continent. France and England were heirs to an ancient quarrel originating far back in feudal ages and kept alive by frequent collisions.

While the French power in America seemed to be confined to a narrow strip of territory along the St. Lawrence and the Lakes, the remote north-eastern portion of the continent, and in the western wilderness to very distant missionary stations, very little apprehension of real danger to their colonies was felt by the English; but when, after the French lost Louisburg in 1745, they built strong vessels at the foot of Lake Ontario; made stronger their little trading fort at Niagara; built a cordon of fortifications, more than sixty in number, between Montreal and New Orleans; claimed dominion over all the territory drained by tributaries of the Mississippi, with the plausible plea that the French were the discoverers of a greater portion of that stream, and were negotiating treaties with the powerful Delawares and Shawnoese, on the frontiers of Pennsylvania and Virginia, the English perceived real and impending danger. The American colonists saw it first, and were alarmed; hence the proposition to plant an English settlement west of the Alleghanies. It was at that moment, when there appeared the plausible pretext of a necessity for united action, under a single head, against the French, that the British government resolved to assert its supreme authority in the colonies. Governor Shirley, a thorough royalist, proposed the building of frontier forts, under the direction of royal officers and engineers, at the expense of the colonies, and demanding from them the levying of a tax sufficient for the purpose. The crown officers of New York approved the measure. Shirley went to England to perfect his schemes, and found the government eager to do anything to check the democratic spirit in America which was evidently aiming at legislative independence, if not the setting up of an independent sovereignty. The English-Americans found themselves in the critical position of being compelled to fight the French and Indians for the preservation of their domain, and to contend with the mother country for their chartered rights and natural liberties. The French were their political and religious enemies, and menaced them with open hostility; their British brethren were their social foes, nestling in their bosoms, and seeking to conquer their noble and holy aspirations under false pretences. Yet the Americans were hopeful and firm. When the Lords of Trade induced the parliament to attempt to assert its supremacy in the colonies, and royal governors, under instructions, demanded of the colonial assemblies, in haughty words, the money and the rights of the Americans, their demands were met by a quiet defiance in the form of positive refusals and energetic protests of an indignant people. These had, many of them, been driven from England by persecution; had founded homes and built up states without England's aid, and had spent blood and treasure freely for England's honor and glory without even the poor return of thanks; therefore this insidious attempt to enslave them gave vehemence to their determination to assert their right to local self-government at all hazards. Their bold attitude at this time made the imperial government pause, and reserve its wrath for a more convenient season.

The words of young Mahew went forth from his pulpit in Boston, at that time, with the seeming unction and authority of the ancient prophets, "Thus saith the Lord"—when, with fervid eloquence, he denounced the unholy alliance of church and state for stamping out the freedom of Americans. It was then no secret that the English hierarchy were conspiring with the crown for the establishment of an episcopacy in America, and making the liturgy of the Church of England the state form of public worship. It was a part of the plan for enslaving the Americans. Whitefield had sounded the alarm-bell in New England, and Mahew was among the first to openly avow the public dissatisfaction. He vehemently reproved the "impious bargain between the sceptre and the surplice." "Resist the small beginnings of civil tyranny," he said, "lest it should swell to a torrent and deluge empires." "The divine right of kings, and non-resistance," he said in a sermon in 1750, "are as fabulous and chimerical as the most absurd reveries of ancient or modern visionaries. . . . If those who bear the title of civil rulers do not perform the duty of civil rulers—if they injure and oppress—they have not the least pretence to be honored or obeyed. If the common safety or utility would not be promoted by submission to the government, there is no motive for submission." And he declared that disobedience, under such circumstance, became "lawful and glorious." The sentiment of the colonists was responsive; and the temper manifested by the people then was the herald of that flame of feeling which, a quarter of a century later, kindled the old war for independence. It aroused the animosity of the crown and its creatures against the Americans, and history was repeated. Demosthenes said to the Thebans two thousand years before:

"We are well aware of that inextinguishable hatred which kings and the slaves of kings have ever felt towards nations which have plumed themselves on being free."

A crisis was now at hand. The disputes between the French and English in America ripened into action.

The French were offended by the planting of Halifax, in Nova Scotia; and a partisan named La Corne, professing to act under the orders of Joncaire, chief captain in Canada, took possession of the isthmus that connects the peninsula with the main, with a large force of French and Indians. He summoned the Acadians to renounce their allegiance to the English and take refuge with the French; and that poor people were at their wits' end. He held a village (now Fort Lawrence), and compelled the inhabitants to take an oath of allegiance to France.

When Cornwallis heard of this he called upon Massachusetts to help in dislodging the intruders. The Assembly replied: "By the constitution of this province we must first be convinced of the necessity of raising supplies." So they politely refused, and Cornwallis was compelled to rely upon the slender means at his command. With four hundred soldiers he appeared in transports before the town. The alarmed Jesuit priest set fire to the church, and compelled the bewildered inhabitants to lay their houses in ashes and flee across the river. The French were too strong for the English, and the latter withdrew. A second expedition, a few months later, was successful. Fort Beau Sejour, which the French had built opposite the desolated town, was captured, with loss of life. This was the first blood they had shed in war since the treaty at Aix-la-Chapelle. It was now August, 1750.

This event was followed by the capture of French vessels by an English man-of-war off Cape Sable. The French government, exasperated by these insults to their flag, broke off negotiations for a peaceful settlement of boundaries in America, and resolved to appeal to the arbitrament of the sword. At near the head of the valley of the Ohio was the theatre of the first passage at arms.

The Ohio Land Company took measures for defining and occupying their domain. Thomas Lee, Augustine and Lawrence Washington, and other leading Virginia members of the Company, ordered goods to be sent from London suitable for the Indian trade; and as no attempt at settlement could be safely made without some previous arrangement with the Indians, the Company petitioned the Virginia government to invite the savages to a treaty council. As a preliminary movement, the Company took measures to obtain information concerning the best lands beyond the mountains. English traders with the Indians had traversed the passes through them, and spoke of the beauty and fertility of the country beyond, but the Company wished more definite knowledge. In the autumn of 1750, Christopher Gist, from the borders of the Yadkin, was in Virginia. He was a bold and skillful woodsman, and acquainted with Indian life; and he was employed to cross the great hills and spy out the land. He was instructed to observe the best mountain passes; to explore the country as far down as the Falls of the Ohio (Louisville); examine the most useful streams and count their falls; search out the fertile level lands; ascertain the strength of the Indian tribes, and make as accurate a chart of the region as his observations would allow.

GIST EXPLORING THE WILDERNESS.

Gist left Alexandria on horseback at the close of October; crossed the Blue Ridge and the Shenandoah Valley; waded through snow-drifts in the Alleghany Mountains; swam his horse across the Ohio River, and made his way through a rich narrow valley to Logstown, where it was proposed to hold the Indian council. He presented himself as an ambassador from the British sovereign. As such he was respected by the chief, but the savages received him with coolness. "You are come to settle the Indians' land," said the chief; "you never shall go home safe." Undaunted by this covert threat, Gist pressed forward to the Muskingum, stopping at a village of Ottawas, who were friends of the French. The Wyandots at Muskingum received him cordially, and there he found George Croghan, an emissary of the Pennsylvanians who were jealous of the Ohio Company, regarding them as rivals seeking a monopoly of the trade with the Indians of the northwest.

Gist crossed the Muskingum as he had crossed the Ohio—the "beautiful river," in the language of the Iroquois—and pushing on with Croghan and other traders through the stately forests and across savannahs then white with snow, he reached the Scioto River a few miles from its mouth. There dwelt some Delawares; and a short distance below the Scioto there were Shawnoese on both sides of the Ohio. Both professed friendship for the English, and a willingness to attend a general council at Logstown.

Northward lay the beautiful land of the Miamis, a confederacy really more powerful than that of the Iroquois, with whom they were friendly. Thither the representatives of Virginia and Pennsylvania went. They were kindly received. Strings of wampum were exchanged as tokens of friendship. A treaty of peace and alliance was concluded with the confederacy, and arrangements were made for all the friendly tribes to meet at Logstown in grand council.

Just as the treaty was signed, four Ottawas came with presents from the French. The Indian sovereign, who presided at the council, immediately set up the flags of France and England side by side. Addressing the Ottawas, he said: "The path of the French is bloody, and was made so by them. We have made a road plain for our brothers, the English, and your fathers have made it foul and crooked, and have made some of our brethren prisoners. This we look upon as an injury done to us." Then suddenly turning his back upon the Ottawas, he left the council. The French flag was removed, and the emissaries who bore it were ordered to return to their Gallic friends at Sandusky.

Gist viewed the magnificent country he was in with deepest admiration, and bidding his English companions and the dusky barbarians farewell, he went down the valley of the Little Miami to the Ohio and along that stream almost to the Falls. Then he penetrated the famous blue-grass region of Kentucky, with its marvellous forests; climbed over the mountains to the headwaters of the Yadkin and the Roanoke, and at the end of a journey of seven months, he stood before Lawrence Washington, at Mount Vernon, then chief director of the Ohio Company, with a vast amount of valuable information.

The promised council of the western tribes was not held until June, 1752. Gist was there as the agent of the Ohio Company, and Colonel Fry and two other commissioners represented Virginia. Friendly relations with the Western Indians were established by the treaty, but the barbarian chiefs steadily refused to recognize any English title to lands west of the Alleghany mountains. On that point they had been equally firm with the French, and resisted the importunities and claims of both. A shrewd

Delaware chief said to Gist: "The French claim all the land on one side of the river, and the English claim all the land on the other side of the river; where is the Indians' land?" It was a question difficult to answer. Gist did not attempt it, but said: "Indians and white men are subjects of the British king, and all have an equal privilege of taking up and possessing the land, in conformity with the conditions prescribed by the sovereign."

The Ohio Company sent out surveyors to explore the country, make definite boundaries and prepare for settlements. English traders penetrated the Ohio country to the domain of the Miamis and beyond, and the Indians found profit by their friendly relations with them. The jealousy of the French was aroused. They regarded the English as intruders. They saw with alarm the waning French influence among the tribes of the upper Ohio Valley, and presaged the ultimate destruction of their fortified line of communication between Canada and the Gulf of Mexico. Finally, in 1753, they seized and imprisoned some of the surveyors and traders; and about twelve hundred French soldiers were employed to erect forts in the wilderness between the upper waters of the Alleghany River and Lake Erie. One of these was erected at Presq'-isle, now Erie, on the southern shore of the lake of that name. Another was reared at Le Bœuf, on French Creek, now Waterford; and a third was constructed at the junction of French Creek and the Alleghany River, on the site of the village of Franklin.

The Ohio Company complained of these hostile demonstrations. Their lands lay within the chartered limits of Virginia, and the authorities of that colony felt it their duty to interfere in defence of the rights of the Company. Already the governors of Virginia and Pennsylvania had received instructions from England to repel the French by force of arms, if necessary. Robert Dinwiddie, one of the Company, and now governor of Virginia, determined to first send a letter of remonstrance to M. de St. Pierre, the French commander. Now, George Washington, who was destined to occupy a conspicuous place in the history of our country and of the world, first appeared on the theatre of public action, at the very opening of that illustrious drama whose closing scene was the founding of a mighty nation.

Young Washington was then a little more than twenty-one years of age. He was of an excellent and honorable family, whose roots lay far back in English history. He was a sort of foster-son of old Lord Fairfax; and as a public surveyor and skillful hunter, had traversed the forests of Virginia far and near, in the direction of the Ohio. At the age of nineteen years he had been commissioned a major of militia, charged with defending the colony against incursions of the Indians, and had entered upon the duties of his office with alacrity and zeal. Fraternal affection had called him from them to attend upon a dying brother, but he had evinced, during his short service, such an aptitude for military pursuits, and such faithfulness in performance, that he was marked for promotion.

Dinwiddie sent for Major Washington. He appeared promptly at the room of the governor (more exactly the lieutenant-governor) in the old state-house at Williamsburg, late in October, 1753. Dinwiddie was a bald-headed Scotchman, sixty-three years of age, with thin sandy hair, stout built, and so extremely nervous that his writing bore the marks of a trembling hand. Young Washington was full six feet in height, strongly built, with a florid complexion and every indication of high health and physical strength. The governor then first revealed to the major the object of his summons, and received his cheerful agreement to perform whatever duty might be required of him. The governor gave him a commission and instructions to proceed to the quarters of the French commander, and present to him in person a letter from Dinwiddie, in which the governor inquired by what authority French troops had presumed to intrude upon the territory of the British monarch, and what were his designs. It was a mission of great delicacy, and was accompanied by not a little peril. Discretion, ability, courage, physical endurance, experience in wood-craft and a knowledge of Indian manners, were requisite. Believing young Washington to be possessed of all of these, in an eminent degree, the governor chose him to be his ambassador, out of hundreds of the more pretentious aristocracy of Virginia. The result was creditable alike to the character of Major Washington and the sagacity of Governor Dinwiddie.

Washington was directed to proceed to Logstown (on the right bank of the Ohio, about fourteen miles below the site of Pittsburgh); convene influential Indian chiefs there; tell them the object of his visit, and request them to furnish him a competent escort as a safeguard to the headquarters of the French commander. There he was to demand an answer to Dinwiddie's letter in the name of his king; to observe, with caution, the number of troops that had crossed the lake; perceive the strength and number of their forts, and their distance from each other, and gain all information possible concerning the French on the English frontier. With these instructions Washington left Williamsburg, the Virginia capital, on the thirty-first of October, and was joined by John Davidson as Indian interpreter, and Jacob Van Braam, a Hollander by birth, and acquainted with the French language, to assist him in his intercourse with the people he was going to see. On his way he was joined by Mr. Gist, who acted as guide. With these, and four other men (two of them Indian traders), with horses, tents and baggage, they left the borders of civilization at the mouth of Will's Creek (now

MAJOR WASHINGTON ON HIS MISSION TO THE FRENCH COMMANDER.

Cumberland, Maryland), and made their way over the Alleghany Mountains, then covered with snow. They endured every hardship incident to a dreary wilderness and the rigors of winter. The streams in the valleys were full to their brims. Over the large ones they passed upon frail and rudely constructed rafts, wading and swimming their horses through the floods of the smaller streams. Late in November they reached the forks of the Ohio, on the site of Pittsburgh, where they rested a few days, and then proceeded to Logstown, accompanied by an influential sachem of the Delawares.

The headquarters of M. de St. Pierre was one hundred and twenty miles from Logstown. A bold and patriotic chief named Half-King, who, when the French came with arms and built forts in his country, had vehemently protested against the invasion of the rights of the Indians, and had been treated with disdain, volunteered, with two other chiefs and a skillful hunter, to escort the English company of eight to the headquarters of the French. In the simplicity of his heart he thought the English were only seeking to establish a trade with the tribes for mutual benefit. He and his people soon found that the French and English were equally governed by the ethics of the mailed hand—"Might makes Right," and came to deprive them of their domain and liberty.

After braving perils and hardships, the little company found themselves, early in December, at Fort Venango (now Franklin), the French outpost commanded by M. Joncaire. He received the English with civility, but tried to detach and detain the Indians. He remembered the patriotic speech of Half-King at a previous meeting, when the chief said: "The Great-King above allowed the land to be a place of residence for us, so I desire you to withdraw, as I have done our brothers, the English; for I will keep you at arm's length. I lay this down as a trial for both, to see which will have the greatest regard to it and make equal sharers with us." Joncaire hoped to gain his confidence by shaking his faith in the English, but did not succeed.

Further up the French Creek, Washington found St. Pierre, at Fort Le Bœuf. Here was the end of the Virginia ambassador's journey of forty-one days. The French commandant received him and his companions with great politeness. He was an elderly and courtly knight of St. Louis who, in his early years, had served in the army of Louis the Great, and had escaped the corruptions of the licentious court of his successor. He received the governor's letter with thanks; entertained the bearer and his friends four days, and then delivered into the hands of Major Washington a sealed letter in reply to Dinwiddie's. With this letter and much useful information respecting the forts and forces of the French, gathered by himself and

34

his associates, Washington returned to Williamsburgh at the middle of January.

The return journey was more perilous and fatiguing than the first. A greater portion of it was performed by Washington and Gist alone and on foot. At one time they were fired at by Indians supposed to have been incited to the deed by Joncaire. On another occasion, after working a whole day in constructing a raft, they attempted to cross the swift and swollen current of the Alleghany River upon it. The stream was filled with

WASHINGTON AND GIST AMONG THE ICE.

floating ice. They embarked at twilight, each with a pack on his back and gun strapped to it. They soon found themselves buffeting great perils. Washington, with a setting pole, was trying to hold the frail structure that the ice might pass by, when he was jerked off into water ten feet deep, and saved himself from drowning by catching hold of a raft-log. The raft was crushed, and the travelers, thoroughly drenched, were cast upon a desert island, where they lay upon the snow all night, hungry and half-frozen. Mr. Gist had all of his fingers and some of his toes frozen. Fortunately the ice was so thick over the channel in the morning that they crossed to the main, and toward evening, suffering with cold, they reached the cabin of a Scotch settler, near the spot where, a year and a half afterward, Braddock fought the French and Indians in the battle of the Monongahela. The island on which the travelers were wrecked is directly opposite the United States Arsenal, at Lawrenceville, Pennsylvania, and is known as Washington's Island.

After this adventure, Major Washington and his companion rested two or three days for their own refreshment and to procure horses. During that time the major paid a complimentary visit to the Indian Queen Aliquippa, who resided at the confluence of the Monongahela and Youghiogany rivers, in the southeastern part of Alleghany county. She had complained of his neglect in not calling upon her when on his outward journey. Young Washington explained the circumstances that prevented him, and with an apology he gave her a coat and a bottle of rum. The latter, Washington wrote, "was thought the much better present of the two," and harmony of feeling was restored. Aliquippa, who was a woman of great energy, and had performed some brave deeds, was held in respect amounting almost to reverence by the Indians in Western Pennsylvania.

CHAPTER XVIII.

REPLY TO DINWIDDIE'S LETTER—VIRGINIA PREPARES FOR WAR—A FORT COMMENCED ON THE SITE OF PITTSBURGH—THE FRENCH SEIZE IT AND NAME IT FORT DU QUESNE—WASHINGTON LEADS TROOPS TO RECOVER IT—ATTACKS AND DEFEATS SOME FRENCH TROOPS—COMPELLED TO SURRENDER TO THE FRENCH AFTERWARD—COLONIAL CONVENTION AT ALBANY—PLAN OF UNION ADOPTED—IT IS REJECTED BY THE BRITISH MINISTRY AND COLONIAL ASSEMBLIES—AMERICAN AFFAIRS IN ENGLAND—A MAD MILITARY SCHEME ABANDONED—WASHINGTON LEAVES THE MILITARY SERVICE IN DISGUST—BRADDOCK SENT TO AMERICA WITH TROOPS—PLAN OF THE CAMPAIGN FOR 1755 ARRANGED.

ST. PIERRE'S letter in reply to Governor Dinwiddie's caused immediate preparations for war. It was soldierly in tone and courteous in expression. He said it did not become him as a soldier to discuss civil matters; that Dinwiddie's letter should have been sent to the Marquis Du Quesne, then governor of Canada, by whose orders he acted and whose instructions he should carefully obey; and that the summons of the governor of Virginia to the French to retire from the country immediately could not be complied with.

Dinwiddie laid this letter before his council. The burgesses had shown themselves indifferent to the alleged dangers from the French; and the chief magistrate and his advisers determined not to wait for the assembling of the legislature. Under the general instructions from the king, they authorized the enlistment of two hundred men to march to the Ohio River and build two forts there before the French could descend that stream or its tributaries in the spring. Major Washington was commissioned a lieutenant-colonel, and placed in chief command of the troops to be raised; and the journal of his mission to the French commander was published to arouse the people to action. Washington made his headquarters for recruiting at Alexandria, and authorized Captain Trent to enlist men among the traders and frontier settlers.

Governor Dinwiddie now convened the legislature, and sent an appeal to the other colonies for help in the work so gallantly begun by Virginia. All hesitated excepting North Carolina, whose Assembly immediately voted men and money for the purpose. The royal governors and colonial assemblies were then wrangling fiercely about the supremacy of parliament and the rights of the Americans. The former insisted upon the exclusive right of parliament to fix quotas, direct taxation and disburse moneys through the agents of the crown in the colonies; the latter insisted upon their right to do these things themselves in their own way. Universal jealousy produced perilous procrastination. The danger was imminent. The warm spring days were approaching, when the snows and ice would disappear, and the French might be seen upon the waters of the "Beautiful River."

After much debate, the Virginia House of Burgesses, who, as Dinwiddie complained, were "in a republican way of thinking," voted men and money. They authorized the raising of a regiment of six companies, and appointed Joshua Fry, an English-born gentleman, colonel, with young Washington as his lieutenant. To stimulate enlistments, Dinwiddie was authorized to offer as a bounty two hundred thousand acres of land on the Ohio, to be divided among the soldiers who should engage in the expedition.

Alexandria was made the place of military rendezvous. On the recommendation of Washington, the Forks of the Ohio—the site of the city of Pittsburgh—was chosen the place on which to build the first fort; and Captain Trent was instructed to employ his recruits in its construction. As the spring was passing away, Washington, who was yet at Alexandria, was ordered to join Trent with the advance of the military force and assist in the speedy completion of the fort. He was instructed to "drive away, kill and destroy, or seize as prisoners all persons not the subjects of the king of Great Britain, who should attempt to take possession of the lands on the Ohio or any of its tributaries."

Early in April, Lieutenant-Colonel Washington left Alexandria with a small force, and reached Will's Creek (now Cumberland) on the 20th. On the way he was met by a swift runner sent by the friendly Half-King on the Monongahela, bearing a wampum-belt and this message from the chief: "Come to our assistance as soon as you can; come soon or we are lost, and shall never meet again. I speak it in the grief of my heart." The French had been seen embarking on the Alleghany at Venango, and news of the movement had spread alarm among the barbarians friendly to the English. After giving the heated Indian runner food and a flask of rum, Washington sent him back with a belt and the words: "Your friend and brother is coming; be strong and patient."

As he approached Will's Creek, Washington was met by another runner, who said the French were at the Forks; and the next day an ensign from Trent's company came with the startling news that the French, a thousand strong, with eighteen cannon, sixty bateaux and three hundred canoes, had come down the Alleghany, under the command of Captain Contrecœur, and taken possession of the unfinished fort. These numbers were exaggerations, but the fact remained that the French were occupying the important position at the Forks of the Ohio. They immediately finished the fort on a stronger plan, and named it Du Quesne in honor of the governor of Canada.

Colonel Fry had not yet joined the advance. The young lieutenant-colonel assumed the responsibility of pressing forward with his handful of

PASSING OVER THE ALLEGHANY MOUNTAINS.

raw recruits—not more than one hundred and fifty in number—and a few pieces of light artillery. Leaving the borders of civilization on a cool morning in April, these pioneers penetrated the wilderness in the direction of the Ohio. Without shelter from cold and rain; in scanty clothing and with a small supply of provisions, they dragged the cannon over the great wooded hills; felled trees; bridged streams; made causeways over marshes, and removed rocks, to make the march of the main army easier; and late in May they stood on the banks of the Youghiogany, within forty miles of Fort Du Quesne. There Washington received a message from Half-King, saying: "Be on your guard. The French are near, and intend to strike the first English whom they shall see." On the same day this report was confirmed. Ignorant of the number of the French, Washington fell back to a fertile plain which he had crossed, called the Great Meadows, and there built a stockade and named it Fort Necessity. It was near the modern national road between Cumberland and Wheeling, in the southeastern part of Fayette county, Pennsylvania. There Mr. Gist, who had a settlement near, came to him and reported that he had discovered the tracks of the French within five miles of the Great Meadows.

At about nine o'clock in the evening of the same day, a message came from Half-King, who was about six miles distant, saying that a party of armed Frenchmen were lying in ambush not far away. Notwithstanding the night was intensely dark and the rain was falling copiously, Washington immediately set off with forty men, in single file, for the camp of the friendly Mingo Chief, with whom he made arrangements to surprise the common foe and jointly strike him. The night had been consumed in the difficult journey to the Mingo camp, and it was after sunrise when the English and Indians, each marching in parallel lines, in single file, sought the hiding-place of the foe. It was found among some rocks. Washington, who was at the head of the party and carried a musket, when he saw the Frenchmen, shouted *Fire!* and at the same moment discharged his own gun among them. The volleys of the assailants were returned with spirit. After a fight for about fifteen minutes, when Jumonville, the commander of the French party and ten of his men were killed, the conflict ceased. Only one Virginian was killed. Twenty-two Frenchmen were made prisoners, taken to Fort Necessity, and then sent over the mountains into Eastern Virginia. Of the fifty followers of Jumonville, only fifteen escaped.

This was the first blood shed in the *French and Indian war*. So was opened by young Washington, who fired the first gun, that long and bitter contest for the rights of man which, like an earthquake, shattered into fragments the institutions of feudal ages which had been transplanted in our country, and shook the foundations of society in Europe.

This skirmish, which occurred on the 28th of May, 1754, made a profound impression. It was exaggerated by French publicists and diplomats. France and England were then at peace, and were saying sweet things to each other, disguising bitterest hatred with a cloak of false professions of friendship. The attack on Jumonville was denounced as an outrage by the

French. It was alleged that Jumonville was a civil messenger, bearing a peaceful despatch, and therefore Washington was a murderer. This fiction passed into French history, and has never been expunged. There is no clearer point in national annals than the fact that Jumonville was the bearer of a hostile summons, and his skulking in ambush is proof of his hostile intention. Contrecœur had begun war by capturing the fort at the Forks; and every circumstance justified the conduct of Washington.

Two days after this event, Colonel Fry died at Will's Creek, leaving Washington in chief command. A few troops pressed forward to join him, and he was burdened at Fort Necessity with about forty families of friendly Indians, among them those of Half-King and Queen Aliquippa. With his little army swelled to about four hundred men, he moved toward Fort Du Quesne, when news came that M. de Villiers, brother of Jumonville, had marched with some Frenchmen and more than a thousand Indians to avenge the death of his kinsman. Washington fell back to Fort Necessity and strengthened it. There he was attacked on the 3d of July by six hundred Frenchmen and about three hundred Indians, a reserve being concealed in the woods. After a conflict for about nine hours, De Villiers, finding his ammunition to be failing, proposed a parley. It was now twilight. Washington, whose force was much inferior, agreed to surrender the fort and troops on the condition that he and his men should retire from the stockade with the honors of war and return to the inhabited portion of the country; the Virginians agreeing to restore the prisoners taken from Jumonville's party, and not to erect any establishment west of the mountains for the space of a year.

On the morning of the 4th of July, the two commanders, seated upon a log outside of the fort, with Indian chiefs and Virginia officers looking on, signed the capitulation. Then the troops moved away, re-crossed the mountains to Will's Creek, and returned to their homes, while their commander hastened to Williamsburg to report to the governor. The conduct of Washington and his men was highly approved; and when the House of Burgesses met, the thanks of the colony were voted them "for their bravery and gallant defence of their country." So ended the first campaign of the French and Indian war.

Meanwhile a civil movement in the colonies of great importance had taken place. It was a movement in the direction of a national union. For some time there had been indications that the Indians, and particularly the Six Nations, influenced by French emissaries, were becoming alienated from the English. The colonists were uneasy; and the British government, acting upon the advice of the colonial governors, took measures to strengthen the good-will of the barbarians. The British Secretary of State issued a circular-letter to the various colonial assemblies proposing a convention to be held at Albany, composed of committees from the several assemblies, and representatives of the Six Nations. To this proposition seven of the assemblies cheerfully responded, and on the 19th of June, 1754, twenty-five delegates from these colonies met in the old City Hall in Albany. James De Lancey, acting-governor of New York, was chosen to preside, and he was authorized by the Virginia Assembly to represent that colony in the convention. It was an assembly of remarkable men, such as had never

WASHINGTON SIGNING THE CAPITULATION.

before been seen on the continent. The most remarkable man of all was Dr. Franklin, of Philadelphia, then almost fifty years of age.

The chiefs of the Six Nations were there in very great force. Among them, as chief orator, was "King Hendrick," the eminent Mohawk sachem who was killed near Lake George, the following year, while battling for the English. These barbarians received the first attention in the convention. The proceedings were opened by a speech to them by De Lancey, to which Hendrick responded. While they accepted the belts of wampum as tokens of alliance and friendship, there was evident dissatisfaction with the conduct of the English, whom the orator frankly reproved. Standing in the midst of the council, he spoke of the injustice and want of spirit of the English, with significant gestures. "We thank you," he said, "for renewing and brightening the covenant chain. We will take this belt to the Onondagas, where our council fire always burns, and keep it so securely that neither the thunderbolt nor the lightning shall break it. Strengthen yourselves, and bring as many as you can into this covenant chain." Then, with his dark eyes flashing with scorn and indignation, he raised his voice, and with impassioned manner, he exclaimed: "Look at the French; they are men; they are fortifying everywhere; but, we are ashamed to say it, you are like women, bare and open, without any fortifications." "It is but one step," he said, "from Canada hither, and the French may easily come and turn you out of doors." Already many of the Onondagas had settled at Oswegatchie (now Ogdensburgh, on the St. Lawrence), under the protection of the French; and some of the Mohawks complained bitterly of the seizure of lands in the west, by New Englanders, that belonged to the Indians; but the conference closed amicably, and, on the whole, satisfactorily to both parties.

The Massachusetts delegation had come to the convention prepared to suggest business quite as important as a treaty with the Indians. They were authorized to invite the convention to a consideration of the question whether a union of the colonies for mutual defence was not desirable. They were also authorized by the General Court to agree to articles of union or confederation. The proposition when submitted was favorably received by the convention, and a committee, composed of one member from each colony represented, was appointed to draw up a plan. That committee consisted of Hutchinson, of Massachusetts; Atkinson, of New Hampshire; Pitkin, of Connecticut; Hopkins, of Rhode Island; Smith, of New York; Franklin, of Pennsylvania; and Tasker, of Maryland.

The fertile brain of Dr. Franklin had conceived a plan before he went to the convention. It was similar in its leading features to those proposed by William Penn and Daniel Coxe, already mentioned. He submitted it to the committee in writing, and it was adopted after slight modifications. It was debated in the convention day after day, for almost a fortnight, "hand-in-hand with the Indian business," Franklin wrote, and was agreed to on the 11th of July by all but the delegates from Connecticut, William Pitkin, Roger Wolcott, and Elisha Williams. The union was "for the general defence of his majesty's subjects and interests in North America, as well in time of peace as of war."

Franklin's plan proposed a grand council or congress of forty-eight members, chosen by the several assemblies, the representatives of each colony to be, in number, in proportion to the contribution of each to the general treasury; that the congress should choose their own speaker and have the general management of all civil and military affairs, and to enact general laws in conformity to the British constitution and not in contravention of acts of the imperial parliament; to have a President-General (with Philadelphia the seat of government) appointed and paid by the crown, who should bear a negative or veto power on all acts of the congress, and to have, with the advice and consent of the congress, the appointment of all military officers and the entire management of Indian affairs, the civil officers to be appointed by the congress with the approval of the President-General. This plan of government was similar, in its leading features, to our National Constitution, in the framing of which Dr. Franklin bore a conspicuous part more than thirty years after the convention at Albany.

Franklin's thoughts had been occupied with the topic of union for some time. Several weeks before, he had published the following paragraph in his newspaper, the *Pennsylvania Gazette*, in an account of the seizure, by the French, of the position at the Forks of the Ohio: "The confidence of the French in this undertaking seems well-grounded in the present disunited state of the British colonies, and the extreme difficulty of bringing so many different governments and assemblies to agree in any speedy and effectual measures for our common defence and security; while our enemies have the very great advantage of being under one direction, with one council and one purse." At the close of the article was a rude wood-cut representing a serpent, the ancient emblem of *vigor*, separated into as many parts as there were English-American colonies, and under it, in large letters, the words JOIN or DIE. This significant device, which seems to have been first used by Franklin, figured conspicuously at the opening of the Revolution twenty years afterward.

The *Plan of Union* adopted by the convention was submitted to the Lords of Trade and Plantations. That body did not approve of it, nor even recommend it to the consideration of the king. Neither was it favorably received by the assemblies, partly because the royal governors at first warmly recommended it. In endeavors to please both royalists and republicans, the convention utterly failed. Franklin wrote: "The assemblies all thought there was too much *prerogative* in it, and in England it was thought to have too much of the *democratic*," and it was rejected.

When intelligence of the expulsion of the English from the Ohio Valley reached the royal cabinet, measures were taken for the recovery of what had been lost, and for the creation of a new colony west of the Alleghany

Mountains for its security in the future. The Earl of Albemarle was then governor-in-chief of Virginia, with Dinwiddie as his lieutenant. He instructed the latter to grant lands to any persons desiring to settle in the Ohio region, not more than a thousand acres to each. So it was that Virginia became the pioneer in the extension of the colonies westward, and the mother of States in the great basins of the Ohio. At the same time the ministry were eager to regain, by military power, what had been lost. They could not wait for the slow process of colonization. Indeed the exigencies of the case would not permit. The direction of American affairs was left to the warlike Duke of Cumberland, then captain-general of the British army, and by his orders Dinwiddie prepared for a winter campaign against the French. He ordered Washington to join his regiment at Alexandria, to fill up the companies by enlistments, and to hasten to Will's Creek, where Colonel Innis was building Fort Cumberland, and with his own troops, and the remnants of companies from other colonies, march over the Alleghany Mountains and drive the French from Fort Du Quesne. It was so late in the year that the mountains would be impassable on account of snow-drifts by an army inadequately supplied with food, clothing, and transportation. Washington knew this; and in a letter to one of the governor's council, he vehemently remonstrated. His words were heeded, and the mad scheme was abandoned.

Meanwhile French emissaries were busy among the savage tribes west of the mountains, inciting them to a war of extermination against the English. The same influence had caused a murderous Indian raid upon the frontiers of New England; and yet, in full view of the impending danger, some of the colonies were strangely apathetic. Governor Shirley put forth energetic efforts in Massachusetts to avert the evil. New York subscribed twenty-five thousand dollars for military service, and Maryland thirty thousand dollars for the same. The British government sent over fifty thousand dollars to aid the colonists, and Virginia made an appropriation of the same amount.

The crown appointed Governor Sharpe, of Maryland, temporary commander-in-chief of all the colonial forces. This led to injurious disputes about military rank and precedence among the Virginia officers, when Dinwiddie, more zealous than wise—more rash than discreet—having a large sum of money at his disposal, and entirely ignorant of military affairs, assumed the responsibility of arranging these affairs in his colony as he pleased. He enlarged the provincial army to ten companies of one hundred men each and broke it up into companies, so that the highest rank in that little army was captain, and at the same time inferior in position to the same rank of those commissioned by the crown. Washington would not submit to the degradation, but resigned his commission and retired from the military service.

Knowing the value of Washington's services at that critical time, Governor Sharpe urged him to remain in the army, and intimated that he might hold his former commission. "This idea," wrote the indignant young Virginian, "has filled me with surprise, for, if you think me capable of holding a commission that has neither rank nor emolument annexed to it, you must entertain a very contemptible opinion of my weakness, and believe me to be more empty than the commission itself." He declined the appointment and added: "I shall have the consolation of knowing that I have opened the way, when the smallness of our numbers exposed us to the attacks of a superior enemy; and that I have had the thanks of my country for the services I have rendered."

DISCUSSION BETWEEN FRANKLIN AND SHIRLEY.

The early portion of the ensuing winter was spent by the colonists in anxious solicitude. France and England had been coquetting, with mutual professions of friendship, while every movement of the French in America indicated hostile intentions. The necessity of a colonial union was never more apparent than then, and Franklin, who had set his heart on the project, visited Shirley to confer with him on the subject. At the governor's house in Boston they discussed the topic long. Shirley was favorable to union, but it must be effected by the fiat of the British government, and not by the spontaneous act of the colonists. Franklin's love of popular liberty would not consent to such a union, and he parted from Shirley with the assurance of the latter that he would immediately recommend not only a union planned by parliament, but a tax.

Meanwhile the British government, perceiving the peril of English dominion in America, resolved to send military aid to the colonists. Edward Braddock, an Irish officer of distinction then in Ireland, was appointed commander-in-chief of all British forces in America, and was ordered to proceed immediately to Virginia with two regiments of regular troops. He was a man soured by broken fortunes; haughty in spirit; brutal in manners; conceited and brave. He was ordered to call a council of royal governors on his arrival in America, and to exact a revenue from the colonies for military service. They were also to be informed that it was the king's pleasure "that a fund be established for the benefit of all the colonies collectively in North America"—a financial union—and that the general and field officers of the provincial forces should have no rank when serving with the general and field-officers commissioned by the king.

Braddock sailed with his two regiments. "What does that mean?" inquired the French minister. "Only defence, that the general peace may not be disturbed," replied the perfidious Duke of New Castle, of whom it had been written:

> "He makes no promise but to break it;
> Faithful to nought but his own ends,
> The bitterest enemy to his friends;
> But to his fixt, undaunted foe,
> Obsequious, base, complying, low.
> Cunning supplies his want of parts;
> Treason and lies are all his arts."

Each government, evidently playing false toward the other, made friendly propositions for mutual concessions that were simply impossible; and so the matter stood when Braddock arrived in Chesapeake Bay, with his two regiments borne by vessels under Admiral Keppel. He first visited Governor Dinwiddie, at Williamsburgh, and then repaired to Alexandria, on the Potomac, with the admiral, where, at the middle of April, he held a council with royal governors at the fine house of Jonathan Carey. The governors present were Shirley, of Massachusetts; De Lancey, of New York; Sharpe, of Maryland; Morris, of Pennsylvania; Dobbs, of North Carolina; and Dinwiddie, of Virginia. These crown-officers told Braddock at the outset that the Assemblies would not comply with his demand for a revenue, nor the wishes of the king for a general fund for military purposes; and they agreed that it would be proper to recommend the government to take measures to force the colonies to bear their share of the expenses of the regular troops sent here. A communication to that effect, signed by the governors and the general, was sent to the ministers; but events would not wait on governors nor legislation. The council at Alexandria were compelled to take immediate action, or all would be lost. The warm weather was coming, and so were the French and Indians. So the council planned the campaign for 1755, depending upon the imperial government and the free-will of the colonists for the necessary supplies in executing it. Three separate expeditions were planned. One was to proceed against Fort Du Quesne, led by General Braddock; a second was to attack Fort Niagara at the mouth of the Niagara River, and Fort Frontenac at the foot of Lake Ontario on the site of Kingston, and was to be led by General Shirley. A third expedition, led by William Johnson (a nephew of Admiral Sir Peter Warren, and then the government superintendent of Indian affairs among the Six Nations), was to attempt the seizure of Crown Point on Lake Champlain. A fourth expedition had already been planned in the East, for the expulsion of the French from Nova Scotia, and possibly the recapture of Louisburg.

The colonists were delighted by evidences that the imperial government intended to help them in their unequal contest with the French and Indians. They laid aside their grievances, and with zeal and patriotism joined the government in preparations for war. All of the colonial legislatures, excepting Pennsylvania and Georgia, voted men and supplies for the impending conflict. The Quaker Assembly of Pennsylvania were conscientiously opposed to military movements, and Georgia was too indigent in men and money to do anything.

CHAPTER XIX.

THE ENGLISH BEGIN HOSTILITIES ON THE SEA—EXPULSION OF THE ACADIANS FROM NOVA SCOTIA—HATRED OF THE ACADIANS BY BRITISH OFFICIALS—BRADDOCK'S PRIDE AND FOLLY—HIS ARMY MOVES SLOWLY TOWARD FORT DU QUESNE—WASHINGTON ON BRADDOCK'S STAFF—GIVES GOOD ADVICE—A DETACHMENT OF THE ARMY MOVES MORE RAPIDLY—WASHINGTON'S WISE ADVICE REJECTED—BRADDOCK'S ARMY DEFEATED IN BATTLE AND HIMSELF SLAIN—RETREAT OF THE ARMY—WASHINGTON MARVELLOUSLY PROTECTED—SHIRLEY'S EXPEDITION A FAILURE—EXPEDITION UNDER JOHNSON AT THE HEAD OF LAKE GEORGE—APPROACH OF A FRENCH ARMY.

THE French, false themselves, did not believe Newcastle's assurance; and when Keppel sailed with Braddock's troops, they sent a fleet with soldiers, under the veteran Baron Dieskau, to reinforce their army on the St. Lawrence. With Dieskau went Vaudreuil, the successor of Du Quesne as governor of Canada. Admiral Boscawen, with some English ships, pursued the French fleet, and they came together south of Newfoundland. "Are we at peace or war?" asked the French. They were answered by the thunder of Boscawen's cannon. Two of the French ships were captured; the remainder escaped and landed the governor, with Dieskau and his troops, at Quebec, late in June.

Meanwhile the eastern expedition had moved. Three thousand men sailed from Boston on the 20th of May, 1755, under the command of General John Winslow, a great grandson of Edward Winslow of the *May-Flower*, and then major-general of the Massachusetts militia. They landed at near the head of the Bay of Fundy, where they were joined by Colonel Monckton and three hundred British regulars and a small train of artillery from a neighboring garrison. The French at Beau-Sejour and other military posts on the peninsula were ignorant of the hostile preparations of the two governments, until the appearance of this armament. Resistance would have been in vain. The peninsula became an easy prey to the English before the close of June. The French soldiers were sent to Louisburg, and the Acadians, who had been forced into the service, were granted an amnesty. But a sad fate awaited them.

The simple Acadians expected forbearance and went on cultivating their lands. They readily took an oath of allegiance, but could not pledge themselves to bear arms against their kindred in nation and religion. The English coveted their fertile lands, and made their refusal a pretext for possessing them. A technical question in law was raised, whether one who refuses to take all required oaths could hold lands in the British dominions. It was referred to the chief-justice of Nova Scotia, who decided against the Acadians; when it was determined to drive them out of the province and force them to settle in the English colonies. Not a word of suspicion reached the ears of the intended victims until the cruel plot was ripe for execution. The command went forth for their distribution among the English colonists. The French government asked for them the privilege of leaving their lands, taking with them their effects, and choosing for themselves their future home. "No," was the reply; "they are too useful subjects to be lost; we must enrich our colonies with them." A touching memorial to the council at Halifax was borne by a deputation of educated men, in which they asked for the restitution of the guns and canoes of the people for domestic use, and promising fidelity as the ransom for them. The document was read in an humble manner by the leading deputy, to the governor. That official treated it and its bearers with scorn. "It is highly arrogant, insidious and insulting," said Governor Lawrence. He charged them with intending to carry food to the enemy in their boats, and reminded them that a law of the British realm forbade all Roman Catholics having arms in the houses. He scolded the deputies without stint. "It is not the language of British subjects," he said, "to talk of terms with the crown, or capitulate about their fidelity and allegiance. What excuse can you make for your presumption in treating this government with such indignity as to expound to them the nature of fidelity? Manifest your obedience by immediately taking the oaths required, before the council." The deputies meekly replied: "We will do as our people may determine," and asked leave to return home and consult them.

On the following day they saw the peril of themselves and their people, and offered to take the oaths. "By a law of the realm," said the governor, "Roman Catholics who have once refused to take the oaths cannot be permitted to do so afterward, and are considered Popish recusants;" and as such they were cast into prison. The chief-justice insisted that all the French inhabitants—hundreds of innocent families—were rebels and Popish recusants; that they stood in the way of English interests in the country; that they had forfeited their possessions to the crown, and advised against the receiving of any of the French inhabitants to take the oath, and also the removing of all of them from the province.

Execution of the cruel measure recommended speedily followed the utterances of the opinion of the chief-justice. A general proclamation was issued ordering all the Acadians, "old men and young men, and lads ten years of age," to assemble at designated places, on the 5th of September, 1755. They obeyed. The proceedings at one place afford a fair picture of those at all others. At Grand Pré, four hundred and eighteen unarmed men were assembled. They were marched into the church, where they were addressed by Winslow, the Massachusetts militia general. He told them they had been called together to hear the decision of the King of England

THE ACADIANS DRIVEN INTO EXILE.

in regard to the French inhabitants of the province. "Your lands and tenements," he said, "cattle of all kinds, and live-stock of all sorts, are forfeited to the crown, and you, yourselves, are to be removed from this, his province. I am, through his majesty's goodness, directed to allow you liberty to carry off your money and household goods, as many as you can, without discommoding the vessels you go in." Then he said, "You are now the king's prisoners."

Consternation suddenly filled every household in Grand Pré. Nineteen hundred and twenty-three men, women and children were driven on board British vessels at the point of the bayonet, from Grand Pré alone. The men and boys assembled at the church, went first; the sisters, wives and daughters had to wait for other transports. They marched from the church to the water's edge, some in sullen despair, others with hands clasped and eyes uplifted, praying and weeping, and others singing hymns, while on each side of the sad procession was a row of women and children on their knees imploring blessings upon the heads of the dear ones.

The fate of the people of Grand Pré was the fate of all. The wrath of the English excited against the French for their long and cruel warfare upon the frontier settlements of New England, with their savage allies, was poured out in full measure upon the heads of this innocent pastoral people, who had never voluntarily lifted sword nor spear nor firebrand to harm the English. Many, forewarned, tried to escape. A hundred families near Annapolis fled to the woods, where they were hunted by the troops like noxious wild beasts. Many were shot dead by watching sentinels. An English officer wrote in cool blood: "Our soldiers hate these French Catholics, and if they can find a pretext to kill them, they will." Some hid in the forests and among the rocks in remote parts of the peninsula; some found their way to Quebec, and many were sheltered from the English and fed in the wigwams of the so-called savages. But seven thousand were borne away by English ships, and scattered among the English colonies. To prevent their return, their villages and rural homes in Nova Scotia were laid waste by flames, and their live-stock was used by English officials. A large, beautiful and fertile tract of country became a solitude and desolation—a precious offering upon the altar of greed, hatred, bigotry and fear.

The sufferings of the Acadians were acute in exile. Many families, separated at the outset by the cruel arrangements for their transportation, were never re-united, and the English colonial newspapers contained advertisements seeking information about parts of dismembered families. They were dropped along the shores of the colonies from the Penobscot to the Savannah without resources, and ignorant of the language of the people among whom they were cast excepting in South Carolina, where they received great kindness from the Huguenot families there. They abhorred the almshouse, and dreaded servitude in English families. They yearned for their native land with sadness as intense as that of the Hebrews on the borders of the rivers of Babylon; and many wandered through the forests to Louisiana and Canada—men, women and children—sheltered by bush-camps and partaking of the hospitalities of the Indians, that they might rest under French dominion. Some families actually went to sea in open boats, to find their way back to Acadié, and coasting along the shores to

New England, were there met by orders from Nova Scotia to stop all returning fugitives.

Many touching stories are told of parents seeking and finding children; of children seeking and finding parents, and of the wanderings of lovers in search of each other, and of unexpected meetings. This portion of the history of these captive exiles lends beauty and pathos to many a page of *Longfellow's Evangeline*. When I was in Montreal, many years ago, the following well-authenticated story was told to me:

A beautiful maiden, daughter of a wealthy citizen of Grand Pré, was to be married in the church there, to a son of the local magistrate of that village, on the day when Winslow pronounced the doom of the colony. They were dressed for the nuptials that were to be celebrated immediately after the conference with the English officers, in the presence of the "old and young men and lads of ten years," there assembled. Alas! the young man was among the prisoners then made and doomed to perpetual exile. As he passed to the ship in the sorrowful procession, he kissed the kneeling, weeping, heart-broken maiden, and said hurriedly: "Adele, trust in God and all will be well!" He was landed at the city of New York, and made his way to the St. Lawrence, where he became a trader with the Indians. The maiden and her mother followed a fortnight later, and were also landed at New York. They accepted the hospitalities of a Huguenot family far up the Hudson River. Soon afterward a band of Mohawks, because of some affront, made a raid into the settlement, and the maiden was carried away captive by an old chief who led the band, into the deep wilderness of the Saeondaga.

Meanwhile Jean Baptiste Le Cœur, the young Acadian, had never lost his faith in the prophecy of his heart at parting, that he and Adele would meet again and be happy. He was now trading with some Mohawks at the French mission at Crown Point. One of the young barbarians told him that a beautiful French girl, the captive of an old chief, who treated her tenderly as a daughter, was then in the Scarron (Schroon) Valley. Le Cœur was instantly impressed with the belief that she was his lost Adele. He accompanied the young Mohawk to the borders of Scarron Lake, where he found the lodge of the chief. As he approached it, in the shadows of the forest, he saw a young woman, with her back toward him, sitting on a mat at the door of the wigwam feathering some arrows. On her head was a French cap. Her neck was fair. He approached her gently. Their eyes met. The maiden sprang from the mat, and uttering a wild cry of *Jean!* she fell, fainting, in her lover's arms. It was a moment of supreme joy. The prophecy of Le Cœur's heart was fulfilled. The old chief, touched with mercy and compassion, gave away his pale-faced daughter before the altar at Crown Point, where the affianced at Grand Pré were married by a revered priest of the beloved church, in the bosom of the wilderness. Descendants of Jean Baptiste and Adele now occupy a high social position in Montreal.

The English officials pursued the smitten Acadians with a rod of hatred, after their expulsion. When Lord Loudon was commander-in-chief of the British forces in America, some of the Acadians, settled in Pennsylvania, ventured to address a respectful petition to him. The cold-blooded earl, offended because the document was in the French language, brutally seized five of the leading men who signed the petition, and who had been persons of wealth and distinction in Nova Scotia, and sent them to England with a request that, to prevent their being troublesome in the future, they should be consigned to hard service as common sailors in the British navy. The king appears to have approved the measure; and the Lords of Trade, when the exodus from and the desolation of Acadia was completed, congratulated the British monarch—the profligate Hanoverian—that "the zealous endeavors of Lawrence [governor of Nova Scotia] had been crowned with entire success." The annals of the most barbarous nations can afford nothing more exquisitely cruel than the treatment these poor people received from their English conquerors. "We have been true to our religion and to ourselves, yet nature appears to consider us only as objects of public vengeance," said some of them who remained in Nova Scotia, sadly, in a petition to the local government for relief.

MEETING OF THE ACADIAN LOVERS.

During these movements in the East, the expedition against Fort Du Quesne had begun and ended. Braddock, sanguine and dogmatic, had written to Newcastle from Williamsburgh, that he should be beyond the Alleghanies before the close of April. In an interview with Dr. Franklin at Frederick, Maryland, he told the statesman, in a boastful manner, what he should do elsewhere in America, after he had captured the Ohio fort. He saw no serious obstacles in his way. The philosopher, seeing how shallow was the general's knowledge of the impediments before him, ventured to say at the commander's dinner-table that the mountains were hard to pass with troops and their supplies, and that the Indians were dexterous in laying and executing ambushes. "The savages," said Braddock haughtily, "may be formidable to your raw American militia; upon the king's regulars and disciplined troops, it is impossible they should make any impression." This remark was a key to the secret of his subsequent misfortunes.

The army for the recovery of Fort Du Quesne assembled at Alexandria. Colonels Dunbar and Sir Peter Halket were Braddock's chief lieutenants. There Colonel Washington, who had been invited by Braddock to join his military family as aid, and retain his title, and had agreed to accept the position, but as a volunteer only, had his first interview with the general. The young Virginian joined the army at Will's Creek (Cumberland) in May, where it had been detained by lack of horses and wagons for transportation, which Dr. Franklin, when called upon, promptly supplied from Pennsylvania. The whole force gathered there, regulars and provincials, each in about equal numbers, was two thousand men. Braddock looked upon the latter with contempt, and wrote to ministers that he did not expect much from them because they had "little courage or good-will." In his petulance because of frequent breaches of promise on the part of contractors, he charged the whole American people with a want of ability, honor and honesty, and raved at times like a madman. Washington found him, as he wrote to William Fairfax, "incapable of arguing without warmth, or giving up any point he asserts, be it ever so incompatible with reason or common sense."

The distance from Cumberland to Fort Du Quesne was about one hundred and thirty miles. At the close of May, five hundred pioneers were sent forward to clear the pathway and collect stores at Fort Necessity; but the main army was not ready to move until the 10th of June. This delay gave the French time to gather their barbarian allies and well-prepare to receive the English. Washington was impatient; and at the middle of June, he ventured to advise Braddock to detach a part of the army in light marching order, with the artillery, and send them forward, leaving the remainder to move more slowly. The general consented, and with twelve hundred men under Sir Peter Halket, he pushed forward on the 19th of June. The provincials in the advance were entrusted to the command of Washington, and were eager to press on, but were restrained by the regulars; and it was the 8th of July before the advanced division of the army reached the forks of the Monongahela and Youghiogany rivers, where they rested until the morning of the ninth. They were then about a dozen miles from Fort Du Quesne.

The English forded the Monongahela on the morning of the 9th of July, and advanced along its southern shores. Washington knew the perils of their situation, for the troops were disposed in solid platoons, after the fashion of European tactics. He ventured to remonstrate with Braddock

FLIGHT OF THE ENGLISH TROOPS.

and advise him to dispose his army in open order, and employ the Indian mode of fighting in the forests. The colonel was silenced by the general angrily saying, "What! a provincial colonel teach a British general how to fight!"

The army moved on, re-crossed the Monongahela to the north side, and were marching in fancied security on the part of the regulars at about noon on that hot July day, when they were suddenly assailed by volleys of bullets and clouds of arrows on their front and flanks. They had fallen into an ambush against which Washington had vainly warned the haughty general.

De Beaujeu, the commander of a party of less than three hundred French and Canadians, and little more than six hundred Indians, had been sent from the fort by Contrecœur to meet the advancing English. They came upon the latter sooner than De Beaujeu expected, but the ambush was quickly and skillfully formed. He fought bravely and fell in the first deadly onslaught between the combatants. The suddenness of the attack and the horrid war-whoop of the Indians, which the regulars had never heard before, so frightened them that they were disconcerted and thrown into confusion; and nothing saved the little army from total destruction or capture but the more skillful manœuvres of the provincials under Washington, who fought as the Indians did.

The British officers behaved nobly and did all in their power to encourage their men, until they were disabled; but the regulars soon became unmanageable. Braddock, seeing the peril, was in the front of the fight rallying his recoiling troops, and inspiring them with what courage he might by his own example. For more than two hours the battle raged. Of the eighty-six English officers, sixty-three were killed or wounded; among the former was Sir Peter Halket. One-half of the private soldiers was also killed or wounded. All of Braddock's aids were disabled; and Washington alone was left unhurt, to distribute the orders of the general. Braddock had five horses shot and disabled under him, and finally a bullet entered his body, and he, too, fell mortally wounded. So bravely did the provincials maintain their ground that they were nearly all killed. Of three Virginia companies, only about thirty men were left alive. "The dastardly behavior of those they call regulars," Washington wrote to his mother from Cumberland, "exposed all others that were inclined to do their duty to almost certain death; and at last, despite of all the efforts of the officers to the contrary, they ran, as sheep pursued by dogs, and it was impossible to rally them."

Washington, perceiving that the day was lost—his dying general carried from the field, and the British regulars running for their lives—rallied the provincial troops, and gallantly covered the retreat. The French and Indians did not follow. Colonel Dunbar, in the rear, received the broken army on the 12th of July. Then they all fled first to Fort Cumberland, which was abandoned, and thence marched to Philadelphia. Washington and the southern provincials went back to Virginia; and so ended the second expedition of the campaign of 1755.

The British had left their cannon and their dead on the battle-field; and the body of Braddock, from which life had departed three days after the conflict, was buried in the forest more than fifty miles from Cumberland. It was borne to the grave and interred by torch-light on the evening of the 15th of July, when Washington, surrounded by sorrowing officers, read the impressive funeral service of the Church of England. That grave may be seen near the National Road, between the 54th and 55th mile-stones.

The protection of Washington from harm during that battle was wonderful. "I luckily escaped without a wound," he wrote to his mother, "though I had four bullets through my coat, and two horses shot under me." At

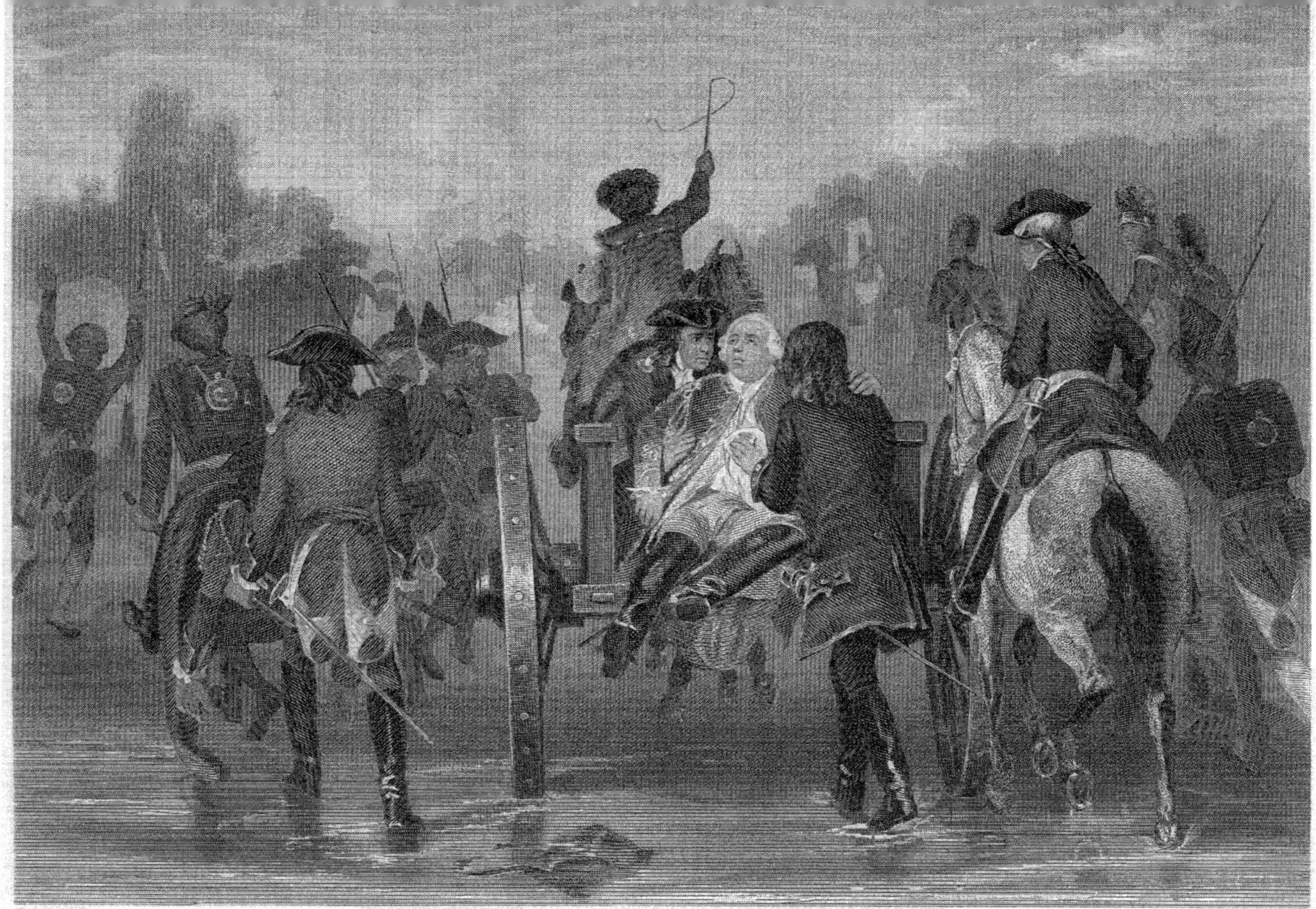

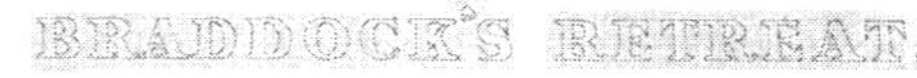

Painted by Alonzo Chappel

Entered according to act of Congress A.D. 1877 by Johnson & Miles, in the office of the Librarian of Congress at Washington.

BRADDOCK'S RETREAT.

Johnson & Miles, Publishers New York

one time an Indian chief singled him out for death by his rifle, and directed his followers to do the same. Fifteen years afterward, when Washington was in the Ohio country, that chief traveled many a weary mile to see the man at whom he said he had fired more than a dozen fair shots, but could not hit him. "We felt that some Manitou guarded your life," said the chief, "and we believed you could not be killed." "By the all-powerful dispensations of Providence," Washington wrote to his brother John Augustine, "I have been protected beyond all human probability or expectation. Death was levelling my companions on every side." At Cumberland, he heard a circumstantial account of his death, and his "dying speech." Washington was never wounded in battle.

Governor Shirley was appointed Braddock's successor in the chief command of the British forces in America. The expedition led by him to operate against Forts Niagara and Frontenac was not exposed to great perils nor suffered serious disasters. Nor did it accomplish much. After a very fatiguing march through the wilderness from Albany to Oswego on the southern shore of Lake Ontario, he arrived at the latter place in August, his little army of fifteen hundred men reduced by sickness and dispirited by the news of Braddock's disaster. The Assembly of New York had freely voted men and money for the expedition, and the Six Nations had promised many warriors; but on the first of September, not more than twenty-five hundred able-bodied men were in camp at Oswego.

The energetic Shirley was not disheartened. There was a small, dilapidated fort at Oswego. He at once began to strengthen the post by erecting two stronger forts, one on each side of the Oswego River, which there enters the Lake between high banks. Fort Pepperell (afterward Fort Oswego), on the west side, had a strong stone wall, with square towers; Fort Ontario on the east was built of huge logs and earth. Shirley also constructed vessels to bear his troops over the bosom of the Lake to their future destination. But reinforcements did not come. He waited all through September. Storm after storm swept over the Lake, threatening any flotilla that he might launch upon it with great peril, if not actual disaster. The breath of approaching winter began to be keenly felt, and, disappointed, he was compelled to abandon the expedition for a season. Leaving seven hundred troops to garrison the fort, the general marched back to Albany with the remainder, where he arrived late in October. There he made vigorous preparations for reinforcing and supplying the garrison at Oswego, for the Marquis de Montcalm, a distinguished French soldier, was then governor of Canada, and would be likely to pursue aggressive measures the following spring. Colonel John Bradstreet was appointed commissary-general at

Albany, with Captain (afterward General) Philip Schuyler as his chief assistant. Then Shirley returned to Massachusetts, leaving William Alexander (Lord Stirling), his secretary, in New York.

In the meantime, the expedition entrusted to the leadership of William Johnson (then swaying immense influence over the Indians in the Mohawk Valley), and destined for wresting the strong post of Crown Point, on Lake Champlain, from the French, had been more successful than either that of Braddock or Shirley, although it did not achieve its intended object. His army consisted chiefly of New England militia and Indians—the former from Connecticut, Massachusetts and New Hampshire, and the latter from

IDLE SOLDIERS AT LAKE GEORGE.

the Mohawk Valley. These were assembled at Albany, the New England men having Phineas Lyman for their chief commander. There were also some New York and New Jersey militia, with the army, when, in July, it was at the head of small-boat navigation on the Hudson, fifty miles above Albany, and numbering about six thousand able-bodied men. Among them were Putnam and Stark, who afterward became famous leaders in the war for independence.

General Lyman was a graduate of Yale College, an acute statesman and brave soldier. While waiting on the banks of the upper Hudson for Johnson to join him, he employed his troops in the construction of a strong fort of logs and earth, which they insisted upon naming Fort Lyman, in honor of their beloved commander. When Johnson came in August, he deprived the general of that honor, and gave it the name of Fort Edward, in compliment to a royal scion. That act has been attributed to the jealousy of Johnson, who doubtless did not relish the popularity of his lieutenant; but it is more probable that it was done to gratify his passion for flattering royal persons. He took command of the troops on his arrival, and with the main body he marched to the head of a beautiful lake, more than a dozen miles distant, which the French had named Holy Sacrament, but which Johnson, in compliment to the king, named Lake George. There he formed a camp for five thousand men, protected on the north by the lake and on both flanks by impassable morasses and tangled forests. There the troops sat down in idleness waiting for the coming of wagons with stores and cannon for the expedition. It was a beautiful summer camp; but no trench was dug, no mound was raised, as a defence against an active and skillful foe. The three hundred Mohawk warriors, under "King Hendrick," were allowed to roam the forests at pleasure, for Johnson did not dream that a French army, like a wily serpent, was stealthily moving toward his camp.

While the English provincials were thus making feeble preparations for seizing Crown Point, the French had been busy in the execution of measures to defend that post. Vaudreuil, the governor of Canada, had called to arms every able-bodied man in the vicinity of Montreal, and invited laborers from below to come up and gather the harvests. With these recruits, sixteen hundred strong, seven hundred regulars and as many savages (almost half of them emigrants from the Six Nations), the French were prepared to defend their fortress at Crown Point. A greater portion of them were placed under the command of the Baron Dieskau, who proceeded to the head of Lake Champlain, whence he intended to make a swift march upon Fort Edward, and capture it and its garrison by surprise. Four days, as secretly as possible, he traversed the woods, when it was found that his guides had lost their way, and that he was in the path to the head of Lake George, and four miles from Fort Edward. Indian scouts had told his savage followers of the great guns at Fort Edward, and that there were more in the camp on the borders of the lake. The barbarians, afraid of cannon, refused to attack the fort, but were willing to fall upon the exposed camp at the head of the lake.

CHAPTER XX.

MILITARY EVENTS AT THE HEAD OF LAKE GEORGE—HONORS WRONGLY BESTOWED—AN OPPORTUNITY FOR SUCCESS LOST—PERFIDY OF THE BRITISH CABINET—THE PROPHECY OF JOHN ADAMS AND ITS FULFILLMENT—PLANS FOR THE CAMPAIGN OF 1756—FRANKLIN IN MILITARY LIFE—WASHINGTON'S EMBASSY TO BOSTON—HIS LOVE AFFAIR IN NEW YORK—LORD LOUDON COMMANDER-IN-CHIEF — ABERCROMBIE AT ALBANY — HIS FOLLY AND SUPINENESS — BRADSTREET'S EXPEDITION—THE FRENCH CAPTURE OSWEGO—LOUDON'S IMBECILITY ILLUSTRATED—THE RESULTS OF THE CAMPAIGN OF 1756—LOUDON'S IGNOBLE VICTORIES.

IT was a beautiful evening—the 7th of September, 1755—when an Indian scout came to Johnson's camp, at Lake George, with the startling news that a French army had been seen landing at the head of Lake Champlain, near the site of the village of White Hall. This messenger was followed by another at midnight, with the more alarming news that French and Indians were making a rapid march toward Fort Edward. Early in the morning a council was held, and it was proposed to send out a small party in three divisions to meet the foe. The shrewd Mohawk sachem and chief, King Hendrick, said: "If they are to fight, they are too few; if they are to be killed, they are too many." Then taking in his hands three strong sticks, he said: "Put them together and you cannot break them; take them separately and you can break them easily." His logic was apparent, and it was approved by the general, who ordered twelve hundred men in one body to hasten to the relief of Fort Edward. Colonel Ephraim Williams, of Massachusetts, was the chosen commander of the expedition, and with him went Hendrick and two hundred warriors of the Six Nations. Before their departure the white-haired chief, whose snowy locks covered his shoulders, mounted a gun-carriage and harangued his braves with his powerful voice, in eloquent words, exhorting them to be strong and true to their allies. A provincial officer, Lieutenant-Colonel (afterward General) Pomeroy, who was present, declared that while he could not understand a word of the old warrior's language, such was the power of his voice, his gestures and his whole manner, that his speech affected him more deeply than any other he had ever heard.

The detachment had marched in fancied security to a defile at Rocky Brook, about four miles from camp, when they were assailed in front and flank by musketry and arrows. The French and Indians, who had been misled toward Johnson's camp, apprised by scouts of the march of the English, had formed an ambush in semi-circular shape, the centre cut by the path along which Williams' detachment was moving. The latter had fallen into the fatal trap. The attack was sharp and destructive. Williams and Hendrick were the only mounted men, and both were killed at the first volley. Williams fell dead, and Hendrick died soon afterward. The smitten detachment fled back to camp in a quick but orderly retreat conducted by Nathan Whitney, of New Haven, Connecticut. Colonel Williams was then about forty years of age. While he was passing through Albany on his way to join Johnson, he had made a will, by which he bequeathed his moderate estate to found and maintain a free school in Western Massachusetts. Such was the foundation of Williams' College, at Williamstown. When Hendrick's son heard of the death of his father, he placed his hand over his heart and said: "My father still lives here. The son is now the father, and stands here ready to fight." The travelers on the highway between Glenn's Falls and Lake George may see a monument near the road, erected to the memory of Colonel Williams, not far from the spot where he fell.

KING HENDRICK SPEAKING.

With strange apathy Johnson had made no preparations for the defence of his camp. It was not until Williams had marched on the morning of the 8th, that he began to construct some breastworks of felled trees, and placed two or three cannons upon them. The firing at the ambush had been heard at the camp, and three hundred men were sent to the relief of the first detachment. These met the flying provincials, and joining in the retreat, they all rushed pell-mell into the camp, pursued by the French and Indians, who had cast many of their slain foes into a slimy pool which is still known as "Bloody Pond."

Dieskau intended to rush into the camp with the fugitives and capture it, but his Indians, fearing cannon, halted on the crest of a hill from which they could see the dreaded great guns. So likewise did the intimidated Canadians. Dieskau, whose armorial legend was, "Boldness wins," pressed forward with his regulars, and at near noon a battle began. The French had no artillery, and their musket-balls had no effect upon the breastworks. The Canadians and Indians tardily took positions in sheltered places on the flanks, and did little service. The New Englanders had only their fowling-pieces. There was not a bayonet among them. They were good marksmen, and kept their enemies at bay during a conflict of more than four hours. Fortunately for the provincials, Johnson was slightly wounded in the thigh at the beginning of the action, and retired to his tent. He was not a skillful and experienced soldier like General Lyman who had just joined him, and into whose hands the conduct of the battle now fell. Lyman directed it with skill and bravery, until a greater portion of the French regulars were killed or wounded. A bomb-shell thrown by a howitzer from the provincial camp among the Canadians and savages had made them fly in terror to the woods, when the provincials, leaping over their breastworks, and clubbing their muskets, scattered the living remnants of the assailants. Dieskau, who had been three times wounded, would not retire, but sat upon a stump of a tree, with his saddle by his side, faint from loss of blood, when, from a musket discharged by a renegade Frenchman, he received an incurable wound. He was carried into the camp, where he was tenderly treated by General Johnson and his family. This kindness inspired the warmest gratitude in the breast of the baron, who, before he left America for France, presented an elegant sword to Johnson in token of that sentiment. The baron died in France, from the effect of his wounds in 1757.

This repulse was lauded in England as a great victory. Johnson had very little to do with it, personally. It was the work of General Lyman and his New England troops. Yet the services of Lyman were overlooked. Johnson did not even mention him in connection with the battle, in his despatch. The king created Johnson a baronet, and parliament voted him thanks and the sum of twenty-five thousand dollars wherewith to support the dignity of the title. The recipient being a nephew of Admiral Sir Peter Warren, the influential friends of that officer, at court, secured the honor for Johnson.

For reasons inexplicable just now, the provincial commander remained at the head of Lake George, instead of pursuing the shattered remnant of Dieskau's army and driving the French from Ticonderoga, which they were fortifying. It was possible also, immediately after the panic produced by the repulse at Lake George, to drive them from Crown Point, the ultimate object of the expedition. General Lyman and others urged Johnson to pursue. The Mohawks were burning with a desire to be revenged for the loss of their beloved chief; and the Oneidas were willing to join them if immediate pursuit should be made. But Johnson refused to move. The Oneidas, three days after the battle, left him and returned home; and the only harm which the French and their allies experienced after leaving the lost battle-field was a severe smiting by some New Hampshire militia under Captain McGinnes, and a small body of New York militia under Captain Folsom, who were making their way to the Lake from Fort Edward. They compelled the French to leave all their baggage and fly for their lives. In the affray McGinnes was mortally wounded, and his name was added to the list of the provincials, more than two hundred in number, who were killed that day. There were almost a hundred wounded. Among the four hundred lost by the French was M. de St. Pierre, the Knight of St. Louis, and the commander to whom Washington was sent on a mission at the close of 1753.

THE WOUNDED DIESKAU.

Johnson lingered at the head of Lake George all the autumn, and employed his men in the construction of a fort which he named *William Henry*. When the breath of approaching winter came from the north, he dismissed the New England militia to their homes, and leaving garrisons at Forts Edward and William Henry, he retired to his fortified stone mansion on the banks of the lower Mohawk, which he called "Fort Johnson." It is yet standing not far from the village of Amsterdam. So ended military operations in America in the year 1755.

France and England were still at peace with each other. The British cabinet was then controlled by absurd men, who were likely to embroil the nation in useless war at any time by their folly or by acts deserving a harsher name. They did so by rank perfidy. Secret orders were suddenly issued to the commanders of all British men-of-war to seize all French vessels, public or private. The British king's share of the spoils gathered under the operations of this order was three and a half million dollars; and eight thousand French prisoners were made captives. "What has taken place," indignantly exclaimed a French minister, "is nothing but a system of piracy on a grand scale unworthy of a civilized people." He was right. "Never," said the French monarch, "will I forgive the piracies of this insolent nation;" and in an autograph letter to the British king, he demanded full reparation for the insults offered to the French flag, and the injury done to the French people. But Great Britain then arrogantly claimed, and with reason, that she was "*Mistress* of the Seas;" and Thomson had lately uttered the sentiments of the proud British nation in his stirring song, "Britannia rules the Waves," saying boastfully:

"When Britain first at Heaven's command,
Arose from out the azure main,
This was the charter of the land,
And guardian angels sung the strain;
Rule Britannia, Britannia rules the waves!
Britons never shall be slaves."

The exploit of the British ships-of-war in capturing so many French vessels was boasted of in the British parliament, and the people, rejoicing in their strength, were almost unanimously in favor of war with the French. That spirit prevailed for three-quarters of a century until the mistressship of the seas was successfully contended for by the Americans in the war of 1812–15.

The home governments of the two nations now took up the quarrel. The campaign of 1755 had assumed all the features of regular war between their respective subjects. When the flowers bloomed in the spring of 1756, the British ministry and people had resolved to make war, and the French were compelled to accept the issue. On the 17th of May, 1756, a declaration of war went forth from the British cabinet. This action was reciprocated by the French cabinet on the 9th of June following. The die was then cast. The peace solemnly guaranteed at Aix-la-Chapelle was ruthlessly broken to gratify a lust for power. While these two potential nations had been preparing, for several years, for the impending strife for dominion, the thoughtful men among the English-American colonists, who loved liberty more than power, had been musing upon the glorious probabilities of their future. John Adams, a school-teacher in Worcester in 1755, in a letter to Nathan Webb, wrote: "Mighty states and kingdoms are not exempted from change." "Soon after the Reformation, a few people came over into this new world for conscience sake. This apparently trivial incident may transfer the great seat of empire into America. . . . . . If we can remove the turbulent Gallics, our people, according to the exactest calculations, will, in another century, become more numerous than in England itself. The united force of Europe will not be able to subdue us. The only way to keep us from setting up for ourselves, is to disunite us." This dream became a prophecy. Less than thirty years afterward, the dreamer stood before the monarch of England, as the representative of an American Republic where, only ten years before, were flourishing English colonies. And just a century after that dream, the number and strength of the people here exceeded the calculation of the dreamer. The population was more than double that of England; and while his country was fiercely torn by a savage civil war, its government defied the powers of Great Britain, France, Spain, the Papal States and other European nations whose rulers were the enemies of our free institutions. In the utterance of that defiance, a grandson of John Adams bore a conspicuous part. That government lives to enjoy the respect of the civilized world. In 1765, Lord Kames uttered a prophecy similar to that of young Adams.

Shirley, the commander-in-chief of the British forces in America, called a convention of royal governors at New York, late in 1755, when a plan for a splendid campaign in 1756 was arranged. It included the capture of Quebec, Forts Du Quesne, Frontenac, Niagara, Detroit, and other French posts in the northwest. They again urged the parliament to take vigorous measures for compelling the colonists, by a tax, to furnish a general fund for military purposes in America, and that body was disposed to do so, when the question assumed minor importance in the presence of grave dangers. The Indians were threatening the frontier settlements of Virginia, Maryland and Pennsylvania with desolation; and very soon whole families were flying back to the older settlements, leaving their dwellings and crops to the mercy of the savages. The authorities of those colonies took action to stay the flood of desolation surging upon their frontiers. Those of Virginia appointed Washington commander-in-chief of all her forces; those of Pennsylvania gave Dr. Franklin the commission of colonel, with instructions to raise troops and construct a line of forts or block-houses along the frontier, which he did. Those of Maryland joined in measures for the common defence. But the selfish claims of the proprietaries of Pennsylvania, and the absurd and arrogant assumption of inferior officers commissioned by the crown, to superiority over provincial officers of much higher rank, stood in the way of efficient action. Delays were dangerous to the public good, and Washington was chosen by his brother provincial officers to go as an ambassador to General Shirley to seek a removal of the latter-named difficulty. Early in the month of February, 1756, he set out on a journey to Boston, five hundred miles distant, on horseback, accompanied by Captains Mercer and Stewart, the former being his aide-de-camp. His fame had preceded him, and he received much attention in the several

A FAMILY FLYING FROM THE SAVAGES.

cities through which he passed. His mission to Shirley was successful, and at the end of seven weeks after his departure, he returned to Williamsburgh with a satisfactory arrangement for the future.

While he was on his way to Boston, Colonel Washington tarried a little in New York, where he was the guest of Beverly Robinson, son-in-law of the Lord of the Phillipse Manor on the Hudson. There he met Mrs. Robinson's sister Mary, who was young, vivacious, accomplished and beautiful. This maiden's charms made a deep impression on the mind and heart of the young hero. Her musical culture was displayed by the singing of sweet songs accompanied by a spinet; and in every aspect of her character, she was a charming young lady. The day-dreams of the young Virginian, while on his way to Boston and back, were of her; and at their second meeting at Mr. Robinson's (where he was a guest on his return), he was still more deeply impressed with the charms of the heiress of money and broad acres. He left her with a resolution no doubt formed, but not expressed, to offer her his hand and heart. But a rival soon appeared in the person of Colonel Roger Morris, Washington's companion-in-arms in the field when Braddock fell, and he won the fair lady and her splendid fortune. All but the lady was lost in the fires of the Revolution that burst out twenty years later, for Morris was a Tory and so were his wife's family, and their property was swept away by remorseless confiscation. The colonel and his family were compelled to fly from the elegant mansion built on Harlem Heights (yet standing) with the money of Mary Phillipse, and it was used as headquarters by her Virginia lover in the autumn of 1776.

Shirley did not long remain commander-in-chief. The Earl of Loudon, a cold-hearted, bilious, indolent and inefficient peer, who was a zealous advocate of the prerogatives of the crown and despised republicanism, was appointed the successor of Shirley, and governor of Virginia. As an attempt to establish centralized royal government in America had failed, it was now determined to place the colonies under absolute military rule. The commission of Loudon and his instructions, carefully drawn by the Chancellor of England, did establish such rule throughout the continent, making it independent of and superior to the authority of the royal governors. This commission, so contrary to the spirit of the British constitution, remained a precedent for others until the general revolt of the colonies.

Procrastination marked every step of the campaign on the part of the English. Loudon did not send General James Abercrombie (his lieutenant) with troops until near the close of April. The ship with money was not dispatched until the middle of June, at which time Abercrombie arrived; and the commander-in-chief did not reach our shores until past midsummer. The plan of the campaign called for ten thousand men to attack Crown Point; six thousand to proceed against Niagara; three thousand against Fort Du Quesne, and two thousand to cross the country from the Kennebeck to the Chaudière—a feat performed by Arnold and a few followers, twenty years afterward—to attack some French settlements in Canada. Many of those destined for Crown Point and Niagara were already at Albany when Abercrombie arrived. He was not remarkable for either vigor or forethought. He loved his ease, and was a great stickler for the assertion of royal authority; and instead of stimulating the provincials with hope and patriotism, he depressed them with disappointment and disgust. Seven thousand troops were there, under General Winslow, impatient to be led to Lake Champlain; and another party were anxiously awaiting orders to hasten to Oswego, for rumors came down through the forests from the St. Lawrence that the French were about to move in large force against the English frontiers.

WILLIAM SHIRLEY. WASHINGTON, AGED 40. GENERAL BRADDOCK.
KING HENDRICK. WILLIAM JOHNSON.

But the Scotch general seemed more intent upon asserting royal authority by forcing the colonists to have the regular troops quartered upon them, than in pressing forward against the enemy; and he cast a firebrand into the army at Albany (composed of regular and provincial troops, about ten thousand strong), by compelling the officers of the latter to obey the commands of those of the former of equal rank. He and Mayor Sybrant Van Schaick had many stormy interviews about the billeting of regulars upon the people. On one occasion, there was an open quarrel between the lean Scotchman and the burly Dutchman, when the mayor, terribly excited, shook his fist at the general and exclaimed: "Go back again with your troops; we can defend our frontiers ourselves." The general triumphed; and he sent to his superiors, at a time when Crown Point should have been in his possession, and the garrison at Fort Niagara his prisoners, a shout of exultation because of his victory, saying: "In spite of every subterfuge, the soldiers are at last billeted upon the town." This victory cheered the hearts of the Lords of Trade, who now believed that the absolute submission of the colonies was an event near at hand.

Abercrombie loitered in Albany, waiting for the arrival of Loudon, when he predicted mighty things would be done. He would go neither backward nor forward, but wasted strength there in constructing useless fortifications, when the best defence for that city would have been the security of the frontier posts. Meanwhile the brave and active Colonel John Bradstreet arrived from Oswego with the startling news that the French and Indians were threatening the forts there, and that a strong force was actually moving at the foot of Lake Ontario for the capture of the post. But Abercrombie was unmoved, and the ten thousand men, chafing with impatience and suffering from sickness, were kept at Albany.

Bradstreet had gained laurels at Louisburg eleven years before, and had been made lieutenant-governor of St. Johns, Newfoundland. Knowing his worth, Shirley had called him into active military service, and sent him from Albany, with a competent force, to provision the garrison at Oswego. With two hundred provincial troops and forty companies of boatmen, he crossed the country by way of the Mohawk River, Wood Creek, Oneida Lake and the Oswego River, and placed in the fort at Oswego provisions for five thousand troops for six months. He was accompanied by Captain (afterward General) Schuyler, as commissary.

Bradstreet had observed that his descent of the Oswego River had been watched by French and Indian scouts. He had gone only nine miles up that stream on his return, when he was attacked by a strong party of French regulars, Canadians and savages. The provincials drove some of them from an island in the river, and there Bradstreet made a defensive stand. One of the Canadians, too badly wounded to fly with his companions, remained, and a boatman was about to dispatch him, when young Schuyler saved his life. Soon afterward Bradstreet abandoned the island and drove the assailants back into the forest. Owing to accident, there was only one bateau left at the island when the colonel ordered his men away. It was hardly sufficient to carry the commander and the little party with him. The wounded Canadian begged to be taken in, but he was refused. "Then throw me into the river," he cried, "and not leave me here to perish with hunger and thirst." The heart of Captain Schuyler was touched by the poor fellow's appeal, and handing his weapons and coat to a companion-in-arms, he bore the wounded man to the water, swam with him across the deep channel, and placed him in the hands of a surgeon. The soldier survived; and nineteen years afterward, when Schuyler, at the head of the northern army of the Revolution, sent a proclamation in the French language into Canada inviting the inhabitants to join the patriots, that soldier, living near Chamblée, enlisted under the banner of Ethan Allen, that he might see and thank the preserver of his life. He went to Schuyler's tent, on the *Isle aux Noix*, and kissed the general's hand in token of his gratitude.

After a sharp fight in the forest near the Oswego River, Bradstreet dispersed his motley foe, and hastened to Albany with the startling news just mentioned. Meanwhile the more active French had been preparing for an attack on Oswego. So early as March, three hundred Frenchmen, led by Indian guides, had made their way on snow-shoes along the bases of the Adirondack Mountains, on the north and west, to the vicinity of Oneida Lake, destroyed a small English stockade there, called Fort Bull, and returned with thirty prisoners. Late in May, eight hundred men under De Villiers, pushed forward to Sandy Creek, at the eastern end of Lake Ontario, and from that party went the detachment that assailed Bradstreet. At about the same time, Field Marshal the Marquis de Montcalm arrived at Quebec as governor-general and commander-in-chief. He was small in stature, but very energetic in mind and body. He instantly surveyed the field of his future operations. By journeying night and day, he penetrated to Ticonderoga, where the French had built Fort Carillon. He saw the value of that position, as well as Crown Point, and hastening back to Quebec, he prepared an expedition, secretly, against Oswego. At the head of three regiments, he ascended the St. Lawrence to Fort Frontenac, and was joined at Montreal by a large body of Canadians and savages. With this force, about five thousand in number, he crossed the lake in bateaux and canoes, and anchored in what is now Sackett's Harbor, early in August.

Fort Oswego, on the west side of the river, was a strong work. Fort Ontario, on the east side, was weaker, and was considered an outpost to the other. Against Ontario, Montcalm led his forces. Behind Four-Mile Point, a long wooded cape eastward of Oswego, he landed his troops, unobserved by the English scouts, and was in full march through the woods before he was discovered. Colonel Mercer, the commander of the little garrison of one thousand men, at Ontario, prepared to receive the foe, who invested the fort in full force, with thirty pieces of cannon, some of which had been taken from Braddock the year before. Finding sharp resistance, Montcalm began a regular siege, and on the 14th of August, when he was about to storm the works, Colonel Mercer, who saw that further resistance would be useless, agreed to surrender the post to the French. One hundred and twenty pieces of artillery, six vessels of war, three chests of coin and a large quantity of ammunition and stores, were the spoils of victory. To allay the jealousy of the Six Nations, Montcalm destroyed both forts; and the priests who accompanied him erected a cross, on which they placed the words, "THIS IS THE BANNER OF VICTORY." Close by it they raised a wooden column, on which was placed the arms of France and the inscription: "BRING LILIES WITH FULL HANDS." Then Montcalm descended the St. Lawrence, with his prisoners, and sent the captured English flags to decorate the churches of Montreal and Quebec. The destruction of the forts at Oswego was an admirable stroke of policy on the part of the French commander. It pleased the savages, and, as he hoped, caused them to assume a position of neutrality toward the belligerents. French emissaries soon seduced the Oneidas, Onondagas, Cayugas and Senecas from the British interest.

Loudon arrived just in time to hear of the loss of Oswego, as the first military news that reached him. He congratulated the country because of its escape from greater disasters. "If the attack had been made on the provincials alone," he said, "it would have been followed with fatal consequences." He would not allow any merit in the character of a provincial soldier. For them he had nothing but contemptuous words. Notwithstanding the provincials had saved the remnant of Braddock's army, in spite of the cowardice of the regulars and the obstinacy of their general; had conquered Acadia; defeated Dieskau, and had performed nearly all of the really useful military service against the French, he praised the British regulars and disparaged the Americans. Pleading the danger of another attack from the French, in greater force, as an excuse for his imbecility, he left the enemy to build a stronger work at Ticonderoga, dismissed the provincials to their homes, and placed the regulars in winter-quarters.

Under his instructions, Lord Loudon demanded of the city of New York, free quarters for himself, his officers, and a thousand men. "Your demand is contrary to the laws of England and the liberties of America," said the mayor of the city. "Free quarters are everywhere usual; I assert it on my honor, which is the highest evidence you can require," answered the haughty earl. The mayor was firm, and Loudon determined to make New York an example for the rest of the continent. When the citizens, by the lips of the mayor, pleaded their rights as Englishmen, his lordship, with a vulgar oath, said to the magistrate: "If you don't billet my officers upon free quarters, this day, I'll order here all the troops under my command, and billet them

LORD LOUDON.

myself upon the city." A subscription for the purpose was raised, the officers were billeted on the city, and Loudon won his first victory. A similar contest, with a similar result, occurred in Philadelphia, and there Loudon won his second victory.

In the meantime the provincials had won a substantial victory on the

Alleghany River, in Pennsylvania. We have observed that Dr. Franklin had superintended the construction of a chain of small posts along the Pennsylvania frontier, from the Delaware to the borders of Maryland, as a defence against hostile Indians. But the savages continued to harass the remote settlements, until, on the borders of Pennsylvania and Virginia, almost a thousand white persons had perished, and much property had been plundered or destroyed. Franklin was satisfied that he was not in his right place, and abandoned military life forever. Colonel John Armstrong, of Pennsylvania, took his position, and with three hundred men, accompanied by Captain Mercer of Virginia, he proceeded, in the night of the 7th of September, 1756, to chastise the hostile Delawares at Kittaning, one of their principal villages (now in Armstrong county), within thirty-five miles of Fort Du Quesne. Stealthily, Armstrong and his followers passed the Alleghany Mountains and took post not far from Kittaning, at midnight, when the savages were sleeping without a dream of danger near. It was a warm night, and some were reposing in the open air on the outskirts. Upon them the provincials came at dawn. The savages sprang to their feet, gave the war-whoop, and flew to the village, closely pursued by the provincials, who killed many of their chiefs and utterly destroyed the town. Not a vestige of a dwelling was left. The chastisement was effectual. It inspired the Delawares with such fear of the white man, that they were completely humbled, and the frontier had peace. So ended the campaign of 1756. The chief results of that campaign were a gain of strength and territory by the French; two victories in battle over the common foe by the provincials, and the bloodless conquest of the unarmed English cities of New York and Philadelphia by Lord Loudon and his British regulars, the spoils of his victories being free food and lodging for a few months and the contempt of the people. Fifteen hundred volunteers and drafted militia, under Colonel Washington, were placed in stockades during the ensuing winter, for the defence of the frontiers of Pennsylvania and Virginia; and on the western borders of the Carolinas, several military posts were established as a protection against the Cherokees and Creeks, and their neighbors, among whom French emissaries were at work.

CHAPTER XXI.

CHARACTER OF LORD LOUDON—THE CONDITION OF ENGLAND—PITT CALLED TO THE CABINET—HIS DISMISSAL FROM IT—PLAN OF THE CAMPAIGN OF 1757—EXPEDITION AGAINST LOUISBURG A FAILURE—IMBECILITY OF LORD LOUDON—DISGUST OF THE INDIANS—THEIR ALLIANCE WITH THE FRENCH—MONTCALM ON LAKE CHAMPLAIN—STARK'S EXPLOITS—FORT WILLIAM HENRY THREATENED—CAPTURE OF FORT WILLIAM HENRY BY THE FRENCH—A MASSACRE—COWARDICE OF GENERAL WEBB—PUBLIC DISCONTENT IN ENGLAND—PITT RECALLED TO THE CABINET—HIS POLICY AND ITS EFFECTS—PREPARATIONS FOR THE CAMPAIGN OF 1758.

NO better instrument could have been selected by the British government to render that government odious to the colonists than the Earl of Loudon. He was devoid of genius either civil or military. Imperious and undignified in his deportment; quick to threaten but slow to execute; possessing no semblance of public virtue; unsympathetic with anything noble or generous in human character; always in a hurry and hurrying others, but excessively dilatory in the performance of duties, he excited the disgust, jealousy, dislike and contempt of the colonists. He could not understand how a public officer could be unselfish and honest. When Dr. Franklin urged him to reimburse money which the latter had spent for the public service, the earl told him he could afford to wait, as he had doubtless taken care to fill his own pockets in his public transactions. When Franklin repelled the insinuation by declaring his integrity, the corrupt earl spoke of it as a thing incredible. "I wonder much," wrote Franklin, "how such a man came to be intrusted with so important a business as the conduct of a great doing; but having since seen more of the great world, and the means of obtaining and motives for giving places and employments, my wonder is diminished." Referring to Loudon's hurry and tardiness, a person said to Franklin: "He is like St. George on a sign-post; always on horseback, but never goes forward."

Events equally disgraceful in England and America occurred during the year 1756. Quarrels, scandals, intrigues, corruptions and imbecility had marked the court and administration of the British monarch. The king's mistress governed the realm. Patriots trembled for the fate of their country. Satire and caricature assailed its governing ministers; and Hogarth arose in reputation. The only hope for the future of England, in the minds of thinking men, was given late in the year, by raising William Pitt, the great Commoner, to the dignity of Secretary of State. The English people were with the untitled minister; the English aristocracy were against him. The latter, in power, stood in the way of every wise and generous plan of Pitt. When he proposed to pursue a just and liberal course toward the American colonies, he was met by churlish cavils from the Lords of Trade, and demands for the taxation of the Americans. When he was pressed to recommend a stamp-tax for America, he replied: "With the enemy at their back, and British bayonets at their breasts, in the day of their distress, perhaps the Americans may submit to the imposition." Pitt understood the Americans better, and had a clearer conception of justice and its wise policy, than any public man in England. He would not yield his country to the persuasion nor threats of the aristocracy; he would not resign the office which he knew the English people desired him to fill; and in the spring of 1757, he was dismissed by the king, with other good members of the cabinet. The government of England was in a state of anarchy for several weeks, and Loudon was making infinite mischief in America.

In January, 1757, Loudon held a council in Boston. The governors of Nova Scotia and New England were there. The earl's behavior was that of an autocrat. His opinions, dogmatically expressed, swayed the council and determined its decisions. Better men acquiesced in his plans in violation of their wiser convictions, because they feared less injury from his imbecility than from his uncontrolled resentment. It was decided to confine the military operations of the campaign to the capture of Louisburg; an object of far less importance to Great Britain and her colonies at that time, than the expulsion of the French from the frontier posts and from Montreal and Quebec. The New England people were disappointed and alarmed, New Yorkers were amazed. Pennsylvanians and Virginians were distressed because of the exposed condition of their frontier settlers to the sanguinary visits of the savages and their allies. Yet the colonists responded generously to calls for men and supplies, and at the first of June, 1757, Loudon found himself at the head of an army of provincials who, alone, were competent, under a good commander, to crush French dominion in America.

The earl resolved to lead the expedition against Louisburg in person. His officers easily foretold the result. Before his departure he made precautionary provisions. He ordered Colonel Bouquet to watch the Carolina frontiers with a few troops. General Stanwix was ordered to guard the western frontiers with two thousand men; and General Webb was sent with six thousand troops to defend Forts Edward and William Henry. Washington spent the summer with a few Virginia troops, in skirmishing with Indians and building a fort at Winchester, his headquarters.

The earl was ready for his eastern campaign late in June. Having exasperated the people of the whole country by impressing into the British service, at New York, four hundred men, he sailed from that port with a considerable force, and arrived at Halifax on the 30th of the month. There he was joined by ships under Admiral Holborne and six thousand troops commanded by George Viscount Howe. On the 9th of July he assembled his whole armament, composed of ten thousand soldiers, sixteen ships of the line, and several frigates and transports. It was supposed that an immediate attack upon Louisburg was intended, but the hope was delusive. The troops were landed. They were made to level the uneven ground for a parade; and for almost a month they were employed in the cultivation of a vegetable garden and exercises in sham fights and sieges. The army was dispirited, and the patience of the officers was exhausted. Major-General Lord Charles Hay could no longer repress expressions of his indignation. One day while he was sitting under a tree near the seashore, discussing army matters with some fellow-officers, he sprang to his feet, and blazing with indignation, he said, as he pointed toward a noble ship lying near, and to the idle camp not far off, "See how the power of England is held in chains by imbecility! Her substance is wasted by indecision! With such ships and such men as we have here, led by an energetic and competent commander, Cape Breton and its fortress, and all this eastern region, might have been a part of the British empire a month ago." For these brave words, his lordship was arrested, sent to England and tried by court-martial, and was acquitted. At that trial, there was a tragical event.

LORD CHARLES HAY INDIGNANT.

The President of the Board, while putting a question to Lord Hay, fell from his seat in an apoplectic fit, and died.

Stung by Lord Hay's remarks, Loudon bustled about a few days and embarked his troops as if for Louisburg. During the delay at Halifax, that fortress had been reinforced, and ships had been added to the French fleet there. A reconnoitering vessel brought word to the earl that his enemy had one more ship than he; so his lordship abandoned the expedition and sailed for New York. The army was amazed and thoroughly disgusted. On the 10th of August, when the fleet had voyaged westward only two days, an express sloop was met. A messenger from her came in haste to Lord Loudon with a despatch, telling him that the French, in large numbers, had closely invested Fort William Henry, on Lake George. The earl immediately sent orders back for troops that he had left behind, to follow him to New York. When he arrived there at near the close of August, he was met with the news that the French were in possession of Fort William Henry and all northern New York. The province was trembling with alarm. That alarm was intensified fourfold when the stupid and stubborn earl proposed to encamp his forces on Long Island for the defence of the continent!

For more than a year the English in America had acted so much "like women" that the Indians were disgusted. They admired the different spirit of the French, and warriors from more than thirty "nations" were at Montreal at the beginning of the summer of 1757. Governor Vaudreuil told them of glory and plunder surely to be won by alliance with the French. Montcalm danced their wild war-dances with them; he sung their fierce war-songs with them, until their affection for him and enthusiasm for the cause of the French became intense, and they were ready to follow wherever that general might lead. He commanded them to meet his regulars and Canadians at St. Johns on the Sorel, for a voyage over the Lake. They went, in a wild, tumultuous march for Montreal, accompanied by priests who chanted hymns and anthems in almost every Indian dialect. In canoes and bateaux the motley army, led by Montcalm, went up Lake Champlain and landed at Ticonderoga. It was hot July. Under a wide-spreading oak high mass was celebrated, and voices chanting sacred hymns were mingled with the martial music of French instruments. Scouts were sent out and returned with prisoners and scalps. When Marin, who had destroyed the hamlet of Saratoga a dozen years before, came back from the hills near Fort Edward, and pointed to his canoe moored at the shore, in which lay a solitary prisoner and more than forty scalps, the savages set up a yell of exultation that awakened the echoes of Mount Defiance and Mount Independence, then bearing Algonquin names. Very soon the whole body of Montcalm's force moved to the foot of Lake George, for their destination was Fort William Henry, at the head of the Lake. "His sailing," wrote Malartie from Montreal, when Loudon departed for Halifax, "is a hint for us to project something on this frontier." The expedition against Fort William Henry was the result of that hint.

During the previous winter, the Rangers commanded by Major Rogers, at Fort William Henry, had not been idle. The active and intrepid Lieutenant Stark (afterward the hero of Bennington), who commanded the Rangers when Rogers was absent, was frequently out, at the head of scouts, watching the foe and striking them a blow now and then near Fort Carillon

FRENCHMEN ATTACKED BY STARK.

—a name suggested to the French by the rushing waters of the outlet of Lake George, and which also suggested to the Indians their name of *Che-on-de-ro-ga*—"Sounding Waters"—the origin of Ticonderoga. These Rangers glided over the frozen waters on skates, or traversed the pathless forests on snow-shoes. On one occasion a party of Frenchmen were traveling merrily on the lake between Ticonderoga and Crown Point, on rude sledges drawn by Canadian ponies, when Stark and his followers rushed from the woods, and made some of them prisoners. Others were borne beyond danger by the frightened ponies, which fled over the ice with the fleetness of the wind. As Stark touched the shore with his prisoners, he was assailed by a large body of Indians in the edge of the woods. An unequal fight was kept up until dark, when Stark, leaving twenty of his men behind—killed, wounded, and missing—made his way back to the fort.

Meanwhile, fifteen hundred French regulars and Canadians followed the younger Vaudreuil from the St. Lawrence to Lake George, to capture Fort William Henry by surprise. They traveled on snow-shoes; their provisions were carried on small sledges drawn by dogs, and their beds were bear-skins spread upon the snow. Stealthily they went over the frozen lake, and appeared before the fort at midnight. The garrison were on the alert. The invaders set on fire the vessels there frozen in the ice, the store-houses and some huts, and escaped by the light of the conflagration. That was the night succeeding St. Patrick's day, in March, 1757. From that time until early in August, the garrison suffered very little molestation.

At the close of July, the garrison at Fort William Henry was composed of less than five hundred men under the brave Colonel Monro. A short distance from the fort, on a gentle rocky eminence, where may now be seen the ruins of the citadel of Fort George, seventeen hundred men lay intrenched.

A little more than a dozen miles distant was Fort Edward, where lay the timid General Webb, with about four thousand troops. At the same time Montcalm was at the foot of Lake George with six thousand French and Canadians, and about seventeen hundred Indians. There he held a grand council, and then he moved over the waters and along the western shore of Lake George. In a skirmish on the Lake, a great Indian warrior had been killed, and his body borne away by his comrades. Funeral honors were paid to it. It was dressed in full war-costume, and painted as if for the war-path. Brilliant ribbons, and glittering belts in which were his tomahawk and scalping-knife, and earrings and nose-jewels, adorned the dead body, which was placed upright on the green sward. In his hand was a lance; at his lips was a pipe, and by his side a filled bowl. In this presence there was an oration; then followed the death-dance and the death-song, accompanied by the low music of a softly-beaten drum and the tinkling of little bells. Then the body was placed in a grave, in a sitting posture, with plenty of food, and covered with earth; and the spirit of the warrior was dismissed to the happy hunting-grounds beyond the setting sun.

On the 2d of August, Montcalm, who had passed up the Lake with the main army, on bateaux, landed, with a heavy train of artillery, not far from the site of the village of Caldwell, and at once constructed siege batteries. La Corne, with Canadians, had landed on the east side of the Lake, and taken position across the road leading to Fort Edward; and De Levi, with French and Canadians, formed a camp northwest of La Corne.

This sudden appearance of so large a force was a surprise to the commander of the garrison. General Webb had come up from Fort Edward a day or two before, under an escort of Rangers led by Major Israel Putnam. He examined the fort and the intrenched camp, and sent Putnam on a scout down the Lake, who discovered a large force of French and Indians. This fact Webb concealed from Colonel Monro, and immediately returned to Fort Edward, with the same scout. Not doubting the intention of his superior to give him all the aid in his power, the veteran, when, on the 4th of August, Montcalm demanded an instant surrender of the fort, refused compliance in a defiant tone. The siege was then prosecuted with vigor, but Monro held out, in continual expectation of aid from General Webb. Express after express was sent through by-ways to Fort Edward, imploring aid; but Webb, fearing an attack upon that post, would not spare a man. Finally, when Sir William Johnson was allowed to march with Putnam and his Rangers and some provincials to the relief of Monro, the whole force was recalled when within three miles of Fort William Henry. Instead of forwarding relief to the beleaguered garrison, Webb sent a letter to their commander, in which he gave an exaggerated estimate of the numbers of the French and Indians, and advised him to surrender to prevent the massacre of his whole force.

This letter was intercepted by Montcalm, at a moment when he was about to abandon the siege and return to Ticonderoga, for his ammunition and provisions had become almost exhausted during a siege of several days. He sent the letter in to Monro, with a summons for him to surrender. That commander perceived the hopelessness of his situation. His own means for defence were almost exhausted, and he could not expect aid from Fort Edward. He yielded reluctantly, after honorable terms had been agreed upon. The garrison were to march out with the honors of war, carrying with them their baggage and small arms, and one cannon in recognition of their gallant defence of the fort, Monro agreeing that his men should not bear arms against the French for the space of eighteen months; also to deliver at Ticonderoga, all the French and Indian prisoners in the hands of the English. Montcalm pledged himself to furnish them with a strong escort half-way to Fort Edward. All this had been arranged at a council in which the Indians were represented. On the 9th of August, the French entered the fort and the English left it.

It was now near evening. Montcalm had kept intoxicating liquors from the savages, and admonished the English to do likewise. They did not heed the admonition, but supplied the Indians with rum. After a night's carousal, the savages were ready for any mischief. At daybreak they gathered

MONTCALM TRYING TO STOP THE MASSACRE.

around the English camp with hostile menaces. When the garrison began their march toward Fort Edward, the infuriated Indians fell upon them, plundered nearly all of them, murdered a large number of the soldiers and women, and made many prisoners. Montcalm and his officers did all in their power to arrest the fury of the savages. He and De Levi rushed in between them and their victims, at the peril of their own lives, and finally stayed the massacre. The survivors were sent to Fort Edward under a strong escort, and the prisoners were afterward ransomed in Canada.

MASSACRE AT FORT WILLIAM HENRY.

The fort and all of its appendages were immediately destroyed by fire and pick, and its conquerors moved down the Lake the same day. Putnam, who visited the ruins as soon as the French had left, described the scene as appalling. He saw the bodies of murdered Englishmen scattered in every direction, many of them half-consumed among the dying embers. He counted the bodies of more than one hundred women shockingly mangled, and some of them scalped. The fort was never rebuilt. An irregular line of low mounds—the remains of Fort William Henry—might have been seen on the borders of the Lake until 1854, when the site was covered by a large summer-hotel, already mentioned.

General Webb, at Fort Edward, with almost six thousand men, expecting to be attacked at any moment, sent off his private baggage to a place of safety, preparatory to a retreat to the Hudson Highlands. But his dreaded foe, having accomplished the chief object of his expedition, returned to Lake Champlain to rest upon his laurels. So ended Loudon's campaign in 1757. It was more inglorious than that of the preceding year. The British aristocracy had weakened British power; and their representative in America had disgraced the British arms. The English had been expelled from the Ohio basin; they had been made powerless in northern New York, and contemptible in Nova Scotia; and the French bore undisputed sway over the St. Lawrence and the Great Lakes, and the Valley of the Mississippi. At that moment, French territory in America exceeded that of English full twenty-fold. The colonists were humiliated and exasperated. But they were learning, in a degree, the measure of their strength in union. It was a lesson of vast importance to them in their impending struggle with a power that sought to enslave them.

The position of American affairs alarmed the English people. "We are undone at home with increased expenses; abroad, by ill-luck and incapacity," exclaimed Chesterfield, one of the most enlightened of the English aristocracy. He uttered the opinions of the British nation outside of that aristocracy, and their rulers were soon compelled to listen. Light concerning the Americans was spreading over England. Thinking men saw justice in their demands for local self-government, and reason for their restiveness and irritation because they were continually plagued by the rapacity and haughty bearing of many of the royal governors and the unjust exactions of the British ministry. They saw the danger of the Americans being driven to the renunciation of their allegiance to Great Britain, if a more just policy toward them should not be speedily exercised; and the English people became so clamorous for a change in the administration, that the alarmed king, after suffering England to be eleven weeks without a ministry, was compelled to recall Pitt to the cabinet in June, 1757, invested with powers which made him, in fact, prime minister of the realm. To him was intrusted the supreme direction of military and foreign affairs. He wielded his power with wisdom, and won glory for his country.

While Loudon was trying his best to conquer the Americans by overawing their assemblies and bringing the people into submission to the royal will, Pitt was devising plans for conciliating them by just and generous treatment. When, late in the year, Bostonians refused to submit to the billeting of royal soldiers upon them, the imperious earl sent a manifesto to the authorities of that city, saying: "I have ordered the messenger to wait but forty-eight hours in Boston; and if, on his return, I find things not settled, I will instantly order into Boston the three regiments from New York, Long Island and Connecticut; and if more are wanted, I have two in the Jerseys at hand, besides three in Pennsylvania." When that message was on its way to the New England capital, another from Pitt was crossing the Atlantic for the recall of Loudon, for the minister could "never hear from him, and did not know what he was about." So the Americans were relieved.

"Give me your confidence," Pitt said to the king, "and I will deserve it." The monarch replied: "Deserve any confidence and you shall have it." Upon this foundation Pitt began his brilliant administration, in the summer of 1757. American affairs demanded and received his early attention. General Abercrombie was appointed the successor of Loudon in chief military command in America. Relying upon the cheerful patriotism of the colonists, Pitt invited them to raise as many men as possible for an expedition against Montreal and Quebec. He assured them that England would provide arms, ammunition and tents, and that nothing would be required of them but the levying, clothing and pay of the men, for which expenditures the king would recommend parliament to grant a proper reimbursement. By order of the king, he sent instructions for all provincial officers no higher than a colonel to have equal command with officers of the same rank commissioned by the crown, according to the date of their respective commissions. These were cheering omens for the Americans, and they prepared for the campaign of 1758 with alacrity. In these liberal schemes Pitt was opposed by the aristocracy, because they yielded to the notions of independence cherished by the Americans, and the law-lords opposed the concessions as being contrary to the spirit of the British constitution. The great Commoner met their decisions with this telling maxim: "The lawyers are not to be regarded in questions of liberty."

Preparations for the campaign of 1758 were pressed with vigor. A strong naval armament was placed under the command of Admiral Boscawen, and twelve thousand additional English troops were allotted to the service of America. Equal vigor and more enthusiasm was observed in the colonies. Pitt asked for twenty thousand provincial troops. An excess of levies soon appeared. New England, alone, raised fifteen thousand. In Massachusetts the zeal of the people was unbounded, and the sacrifice of personal interest for the public good was marvellous. Public and private advances in that colony amounted to more than a million dollars, during the year 1758. In order to raise money, enormous taxes were levied and cheerfully paid. In many instances the tax was equal to two-thirds of the income of the tax-payer. It was *levied by their own chosen representatives*, and the people were content.

New York furnished twenty-seven hundred men; New Jersey, one thousand; Pennsylvania, three thousand, and Virginia, two thousand. Some came from the more southern provinces; but to the people of that region was intrusted the defence of their frontiers, and, if opportunity should offer, the expulsion of the French from Louisiana. When Abercrombie took command of the army in May, 1758, he found fifty thousand men at his disposal—a number about equal to the entire masculine French population in America at that time.

The plan of the campaign was a renewal of that of General Shirley for 1756, spoiled by Loudon. It included expeditions against Louisburg, Fort Du Quesne, the strong posts on Lake Champlain, and Montreal and Quebec. To Sir Jeffery Amherst, a veteran soldier then about forty years of age, with the accomplished James Wolfe, ten years his junior, as his lieutenant, was intrusted the leadership of the expedition against Louisburg, in connection with Boscawen's fleet. General Joseph Forbes was placed in command of the troops that were to attempt the conquest of Fort Du Quesne and the Ohio Valley; and General Abercrombie, with young Lord Howe as his lieutenant, was directed to sweep the French from Lake Champlain, and attempt to expel them from Montreal and Quebec. To Wolfe and Howe Pitt looked for success, more than to Abercrombie and Amherst. They were both young men; experienced in military life; judicious, magnetic, and full of energy.

CHAPTER XXII.

THE SIEGE AND CAPTURE OF LOUISBURG—EXPEDITION AGAINST TICONDEROGA—CAPTURE OF FORT FRONTENAC—ACTIVITY OF THE FRENCH—ADVENTURES OF PUTNAM—EXPEDITION AGAINST FORT DU QUESNE—WASHINGTON'S DEEDS AND MARRIAGE—PLAN OF THE CAMPAIGN OF 1759—WISDOM OF PITT—THE FRENCH IN CANADA—EXPEDITION AGAINST CROWN POINT—EXPEDITION AGAINST FORT NIAGARA—EXPEDITION AGAINST QUEBEC—ARRIVAL OF THE ENGLISH THERE, AND THEIR OPERATIONS.

THE campaign of 1758 opened with the siege of Louisburg. Admiral Boscawen arrived at Halifax early in May, with a fleet of almost forty vessels, bearing an army of ten thousand effective men led by Sir Jeffery Amherst, with General James Wolfe as his chief lieutenant. At near the close of May the whole armament left Halifax for Cape Breton, and landed on the shores of Gabarus Bay, not far from Louisburg, on the 8th of June. The surf was running high and breaking in foam on the rugged shore. Wolfe, at the head of the first division, ventured among the turbulent waters before the dawn. Several of his launches bearing troops were upset or shattered. When he reached shoal water, the impatient young general leaped into the sea waist-deep, drew his sword, and in the morning twilight led his soldiers against breastworks and *abatis* in the face of a sharp fire from batteries. The French were driven from their outworks into the fort, and the siege immediately began. It lasted almost fifty days.

The garrison at Louisburg was composed of twenty-five hundred regulars and six hundred militia, under the command of Chevalier de Drucourt. In the harbor were several ships of the line and some frigates; and vessels were sunk at the entrance of the harbor to prevent the ingress of an enemy. Wolfe was the soul of the expedition. Four days after the landing, he led some infantry and Highlanders to the capture of a battery on the northeast side of the harbor; and smaller works were soon secured. The English cannon were placed in battery and soon began to play upon other outworks, the fort, the town, and the vessels in the harbor. Four of the latter were burned and one was carried off by the English, late in July. The town of Louisburg was then reduced to a ruin. Almost all of the cannon of the fort had been dismantled by English shot and shell; and the French were compelled to capitulate on the 26th of the month. The next day the English took possession of the fort and town, with the islands of Cape Breton and Prince Edward; and all the coast nearly to the mouth of the St. Lawrence passed into the possession of Great Britain. The spoils of victory were about five thousand prisoners and a large quantity of munitions of war. After that victory, the French power in America began to wane. The attempt to capture Quebec was deferred until another year, and Wolfe returned home and received the plaudits of the nation.

Activity now prevailed throughout the colonies. The generous voice of Pitt had inspired the Americans with hope and enthusiasm. While Amherst and Wolfe were conquering in the East, Abercrombie and young Lord Howe were leading seven thousand regulars and nine thousand provincials through the forests of the upper Hudson, and over Lake George, against

WOLFE LANDING NEAR LOUISBURG.

Ticonderoga. At the beginning of July, the whole armament, fifteen thousand strong, were at the head of Lake George.

Like Wolfe in the East, Lord Howe was the soul of the expedition in the North. He was a military Lycurgus, and introduced sweeping reforms. He abolished ornament in dress; caused the hair of his men to be cut short to prevent maladies engendered by wet locks; shortened the muskets to make them more convenient in tangled woods, and had their barrels painted black to prevent discovery by their glitter; made his men wear leggins, like the Indians, to ward off briers and insects, and forbade the carrying of chairs and tables and other useless things. In these reforms his lordship led by his personal example. One day he invited officers to dine with him. He received them cordially in his tent. The ground was covered with bear-skins. For each guest was a log for a seat, such as his lordship occupied. Only pork and beans were served. He drew a sheath-knife and gave one to each of the officers, and told them to eat. His example was cheerfully followed.

Early on the 5th of July, 1758, Abercrombie's army moved down Lake George in more than a thousand bateaux and whale-boats, accompanied by artillery on rafts. Just at twilight they landed on a long, grassy cape for rest and refreshments, after a sultry day. It was Saturday evening. The soldiers strolled over the cape, and Lord Howe spent hours in his tent in consultation with Stark and other provincials, who knew the country well, concerning the situation of Ticonderoga and the region between it and Lake George. At a little before midnight, the soldiers were re-embarked. A most inspiring scene was presented. Howe, in a large boat, and surrounded by Rangers as a guard, led the van of the flotilla. The regulars occupied the centre; the provincials, the wings. The sky was starry and serene. Not a breeze ruffled the waters sleeping quietly in the shadows of the mountains. The oars were muffled; and so silently did the army move over the waters in the darkness, that not a scout upon the hills observed them. Day dawned just as they were abreast the Blue Mountain, four miles from their landing-place; and the first intimation which the outposts of the enemy there had of the approach of the English, was the apparition of scarlet uniforms as the boats swept around a point and the army prepared to land.

In four columns—the regulars in the centre—the army moved forward as soon as they were landed, leaving their provisions, artillery and baggage behind. They were soon in a dense forest with incompetent guides. Suddenly the advanced guard, led by Lord Howe, fell in with a party of French soldiers, who had lost their way. A sharp skirmish ensued, and Howe was killed by a musket-ball. The whole army fell into confusion because of his death, and Abercrombie led them back to the borders of the Lake. The next day pioneers, under the command of the brave Colonel Bradstreet, opened the way to the Falls, and on the morning of the 8th, Abercrombie moved forward with his whole force, leaving his artillery behind, to attack the outworks of the French at Ticonderoga. That fort was then occupied by Montcalm with about four thousand men.

Relying more upon the reports of his own officers than upon those of the despised provincials, Abercrombie was deceived concerning the outworks and the men behind them. His troops, moving in three columns, were ordered to scale the works, without co-operating artillery. Four hours they were endeavoring to cut their way through felled trees, and attempting to gain the intrenchments, in the face of a heavy fire, when they were compelled to retreat. Back to Lake George, Abercrombie fled, leaving two thousand men (chiefly regulars) dead or wounded in the forest. He had kept himself away from danger during the struggle, and when he was needed to soothe and lead his defeated troops, he could not be found. Montcalm had been continually with his men, conducting every movement in the contest. The alarmed Abercrombie did not cease flight until his whole army had reached their old encampment at the head of Lake George. From that point Colonel Bradstreet was allowed, after earnest solicitation on his part, to lead three thousand men against Fort Frontenac (on the site of Kingston, Canada), which they captured late in August, with the shipping there. The garrison surrendered on the 27th of that month; and so English dominion over Lake Ontario was secured. Bradstreet lost only three men in the fight, but five hundred were destroyed by a fearful camp-fever that broke out soon afterward. With the remainder he assisted in building Fort Stanwix, on the site of the village of Rome, on the upper Mohawk. Meanwhile, Abercrombie, after garrisoning Fort George, which had been built near the head of the Lake, returned with the remainder of his troops to Albany. The body of Lord Howe was conveyed to that city by Captain Philip Schuyler, and placed in his family vault. When, in after years, the remains were removed to their final resting-place, under St. Peter's Church in Albany, it was found that his lordship's hair, which was short when he fell, had grown several inches in length, and was smooth and glossy.

Montcalm did not follow the retreating English, but he was not idle. He strengthened Ticonderoga, and sent out scouting parties to annoy the English and capture their foragers. These parties were watched by Major Rogers, of New Hampshire, and his Rangers, of which Israel Putnam was second in command. They were often actors in exciting scenes. On one occasion, not long after the attack on Ticonderoga, a party of French and Indians, under Captain Molang, captured a convoy of English wagoners. Rogers and Putnam hastened to intercept them on their return. Not far from the present village of Fort Ann, they fell into an Indian ambush, and a severe skirmish ensued. Putnam and some of his party, separated from the rest, were made prisoners. His comrades were scalped, but he was reserved for a more cruel fate. His captor bound him to a tree, where he remained during the rest of the fight, and his clothes were riddled with bullets by the cross-firing of the combatants. Before he was released, a young warrior amused himself in throwing his keen tomahawk as near Putnam's head as he could without hitting it. When the major was unbound, he was led deeper into the forest, and tied firmly to a tree. Faggots were piled around him; a torch was applied, and the flames were crackling, when a furious thunder-storm burst over the country. The rain almost extinguished the fire, but it was soon revived with greater intensity. The victim had lost all hope, when

Molang, who had heard of the scene, rushing through the band of Indians, released Putnam and conducted him to Ticonderoga.

Putnam had many other hair-breadth escapes from death in that region. He spent the winter of 1756–7 on an island in the Hudson, near Fort Edward. The barracks of the fort took fire. The flames spread rapidly toward the magazine, in which were three hundred barrels of gunpowder. Putnam hastened from the island to assist in putting out the fire. Nearer

PUTNAM IN PERIL.

and nearer it crawled toward the magazine, when the intrepid major mounted to the roof and ordered buckets of water to be handed up to him. His labor seemed vain. The fire was charring the external planks of the magazine, and Colonel Haviland, the commander of the garrison, ordered Putnam to come down from his place of imminent danger. But the major persevered and put out the fire. He was several weeks recovering from the burns he then received. It was at this post, and just before this occurrence, that Putnam had his famous duel with a regular officer. That officer challenged the major to fight. As the challenged had the right to choose weapons and methods, Putnam proposed that each should be seated upon a keg of gunpowder with a fuse attached; that the fuse of each should be lighted at the same time, and that he who should sit longest should be regarded as the bravest man. Two kegs were brought from Putnam's quarters. The principals were seated upon them, and the fuses lighted by the seconds. The fire flashed along the trains for a few moments, when the British officer arose in haste and fled from the fatal keg. Putnam walked leisurely to his antagonist's fuse and put it out, and then seated himself again on his own keg, with perfect unconcern, cheered by his comrades. The kegs contained nothing more destructive than *onions*.

When Amherst, at Cape Breton, heard of the disaster at Ticonderoga, he sailed for Boston with four regiments and a battalion, and made forced marches across New England to Albany. He reached the camp of Abercrombie in October, and the following month he received a commission appointing him commander-in-chief. Abercrombie returned to England, and to divert public censure from himself, he roundly abused the provincials.

While disaster was attending the army in the North, General Joseph Forbes had gathered about six thousand men at Fort Cumberland, in Maryland, preparatory to a march against Fort Du Quesne. Washington was there with about two thousand Virginians; and Colonel Bouquet had come up from the Carolinas with over a thousand Highlanders, three hundred royal Americans, and a body of Cherokee Indians. It was known that Fort Du Quesne was feebly garrisoned, and Washington advised an immediate advance over Braddock's road. It was then July. In less than thirty days the fort might have been taken. But other counsels prevailed, and Forbes, who was so ill that he was carried on a litter, determined to construct a new road for his troops over the Alleghanies. It was an almost fatal mistake. When autumn came, and it was known that the capture of Frontenac by Bradstreet had discouraged the Indians and caused many of them to leave the French, the army was yet creeping slowly over the mountains. Washington was impatient and indignant; and he wrote to the Speaker of the Virginia Assembly, saying: "See how our time has been misspent! Behold how the golden opportunity has been lost, perhaps never more to be regained!"

At about that time Bouquet was sent forward, with two thousand men, to Loyal Hanna, in Westmoreland county, Pennsylvania, to build a fort. Bouquet, anxious to win renown, sent out Major Grant, with eight hundred Highlanders and some Virginians under Captain Bullitt, to reconnoitre Du Quesne. Grant took post on a hill near the fort, and dividing his force, tried to draw the garrison out into an ambush. They made a sortie in force, for four hundred men had lately been added to the garrison. They kept the English divided and defeated them in a severe skirmish, killing and wounding many, and taking some prisoners. As in the case of Braddock's defeat, the regulars gave way on this occasion, and the little army was saved from total destruction or capture only by the gallantry of Captain Bullitt and his provincials. The French, elated with their successes, proceeded to attack Bouquet at Loyal Hanna, but after a fight of four hours, they were repulsed with considerable loss.

Washington had anxiously desired to be in the advance. He was now sent forward to Loyal Hanna, where he was placed at the head of a brigade composed of a thousand provincials, and ordered to move in front of the army. But it was November before General Forbes, with the artillery and main body, reached that point, and full fifty miles of rugged way lay between the army and Fort Du Quesne. A council of war was held, when it was decided that the lateness of the season made it prudent to defer the attack upon Fort Du Quesne until another season. Fortunately Washington, just at that time, heard of the desertion of the French by their Indian allies, and the weakness of the garrison at Fort Du Quesne. He obtained permission to push on with his brigade. The main army followed. The provincials, inspired with the zeal of their young leader, overcame every obstacle with alacrity, and very soon they stood upon a hill overlooking the object of their destination. The garrison, only five hundred in number, alarmed at their approach, set fire to the fort that night and fled down the Ohio in boats by the light of the conflagration. The ruins were entered the next day (November 25, 1758), and over the charred remains the British standard was unfurled. In honor of the great English statesman, the name of Fort Pitt was given to Fort Du Quesne, and the little village that soon grew around it was called Pittsburgh. Two Virginia regiments were left there as a garrison, and the main army returned to the borders of civilization. The great object of the war in the middle colonies was accomplished. The basin of the Ohio was secured to the English.

Washington marched the remainder of his troops to Williamsburgh, where he took leave of them with the intention of quitting military life. He had been elected a member of the Virginia Assembly, and was affianced to the charming widow of Daniel Parke Custis, who was about his own age—twenty-six years. They were wedded at the "White-House," the residence of the bride, on the 17th of January (6th, Old Style), 1759, by the Rev. David Mossom, for forty years rector of St. Peter's Church, New Kent, near by. Then Washington took his seat in the Assembly at Williamsburg; and at about the close of their honey-moon, the Speaker of the House, by its order, rising from his chair, thanked the young colonel in the name of Virginia for his public services. Washington, surprised, arose to reply, but could not summon words. His face flushed with confusion, when the Speaker relieved him by saying: "Sit down, Colonel Washington; your modesty is equal to your valor, and that surpasses the power of any language I possess." That Speaker was Mr. Robinson, father of Beverly Robinson of New York, at whose house Washington met Mary Phillipse about ten years before.

With the expulsion of the French from Fort Du Quesne, the campaign of 1759 was ended. It had been a successful one for the English. They had captured three of the most important of the French posts—Louisburg, Frontenac, and Fort Du Quesne. The faith of the Indians in the invincibility of the French was eclipsed; and at a great council held at Easton, on the Delaware, in the autumn of 1758, several powerful tribes were present, and joined the Six Nations in making treaties of friendship and neutrality with the English. The right arm of French power was thus paralyzed, and peace was secured to the frontiers of Pennsylvania and Virginia. The people of Canada were discouraged. Their resources were almost exhausted, and they cried for peace. Montcalm wrote to Vaudreuil: "I am not discouraged, nor are my troops; we are resolved to find our graves under the ruins of the colony."

The final struggle for dominion in America was now at hand. Pitt had studied the geography of North America with diligence, and based his plans upon its teachings. Encouraged by the results of the campaign in 1758, in America and in Europe (where the victorious Frederick the Great of Russia, who had opened the Seven Years War on the continent in 1756, was the ally of the English), Pitt conceived a magnificent scheme for conquering all Canada, and crushing French power in America forever. That dominion was now confined to the region of the St. Lawrence, for the settlements in the West and South were cut off from co-operation with the Canadians.

Pitt had the rare good fortune to possess the confidence of all parties at home and in the colonies. The English people were dazzled by his real greatness; the colonists were deeply impressed by his justice. He had promptly reimbursed all the expenses of the last campaign incurred by the colonial assemblies, amounting to about a million dollars, and they as promptly seconded his scheme of conquest, which had been communicated to them under an oath of secrecy. Whatever he asked for he obtained. When he asked for sixty million dollars, and an immense force for service on sea and land in 1759, in Europe and America, the parliament almost unanimously granted his request. "He declares only what they would have them do, and they do it," wrote Chesterfield.

The general plan of operations against Canada was similar to that of Phipps and Winthrop, almost seventy years before. A strong land and naval force, under the command of General Wolfe and Admiral Saunders, were to ascend the St. Lawrence and attack Quebec. Another force, led by Amherst, was to drive the French from Lake Champlain, seize Montreal and join Wolfe at Quebec; and a third expedition, commanded by General Prideaux, was to take possession of Fort Niagara, and then hasten over Lake Ontario and down the St. Lawrence to Montreal. To General Stanwix was intrusted the task of completing the occupation of the posts in the West from Fort Pitt to Lake Erie.

Pitt would not listen to the vicious twaddle about enforcing royal authority in America, that fell from the lips of the Lords of Trade. "We want the limited co-operation of the Americans," said the wise minister, "and to have it we must be just and allow them freedom." These words ran like an electric thrill through the hearts of the colonists, and there was eagerness everywhere to manifest loyalty and to help the cause. Men and money were freely given; while the French in Canada, growing poorer and diminishing in numbers, received scanty aid and little encouragement from France. "The king relies on your zeal and obstinacy of courage," the French minister wrote to Montcalm. "Without unexpected good fortune or blunders on the part of the English," the general plainly replied, "Canada must be lost this campaign, or certainly the next." But France could do no more for her distant colony, for her wars nearer by had exhausted her treasury. With these relative prospects, the belligerents entered upon the contest in the early summer of 1759.

Late in June, Amherst was at the head of Lake George with about twelve thousand men, regulars and provincials in equal numbers. There he lingered for about a month, and then passed over that beautiful sheet of water with banners flying and martial music resounding, for he felt strong and did not seek concealment. On the 22d of July, he appeared before Fort Carillon, at Ticonderoga, with about eleven thousand men. Boulamarque, the French commander there, had just heard that Wolfe and Saunders were before Quebec. Seeing no chance for successful resistance nor reinforcements, he actually destroyed the fort and fled with his garrison down the Lake to Fort Frederic, on Crown Point, on the 26th. Amherst pursued, and on his approach on the 1st of August, the French abandoned that post also and fled to *Isle-aux-Noix* in the Sorel River, the outlet of Lake Champlain. Amherst took possession of Crown Point, without opposition; and if he had still pursued as he intended to do, he might have unfurled the British flag in triumph over the walls of Montreal before the close of September. The country between Lake Champlain and the St. Lawrence had been shorn of men to reinforce Montcalm at Quebec, who called loudly for troops to avert impending danger there. Old men, women and children were compelled to gather in the harvests near Montreal, to avoid starvation, and the Indians with the French army had deserted their allies. But Amherst, deceived by reports of the strength of the French at the foot of the Lake, and of a strong-armed flotilla there, lingered at Crown Point until October, causing repairs to be made to the fort at Ticonderoga, and constructing a new one on the promontory where he was encamped.

FEEBLE ONES HARVESTING.

He had, meanwhile, been building vessels to transport his troops down the Lake. On these he embarked his army at the middle of October, when heavy storms sweeping over the waters, and a message from Quebec, caused him to turn back and put his army into winter quarters at Crown Point. Captain Loring, with a little squadron of armed vessels, defying the storms, went down the Lake and destroyed the French flotilla, and so gained the mastery over that important sheet of water. The troops at Crown Point built there that strong fortification whose picturesque ruins still attract the attention of the summer tourist on Lake Champlain.

Prideaux's little force, destined to capture Fort Niagara, sailed from Oswego on the first day of July, leaving Colonel Haldimand to repair the works there. The troops that embarked consisted of two New York battalions, one of Royal Americans, two British regiments, a detachment of artillery, and Indian auxiliaries under Sir William Johnson. They moved slowly along the southern shores of Lake Ontario, and on the 15th of July, landed six miles east of Fort Niagara without opposition. The siege was commenced immediately. The fort stood near the bank of the Lake at the mouth of the swift-flowing Niagara River, where La Salle planted his stockade. The garrison was composed of a little more than six hundred soldiers. The commander, aware of danger, had sent for forces to be drawn from the posts between there and Fort Du Quesne and from the South, and they were on the way, almost three thousand strong, of whom one-half were Indians.

At the beginning of the siege, Prideaux was killed by the bursting of one of his own cannons, and the command devolved on Sir William Johnson. He disposed his force so as to meet the approaching army for the relief of the fort. They came in collision on the 24th of July. A severe fight occurred, when the French and their allies were defeated and dispersed, leaving their killed and wounded lying in the forest. On the following day the fort and its dependencies, with the garrison, were surrendered to the English, and British dominion was immediately extended along Lake Erie to Presque Isle, now Erie. The connecting link between Canada and Louisiana was now broken, never to be restored.

Sir William was so encumbered with his prisoners, and being unable to procure a sufficient number of boats for transportation, he could not proceed to Montreal, according to the original plan, to co-operate with Amherst, so he garrisoned Fort Niagara and returned with the remainder of the troops to Oswego, and thence to Albany. These events drew De Levi, Montcalm's second in command, from Quebec, with a body of troops to prevent the Americans descending the St. Lawrence. For awhile he watched the passes at the rapids below Ogdensburg, when he returned to Quebec.

The great event of the campaign was impending while those just described were occurring. The fleet of Admiral Saunders (whose lieutenant was Admiral Holmes), consisting of twenty-two line-of-battle ships and as many frigates and smaller vessels, and bearing eight thousand troops under General Wolfe, ascended the St. Lawrence as soon as the ice had left that stream, and anchored off the beautiful island of Orleans, a few miles below Quebec, and in full view of the city. Upon that island the troops landed on the 27th of June. Among the subordinate naval officers was James Cook, who afterward circumnavigated the globe and discovered the Sandwich Islands. Among the commanders of land troops were General Robert Monckton, afterward governor of New York; the impetuous Col. Murray;

General George Townshend, who soon became a peer of the realm; Colonel Guy Carleton, in command of grenadiers, and Lieutenant-Colonel William Howe, a leader of light infantry, both of whom were conspicuous in the royal service in our war for independence.

Quebec was partly on a high rocky promontory at the confluence of the St. Lawrence and St. Charles rivers, and upon a plain on the borders of the latter. The upper town was surrounded by a strong wall with five gates. Two of these opened out upon an elevated plateau, on the southwestern side, called the Plains of Abraham, whose border on the St. Lawrence is marked by steep declivities. The shores of that river were lined with batteries above and below the city, and the town was strongly garrisoned. Along the St. Lawrence between Quebec and the Montmorenci River, a distance of some miles, lay Montcalm, with a force of French Canadians and Indians, in an intrenched camp, a larger portion of the former having been impressed into the service.

Wolfe prepared for a siege with amazing skill and vigor. On his left lay his proud fleet at anchor, and the beautiful island was dotted with the white tents of his army. During the day after his arrival, clouds gathered in ominous blackness. The evening was dark and tempestuous, lighted only, until about midnight, by flashes of lightning. Suddenly a lurid glare shot across the billows as a fleet of fire-ships went blazing down the river in wrath toward the English shipping. The skillful British seamen caught each vessel as it came, and turned it away from the English ships. Their flames expired in darkness far below Orleans, as they drifted on the current.

The English, under General Monckton, now proceeded to take possession of Point Levi, opposite Quebec. There, on the 30th of June, they began to erect batteries within a mile of the town. From there red-hot cannon balls and blazing bomb-shells were hurled upon the city. These set fire to fifty houses in one night in the lower town, but the citadel, crowning Cape Diamond, the highest part of the promontory, was beyond the reach of their missiles, and the real military strength of Quebec remained untouched. It was upon this natural strength of the position that Montcalm relied for final victory, more than upon his exhausted troops and unwilling conscripts. Wolfe knew this, and resolved to attack the French commander in his fortified camp, and for that purpose he first landed a strong force, under Generals Murray and Townshend, below the Montmorenci, on the 10th of July, and formed an intrenched camp there. But when he looked for a place to cross that stream, he found the only fordable spot three miles from its mouth, and the opposite bank, steep and wooded, strongly fortified by the vigilant Montcalm.

The impatient Wolfe now reconnoitered the shores from the Montmorenci to Quebec, and along the craggy base of the Plains of Abraham far up toward Sillery. Everywhere military preparations for defence met his eye. He returned to the Montmorenci chafing with zeal, but conscious that he had made no advance toward the capture of the walled city which he had threatened for almost a month. Fire-ships again came blazing down the river, but were again turned away harmless. He saw danger in delay, and resolved to risk more; so, at the close of July, he ordered Monckton to cross over with his regiments, grenadiers and other troops, and land upon the beach at the foot of the cataract of Montmorenci, where that stream, after passing for a mile over a rocky bed in continuous roaring rapids, leaps into a dark chasm, at one bound, two hundred feet below.

Murray and Townshend were now ordered to force a passage across the Montmorenci below the falls at low tide, and co-operate with Monckton, on his arrival, in an attack upon the French lines. Wolfe selected the spot for the landing and attack. A signal was given, and boats from the fleet went swiftly across the St. Lawrence from Point Levi, and first landed grenadiers and Royal Americans, under cover of a fire from some of the English vessels. Monckton's regiments followed. Owing to confusion in landing, there was delay, when the grenadiers, impatient, would no longer wait for the troops across the Montmorenci, who were to support them, and rushed up the acclivity to penetrate the French camp. Already their foes had kept up a sharp fire of musketry and great guns for some time; now they were concentrated, and poured such a destructive shower of lead and iron upon the assailants, that the English were repulsed with much slaughter. They fell back in confusion to the shelter of a battery and block-house on the beach. Wolfe ordered a retreat, but a terrific thunder-shower that burst upon them at that moment detained them until darkness came, when the tide came roaring up against the current of the St. Lawrence, threatening to submerge the troops on the narrow beach. Monckton, with great coolness, embarked the shattered army in boats, and most of them were saved. They had lost between four and five hundred of their companions in the contests of the day.

When news of these events reached England, conservative men shook their heads and declared that Wolfe was mad. "Mad!" exclaimed the king, "Wolfe mad! I wish he'd bite some of the other generals."

CHAPTER XXIII.

WOLFE'S ILLNESS AND DESPONDENCY—PREPARATIONS TO ATTACK QUEBEC—BATTLE, AND DEATH OF WOLFE AND MONTCALM—SURRENDER OF QUEBEC—ATTEMPT TO RECAPTURE IT—SURRENDER OF MONTREAL AND ALL CANADA—ROGERS' EXPEDITION TO DETROIT—INTERVIEW WITH PONTIAC—CAPTURE OF DETROIT—WAR WITH THE SOUTHERN INDIANS—WAR CONTINUED ABROAD—TREATY OF PARIS—DISCONTENT OF THE INDIANS—CONSPIRACY OF PONTIAC AND ITS EFFECTS—FATE OF PONTIAC.

WOLFE soon heard, with joy, news of the capture of Fort Niagara and the expulsion of the French from Lake Champlain. He now listened eagerly for the drums of Amherst, for he expected that general would speedily join him. He sent Murray above Quebec to destroy the French shipping, and open communication with Amherst. But that general did not appear, for reasons already mentioned.

Chagrin because of his failure at Montmorenci, fatigue, anxiety, disappointed hopes, and the extreme heat of the weather, prostrated Wolfe with fever and dysentery. For almost a month his life was in great peril. Early in September he was able to hold a council of war at his bedside, and on the 9th he wrote a desponding letter to the Earl of Holderness, in which he mentioned the critical situation of the army and of himself. "My constitution," he wrote, "is entirely ruined, without the consolation of having done any considerable service to the state, or without any prospect of it." But he had told the earl that a council of war had decided that his shattered army should attack the foe. His letter reached London at the middle of October. The result of the promised attack was awaited with intense anxiety, for the young commander's epistle had created anger and consternation in England. It was followed three days later by news of that result, and the hearts of Wolfe's countrymen throbbed quickly with emotions of joy and grief.

It was determined to land a large body of troops above Quebec, for the purpose of drawing Montcalm from his intrenchments into an open field fight, in which the English would have the advantage. Wolfe, with some companions, in a boat, reconnoitered the shores, and selected the cove that yet bears his name, for the landing-place. From that cove a narrow path through a ravine tangled with vines and brambles led up to the Plains of Abraham; and along that perilous way it was resolved the troops should climb stealthily in darkness, if possible. The fleet was prepared to co-operate with the army, and on the 12th of September (1759) everything was ready for the execution of the dangerous and even desperate enterprise.

In the afternoon of that day, a feint was made in the direction of Montcalm's camp by the ships and some troops, to divert the attention of the foe from the real point of attack. At nine o'clock in the evening Wolfe and his

LORD HOWE. LORD AMHERST. GENERAL WOLFE. GENERAL ABERCROMBIE.

main army were embarked on flat-boats above Point Levi, and floated up the river with the flood-tide, some distance above the selected landing-place, followed by the ships. There was joy in Quebec and the French camp, for it was believed the English were retreating.

The evening was warm and star-lit. Wolfe seemed in better spirits than usual, and at the evening mess, with a glass of wine in his hand, and in the light of a lantern, he sang impromptu that little campaigning song which has been often chanted in the tents of British soldiers since, beginning—

> "Why, soldiers, why,
> Should we be melancholy, boys?
> Why, soldiers why,
> Whose business 'tis to die!"

But a cloud of presentiment that his end was near evidently shadowed the young hero's thoughts; and when, at past midnight, black clouds had gathered in the sky, and the boats were floating silently back, with muffled but unused oars, upon the ebb tide, to land the troops under cover of the darkness at the selected place, he repeated, in a low musing tone to the officers around him, that touching stanza in Gray's "Elegy in a Country Churchyard"—

> "The boast of heraldry, the pomp of power,
> And all that beauty, all that wealth e'er gave,
> Await, alike, the inevitable hour—
> The path of glory leads but to the grave."

"Now, gentlemen," said Wolfe, as he closed the verse, "I would prefer being the author of that poem to the glory of beating the French to-morrow."

In the darkness, sixteen hundred troops landed at Wolfe's Cove, and others speedily followed. The general led the way, with Monckton and Murray, and Lieutenant-Colonel Howe. They hastened up the acclivity in the face of shots from startled sentinels along the brow of the cliff, and reached the Plains of Abraham at early dawn, three hundred feet above the St. Lawrence. At sunrise, about five thousand British troops were standing in battle array, on the open plain before Quebec. News of the surprising apparition had gone into the city like the wind, and thence to Montcalm at Beaufort. He supposed, from the first account received, that it was only a small party who had come to burn a few houses and retire; but when later information reached him, he marched a greater portion of his army from his camp to attack the British, saying: "If it is necessary to fight them, it is necessary to crush them."

At ten o'clock the two armies stood face to face on that lofty plateau, the French on the higher ground near the city wall. Neither party had much artillery—the English only a six-pounder, which some sailors had dragged up the ravine. They were stronger than Montcalm imagined. He sent a messenger to his camp for fifteen hundred reserves, and another after a detachment that had gone up the river. The two armies were about equal in numbers then, and the impatient Montcalm began the attack without waiting for his reinforcements. Wolfe was at the head of the grenadiers who had been repulsed at the Montmorenci. They burned with a desire to wipe out the stain of that event, for their beloved commander had censured them for their rashness. He ordered his soldiers to double-shot their muskets and reserve their fire until the enemy should be very near.

A short and severe battle now ensued. Terrible were the volleys of the double-shotted muskets at close quarters. The French were thrown into confusion, when they were attacked by the bayonet so terrible in the hands of English soldiers. The general was urging on the bayonet charge, when a bullet slightly wounded him in the head. Another soon wounded him in the abdomen; and a third pierced his breast with deadly effect. "Support me," said the general to an officer near him; "Do not let my brave soldiers see me drop; the day is ours—keep it." He was borne to the rear in a dying condition, when the officer, on whose shoulder he was leaning, cried out, "They run! they run!" "Who runs?" feebly inquired Wolfe. "The enemy, sir; they give way everywhere," said the officer. The general then gave an important order for a movement to cut off the fugitives, and feebly said: "Now, God be praised. I die happy!" He never spoke again, and soon afterward expired. Montcalm had also been

WOLFE MORTALLY WOUNDED.

mortally wounded, and died the next morning. His body was buried in the grounds of the Ursuline Convent at Quebec. In its chapel a small mural tablet commemorates him; and there I saw, a few years ago, the skull of that French commander, its base covered with a blue velvet and gold-laced military coat collar. Wolfe's remains were taken to England, and his grateful government erected a monument to his memory in Westminster Abbey. Almost seventy years afterward an English governor of Canada caused a noble granite obelisk to be reared in the city of Quebec, and dedicated "*To the Memory of Wolfe and Montcalm.*"

General Townshend succeeded Wolfe in command of the army. With unparalleled selfishness and meanness, he tried to arrogate to himself the glory of the victory. He did not even mention Wolfe's name in his narrative of the battle. But others did, and public justice was quick to award honor where honor was due, and Townshend disappeared in a peerage. Five days after the battle, Quebec was surrendered to the English. The news reached England a month afterward—three days after Wolfe's desponding letter to Holderness, as we have observed. The joy of the people was intense; then grief because of the death of the hero was deep and heartfelt. "They despaired—they triumphed—they wept," wrote Horace Walpole, "for Wolfe had fallen in the hour of victory! Joy, grief, curiosity, astonishment were painted on every countenance; the more they inquired the higher their admiration rose." Exultation stirred every heart in the colonies. Illuminations, bonfires, cannon-peals and oratory everywhere expressed the general joy, and thanksgivings were uttered by every lip.

It was the 18th of September, 1759, when the city of Quebec, its fortifications, shipping, stores and people, passed into the control of the English, and General Murray with five thousand troops occupied it. The English fleet, with prisoners, sailed for Halifax. The campaign was ended, but Canada was not conquered.

De Levi succeeded Montcalm in command of the French forces. Early in the spring of 1760, Vaudreuil, governor of Canada, sent him to recover Quebec. Murray, boastful and rash, marched out to meet him; and at Sillery, three miles above the city, they met and fought one of the most sanguinary battles of the war. De Levi led nearly ten thousand men; Murray was at the head of over six thousand men. The English were defeated with the loss of a fine train of artillery and a thousand soldiers, and fled back to the walled town. The French besieged the city, and the condition of the English was perilous, when, early in May, a British squadron with provisions and reinforcements, sent by the sagacious and provident Pitt, ascended the St. Lawrence. Two of the ships that arrived first at Quebec destroyed the French shipping there. De Levi supposed them to be the vanguard of a large armament, and at the middle of May he raised the siege, abandoned most of his artillery and stores, and fled with the greatest celerity toward Montreal. Murray pursued, but could not overtake the fugitives. Montreal was now the last remaining stronghold of the French on the continent; Amherst might have had possession of it before De Levi besieged Quebec, but he spent the whole spring and summer in preparations for a regular invasion of Canada. Meanwhile Vaudreuil had collected all of his available forces at Montreal for the final struggle.

Amherst, though slow, was sure. He moved three armies against Montreal with so much precision that they arrived there almost simultaneously. With about ten thousand men he marched to Oswego, where he was joined by a thousand warriors of the Six Nations, under Sir William Johnson. He went over Lake Ontario and down the St. Lawrence, and appeared before Montreal on the 6th of September, having taken Fort Presentation at Oswegatchie (now Ogdensburg) on the way. On the same day General Murray arrived there from Quebec with four thousand troops, and on the following day Colonel Haviland appeared on the St. Lawrence, opposite Montreal, with three thousand soldiers. He had marched from Crown Point, and had driven the French from *Isle aux Noix*. Within the space of thirty hours, over seventeen thousand English troops had gathered around the doomed city. Vaudreuil saw that resistance would be foolish and vain, and he surrendered. On the 8th day of September, 1760, all Canada passed under the dominion of Great Britain, with no stipulations for civil liberty. The pleasure of the king was the law of the land. That king—George the Second—died suddenly a few days after the glorious news of the conquest of Canada reached London, when he was seventy-seven years of age, and was growing blind and deaf. He left England the foremost nation of the world in military fame and moral grandeur.

General Gage was made military governor of Montreal, and General Murray was sent to garrison Quebec with four thousand men. Joy spread over the English-American colonies, for peace in the future seemed to be secured. The people everywhere assembled to utter public thanksgiving to Almighty God for the great deliverance. But there was something yet to be done to make the conquest complete. The flag of France yet waved over the fort at Detroit, and other places in the West. Amherst could not allow the French lilies, emblazoned on that flag, to be seen anywhere in the conquered domain. A few days after the surrender of Montreal, he sent Major Rogers, with two hundred Rangers, to plant the British standard at Detroit and elsewhere. They went by the way of Frontenac, and along the northern shores of Lake Ontario around to Niagara. At the latter place they furnished themselves with a costume suitable for the wilderness, and voyaged over Lake Erie in the chilly days of October and November. At the mouth of a river on its southern shore, they met a deputation of Ottawa chiefs, who told them to remain there until Pontiac, their emperor, should arrive, for he desired to see them with his own eyes.

Pontiac soon came. He was a fine specimen of a North American Indian, and was ruler over a magnificent domain in Ohio and Michigan. His people (the Ottawas) revered him, and the tribes over whom he reigned admired him for his wisdom and bravery. He met Rogers with a princely air, and demanded why he had entered his dominions without his leave. Rogers explained that the English had conquered Canada, and that he came only to drive out the French, their common enemy, and then gave the emperor a belt of peace. Pontiac returned it, saying: "I stand in the path until morning." Turning on his heel, he left Rogers in doubt concerning the chief's intentions. His men kept watch for treachery all night. In the morning, Pontiac sent them some food. He soon followed, and gave Rogers assurances of his friendship. He had been the ally of the French, but was too shrewd to adhere to a waning cause. He was willing to court the favor of the English; so he and Rogers sat upon a log and smoked the calumet. He sent word to the tribes south and west of Lake Erie that the strangers had his permission to cross his dominions. Rogers marched on, and on the 29th of December, 1760, he unfurled the British flag at Detroit. The garrison were made prisoners, but the French settlers were allowed to remain on the condition of taking the oath of allegiance to the British crown.

When Canada was falling prostrate at the feet of British power, the storm of war lowered darkly along the Carolina frontiers. There had been strife with the Indians there for years. The Cherokees, the treaty friends of the English, strove hard to maintain peace. They were the hardiest and most enlightened of the savages in that region. These mountaineers, occupying the hill country of Georgia, exerted a powerful influence over the surrounding tribes. But their patience was exhausted by wrongs which they and their friends had suffered at the hands of frontier Virginia Rangers, and the treachery of the royal governor of South Carolina, and in the spring of 1760, they flew to arms with the tribes of Tennessee, Alabama and Georgia as allies. In the space of a few weeks the western frontiers of the Carolinas were swept with the fiery besom of desolation. French emissaries had worked powerfully upon the Indian mind, and military stores had been sent to the Cherokees from Louisiana. The smitten and menaced people called

CONFLICT WITH THE INDIANS ON THE SOUTHWESTERN FRONTIERS.

loudly for help. Amherst heeded their supplications, and early in April, he detached Colonel Montgomery (afterward Lord Eglintoun) from the army of Stanwix, with six hundred Highlanders and as many Royal Americans, to strike the Cherokees. He was accompanied by Colonel Grant, who had been assailed by the garrison of Fort Du Quesne a few months before. In the western part of South Carolina, beyond the Saluda, they were joined by seven hundred Carolina Rangers, among whom was Moultrie, who afterward figured in the American war for independence.

On the first of June the English were ready to apply the scourge. They penetrated the beautiful Valley of the Keowee, on the western borders of Anderson District, in which well-built houses and cultivated fields gave tokens of a semi-civilization. That valley they plundered, and desolated it with fire, driving the families to the wooded hills, where they looked down upon their possessions utterly ruined. Onward the English marched over the hills and the headwaters of the Savannah to the Valley of the Little Tennessee. Down that valley they marched, compelled to fight almost every inch of their way in the heart of the Southern Alleghany Mountains. The whole country was aroused. The patriotism of the Cherokees gave intensity to their anger. The English were in serious peril, and Montgomery wisely retraced his steps. This movement left the English garrison at Fort Loudon, on the Tennessee, at the mercy of the savages, who murdered a part of them after they had surrendered, and scattered the remainder, as prisoners of war, among the tribes. Montgomery hastened to Charleston, and regardless of the prayers of the people, who feared the ire of the exasperated Cherokees, he embarked for Halifax.

The Cherokees were not subdued, but were more fiercely inflamed against the English. They prepared for the war-path the next year, when Colonel Grant appeared with a stronger force, and compelled them to stand on the defensive. He burned their villages, desolated their fields, and killed many of their warriors. Finally, the nation, dispirited, humbly sued for peace in June, 1761, and a treaty to that effect was made.

Although the war had ceased in America, the French and English continued it upon the ocean and among the West India islands, with almost unbroken success by the latter. It was ended by a treaty of peace negotiated in 1762, and signed at Paris on the 10th of February, 1763. By its terms France ceded to Great Britain all her claimed territory in America eastward of the Mississippi River, north of the latitude of the Iberville River, a little below Baton Rouge. New Orleans, and the whole of Louisiana, was ceded by France to Spain, at the same time; and so her entire possessions in North America, for which she had labored and fought for more than a century, were relinquished. Spain, with whom the English had been at war for a year previously, ceded East and West Florida to Great Britain, at the same time. Now the English held undisputed possession (excepting by the Indians) of the whole continent from the shores of the Gulf of Mexico to the Frozen Sea, and by claimed prescriptive right, from ocean to ocean. The domain wrested from the French had been procured at a cost to Great Britain and her American colonies of five hundred and sixty million dollars.

The storm in the south had scarcely ceased when another, more portentous, was seen gathering in the northwest. All over the land from the Shenandoah Valley to Lake Superior, from Western New York and the line of the Alleghany Mountains stretching into the Carolinas, to the Mississippi River, a deep-rooted jealousy of the English appeared among the Indians after the conquest of Canada. They regarded the English as a nation of amazing power, who were ready to rob them of their lands and destroy their race. The treatment of the natives by the English was so cold and unfriendly when compared with the French, that the savages could feel no real friendship for the British, and it was only fear or policy that caused the Indians to make treaties with them. The chiefs were treated with contempt by the British officers, and so their pride was wounded; they treated the people as children or slaves, and so lost their respect. Traders cheated them and aroused their anger. In every way they were made to feel, by contrast with the conduct of the French, the meanness and wickedness of the English. The jealousy of the savages was crystallized into implacable hatred, and in 1761, they began to form confederacies and plotted conspiracies for the destruction of their English masters.

When, after the treaty of Paris in 1763, the tribes were informed that France had ceded the country to Great Britain, without asking their leave, there was wide-spread indignation among them. The arrogance of Amherst in his official intercourse with them fanned the flame, and a vast confederacy was formed for the purpose of attacking all of the English forts on the frontiers on the same day, to destroy their garrisons and to desolate their settlements, westward of the Alleghanies.

At the head of this conspiracy was the great Ottawa chief, Pontiac, then about fifty years of age. He was conspicuous for courage, resolution, energy, and magnetic attraction and vehement ambition, and ruled many tribes with almost despotic power. He had fought on the side of the French in the war just ended, and was their friend until his interview with Major Rogers. He trimmed his sails so as to catch the favoring breeze of the power he held to be the most potential, but his pride was soon deeply wounded by the

PONTIAC IN COUNCIL.

arrogance and neglect of the English. He saw his race divided, weak, and powerless before a great nation. He saw the English rapidly spreading their settlements over the hunting-grounds of the Indians, and driving them steadily toward the setting sun. In his horoscope of the future, he saw the last of his race, naked and famishing, driven into the Pacific Ocean, of which he had vague ideas. Ambition and patriotism urged him to lead a conspiracy for the salvation of his country and his race. He did so, with marvellous skill and energy.

Late in 1762, Pontiac sent ambassadors to the tribes around the lakes, and all over the country southward far toward the Gulf of Mexico. Each bore the wampum war-belt and a hatchet painted red in token of hostilities. Each delivered the stirring words of Pontiac, calling them to the defence of their country and their lives; and everywhere his words were approved. He called a general council at a spot near Detroit, designated by him, and there the tribes were assembled in April, 1763—the Ottawas, Miamis, Wyandotts, Chippewas, Pottawatomies, Mississaugues, Shawnoese, Foxes, Winnebagoes and Senecas—the latter the most warlike of the Six Nations. Pontiac was there with his squaws and children, and the meadow in which the council was held presented a gay and animated scene. The idle young warriors gathered in groups to feast, smoke, gamble, and tell stories; many of them bedizened with beads, feathers, hawks' bills, and other tokens of foppery. "Here, too," says Parkman, "were young damsels radiant with bears' oil, ruddy with vermilion, and versed in all the arts of forest coquetry; shrivelled hags, with limbs of wire, and the voices of screech-owls; and troops of naked children, with small, black, mischievous eyes, roaming along the outskirts of the woods."

The council was convened on the 27th of April. All were seated on the grass in a wide circle, row within row, a grave and silent assembly. When pipes had been lighted and passed from hand to hand, Pontiac arose, plumed and painted, in full war-costume, and with loud voice and impassioned manner, addressed the multitude. He recounted the wrongs of the red race, and spoke of the danger to be apprehended from the sovereignty of the English. He held out a long and broad belt of wampum, which, he said, he had received from the king of the French, and that the fleets and armies of that monarch would soon come back to reconquer Canada, when the Indians would once more fight by their side. He appealed to the superstition of his hearers by reciting an Indian legend, and in various ways he excited them with a burning desire for immediate action.

Treachery was to be the first movement of Pontiac and his followers in the execution of the sanguinary scheme. He was to begin the tragedy at

Detroit. Under the pretext of holding a friendly council with Major Gladwin, the commander of the fort, he entered it in May, with about three hundred warriors, each carrying a knife, tomahawk and short gun, concealed under his blanket. When Pontiac should arise and show the green side of a belt, the massacre of the garrison was to begin. A friendly Indian had warned Gladwin of the danger the day before, and it was averted by the appointment of another conference. The gates were shut upon Pontiac after he and his warriors had retired, and he began a siege of the fort that

PONTIAC IN COUNCIL.

continued more than a year. By similar acts of treachery, or by sudden and unexpected assaults, every post west of Oswego, excepting Niagara, Fort Pitt and Detroit, fell into the hands of the dusky confederates within a fortnight afterward, for the work was performed at different points almost simultaneously.

At Michillimackinack, Indians came to the fort at the close of May, as if to trade. Every day they engaged in the exciting pastime of ball-playing on the plain near the fort. On the 2d of June their squaws came with them, entered the fort, and stayed there. The commander and a lieutenant, unsuspicious of any danger, stood just outside the gate, watching the game. At length the ball was sent near the gate, and two or three Indians pursuing it, went behind the officers, seized them, and carried them off to the woods. The other Indians rushed into the fort, seized hatchets which the squaws carried under their blankets, and murdered a part of the garrison, making prisoners of the remainder.

Captain Dalyell, aide-de-camp to General Amherst was sent in a vessel with reinforcements and supplies for the garrison at Detroit. They ran up the river in the night at the close of July, and succeeded in getting both into the fort. Dalyell at once proposed to make a sally from the fort and attack the besiegers, who lay about a mile up the river. Gladwin thought it would be imprudent. Dalyell persisted, and with two hundred and forty chosen men, he marched in the darkness at three o'clock in the morning of the 31st of July, to surprise Pontiac. The chief was on the alert, and at a small stream at the northern verge of the city of Detroit, the English, furiously assailed, were forced to make a precipitate retreat, leaving twenty of their comrades killed and forty-two wounded, on the borders of the brook, which, to this day, bears the name of Bloody Run. Dalyell was slain while trying to carry off the wounded, and his scalp was an Indian's trophy.

This victory encouraged the Indians, and they swarmed around Detroit and Fort Pitt. For the relief of the latter, Colonel Bouquet was sent with a force of regulars from Pennsylvania. Early in August he approached the fort, when the besieging savages attacked him. He had two desperate fights with them, in which he lost about one-fourth of his command and all of his horses, but he drove the assailants away and entered the fort with the remainder. Detroit was relieved the next summer by a force under Colonel Bradstreet.

The power of the Indian Confederacy was now broken, and chiefs of the hostile tribes sued for pardon and peace. The haughty Pontiac would not yield. He tried to rally the confederate tribes, but in vain. He went to the Illinois country where no Englishman had been, and where the French flag yet waved. Among the tribes there he exerted his eloquence to induce them to make war on the English. He sent an ambassador to New Orleans to ask the French to aid him. His efforts were vain. The cause that lay next to his heart was ruined. Afterward we find him holding a friendly conference with Sir William Johnson at Oswego; then he is seen at

St. Louis trying to arouse the French people there to drive the English out of the Illinois country, which they had seized. At last, in 1769, this haughty Indian prince—this Catawba prisoner adopted by the Ottawas—who had swayed almost unbounded power over thousands of square miles of territory, was slain near Cahokia. A strolling Indian was bribed by an English trader to murder him. That savage, for the gift of a barrel of rum, stole softly behind Pontiac in the forest and buried his hatchet in his brain.

DEATH OF PONTIAC.

END OF BOOK III.

BOOK IV.

THE

WAR FOR INDEPENDENCE,

OR

THE POLITICAL REVOLUTION.

FROM 1760 TO 1789.

www.ingramcontent.com/pod-product-compliance
Lightning Source LLC
LaVergne TN
LVHW021054110826
845150LV00001B/72